BOOKS BY PETER WYDEN

Wall—The Inside Story of Divided Berlin
The Unknown Iacocca
Day One—Before Hiroshima and After
The Passionate War—The Narrative History of the Spanish Civil War
Bay of Pigs—The Untold Story

WALL

THE INSIDE STORY OF DIVIDED BERLIN

PETER WYDEN

SIMON AND SCHUSTER
New York   London   Toronto   Sydney   Tokyo

Simon and Schuster
Simon & Schuster Building
Rockefeller Center
1230 Avenue of the Americas
New York, New York 10020

Designed by M. B. Kilkelly/Levavi & Levavi
Manufactured in the United States of America

1   3   5   7   9   10   8   6   4   2

Library of Congress Cataloging in Publication Data
Wyden, Peter
Wall: the inside story of divided Berlin/Peter Wyden.
p.   cm.
Includes bibliographical references.
1. Berlin Wall (1961-   ) I. Title.
DD881.W93   1989
943.1′55—dc20   89-36905
CIP
ISBN 0-671-55510-3

To Elaine

CONTENTS

Contents   *11*

The Berlin Wall is people, people caught for nearly thirty years between two armed camps not of their making. As this is written, their captivity continues, but perhaps not for much longer.

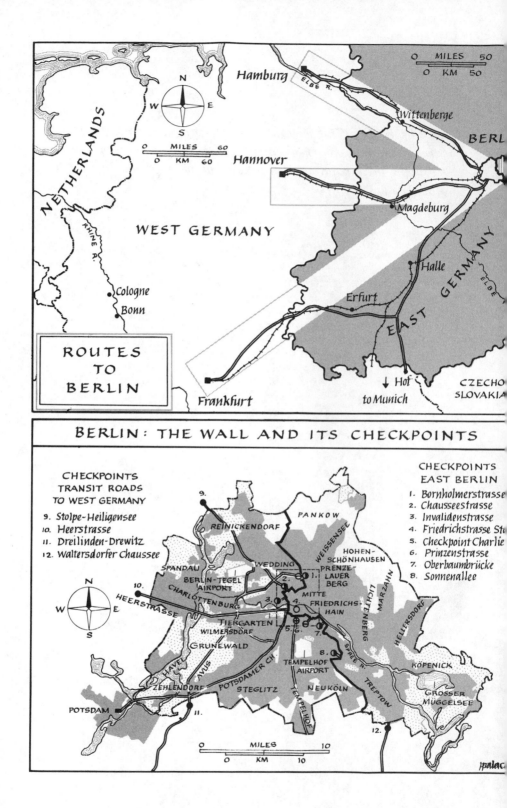

ROUTES TO BERLIN

NETHERLANDS

WEST GERMANY

Hamburg

Hannover

RHINE R.

Cologne

Bonn

Frankfurt

ELBE R.

Wittenberge

BER

Magdeburg

EAST GERMANY

Halle

ELBE

Erfurt

↓ Hof
to Munich

CZECHO
SLOVAKIA

N
W E
S

MILES 50
KM 50

MILES 60
KM 60

BERLIN: THE WALL AND ITS CHECKPOINTS

**CHECKPOINTS
TRANSIT ROADS
TO WEST GERMANY**

9. Stolpe-Heiligensee
10. Heerstrasse
11. Dreilinden-Drewitz
12. Waltersdorfer Chaussee

**CHECKPOINTS
EAST BERLIN**

1. Bornholmerstrasse
2. Chausseestrasse
3. Invalidenstrasse
4. Friedrichstrasse St
5. Checkpoint Charlie
6. Prinzenstrasse
7. Oberbaumbrücke
8. Sonnenallee

N
W E
S

PANKOW

REINICKENDORF

WEISSENSEE

HOHEN-
SCHÖNHAUSEN

SPANDAU

WEDDING

PRENZE-
LAUER
BERG

BERLIN-TEGEL
AIRPORT

CHARLOTTENBURG

MITTE

LICHTENBERG

MARZAHN

HELLERSDORF

HEERSTRASSE

TIERGARTEN

FRIEDRICHS-
HAIN

WILMERSDORF

GRUNEWALD

SPREE R.

HAVEL

AVUS

POTSDAMER CH.

TEMPELHOF
AIRPORT

KÖPENICK

ZEHLENDORF

STEGLITZ

TEMPELHOF

NEUKÖLN

TREPTOW

GROSSER
MÜGGELSEE

POTSDAM

MILES 10
KM 10

palac

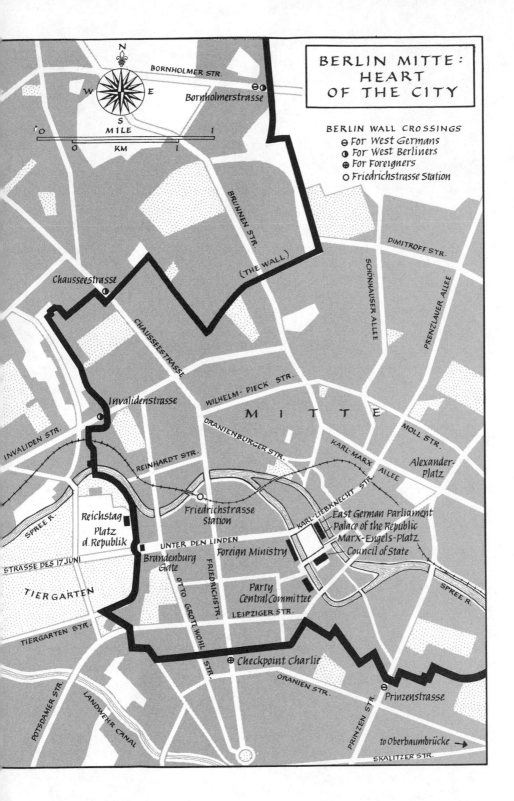

BERLIN MITTE:
HEART
OF THE CITY

BERLIN WALL CROSSINGS
⊖ For West Germans
◐ For West Berliners
⊕ For Foreigners
○ Friedrichstrasse Station

N
W E
S
MILE
0   1
KM
0   1

BORNHOLMER STR.

Bornholmerstrasse

BRUNNEN STR.

DIMITROFF STR.

(THE WALL)

SCHÖNHAUSER ALLEE

PRENZLAUER ALLEE

Chausseestrasse

CHAUSSEESTRASSE

WILHELM- PIECK STR.

M I T T E

MOLL STR.

Invalidenstrasse

ORANIENBURGER STR.

KARL-MARX ALLEE

Alexander-
Platz

INVALIDEN STR.

REINHARDT STR.

KARL-LIEBKNECHT STR.

SPREE R.

Reichstag
Platz
d.Republik

Friedrichstrasse
Station

East German Parliament
Palace of the Republic
Marx-Engels-Platz
Council of State

STRASSE DES 17 JUNI

UNTER DEN LINDEN

Brandenburg
Gate

Foreign Ministry

SPREE R.

TIERGARTEN

FRIEDRICHSTR.

Party
Central Committee

OTTO GROTEWOHL STR.

LEIPZIGER STR.

TIERGARTEN STR.

⊕ Checkpoint Charlie

POTSDAMER STR.

LANDWEHR CANAL

ORANIEN STR.

PRINZEN STR.

⊖ Prinzenstrasse

to Oberbaumbrücke →

SKALITZER STR.

PART I

KENNEDY CONFRONTS KHRUSHCHEV OVER BERLIN: HISTORY'S FIRST NUCLEAR CLASH

1

KHRUSHCHEV: "THE WEST WILL STAND THERE LIKE DUMB SHEEP"

**West Berlin,
Winter 1987**

Walking along the west bank of the Spree River with her daughter Sulamith, age six, Bärbel Grübel was encircled by history. Behind Bärbel and Sulamith towered the cupola of the Reichstag, the parliament killed off by Adolf Hitler's rantings. To the East across the water ran that contemporary monument to dictatorship, the Berlin Wall.

But Bärbel Grübel faced more than impersonal landmarks in this neighborhood. Across the river, within easy vision, was Reinhardtstrasse. There, Bärbel grew up and there her parents still lived, separated from the rest of the family by the Wall. The parental apartment was only a few hundred yards—yet worlds—away from where Bärbel and Sulamith were standing.

"Why can't I see Grandma and Grandpa?" asked Sulamith, having asked the question often before.

"I've told you and told you," Bärbel said. "Until that damned Wall comes down, you can't see them, you can just talk to them on the phone."

"So when will the Wall come down?" asked Sulamith, as she had asked many times.

"I don't know, dear, but soon, I think."

That damned Wall. Its future was wrapped in secrecy, just like its beginnings.

Bärbel Grübel walks with her six-year-old daughter Sulamith on the west bank of Berlin's Spree River, winter 1987. Across the water to the east is the Wall—and somewhere behind it, Bärbel's two older children.

**Moscow,
Thursday, August 10, 1961**

The party was small, the mood jolly. The Soviet Union's highest military leaders had gathered in their richly bemedaled regalia to celebrate the sixty-second birthday of Sergei S. Varentsov, whose formal title did not adequately reflect his crucial function. As Chief Marshal of Artillery, Varentsov was in charge of more than cannons. He oversaw the entire Russian missile program, and in the current summer of the unprecedentedly acute crisis over Berlin the Soviets for the first time were threatening the West all too persuasively with the use of nuclear weapons on a global scale.

The threats kept being bellowed by the short, bulky, bullet-headed Soviet Premier, who had promised to "bury" the West with Varentsov's missiles. So it was not surprising that this intimidating head of state, Nikita S. Khrushchev, was putting in a personal appearance at his chief missile marshal's birthday party in the Defense Ministry. It was, moreover, an appropriate occasion for the Commander in Chief to treat his assembled insiders to an electrifying announcement.

"We're going to close Berlin," Khrushchev said. "We'll just put up serpentine barbed wire and the West will stand there like dumb sheep. And while they're standing there, we'll finish a wall."

The brass and their wives applauded with enthusiasm, but for one of the group's officers Khrushchev had just created a dilemma. He was Oleg Vladimirovich Penkovsky, fifty-two. Although Penkovsky was only a colonel in the GRU (Soviet Military Intelligence), his superb connections made up for his lowly rank. The chief of the GRU, General Ivan Serov, had made Penkovsky his protégé. And today the colonel was a guest at Chief Marshal Varentsov's party because the marshal considered him as close as a son. Varentsov had sent Penkovsky to Guided Missile School (where the colonel graduated first in his class). Later, the marshal had helped him land a job with the elite GRU, for which Penkovsky traveled widely with orders to pilfer foreign scientific intelligence. Officially, the colonel worked for the State Committee for Science and Technology at 11 Gorky Street.

Penkovsky was the least conventional of Russians. He was flashily brilliant, effusive, and hyperenergetic. His noisy enthusiasm was infectious. Measuring five feet eight inches, he moved very rapidly. He was an obsessively neat fitness fanatic with a ramrod back and

Soviet Premier Nikita S. Khrushchev harangues the United Nations in 1960. "We're going to close Berlin," he told his generals a year later. "We'll just put up serpentine barbed wire and the West will stand there like dumb sheep."

exceptionally powerful, well-conditioned muscles. His combed-back reddish hair was receding, and the enormous forehead heightened the effect of the deep-set eyes, which, an associate would recall, "were magic to women." He spoke passable English and French, and moved as easily in London and Paris, where Soviet espionage assignments often took him, as he did in Kremlin society.

Penkovsky could easily differentiate between routine intelligence fodder and a secret of the very first rank. Khrushchev's disclosure of the Soviet surprise plan for Berlin obviously belonged in the latter category. This made Penkovsky's quandary painful, because he was a double agent, almost certainly the most productive agent in place ever to feed secrets to the Central Intelligence Agency—thousands of documents and orally transmitted morsels, tens of thousands, in bewildering profusion. And although he was active for only nineteen months, his service happened to coincide precisely with the dangerous times of the Berlin Wall in 1961 and with the Cuban Missile Crisis in 1962.

Penkovsky was almost too much of a good thing, a one-man avalanche. The sheer volume of his "take" created migraines for his handlers in the CIA and the cooperating British MI6.* And since his pride and ego were mountainous, he was given considerable latitude as to when and how to spirit his treasures into Western hands.

Now he possessed a highly perishable nugget about Berlin. What should he do with it?

Several kinds of "drops"—"dead" and "live"—had been arranged for this spy-of-spies within Moscow. But he had always considered them terribly risky. He had also been given a series of nonverbal signals—prearranged patterns of rings on certain phones of the American Embassy—but these were to be strictly reserved for the most extreme emergencies, such as imminent capture.

The greatly preferred delivery system, the surest, was also the slowest. It was Penkovsky in person, handing over masses of photographed documents and hoarsely haranguing his Western debriefers with his recollections in frantic all-night sessions in Paris

---

* Penkovsky's take was so huge, and his handlers were so determined to keep even the CIA staff from guessing his identity, that the materials coming in from him were divided up in Washington so they could be variously attributed to twelve different sources.

and London hotel rooms during his periodic trips on behalf of his Soviet bosses.

Penkovsky had returned from a London mission only a few days before Khrushchev's birthday party for Chief Marshal Varentsov. His next trip was scheduled for Paris, but not until September. So today, Thursday, August 10, it was up to him—and up to him alone—to decide how useful it would be for the West to receive a four-day advance warning of the Berlin Wall.

For better or for worse, he decided to do nothing.

"I knew you'd want to know," he would tell his partners in Paris in September. "But I could tell you only at great risk to me and I knew it would be impossible for you to do anything about it."

This was not necessarily so, but it was consistent with Penkovsky's personality. He was a man of firm opinions. Also, he was entitled to believe on Thursday, four days before the first signs of the Wall appeared, that the West with its enormous resources would receive other leaks of such a major military move, involving massive deployment of forces.

But this was not to be. Few secrets were ever better kept.

Hyannis Port, Massachusetts, Sunday, August 13, 1961

The West was on holiday, and the tall, thin man looked like a vacationer in his beach clothes. Only his face showed tension.

"This is Watchman," he said into his walkie-talkie. "I've got a top-priority message from Washington. You must turn the President around and come back to shore."

Fifteen minutes later, at about 1 P.M. on this bright and refreshingly breezy summer Sunday, President John F. Kennedy, wearing white ducks, a polo shirt, and a frown, stepped off the cabin cruiser *Marlin* at the dock of the Kennedy family compound in Hyannis Port on Cape Cod, plainly displeased by this interruption of his holiday.

"Watchman," the code name for Brigadier General Chester V. (Ted) Clifton, the President's military aide, handed him a yellow one-paragraph telex message from the White House Situation Room.

"How come we didn't know anything about this?" demanded Kennedy, looking surprised and angry. "Couldn't a tunnel have found this out?"

President John F. Kennedy relaxes with his wife Jacqueline and his father Joe aboard the cabin cruiser *Marlin* off Hyannis Port, August 1961. "How come we didn't know anything about this?" he demanded angrily when word of the Wall finally reached the Kennedy family compound.

A tunnel? Clifton retained only a dim recollection that the CIA had once tapped into Communist communications from a tunnel under Berlin. That had been in the 1950s and the Soviets had blown the secret years ago.* But Clifton understood what was happening in the President's mind. He was letting off steam and collecting his bearings. Within moments Kennedy was on the phone to Secretary of State Dean Rusk in Washington.

"What the hell is this?" he demanded. "How long have you known this? Was there any warning in the last two or three days?"

The telex said that East German troops were erecting a barbed-wire "barrier" along the East-West border in central Berlin. Traffic by foot, vehicles, and public transport had been stopped between Western and the Communist sectors of the city. Soviet divisions were on the move all around the area.

Since the end of World War II there had been talk of an "Iron Curtain" dividing East and West. The term had been symbolic. This Sunday, suddenly, the split was physical, visible, real.

General Clifton understood the President's anger. For months, Berlin had been the highest-priority trouble spot on Kennedy's agenda. His personal concern was so consuming that State Department officers had nicknamed him "the Berlin desk officer." Nobody questioned that Berlin was by far the world's most volatile flash point.

A perilous confrontation was building between the two most powerful leaders on the globe, men who could not have been less alike, each representing a system of government, a way of life, that seemed irreconcilable with the other: Kennedy commanding the Western camp, Khrushchev the East. And for the first time in history, both sides were brandishing nuclear weapons at each other and appeared ready to use them.

Khrushchev's announced willingness to wage nuclear war over Berlin was a threat of unprecedented and breath-stopping new dimensions. It had to be dealt with at once.

Yet at 1 P.M. on this vacation Sunday, the flow of information

---

* Kennedy had good reason to be thinking of the Berlin tunnel and its builder, William King Harvey, in that summer of 1961. Harvey, probably the most flamboyant of all CIA agents, had recently been placed in charge of plans to assassinate the dictator Kennedy considered to be his enemy number one, Fidel Castro (see page 95).

reaching the President was maddeningly sluggish and incomplete. An almost incredible length of time—seventeen hours—had already elapsed since the border was closed. And still the President was unable to tell: what was going on in East Berlin?

2

THE BOOK OF BÄRBEL: GROWING UP AT THE WALL

**East Berlin,
August 1961**

"Let's see your papers!"

Bärbel was not yet accustomed to hearing the command. Her neighborhood in Berlin Mitte, the grimy, gloomy center of the city, had suddenly been transformed into an armed camp. Often she heard shots, especially in the night. Policemen kept asking for her student identification card. Their snooping made her angry. Why had they become so suspicious? And if they were questioning her identity, that seemed crazy. She was who she was, Bärbel, born in the neighborhood, twelve years old and small for her age.

This time the barked demand for papers turned out not to be directed at her at all. Bärbel had been helping her mother, as usual, by standing in line at the little butcher shop on her street, Reinhardtstrasse; just as she was leaving, an officer happened to challenge an elderly man who stood waiting near the door.

The shop was at the end of Bärbel's newly truncated world, a few yards within East Berlin. Beyond lay the now forbidden West. The boundary, wide open during all of Bärbel's life, had just been barricaded by barbed-wire fencing and, at the street crossings, by three-foot-high stacks of large cement slabs—square, gray, impenetrable.

The elderly man standing in front of the butcher's looked in surprise at the pink-cheeked teenaged officer in the green *Vopo*

(*Volkspolizei*—People's Police) uniform who had demanded to see his papers.

"Why should I show my papers?" he asked. "I'm waiting for my wife. She's at the butcher's. She'll be right out."

Bärbel started back toward her apartment house, number 37, at the near corner of the next block. Passing a group of children playing on the sidewalk, she noticed that the man from the butcher shop was walking behind her. He moved slowly and looked frightened.

"Stop or I'll shoot!" came the command.

The elderly man broke into a very slow trot.

"Stop or I'll shoot!" Bärbel heard again.

The man kept lumbering down Reinhardtstrasse.

Bärbel crossed the street and turned around. Two *Vopos* came running. One stopped and shot the elderly man in the leg; he fell writhing to the pavement. The other cop, very fat, put his rifle to his cheek and, from perhaps twenty yards away, shot the injured man in the stomach.

Bärbel was so profoundly shocked that she could not think of getting away. Frozen to the sidewalk, she watched a group of workmen come running. They had obviously heard the shooting. Emerging from the small mustard factory that adjoined the butcher shop, they were about to pounce on the fat cop when four truckloads of *Vopos* pulled up, fell upon the workers with truncheons, and beat them back into the factory. Only after the street had been cleared was the wounded civilian driven to the Charité, half a block distant. The two-thousand-bed hospital was East Germany's most distinguished, but its surgeons could not save this patient. Political murder had come to Reinhardtstrasse.

At home there was almost no talk of the shooting. Bärbel was not surprised by the silence. Precocious and perceptive, she had learned to read her parents better than most children. Like the wise monkeys of ancient legend, her mother and father heard, saw, and spoke no evil. Gentle and passive, they found life tolerable and wanted only to be left in peace. Bärbel knew that many East Germans were not so passive. Until that August of 1961—specifically, until Sunday the thirteenth, a date that all Germans remember the way Americans remember the Sunday of Pearl Harbor—two thousand and more had been fleeing to the West each day. All told, four million had turned their backs on the repressive Communist regime that reminded them in so many ways of the terrible days under Hitler. Bärbel's parents would not join the refugees. Bärbel, ever the activist, was furious.

She blamed her father, Franz, who could not separate himself from his beloved work as administrator of the urology clinic at Saint Hedwig's Hospital. One of the doctors who escaped to the West had wanted to take Franz and the family along. He had offered Franz similar work at much greater pay. But that was not for Bärbel's father. Saint Hedwig's was *his* hospital, the patients were *his* patients; he could not desert them.

Overnight, in the muggy early morning hours from Saturday, August 12, to Sunday, August 13, it became too late, although Bärbel did not realize it that weekend. She was at her school's summer camp, a huge tent village in the woods near rural Neu-Brandenburg. Early Sunday morning the camp loudspeakers came alive with a brief announcement that startled everyone: the DDR (Deutsche Demokratische Republik, the official designation of East Germany) was "firmly" sealing its western border as a protective measure.

Campers and counselors became absorbed in heated discussion. The closure was inevitable, Bärbel heard people say. The brain drain westward, the exodus of doctors, academics, engineers, and others with vital skills, could not be permitted to continue. And what about the *Grenzgänger,* the forty thousand East Berlin "border crossers" who went to jobs in West Berlin each morning and returned after work to spend their West marks—worth four to five times more than the Eastern currency—buying up scarce goods? Wasn't that unpatriotic sabotage?

The split can't last, said others. Actually to cut up a city, a nation, not to speak of countless families—it can't be done. People won't stand for it, not those in the East nor those *drüben,* "over there" (as people referred to the West). Who could even remotely visualize such a bizarre fissure of the world?

Bärbel couldn't. Among the forests of Neu-Brandenburg it seemed unreal. All her life she had casually gone over to the West, often several times a day. There was no place to play on her block, so Bärbel and her friends ran and skipped across the border into the Tiergarten, Berlin's vast Central Park, three minutes away. No more Tiergarten? It couldn't happen.

Emerging from the subway a few days later, back from camp, and running up Reinhardtstrasse toward her house, she saw that it could and had. The guards had come and the barbed wire and so had the piles of cement slabs and the police demands to see her identity card. The way to her green play world, the Tiergarten, was blocked.

Frantic, she tore upstairs—five flights with no elevator—and confronted her mother, Eva, in the kitchen. Always a sensitive, book-loving child, Bärbel looked nothing like the rebel that she also was. She was a fragile, small-boned little thing, her pretty narrow face framed by silky, long, dark hair and dominated by disconcertingly large, piercing, dark eyes. Voices were rarely raised in her home, but Bärbel was uncontrollably enraged by her sudden confinement in the East, the grotesque split of her universe.

Why hadn't they left before all this happened, the way so many others had quit? Why?

Patiently, Eva reminded her that her father was a responsible person who could not be expected to abandon his patients, the two elderly grandmothers, the family home with all their possessions, to take a wife and four young children and run off with no more than the clothes on their backs, off into the unknown, where conditions might not be as rosy as promised. As the oldest child Bärbel should be sensible and understand.

Bärbel understood but could not agree.

"Now we'll never get out of here!" she screamed.

For Bärbel it wouldn't be never. It would take her twelve years to get out and the consequences would shatter her life forever.

Trapped, Bärbel embarked on the same venture that was becoming—and would remain—an obsession among her countrymen: the hunt for an escape hatch in the border. Gradually, an eleven-foot-high cinder-block wall was taking shape along the twenty-six-mile frontier zigzagging through Berlin. But it was a curious, makeshift obstacle—ugly, uneven, less monolithic yet more ingenious and escape resistant than outsiders could imagine.

The East German authorities, short of everything except gall and cunning, took advantage of all existing construction and natural barriers. In Bärbel's neighborhood the first hurdle was the Spree, Berlin's Hudson River, some four hundred feet wide. Several electrified fences, spaced well apart, came next, and then the dark redbrick wall of the 275-acre Charité Hospital complex. The entire area was overseen around the clock by *Vopos*, always two working as a team, with one keeping an eye on the other while they peered from a chain of new observation towers.

Bärbel faced not one obstacle but an intricate network of inter-locking fortifications.

The hospital's thick, ancient wall stretched within easy running distance of the river, and so night after night, for months, Bärbel crept past the bricks, probing for weak spots in the masonry. She found none. All the time the border around her became more tightly sealed. The work would never stop.

The bridge across the Spree was blown up. The Reinhardtstrasse subway stop was barricaded. The rupture of Bärbel's East-West universe was complete. Tall new lamps and batteries of search-lights turned night into day. Old structures near the water were gradually razed; sand was carted in and spread to create a no-man's-land more than one hundred feet wide; the death strip was regularly raked to reveal any footstep.

Feeling hopelessly imprisoned, Bärbel abandoned her attempts to get out and concentrated on organizing resistance from within. It did not strike her as quixotic that a twelve-year-old was challeng-ing a police state. She modeled her life after books in which such things were done. Years later, behind the bars of East German prisons, she thought of literature as her vicarious existence. She called it her "substitute life."

Back in August of 1961 her use of reading was anything but vicarious. The book that stirred her most at the time was *Each One Dies His Own Death,* a novel by Hans Fallada.* Published right after World War II, the novel chronicled the revolt of Otto Quangel, a carpenter, and his wife, Anna, who confessed under Gestapo tor-ture that they had handwritten 259 subversive cards and eight letters and stuck them under the doors of Berlin householders between 1940 and 1942 to protest the death of their son at the front.

"The Führer has murdered our son," said the cards. "The Führer will murder your sons too."

---

* Fallada had gained international prominence with his 1931 novel, *Little Man, What Now?* The title gained prominence as a slogan in pre-Hitler Germany. It lamented the ordinary individual's inability to decide his own fate and therefore leaving its determination to the totalitarian state. In World War II, the phrase *"kleiner Mann"* ("little man") regained currency among Germans trying to excuse their lamblike willingness to follow Hitler's orders. *"Ich bin ja nur ein kleiner Mann"* ("I'm only a little man") was the defensive denial of responsibility that we heard from ranking officers during prisoner-of-war interrogations. This was the go-along-get-along philosophy that Bärbel Grübel refused to adopt to make life easier for herself in the DDR.

Otto Quangel was executed by guillotine. His wife died in prison during an aerial bombing.

Bärbel decided to improve the couple's methods and put her refinements to work in real life, against the contemporary counterparts of the Nazis, the DDR Communists.

In a stationery store she located a primitive typesetting and printing kit. She also bought a stack of cheap paper and a pair of thin gloves. While her family was asleep, she put on the gloves to be sure she would leave no fingerprints and, pecking out her text letter by letter, spent all night composing and printing some three hundred leaflets. In childish phrases she demanded the assassination of Walter Ulbricht, the dictator of the DDR, the man responsible for the hated Wall and the shootings on Reinhardtstrasse. Bärbel called him "the bloodhound." To her, he was like Fallada's Hitler.

At dawn she stuffed the leaflets into her school bag and dropped copies in neighborhood mailboxes, making sure not to leave out her own house. Fallada's book had taught her that failure to include it would identify it as the likely source of the illicit literature.

As she ducked out of one apartment building, she encountered two *Vopos,* who asked for her papers. She bolted and ran, the police in pursuit. Bärbel was fast on her feet and knew the neighborhood hallways and rear exits. In one of the backyards she quickly heaved her remaining leaflets into a garbage can and dashed into the byways of the Charité Hospital grounds. Eventually she lost the soldiers, who were slower, but she never dared to distribute literature again.

If she couldn't call on the neighbors to do away with Ulbricht, she would personally try taking on the job of eliminating him.* She knew the shelf where the school chemistry lab kept a bottle of nitroglycerin. She would use the explosive to blow up the Volkskammer, the rubber-stamp parliament chaired by Ulbricht. That would catch him and his party cronies. But the lab was locked and Bärbel could not gain possession of the explosive.

Next she decided to try civil disobedience. She felt this tactic would work better if she had allies, so she again attempted to enlist the neighbors. The ideal time and place for her recruiting cam-

---

* Bärbel was not alone in her thinking. The West German intelligence service (BND) proposed the assassination of Ulbricht to the CIA, but the Americans were busy trying to assassinate Fidel Castro and other undesirable statesmen and declined.

paign was in the shops, when everybody was standing in line, impatiently and interminably (or so it seemed), for the basics of life. Vegetables and fruit were of poor quality and available only sporadically. Such luxuries as real coffee were extremely expensive, unaffordable for many. Shoppers muttered and cursed, unloosening the candor and black humor endemic to Berliners, the cockneys of central Europe.*

Bärbel used her place in the lines to stir up the resentment of the shoppers by offering them her ideas of economic sabotage, including a buyers' strike against coffee prices. Nobody betrayed interest in her notions, especially since they came from a twelve-year-old. Grumbling sufficed as an outlet for the shoppers' anger. In all the long time while Bärbel was speaking up to foment resistance, nobody reported her illegal conduct to the authorities, but the cowardice of the neighbors reinforced her mounting disenchantment over the passivity of all the adults she happened to know, going back years before the Wall went up.

Her rebellion had begun as childish muscle-flexing against authority. En route to play in the Tiergarten (Was there ever grass greener on the other side of the fence?) Bärbel and her school comrades had made a habit of annoying the Eastern cops at the border.

"Nyeh, nyeh, nyeh," the children taunted them while running across the invisible line between East and West. "You can't get at us over here!" It was a richly satisfying game.

From the Western border police Bärbel expected sympathy but received none. Perhaps the officers were embarrassed when she mentioned touchy topics. Perhaps they were instructed to stay neutral, to steer clear of controversy. Bärbel was an inconvenient child. She was a veritable walking questionnaire, firing questions at every opportunity. *Why* was Berlin divided into two political systems? *Why* was life in her area, and all over the East, so much more

---

* Food supplies have much improved since the 1960s, but shortages and waiting in line remain trademarks of life and political jokes in the DDR. Typical is the dialogue between a woman and a mechanic whom she has asked to fix her car. "Of course," he replies, "but only if you give me a night in return." The woman reluctantly agrees. "Fine, then get in line at the grocery store—they've got onions! I'll relieve you in the morning."

deprived and restrictive, almost as if World War II had never ended? The Western cops were not informative.

When Bärbel and her friends, at the ages of seven and eight years, ventured into the shopping districts of West Berlin, they were dazzled by the opulence, the noise, the incredible volume of traffic, the lavish neon lights, all so different from home, all unexplained. Poorly dressed, feeling like country bumpkins, they tried to understand the riches flung at them by the West. Nobody helped to explain the why, why, why, the bane of all children. The adults, those wise heads expected to know all answers, failed Bärbel and her friends.

One morning, without warning, the children's favorite teacher did not come to school. Word leaked out that she had defected to the West. To their delight, Bärbel and her friends were able to locate the teacher's new apartment in West Berlin, and they dropped in. It was a bittersweet encounter. Bärbel found it frustrating. She asked the teacher *why* she had found it possible to leave her work, her students; *why* she had chosen to take a chance on making a fresh start in the more impersonal, much more competitive, money-oriented West.

Was the teacher taken aback at the sophistication of the questions? Did she think these children were too young for answers in depth? Did she fear that the real answers would make the lives of her former charges intolerable back home? Bärbel never found out. She remembered only that the teacher's answers were banal, not truly responsive; that she talked mostly of the material comforts, the prosperity of Western life, of nothing that Bärbel didn't already know. When another popular teacher went West—he was an older man—Bärbel didn't trouble to trail him.

Bärbel had her first encounter with physical danger two years before the Wall, in 1959, when she was ten and it had already been long forbidden to import Western books, newspapers, and magazines to Reinhardtstrasse. Not daring to flout the law, Bärbel's parents, as well as the parents of her friends, asked their children to smuggle in such forbidden items. It was another custom that eroded Bärbel's esteem for adults.

The smuggling was a hide-and-seek game until a *Vopo* stopped her one afternoon after she had slowly walked across the border with a suspiciously distended belly. She ran, terrified. Her magazines fluttered to the ground. Would they shoot at a child? It seemed unlikely but not impossible. When she reached the door of her apartment house, shaking, she tucked herself behind the entrance. It was an absurdly obvious hiding place, which was probably why several *Vopos,* bustling up and down the stairs and barging into apartments, never found her. After they left, Bärbel hid behind the door for a very long time before daring to go to her apartment.

By then she had read the nonfictional *Diary of Anne Frank* and learned the fate of young girls who incurred the displeasure of German authorities. She had also made it her business to read other accounts and watch films about Hitler's Third Reich. The parallels between then and now appeared uncanny and quite obvious to her.

Bärbel only had to keep her eyes open in her neighborhood to spot the similarities, and she was good at using her eyes. She watched as neighbors were led away by men wearing dark leather coats, just as the Gestapo had done. Only the name of the secret police had changed. Now it was nicknamed *Stasi* (for *Staatssicherheit,* or State Security), but its agents were equally dreaded.

The torchlight parades and rallies of the ruling political party were as noisy and frequent as under the Nazis; only the initials of the party were different: it used to be called the NSDAP,* now it was the SED.† Both used the label "socialist" fraudulently. Hitler's party was Nazi, Ulbricht's was Communist. Both were repressive, neither tolerated opposition.

Then and now enormous banners fluttered from major buildings and carried much the same messages. Under Hitler, the huge block letters exhorted, "Germany, awake!" Under Ulbricht, they demanded that workers exceed their production quotas. Both regimes made every banner red, always red, bloodred.

And the parallels between then and now invaded life on Reinhardtstrasse.

Just as Anne Frank's parents had taken Anne to Holland, more and more East Berliners had immigrated to West Germany, and as the exodus of Bärbel's neighbors grew, it became more noticeable in the neighborhood. Whenever a family left, their apartment was

---

* Nationalsozialistische Deutsche Arbeiterpartei (National Socialist German Workers Party).

† Sozialistische Einheitspartei Deutschlands (Socialist Unity Party of Germany).

searched and the door was shut off with a large official red seal. In the years before 1961 Bärbel had seen a great many such seals along Reinhardtstrasse. They looked ominous, all the more so because in films about the Nazis, Bärbel had seen Gestapo agents place similar red seals on the apartment doors of Jews who had fled or been herded into concentration camps.

Bärbel watched the reactions of the adults who stayed behind, especially when they passed by the sealed doors of the families who had committed the crime known as *Republikflucht* (flight from the Republic). The grown-ups would scurry quickly past these doors as if the homes were contaminated by a contagious virus. They would not even look in the direction of the doors.

Bärbel was disgusted and concluded that grown-ups must have acted in the same way when they passed the apartments of Jews in Hitler's time. It made Bärbel feel terribly alone, but she was pleased to have found an answer to one of her many questions: she had figured out how Hitler had managed to remain in power until the Allies defeated him in war. Fear. Indifference. Man's inhumanity to man. All had served Hitler then, as they were serving Ulbricht now.

After the Wall came into Bärbel's life, the Ulbricht regime turned into a palpable presence right in her home. Regularly, on Monday morning, men in long leather coats picked up her father in an unmarked car. They were from the *Stasi* and they took Franz to the Alexanderplatz for hours of interrogation. Several Western doctors were working at his hospital—his department chief was Swiss—and the police wanted Franz to spy on them. He refused, telling his interrogators that his work was his sole interest, which was true, and that the doctors were doing nothing wrong, which was true insofar as Franz knew.

The *Stasi* summonses continued every Monday for months, Bärbel's family never being sure that Franz would be permitted to come home that night. Eventually the interrogations ceased, the police evidently having given up on Franz as innocent and hopeless.

But one Monday afternoon Bärbel returned home from school and saw her family sitting, as if paralyzed, around the dining-room table. Nobody uttered a word. Several *Vopos* had just barged in, and the leader was announcing that they had come to search the apartment.

Bärbel's parents were easily frightened. They abhorred controversy and invariably evaded Bärbel's questions about politics. They
wanted to stay uninvolved, neutral. Bärbel never ceased to hate
them for being so different from the few feisty souls who had resisted the Nazis, the heroes in her books. Yet even her obedient father and mother violated DDR law in small ways. Not satisfied with
the clichés of the party press, they loved the forbidden *Westlitera-
tur* (Western literature) that their kids smuggled across the border.

Bärbel had not been spotted that Monday afternoon when she
entered the apartment and heard the voices of rummaging policemen, so she ducked from room to room, hiding incriminating
books and journals (even West Berlin fashion magazines were forbidden), and she managed to keep the house search cursory by a
clever trick. Every home was constantly flooded with Communist
propaganda, so she pulled some of these tracts off the shelves and
scattered them about, quickly opening up some of the pages to
make it appear as if the handouts were being eagerly studied.

When the searchers departed, Bärbel felt triumphant. She had
led Ulbricht's detested henchmen around by the nose. And she
had done it, again, alone.

Continuing her campaign to recruit allies, Bärbel tried to persuade schoolmates to form an underground conspiracy. Nobody
mustered enough nerve to join her. Some youngsters did pitch in
by drawing goatees on school posters of Communist heroes. The
goatee had become a national symbol (Ulbricht wore one and indeed was nicknamed "the Goatee," which qualified this mischief as
an act of opposition). *Stasi* agents came to Bärbel's school and investigated. Although their snooping did not uncover anything, it
served to squelch further opposition at the school.

Eventually she linked up with a like-minded comrade, after all.
Her friend Petra also lived on Reinhardtstrasse, also in a top-floor
apartment, but Petra's corner building directly overlooked the border, from hardly fifteen feet distant. The DDR's desperate housing
shortage notwithstanding, the building would eventually be razed,
like a great many others all along the border, to open up more
space for the still-proliferating frontier fortifications. During the
years of Bärbel's adolescence, however, Petra's apartment remained an amphitheater that offered spectacular viewing to the
girls.

Westward from the living room they looked across the Wall into their former playground: the British sector and the expanse of the Tiergarten, with its sunbathers, picnickers, and young trees—reminders of the war's bomb damage and the later hardships when every surviving tree was carted off for firewood. Looking north from the kitchen, the girls' view took in the Charité Hospital grounds, the Spree River, and the Wall meandering for miles toward the French sector.

In Petra's room, facing south and southwest, the girls had front-row seats to a sweep of German history, a carpetful of landmarks too crowded to be absorbed all at once.

The ministries of governments, dating from before the glory days of the Kaiser to Ulbricht's Spartan rule; the unmarked sites where Hitler was anointed Führer by torchlight and where he killed himself amid smoking ruins; the broad, tree-lined Unter den Linden, with its embassies, theaters, museums; the golden cupola of the Reichstag, the parliament that became an international cause célèbre when a demented Dutch arsonist torched it; and the two-hundred-year-old symbol of the city, the Brandenburg Gate, topped with the chariot driven by (Who was mocking whom here?) the goddess of victory.

Beyond the dozen Doric columns of the Gate, Bärbel and Petra could see far into the West, the island of their fantasies, to the restored spire of the Kaiser Wilhelm Memorial Church; at night the sea of lights, so lavish and shiny, clearly distinguished the American sector. There—it was the wish that dominated their lives like an unstilled appetite—they hoped their future would lie.

Bärbel appreciated her access to Petra's apartment as a gift almost too lucky to be true. For years, often several afternoons a week, she kept gazing down upon her schizoid world, moving from windowsill to windowsill, scanning in three directions like a private radar beam. It was the prisoner's view through the bars of her cell. The scene mesmerized her and drew her into the action between the players moving about directly below.

She knew that she must not be suspected of spying, so she usually stayed far enough away from the window to remain hidden from the binoculars of the *Vopos* in the observation towers. At the same time she wanted to demonstrate whose side she was on, so she sometimes stepped up to smile and wave to the Western military police patrolling in their Jeeps along the Tiergarten side of the river. Whenever an MP spotted her and waved back, she squealed with delight; her sympathies had been recognized.

Bärbel and Petra also lived with the Wall from a ground-level perspective, learning with envy that certain people slipped through the concrete all the time at will, back and forth. During lunch recess, the girls raced from their school on Hannoversche Strasse to the nearest border checkpoint and stood staring at these higher beings—mostly diplomats and lawyers—who were immune to the laws that kept plain mortals confined to the lesser side of the world. How easily these privileged classes moved between East and West, as if the Wall did not exist!

The undiminished eagerness of Bärbel's less fortunate fellow citizens to seek their exit was one of the best-publicized secrets of the DDR. West German TV never stopped crowing about the ingenuity of successful escapes. Bärbel knew what was happening without needing evidence of TV pictures or the hair-raising (and usually true) tales that made the rounds by word of mouth. She merely circulated in her neighborhood and kept surveying the scene through Petra's panoramic windows.

In her eyewitness experience, few of these ventures wound up with happy endings. Peering north from the kitchen one afternoon, she spotted a male civilian hurriedly taking off his clothes on a hillock near the Charité Hospital. Dumbfounded, she saw a *Vopo* atop the nearest guard tower getting ready to fire his Kalashnikov automatic submachine gun. His movements seemed deliberate, casual; he was in no rush. Then the scene exploded. The man jumped into the Spree River; Bärbel screamed; gunfire sounded not from one but three nearby guard towers. The man thrashed his arms and sank.

Several open reconnaissance vehicles arrived momentarily. *Vopos* fished the body out of the water. Shortly afterward Bärbel could see the man being driven down Reinhardtstrasse, bleeding all over but still moving. The next day the paper reported that a thirty-five-year-old "criminal" had tried to flee the country and had died in the attempt.

Violence never left Bärbel's life after that. Walking home from Petra's house, she saw a Jeep dashing away from the border and turning the corner toward the Charité. Next to the driver a man lay sprawled with a copiously bleeding hole in his head, another intercepted border crosser. Some *Vopo* victims did not even have escape on their minds. Petra and her mother watched the shooting of two lovers who had made the mistake of picking a spot near the Charité for a tête-à-tête. Their crime was necking.

Nights were the worst times. There was little to see, too much to hear and to imagine. Sometimes shots came from signal pistols whose rockets only lighted up the border area, but scattered firing was Bärbel's bedtime music. The café on the ground floor had to close, to be turned into a *Vopo* post. After the officers had a few beers, they belted out marching songs and kept the neighborhood awake until very late. During the night Bärbel would be awakened by more shots. She would rush to the window and see the lights of police vehicles careening about.

She did not believe in God, yet every night she prayed for her personal terror on Reinhardtstrasse to end. It never did. After she had married and moved around the corner from her parents' house, the shooting, by then less frequent, kept awakening her own children, the third generation forced to live with the Wall.

3

"THE DISAPPEARING SATELLITE"

**West Berlin,
mid-March 1961**

Some crises break like sudden thunderstorms with little or no warning. Others emit wispy smoke signals in advance. The coming of the Berlin Wall was more palpable. It was, in fact, practically visible to my old friend, the bearlike, bass-voiced George Bailey, and he described it five months ahead of time. He did so in a prestigious and very public place, and his fantasy was quite precise.

Bailey covered Germany as a correspondent for *The Reporter,* then a political magazine respected and carefully read by Washington insiders, including President Kennedy. Bailey was known to know his way around. He was a former U.S. Army intelligence officer, a graduate of Columbia and Oxford, multilingual, a man-about-Europe.* His prophetic article in the March 16 issue of *The Reporter,* titled "The Disappearing Satellite," vividly described all

---

* Bailey's versatility is a rarity among born Americans. A native of Milwaukee, Bailey is fluent in German, Russian, and several other Eastern languages. He is also a certified right-winger and passionate anti-Communist, whom the Reagan administration made director of the American propaganda station in Munich, Radio Liberty, where he presided over a clique-ridden staff of balky refugees. My friends and I considered Bailey an honorary Jew as well, because he married Beate Ullstein of the illustrious German-Jewish publishing clan.

but the Wall's concrete: "Khrushchev will . . . ring down the Iron Curtain in front of East Berlin—with searchlights and machine gun towers, barbed wire, and police dog patrols. Technically this is feasible."

Bailey mustered a convincing case. He cited a 1958 speech by Otto Grotewohl in which the East German Prime Minister conceded with surprising candor that the "continuing flight from the Republic is Problem Number 1" and that it "cannot go on." The Communists were clearly desperate, and Bailey's analysis of their situation was shrewd.

Perhaps because the flow of refugees had been in progress for so long, its explosive nature had never been fully appreciated. This was no emigration problem. It was a population emergency, a national bloodletting. The four million East Germans who had left their homeland since the end of the war constituted the greatest voluntary mass migration in recorded European history. And the wave of migrants was more or less undiminished as it continued into its seventeenth year. In 1960, almost 200,000 had left the DDR. In 1961, there might be more, because 16,700 had crossed into the West in the cold of January alone.

The hierarchy of reasons given by the refugees for leaving their country was fascinating and largely unknown until Bailey reported their priorities. "Political pressure" was only the third-ranking factor reported by the migrants. The second reason was "lack of opportunity to travel abroad." The principal cause was "unsatisfactory or insufficient education of children." The refugees were not so much objecting to the favoritism shown to "workers' and peasants' offspring" or the increasing lack of qualified teachers; when questioned in detail, the migrants made clear that they simply did not want their children educated along Communist lines.

Ideology was their motivator, not Western affluence.

Throughout the 1950s, experts had remarked upon the relatively large number of highly qualified professionals among the refugees. In "The Disappearing Satellite," Bailey documented that the defections in some categories were creating consequences of catastrophic dimensions. The shortage of doctors was especially worrisome to the DDR authorities. In 1960, 698 physicians had left. Since 1954, 3,100 doctors had fled—about one fifth of all doctors practicing in East Germany when the DDR was formally established in 1949! In some rural East German areas, no doctor was available within forty miles.

Most critical of all, as Bailey pointed out, was the effect of the

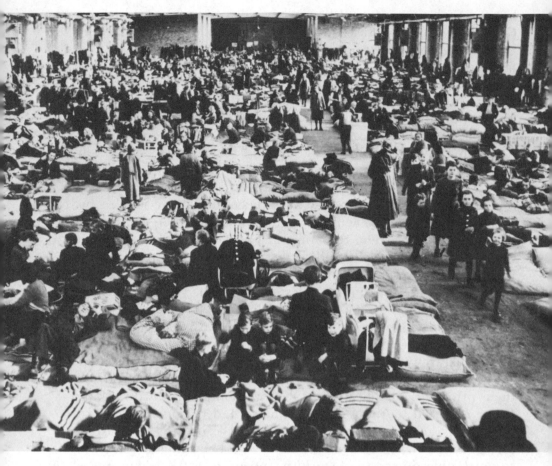

East German escapees crowd a West Berlin refugee center, summer 1961. Between 1945 and 1961, well over four million East Germans left their homeland for the West, the greatest voluntary mass migration in recorded European history.

exodus on the aging of the DDR population as a whole. The country was threatened with extinction by death as well as defection.

"The striking aspect of the refugee flow is its uniformity," Bailey explained. "Throughout the past sixteen years, fifty per cent of the annual total of refugees have always been under 25, seventy-four per cent under 45, and ninety percent under 65. The effect of these numbers on the population structure of East Germany has been staggering. . . . The mass of the population has either retired or is approaching retirement. . . ."

This satellite was truly disappearing. Grotewohl was right. If his nation was to survive, the flow absolutely had to stop, and Bailey saw signs that the East was about to act. He wrote: "There are some indications that the Soviet Union and its East German minions have finally drawn the ultimate conclusion: the only way to stop refugees is to seal off both East Berlin and the Soviet Zone by total physical security measures. The regime has already alerted specialized Communist formations to man the East Berlin sector boundary sometime this spring—bringing up surly Saxons to replace good-natured Berliners along the sector patrol routes. They are transferring tough and experienced customs officers from zonal border duty to check points in the city. . . ."

Although Bailey did not know it until years later, Kennedy read the article and had its facts and conclusions checked.

The secret Wall was no secret. In their own convoluted way, even the East Germans were talking about it.

East Berlin,
Thursday, June 15, 1961

Some 350 correspondents gathered in the former Hermann Göring Air Ministry for one of Walter Ulbricht's rare press conferences—and missed the news he made.

Annamarie Doherr, short and heavy but canny and experienced, asked on behalf of the West German *Frankfurter Rundschau* whether the boss of the DDR intended to shift the border of his country to the Brandenburg Gate in the center of town.

Icy as usual, Ulbricht replied: "I understand your question to imply that there are people in West Germany who would like to see us mobilize the construction workers of the capital of the DDR for the purpose of building a wall. I am not aware of any such intention. The construction workers of our city are for the most part busy building apartment houses, and their working capacities are fully employed to that end. Nobody intends to put up a wall. . . ."

Eventually, this statement would be exhumed and autopsied by intelligence experts and scholars like a freshly discovered coded signal from Mount Olympus. Why would Ulbricht drop a reference to a "wall" when no one had mentioned the concept? Had this most deliberate of dialecticians committed a Freudian slip? Such afterthoughts came later. At the time, Ulbricht's maneuver was overlooked by the press and Western intelligence.

One exception was a group of four émigré television viewers gathered in West Berlin to catch their archadversary's press conference on the evening network news. Fritz Schenk was among them. He and his friends were knowledgeable former officials of the DDR.* The moment Ulbricht denied his intention to build a wall, they broke into derisive shouts and laughter. In 1985, Schenk told me: "We were sure that he'd build one."

---

* The other insiders were Erich W. Gniffke, once Ulbricht's executive assistant; Wolfgang Leonhard, who had come with Ulbricht from Moscow in 1945; and Heinz Brandt, a union leader who had spent years in Ulbricht's prisons.

4

KENNEDY AT THE VIENNA SUMMIT CONFERENCE: "ROUGHEST THING IN MY LIFE"

**Vienna,
Tuesday, June 6, 1961**

"Miscalculation" had been one of John Kennedy's favorite words long before he became President. As a Harvard student he had taken a course on the origins of World War I and had been shocked by how easily one nation's misinterpretation of another's intention could set them sliding into war.* As President, he often lectured his staff on the fatal miscalculation known to experts as "accidental war." Kennedy's point was evident: he was determined not to add to the long history of misjudging an adversary; he would not let inadvertence lead him into battle, especially not battle of the nuclear variety.

The Berlin crisis of 1961 would never be recognized as a time of acute nuclear danger. Yet it was. It was the first time that a major power openly threatened another with nuclear annihilation. Only Khrushchev himself knew whether his bark about his arsenal of missiles might actually lead to an atomic bite.

---

* Kennedy was delighted when *The Guns of August* by Barbara Tuchman further confirmed his discovery. He recommended this brilliant best-seller to his White House staff, but not in time for the 1961 Berlin crisis. The book was not published until 1962, another peak period of the Cold War but the year after the Berlin Wall went up.

With the Wall crisis came a behind-the-scenes debate within the United States government about the when and how of using ultimate weapons whose damage not only would be cataclysmic but, in effect, irreversible. This debate would still remain unsettled toward the end of the century. In 1961 only its outlines were taking shape. And at its center was the appalling risk of one nuclear power misunderstanding the resolve of the other.

The President was barely seated in the gray and red music room of the American Embassy in charming (and neutral) Vienna for his first summit session with Nikita Khrushchev when he introduced this topic to the redoubtable Soviet Premier. It was, after all, crucial.

Kennedy had entered the deceptively gracious Vienna setting in the belief that he was not misjudging his bulky adversary. In his choleric way, this onetime Ukrainian farm boy had lately taken off his shoe and banged it on his desk at the United Nations to protest a Western delegate's speech.* The President's preparations for the encounter with this quaint figure had, in consequence, been clinically precise.

CIA psychologists had briefed Kennedy to beware of an abrupt Khrushchev maneuver; the Russian liked to switch with dramatic suddenness from a "hearty and appealing personality" to apparently uncontrolled rage. The President had also been warned against "getting Khrushchev too tired." Kennedy was to keep an eye on the Russian's left temple vein; its swelling would betray that Khrushchev was getting irritated.

But subtle clues quickly proved irrelevant. Everybody, it seemed, had underestimated (miscalculated) the Russian's intransigence. The very term "miscalculation" enraged him.

"Khrushchev went berserk," Kennedy told an aide while soaking his sore back in the bathtub afterward. "He started yelling, 'Miscalculation! Miscalculation! Miscalculation! All I ever hear from your people and your news correspondents and your friends in Europe and everyplace else is that damned word "miscalculation"! You ought to take that word and bury it in cold storage and never use it again! I'm sick of it.' " The concept, Khrushchev said, was too vague and "Western," just another "clever way of making threats."

---

* The Soviet delegation was fined $10,000 for this rupture of UN etiquette.

Khrushchev and Kennedy meet in Vienna, June 1961. The American President was shaken by the Soviet Premier's nuclear ultimatum.

Walking with the President in the garden after their first session, Khrushchev kept up the heat, circling around Kennedy, snapping at him like a terrier, shaking his finger. And from this tempestuous beginning the tone of the three-day summit turned more and more specifically threatening until Khrushchev unleashed the world's first nuclear ultimatum. His target was Berlin, and the confrontation was unprecedented at several levels.

The ideologies of the two men could not have been more totally polarized, nor could the disparities between their personalities have been more dramatic: the elegant, sophisticated product of wealth faced the earthy primitive. The clash of cultures was equally radical: the carefully calculating technocrat was pitched against the moody emotionalism, the "soul" that the Russians loved to talk about.

Miscalculation? These two leaders were made for it.

And overshadowing their jousting hung the question never posed before with such stark immediacy: would either of them actually *use* nuclear weapons, and upon what provocation?

For the President, the Vienna Summit came at an unfortunate time. Only seven weeks earlier, the champagne air of "Camelot"—his heady first days in the White House—had dissipated when the covert operations of the CIA led him into the first great miscalculation of his presidency, the invasion of Castro's Cuba at the Bay of Pigs.

"How could I have been so stupid to let them go ahead?" he fumed contritely at his counsel Theodore C. Sorensen.

This was a fulmination; stupidity had little to do with the humiliating defeat at the Bay of Pigs. As Kennedy knew by then, and as I had occasion to trace in detail many years later,* the causes of this quixotic setback were less abstract and more complex. The expedition failed principally because the CIA was not qualified to orchestrate such a relatively large military operation in secret, and because the agency kept lying to the President, especially when it promised a revolt inside Cuba and assured him that this invasion force could make a getaway in case of disaster. Supposedly it could "melt into the mountains" (which were in fact much too distant).

---

* My postmortem was the book *Bay of Pigs—The Untold Story* (Simon and Schuster, 1979).

Fundamentally the venture miscarried because the inexperienced President didn't know how to get the best advice out of his staff and because he had, in effect, no secretary of state—a void that would plague him throughout the Berlin crisis and beyond.

Kennedy had quite deliberately designed the functioning of his White House in that pattern. It suited him. The Eisenhower staff style had struck him as too rigid, too hierarchical, too cluttered by committees, too dependent on a strong Chief of Staff, and so JFK dimantled the general's pyramid and substituted a wheel, for which he was the hub. The system was working superbly by 1962, after Kennedy had learned to tame it creatively, and generated shrewd counsel for the Cuban Missile Crisis. In 1961, however, during the Bay of Pigs, it led him to rely excessively on self-serving specialists while cutting him off from the common sense of analytical generalists, notably his brother Robert and his intimate Ted Sorensen, loyalists who had no parochial axes to grind.

The job of secretary of state—the most senior member of the cabinet and normally the architect of foreign policy, the field by which modern presidents tend to be judged—was effectively left vacant from the start. Kennedy considered the post so crucial that he wanted to be his own secretary of state.

Robert Lovett, the elder statesman who initially advised JFK on cabinet selections, elicited the admission that this was the premeditated choice of the President-elect.

"Do you want a secretary of state, or do you really want an *under* secretary?" Lovett asked Kennedy.

Kennedy laughed and replied, "Well, I guess I want an under secretary."

In that case Dean Rusk would be ideal, Lovett said. Then president of the Rockefeller Foundation, Rusk, fifty-two, was the quintessential staff functionary—unflappable, subdued, cautious, endlessly patient, tirelessly hardworking, master of technical detail on a staggering encyclopedia of subjects. He was an Oxford scholarship graduate and intellectually brilliant, although his bald, round head and his bland face made him look, depending on the observer, like a bartender or a Buddha.

"Rusk is the best explainer of things I know," Lovett told Kennedy, and indeed nobody excelled the Secretary at articulating a consensus reached by others. He liked to define, not to decide. A team player, he got along with everyone, even the most reactionary senators. It helped that Rusk could outsit and outrepeat any opponent in any negotiation. He was not, however, a leader of any sort or an incisive counselor, being chiefly interested in his own survival. Worse, his devotion to the chain of command—or his lack of self-confidence—often nudged him into exercising discretion to a point that could only be called furtive. The President and some of his colleagues found this withdrawal infuriating.

Mac Bundy, the National Security adviser, liked to tell the disdainful fiction of six officials meeting with the President and being asked by Rusk to leave so the Secretary could tell the Chief Executive what he thought. Once the others had departed, the President asked Rusk for his views, whereupon the Secretary supposedly said, "Well, if there weren't so many of us in the room . . ."

It was far more than the nuances of organization and personality that shook up the Soviets about the Bay of Pigs episode and encouraged them to bluff at Vienna, and again during the Berlin Wall crisis and beyond. Abram Chayes, a Kennedy appointee who was legal adviser to the State Department, analyzed the fallout of the Cuban adventure on the Russians in this way:

> First, I think it gave [them] the sense that there wasn't a totally responsible team in charge here, that they [Americans] were erratic and you couldn't really predict what was going to happen and therefore you better be pretty darn rough to make sure they didn't do something irretrievable. Secondly, I think the Russians could not possibly understand why, having undertaken this and gone and done what we did, we didn't finish it off. That, I think, raised at least the possibility in the minds of many Russian leaders that there was some failure of nerve here to be played upon.

The dual role of Berlin had become very clear to Kennedy back then: the city was a symbol of American commitment; it was also a bargaining chip in the East-West poker game. He mentioned this perception to former Vice President Richard Nixon, who called on him right after the CIA's pitiful 1,400-man brigade of Cuban immigrants had been taken prisoner. Nixon suggested that the President respond with a full-scale invasion of Cuba by American troops.

"I would find proper legal cover and I would go in," Nixon advised.

"There is a good chance that if we move on Cuba, Khrushchev will move on Berlin," Kennedy countered. It was not his most important reason for shuddering at Nixon's idea. Mostly he did not want to escalate a retrievable disaster into a possibly irretrievable one. Yet he was telling Nixon the truth: Berlin figured in his thinking about any number of other, seemingly unrelated, headaches.

"He's imprisoned by Berlin," said Interior Secretary Stewart Udall after trying to talk to the President about conservation. Others noted that the subterranean depth to which JFK penetrated the Berlin scene was astonishing. He tracked incoming cables and cleared many messages before they went to the Secretary of State for signature. He read transcripts of every conference. Once he questioned Mayor Willy Brandt about the politics of the East Berlin mayor's brother; Brandt did not even know the man *had* a brother.

After the Bay of Pigs, Kennedy accused himself of listening too uncritically to the terrible advice he got from the CIA experts ("all my life I've known better than to depend on the experts"). And still more bad advice kept coming. For Vienna, much of his expert counsel was as wrong on Khrushchev's strategy as it was on the Russian's personality. The official State Department briefing paper told JFK that Khrushchev was "likely" to assume "an attitude of reasonable firmness, coupled with a pitch for improved U.S.–Soviet relations." The experts said that the Soviet leader "would prefer that the talks end on a note of accord."

Briefed to expect that Khrushchev would "probably" display "considerable flexibility," Kennedy in fact found the Russian unyielding in the "irrevocable" demand that America get out of West Berlin. To this end the Soviet Union would, before year's end, sign a peace treaty with the DDR (whose existence the United States did not recognize).

Kennedy asked: Would this mean that American access to West Berlin would be blocked? It would, said Khrushchev. Kennedy gave no ground. He said this was not acceptable.

"I want peace," said Khrushchev, "but if you want war, then that is your problem."*

---

* Khrushchev had rattled his missiles over Berlin before. After the battle for the city first began to heat up, in 1958, he told Ambassador Averell Harriman: "Your generals talk of maintaining your position in Berlin with force. That is bluff. If you send in tanks, they will burn and make no mistake about it. If you want war, you can have it, but remember, it will be your war. Our rockets will fly *automatically*" (emphasis added). Allied nuclear strategists shuddered. They figured that Khrushchev was the bluffer, but then they set to wondering how much of the human command and control over their nuclear weapons the Soviets had aban-

"If that is true," Kennedy responded, holding firm in the face of the ultimate threat, "it is going to be a cold winter."

The next evening, Khrushchev sang, danced, and beat the drums at a reception in Moscow.

Kennedy's aides found the President "deeply disturbed."

"Is it always like this?" he asked his Ambassador to Moscow.

"Par for the course."

"Pretty rough?" the President was asked by James Reston, the influential *New York Times* columnist.

"Roughest thing in my life," said Kennedy. "He just beat the hell out of me."

Some of JFK's aides believed he was overreacting. Kennedy thought that Khrushchev was overreacting; the Russian obviously thought the President was too soft and inexperienced to stand up to the Soviets—another chilling example of "miscalculation."

"I've got a terrible problem," JFK told Reston. "If he thinks I'm inexperienced and have no guts, until we remove those ideas we won't get anywhere with him. So we have to act."

The President now calculated there was one chance in five that Berlin would lead to nuclear war. But who could be sure? Perhaps the risk was greater?

The President was using the press to convince Khrushchev that he was serious about the defense of Berlin and that he was willing to use nuclear weapons if he was pushed too far. "If Khrushchev wants to rub my nose in the dirt," he told his friend the columnist Jimmy Wechsler, for publication in the (then liberal) *New York Post,* "then it's all over."

Privately, Kennedy was of a less (but not much less) apocalyptic mind about Khrushchev's intentions. Despite the Russian's outrageous behavior at Vienna, Kennedy was certain of one conclusion: the man was sane. On the last day of the summit, the President told one of his closest personal assistants, Kenneth P. O'Donnell, "Anybody who talks the way he did today, and really means it, would be crazy, and I'm sure he's not crazy."

---

doned and delegated to computers. When the Chinese invaded Korea in 1950, President Truman, a noted poker player, displayed not much more respect for "nuclears." He told the press that the use of atomic weapons was being "considered" and that he would not involve himself in the heart of such a move: the targeting. "It's a matter that the military will have to decide," he said.

So to what extent was Khrushchev bluffing? The President thought that the threat of signing a separate peace treaty with the East Germans was not serious. But was the Russian also faking when he said he would use nuclear weapons? That seemed less likely.

On the plane from Vienna to London, Kennedy called O'Donnell into his private cabin. For more than an hour, the two men sat alone while the President poured out his heart about the danger that seemed so plausible and possibly imminent: nuclear war. It was a most unusual session. Kennedy almost never revealed his innermost feelings. Much less did he talk about them at any length, as O'Donnell was well aware. He was one of Kennedy's most long-standing henchmen from the Boston days, a tough-minded, taciturn former FBI agent, without sentiment and with no background in foreign affairs, but utterly loyal and a shrewd listener.

Again the President was preoccupied by the dreadful risk of miscalculation. "All wars start from stupidity," he said. "God knows I'm not an isolationist, but it seems particularly stupid to risk killing a million Americans over an argument about access rights on an Autobahn in the Soviet zone of Germany. . . ."

In talking about a million American deaths, the President was either bandying about figures too loosely or O'Donnell's memory of the conversation was wrong. What would in fact have happened in a nuclear war as of mid-1961 is almost beyond comprehension. According to the most optimistic estimate Kennedy was given by the Air Force, American casualties might possibly have been kept as low as ten million, but only if the United States had struck the first blow. In the event of an all-out nuclear "exchange" at that time, the outlook for the survival of an American civilization seemed dubious because of the "missile gap" made famous by the President during his election campaign the preceding year.

According to most estimates, the Soviet Union was said to be ahead in the readiness of intercontinental ballistic missiles. The numbers were very uncertain. The Soviets were thought to have between 50 and 100 ICBMs, possibly 125. The CIA was launching increasingly sophisticated reconnaissance satellites to refine these guesses. The launches were proceeding at a feverish pace, but there could be no certainty until the second half of September. Until then, the life-or-death question would remain open: was the missile gap real?

Meanwhile, the President obviously had to be extra careful to make sure that some inadvertence would not trigger catastrophe.

O'Donnell remembered the President's final remarks as the plane descended toward London. "If we're going to have to start a nuclear war," Kennedy said, "we'll have to fix things so it will be started by the President of the United States, and nobody else. Not by a trigger-happy sergeant on a truck convoy at a checkpoint in East Germany."

To tread lightly. To avoid moves that might be considered provocative by the other side. Such intentions were not simple to execute. They were especially knotty because Khrushchev started to turn up his pressure as soon as the summit was over. He talked of his intention of "freeing" West Berlin from its "occupation regime." Walter Ulbricht announced that a treaty would soon enable him to close West Berlin's refugee centers, its radio station, Tempelhof Airport, and thereby Western access to the city.

Kennedy had a terrible problem indeed: how to make his firmness credible to a bully like Khrushchev.

To know the problem was to begin to know the answer, at least in principle.

"That son of a bitch won't pay attention to words," the President told his staff. "He has to see you move." So Kennedy would move. His objective was to avoid a heart-stopping miscalculation by the Russian. But exactly how could the President credibly demonstrate the presence of a risk to an opponent who was so uncompromising that he refused even to discuss the concept?

The true enormity of the risk implicit in the Kennedy-Khrushchev confrontation after Vienna would not emerge until amost thirty years later. At that time, one Soviet politician with access to Khrushchev in 1961, Fyodor Burlatsky, recalled that the Russian leader thought Kennedy "too young, too intellectual" to be a "real decision maker."* Khrushchev equated Kennedy's sophistication with weakness.

The Russian was viewed by his own people as practicing the risky

---

* Burlatsky wrote speeches for Khrushchev and traveled widely with him. In 1988, he was an editor of *Literaturnaya Gazeta* and head of the Department of Philosophy in the Academy of Social Sciences, which operates under the Central Committee of the Soviet Communist Party. American scholars considered him to be a knowledgeable source. I interviewed Burlatsky on September 27, 1988, in the course of a seminar on the Berlin crisis at Harvard University's John F. Kennedy School of Government.

style of a daredevil pilot or a gamesman. According to them, Khrushchev played politics not in Kennedy's chesslike manner but enjoyed the less rational hopscotch of checkers.

When I asked Burlatsky whether this style indicated Khrushchev's willingness to use nuclear weapons in 1961, the Russian laughed, waved his arms in the air, and said in his heavily accented English: "That is the usual mistake of the West at that time. They think of Russians as rational people, that we plan everything, the first step, the second step. . . ."

Burlatsky shook his head at my naïveté and said that the chance of Khrushchev's resorting to nuclear weapons in 1961 was so remote as not to be worth discussing. He was just playing his games.

So what happened that year seemed clear at last. Kennedy thought Khrushchev might use nuclear weapons and he was wrong. Khrushchev thought Kennedy was too weak to use nuclear weapons and he was wrong. Both miscalculated. The world survived by luck.

5

"COULD NUCLEAR WAR BEGIN BY ACCIDENT?"

**Washington,
late June 1961**

Kennedy was wrestling with Khrushchev at the very time I experienced my own first confrontation with the proposition that "miscalculation" could plunge us into nuclear war. I had become an editor of *The Saturday Evening Post* and had written the lead article of the June 3, 1961, issue, "Could Nuclear War Begin by Accident?" It was—and remains—the scariest writing of my life.

Such terms as "accidental war," "escalation," or "scenarios" that charted future wars were still unknown to the public. In the line of journalistic duty I had become acquainted with some of the exotic new specialists who thought about such things on behalf of the White House and the Pentagon. They were called "defense intellectuals" and worked in "think tanks," then also a novel notion. These strange men, and they were almost all men, personified the wisdom that war was too important to be left to generals. Lately it had also become too technical, too complex.

I first heard about the reality of accidental war from Herman Kahn, a misunderstood physicist genius from the Rand Corporation think tank in California, whom I had befriended and who had written a hair-curling primer entitled *On Thermonuclear War*. It was overflowing with cataclysmic formulas suggesting an infinite variety of ways for victims—that is to say, all of us—to get incinerated by the tens of millions if we were lucky, by the hundreds of millions if we were not.

Few books have been more thoroughly deplored, mostly because Herman managed to sound as if he loved nuclear war. Actually, he loved it no more than an oncologist loves a cancer virus. Herman did insist that people should "think about the unthinkable." People didn't much care to do that, so they called Herman crazy. This diagnosis was not widely resisted, because he weighed about 300 pounds and thoughts popped so rapidly within his brain that his speech often jammed and he sounded like a machine gun with bronchitis.

Before too long some people did start taking Kahn seriously, because leaks suggested that the risks of nuclear miscalculation were *more* unnerving than Kahn—or I, writing in the *Post*—were allowed to hint in public. Kahn was muzzled by security rules; I was kept largely ignorant by them, and consequently my article, I'm embarrassed to concede, makes naïve reading in retrospect. I did get the overriding points right. American nuclear strategy was totally unsettled; no issue was giving the President greater difficulty; and it was Berlin that was pressuring him for answers.

Not that my report made restful bedtime reading. It asked what would happen if junior officers manning the "commit buttons" at our missile bases were to "go ape" (so ran the jargon of the officers in charge of "human reliability"). I showed that in a crisis our top-level "command and control" system might find itself with the wrong kind of command and no control. I reported that some unfortunate "holes" had just been located in the "fail-safe" devices of the launching systems and that a search had been begun for more "holes." I had found top technical people in the Pentagon who were demanding new interlocks to render all nuclear weapons inert pending presidential release.* And I sketched one of the many possible sequences whereby a Berlin crisis could set off fatal miscalculations:

---

* Such a lock was later invented and was to be built into (or attached to) every nuclear weapon. It was called "Permission Action Link" (PAL). Between four and twelve numbers had to be fed into each weapon's triggering system before it could detonate. In case of tampering, the arming mechanism would self-destruct. So, at any rate, the technicians promised. No opportunity arose to learn how the system would work beyond a test scale. The military opposed the locks as excessively restrictive, and in 1964 it was decided not to install them widely.

What if the Russians move to take over Berlin and we alert our missiles and send some of our bombers to their fail-safe points (points of no return) while ultimatums are exchanged and considered? Will the Russians then count down their missiles and send off bombers? Will we then send off more bombers? Can this game of "chicken" be stopped or would it set off an inadvertent war by what professionals call "self-fulfilling prophecy"? There are no firm answers. . . .

There surely were not. It was many years, however, before I found out how infirm the system was at the time.

Kennedy, though, found out quickly, for he was learning his new job in a near-continuous blitz.

Four days after he assumed office, in January 1961, a B-52 bomber carrying two 24-megaton H-bombs disintegrated over North Carolina. One of the bombs ticked to within a hair of exploding on the ground. It was, the administration discovered, just another in a chain of accidents, including inadvertent missile launches and false alarms of Soviet attacks caused by geese, radar blips, and misunderstandings.

In February, fifteen days after Kennedy's inauguration, the administration started up the permanent operation code-named "Looking Glass"; a modified Boeing 707, known as an EC-135 and equipped as a communications headquarters, would stay aloft twenty-four hours a day, with a general aboard, to render command and control over nuclear weapons less vulnerable, although the plane carried a crucial antenna that had a tendency to fall off.*

In March, Secretary of Defense Robert McNamara reported in the Oval Office on the briefing he was given in the underground War Room of the Strategic Air Command (SAC) in Omaha. Eye-

---

* The question of who *actually* might order a release of nuclear weapons in a crisis (and under what circumstances) has never ceased to bedevil planners. This most delicate issue kept growing more complicated because of the increased computerization of weapons and shrinking lead times. An EC-135 can get missiles fired on its own, but the aircraft isn't hard to track, and by the 1980s it was considered possible for enemy action to eliminate all credible human commanders at the very time when effective command would be most vital. This conundrum was graphically named "Decapitation." Measures that, hopefully, might prevent such an ultimate catastrophe remain the nation's most closely held secret. None of these and related problems were assigned priority attention until 1961 and the Berlin Wall crisis.

witnesses would recall that the normally computer-cold Secretary had been "stunned" by the cavalier way the SAC generals contemplated applying their war plan bible, the SIOP (Single Integrated Operational Plan), in one grand nuclear spasm that could spell death for 350 million Russians.

If he received a call from the SAC commander announcing that the country was under Russian attack—so McNamara advised the President—Kennedy should take time out to fly, with the general, to the area where the first bomb supposedly would land in order to make certain—regardless of the delay this would cause in an American response—that the hit was no accident.

Kennedy's reaction to this extreme cautionary suggestion was noncommittal. But he responded enthusiastically to a new and potentially dicey proposal to change the SIOP—a radical departure tailor-made for containing a Berlin crisis.

The present SIOP was hair-raising. In the event of a Soviet move on the city, the military's contingency plan called for "probes" by several American brigades down the Autobahn from West Germany. If these troops were pushed back, which was probable, the United States was scheduled to unleash an immediate all-out nuclear strike. SIOP-62 prescribed this wildly lopsided blow in line with former President Eisenhower's long-standing policy of "massive retaliation."

Kennedy dismissed this choice as giving him no choice at all. He was condemned to pick, he often said, between "holocaust and humiliation." There had to be more and better alternatives, a less lemminglike solution. And so began the search for ways to meet the sharpening Berlin crisis with a new policy, eventually known as "flexible response."

The debate on how to lengthen the nuclear fuse for safer crisis management was far from abstract and would take more than a year to settle. Ultimately it would flush up ways for Kennedy to display credibility combined with effectiveness. It was Khrushchev's pressure on Berlin that taught Kennedy how to *move* ("The son of a bitch has to see you move") without wiping out 350 million Russians.

Well over half a year before "flexible response" became everyone's hobbyhorse in the defense establishment ("It was like sex in a harem," recalled one planner), the idea threatened to torpedo the career of DeWitt (Dee) Armstrong. A short, peppery bantam rooster educated at West Point, this lieutenant colonel had developed an early respect for nuclear weapons while loading A-bombs onto planes. In 1960, returning to the Pentagon after getting a Ph.D. in international relations at Princeton, Armstrong composed a very long and very heretical scenario.

Having asked himself, "How do you display resolve?" he constructed a chain of successive military actions, each step intended to impress the Soviet Union as a symbol of American commitment in a crisis. This scale of mounting pressures would signal to the Soviets their repeated opportunities to break the rising tension.* The Pentagon was no place to sell this brainstorm. His bosses thought Armstrong was "a Bolshevik." He remembered, "They were apprehensive about anything you did that would erode the credibility of our nuclear deterrent."

Hoping for a cozier reception at the State Department, Armstrong personally smuggled his top-secret baby to an influential friend in Foggy Bottom. No sale. "We can't push this just yet," the friend said.

The incoming Kennedy administration, Armstrong thought, would be a more receptive customer, and, sure enough, in March 1961 he managed to be appointed as the Berlin contingency planner in the Pentagon's Office of International Security Affairs. Its chief, Paul Nitze,† was shopping for ideas to make the newly respectable "flexible response" system work.

Rich, handsome, tough, brilliant to the point of intimidation, Nitze represented, like his friend and former boss Dean Acheson, that rare species, the American aristocrat with a lifelong passion for public service. He had served as adviser on national security problems to every President since Roosevelt. With his tailored pinstripes, his flashing steel blue eyes, and his cutting manner, Nitze personified the hard-line wing of Establishment Washington. His anti-Communism, like his persona, was civilized and open to accommodation. Nitze was a searcher.

Nitze was delighted by the smorgasbord versatility of the Armstrong scenario but appalled by its bulk. It was a ledger sheet

---

* Armstrong learned the importance of reading "signals" from one of the very few female defense intellectuals, Roberta Wohlstetter, who used the concept effectively in her pioneering study of Pearl Harbor.

† In 1988, at the age of 82, Nitze still reigned as Special Adviser for Arms Control to President Reagan and played a mean game of tennis. "My body does what I tell it to," he said.

Arms negotiator Paul Nitze wanted a "poodle blanket," not a "pony blanket."

crammed with column after column of Armstrong's precise little hand-printing. The quaint document was some two feet wide, more than twenty inches deep, and too overwhelming to be salable to policymakers.

"It's a pony blanket," Nitze wisecracked. He said he wanted it condensed into a "poodle blanket."

The term took hold. Armstrong delivered the less formidable-looking poodle blanket. Whoever could converse knowledgeably about the poodle blanket that spring and summer was an accredited insider.

The triumphal moment of Dee Armstrong's career came at a luncheon in Secretary McNamara's private dining room. Dressed in a civilian suit, the lieutenant colonel sat at the end of the table. Closer to McNamara sat former Secretary of State Dean Acheson and future Secretary of State Henry Kissinger, both of whom had been recruited by Kennedy to advise him about Berlin.

The subject of the luncheon was the poodle blanket, and McNamara's reaction was pivotal.

"My God, this is extremely risky," he said.

"Mr. Secretary," said ex-Secretary Acheson archly, "we're not in the happy position where we can have a policy with no risk."

"This was the moment McNamara bought the poodle blanket," Armstrong would remember.

Not really. At least not the blanket's ultimate implication.

"The issue was 'Where is this leading?' " So McNamara summarized the weeks of discussions when I talked to him in 1986. "We could take step one, two, three, four, and they could do one, two, three, four. What happens then? I was told, 'Then we have to use nuclear weapons.' I said, 'This is insane.' "

Whereupon I asked McNamara, "Would there have been no point when nuclear weapons would have been used to defend Berlin in 1961?"

"Absolutely none," said McNamara.

"Might we not have threatened the Soviets with nuclear weapons as a psychological warfare ploy?"

"Inconceivable," said McNamara.*

---

* No doubt these were McNamara's thoughts at the time and in 1986. What he *said* in public in 1961, in stark contrast, bristled with martial briskness. "We will use nuclear weapons whenever we feel it's necessary to protect our vital interests," he said then. What Kennedy *said* and *thought* also differed. What Kennedy might in fact have *done* in the face of an actual emergency was still another matter (see

. . .

Perhaps. As long ago as June 1961, McNamara spoke out at a dramatic private Pentagon luncheon against even a small-scale use of relatively low-yield tactical weapons. "They're the same thing, there's no difference," he said with apparent passion. "Once you use them, you use everything else. You can't keep them limited. You'll destroy Europe, everything."

This was a sensationally soft view for a secretary of defense to hold. Nuclear retaliation being the cornerstone of the American defense policy, McNamara's position would have made his post untenable if word of it had leaked.

Only two men attended the luncheon: Adam Yarmolinsky, McNamara's closest confidant on his personal staff, and Daniel Ellsberg, the brilliant thirty-year-old former Marine officer turned Pentagon strategist. In 1971, Ellsberg would become famous for leaking the secret "Pentagon papers" about the Vietnam War to *The New York Times,* but at the time of the 1961 luncheon with McNamara he was still a hard-liner holding twelve security clearances higher than top secret.

Two things impressed Ellsberg about McNamara's tirade against the nuclears. First was the strange circumstance that any secretary of defense would hold such views at all. Secondly, McNamara was putting on a remarkable daily performance to hide his feelings before the military. How could a secretary feel so strongly against these weapons and still preside over their routine deployment?

Right after the luncheon, Yarmolinsky called Ellsberg. "You must not speak of this lunch to anyone," he said. "It is of the highest importance. Not to anyone. It must not get around." Ellsberg promised to keep the secret. But, incorrigibly inquisitive, he asked whether the President felt the same way.

"There is no difference between them at all," Yarmolinsky replied.

---

page 246). And how the Soviets might decode this maze of feints and flourishes had to be anybody's guess.

6

KENNEDY GETS READY: "ARE YOU CHICKEN OR NOT?"

**Washington,
July 1961**

Ever since the Bay of Pigs, John Kennedy had been struggling to put his administrative house in crisis-tight order. It was a vexing chore. He fired Richard Bissell, the CIA executive in charge of the ill-fated operation, and his boss, the legendary Allen Dulles. The President's executive style tightened. He asked more and sharper questions and relied more on his White House inner circle. He never warmed to Rusk—the Secretary was the only cabinet member with whom Kennedy was not on a first-name basis—and his wary relations with State turned into guerrilla warfare that would endure throughout his administration.

The charges and countercharges were common gossip. Kennedy and his henchmen complained that State was exasperatingly sluggish and produced no fresh ideas. "The Secretary never gives me anything to chew on," the President complained. "You never know what he is thinking." More and more, Mac Bundy and his National Security staff took on Rusk's functions. Inevitably the department's bureaucrats complained that the White House crowd was meddlesome and sloppy. Why, they even lost some of the most important papers.

"As far as Berlin is concerned, the Soviet Union is the enemy, not the State Department," a man from the Berlin Task Force tried to remind a White House assistant.

"I'm not so sure," said the White House man, glowering.

State's bureaucrats became increasingly rattled by the President's preoccupation with them, his prodding, his phone calls to underlings way down the line, his disrespect for tradition, his unconcealed exasperation.

"What's wrong with the State Department?" Kennedy asked the veteran Soviet expert Charles E. (Chip) Bohlen as the feuding escalated.

"You are, Mr. President," said Bohlen, and he was not wholly facetious or wrong.

Frustrated by his Secretary of State, Kennedy turned for in-depth help with his Berlin problem to the last Democratic Secretary, the imperious Dean Acheson. The two Secretaries could hardly have been less alike, the differences beginning with their earliest backgrounds. Rusk grew up by the light of kerosene lamps in the poverty of rural Georgia. He sometimes had to go barefoot and his underwear was made from flour sacks. His school had canvas coverings instead of exterior walls. He liberated himself on his own, escaping into academia and ultimately into the State Department, by applying the brains that made him a Rhodes scholar. He was as aloof and dowdy as Acheson was gregarious, privileged, and elegant.

Rusk had no class. Acheson *was* class. Rusk courted power. Acheson *was* power. He looked it, too, resembling a haughty, elegant British general. At State, they called him "the Big Mustache." To his followers he was a deity. His intellect cut knifelike, his sarcasm was feared. He had arrived out of Groton, Yale, and Harvard law, where he had been selected for the *Law Review* and had graduated fifth in his class.

Nevertheless, he admired Rusk, his feelings dating back to 1950, when Acheson had been Secretary of State and Rusk had worked for him as Assistant Secretary for Far Eastern Affairs. The Korean War was that year's crisis and Rusk measured up when many did not. Later it was said that the war might have ended differently if Rusk hadn't been the consummate good soldier. He stood up for American troops crossing the 38th parallel, and when the war went poorly, he counseled that the United States should hold firm and follow the example of the British stand against the Nazis in 1940.

Acheson gratefully remembered Rusk's pluck and loyalty and recited the details explicitly when John Kennedy came to his house on P Street in Georgetown to consult about the position of Secretary on JFK's New Frontier team. Kennedy hadn't known Rusk, and Acheson's own relations with JFK were problematic. Kennedy tended to be ill at ease with the elder statesman, possibly because he knew that Acheson had detested old Joe Kennedy and had been heard to say around Washington's Metropolitan Club that the father had bought a congressional seat for his spoiled son. Robert Kennedy would recall that his brother found Acheson's manner "irritating."

More to the immediate point, Acheson badly wanted his old job back and knew that he couldn't have it. JFK had told intimates that Acheson had made too many enemies in his own party over the years, not to speak of the Republicans, many of whom considered the onetime Secretary ideologically too far to the left, soft on domestic Communists. So Acheson was resigned to recommending Rusk, and Kennedy was reassured to get an endorsement from an experienced old hand.

The President did feel that Acheson was the right man to stand up to Khrushchev on Berlin. Kennedy had been extremely irritated when Acheson, addressing a Foreign Service Association luncheon, dismissed JFK as an "uninformed young man," at best "a gifted amateur" wielding a boomerang. But the President could live with Achesonian quips. Acheson had his uses, and the former Secretary's good judgment had been freshly validated when Kennedy asked his view on the proposed Bay of Pigs expedition.

Acheson had pronounced himself "very alarmed" by the CIA plot and told Kennedy he hoped that JFK "wasn't serious about it." This was followed by another Acheson jab: "I did not think it was necessary to call in [the accounting firm of] Price Waterhouse to discover that 1,500 Cubans weren't as good as 25,000 Cubans." Withal, Acheson was persona grata around the White House in this season of quandary about Berlin.

Kennedy had been in office just under one month when the Soviets catapulted his administration into the Berlin hornet's nest. On February 15 they delivered an aide-mémoire to the Bonn government, claiming that a German treaty could not wait until the West German elections in September. That meant that the Western Allies would probably have to quit Berlin. Promptly, the President appointed an "Acheson Review Group" to study available options.

British Prime Minister Harold Macmillan visited Kennedy in

Washington in early April, and by then Acheson bristled with pugnacious ideas. To the horror of the British delegation, the "brilliant exposition" of the former Secretary skipped over possible diplomatic and economic steps and focused instead on a formidable list of military measures climaxed by the proposal to send all of an entire division rumbling down the Autobahn to West Berlin. While the President listened with a poker face, his closest White House staff advisers revealed how deeply divided they were—as they would be throughout the Berlin crises over the years—between hard-liners and soft-liners.*

"Maybe Dean is right," mused UN Ambassador Adlai Stevenson after the British visitors had departed, "but his position should be the conclusion of the process of investigation, not the beginning. He starts at a point which we should not reach until we have explored and exhausted all the alternatives."

The same hard-line/soft-line division split the State Department, with Secretary Rusk treading so lightly that nobody could fathom where he stood.

Moreover, the British weren't the only Allies discomfited by Acheson's ebullience. In late May, Kennedy paid his respects to the majestic Charles de Gaulle in Paris and found him in favor of preparing for a new defensive "air bridge" to fend off another Berlin blockade. "Le Grand Charles" was relieved when the President assured him that the U.S. Air Force's new C-130 turboprops gave the West an airlift capacity at least five times greater than the slower C-47s and C-54s had supplied during the blockade of the 1940s. New antijamming devices would increase the safety provided by radar landing equipment.†

The possibility of having to order an airlift for a newly blockaded Berlin continued to worry the President on his return from Europe. Still immersed in contingencies to the last detail, he asked the Pentagon for a status report on supplies stockpiled in the island city. On June 14 word reached Kennedy that nonperishable food was on hand to last 180 days and motor gasoline for 300 days, but aviation gas for only 150 days was available, clearly insufficient for another long-term airlift. So on June 21 the President ordered his military aide to prod the chairman of the Joint Chiefs of Staff to

---

* The terms "hawk" and "dove" did not become popular until later.

† There was also a fresh drawback. The Berlin air corridors were threatened by newly installed SAM antiaircraft missiles.

"do something *immediately* re gasoline" for Berlin. The highest-ranking "Berlin desk officer" was making his influence felt.

In the wake of the fiasco at the Vienna Summit Kennedy had again asked Acheson to recommend policy for Berlin, and on June 29 the elder statesman delivered, before the President and the National Security Council, a powerful, brilliantly reasoned five-part paper entitled "The Berlin Crisis." The crisis wasn't about Berlin at all, he argued. Khrushchev was testing America's will to resist, hoping to shatter American power forever. A stark conflict of wills was in the making. There was nothing to negotiate, so any sign of willingness to go to the conference table would be received as a show of weakness and had to be avoided.

Acheson listed the long-sacred "three essentials" to be preserved in West Berlin: (1) the Allied garrisons; (2) freedom of air and surface access; (3) the city's freedom and viability.* By ignoring freedom of movement through *all* of Berlin, Acheson was in effect writing off any Western interest in the Soviet sector. To defend these Allied interests he proposed a rapid buildup in conventional forces, with two or three new divisions to be stationed in West Germany, not in vulnerable Berlin, plus an increase in the U.S.-based reserves; finally Acheson wanted the President to declare a national emergency.

Concurrently, during the daily planning meetings of the Berlin Task Force in the seventh-floor Crisis Room of the State Department, Acheson was at the top of his hawkish form. "Dean was riding high," remembered Abe Chayes, State's legal adviser. "He had the feeling that he was in control."

Acheson, well aware of JFK's problems with Rusk, scented a leadership void. When Supreme Court Justice Felix Frankfurter asked him who held "the helm of the Ship of State," he snorted, "Often no one." At the White House the President was leaving

---

* These "essentials" were originally drafted by the State Department in its efforts to deal with the ground-breaking Khrushchev ultimatum of 1958. In a Moscow speech on November 10 of that year, the Soviet Premier demanded the elimination of the four-power status for Berlin. He designated it as the "capital of the DDR" and said that the Soviet Union would transfer the Soviets' control functions to the East Germans. Historians generally pinpoint this ultimatum as the launching move of the ensuing Berlin crises, including the Berlin Wall problem. The American "three essentials" remained an internal understanding until the West Germans learned of them at a NATO meeting in Oslo on May 8, 1961. Willy Brandt's man Egon Bahr exploded, "This is almost an invitation for the Soviets to do what they want with the Eastern sector." That was an incisive assessment.

several control wheels scattered about, Acheson elaborated scornfully. These "are not locked up at night, so that Caroline and some of the other children around there often play with them." Another wheel was in the hands of Acheson's former subordinate. "Dean Rusk has one in the State Department," the former Secretary scoffed, "but he hasn't learned how to work it very well."

At the age of sixty-eight, Acheson was an aging outsider, lifting his nose in bitterness at the young whippersnappers of the New Frontier and letting his prejudices lead him into misjudgments. Actually, Rusk knew a good deal about the wheel of state; his inhibitions just would not let him operate it. The President wasn't abdicating; he just needed more time to learn his part as the first Chief Executive to face Soviet aggression under the cloud of nuclear war. As for JFK's youthful stewards in the White House, they were mobilizing to resist Acheson.

The warlike fumes rising from the latest efforts to cope with the Berlin problem reminded one aide, the historian Arthur Schlesinger, Jr., uncomfortably of the preparations for the Bay of Pigs invasion, and so he handed the President a cautionary memorandum before lunch on Friday, July 7. He knew that Kennedy was to meet with Rusk, McNamara, and his military adviser General Maxwell Taylor about Berlin the next day at Hyannis Port.

"Are we not running the risk of directing most of our planning to the least likely eventuality—i.e., an immediate blockade of Berlin?" asked the memo. As in the case of Cuba, Schlesinger warned, the President's advisers were defining the issue, "to put it crudely, as: Are you chicken or not?" This formulation was limiting Kennedy's political options. "People who had doubts about Cuba suppressed these doubts lest they seem 'soft,'" Schlesinger reminded his chief. "It is obviously important that such fears not constrain free discussion of Berlin."

Kennedy typically read the memorandum at once, agreed that Acheson's paper was far too narrowly focused on military steps, and asked Schlesinger for another note, unsigned, analyzing the unexplored issues. The President wanted ammunition for the weekend discussions. Schlesinger left to look for Chayes and Henry Kissinger. Both were specialists at negotiations and both were at lunch. Not until after 3 P.M. could the three strategists turn to the task. Chayes and Kissinger talked. Schlesinger typed furiously. The President's helicopter was leaving at five o'clock. The trio barely made the deadline.

Their memo attacked the Acheson paper ferociously, along a

sweeping front. Acheson proposed no immediate political moves, they pointed out, and such rigidity was bound to make the U.S. look unreasonable once an acute crisis developed. The former Secretary set out no political objective (Schlesinger typed, "It is essential to elaborate the cause for which we are prepared to go to nuclear war"). Acheson covered only one eventuality, interruption of access to West Berlin, whereas many forms of harassment were possible. He failed to define possible gradations of American nuclear response in case of all-out war. And he didn't place American strategy in the context of the NATO partners (Schlesinger & Co. queried, "What happens if our allies decline to go along?").

With battle lines thus drawn between the disagreeing factions of the split administration, the President set off a succession of moves to counteract Acheson's hard-lining.

July 8. Once a hot sun had burned through the clouds of a chilly, gloomy Cape Cod morning, the Chief Executive took Rusk, McNamara, and General Taylor sailing on the *Marlin*. While the general and the Defense Secretary went swimming, the President angrily confronted Rusk on the fantail. Why wasn't a reply ready to Khrushchev's Vienna aide-mémoire? Why hadn't State prepared proposals for the negotiation option? Rusk, still in a business suit, was given ten days to deliver (the deadline would pass without the stipulated action). When McNamara returned from his swim, the President sailed into him next. The U.S. armed forces were not, as Kennedy had been assured earlier, adequate for nonnuclear resistance to fight off a Soviet grab for Berlin. The President wished for "a wider choice than humiliation or all-out nuclear war." Specifically (as Ted Sorensen stipulated later), he wanted "a true 'pause,' a month instead of an hour, before choosing nuclear war or retreat." McNamara, too, was given a ten-day ultimatum. Time was demonstrably of the essence: that very day Khrushchev announced in Moscow that he was halting the planned demobilization of his forces and increasing his military budget by one third.

July 13. A formal session of the National Security Council in the White House Cabinet Room opened with Secretary Rusk, surprisingly, siding with Acheson on the issue of not opening negotiations with Khrushchev. The U.S. was "not currently in a good position" to assert itself in such talks, Rusk said. He counseled caution, meaning waiting.

McNamara spoke up in favor of a program of tough measures to put teeth into Acheson's perception of the crisis. The Defense Secretary wanted to declare a national emergency; call up the reserves and the National Guard; extend the service of those on active duty; return service families from Europe; and increase defense expenditure by $4.3 billion.

Acheson rallied to McNamara's support. So did Vice President Lyndon Johnson. Nobody else did. Resistance centered on the declaration of a national emergency, the ultimate signal of national alarm. Such a step might have been an overreaction, a risk that did not appeal to Rusk. So he parted company with his old boss, Acheson. A national emergency "would have a dangerous sound of mobilization," Rusk cautioned.

Acheson cut in archly: "We must do what is sound and necessary in itself, and not act for the sake of appearances. If we leave the call of reserves to the end, we would not affect Khrushchev's judgment of the shape of the crisis any more than we could do so by dropping [nuclear] bombs after he had forced the issue to the limit."

No major decisions were reached, but one crucial position was crystallizing. At an informal session of the smaller Berlin Steering Group immediately afterward in the Oval Office, the President clarified his policy on the status of *East* Berlin. The U.S. would respond with military means only if *West* Berlin were directly threatened, he instructed McNamara. Addressing a query by Rusk, the President said that only "two things" mattered: "our presence in Berlin" and "our access" to the city. By omission, it was finally clear that East Berlin was the East's business.

July 14. Dean Acheson was disgusted. "I find to my surprise a weakness at the top—all but Bob McNamara, who impresses me as first class," he wrote to his former boss, ex-President Harry Truman. He thought Kennedy was like a shortstop, so eager to make sure he "looked good" that he muffed fielding a ball. "We ought to be acting now to bring home to Khrushchev that we are in deadly earnest about Berlin, which is only a symbol for our world position." But Acheson's influence was waning. On the same day Henry Kissinger sent a memo to his boss, Bundy, warning against any one dramatic gesture. The Soviets might find it "unnecessarily bellicose, perhaps even hysterical." A sustained American improvement of military readiness would impress the Kremlin more. Kissinger also counseled the administration not to "shy away" from the negotiating table.

July 17. The boyish, sober-faced Ted Sorensen—he had been advising Kennedy since 1954, longer than anyone except the President's brother Robert—weighed in with a lucidly reasoned memo arguing against "drastic" military steps. Military threats would "engage Khrushchev's prestige to a point where he felt he could not back down from a showdown." The exceptionally influential Sorensen proposed that Kennedy appear on national television to explain to American voters our "intent to defend Berlin at all costs" but that "endurance rather than emergency actions" was required. This stance would give the Soviets "an opportunity to negotiate before the nuclear stage is reached." It was the way to achieve the desired pause of weeks or months, instead of hours or minutes, before either side might feel compelled to reach for atomic weapons. As the President's longtime principal speech writer, Sorensen also reasoned that the process of assembling a major speech would speed up the administration's internal decision making by forcing the White House machinery to forge policy and finally to settle such open questions as whether to declare a national emergency.

July 19. The impending TV speech was drumming the administration into line. At 3 P.M. the President crisply ticked off his decisions to the Berlin Steering Group in the second-floor living quarters of the executive mansion. No national emergency would be proclaimed. Additional military spending would be $3.2 billion —not $4.3 billion, as proposed by the Pentagon. The President would triple draft calls and ask Congress for standby authority to call up the reserves, but no mobilization would be announced. West Berlin would be prepared for an airlift. Bombers on ground alert would be increased by 50 percent. Six additional divisions would gradually be readied for later deployment to Europe. An overambitious civil defense program would be launched. Sorensen would articulate this buildup—substantial but tempered—in a speech to be delivered on Tuesday, July 25. Suggestions for language suitable in the address would be welcome from ranking members of the presidential staff. The meeting closed with no significant dissents. Then, in the Cabinet Room at 4 P.M., the same program was adopted for the record, this time over anguished protests from Acheson. His objections were forcefully rejected by, of all people, Bob McNamara.*

---

* The President and his closest associates took delight in watching McNamara's nimble performance as a team player. He could wax remarkably convincing on both sides of a question. Earlier he had argued that the declaration of a national emergency would be the nation's *only* course. Once the President had ruled against him, he spoke out against the idea with equal vehemence. Acheson, on the other hand, was a bitter loser. To a meeting of the Berlin Task Force he

Officially, Acheson's career as a Kennedy adviser would continue for some time. Essentially it was over. He was the hare who lost to Rusk the turtle. By keeping his head largely hidden in his shell, Rusk would survive as Secretary of State for nine more years, straight through the reign of the explosive Lyndon Johnson. That was longer than any Secretary in memory, as Rusk would always be pleased to point out.

July 21. One of the first suggestions for the President's text came from Edward R. Murrow, the broadcaster JFK had picked to head the United States Information Agency. Known for his vivid touch with words, he suggested that the East Germans fleeing West in such large numbers were "voting for self-determination with their feet"—a phrase that would ring for a long time across all Europe.* Murrow also contributed: "We cannot negotiate with those who say, 'What's mine is mine and what's yours is negotiable.'" General Taylor proposed the paragraph arguing emotionally against his own pessimistic analysis as he had expressed it in internal debate: "I hear it said that West Berlin is militarily untenable. And so was Bastogne. And so, in fact, was Stalingrad. Any dangerous spot is tenable if men—brave men—will make it so." Mac Bundy drafted passages recognizing the "enormous losses . . . bravely suffered by the Russian people" in World War II. Over the weekend of July 22 to 23, Sorensen would pound out a draft of the President's text at the home of friends, Joe and Polly Kraft, on Long Island.

July 22. Walt Whitman Rostow liked to dazzle the President with phrases. This time it might be useful to come up with something catchy, not for television but as personal imagery to stiffen the Chief Executive's backbone in case of a nuclear shootout. Rostow, Bundy's deputy in managing the National Security Council, was an MIT economics professor of brilliance but little professorial reserve. A bantam rooster by temperament, appearance, and vocabulary, he was a wizard with words, and Kennedy was a connoisseur, a collector of punchy slogans. Rostow had christened the "New Frontier" during JFK's election campaign. It was he who had sounded his verbal trumpet to "get the country moving again." Lately, in the internal arguments about Berlin, Rostow had tossed

---

announced, "Gentlemen, you might as well face it. This nation is without leadership."

* German politicians later maintained that the phrase was coined by Ernst Lemmer, the flamboyant former newspaperman who was Minister for All-German Affairs in the Adenauer cabinet.

away the DDR as "the dead rat" of Eastern Europe.* During the
crucial weekend before the President would revise the draft for his
speech, this militant adviser sent Kennedy a colorful memo visual-
izing an imminent "high noon" in Berlin. He argued that the hesitant mood of the Western Allies was no reason for the United
States to pull its nuclear punch, to fear the "atomic trigger." Admittedly, the President might face a "relatively lonely stage." But if
the Allies deserted him, so the little professor prodded, Kennedy
ought to act out his solitary role with the aplomb of poker-faced
Gary Cooper, the sheriff in the film *High Noon.* "We ought to
accept it without throwing our sheriff's badge in the dust," Rostow
wrote. Before giving his TV speech, the President could stand a
booster shot of courage, the old-fashioned pluck that harked back
to the frontier West. Or so his administration's hard-liners
thought. *They* wouldn't have to pull the atomic trigger.

July 24. Back from his weekend labors over the draft of the
President's address, Ted Sorensen faced a frontal attack from Berlin's most ferocious defenders, the parochially famous "Berlin
Mafia," in the person of James P. O'Donnell. Like the other partisans in this unofficial pressure group of Berlin insiders (its enemies
said they were afflicted by incurable "Berlinitis"), the Boston-born
O'Donnell breathed fanatical loyalty to the city where he had lived
more or less continuously since 1945. A onetime *Newsweek* and
Saturday Evening Post correspondent, O'Donnell was currently in
the State Department, writing speeches for Under Secretary
George W. Ball. But regardless of his incarnation, O'Donnell perceived every threat against Berlin as an act of violence against his
fiery Irish self.

Sorensen did not realize what onslaught awaited him when
O'Donnell accompanied Sorensen's brother Tom, the number
three man in the United States Information Agency, to lunch at
the Mayflower Hotel on Monday, the day before the President's

---

* Not all animal analogies play well in history. More than thirty years after Rostow
floated his "dead rat," the DDR could point to its economy as the strongest in
Eastern Europe. Some politicians were served better by the animal kingdom.
When French generals predicted in the darkest hours of World War II that "in
three weeks England will have her neck wrung like a chicken," Prime Minister
Winston Churchill replied in a famous speech, "Some chicken; some neck!"
Khrushchev, on the other hand, refused to outwait Allied resistance against his
policies "until shrimps whistle."

Berlin speech. O'Donnell knew enough about the text to keep his passionate argument going for more than an hour. He praised its undertone of steadfastness ("We do not want to fight—but we have fought before"). What incensed him were repeated references to West Berlin, rather than to the city as a whole.

The implicit omission of East Berlin seemed to cede that part of the city to Ulbricht and the Russians, which fit Kennedy's policy but ignored the long-standing four-power agreements covering the entire city. Both Sorensens argued that the Russians had not observed these pacts for more than a decade. They had gotten away with that, which was exactly what made O'Donnell so furious. He suggested leaving out the word "West" from most of the places where it was used in front of "Berlin." Ted Sorensen declined. The Berlin Mafia was not in the policy-making loop.

July 25. When Sorensen took the reading copy of the President's 10 P.M. talk to the living quarters of the White House at 8 P.M., he found the President sitting up in bed, a hot pad pressed against his chronically painful back, scribbling closing words for the text. He composed nothing dramatic ("I need your good will and . . . your prayers"), but this was a historic speech and he wanted it to end on a personal note. It had turned into an unusually somber address and not one of his best.

"We cannot and will not permit the Communists to drive us out of Berlin, either gradually or by force," the President warned the nation, and he outlined the contingency measures that he and his advisers had hammered out. Even Walt Rostow's high noon imagery found an echo when Kennedy observed, "As Americans know from our history on our own old frontier, gun battles are caused by outlaws, and not by officers of the peace."

The air-conditioning in the Oval Office had been turned off to improve the microphone pickup; Kennedy tensed, flubbed a couple of lines, and began to sweat profusely under the floodlights. It was an omen, although the heat proved mild compared to the temperature of Khrushchev's reaction.

**The White House,
Washington, Monday, July 31**

John J. McCloy had been an eyewitness to much history during his sixty-six years. During World War II he had counseled President

Truman on the decision to drop the atomic bomb. After the war he had been president of the World Bank and United States High Commissioner in Germany. Now he witnessed, horrified, a unique spectacle: overnight, Nikita Khrushchev had undergone a metamorphosis from Dr. Jekyll to Mr. Hyde.

The drama began as a pleasant summer interlude at Khrushchev's dacha in Sochi on the Black Sea. McCloy, having been recalled into the government by Kennedy from his Wall Street law practice to advise on disarmament problems, had been visiting Moscow to lay the groundwork for an East-West conference on nuclear weapons. Khrushchev had invited him to share his vacation for two days, and their first day together, July 26, had been idyllic.

Khrushchev lent McCloy a pair of too-big black swimming trunks. The statesmen splashed in the pool and in the sea and played tennis. McCloy diplomatically restrained his game in deference to his portly and slower opponent's handicap. Khrushchev's substantive comments were few and easygoing. The continuing exhange of diplomatic notes about the settlement of the German question was like kicking a football back and forth, he remarked, and "would probably continue until a treaty was signed." His tone was relaxed.

The next day, so McCloy cabled Kennedy, "the storm broke." Khrushchev had studied the President's television address. He was livid. Emotionally, the Premier branded the speech a "preliminary declaration of war." The Soviet Union would never sit still for such an ultimatum. It would sign a German peace treaty "no matter what." Western access to West Berlin would cease. If the Allies attempted to force their way into the city, there would be war. The conflict would "be thermonuclear," Khrushchev lectured. America and the Soviet Union might survive, but America's European allies would not.

This scenario largely matched what Khrushchev had been threatening right along. But for McCloy he pulled out a new menace. Since a war would be decided by the biggest rockets, McCloy should keep in mind that the Soviets could deliver onto American territory a hundred-megaton "superbomb." Khrushchev's scientists were "eager" to test it. This was the strongest hint yet of how far the Soviets would go to intimidate the West.

Khrushchev also offered McCloy a scenario of how war might start at any moment without America as initial aggressor. The exodus of East Germans to the West could trigger a revolt, such as the short-lived workers' rebellion of 1953, Mr. K. hypothesized. Such an outbreak might be followed by a West German attack on the DDR. McCloy tried to defuse the Premier's fear, assuring him that the West Germans were under American control through NATO. Khrushchev would have none of this. "The old Nazi generals," he said, could not be trusted. They would take advantage of a temporary weakness in the DDR.

Khrushchev would have to end the mass exodus of East Germans, he said, but he didn't reveal how.*

Gradually, he calmed down. War could be avoided if both sides showed "reasonableness," he said. He believed in the President's good sense. The West would not fight to protect occupation rights in West Berlin. Repeatedly he asked why Moscow and Washington couldn't work out their differences over Germany.

Alarmed by Khrushchev's "rough warlike language," McCloy presented Kennedy with a dilemma. On July 29 he cabled from Moscow that the Berlin situation was, in his view, "not yet ripe for any negotiation." On the other hand, it was "too dangerous" to be allowed to "drift." The President received the word at Hyannis Port. McCloy was about to leave for Paris for more disarmament talks. Kennedy messaged him to cancel his plans and return to Washington for a personal report immediately. The flood of DDR refugees was obviously forcing Khrushchev's hand. It was he who could not afford to let that situation drift, and the President was not the only policymaker in Washington who sensed imminent action.

On Sunday, July 30, J. William Fulbright, chairman of the Senate Foreign Relations Committee, was asked on a national TV program whether he was "willing to accept any concession on the part of the West which closed West Berlin as an escape hatch for refugees."

"The truth of the matter," the Senator responded, is that the "Russians have the power to close it in any case." They could do so next week "without violating any treaty." Fulbright, the only ranking politician who had resolutely opposed the Bay of Pigs invasion, wanted to remove Berlin from the list of the world's tinderboxes. He observed, "I don't understand why the East

---

* This Khrushchev monologue was one of the seedbeds of subsequent rumors that the Soviets had tipped off the United States in advance to its plans for building the Berlin Wall. In fact, Khrushchev had not even authorized the Wall when he entertained McCloy.

Germans don't close their border, because I think they have a right to close it."

In East Berlin, banner headlines hailed the statement as a "compromise formula." And in the Kremlin, Khrushchev and Ulbricht were preparing to apply it.

PART II

MOVING TOWARD THE WALL

7

THE KREMLIN SIGNS ON: "BUT NOT ONE MILLIMETER FARTHER"

**Moscow,
Saturday, August 5, 1961**

The ranking leadership of the Warsaw Pact satellites, assembling for a climactic midafternoon session in the Kremlin, watched closely how Premier Nikita Khrushchev addressed Walter Ulbricht, the DDR boss. Khrushchev's words of greeting were pleasant, but the cordial air evaporated as the discussion of the East German refugees progressed.

"Thanks, Comrade Khrushchev," Ulbricht finally said. "Without your help we could not solve this terrible problem."

"Yes, I agree," Khrushchev responded, "but not one millimeter farther."

According to a conference participant who observed this chilling encounter,* Ulbricht paled. The DDR dictator had been lobbying

---

* The eyewitness was Colonel Jan Sejna (pronounced Shay-na), the thirty-four-year-old chief of staff to the Czech Minister of Defense, a political post. When the Soviets took over Czechoslovakia in 1968, Sejna, by then a major general, used his diplomatic passport to cross the Czech-Austrian border in his Mercedes. He requested asylum at the American consulate in Trieste and was flown to the United States. His CIA debriefings took "a long, long time," the short, square-faced general told me with a thin smile when I interviewed him in an Arlington, Virginia, hotel lobby in 1986. Our meeting was arranged by a retired CIA officer.

the Soviets to assume jurisdiction over the westward Allied air corridors from Berlin. He also wanted to seize control of the city's Western sectors. Khrushchev had evidently decided against both of these recommendations to solve the "terrible problem" of the refugees. And he enjoyed announcing his veto even before the ultrasecret session of the more than forty Soviet bloc leaders got under way. It began to look as if five months of Ulbricht's frantic shuttle diplomacy between East Berlin and Moscow had been fruitless.

His first pitch, delivered at a similar Kremlin conference on the morning of March 29, had drawn a negative reception.* Ulbricht had then proposed erecting barbed wire and increasing the border patrols along the sector frontier without mentioning his plan to reinforce this barrier later with a concrete wall. The Hungarians complained that visible defensive fortifications would set off unfavorable propaganda. The Romanians worried that it might spark war. Khrushchev thought it was at best premature; if they were to move now, Kennedy might cancel the June summit meeting in Vienna, where the Soviet Premier wanted to size up the President.

Nobody minded giving Ulbricht a hard time, and that included Khrushchev himself. When the Soviet leader had been a commissar with Soviet troops at Stalingrad, he had met this dour German comrade during the battles of 1942 and had not been impressed with Ulbricht's abortive propaganda efforts to talk Nazi troops into surrendering. Over the years since, the Warsaw Pact allies had not overcome their traditional distrust for their German compatriots. Among themselves, the Slavs still muttered that all Germans were "fascists" at heart. And the arrogant Ulbricht made himself particularly unpopular by missing no opportunity to point out that the DDR was Communism's show window to the West and therefore deserved priority treatment in the constant competition for support from Mother Russia.

By evening, Ulbricht had salvaged only one concession from his

---

I never learned Sejna's address or phone number or the name he uses in public, nor the Washington organization where he was said to be doing "research."

* Washington had been alerted to Moscow's concern. Two weeks earlier, Llewellyn Thompson, the American Ambassador to Moscow and a veteran Kremlinologist, had sent home a prescient cable, beginning, "If we expect Soviets to leave Berlin problem as is, then we must at least expect East Germans to seal off sector boundary in order to stop what they must consider intolerable continuation refugee flow through Berlin."

reluctant friends: he was authorized to "prepare everything" to proceed for a possible green light at some subsequent stage.

As soon as he arrived back home, Ulbricht instructed Erich Honecker to assemble the necessary organization, materials, and men. Although it would be one of the more ambitious construction jobs of modern times, the preparations had to be cloaked in absolute secrecy. Honecker was delighted. With his eye on replacing the aging Ulbricht, the former youth leader had already moved on to new responsibilities as secretary for national security. If he could show his peers—and history—that he knew how to solve the "terrible problem" of the refugees, his future would be secure.

Ulbricht made his next sales trip to Moscow on Monday, July 31. The temperature outside was 92 degrees. Within the Kremlin, the atmosphere was cool. The Western Allies were flying hundreds of DDR refugees to the West from Berlin every day, Ulbricht reported; such nose-thumbing at the sovereignty of the DDR was intolerable to him. Khrushchev and his advisers nevertheless did not wish to authorize Soviet fighters to enforce the proposed closure of Western air access lanes; the West might consider this an act of war.

Well, Ulbricht asked, what about a wall to close off the sector border? Khrushchev and the other conferees were still dubious. They agreed only to resume discussion of the "terrible problem" at the upcoming Warsaw Pact leadership meeting scheduled, at Ulbricht's request, for Thursday, August 3.

Backed up by his deputy and his two principal foreign affairs advisers, Ulbricht resumed his lobbying when the allies met again that Thursday. The refugee exodus, he reported, was disrupting the DDR economy; unless it was stopped "here and now," he would be unable to meet commitments to deliver raw materials and manufactured goods to his friends in the East. And his situation was explosive. Any day might see new worker uprisings; this time they might be harder to quell than in 1953.

Reluctantly, Khrushchev and his partners agreed to have Ulbricht put up a wall if, in time for the final session, on Saturday, August 5, the East Germans could make a convincing case on two counts: Could the DDR forces keep the lid on the restless workers of East Berlin? And could the DDR withstand an economic blockade if the West Germans decided to stop interzonal trade?

Those requirements meant homework for Ulbricht and his

team. Having rushed back to Berlin by the early morning hours of Friday, August 4, Ulbricht summoned his six key ministers to his villa in the leadership's golden ghetto in suburban Wandlitz. Ulbricht's deputy, Willi Stoph,* and Honecker would work up the military requirements. The others would attend to the economic questions. They all worked through the night and at 10:30 A.M., joined by three more ministers, they convened in the Ministry of Public Health near Unter den Linden. According to the public cover story, they were considering how to protect the DDR against a reported "polio epidemic" in West Germany. The East Berlin media had been spreading this fake scare story to discourage refugees.

The economic report caused Ulbricht's men no concern. The military appraisal did. According to the review prepared by Willi Stoph and Erich Honecker, the available 8,200 *Vopos* and 3,700 "garrisoned police" could be augmented by 12,000 factory militiamen and 4,500 elite troops of the guard regiment controlled by the State Security *(Stasi)*. But the conferees estimated that an additional 40,000 men might be needed to abort any repetition of the 1953 riots. The 10,000 regular troops with their 150 tanks stationed in the Berlin area would have to be reinforced by militiamen from politically reliable Saxony, and Honecker volunteered the services of his former charges, youth units of the Free German Youth, the FDJ, for border patrol duty.

Honecker's meticulous groundwork to assemble the physical requirements looked good to the leaders, especially since the movement of materials would ultimately be massive and total secrecy could not be broken. Barbed wire, some forty kilometers in length, had already been transported from near the West German border to the large military base at Basdorf. The camp was close to Route 109; the fencing could easily be trucked into East Berlin at the last moment. Concrete slabs and posts had been stored at scattered building sites around the city and could be readily transported to the border for the second phase of the operation.

The question of the exact timing, subject to Khrushchev's final okay, was last on the agenda. D day could not be a busy weekday, when the more than 40,000 detested *Grenzgänger* (border crossers) traveled from the East to their jobs in the West, and 13,000 West Berliners crossed over to jobs in the East. Interference with such

---

* Still a member of the Politburo in 1988.

formidable movements could lead to incidents. A weekend would be ideal, especially in midsummer. The locals would be relaxing. So would the Western authorities. The coming weekend, thirty-seven hours away, was too close to be manageable. They would try for the following one, August 12 to 13.

Back in Moscow in the very early morning of Saturday, August 5, Ulbricht had to cool his heels until midafternoon while Khrushchev disposed of other business. If the German retained some lingering hope that his Soviet protectors would let him march into West Berlin, Khrushchev's greeting ("Not one millimeter farther") snuffed it with finality.

In yet another of his presentations, this time quite emotional, Ulbricht, salesman and supplicant, again appealed to his comrades to let him at the very least seal the border at once. The Americans would do nothing. As evidence, the Goatee cited the July 30 TV pronouncement by Senator Fulbright of the Senate Foreign Relations Committee that the East had the right to close the border.

How much further could the Americans go toward giving Ulbricht virtual permission to go ahead?

Khrushchev rose to agree. He told the Communist leaders that he had been impressed at Vienna by Kennedy's desire to be an independent executive and not to let himself be manipulated by military or industry interests; JFK wanted to be a man of peace. Khrushchev said he had played "cat and mouse" with the President in Vienna. The satellite leaders smiled in unison. There could be no question about the identity of the cat; a Kennedy mouse could hardly threaten a stealthy Soviet feline.

Ulbricht's disclosure that he planned to put up a solid wall, not merely a barbed-wire fence, triggered unease among some of the satellite leaders. Khrushchev offered a compromise. The border would initially be sealed by barbed wire. If, as expected, the West did not respond with force, a wall could replace it.* Under no

---

* Many years afterward, reports were published claiming that sometime prior to the events of August 13, probably after the August 5 Kremlin meeting, the Soviets and the East Germans agreed that the DDR forces were to withdraw 100 meters if the West were to resist the installation of barbed wire. If the West were to push farther, Ulbricht's men were to retreat another 100 meters. If the Allies moved still farther east, the DDR troops were to retreat for the third and last time and call in the Soviet forces that would stand by around the periphery of the city. Communist participants told me that there was no such agreement.

According to his memoirs, Khrushchev was deeply involved in the detailed planning. He remembered asking his East Berlin Ambassador to send him a map

circumstances were Ulbricht's men to venture into Western territory. Soviet officers would be at hand to watch them.*

Attending the conference that day was the bullet-headed, bemedaled Marshal Ivan S. (the Tank) Koniev, a World War II hero who hated Germans and had marched into Berlin in 1945. Khrushchev eventually explained why he had recalled the gruff and tough warrior at the age of sixty-three to take over once again as Commander in Chief of Soviet forces in Germany. The appointment was meant to impress friend and foe, and it did.† But the buttons that would require pushing on Sunday, August 13, were in the hands of little Erich Honecker.

Having been so lengthily belabored by Ulbricht about the East's inability to compete with the dazzle and affluence of West Berlin, Khrushchev decided to see for himself just what was attracting so many DDR citizens across the border and into the arms of capitalism. Chaperoned by the commandant of Berlin's Soviet occupation troops, he traveled West incognito.

"I never got out of the car," he recalled, "but I made a full tour and saw what the city was like." And while he did not record his impressions, he could hardly have failed to register the contrast of the two Berlins as an ideological marketplace.

---

of West Berlin; deciding to put up "antitank barriers and barricades"; and using DDR troops out in front, placing his own men "a few meters" to the rear in order "to give the impression that the whole thing was being carried out by the Germans." He remembered setting August 13 as D day and laughing at the date: "We kidded among ourselves that in the West the thirteenth is supposed to be an unlucky day. I joked that for us and for the whole socialist camp it would be a very lucky day indeed."

* The Russians did this quite literally. Once the fencing was put up, CIA officers saw Soviet officers actually keeping binoculars trained on the DDR forces from vantage points slightly farther east—a case of watchers watching watchers.

† Koniev's recall was psychological warfare. In his 1970 memoirs Khrushchev called it "just an 'administrative' appointment to demonstrate to the West that we regarded the situation as seriously as they did. Our regular commander in Berlin, who was junior in rank to Koniev, remained in charge while Koniev reported to us in Moscow." The Soviet Premier added: "The fact that Koniev afterwards spent most of his time in Moscow proves we weren't expecting the confrontation to escalate into a full-scale military conflict." Initially, Khrushchev had offered the job to the even more honored Marshal Georgi Zhukov, whom Koniev had beaten to Berlin by one day, back in 1945. Zhukov turned down the 1961 propaganda chore, pleading advanced age.

8

THE LEGENDARY MEN BEHIND
THE CIA'S BERLIN BASE

**West Berlin,
Wednesday, August 9, 1961**

"I vote for a wall," repeated the American colonel whom the others called "Von." There was a scuffling of chairs. The men were rising to leave the Commanding General's conference room.

"Von, you're getting panicky," chided the representative from British intelligence, walking out with the colonel from the regular Wednesday afternoon "prayer meeting" of the Intelligence Coordinating Committee, known as the Berlin Watch Committee. This interagency group had finally been organized in June as an exercise in self-defense. It was to bring some measure of coordination to the evaluation of developments and hopefully keep the many Western intelligence collectors from stumbling over each other quite so much.*

In the corridor of the United States Mission, on Clayallee, the committeemen ran into Dave Murphy, one of the senior officers of the Central Intelligence Agency's BOB (Berlin Operating Base). Having already heard how Von had ruffled the meeting, Murphy laughed at the colonel.

---

* Even a U.S. Navy intelligence presence flourished on the landlocked Berlin Watch Committee, under the acronym CINCNAVEURREP BER (Commander in Chief Naval Europe Representative Berlin).

"Von, we hate you, but we love you," he said.

Despite his Teutonic sobriquet, Colonel "Von," whose full name was Ernest von Pawel, was from Laramie, Wyoming. He was forty-six, a professional Army officer with twenty-five years of service, and currently chief of the U.S. Military Liaison Mission to the DDR, with headquarters in Potsdam. What he had done at the August 9 meeting was to face down the almost total opposition of his peers in the Berlin intelligence community.

The CIA representative, John P. Dimmer, Jr., the small but very vocal deputy chief of his agency's base, said that a wall would represent "political suicide" for Walter Ulbricht. He considered it more likely that all of Berlin would be sealed off. Others rejected a wall through Berlin as "impractical" and the "least likely" method for the DDR to cut off the flow of refugees.

Defending his lonely position, von Pawel had reminded the committee of the infamous wall that the Nazis had put up in World War II to seal off the Jewish ghetto in Warsaw. The colonel conceded that he lacked hard evidence of present Communist intentions, but he spoke up stoutly for his hunch.

"If you think a wall is the least likely option, then that is where I place my bet, because we've never outguessed the Soviets before," he argued.

Von Pawel was able to muster one ally: Lieutenant Colonel Thomas McCord, chief of the Army's 513th Military Intelligence Group, Berlin, the officer principally responsible for gathering tactical enemy data in the area. When the Watch Committee chairman, yet another Army colonel, turned to McCord and asked, "Do you think they plan to build a wall, Tom?" McCord, a burly, popular Texan known for his no-nonsense manner, said yes.

To him it was pretty much a certainty. Ulbricht absolutely *had* to stop his people from fleeing. Two methods were open to him: a physical barrier or a human one. McCord thought a human fence would be useless; the guards themselves would run away. That left a wall as the only realistic alternative. And unlike von Pawel, McCord possessed more than a hunch. He had evidence in hand.

The intelligence people were operating that week as if Berlin and Washington were on different planets. While President Kennedy was unaware that drastic Communist action was almost certain in Berlin—the term "wall" was not even breathed in Washington's intelligence community—Western espionage professionals at the scene talked of almost nothing else. McCord had received several graphic tips from German sources; one of these even pinpointed the correct target date.

The report had reached him around 4 P.M. on the previous Sunday, August 6. The source was new: a physician in Berlin's rural outskirts who also served as a functionary of the SED Executive Committee in his district. This was the doctor's first report and it was sensational. His committee had been informed of "drastic measures" to seal off West Berlin *the next weekend.* Several DDR and Soviet divisions would participate. Local emergency measures included slaughter and storage of livestock.

McCord and two other colonels met with the CIA base chief, the redoubtable and universally respected William J. (Bill) Graver, thirty-nine, six feet four inches tall, and nicknamed "El Supremo." Together they dissected the doctor's report. The results, which McCord communicated to the Watch Committee at its August 9 meeting, were unfortunate. The evaluators were disturbed because the source had not been previously tested; the number of head of livestock he had mentioned seemed excessive for his district; and one of the Soviet divisions reported by him had been incorrectly labeled. The group therefore decided to forward the report to higher headquarters, with a classification that consigned it automatically to a wastebasket.

Similar reports met with the same fate at the hands of other Allied intelligence services. The French learned from their best agent in East Berlin, Dr. Hartmut Wedel, a dentist, that several patients prominent in the SED leadership had told him, while sitting in his treatment chair, that the DDR was planning a major strike against West Berlin. The doctor was given no details about timing; otherwise his information was explicit.

"They're going to erect barriers right in the middle of Berlin," he advised his French case officer.

The men around the conference table of the Berlin Watch Committee on that Wednesday before the advent of the Wall considered themselves supremely qualified to master any crisis of their craft. They were, as they saw themselves, the best in the business and the inheritors of a proud tradition. Their patron saint was that memorable figure, William King Harvey, the CIA base chief during much of the 1950s. Bill Harvey was a legend-among-legends throughout the agency and had taught the intelligence business to many Berlin hands, including El Supremo, Bill Graver.

Graver was, among other attributes, something of an intellectual snob. He disdained attending the Berlin Watch Committee, for example, dismissing its deliberations as just "another cultural event." But even Bill Graver revered—yes, revered—Bill Harvey, the spy boss who fit into Berlin much as a baby belongs in a playpen.

During its Wild West era, starting in the late 1940s but especially throughout the 1950s, Berlin was Espionage Central. "There were more agents per acre in the town than any other place in the world," recorded Kennedy's military adviser General Taylor. Counting the delegations from Greece and Norway, eighty-six separate intelligence operations stumbled over each other's tracks. Inconvenient adversaries vanished in routine kidnappings.* "Informations," most of them fake or designed to mislead, were standard merchandise hawked in the cafés along Kurfürstendamm.

"It was an absolute bedlam," I was assured by one American agent, an imperturbable type with seventeen years of operational experience in an entire city gone berserk. Among colleagues in "the agency," the operatives of the CIA's Berlin base were appropriately called "the Berlin Cowboys." † CIA service in this city of direct action was prized. This was what intelligence work was supposed to be all about. To be an alumnus of Berlin looked promising in one's personnel file. Also, it was great sport. Agency old-timers used to reminisce about those days with German colleagues, and sooner or later someone would sigh and remark, *"Damals war's schön!"* (It was beautiful in those days!)

Within the bubbly chaos, one operator and one operation stood out in the minds of initiates: base chief Bill Harvey and his master creation, "Operation Gold," the famous "Berlin tunnel." For eleven months and eleven days in 1955 and 1956 the listening devices in "Harvey's hole" underneath East Berlin—it measured 20 feet deep, 1,476 feet long, and 6½ feet in diameter—tapped every Soviet communication not only in all of East Germany but throughout the Eastern bloc satellite nations and the lines from East Berlin headquarters in Karlshorst to Moscow.

---

* Police records registered 229 actual and 348 attempted Communist kidnappings in West Berlin between 1945 and the construction of the Wall. No reliable statistics are known for kidnappings by Western agents in Communist territory.

† The nickname was chosen to contrast Berlin methods with the gentler ways of the CIA contingent in the Austrian capital, known as "the Vienna Choirboys."

The Communist communications happened to be centralized to permit such a gigantic "take," but its magnitude buckled the CIA's capacity to translate all incoming tapes without delays, which could make the "gold" obsolete and therefore worthless.* The cost exceeded twenty-five million preinflation dollars, but nobody complained, since the tunnel presumably revealed the intentions of the enemy in advance—the highest function of all espionage.

The revered General George C. Marshall had pinpointed this priority most aptly back in 1947 when he was Secretary of State and the CIA was founded. "I don't care what the CIA does," he said, "all I want from them is twenty-four-hours' notice of a Soviet attack."

Understandably, the Berlin tunnel was the Las Vegas, the overflowing jackpot of intelligence collection, that popped into President Kennedy's mind when he learned seventeen hours late, on August 13, 1961, that the Communists had brought off a huge undetected military move in East Berlin. How could such a surprise have come about? East Berlin was supposed to be as transparent as window glass. Bill Harvey had made it so, hadn't he?

And Harvey was a lot more than memorable history. He had been personally introduced to President Kennedy, a James Bond fan, as the American 007. One of the favorite spooks of the Kennedy brothers, Brigadier General Edward Lansdale, took Harvey into the Oval Office. As Lansdale told the story, which Harvey later denied, the general barely kept the agent from carrying two hidden guns into the presidential presence, one in a shoulder holster and a "backup piece" strapped to the belt in the small of Harvey's back.

Starting in that very summer of 1961, the administration was depending on Harvey to rid it of the Kennedy brothers' most inconvenient and obsessively hated adversary, Fidel Castro, the victor of the Bay of Pigs. Since earlier "disabling operations" had failed to produce the desired "health alteration" of the Cuban leader—poison pills couldn't be slipped into his meals, as planned—the agency placed Harvey in charge of a new "executive action" program whose key employees were Mafia mobsters. It was codenamed ZR/RIFLE, and it included "a capability to perform assas-

---

* The processing of the backlog was not completed until two years and five months after the Soviets shut the tunnel down.

sinations," as Harvey eventually admitted to a Senate investigating committee.

One CIA director after another was tempted to fire Bill Harvey, but only his first boss pushed himself to do it, and that was long ago. In 1947 the puritanical J. Edgar Hoover dismissed Bill as an FBI counterintelligence agent. The cause: drunkenness. Bill *was* a chronic drunk, a highly visible one who consumed three martinis at lunch (two of them were doubles), drank Scotch neat by the water glass, and often fell asleep in his office in the afternoon. He was so corpulent that the agency gave him medical dispensation to fly first class so he could fit into airplane seats. Harvey was also paranoid, always packing a gun or two, keeping a weapon on his desk even at CIA headquarters in Langley, Virginia, and sometimes loading it and practicing with the trigger in front of nervous visitors.

"If you ever know as many secrets as I do, then you'll know why I carry a gun," he explained in his raspy voice.

His attitude toward the Germans was not what one would expect from a ranking American representative who had constant dealings with officials of the host country. "He hated the goddamned Krauts," one of his admirers said evenly. "He wanted nothing to do with them." Sometimes Harvey looked at a local newspaper to encourage the belief that he knew some German. He didn't, and he refused to learn.

Still, Harvey's reputation as a superagent was deserved. The man had scope. It was Bill who unmasked Kim Philby, the British traitor whom Allen Dulles considered the most dangerous Soviet spy ever to penetrate Western intelligence. And the Berlin tunnel showed Harvey at his most imaginative and dogged best. Senior agency officers were certain that Dulles would never have gone ahead with such a monumental and risky undertaking—the CIA director ordered that "as little as possible concerning the project be reduced to writing"—if Harvey hadn't been in charge in Berlin.

The assignment would have overtaxed a less obsessed man. Before 3,100 tons of dirt could be excavated, Harvey conceived the idea to build a warehouse over the mouth of the tunnel near Schönefelder Chaussée in Lichtenberg and to disguise it as a radar intercept station. After a CIA soil mechanic overcame underground water problems, 125 tons of steel liner plates, shipped from the U.S. in crates marked "spare parts," were bolted together to form the walls.

Harvey conducted frequent inspections at night, cautiously

Bill Harvey's famous Berlin tunnel *(above)* allowed the CIA to listen in on Soviet and East German telephone circuits in the mid-1950s. What Harvey *(far right)* didn't know was that, because of the British mole George Blake *(near right)*, the Kremlin had long been aware of the tunnel and the wiretaps.

changing cars en route so he would not be followed. When the tunnel was finished, he walked to a steel-and-concrete door that marked the border and where he had ordered a sign to be put up with lettering in German and Russian: ENTRY IS FORBIDDEN BY ORDER OF THE COMMANDING GENERAL.

The taps that led into 172 Soviet and East German circuits, each carrying eighteen or more channels, were installed by British operatives; they were more experienced than the Americans in this line of work. Tapes of recorded phone conversations were shipped to London for translation. The take from wire traffic and other sources was processed in a shabby temporary building left over from World War II near the Washington Monument in Washington. It was T (for "Tempo") 32, known as "the Hosiery Mill" because it nearly drowned in its many threadlike wires.

Internal CIA postmortems questioned the value of the tunnel's intelligence feast. No great scoops were uncovered. The "OB boys" were happy because the tunnel produced mountains of "order of battle" data on the secret but transitory movements of Communist military assets. The bulk of the take was curiously marginal, however, and the official CIA version of the tunnel's discovery on April 21, 1956, sounded mundane enough to be either true or grossly naïve. Supposedly, unusually heavy rainfall damaged a Soviet wire that was already in poor shape, and the repair crews stumbled across the taps. Somebody hung a black wreath on Harvey's office door that day.

The Soviets turned the tunnel into a propaganda showpiece. The Berlin press corps was invited for a tour and a briefing, and the Soviet end became a tourist attraction with a snack bar. The American press was enchanted by Harvey's audacity ("The stuff of which thrill films are made," said the *New York Herald Tribune*). Abroad, the United States stood exposed for overambitious snooping, but the ultimate outcome of the tunnel caper was more embarrassing.

"From the beginning it was realized that the duration of this operation was finite," said a CIA report on Operation Gold. But even though Dulles, Harvey, and their colleagues had reckoned with the eventual discovery of the tunnel, they were convinced that its take made the effort worthwhile. Unfortunately, it developed five years later, over the Easter weekend of 1961, that the fabled tunnel had been a farce, an exercise in total futility.

The Russians had known about it all along. It had operated only at their sufferance. They left it alone for a while to protect their mole in Harvey's Berlin kingdom: the Soviet agent who tipped them off. Meanwhile they felt secure because the Allies were learning little of intrinsic value.

"The Soviets knew that the tunnel's chief value was early warning, and they also knew that they weren't going to attack," one ranking CIA chief dolefully observed to the Washington correspondent David C. Martin after the crushing news of the duplicity broke.

Harvey's reputation did not suffer because of the tunnel's uselessness, especially not in Berlin. "Harvey was gone from Berlin for more than a year when the Wall was built," the base reports officer told me, "but those who followed were his lieutenants. They all held Harvey in awe."

Out of the frenetic Berlin base, Harvey and his case officers also controlled the East European agents who delivered secrets by courier or personally, sometimes by the suitcaseful. It was useful to be Harvey's protégé. His graduates tended to do well, nobody more so than El Supremo, Bill Graver, also known as Der Lange (the Tall One) because of his remarkable height.

Hyperenergetic, hyperambitious, fidgety to the point of jumpiness, poker-faced yet exploding with expressive body language, Graver became known in the agency as an elegant handler of bureaucratic power. He was a sardonically witty, incisive briefer whose performances impressed superiors, an animated mimic, a take-charge fellow, an obvious leader; but above all he ranked as a politician, never hesitating to cut a corner or two for political advantage. He seemed to venture no move without taking its measure against the long-term implications for his career.

Graver was a Bill Harvey acolyte, no question. He would speak of his "fondness" for Harvey. He especially admired Harvey's fearlessness, not so much the sangfroid attitude toward the external opposition, the Communists, but Harvey's fuck-you manner toward the enemy within, the opposition that was much harder to handle than the Reds—the bureaucracy that ran the agency and handed out the money, the assignments, the promotions. The success of Harvey's tunnel was debatable, but the way Harvey charged up the hill, taking Project Gold right to the pinnacle to Dulles and Bissell, the great doubters who controlled the appropriations, never taking no for an answer, and coming back to charge uphill again and again after rejections along the way—*that* was unassailable heroism to Bill Graver.

Graver observed Harvey closely during the creation of the mighty tunnel—watching and learning how Harvey brushed past complexities; how Harvey's memory allowed him to go to a file drawer and instantly fish out a paper everybody had forgotten years ago; how Harvey would roar through a report and mark it up, stabbing viciously at every weakness.

"Harvey should be the only person in the world allowed to put comments on the margins of reports," marveled one of his Berlin case officers during the glory time of the 1950s. How Harvey's disciples loved him!

Graver's veneration of Harvey did have significant limits. El Supremo, agile and forever the boyish elitist, came out of the more sophisticated tradition of a brief career as a college instructor and five years of service with the CIA "Choirboys" in Vienna. Graver's style was much more orderly, more button-down, in dress as well as manner. He spoke German well, he didn't drink or cuss to excess, and he wielded a rapier, not a fuck-you sledgehammer. Graver was at heart a wary warrior, careful to sit in a corner chair where nobody could sneak up on him, never walking under construction scaffolding where an ill-wisher might discharge a two-by-four on his head.

While most of his people thought highly of Graver, they did not adore him. He did not inspire emotional fealty, and some resented his corner cutting and his way of sometimes not looking at you when he talked to you. But the payoff of his Teflon management skill was gratifying. Graver was the spy-in-charge who totally missed the Berlin Wall, yet he wound up as chief of London Station, the CIA's most prestigious overseas assignment.*

Another of Harvey's students was Theodore Shackley, tall, with an elegant Boston accent, and so furtive that his agency colleagues came to call him "the Blond Ghost." For Harvey's tunnel, he handled liaison with the British MI6 agents headquartered in the Olympic Stadium way uptown. After Berlin, Shackley, thirty-four, worked once more with Harvey, this time out of Miami in the campaign against Castro. There, Ted had become chief of the

---

* He was still active at sixty-six in the fall of 1988, looking boyish as ever, after more than forty years as an intelligence officer.

JM/WAVE Station, whose more than six hundred American agents made it the largest CIA operation in the world. Odds makers in the agency thought Shackley would one day become CIA director, but the Blond Ghost sabotaged himself and fell from grace.*

Bill Harvey could not think back upon his Berlin days without regret, indeed a sense of personal betrayal. Ironically, he never trusted the British and called them "untrustworthy motherfuckers" to their faces. It turned out that as far back as 1953, when he first started planning the tunnel with his British counterparts at conferences in London, the double agent, an MI6 man named George Blake, participated in the top-secret discussions. He even took minutes of the meetings. Later, working for four years from the Olympic Stadium in Berlin, Blake was in touch with the tunnel operations step by step.

Eventually suspicion fell upon Blake's unorthodox history. Born as George Behar of Egyptian parents in Rotterdam, he began to display a flair for intelligence work as a very young man during World War II. A member of the Dutch underground, he arrived in England with a warning that the Germans were secretly controlling nearly all British intelligence teams in Holland. In 1950, as MI6 station chief in Seoul, he was captured when the North Koreans invaded the South. After three years in prison, officially a stoic hero but presumably subject to Communist brainwashing, he was repatriated to London via East Berlin and resumed his career with MI6.

The case against Blake was flimsy. British counterintelligence

---

* High executive status notwithstanding, Harvey and Shackley did not lose their touch as operatives. To support continuing CIA schemes for eliminating Castro, they rented a U-Haul truck, filled it with explosives, detonators, and guns, and drove it to a parking lot, where they handed the keys to one of their hired Mafia killers, Johnny Rosselli. A year later, Rosselli's body, its legs cut off, was found stuffed in an oil drum floating in the ocean off Miami. Shackley and Harvey left their intelligence careers alive but out of favor. Shackley's reports were no longer trusted. After rising to the number two post in the directorate for clandestine operations, he was, in effect, forced out of the CIA because of his contacts with Edwin P. Wilson, a rogue CIA man who went to prison for supplying a terrorist capability to Colonel Qaddafi in Libya. In 1987 Shackley appeared in the Iran-Contra affair as a middleman negotiator. Harvey's drinking finally so embarrassed the agency in his last post, as station chief in Rome, that he "resigned." He died in 1976, aged sixty, in Indianapolis, where he was keeping himself afloat as a $9,000-a-year editor with a small publishing house.

discovered that their man had a cousin who was one of the founders of the Egyptian Communist Party; that he had spent time in Moscow en route back from Korea; and that he sometimes asked his secretary to type an extra copy of reports "for the files." The chief interrogator, bluffing, stacked a huge pile of papers on his desk and told Blake that it represented the case against him. The ploy worked. The mole broke and confessed.

"Blake was lashing back at British society and British life for injuries, real or imagined," a CIA officer told David Martin. "The amount of damage he was able to do was almost on a monumental scale." More than fifty American and British agents were betrayed by him. Sentenced to forty-two years, the longest prison term ever handed down by a British court, Blake served only five years, in Wormwood Scrubs, before making a daring escape to Moscow, where he received the Order of Lenin and reminisced about the Berlin tunnel to *Izvestia*. It still pleased him to gloat about how he had fooled the great Bill Harvey and the Berlin Cowboys.

"Many people made a career for themselves in connection with this notorious tunnel," he said.

A KGB mole of even more devastating order was caught during the same period because a double agent for the CIA passed along a bit of gossip in Berlin. He had picked it up from his Soviet boss, the chief of KGB counterintelligence. The Russian had bragged about one of the six West German intelligence officials who had received "orientation" at CIA headquarters in the United States at CIA expense four years earlier, in 1956. The visitor to Washington had been a Soviet agent.

This item rang like a burglar alarm in the ears of a senior CIA officer, Clare Edward Petty, who had been running a largely dormant investigation named Operation DROWZY. Petty was an exceptionally intense and hypersuspicious counterintelligence man,* and his effort was fallow for lack of hard evidence.

---

* Petty, whom I found calm and congenial in retirement at Annapolis, Maryland, later became famous within the CIA as the author of an enormous report suggesting circumstantially that James Jesus Angleton, the venerable director of CIA Counterintelligence, one of the agency's Grand Old Men, was actually a Soviet mole. It was a little like a parish priest accusing a cardinal of rape. The charge was never substantiated, although Angleton was eventually fired for having

For eight years Petty had been performing liaison with General Reinhard Gehlen's BND, the German Bundesnachrichtendienst (Federal Intelligence Service), headquartered in Pullach, outside of Munich.* The BND's fearful losses of "assets" had convinced him that "the Org," as the agency was called, had to be infested by a double agent at its highest level. Eventually Petty became convinced that the traitor was *Oberregierungsrat* Heinz Felfe, nicknamed "Fiffi," the chief of the Soviet Section in Department III/F (counterintelligence). It galled Petty that he hadn't been able to prove it, and after the Berlin tip from the double agent he was even more furious because he himself had been the CIA official who guilelessly escorted Felfe and his associates during their Washington inspection.

Felfe had embarked on his intelligence career in the Nazi Berlin of the 1930s as an SS *Ober-Sturmführer* in Heinrich Himmler's *Reichssicherheitshauptamt* (RSHA), Hitler's security agency. It was the sort of professional experience General Gehlen appreciated in his key officers after the war, and for eleven years Felfe—quiet, bald, and professorial—built an astounding record in the BND. He established a network of informers in Moscow led by a Soviet colonel. He collected minutes of the East German Politburo in Berlin. He identified Communist spies by the dozen and uncovered their drops, couriers, and safe houses. He produced Soviet documents and codes. He told Gehlen that he had defused plans to kidnap or assassinate the general.

Gehlen came to trust Felfe totally and placed him in charge of *Operation Panoptikum* (Wax Works), thereby sabotaging the Org's elaborate scheme to neutralize Soviet penetration of the BND. Fiffi was a star, and the general loved showing high-level visitors the pièce de résistance in Felfe's office: a gigantic, constantly updated multicolored plan of KGB headquarters in Karlshorst, including

---

turned too inconveniently paranoid. He thought that just about everybody was a mole.

* In those times the BND was pretty much a wholly owned subsidiary of the CIA. Its director, Gehlen, a tiny, vain martinet of a general, may have been the most overrated secret service boss of modern times. He was, however, an excellent salesman. With his closest aides and fifty steel cases of Nazi intelligence files, this *Abwehr* general engineered his instant renewal by insinuating himself into the hands of Allen Dulles at the end of World War II. In the ensuing years Gehlen politicked resourcefully with a succession of West German chancellors until, after one scandal too many, he was ousted in 1968.

every parking space and the lavatory used by the commanding general. As an intelligence tool, this display was a useless conceit ("nonsense," *Schwachsinn*, Felfe called it years afterward), but it reinforced the impression that Fiffi was omniscient.

In a way he was, because his extraordinary intelligence achievements were *Spielmaterial,* material for games, sophisticated fakes concocted by the KGB in Karlshorst for consumption in the gullible West. The Soviets had recruited Felfe even before he went to work for Gehlen. They referred to him as "Paul" or "P-33." Felfe was in daily touch with Karlshorst via his A-3 radio and he supplied more than 300 Minox films (containing pictures of 15,661 documents) via another double agent, one of his oldest friends, a bull-necked former Gestapo agent who worked for the BND in Bonn. With Felfe regulating the pipelines carefully—supplying "not too much and not too little," as he explained later—the two men transmitted the weekly and monthly reports of the BND and a steady flow of other timely secrets. They penetrated the Chancellor's office in Bonn, tapped into some operations of the CIA base in West Berlin, and tipped off the KGB when Soviet spies were about to be arrested. Over the years, ninety-four BND agents were "blown" by Felfe in the DDR.

The CIA could tell that something was very wrong inside German intelligence, but they couldn't place a finger on any specific rotten apple and so they confined themselves to fuming at this entire outfit of leaky allies. "They fucked up in World War II and they were fucking up now," said one of the CIA managers in Berlin. "The only good thing was that they speak fluent German."

Felfe was special, though. He was a virtuoso.

His relationship with his Soviet bosses was personal and congenial. Felfe frequently had to be in Berlin on BND business, and he used some of these occasions for brief detours eastward to report progress and to receive instructions from his controllers at Karlshorst over caviar and champagne.

For his dual diligence Felfe was showered with appreciation and money by both his employers. In his best years he collected two hefty salaries totaling about 300,000 marks a year, including Christmas bonuses. About two thirds of his compensation came from the East. For his tenth BND anniversary in 1960, General Gehlen officiated at a celebration in his office and presented Felfe with a silver plaque: FÜR TREUE DIENSTE (For Loyal Service). It showed Saint George killing a dragon that symbolized the KGB. The Russians gave him an extra bonus of 20,000 marks.

Felfe loved living well—he acquired an elegant home in a Bavarian mountain resort and a farm where he raised cattle—but money was only one of the forces that drove him. In their youth, he and his partner in Bonn had come from Dresden and they wanted revenge for the friends and family members who died in the Allied saturation raids on that city. A third ex-Nazi, who shuttled as a BND courier between West Germany and Berlin and carried documents from Felfe to the KGB on the same trips, also was one of Fiffi's prewar cronies from Dresden.

Felfe was moved by something more, however, and Clare Petty, the CIA agent responsible for his downfall, was struck by this extra dimension. "They were all mad about Dresden," he told me, "but a central feature was that Felfe wanted to show his intellectual arrogance. It gave him fantastic personal satisfaction to put one over on Gehlen. He took great pleasure in that."

The end came quickly. The BND finally placed a tap on Felfe's phone and discovered an unusually large volume of calls to his partner in Bonn. The Bonn agent was tailed, and he appeared to be in communication with the Soviets. One Friday in November 1961 he called Felfe and complained that he had been unable to decode a message. Felfe told him to forward the signal by registered mail. BND security agents found that it contained instructions from Felfe's Soviet case officer in Berlin. They resealed the letter; when it was delivered to Felfe on Monday, he tried—unsuccessfully—to swallow the note as police burst into his office and wrestled him to the floor.

Taken before the BND official in charge of the investigation, Felfe carried a black attaché case, which he placed casually on the officer's desk. Later it turned out to contain fourteen microfilms of documents and one tape that he was about to forward to Karlshorst. His audacity did not desert Felfe in prison either. Assigned to wrap and address magazines, he produced extra labels and mailed coded inserts to cover addresses, thereby keeping his Karlshorst handlers abreast of his interrogations. Petty sat in on the first six weeks of the questioning. When the American appeared for the initial session in the top-floor recreation room of the prison, Felfe recognized him instantly. He smiled and stuck out his hand in greeting, one pro to another.

9

ANATOMY OF AN INTELLIGENCE FAILURE

West Berlin,
Thursday, August 10, 1961

The most virulent disease of Berlin as an intelligence playground (my CIA friends preferred the more evocative German word for it, *Tummelplatz*), was rarely mentioned. Perhaps that might have spoiled the sport. The critical ailment was simply surfeit.

"Too much came from too many," I heard from an American intelligence officer who collected intelligence for the U.S. Air Force from the refugees pouring into the Marienfelde reception camp. The sheer onslaught of live information into this oasis, the years-around movable feast of an intelligence smorgasbord, sparked a headlong intramural race for the juiciest interviewees. For years, my Air Force man hand-carried the daily biographical list of fresh arrivals from the camp to headquarters on Clayallee. En route, he opened the envelope, noted the choice names for instant attention by his Air Force bosses, and resealed it to escape "enemy" notice.

Resentment and resistance against the CIA and its elitist snobs (or so perceived) ran especially deep among the numerous competitors within the home teammates. "We didn't need any CIA cover people sneaking around with cameras doing the same things we were doing," E. Allan Lightner, Jr., the ranking State Department old-timer and deputy director of the U.S. Mission in Berlin, bristled at me twenty-five years after the Wall went up.

Berlin intelligence work was like a brawl; a novelist could best convey its feel.*

The bureaucracies tried to cope by using bureaucratic tools. They relied heavily on the many committees and the resulting collective judgments. They attempted to ration secrets by imposing limited access through "compartmental clearances," several of these classifications running higher than "top secret." System, system, everything was supposed to work by system. They even conceived a system to ease the inbred warfare between the oil-and-water factions scrabbling for recognition within every intelligence organization: the natural conflict between the collectors and the analysts.

In CIA theory, officers in the field existed to collect; committees of analysts in Washington lived to interpret. The two functions could never be cleanly separated because, in contrast to church and state, the same hierarchy issued the paychecks. Not every bleep of information could be funneled to Washington. It would have aggravated the existing chaos and would have been physically much too unwieldy. And so a system was created to select, to winnow, to grade, to "prioritize." Every bleep was labeled in one of thirty-six gradations, from A-1 to F-6. The last designation indicated that the item came from a source so obscure that its value was unknown and possibly zero.

Often the turf within the intelligence turf became a battleground of intense internal conflicts. Officers in the "collection side of the house" would feel that the analytical side was ignoring or underrating marvelous morsels acquired at great effort in the field. The analytical side tended to ward off the field people as chronically overexcited wild men. Some of the craftier collection people developed private channels to the analytical side and bypassed the system by communicating choice tips to sympathetic analysts of their acquaintance.

At times, feelings between the field men and the desk men were as sour as if the two groups were enemies, especially when the

---

* "Berlin. What a garrison of spies!" wrote John le Carré in his 1986 novel, *A Perfect Spy.* "We had tunnelers and smugglers, listeners and forgers, trainers and recruiters and talent-spotters and couriers and watchers and seducers, assassins and balloonists, lip-readers and disguise artists. But whatever the Brits had, the Americans had more, and whatever the Americans had the East Germans had five of it and the Russians ten of it. . . . And the committees. . . . Berlin was not safe enough to contain them. . . ."

home office people would, in effect, go on strike and simply refuse to pass along information collected abroad. "The Reports Office took the position that if you can't mangle it, it's not information," recalled one old-timer. "We'd take copies of reports that they wouldn't disseminate and walk them over to the other side of the house."

In addition to the committees at the top of the heap in Langley, Virginia, more committees sprouted around the bottom—such as the Berlin Watch Committee, which was supposed to pool the wisdom, the smell, the hunches, the reputations of military operators like Tom McCord, Ernest von Pawel, and representatives from State and CIA.

It didn't work. Surfeit. Interservice jockeying. Fragmentation. Arrogance. All that, plus the fondness for memories of flawed successes and flawed heroes of a departed era. All this was ballast that the committee and its chiefs carried into the Berlin Wall crisis. Not to mention the cunning of the enemy.

In August 1961 Berlin was still the most productive intelligence collection center in the world. It was the one hole in the Iron Curtain that permitted largely unimpeded passage not only into East Germany but, way beyond, into the entire "denied area" of East bloc nations, including the Soviet Union, and the American effort to tap this mammoth territory for information was organized on an ambitious scale.*

The BOB personnel numbered only about one hundred, but each of the forty case officers, the actual agent handlers, ran about a dozen spies and met with them regularly in West Berlin. Since the Americans were not supposed to expose themselves to enemy interrogation in case of capture, they were not allowed to travel in the East. The hundreds of agents, swarming all over the forbidden countries, were therefore foreign nationals, and much of what they

---

* Although the Communists exploited Berlin much more extensively as a base of operations against intelligence targets in the opposite direction, nothing made them more furious than the manipulations of Harvey, Graver, and their crew. Eventually Berlin's unique status as a seedbed of espionage became a high-level diplomatic issue. When the Soviets brought up this Western "subversive activity" (*Wühlarbeit*) at the 1959 meetings of the Foreign Ministers, the CIA dispatched Bill Harvey to Geneva with a response: a compendium of parallel Communist efforts in the city, lovingly compiled by the counterespionage (CE) contingent of the base. The exchange of sins altered nothing.

gathered in the way of Foreign Positive Intelligence (FPI, in the agency's parlance) was routine economic data that Communist regimes treated as secrets.

Often the agents had to travel no farther than East Berlin, where every Eastern bloc nation maintained central trade offices that covered all needs and sales offers for each entire country. Until the late 1950s, East-West trade had been largely in the hands of smugglers or career criminals, most of them KGB connected. By 1960, fairly respectable Western commission buyers and salesmen had taken over, along with banks and trading companies. From these ranks the CIA recruited many of its agents.

Security precautions were meticulously observed. CIA officers never used their real names in contacts with agents. The Americans carried screwdrivers and exchanged U.S. military license plates on their cars for German ones before driving off to meet a contact. Foreign-born agents would be "fluttered" or "boxed" by an American "poly man," a polygraph operator, every time they returned from a mission in order to ascertain, at least hopefully, whether they had been "turned" (recruited as double agents by the opposition) while operating in enemy territory.* Case officers would hound themselves ruthlessly trying to retrieve papers, if at all possible, within fifteen minutes after agents deposited them for pickup in "dead drops" (unattended public hiding places).

CIA officers never, never met agents except in public or in "safe houses"—apartments or houses operated by the agency and managed by German housekeepers, who were checked by a poly man once a week. Until the Wall curtailed CIA operations, some forty safe houses were operating in the city under such code names as Beach House and Green House. One officer and two assistants were required, full time, merely to administer these hiding places because leases ran out, houses were "blown" by enemy agents, and new acquisitions had to be arranged constantly with the help of civilian newspaper advertisements.

Sometimes the collection of sensitive requirements on the BOB's want list, known as the Related Missions Directive (RMD), depended on luck. I talked to one of Graver's case officers, who, chatting with a fortyish woman at a party, discovered that her East

---

* The insider terms "box" and "flutter" derived from agency cryptonyms for the polygraph, first known as "LCBOX," later as "LCFLUTTER." Although the device fell into disrepute in American courts, I never heard of the CIA questioning its value.

Berlin apartment overlooked a Soviet military parking lot. She could copy the numbers from the license plates of vehicles. This was important Order of Battle (OOB) information, since each Soviet division was assigned its own license designation. If the prevailing identification pattern changed on the parking lot, this probably meant that a division had been moved.

At first the woman brought out lists every week. When this became too much trouble, she received "commo," a means of clandestine communication. My agent friend taught her the art of "secret writing" (SW). She was given a supply of white pills to be dissolved in water and used as invisible ink for sending information in large block letters, usually on the back of harmless cover notes. The woman learned how to steam and rub the secret writing so that the paper's fibers would not look as if they had been displaced.

All these precautions could quickly have become worthless, since iodine fumes can bring out almost any writing, but nobody troubled to apply iodine fumes to the letters that my friend's friend mailed, with a fake return address, to a post office box in Frankfurt. About six months after the Wall went up, the woman got married and moved to Leipzig. Without having been asked, she briefed her apartment's new resident, who continued doing the job without revealing her identity to the CIA. When the new agent ran out of invisible ink, he or she sent out the license numbers "in the clear."

"For all I know they're still doing it," my CIA man said nearly thirty years later.

The Marienfelde Reception Center, where refugees from the East were processed and debriefed, was also helpful for the recruiting of the more important agents in place. With luck and persistence, defectors who passed through the camp became middlemen in arranging for a long-term flow of information to come from friends, relatives, or other contacts who stayed behind. Once a refugee had identified such a potential source of intelligence to an interrogator at Marienfelde, he was instructed, "Get him over here for a visit and we'll have a cup of coffee with him."

If the visitor was well placed to receive useful information, he was then confronted with an attractive enticement. "You can work your way out of the DDR," the CIA recruiter would tell the prospect. "Wouldn't it be nice to have a one-hundred-thousand-dollar nest egg in Frankfurt when you want to leave the country after a while?"

Over the years, case officers learned to recognize what motivations worked best for turning perfectly ordinary people into reliable spies. Ideologues tended to be hotheads who ignored instructions and caused trouble. But a desire for personal revenge —against real or imagined slights—was a powerful asset. An offer of money was usually not effective of itself. Nevertheless, pay was of some help as a persuader, and once a spy had accepted compensation he would be committed or at least implicated.

"You *want* him to take money, it's a handle," was the way one case officer put it to me. "Usually we put an amount equal to five percent of his normal annual income into escrow in a West German bank. He'll be shown the bank records. Operational expenses will also be paid."

Case officer work was not for imperceptive people.

Donald R. Morris, thirty-seven, a former professional Navy lieutenant (Annapolis '44), a linguist and a successful novelist, was the type of case officer the CIA treasured. His mind whirred at top speed, throwing off ideas like electrical sparks (his degree was in electrical engineering). Don Morris ranked his CIA work way ahead of his family, he needed practically no sleep, and his memory operated like a retrieval system of everything he had ever seen or heard. Morris reveled in complexity and arcana (he would soon write the definitive history of the Zulu nation), his patience was infinite, his devotion to detail fanatical.

Hardly the least of his talents was the way he had with people. Don Morris was a wonder with people, canny and enthusiastic, zeroing in on them with empathy, taking them in, taking them over, sometimes for years.

Morris knew that the volume of business at the Marienfelde camp, his favorite hunting ground, always peaked on Friday night because weekend refugees hoped that their absence would not be noticed until Monday. One Saturday morning in January 1960 Morris received a promising call from one of the center's spotters —German agents assigned to tip off case officers about interesting new refugees. Using code numbers, the spotter informed Morris of an East Berlin woman, a late Friday night newcomer, whose job with the East German state railroad somehow involved the Karlshorst *Sperrgebiet,* the Soviet off-limits zone.

Morris's curiosity was automatic. Any data about this Karlshorst ghetto, the forbidden all-Soviet enclave of nearly a square mile, were of interest. But the woman he met at the Beach House in

Dahlem the same snowy morning—he always referred to her as Annie—was a plump, dowdily dressed war widow of fifty-three with a knitting bag who wanted to talk only about her one interest in life—her son, Willy, a machinist who had gone West at age eighteen because he hated the DDR dictatorship, and whom she wanted to join. She missed him woefully, and she was not crazy about the DDR.

Morris let her talk and talk. Only when Annie started on her third cup of coffee with cookies did he steer her gently toward details of her work. She was flattered and amazed. She had done the same chores for more than ten years. The routine was extremely dull. Nobody had ever inquired about it. Each morning, alone in her cramped back room in the cargo depot near the Karlshorst ghetto, Annie received bills of lading for freight shipments from and to the Soviet Union. She had to unpin the sheaves, stamp the papers, redistribute the copies, and call each Russian's office to arrange for pickup or delivery of the crates containing his household effects.

Annie had never realized until Morris pointed it out to her that she had access to the full and authentic name, rank, location, and recent movements for nearly every KGB and GRU officer coming into the DDR or leaving the country, as well as arrivals and departures at the special secret police housing in Moscow. All this was priceless information. To find out what the opposition was up to, it would be handy to tail its operatives. This was supersensitive work that no one could even begin until one knew who and where the opposition was.

Annie's bright blue eyes glistened with animation at hearing the news of her importance. This in turn gladdened Morris, because he knew that it was practically impossible to turn a plain citizen into a good spy unless that person could be convinced that it was in his or her own interest to do what the case officer wanted. Annie would have been insulted if he had suggested she should go back to her job merely for extra pay, even if it was only for a few months and she could stop whenever she wished.

She was not much interested in politics. And she didn't look like an adventurer (often a promising category). She was, however, lonely, and that was helpful.

Her life had little purpose. She had sparkled when Morris had talked to her about her work and had found it fascinating. Now she was no longer alone or useless. Don Morris had found the key to Annie and turned it in the correct direction. Back at the office, when he faced the usual report forms, he paused only briefly before the full blank page marked "Agent's motivation." Then he filled in a single word, "Loneliness."

By that time—that very Saturday afternoon—Annie was back in East Berlin, acting as if she had never left. She had agreed to stay for six months, possibly a year. She would make extra copies of the flimsies she normally prepared from the papers that came to her desk, and in two weeks she was to bring her take to the same S-Bahn *(Stadtbahn)* elevated station on West Berlin's Savigny Platz where Morris had seen her off. She would be carrying them folded and hidden in her bra, a detail that made her smile.

She smiled again when she reappeared two Saturdays later. She laughed when she related how she had flirted with the *Vopos* at the border. She glowed when Morris bought her a new silk dress at the Ka De We department store. She was positively gay when she waved good-bye. Her new life as an agent had lifted her depression, and she took to every twist of her new trade.

More than a year after Annie had begun her trips for Don Morris, he decided to give her a means of "alternate commo," a way to communicate without personal visits. She learned secret writing by way of ink pills hidden in an East German lipstick Morris gave her. He had hesitated for weeks: the rule was to keep dealings with agents simple. Methods popularized in spy movies tended to make amateur agents terribly nervous, usually for good reason. In most homes it wasn't easy to hide helpful accoutrements like a radio transmitter. But the flow of Annie's unique information could not be interrupted for lack of commo. She might become ill, unable to travel. Morris might have to leave town. The border might be closed, a speculation that made them both smile when they considered it; the contingency seemed so remote.

That conversation took place not long before the Wall went up, making Annie wonder whether she would ever see her Willy again.*

Whenever indicated, the BOB's Technical Services department was superbly outfitted to deliver paraphernalia familiar to James Bond fans. Passports, genuine and fake, with identity photos or

---

* Morris did "exfiltrate" Annie through a sequence of complicated ruses, but not for another year.

without, could be ordered like cafeteria lunches. So could weapons, radio transmitters, or identity cards thoughtfully left blank for individual "fill-ins." Theater stubs, used plane tickets, receipted hotel or department store bills, and other telltale "pocket litter" were available to document an agent's presence in just about any locality that he was supposedly frequenting on a particular day or at a particular time. No gimmick was neglected to document a cover story.

To tap the larger perspective of enemy intentions, the BOB was blessed with the take from electronic surveillance, which seemed omnipotent. "We had tremendous technical coverage," claimed one of the senior CIA managers. "It was very deep, very sophisticated, constantly flashing for critical intelligence." Again, Berlin's location as a mini-island in Soviet-controlled territory was helpful. "To get at tactical radio transmissions from the Soviets, you've got to be close," the CIA manager explained.*

And while spy satellites were too new and therefore still too few for reconnaissance against anything less important than nuclear missile bases, Western spying from the air was likewise continual. "The Air Force was doing low-level black [secret] photography from the [Berlin-Helmstedt] air corridors several times a day," said a CIA officer familiar with these missions. "They could count the [artillery] field pieces on the ground."

Direct ground surveillance of the opposition, while legal and vigorously pursued by the U.S. Army, was shakier. On paper the opportunities to track Communist preparations for military surprises looked ideal. Under a 1947 agreement, the three Western powers were still allowed to maintain military reconnaissance outposts in the DDR. In exchange, the Soviets operated three such teams in West Germany. Under the zealous Colonel von Pawel, patrols of the American Military Liaison Mission (MLM) cruised

---

* In 1989, the National Security Agency and the Army's Intelligence and Security Command still employed six hundred men to operate "radar stations" on the Teufelsberg, a 115-meter mountain in the Grunewald excursion woods of West Berlin, built from twenty-five million cubic meters of *Trümmerschutt* (rubble cleaned up from the war). Unfortunately, the take from such operations could be as fatally compromised as the output of Harvey's tunnel. The weak links were traitors like James W. Hall III, an Army warrant officer sentenced in 1989 to forty years for espionage. From 1982 to 1985 he had been paid $300,000 by East German and Soviet intelligence for secrets from the American electronic eavesdropping in Berlin. One program rendered useless by Hall was said to have cost the United States hundreds of millions of dollars.

through the DDR daily, paying special attention to troop movements and military transports along the Autobahnen.

The "coverage" was illusory. "SSD [*Stasi*] tails were with us most of the time," the colonel explained later. "When we thought they were not, we usually were wrong." Often the opposition escorts harassed and detained the Americans. Worse, most of the DDR's area was off limits to von Pawel and his inspectors. "Goose egg" (permanent restriction) maps denied them access to well over half of the country. In addition, they were barred from more than five thousand "restricted areas" that were marked by signs in four languages. And since they were not accredited to East Berlin, they never patrolled there.

That wasn't the end of the ballast afflicting "Von's" missions. To his great annoyance, he was never cleared to receive much of the relevant information to which his superiors had access and that could have helped him and his men do a sharper job of reconnaissance. Regulations specified that officers assigned to opposition territory were not entitled to know sensitive data because they might be forced to give secrets away in case of capture.

This was no marginal handicap. When the men in charge of the CIA's BOB later wondered why they had received not the slightest inkling that a wall was about to go up, some of the blame was assigned to the bureaucratic circumstance that von Pawel and his mission had been inadequately "tasked." In plain English, this meant that the Liaison Mission had been given too few specific instructions on what to look for: such as large transports of the distinctively designed "Spanish rider" tank barriers.

Humility and an appreciation of his limitations were not known assets of Bill Graver, and this hampered him and his officers in several ways. They weren't *looking* for signs of a wall, so they were not too likely to find evidence of preparations even for such an enormous project. Since Washington had written off East Berlin, nobody had reason to worry much about maintaining control over the area. Graver and his colleagues were therefore not greatly upset over their most serious failure: their inability to penetrate the DDR leadership or even to get rudimentary reports from, say, a cleaning woman with entry to the headquarters where Honecker was doing his scheming.

True, the largely leakproof controls imposed by the overwhelming manpower in the security apparatus of the DDR dictatorship made it exceptionally difficult to tap the secrets of the leaders. Penetration was possible, however. Until May 1961, Colonel Tom

McCord and his military intelligence officers maintained a reliable East Berlin source with access to the top echelon of the SED. That mole's information about DDR plans did get through to the top of the American policy apparatus, and he earned a specific commendation from Secretary of State Christian Herter. Unhappily, he was detected violating his *Westverbot** and was never replaced.

More typically, the hard data about the Wall that were obtained by Dr. Hartmut Wedel at his dentist's chair in the French sector evidently got lost in the shuffle of the Allied committee system— the filter that a frustrated CIA veteran of the Berlin base subsequently described to me as "layering, layering, layering." The CIA old-timer went on: "Unfortunately, the dictum of the computer experts applied: GIGO—garbage in, garbage out. The communications system flashed huge amounts of data to the appropriate points; alas, in sum this was not the right data."

The intelligence system had grown too big, too complex, and too clogged to serve the great General George Marshall's lone requirement: twenty-four-hours' notice of a major move by a major enemy.

----

* DDR functionaries with access to sensitive information were not allowed to travel in the West. *Westverbot* was the order that was supposed to keep them from crossing the border.

10

THE SPY OF SPIES: "I LEARNED ABOUT THE BERLIN CLOSING"

Moscow,
Thursday, August 10, 1961

By enormous good luck, the CIA did have its agent in place in Moscow, briefly but during just the right period. He did know the secret of August 13 and he was no run-of-the-keyhole snooper. He was that perfectly positioned colonel of the GRU, Oleg Penkovsky, probably the most productive spy of the century.*

Penkovsky had a dreadful time trying to enlist in the cause of the West; luckily, he was, along with a great many other attributes, very persistent. He finally made the team on the fifth try over six years, his services having been turned down first in Ankara during 1955 when Penkovsky was deputy chief of the GRU in Turkey. The CIA thought he sounded too good to be anything but a provocateur and wanted nothing to do with him then.

On March 10, 1961, at last, the colonel connected. He informed a member of a British commercial delegation that he would soon head a Soviet delegation on a visit to Britain. The visiting British

---

* This view of Penkovsky's value to the West became generally accepted within the intelligence community. In his authoritative book *The Mole,* William Hood, a spy boss in the OSS and the CIA for more than thirty years, judged: "There may have been more important agents, but if one has been detected, his case has not been publicized. Until such an agent is identified, Penkovsky's reports will remain unique in modern intelligence history."

group in Moscow was led by a "businessman" named Greville Wynne, whom Penkovsky handed some papers and a letter addressed jointly to the President of the United States and the Queen of England. Wynne was, in fact, a courier for British intelligence, and on the night of April 20 Penkovsky met with representatives of MI6 and the CIA in the Mount Royal Hotel in London and got his chance to explain himself.

The Western operators could hardly trust their luck as they set about to figure out this "walk-in" agent who had stubbornly walked in for the fifth time. Penkovsky was a puzzler—and hardly a conventional Russian.

"Quality" was the word for the colonel. He really knew how to appreciate quality girls, quality porcelain, nylon sheets, silk shirts, London tailoring, and French cuisine. Compounding the astonishment of the CIA, this high-living bon vivant had no interest in pay. He insisted that his motive was ideological.

He had grown to abhor the Communist regime, particularly Khrushchev, who, Penkovsky was convinced, was quite capable of blundering the world into nuclear war, Berlin being the most likely tinder point. The colonel's background offered some support for his allegations of purity. His parents had been bourgeois civil servants under the czar, and his father had been killed fighting as an officer against the Bolsheviks during the Russian Revolution.

In the beginning, Penkovsky's American and British controllers could be positive of little more than some seductive (but conceivably suspicious) evidence that he was brilliant as well as breathtakingly well connected. His father-in-law had been a most senior political general and a friend of Stalin. His closeness to the chief of the GRU, General Ivan Serov, and to Chief Marshal Sergei Varentsov, the head of the Soviet guided missile program, was authenticated.

The initial Western investment in Penkovsky was small. The men from the CIA and MI6 sent him back to Moscow with a Minox miniature camera, a transistor radio receiver, and good wishes for this equipment's productive use. Penkovsky's response was electrifying. He worked frenetically, and when Wynne returned to Moscow for more trade talks the following month, the colonel met him at Sheremetyevo Airport and handed him, during the drive into the city, twenty rolls of exposed film. In his room at the Metropol Hotel that night Wynne gave Penkovsky thirty rolls of fresh film. It was the start of an astounding flow of precious intelligence, adding up, eventually, to some ten thousand pictures of top-secret documents, mostly about the latest Soviet missiles. The West had never seen anything like it.

When Penkovsky's legitimate GRU business brought him back to London that summer, he met through many nights with his Western controllers. Relays of them grilled him and fed him pep pills. He never had more than three hours' sleep. A whole floor of a hotel at Marble Arch was devoted to pumping Penkovsky dry: tape recorders, coding machines, and a private line to Washington kept his output moving. A doctor was in constant attendance. Every word of these and later debriefings was transcribed and weighed in Washington. Fortunately, Penkovsky's English was up to the tiring task.

Since his take was so outstanding in volume *and* quality, the CIA and MI6 arranged elaborate systems for him to get his material out of Moscow without having to rely exclusively on a single vulnerable courier like Wynne (with whom the colonel quickly developed a hearty friendship). The controllers also wanted Penkovsky to be able to get out messages quickly in case of emergencies.

They introduced him to Janet Chisholm, the wife of a British Embassy attaché in Moscow and mother of three children, who had been picked as his regular live contact. Typically, Penkovsky would come upon her children playing in a sandbox. As the mother watched, he would give the youngsters a box of candy drops containing rolls of exposed film. He would also leave films at agreed-upon dead drops, behind the radiator at the entrance door to 5 Pushkin Street, or at other obscure spots from which Western Embassy personnel would retrieve them after he called certain Moscow phone numbers and left designated signals without having to speak. London would acknowledge receipt of the deliveries by a signal that Penkovsky could pick up on his radio receiver. The colonel was further supplied with telephonic signals for such possible crises as his impending arrest or imminent outbreak of war.

Penkovsky plunged into his new role with an unbridled enthusiasm. In his mind he created a fresh persona for himself. He asked his friend Wynne to call him "Alex." While he preferred British manners, he loved American power, and so he asked to wear a tailored American military uniform at his debriefings. The uniform was held in safekeeping by his mentors, and when it was not immediately available to be worn, Penkovsky was much displeased. But when his request to be introduced to President Kennedy could not be fulfilled, he accepted American citizenship instead, along with a CIA medal. Penkovsky was also made a colonel in the U.S. Army to reassure him that his new work did not involve a loss of rank. These were compensations that enthralled him.*

Although money did not motivate Penkovsky, the CIA, in keeping with normal policy of tying down an agent's loyalty by making him accept compensation, opened a Western bank account for him and paid him at the rate of about $40,000 a year. The colonel never asked for money and never collected any of his pay. He did ask for a stream of expensive gifts from his handlers. These were bought for him and he received them with delight.

From the perspective of his controllers, Penkovsky had but one weakness. Like a reformed drunk railing against the devil alcohol, he hated Khrushchev's Communism so passionately that the CIA analysts considered his political judgment to be clouded. He constantly tried to egg on the Allies to take a tougher stand on Berlin.

"He wanted to start World War Three," I was told by one man privy to his output.

Still another circumstance made his reporting on Berlin suspect in the eyes of the CIA. Berlin was not a technical problem like a missile. Penkovsky's military sources were demonstrably impeccable; moreover, much of his technical information reached the West in the original documentary form. But his political information came from hearsay, often gossip. It could easily have been colored by his own vengeful views. So the CIA analysts were inclined to discount much of the colonel's data on "soft" nonmilitary matters as probably exaggerated.

The evaluators were so determined to remind policymakers of the wheat-and-chaff duality of Penkovsky's output that they created a different secret code name for each category. The hard

---

* The principal CIA debriefer of Penkovsky was a fatherly, bearlike Russian-born agent named George Kisevalter. According to a CIA eyewitness, he would have qualified as a character actor. When Penkovsky's demands to meet President Kennedy became insistent, Kisevalter would assume the facial expression of a parent about to bestow great gifts. He would then extend both arms in a gesture bespeaking patience as well as justified expectations. And he would say nothing. According to Greville Wynne's accounts, the CIA eventually spirited Penkovsky to Washington on a daring eighteen-hour aerial round-trip during which the colonel supposedly talked with the President for thirty minutes and received his "personal thanks and the thanks of the United States." These accounts were accepted as fact in serious books about the CIA as late as 1987. I have been assured by an excellent source in the CIA that the stories were hogwash, that the President never laid eyes on Penkovsky.

material on weapons and technology was classified as "Ironbark." The soft political take was called "Chickadee," the latter label having been deliberately chosen for its similarity to "chickenshit."

When Penkovsky learned about the border closure four days ahead of time and did not pass the news along, he was behaving in an uncharacteristically low-key function. Canny as he was, he had perhaps begun to sense that his handlers were not attaching much importance to his "Chickadee" political gleanings.* No one can say what might have happened if Penkovsky had flashed an alert to the West and if the word had reached the policymakers in Washington in time. It is conceivable, if unlikely, that such a warning might have moved President Kennedy to issue so menacing a warning that Khrushchev might have refrained from going ahead with his Wall.

Relatively, the absence of a Penkovsky warning about the August 13 operation was minor. The big payoff for him and his patient mentors came to the West during the Cuban Missile Crisis the following year. For the time being, Khrushchev was free to maneuver as he wished.

---

* For nearly thirty years, only sixteen mysterious words left a trace of Penkovsky's connection to the history of the Berlin Wall. Three years after his death, the CIA authorized publication of autobiographical notes based on his debriefings (*The Penkovsky Papers,* Doubleday, 1965). Without explanation, this sentence appeared on page 236: "I learned about the Berlin closing four days before the Soviet government actually closed it off." Of course Penkovsky's CIA debriefers knew that the colonel had been tipped off by Khrushchev personally in August 1961 (see page 23). And while they finally told me the story in 1988, the whole business had been considered so sensitive that the debriefers never informed their Berlin colleagues of the agency, not even years after the fact. In the 1970s, at a Washington reunion of old Berlin hands, Allan Lightner, the United States Minister in Berlin back in 1961, asked Bill Graver, the CIA base chief at the time, about the sixteen words in the Penkovsky memoirs, suggesting that Graver had known about the Russian's warning all along. Graver denied knowing of a warning in the memoirs. Yet, at the party Graver came away with the impression that Lightner did not believe him.

11

THE PRESSURE RISES

Paris,
Tuesday, August 8, 1961

Khrushchev kept turning up his pressure valves. On Monday, August 7, an emissary from Amintore Fanfani, the Prime Minister of Italy, appeared in Paris with a message from Khrushchev for President Kennedy. The next day Fanfani's man turned to Press Secretary Pierre Salinger, who was in town with USIA chief Ed Murrow, and Salinger cabled Fanfani's unsettling news to the President in an "eyes only" cable.

Fanfani had been exposed to Khrushchev's extreme belligerence during a series of meetings in Moscow from August 2 to 5, Salinger reported. The Berlin problem had to be settled at once, Khrushchev insisted to Kennedy's Italian ally. About a dozen times, no less, he hammered away with his doomsday threat that a war over Berlin would be a nuclear conflict right from the start. Khrushchev said he was willing to negotiate but urged the President "not to wait too long."

The Soviet Premier had sent Fanfani on his way with a quixotic fulmination harking back to the June summit in Vienna when Kennedy kept warning about the danger of "miscalculation" in Soviet-American affairs and Khrushchev said he was sick of the word. Now the Russian was so disgusted that he told Fanfani he "wished for the return of John Foster Dulles." Dulles's position as an implacable foe of Moscow had at least been unambiguous. Kennedy's "complex foreign policy provided a great problem" for Khrushchev. Or so the Russian leader wanted the President to believe.

No leak anywhere hinted that Khrushchev's historic decision—to cut off the westward flow of refugees—was an accomplished fact by the time Kennedy received Fanfani's warning.

The White House, Washington,
Thursday, August 10, 1961

What did the President plan to do about the East German refugees? He had separate public and private answers to the question.

Publicly, the dilemma brought forth this exchange at his press conference of August 10:

Question: "Mr. President, some members of your administration and others have privately expressed concern that the continued large flight of East German refugees to the West might result in an act of violence. Senator Fulbright suggested that the border might be closed. Could you give us your assessment of the danger and could you tell us whether this Government has any policy regarding the encouragement or discouragement of East German refugees moving West?"

Answer: "Of course, we're concerned. . . . There has been a . . . tremendous speedup of people leaving the Communist system. . . . The United States Government does not attempt to encourage or discourage the movement of refugees. . . ."

It was an answer most notable for what it did not address. It did not assess the "danger" posed by the refugee flow. It did not refer to the right of free movement throughout Berlin. And it did not contradict Fulbright.

"The impression is unmistakable," commented a historian later, "that the United States Government considered the refugee problem a purely East German affair and would make no move should the East Germans act to solve it."

Privately, the President had pronounced such a laissez-faire stand a few days earlier while strolling with his adviser Walt Rostow along the colonnade by the White House Rose Garden. Picking up on what Khrushchev had told McCloy in Sochi, Kennedy told Rostow that the Soviets would have to impose control over the refugees. The Soviets could not let Eastern Europe "trickle away." Fortunately, the DDR was not a vital interest for the United States.

"I can get the alliance to move if he tries to do anything about

West Berlin," the President told Rostow, "but not if he just does something about East Berlin."

Kennedy had no doubt that Khrushchev would act. The Premier "faces an unbearable situation. East Germany is hemorrhaging to death, and as a result the entire East bloc is in danger. He has to do something to stop this. Perhaps a wall."

The fateful word had been uttered aloud, if only in confidence.

**Bonn,
August 1961**

Among some of the leading conservative CDU politicians in the West German capital, fear of Communist *Sperrmassnahmen* (closure measures) at the border was rising, and three influential CDU members of the parliament banded together to lobby Ernst Lemmer, Adenauer's Minister for All-German Affairs, about countermeasures.

"[Axel] Springer [the conservative publisher] keeps plugging his slogan 'Open Up the Gate,' " said one of the deputies impatiently, "but over on the other side they're going to slam the gate shut!"

The meeting stretched on for two hours, and eventually Lemmer got out a large map of Berlin. The politicians crowded around as Lemmer explained to his satisfaction that it was "technically impossible" to close a 150-kilometer border within a city.

Besides, so Lemmer lectured, Ulbricht couldn't afford to lose face by making such a hugely visible admission that his efforts to turn the DDR into a viable nation had failed. If the East Germans wanted to "vote with their feet," Lemmer said, that was their own business. This may have been the first time this picturesque phrase was used. Lemmer, an old newspaperman, bouncy and bulky, had a way with phrases, and in Berlin the pressure of the feet from the East was taking on more and more urgent meaning.

**West Berlin,
Friday, August 11, 1961**

John Mapother had just reported to Berlin as the new Reports Officer of the CIA base, bringing along his wife and four children. A soft-spoken, Kentucky-born alumnus of the intelligence committee civil wars in Washington, Mapother, lanky and cautious, was delighted by his new post, and for the usual reasons. Berlin *was* Espionage Central and very useful for one's career. But when he toured the Marienfelde camp on Friday, August 11, he began to wonder whether he had been wise to bring his children. While Friday night was always a peak time for the arrival of refugees, that last Friday before the Wall was bedlam. Not only was there a sudden and dramatic surge of arrivals (four thousand that day), but the quality of these immigrants—the high percentage of professionals and other affluent citizens who had chosen to give up security, homes, savings, fine careers—was astounding. These people were not simply on the run, they were stampeding. Like antelopes scenting lions, the refugees seemed to know instinctively that "they" were going to close the border, "they" were going to move imminently, "they" were about to shut the gates to freedom. Mapother was overwhelmed by the hysteria that had gripped these obviously intelligent people. But still no one in the East talked about a wall.

12

AT THE BRINK: "SOMETHING IS GOING TO HAPPEN"

"Gentlemen, my name is Koniev," said the bald, pudgy figure in the Soviet marshal's uniform. "You may perhaps have heard of me." His eyes twinkled.

As he stepped up to shake the marshal's hand in the Soviet army's principal German headquarters southeast of Potsdam, Colonel von Pawel of the American Military Liaison Mission was stunned, absolutely floored. He had heard of the marshal all right. Koniev, "the Tank," was conqueror of Prague and Dresden, Marshal Zhukov's fellow conqueror of Berlin, the retired chief of all Warsaw Pact forces, the great tactician of battles against *cities*.

"I am now the Commander in Chief," Koniev said, and von Pawel understood the implications. This was as if the Americans had decided to call Eisenhower out of retirement. Not only was something enormous going to break, the Soviets wanted to be sure to impress the Allies that it was very, very big indeed. And since Koniev was known to detest Germans, his appointment could also serve as a signal to the East Germans that the Russians remained very much in control.

Von Pawel admired how the Soviets had stage-managed their surprise. They all but had Koniev popping out of a cake. Only that very morning, the American colonel and his British and French opposite numbers had been summoned to appear in Zossen at 4:30

P.M. to see "the Commander in Chief." That would normally have been Colonel General Ivan I. Jakubovsky, but he was now standing deferentially in a corner of his own office while Koniev invited von Pawel and his colleagues to partake of the usual champagne and caviar.

No more than banal bonhomie was exchanged, but later the same day the marshal dropped a tantalizing morsel of intelligence at a buffet in his Potsdam villa for the three Allied military commandants of West Berlin. One of the Western generals ventured, "We are hearing about substantial military transport activity in your command."

"Gentlemen, you can rest easy," the marshal replied. "Whatever may occur in the foreseeable future, your rights will remain untouched and nothing will be directed against West Berlin."*

Koniev did not sound or act like a front man, a character actor, yet he was. In his later gleeful admission, Khrushchev spelled out that the marshal's very appointment was a bluff, part of the Soviet Premier's scheme to keep the West off balance. Contrary to what intelligence officers like Colonel von Pawel were led to believe, General Jakubovsky remained in command of Soviet troops throughout the crisis.

East Berlin,
Friday, August 11, 1961

Although the secret of August 13 was very tightly held by the very top echelon of the DDR government, the East Germans administered their security measures with intelligent latitude.

Wolfgang Seiffert, thirty-five, was one of Honecker's bureaucrats who was told in advance that the border would be sealed. Strictly speaking, he had no need to know about this because he

---

* It was the misinterpretation of this assurance that caused the Allies much annoyance for decades to come. Mistrustful West Germans inferred that the East had struck a deal with the West approving—or at least accepting in advance—the construction of the Wall. The concept of such a fictional stab in the back *(Dolchstosslegende)* is popular in German history and nurtured by the paranoid suspiciousness that drives most German politicians. Kennedy once characterized this weakness with his marvelous wit. He said that the Germans were like the wife who kept asking her husband, "Do you love me?" When he keeps saying that he does, she demands, "But do you *really* love me?"—and then has him trailed by detectives.

was not directly involved in the *Aktion*. He was, however, a trusted party man and knew Honecker well. He liked Erich and they had worked harmoniously together, although that had been more than ten years before, when both were leaders of the FDJ (Freie Deutsche Jugend), the SED's youth organization. An agreeable academic type who was working on his doctorate in jurisprudence in his spare time, Seiffert would not have dreamed of claiming that he was a key member of the government.

His job did have a certain sensitivity. Seiffert, bubbly and intense, was a member of the large staff of the party's Central Committee (ZK der SED) and worked in its headquarters on the Werdersche Markt. Seiffert was in the *West* department of the ZK, primarily in charge of relations with Communists in West German trade unions. He also operated a party newspaper for Western trade unionists. These were delicate functions because the Communist Party was illegal in West Germany.

Along with seven or eight colleagues, Seiffert was summoned to a meeting on Friday, August 11, at which his director, an old-time Honecker pal with the cheerful name Erich Glückauf (Good Luck), disclosed the welcome news. A "securing" *(Absicherung)* of the border was about to take place, said Glückauf. No Western military response was expected. The word "wall" was not mentioned; Glückauf spoke of "permanent fortifications." The exact date of the action was not given, but Seiffert surmised that it was imminent.

He was not alarmed. In the line of duty, Seiffert was in touch with knowledgeable sources in the West, and his reading of the mood on the other side convinced him that there would be no war. From the perspective of the DDR, the border closure was, in his view, an essential and stabilizing step. He recognized that a wall constituted a defeat, an admission of weakness by the DDR, but seventeen years would elapse before he broke away.*

---

* In February of 1978, Seiffert, by then a bald, bearded, and bulky professor of international law, was allowed to leave East Berlin by train to accept a guest professorship at the University of Kiel in West Germany. He never returned to the East and has since become a leading and respected authority on DDR affairs.

**Ahlbeck, East Germany,
Friday, August 11, 1961**

"Something is going to happen," said Kollow, the old fisherman. "They're planning something. For two days police units from here have been moving to Berlin. They're pulling together everything they've got."

Kollow was listening to the radio with Klemens Krüger, a vacationing writer from Munich who was renting a room in the fisherman's home. Krüger had fled from the DDR in 1953, and he knew the local Mecklenburg area well, having been born nearby.

The resort coast along the Baltic obviously was more popular than ever. Some ten thousand vacationers were roosting in a tent city stretching for ten kilometers along the beaches. They were brushing their teeth and washing their dishes in the ocean, singing, drinking, and black-marketing the nights through. It was a madhouse.

Krüger was astounded at the sophistication that Kollow and the summer people, isolated on this remote seacoast, were displaying about the implications of what they were hearing on the radio. Without exception they were nervous, arguing about whether to leave the country and when. Whoever wanted to get out had better do it right away, before Ulbricht banged the door shut, they told each other. In the afternoon the women dashed with empty shopping bags to the town square: potatoes had arrived! There had not been any for quite a while. *Vopos* were making sure that nobody photographed the women standing in line.

Before going to bed that Friday night, Krüger listened to the DDR radio, the Deutschlandsender. He heard snappy bulletins, marching music, request concerts for soldiers of the *Volksarmee.* "It's like in Hitler times," he wrote in his diary. His sleep was sporadic. Outside, some youths kept singing over and over again, "Berlin stays free . . . drink Coca-Cola, Berlin stays free . . . drink Coca-Cola . . . *Berlin bleibt frei . . . trinkt Coca-Cola. . . .*"*

---

* For a remarkable number of East Germans, Coca-Cola was a symbol of freedom, even though very few had ever tasted the beverage.

**Ahlbeck, East Germany,
Saturday, August 12, 1961**

Klemens Krüger was watching a DEFA (Communist) newsreel in
the local cinema. When Walter Ulbricht appeared on the screen,
many youths started laughing and jeering. "Look at the Goatee,
look at the Goatee!" they shouted.

The lights went on. "Who was shouting?" called a group of *Vopos,*
rushing into the theater.

Everyone kept a straight face and sat in silence. As soon as the
police disappeared, the noise of the critics resumed. The cops did
not bother to return.

All day Krüger, his writer's curiosity aroused, soaked up the
atmosphere of the East, so different from his usual surroundings
in Munich. The district newspaper was railing against West German "slave traders" and "child kidnappers" and demanded: "The
swamp West Berlin must be dried up!" The guests at his rooming
house kept saying that Ulbricht was about to "shut the gate to the
West," but they expressed faith in Chancellor Adenauer and in
President Kennedy's "promise" to "keep the gate open."

In the countryside, around noon, Krüger saw farmers sitting
and arguing by the side of unkempt cornfields. He had never seen
such a sight at midday during harvesttime, but these were newly
collectivized farmers and they were on an eight-hour day. That
was why potatoes were so scarce.

After the movie that Saturday night, Krüger sat drinking with
some young vacationers who were staying at the seaside tent city
and heard views different from those prevailing among the older
guests at his rooming house. These young people didn't care for
Adenauer and West German conditions, about which they were
remarkably well informed.

"That's for our elders," one of them said. "They're living on
those illustrated magazines they smuggle in, the ones that report
every royal wedding. What we want is a socialist state maybe like
Poland or, better, the Scandinavian type of socialism."

Yet here, too, the urgency of developments that weekend kept
intruding. A young woman asked, obviously frightened, "What'll
happen when Ulbricht closes the sector border?"

PART III

THE WALL GOES UP: SUNDAY, AUGUST 13, 1961

13

EAST BERLIN, HOUR BY HOUR: INSIDE HONECKER'S STAFF

**East Berlin,
Sunday, August 13, 1961**

No wonder Western intelligence could learn nothing about the DDR's preparations for erecting the Wall. All advance moves were kept just about invisible. Perhaps no military operation was ever so compulsively, so tightly held by so minuscule a band of insiders. The CIA would have been dumbfounded:* until about midnight on Saturday, August 12, only some twenty totally trusted leaders knew what was about to happen. All others whose staff work was needed were told only of enigmatic impending "exercises."

The word "wall" was taboo. It was simply mentioned nowhere. The operation carried no code name. Until about 3 P.M. on Saturday, not one telltale word was committed to any typewriter. Orders were either transmitted orally or they existed only in handwritten drafts composed by one man, an obscure police colonel named Gerhard Exner, who had distinguished himself some years earlier by enforcing leakproof secrecy when all of the DDR's currency was called in to be exchanged for new money in order to reduce excess purchasing power.

This weekend, deeply worried about possible Western reaction,

---

* Even at this late date, the agency should be surprised to learn what happened. Most of the information in this section has never come to light anywhere.

the DDR was steeled for any eventuality. Soviet divisions ringed
the city. East German army units were about to line up ten thousand men strong along the Berlin border, though well behind it
and out of sight. A special bilingual Soviet-German liaison staff
would assemble at Russian headquarters in suburban Karlshorst in
case Russian intervention was needed. Overtly, Erich Honecker
and his planners wanted to trivialize their moves. The danger of
war was best minimized by making the border closure look like a
low-key local police action, nothing much more than an effort at
crowd control.

And so the units that made up the front line consisted of some
ten thousand men from the People's Police (the *Vopos*) and the Riot
Police *(Bereitschaftspolizei)*, augmented by factory militia outfits
known (and always referred to in full) as the Battle Groups of the
Working Classs *(Kampfgruppen der Arbeiterklasse)*. The latter were
civilian formations, spottily trained. They were deliberately chosen
to be stationed out in front, the most exposed and visible representatives of the DDR's armed might, because the bearing of these
worker-soldiers tended to be less than trim and snappy. They did
not look too warlike.

Colonel Exner of the Berlin police was assigned to a key planning role in part because, strictly speaking, the border move could
indeed be viewed as less than menacing, a large-scale police maneuver. At least so Honecker decided. The operation would remain locally confined as long as nothing went wrong. And since
the police already had a tight communications network in place,
with every section of the border in instant telephone contact via
the regular precincts, the operation was most conveniently run out
of Berlin police headquarters.

Distances in the DDR being very short, no major movements of
troops or supplies were necesssary until after midnight Saturday.
No sizable quantities of construction materials had to be shipped
until later. On their trucks, the troops transported barbed wire,
Spanish riders, and fence posts as part of their equipment for
"exercises."

To coordinate all operations, Honecker and Exner did form a
special Action Staff *(Einsatzstab)* to work out of the police headquarters, a redbrick postwar building, seven stories high, occupying an entire huge block off Karl-Marx-Allee and the busy
Alexanderplatz. In Western countries, a staff specially organized
to control such a large operation would have been sizable and

probably gossipy. Under Honecker, it numbered exactly eight, including his personal secretary.

His principal executive assistant was Werner Hübner, a member of his personal staff since 1957.* Hübner held the rank (and wore the uniform) of an army lieutenant colonel, but he was much more a civilian, a military adviser of the SED's Central Committee. A compactly built man with a ready smile and a politician's conciliatory manner, Hübner had started out as a locksmith but held a doctorate in history and was the perfect staff man: alert, tireless, and not given to making mistakes.

Honecker's operational plan was designed to convey the impression that absolutely nothing out of the ordinary was about to occur. Special care was taken so that there was almost no time for anyone possibly to discover that anything unusual was brewing at police headquarters. Honecker's staff was crowded into only four rooms on the third floor; Honecker was the only one to have an office and a conference table to himself. Detailed Berlin maps and specially installed communications equipment lined the walls of the other offices.

But it was the *timing* that was most exquisitely scheduled. Hübner and the rest of the tiny staff never used the police headquarters offices until 8 P.M. Saturday, and in the vast building with its nu-

---

* Colonel Exner being in poor health, Hübner on October 25, 1988, became the source for most of the information conveyed here. Now a sixty-year-old major general, he was a section chief in the party's Central Committee, his outfit being comparable to a highly politicized version of the U.S. National Security Council. Hübner had consulted Exner on my behalf in order to refresh his memory of the 1961 events. The Wall operation is still considered so secret in the DDR that almost none of the details reported here—not even Exner's or Hübner's names —appear in the DDR's military histories. Hübner considered himself a civilian. For our interview, however, he appeared in uniform, with wide, bright red stripes running down his trouser legs. He chuckled over his regalia, saying that he almost never wore it and had put it on only in my honor. Exner and Hübner are unknown in the West, and the normally reliable West German intelligence literature is wrong about at least one significant fact concerning the leadership of the DDR's Wall operation. It attributes administrative control to Horst Skerra, an army lieutenant colonel in 1961 and now a lieutenant general in charge of the Leipzig military district. Actually, Skerra in 1961 was merely the operation's liaison man with the army. He was not stationed at police headquarters but at the Defense Ministry in suburban Strausberg.

merous entrances the arrival of such a small handful of people in the dusk of a summer weekend evening caused no stir. Honecker did not begin to use his operations office for the first time until about 10 P.M. The other ranking ministers who came to control the operation drifted in after eleven o'clock. Walter Ulbricht arrived after midnight and stayed for only about an hour.

One group of men, women, and children could have given the show away. They were printers, their wives, and youngsters, and they were Werner Hübner's special charges. It had been one of his tasks to arrange for the printing of posters that would announce the border closure measures Sunday morning on the public *Litfassäulen** of East Berlin. On Saturday, after the posters were printed, Hübner ordered the printers, along with their families, to be kept locked up in their plant until midnight.

As Hübner remembered it later, it was his personal estimate that the chances of the Western powers reacting with countermeasures were no more than 10 percent. If explicit DDR plans existed to deal with such contingencies, he was not told of them, and he was privy to every piece of paper that passed across Honecker's desk. In retrospect he came to believe that any Western steps would have led to no more than the ineffectual standoff of tanks that did occur in October (see page 260).

The ranking officers who had to set the operation physically in motion were told almost nothing, not even at action time. When Lieutenant Colonel Martin Löffler, commanding an 1,800-man regiment in the First Motorized Rifle Division of the National People's Army (NVA), was summoned to his headquarters at Strausberg, about thirty kilometers east of the Berlin suburb Pankow at ten o'clock on Saturday night, he thought he was headed for a party celebrating the birthday of Walter Ulbricht's deputy.

It was a feast of memorable opulence: platters of buttered salmon and caviar sandwiches lined one wall of the large third-floor staff room. Further delicacies included cold veal as well as meat salad. Waiters poured vodka, schnapps, and Crimean cham-

---

* These advertising pillars—tall, fat, round, and scattered throughout the city streets—were a Berlin invention, the idea of a printer of the mid-1800s, Ernst Litfass.

pagne. An Egyptian-made film about the Suez Canal crisis was shown in the garden; the documentary introduced a martial note for the seventy-odd assembled commanders of the units that surrounded Berlin. Shortly before midnight everybody was invited back inside, the white cloth hiding a huge wall map of the area was removed, and the Defense Minister, General Karl-Heinz Hoffmann, wavy-haired and a bit of a dandy, stepped to the rostrum to begin the never-announced briefing.

This was the night, he declared, when they would seal the sector border dividing Berlin, thereby ending the exodus of the disloyal profiteers who drained the nation by fleeing westward. The operation was so closely held, the general disclosed, that even most of Ulbricht's ministers were getting the word only at this very moment. The troops were to be fully combat ready. If the Western Allies resisted, Löffler and his men were to follow standard operating procedures. Löffler knew what this meant: they would fire warning shots into the air and await firing orders *(Schiessbefehl)* from the division commander—unless their lives were at risk, in which case they were to defend themselves at once.

The operations chief stepped up next and he too communicated no instructions that Löffler considered unusual. Commanders whose units failed to meet the schedules would be penalized. Detailed orders with marching routes and maps *(Befehlskarten)* were waiting in the adjoining room. As in the Soviet army, no questions were solicited from the commanders or asked by them. The briefing lasted less than twenty minutes. Nothing explicit was said about any barriers or precautions that Löffler and his men might take to avert (or conceivably delay) the outbreak of World War III. They were to fan out three hundred or more meters behind the sector line. The Border Police, People's Police, and militiamen from the factories would man the border.

Shortly after midnight Löffler and his convoy, using their dark blue blackout lights, were rolling down the Autobahn. Their division was to occupy a fifteen-kilometer stretch along the southern city limits, not far below the DDR's one international airport, Schönefeld. Time was ample. They were not scheduled to take up their station until 4 A.M. Obviously, no trouble was expected before sunrise, at the earliest.

The blustery little thirty-six-year-old Löffler was a professional soldier of the no-nonsense tradition, a son of Ulbricht's Saxony,

A young Erich Honecker (*above*)
inspects his troops. It was
Honecker's total secrecy and
meticulous planning that enabled
the Soviets and East Germans to
spring the Wall on a totally
unsuspecting West.

General Karl-Heinz Hoffmann, the
DDR Defense Minister, briefed his
commanders at the very last
moment.

and he had only one concern about his own risk in the operation.*
The morale of his men, all young volunteers, was a shade too
spirited. They not only loved going to the front, they were eager
to keep right on moving into West Berlin.

In his command post at police headquarters, meanwhile, Erich
Honecker, surrounded by six of Ulbricht's ministers, had signaled
the official onset of the operation at precisely midnight ("0:00
hours"). The first order went to the Minister of Transportation:
stop all elevated and subway trains between East and West Berlin.

It was the only step reaching out beyond the DDR borders that
night.

Disguised internal moves had begun one and a half hours earlier, when Honecker issued coded orders to NVA units in four
outlying provinces to start out toward Berlin on so-called night
maneuvers. The troop movements began quietly until, at 0:01
hours, alert sirens screamed three times at garrisons throughout
the DDR.

At his barracks in Röntgental, forty kilometers from the center
of Berlin, Sergeant Rudi Thurow, twenty-three, awoke with a start.
Soviet T34 and T54 tanks were thundering past his window—he
had never seen so many. At 0:20, his company commander told
the assembled officers and noncoms that the spying and border
crossing in Berlin were about to end. Thurow thought, *Is it war?*

As if the C.O. had guessed what was on the minds of his men,

---

* Although Löffler had received training in the Soviet Union and had worked at
a sensitive post in the DDR Defense Ministry, he was no robot. Slipping away
from his troops during maneuvers at the border on September 8, 1962, he
climbed across two fences in a sector that he knew to be lightly guarded and
walked into the deserted nighttime streets of the West Berlin suburbs looking for
police. He wanted to be led to the American authorities. Two cops happened to
drive by in a Volkswagen and politely asked the "Herr Oberst" for his pistol.
Löffler scoffed, "No cop is going to get my pistol!" At the police precinct he
barked the same refusal at the lieutenant in charge. When two hastily summoned
American civilians arrived, Löffler handed them his pistol but warned them it was
loaded. Shocked, the Americans returned the weapon to Löffler for unloading.
"I was a soldier, not a politician," he said in 1986, and so he had deeply resented
the snooping of two lieutenants in his regiment who were actually *Stasi* spies.
Ultimately Löffler defected because of difficulties with his superiors, who unjustly
blamed him for the increasing defections from his unit after the Wall was built.
Invited to the United States, Löffler served twenty years with the Pentagon's
Defense Intelligence Agency.

he explained they would be part of moves to institute "a reliable watch" and "effective controls" at the border. "Unrest" of civilians was likely but "military conflict" was out of the question. A sergeant next to Thurow muttered, "Are the Allies really going to stand for this?" By 4 A.M. Thurow and his men had occupied the suburban Bernau railroad station. Their mission: turn back all "border crossers" bound for West Berlin.

At his garrison outside Leipzig, Sergeant Georg Grosse, twenty-one, was instructed to wait until the engineer units had moved out; Grosse was told that these men were to "drive barbed wire." He was puzzled; he had no idea what that meant. To his astonishment, he saw engineers load huge rolls of barbed wire, Spanish riders, and concrete posts onto trucks that drove off toward Berlin.

In his encampment at Basdorf, twenty-year-old Private Horst Ewald of the Border Police, standing by in formation to await his unit's trucks, also was perplexed as coils of barbed wire were heaved aboard other trucks. He had seen hoards of this wire around his base and had wondered what it was for. Wire was used in his obstacle course and firing-range exercises, but lately so much of it had been piled up that it covered one fourth of the soccer field. Nobody knew why.

Well after midnight, as his convoy of men and wire rumbled down Prenzlauer Allee en route to central Berlin, Ewald still wondered what this maneuver was about.

In his NVA barracks at Zepernick, on Berlin's eastern city limits, Conrad Schumann, a baby-faced nineteen-year-old Border Police sergeant, was startled to be shaken awake by a buddy who snapped, "Come on, man, we've got to head for the border!"

Bobbing down Unter den Linden in his armored car, Schumann heard another pal muse, "Maybe there'll be war!" Disembarking before the Brandenburg Gate at 1:30 A.M., they were received by an officer whom they didn't know. He told them they were to take control of the border to protect it "against the enemies of socialism." Schumann recalled, "We stood around looking pretty stupid at first. Nobody had told us how that's done: taking control of a border."

Adam Kellett-Long, correspondent for Reuters, the only Western news service permitted to operate in East Berlin, was trying to extricate himself from a professional embarrassment during that night from Saturday to Sunday. His bosses in London were annoyed with him about his alarmist reporting.

On Friday, impressed by the strident tone of resolutions passed by a special session of the DDR's rubber-stamping Volkskammer (parliament), young Kellett-Long had sent a long dispatch reflecting his belief that something radical was about to take place at the border. Even though—as his dispatch carefully recalled—Walter Ulbricht had in June denied any intention to build a wall, maybe the East Germans really would throw up a wall and split the city.

Kellett-Long's desk editors in London had considered such speculation farfetched, even ridiculous. As Saturday went by and nothing happened, they turned increasingly restive and asked their East Berlin man to follow up with a calmer "climbing-down" dispatch for London's fat Sunday papers. So on Saturday night, an automobile tour of East Berlin having convinced Kellett-Long that nothing unusual was afoot, he sat down in his office on Schönhauser Allee to tackle the chore of composing an artful exercise of backtracking. It had to concede that he had been too alarmist on Friday, but hopefully it would not leave him looking like a fool on Sunday.

He was wrestling with this unpalatable enterprise shortly after midnight when the phone rang and an unknown voice said in German, "A small suggestion—don't go to bed tonight!" followed by a ring-off click.

Thus alerted, Kellett-Long got back in his car and drove up Leipziger Strasse toward the Potsdamer Platz and the border. This time, a soldier halted him well before the square by waving a red light and announcing, "The border is closed!"

Kellett-Long rushed back to his office, sent London a dispatch about his latest encounter, and at 1:11 A.M. the ticker of the East German news agency ADN—normally silent after midnight—began to click out a long proclamation from the Warsaw Pact governments. The last paragraph contained the kicker: measures were being taken to organize "reliable supervision and real control" of the sector boundary.

The other shoe had dropped, although Kellett-Long could still not be sure of its shape and size. ADN's phrasing sounded tough but could mean anything. It could even be empty propaganda sound effects. Erich Honecker's security veil was still in place.

· · ·

Lieutenant Colonel Löffler and his motorized regiment of the People's Army were determined to meet their marching orders; indeed, they improved on their schedule, arriving at their southern border perimeter around 3 A.M. instead of the four o'clock deadline. They were eager to do battle and were fully equipped for it. Each man carried more than one hundred live rounds in his ammunition belt and pockets; more was piled up in easy reach on the vehicles.*

Löffler knew he was being watched and who was doing the watching. He had been told that Honecker was in overall charge, and Honecker—always mindful of details and of his personal responsibility for monitoring morale in the ranks—did take time out for appearances along the border during the night, questioning commanders and giving little pep talks.

Honecker, too, knew he was under close scrutiny. Ulbricht and Marshal Koniev could be counted on to pounce the moment anything went wrong. The operation was intricate. Its many parts, deliberately fragmented for secrecy, had to fall smoothly into place as in a jigsaw puzzle. Any small accident might rip away Honecker's security precautions and blow up the element of surprise. It was vital to catch the Western Allies napping.

His army units, with steady professionals like Löffler in charge, were practiced and dependable, but the *Vopos*, the Border Police, and the factory militia lacked experience in military operations. These raw men represented a grave risk to world peace and, equally worrisome, to Honecker's career. If the plan went awry, he would never succeed Ulbricht.

Everything went like clockwork, however. The West had been caught asleep and was not stirring. At 2 A.M., accompanied by Colonel Exner, Honecker left police headquarters to tour his troops all along the border. At 4 A.M. he was back, and he retired to a cot in his office. Shortly after 6 A.M. he told his little staff, "We can leave now," and he departed for his home in the VIP ghetto at

---

* In recent years some DDR military historians began to insist that Communist troops at the border were not issued live ammunition. This is not true, according to eyewitnesses with whom I spoke, as well as published accounts of participants. However, the men in Löffler's unit were considered so trigger-happy that they were ordered on August 16 to hand in their ammunition for safekeeping aboard their vehicles. The same cautionary measure may have been instituted in other units.

suburban Wandlitz, then popularly known as "Bonzograd"—a *Bonze* being the derogatory Berlinese term for "big shot."

For Honecker, it had been a tense but triumphant night. And as crises went, this one had been remarkably brief. His fellow citizens found the events more difficult to digest.

5:00 A.M. In Ahlbeck, on the DDR's Baltic coast, Kollow, the old fisherman, awakened Klemens Krüger, his vacationing roomer from West Germany. "You've got to get up right away," he said. "Ulbricht closed the sector border. You've got to leave! There's going to be war! The Western powers aren't going to tolerate this!" It was daylight. Krüger shook himself awake and went to the living room, where Kollow's daughter was sitting at the radio. Her son had fled to the West six months earlier.

"If there's war they're going to call up my boy," the daughter said. She did not articulate the obvious. If war came, it would be civil war, and her boy would be fighting on the other side.

Other roomers came drifting into the room, including several tourists from East Berlin. A West Berlin radio station reported that Willy Brandt was hurrying home, but nothing was said about any American action.

"Will the Western powers intervene?" someone asked.

"If they want to intervene they've got to do it right away," said Kollow.

"But the Allied troops haven't been alerted."

"They've got to clear away the barbed wire with their tanks," said old Kollow. "Nobody would fire a shot!"

6:30 A.M. Driving up to the sprawl of office buildings that housed the Ministry of State Security (*Stasi*) at Normannenstrasse 22, the tall, nearly bald man known as Karl Hager saw his Soviet controller waiting impatiently at the gate. The Russian was Yuri Vasilyevich Novicov, a highly experienced KGB officer. Prior to his assignment to Russian headquarters in Karlshorst, he had been expelled from the United States for spying out of the Soviet Embassy in Washington. Karl, a native Austrian whose real name was Rupert Sigl, had been a full-time KGB agent for seven years.

Sigl, thirty-two, figured that something special had to be breaking, because he had been awakened at his apartment by the controller at 6 A.M. and instructed to come at once to Normannen-strasse, where he had never been. The KGB considered their East German brethren arrogant and bureaucratic. They also didn't entirely trust the *Stasi*. The KGB operatives thought that their German colleagues lacked "soul." The Russians often talked about their soul. And so Sigl normally met his boss in the official Russian ghetto in Karlshorst, though never at headquarters itself. He was asked to come to the KH (Konspirative Haus, or safe house) at Köpenicker Allee 58, nearby, because the KGB did not quite trust their own foreign agents either.

"So how do you like this new step?" asked Yuri Vasilyevich as soon as Sigl arrived at Normannenstrasse. Yuri was obviously in excellent spirits.

"The surprise really came off," said Sigl.

"You can say that again! Nobody below the rank of general had the slightest knowledge beforehand," claimed the Russian, which made Sigl feel better.

"Now it remains for us to see how the West will react," Rupert said.

"The wastebaskets are ready for the usual protests," scoffed the Russian.

"A shot fired negligently in this situation could trigger more than a paper protest," Sigl cautioned. "I don't think that the tanks have dummy rounds in their barrels and those on the other side certainly not either."

"Nothing will happen," said Yuri Vasilyevich.

7:00 A.M. Klemens Krüger and his fellow vacationers were still sitting around the radio in the living room of Kollow, the Baltic fisherman. They were dredging up phrases they remembered from speeches by Adenauer and Kennedy, speeches about freedom for Berlin. Why wasn't the West making a move? "That would mean war," said Krüger. "Nuclear war." The DDR citizens who surrounded him were making him feel guilty about the West's inaction.

11:00 A.M. Among East Berlin civilians the news was slow to filter out. Nobody seemed to be aware of any unusual occurrence even well after 10 A.M., when a group of Eastern journalists and authors assembled at Schönefeld Airport for a group flight to Varna, Bulgaria. They were to attend a journalists' convention at nearby "Golden Beach."

Quite suddenly, everybody had heard a report about the border closing, probably via the radio, and the journalists were asking themselves questions. Would the Berliners, East and West, accept this quietly? A few tanks could sweep away fencing and bricks. What exactly would the DDR army do if the Allies were to resist? What would the Soviets do? At least one member of the delegation, the novelist Stefan Heym, wondered whether their flight to Varna would leave. If the DDR was preparing for war, wouldn't Schönefeld be required for military purposes?

Some members of the delegation were becoming agitated, but not, after reflection, Heym. Confronted with a power play, the West Germans would knuckle under. The Allies would hardly fight about a border that they had themselves ordained almost twenty years ago. The flight to Bulgaria did leave as scheduled, but a nagging thought occurred to Heym. Born in Germany, he had been a refugee in America but had fled again during the McCarthy witch-hunting days, this time to East Berlin. Although he was a determined left-winger, his writings had increasingly caused him difficulties with the Communist leaders. Theirs was a socialism gone wrong, he believed. They seemed indifferent to the needs of individual citizens. Why did they need a barricade to isolate themselves?

In his memoirs Heym would record that he remembered thinking en route to Bulgaria, *What kind of socialism is it that needs to wall itself in so that its people won't run off?*

Evening. In the rooming house of Kollow, the fisherman, the radio reported that Secretary Rusk was calling for negotiations. Negotiations? The vacationing roomers were bitter. "They've written us off," said a slightly pudgy blond woman from Erkner, an outlying East Berlin suburb. "Over there they think only of their own security. Prosperity is everything to them. . . ."

Monday morning. Deutschlandsender, the DDR radio, was blasting marches and jubilant interviews with Communist soldiers into Kollow's living room. His roomer Klemens Krüger, the vacationing West German writer, was preparing to leave for Munich. Kollow was depressed because the West was doing nothing.

He waxed nostalgic about West Berlin, now closed to him for good. "What a *Fest* it always was for us," the old man reminisced. "Every Christmas we drove to West Berlin and bought shoes, clothes, and stockings. Everything was four times more expensive than here, but at least they had things available. Then we went to the movies and bought some illustrated magazines that we smuggled back in. Now everything is over. . . ."

14

WEST BERLIN, HOUR BY HOUR: WOULD THERE BE WAR?

**West Berlin,
Sunday, August 13, 1961**

1:54 A.M. Clad in his underwear, Acting Commissioner Hermann Beck had just dozed off in the second-floor Situation Center of West Berlin police headquarters on Tempelhofer Damm when the phone next to his cot rang with a report from the Spandau precinct. The elevated train from Staaken into East Berlin had been stopped at the border. All passengers had to leave the train and got their money back.

1:55 A.M. The North precinct was on Beck's phone. At the Gesundbrunnen border station all trains in both directions had been canceled a moment ago, according to a loudspeaker announcement on the platform. Beck wondered what was going on. The entire train system seemed to be in trouble.

1:57 A.M. The chief of the Security Police Command, Erich Dünsing, having just learned that train service was being disrupted all over town, tried to phone Deputy Mayor Franz Amrehn, Mayor Willy Brandt being away to campaign for the West German chancellor's post. Amrehn's phone was busy, but Dünsing remembered that a retired police chief lived in the same building, whom he now called and instructed to run to Amrehn's flat and tell him to clear his line. After mobilizing Amrehn, Dünsing alerted the deputy security officers of the American, British, and French garrison commanders. Without exception, the ranking Allied security men were on vacation.

2:00 A.M. Scribbling notes in his undershirt and shorts, Commissioner Beck abandoned his initial suspicion that Eastern intelligence agents were sabotaging the public transportation system. He was being flooded by ominous bulletins indicating that some sort of a much more general problem was brewing. He was being told: "*Vopos* closing Brandenburg Gate." "Twenty-three trucks with *Vopos,* armed with machine guns and submachine guns, seen on Pariser Platz." "West Berlin tourists reporting large numbers of Soviet tanks reported on Federal Road 5." "Work groups tearing up pavement on Ebert Strasse."

2:30 A.M. Alerted by Beck, the police chief of staff, Günter Dittmann, hurried into the Situation Center. Beck told him that Soviet and DDR military units were encircling Berlin and massing at the border but were making no moves into West Berlin. The officers decided to leave the thick sealed envelope with their secret plan for the defense of West Berlin in their safe. Instead, they dispatched a telex declaring Alert Level E-1 and calling all 13,000 cops to their posts.

2:30 A.M. For Av Westin, events were confirming his fear that war was likely. He was a New Yorker stationed in London as a field producer for CBS-TV, and contrary to his custom he had brought his wife, his daughter, and even her nanny to Berlin while making a documentary on the escalating crisis. Yesterday the filming at Marienfelde had been especially unsettling. More than 2,500 refugees had pounded into the camp propelled by barely controlled panic.* Many were convinced something dreadful was about to

---

* The Germans have a graphic term for such deadline apprehension: *Toresschlusspanik,* meaning panic at the imminent closing of the gates.

happen. Westin was relieved to have his family close to him. If war came, they "might as well be together."

He was relaxing at the Cracked Egg cabaret over a late drink with his on-camera correspondent, the lanky, bass-voiced Daniel Schorr, when one of their German cameramen phoned. A tip had just come in that something strange was happening at the Brandenburg Gate. The details were unclear but sounded ominous.

Within ten minutes Westin and Schorr had raced to the Gate in Dan's silver-gray Mercedes diesel. The scene was eerie. Dazzling white-blue searchlights bathed the area in the brightness of daylight. DDR soldiers were everywhere. Some stood about looking menacing with submachine guns slung across their chests, others strained over the clattering tools that were ripping up the map of Europe right in front of Westin's and Schorr's eyes—the jackhammers.

"Major news events have their own peculiar background sound," Westin wrote years later, "and those jackhammers that night still ring for me in a very frightening way."

The CBS camera crew assembled rapidly and shot historic 16-millimeter footage: holes being dug for concrete posts, barbed wire being dropped off trucks in coils and strung between the posts at intersections, West Berliners pressing against the obstacles, enraged, cursing, shaking their fists, shouting protests at the sullen Communist troops.

But the day of news film being flashed instantly into living rooms had not yet arrived. Photography had to be hauled in string "orange bags" by prop plane to London for jet transshipment, and so the CBS group's work was not shown in the United States until Tuesday night.

Art was imitating life. The Berlin Wall crisis was unfolding in *slow motion.* As yet, it was not even identifiable as a crisis about a wall. There was no wall, nor any sign of an intention to erect one. The cautious Erich Honecker and his helpers had planned their moves that way.

3:00 A.M. Police headquarters, City Hall, and the offices of all three Allies were swamped with messages from every section of the border: everywhere streets were being ripped up, barbed wire was being strung. The telephone receiver never left Commissioner

Beck's ear. With his other hand he pulled on his uniform pants and his blue duty shirt.

3:25 A.M. Radio RIAS interrupted its program of popular music —they were playing a number called "Let's Do It Like the Swallows Do"—and an announcer read a bulletin from United Press International: "Strong forces of the Communist People's Police tonight sealed off the border between East and West Berlin. . . ."

3:30 A.M. What *were* the East Germans up to? Richard Smyser, a member of the U.S. Mission's Eastern Affairs staff, was instructed to investigate. With another State Department man at his side, Smyser reached Potsdamer Platz in his Mercedes convertible at about 3:30. Soldiers were unloading construction equipment. Barbed wire was being strung. After some speech-making by the *Vopos* ("We're not interfering with Allied rights"), enough wire was rolled back to let the Americans through. They were free to look around.

North and south of Unter den Linden, military trucks were moving up more troops and equipment. Steel poles were being carried from trucks. A few blocks farther east military personnel carriers and radio vans were lining up in vacant lots. Residents in nightclothes were peering out of windows, but the streets were generally deserted. The real news was negative and reassuring: the Americans saw no Russian troops or tanks. Nor was there equipment of the kind—artillery, for instance—that would have suggested aggressive intentions. The East Germans were simply digging in.

By dramatic contrast, the Friedrichstrasse station, the most popular exit from the East, was chaos. Hundreds of East Berliners, many of them shouting, some in tears, were trying to storm the platform of the elevated trains, unaware that traffic to the West had been broken off. Officials began circulating leaflets explaining new regulations from DDR Interior Minister Karl Maron: Berlin's mass transit system was being split into two autonomous halves. Smyser tried to elbow himself up the station steps, but the crush was too great.

Leaving through the Brandenburg Gate, Smyser reminded the *Vopo* officer in charge that the Eastern sector of the city was under four-power rule and demanded to see a Soviet officer. The *Vopo* said this was superfluous since he and his DDR people, not the Soviets, were in charge. The Americans were waved through the border. Honecker had made his point: the fledgling DDR government was asserting itself cautiously, but it had to be reckoned with.

3:30 A.M. Wolfgang Vogel, an obscure East Berlin attorney who would shortly emerge as the key mediator between the two Germanys, faced an instant identity crisis. He had been enjoying a convivial evening with his wife, visiting friends in West Berlin—a doctor and his wife who lived on Keithstrasse, near the Ka De We department store, a ten-minute drive from the border.

As the Vogels were about to get into their red Opel Rekord to drive back to East Berlin, some passersby, noticing the car's Eastern license plates, stopped and said excitedly: "Do you have any idea what's happening over there? East Berlin has been closed off!"

Vogel, still in a giddy party mood, said they had to be out of their minds.

"No, no," the strangers insisted, "there are tanks and soldiers and there's supposed to be shooting!"

The Vogels went back to their friends and turned on RIAS. Confirmation of the street rumors was prompt and dramatic: "Since about one A.M. pneumatic drills are rattling and digging a ditch here at the Brandenburg Gate," a reporter was shouting, trying to make himself heard over the drilling noise. "The ditch is about half a meter deep and half a meter wide." The reporter said he was seeing columns of DDR military trucks. Proceeding to Potsdamer Platz, he watched the border crossing being blocked by barbed wire.

Vogel was instantly convinced that war was inevitable. He could not conceive that the Western Allies would passively tolerate what the radio was reporting so unmistakably.

An RIAS announcer advised Easterners who were visiting in West Berlin to stay put and await developments. The Vogels' friends, fearful for the safety of their visitors, also counseled them to wait until the situation clarified. Vogel's wife was uncertain; maybe they should at least await the light of day.

Vogel was grappling with a larger issue. Much of his social and professional life was in the West. If war really came, he could practice law there very comfortably. But he did not belong. His home and heart were in the East, and this was the time to be counted, to declare his allegiance without equivocation.*

At the Brandenburg Gate, the Western police also advised the Vogels to delay crossing the border into uncertainty. Caught by momentary caution, Vogel thought of calling his doctor friend to check whether anything new was developing, but no phone was in sight. There was no turning back. He drove on.

On the East side of the Gate, the *Vopos* were casual. They merely told Vogel to drive home. The atmosphere was tense, however. In the darkness Vogel discerned tumult. Reinforcements were pulling up. Traffic was frozen solid. People were dashing around asking questions that nobody could answer. Just as in the West, the rat-tat-tat of the jackhammers dominated the scene. Like scalpels tearing into connective tissue, the drills were literally separating East from West.

It did sound and look very much like war.

4:00 A.M. For Mayor Willy Brandt, the decisive episode of his turbulent life as a statesman began with a predawn *Blitztelegramm* from his Berlin office. News of the border closure was reaching him, drowsy and hung over, aboard his special campaign sleeping car. It was hooked onto the Nuremberg-to-Kiel express train. He got off at the next stop, Hannover, and took the first plane home.

Brandt had been electioneering hard for the West German chancellorship, held by the foxy old Konrad Adenauer, who was well ahead in the polls. Brandt's American-style barnstorming, hitherto not practiced in Germany, while exhausting, was relieved by occasional fun. Under the influence of good friends and good wine, the mood on his car that night from Saturday to Sunday had been, as Brandt recalled, *ausgelassen* (frolicsome).

Friends worried about Willy's drinking, his sometimes stony moods, the public disclosures of his affair with a vengeful woman, including texts of his cloying love letters to her. Brandt's career faced other delicate liabilities. He had forsaken his homeland for Norway during the war, had even become a Norwegian citizen. The East Germans insisted he was a CIA agent. And word was getting out that he had been born out of wedlock.

---

* Going over these events with me in his office in 1986, Vogel said, *"Ich gehöre hier her, das wollte ich zeigen"* (I belong here, I wanted to show that).

None of this seemed to matter much. It was so easy to forgive Willy. He was so likable. He had the fire, the ramrod posture, the craggy face, the challenging chin, the brains—all the combined cerebral and animal appeal that comforted voters and stimulated them. He was, as his confidant Egon Bahr said, a "liberated German" without guilt feelings. After all, he had not sat on his duff in Scandinavia. He had worked full time in the anti-Hitler opposition. And Brandt was not bound by the postwar clichés; he possessed vision.

Unlike almost everyone else, he had not dismissed the possibility of a wall going up in Berlin. That Saturday in Nuremberg some associates had fleetingly recalled Walter Ulbricht's unexpected press conference comment that "nobody had any intention" of building such an obstacle. When all but one colleague had left by early morning, Brandt ruminated, "Maybe they *are* going to build a wall."

He had not been alarmed, however. Seismic events tended to calm him. And he was hardly alone in the world. At the root of his thinking was his faith in America. Brandt's feelings about the United States had always been warmly admiring. Lately, his friends thought that young JFK had become Willy's role model. Brandt, at forty-eight only slightly older, did feel a special affinity for Kennedy. The President was an ally who could be relied on.

4:00 A.M. George Bailey, representing *The Reporter* magazine and ABC, watched a *Vopo* captain in a plum-colored dress uniform ripping into the pavement at Potsdamer Platz with a pneumatic drill. A cigarette was dangling from one corner of the captain's mouth and he was clearly enjoying his strenuous work, for he was smiling. A group of young people, dressed in their weekend best for a night in the West, walked toward the Brandenburg Gate. As they disappeared between the towering columns, they turned to wave back at the cops, cleaning women, and reporters watching from the West. "We shall never see them again," said a woman next to Bailey. His springtime prediction in *The Reporter* magazine about the travail of the "disappearing satellite" ("Khrushchev will ring down the Iron Curtain in front of East Berlin") had turned into fact.

· · ·

4:10 A.M. Hans Maria Globke sleepily picked up the phone at his home, Diezstrasse 10 in Bonn. Globke, sixty-three, was Chancellor Konrad Adenauer's highly controversial chief of staff.* Ten minutes earlier, when he had been awakened by a night editor of the West German federal press office and told that Berlin was being divided by barbed wire, he had decided to do nothing. But now Franz Amrehn was on the phone from Berlin. Amrehn, acting mayor in Willy Brandt's absence, was a ranking member of the CDU, the party of Adenauer and Globke, and he was alarmed. Globke decided he needed more authoritative information. The supervision of the German CIA, General Reinhard Gehlen's *Bundesnachrichtendienst* (BND), was part of his portfolio. He dialed its secret number in the Munich area.

A voice said only "Hello." Globke identified himself, asked to be called back, and shortly his BND confirmed the border closure, along with its opinion that there was no evidence of danger to West Berlin. Globke decided not to awaken the eighty-five-year-old Chancellor Adenauer, who had returned late that evening from a rugged campaign trip in Schleswig-Holstein and was badly in need of rest.

5:30 A.M. The CIA duty officer at the United States Mission on Clayallee phoned the home of the number two man at the agency's BOB, John Dimmer, chief of operations. "They sealed the border," the duty officer said. Dimmer had not been sleeping long. He had been up late with his chief, Bill Graver, interrogating a Czech defector who had committed a long-unsolved major political murder. As an agency veteran and World War II battalion commander, Dimmer was accustomed to emergencies, and he reflected quickly

---

* Globke was the author of a number of laws that enabled Hitler to seize power in 1933. He was coauthor of the official interpretation of the main body of anti-Semitic "racial" laws, and it was he who initiated the idea of forcing all German Jews to adopt the middle names of Israel or Sarah. The DDR tried him and sentenced him to life imprisonment in absentia as part of a long tug-of-war between the West and East German governments, each heaping abuse on the other, correctly, for employing Nazis in high places. The Germans had a phrase for this sniping: *"Haust Du meinen Juden, hau' ich Deinen Juden"* (If you beat my Jew, I'll beat yours). This expression generally was not considered anti-Semitic. On the contrary, it was said to indicate recognition that Germans traditionally had made scapegoats of Jews.

about the border closure. The CIA had no action responsibility in the situation; that role fell to the Army's G-2 people. Whatever the Communists were actually doing at the border was no crisis, at least not yet. The key question seemed to have been answered in the negative. This was "the Holy Ghost Question" and it ran: "Do you have any indication that an enemy intends to attack the United States?" Dimmer did go to the office and called Graver, no friend of his. "You'd better come in," he said, "it's happening."

6:00 A.M. In the Dahlem guest house of the U.S. Mission, Dimmer got John Mapother out of bed. Having arrived from Washington only a few days before, Mapother was taking over as the Reports Officer. With the usual circumspection practiced by CIA people when they talked on open telephone lines, Dimmer said that Mapother ought to come down to the office. Some matters were going on that he "ought to have a look at." Mapother hurried to his new desk, but found that he had little to do. Dimmer had wanted to be prepared to respond to the wave of alarm messages he expected to come pounding in from Washington. The messages never materialized. "Washington reacted as if they didn't know what hit them," Mapother said later.

6:15 A.M. With some trepidation, Adenauer's chief of staff, Globke, dialed area code 907 and then the number 2867. He was calling the home of Chancellor Adenauer considerably earlier than he would have liked. Adenauer's widowed caretaker picked up the phone. Globke asked her to awaken the Chancellor and have him call back. Five minutes later, the Chancellor was on the phone and Globke summarized the news. "What does Gehlen say?" was Adenauer's only question. Then he asked that he be kept informed and went back to sleep.

7:00 A.M. Huddling with his entourage around the radio in his room at the guest house of the U.S. Mission, Edward R. Murrow scented a very big story in the making. It was good for his spirit to be back in Berlin, exciting, almost like being a reporter again. Berlin stirred Murrow's feel for history and many personal memories. Here, for CBS in the 1930s, he had hired an unknown, broke

Though he was no longer a broadcaster, USIA chief Edward R. Murrow *(above)* still had the reporter's knack for being at the right place at the right time, arriving in Berlin on a routine agency tour just hours before the Wall went up.

Archconservative West German publishing magnate Axel Springer *(above right)* had predicted that Berlin would be divided.

Filming during the crisis, director Billy Wilder *(right)* had to build a fake Brandenburg Gate in Munich for his 1961 Cold War comedy *One, Two, Three.*

newspaperman named William Shirer.* In the war Murrow had flown bombing missions over Hitler's capital, describing the inferno as "orchestrated hell." During the airlift he had shuttled to Tempelhof Airport with thirteen tons of coal aboard.

These days, still tense as a coil, quizzical, chain-smoking three to four packs of cigarettes daily, he found few causes in which to invest his outwardly subdued passions. He didn't fit the role of bureaucrat, running America's limp propaganda arm, the United States Information Agency (USIA).

Kennedy was fond of the chronically morose Murrow. He admired Ed's restraint and folk hero status. Murrow was class. Everybody remembered Ed, microphone in hand, on flaming rooftops during the Blitz, intoning like a heavy bell, "This is *London!*" After the war, Ed radiated integrity on "See It Now" and "Person to Person." Only such a star TV personality could get away with referring to JFK patronizingly as "that young man."

By chance, Murrow had arrived from Bonn at 10 P.M. Saturday on a routine tour of his agency's outposts.† At an official dinner in the West German capital he had been collared by Axel Springer, the newspaper magnate, who urged him to warn the President.

"He's running into an ambush," Springer predicted. "You Americans are so fixated on access over the Autobahn and the air corridors that you're forgetting the Berliners. I have a fear that Berlin is going to be divided. Think of the dilemma then! More than a million Berliners live in East Berlin!"‡

Murrow did not trust Springer. The publisher was an archconservative. His enemies called him vain and power obsessed. His anti-Communism was virulent. There was also much to like about Springer. His emotional commitment to Berlin was sweeping. He treasured the city like a lover. He dominated its newspaper market

---

* Shirer's books *Berlin Diary* and *The Rise and Fall of the Third Reich* would make him the preeminent authority on Germany for two generations of Americans.

† To this day, some West German politicians remain unconvinced that Murrow's fortuitous arrival was a coincidence. They believe it was part of a secret Soviet-American deal whereby the United States would consent to the Wall if the Russians left West Berlin alone. The existence of such an East/West conspiracy has always been convincingly denied by knowledgeable participants on both sides, and no evidence exists to support it, but the story will not die.

‡ In 1988, West Berlin had a population of 1.96 million, East Berlin, 1.2 million. The total was slightly more than in 1945, but about one third less than before World War II.

and had broken ground for a dramatic new skyscraper headquarters on Kochstrasse only twelve feet west of the sector line.

This weekend Springer had been proved prescient, although Sunday morning's radio reports left Murrow confused about the import of the commotion at the border. Several calls to the U.S. Mission produced little enlightenment from officials there, but Murrow decided to stay with the story and to extend his Berlin visit, originally scheduled for only one day.

All good reporters are lucky reporters, according to an old incantation of European journalists, and on this weekend luck had dropped Murrow like a paratrooper straight into a reporter's feast. Better yet, he could do more than report. As the only American policymaker on the spot, he could make his influence felt.

7:30 A.M. It had been an irksome, thoroughly frustrating night for Colonel von Pawel, the head of the American Military Liaison Mission to the DDR. He had planned to spend the weekend resting at the Hilton Hotel in West Berlin, but at 10:45 Saturday night his deputy called from their suburban Potsdam headquarters and asked "Von" to come home so they could "finish the chess game." Von Pawel knew this meant trouble from Marshal Koniev's troops, but what kind? Snooping on his drive to Potsdam, he got as far as Highway 2, where he was stopped by military traffic. He counted one hundred tanks. How long before he could get through? "Several hours," said the *Vopo* in charge. Von turned back to try another route. When he reached Potsdam at 1 A.M., his deputy said that at least two Soviet infantry and one armored division were on the move. But why? One of Von's sergeants hid under a bridge from 4 to 6 A.M. and saw a whole division churn down the Magdeburg Autobahn. Another sergeant counted three hundred fast-rolling tanks on another highway. Still, Von's entire Mission would have done just as well getting their bed rest instead. When the colonel called the area's American commander, Major General Al Watson, at 7:30 in the morning, he reported Soviet divisions tucked into the woods north, south, and east of Berlin, but their intentions remained hidden in the proverbial fog of war.

8:00 A.M. "When are the Americans coming to put an end to this nightmare?" Reaching for Willy Brandt's arm, a man asked that question of the Mayor when Brandt, just off the Hannover plane, inspected the border at Potsdamer Platz and the Brandenburg Gate.

His sleepy eyes hidden behind dark glasses, Brandt could only shrug. He was himself deeply shocked. "Dreadful!" he muttered. *Kampfgruppen* militiamen with submachine guns were lined up elbow to elbow. Spanish riders were being rammed into ground that the jackhammers had ripped open. Not one Allied jeep was in sight. The Western military presence consisted of three British MPs armed with pistols and truncheons.

8:30 A.M. John Kenney was feeling elated. A CIA agent, he had been working extra hours as a "collection officer" interviewing refugees at the Marienfelde Reception Center. This night he had been pacing the floor at the Zehlendorf U.S. Army hospital, where his wife was giving birth to their first child, a daughter. In the morning, eager to share his news, Kenney went to the nearby CIA headquarters. At the hospital he had heard talk about some "trouble downtown," so he assumed that many of his one-hundred–plus colleagues would have been called in to assess the situation. To his amazement, the halls were deserted. The branch chiefs seemed to be working behind closed doors, but there was nobody whom Kenney could buttonhole about his beautiful new daughter. It was just another sleepy Sunday in a U.S. government office.

9:00 A.M. The duty officer at the enormous United States Embassy at Mehlem, overlooking the Rhine in suburban Bonn, arrived at his desk to find a number of urgent NIACT telegrams from Berlin. He marked them "Noted" and put them aside. Ambassador Walter Dowling did not learn of the Berlin developments until he was notified at a Little League baseball game after lunch, more than twelve hours after the crisis began.

9:00 A.M. Reality was playing a dirty trick on Billy Wilder. The famous director was not accustomed to shabby treatment. It worried him.

In films like *Sunset Boulevard* and *The Lost Weekend* he had dealt memorably with life's disasters. With comedies like *The Apartment* and *Some Like It Hot,* he made the world laugh by standing reality on its head. This weekend, in the middle of filming the farce *One,*

Two, Three with Jimmy Cagney in Berlin, the Communists sabotaged him. Humorless bastards.

Wilder was especially miffed because Berlin had been his turf before he emigrated to Hollywood. He had drifted to Germany from Austria in the wild twenties, eking out a living as a free-lance newspaperman. He dated Marlene Dietrich, hung out with the literati at the Romanische Café, and made extra marks in the Eden Hotel as a gigolo, dancing in white tie and tails with fat old ladies (whom he also gave private lessons in the Charleston).

In the sixties, Berlin was decidedly less amusing, notably East Berlin even before the Wall. The Communist film colony had laid on a buffet at Horcher's while filming began for *One, Two, Three,* and the famished Easterners gobbled all the food within minutes. When Wilder was taken to hear a hotel orchestra play "Alexander's Ragtime Band" by Irving Berlin, the rendition was so doleful that he muttered one of his famous wisecracks: the composer must have changed his name to "Irving East Berlin."

Wilder did not even attempt to persuade the Communists to let him film *One, Two, Three* in the East. They would not have appreciated the script. It called for a dour young Communist to be subverted by Jimmy Cagney's dynasty of American Coca-Cola distributors. Eventually, the new capitalist convert, played by Horst Buchholz, another Berliner from Hollywood, defected through the Brandenburg Gate on a motorcycle bearing a yellow balloon with the legend "Russki Go Home."

For Buchholz, the filming was a nostalgic homecoming. The star had grown up in East Berlin and his parents still lived there. He remembered how he had moved to West Berlin as a struggling young actor, taking the subway back and forth with ease and later a little car that he would drive right through the Brandenburg Gate.

Right from the start, Wilder had attempted to finesse the Berlin realities by spending $200,000 on a fake Brandenburg Gate and Unter den Linden, which he ordered constructed on the terrain of a Munich film studio. He also needed overall "long shots," and to film these he had assembled cast and crew in Berlin on Saturday night, August 12. Shooting was to start Sunday, but when he came down to breakfast at the Hotel Kempinski, a lot of civilians were milling around in the lobby and hallways. They were *Grenzgänger,* hotel employees who lived in the East and wondered whether they could (or should) go home.

Wilder tried to push his project ahead anyhow, but when he

began filming with Communist territory in the background, an officer demanded that he stop or face "dire consequences."

The director did not greatly mind having to retreat to his quiescent movie set in Munich. He was much more worried that the audiences might torpedo his movie. In all his years of converting reality into art, he had never had comedy turn into tragedy while in the making. The transformation might not work at the box office.*

Early morning. "I toured East Berlin today and found it an armed camp," Dan Schorr broadcast on CBS radio. "Police and troops with machine guns everywhere hold back the sullen population . . . Russian and East German tanks in reserve. . . . Demonstrations were broken up with the threats of bayonets and dozens of people were arrested. My cameraman and I were arrested and held for ninety minutes, our film confiscated. . . .† I saw hundreds of confused and resentful East Germans being turned away from subway and train stations, some arrested for shouting. . . . I saw plainclothes policemen break up every gathering of more than three persons on the streets. Some had to be pushed. . . ."

11:00 A.M. Willy Brandt was determined to push the Western Allies into some strong action. He failed. When he was allowed to plead his case to the American, British, and French generals who made up Berlin's Allied governing body, the *Kommandantur,* his prospects looked discouraging from the start.

The *Kommandantur* had become a fiction. Its generals were prohibited from taking political action without orders from their respective governments. Its military muscle was laughable; the combined Western garrisons of 11,000 faced a force of more than 500,000 Communists. The pretense that the *Kommandantur* was still a four-power commission was carefully kept alive even though it was absurd.

When Brandt walked into the conference room on Kaisers-

---

* It didn't. When *One, Two, Three* was shown in Berlin in December, critics responded bitterly. *BZ am Mittag,* one of the papers for which Wilder had written in the twenties, mourned: "What tears our hearts apart, Billy Wilder finds funny."

† Another CBS photographer, John Tiffen, was held all night and not allowed to go to the bathroom.

werther Strasse in Dahlem—he had never been in the building
before—he was struck by two bizarre anachronisms. A vacant
fourth chair was kept reserved for the Soviet commandant, and a
portrait of the last Russian general to attend these meetings remained on the wall. Nothing indicated that he had walked out
thirteen years ago and that the Soviets had boycotted the *Kommandantur* ever since.

By now Brandt was boiling. His normally explosive temper had
not been calmed by having been kept waiting for fifteen minutes.

"You let Ulbricht kick you in the rear last night!" he burst out
right off.

The reaction was icy silence. Later, a British official wondered
aloud before reporters whether the Mayor had been entirely
sober.*

Eventually the commandants coldly requested that Brandt address himself to the facts.

"What happened last night is an illegal breach of the existing
four-power agreement concerning free movement in all of Berlin,"
the Mayor began. He demanded—"at the least"—an immediate
sharp protest to Moscow.

More silence.

Brandt asked what means were available to the Allies to prevent
further Communist measures to "liquidate West Berlin."

More silence.

"You must do something!" Brandt exclaimed, highly agitated.†

---

* Brandt's physical state at the meeting was still controversial in the 1980s. He
was never a "morning person," and in his memoirs (1978) he conceded that "in
those days" he failed to make his points "with anything like enough force and
clarity."

† Some eyewitness accounts of this meeting describe it differently. Howard
Trivers, the number two man of the Berlin U.S. Mission, more than a decade
later asserted in his memoirs: "Brandt was a subdued and reflective man at the
meeting. . . . He did not plead for energetic action; he did not ask for 'an immediate show of force.' " The Reverend Heinrich Albertz, then Brandt's chief of
staff and later his successor as Mayor, told an interviewer in 1974: "That was no
conference, it was people facing each other helplessly." It is a commonplace that
many factors—fading and selective memories, varying attention spans, personal
and political prejudices, and such circumstances as participants entering a meeting room late or leaving it early—can retrospectively produce a *Rashomon* effect
of apparent conflicts. My account of the meeting at the *Kommandantur* is based on
Brandt's memoirs and on conversations with four reliable German and American

"Is that the view throughout the city?" asked the British commandant.

"Yes!"

And yet what *could* these three toothless generals be expected to do? Brandt had no way of knowing that they had already reached a do-nothing decision during two hours of prior deliberations. They had never done anything important without first consulting their governments. This Sunday morning (it was now around 4 A.M. in Washington), the failure of the capitals to respond to the wire service bulletins was proof that the governments were not interested in being awakened for consultations. And so the generals retreated into another handy fiction: Honecker's sealing of the border was an internal Eastern matter. Since it did not threaten Western access to Berlin or any other Western rights, the responsibilities of the generals were not involved.

So what to do? Nothing!

Desperate to salvage something from this infuriatingly frustrating confrontation, Brandt pleaded, "At least send some patrols to the sector border immediately to combat the sense of insecurity and show the West Berliners that they are not in jeopardy!"

That made the commandants come to life, though not in the way Brandt had hoped. A show of military force was out of the question, they said. It would elevate the events to the very level of *international* significance that the commandants did not wish to recognize. The Mayor should send enough West Berlin police to the border to keep their own citizens in line.

Brandt tried again: Would the generals personally deliver a protest note to their Soviet opposite number at his Karlshorst headquarters? No, ruled the commandants; the general probably wouldn't be in the office on Sunday and the Westerners would be made to look foolish.

How about circulating a protest through the media? Once more the commandants refused; they could not protest without consulting their capitals.

Exhausted and depressed, Brandt took his leave. He could not resist sniping at the inaction of the generals. "The entire East is going to laugh from Pankow to Vladivostok," he told reporters

---

participants. I conclude that some memories of Brandt's fervor were derailed because the long meeting turned increasingly desultory as it dragged on without resolution.

outside the *Kommandantur*. To his confidant Egon Bahr, he delivered a more pointed judgment later that day: "*Kennedy* is making mincemeat out of us."

Kennedy. In the end, everything depended on the willingness of one man to recognize his stake in the crisis, and that was Kennedy, the de facto leader of the Western alliance. Kennedy's failure to respond quickly and vigorously to the Communist challenge that week devastated Brandt personally and politically. It was a painful human disappointment to be abandoned by a trusted ally. As the elected protector of *Frontstadt* Berlin, Brandt suddenly felt very much alone.

Friends would remember this American desertion as *the* key incident of Brandt's life and a watershed in German history.

"On August thirteenth we became adults," Egon Bahr told me years later. "Too bad it had to happen that way."

While Brandt, like many Europeans, could never bring himself to dislike Kennedy or the Americans, he weaned himself away like a son growing apart from his family. The adversity would lead him to great new heights, to his *Ostpolitik* of rapprochement with the East, to the chancellorship and the Nobel Peace Prize. It would kindle antinuclear sentiment in West Germany, a new pacifism, a yearning for disarmament that bedeviled American policymakers until disarmament began to become fashionable and beyond.

All that evolved years afterward. As Brandt remembered that week of August 1961, he experienced it as a denouement, an hour of lonely truth. He phrased it graphically: "The curtain went up and the stage was empty."

Noon. "I was boiling," remembered Sydney Gruson. "It was almost unforgivable." *The New York Times'* senior correspondent in Germany was incensed by his paper's limp initial coverage of the crisis. A hardened war reporter, Gruson scented major news, conceivably even war. The onset had caught him in the Bonn bureau. His plane did not land in Berlin until midday Sunday, but Gruson was determined not to let the *Times* underplay events.

12:30 P.M. Would there be war? Unanimously, the foreign policy commentators pondering this momentous question on Germany's most influential television program did not think so, but they divided sharply on how the West should respond to the border closure. For years, the "Frühschoppen" show had been a national habit at noon on Sunday, though its panel had never been handed the opportunity to dissect news so fresh, so big, so close to home.

Most of the panelists on the dais at the Westdeutsche Rundfunk studios in Cologne recommended negotiations with the Communists. Some thought the crisis should be taken to the United Nations. One member of the group did demand strong action, and he had gained his expertise on Communism at first hand.

Intense and bubbly, Professor Wolfgang Leonhard, the historian and later a professor at Yale University, had, in the 1940s, been the youngest functionary of the new East German Communist government. The Soviets had imported him from Moscow with Walter Ulbricht's famous immigrant group when Berlin was about to fall. Now Leonhard argued impatiently that there was no time to wait for the United Nations to act. Khrushchev was bluffing. The West should take military action at once—carefully. It should move tanks all the way up to the border—"up to the last centimeter," said Leonhard. The Soviets would surely stop constructing fortifications under the heavy breath of such pressure, he lectured.

The West should remember Hitler's illegal 1935 occupation of the Rhineland, the historian pleaded. The German dictator's aggression succeeded unopposed; later it developed that his officers carried blue envelopes instructing them to withdraw immediately in case of opposition. Leonhard's history lesson drowned in the shocked protests of his fellow panelists who trivialized him as a Cold War monger.

1 P.M. David Brinkley's eyewitness film from Friedrichstrasse station and Bernauer Strasse managed to make the one o'clock plane to London to be aired on NBC's popular "Huntley-Brinkley Report." The easygoing Brinkley hadn't been too interested in going to Berlin. Nothing much was going on there. It merely happened to be on his way to Austria, where he was to make a light feature, "Our Man in Vienna." Reuven Frank, the show's producer, didn't want the audience to think that his stars didn't get about, so he was taking them around the world from time to time to be seen against backgrounds where news was made. "If we don't go to Berlin, we'll look like jerks," Frank had told Brinkley. They went and they were looking terrific.

. . .

Late afternoon. Eager like a cub reporter to see the action at the border, Ed Murrow got into a black Chevrolet with three of his USIA colleagues and drove to Potsdamer Platz. They recognized Dan Schorr, who was talking into a microphone describing the stringing of more barbed wire, and Robert Lackenbach of Time-Life, who told Murrow that the mood of the West Berliners was very ugly.

At Checkpoint Charlie, Murrow's group stopped to show their papers, but Ed was not letting himself be delayed by teenaged *Vopos.*

"Go ahead," he commanded the driver before formalities were completed. One of the USIA men, James Hoofnagle, "expected a bullet in the back," but there was no trouble.

Vopos, Kampfgruppen militia, and clusters of clearly agitated East Berlin civilians jammed the normally deserted streets.

The Americans settled in at the shabby surviving rear wing of the historic Adlon Hotel, where Murrow had hired Bill Shirer a quarter of a century earlier. Chain-smoking, his brow deeply furrowed as usual, Ed reminisced about the days when Hitler's elite operated here in style. The Adlon had been one of the world's most opulent hotels. Its fans at one time included the Kaiser himself. This weekend the beer was thin, and the clearly audible death rattle of the jackhammers from the nearby Brandenburg Gate kept reminding the American propagandists that Berlin, inescapably, was caught by yet another sweeping change in the winds of world power.

"I wonder if the President realizes the seriousness of this situation," Murrow mused after the group returned to the West.

Evening. Bill (El Supremo) Graver of the CIA felt enormous tension, indeed a state of shock. Were the Russians going to attack? He was not at all convinced that his Berlin outpost was safe. Although he was *the* intelligence authority in place, having served in the city under Bill Harvey from 1954 to 1958 and as chief of the German desk at Langley headquarters until his transfer back here a few weeks ago, he was distressed by what he was finding out for the first time, now that great danger was upon him. An evacuation plan existed for his unit, but it was worthless. If the Soviets were to send raiding teams against the Clayallee headquarters, the protec-

tion supplied by the Army—no more than a handful of GIs—
would be overrun at once. Provisions for the burning of sensitive
CIA documents were totally inadequate. He would have to install
vats with powerful chemicals, but that would take time and they
would have to be placed outside; carrying papers out of the offices
would slow the destruction process. The entire setup was a security
mess, and a highly risky one.

Late night. Increasingly agitated by the explosive mood of the
Berliners and the tepid reaction from Washington, Ed Murrow
decided to cable President Kennedy his personal impressions.

Joe Phillips, a former *Newsweek* columnist and now USIA's director for Europe, sat at the typewriter and Murrow dictated a heartfelt wake-up call. The first draft did not satisfy him and he spent
another two hours rewriting. The cable he dispatched after 2 A.M.
zeroed in on the situation from the perspective of Murrow's own
policy responsibilities for psychological warfare. It could hardly
have hit harder: "If Washington continues to react as it has until
now, U.S. policy in Berlin faces a fiasco. The mood of the population is miserable. If Washington doesn't act immediately, we are
threatened with a political catastrophe."

15

WASHINGTON, HOUR BY HOUR: EVEN THE NEW YORK TIMES WAS HALF ASLEEP

**Washington,
Sunday, August 13, 1961**

Midnight (5:00 A.M. Berlin time). Almost all of Washington was asleep. Having just left a party in Georgetown, Lothar Loewe was driving across the Memorial Bridge when he turned on the NBC radio news and heard a vague bulletin about the border closing. A born Berliner, Loewe was a rambunctious but exceptionally well-connected and well-liked West German television correspondent. Instead of heading home, he turned around and raced to the State Department. His lightning response failed to pay off with any story. A small handful of his usual contacts were at their posts on the seventh floor of the department, but they knew nothing that Loewe hadn't already heard on his car radio. They said that their information was meager and difficult to interpret. Loewe asked whether they had telephoned Berlin. He was told that this wasn't feasible. They had no secure telephone lines to Berlin and calls on open phones were unauthorized.

Midnight. John C. Ausland, forty-one, the duty officer of the State Department's Berlin Task Force, was asleep when the phone rang at his home. Ausland knew Berlin well: he had been stationed there for two years as a junior Foreign Service officer; in the 1950s he had headed the East German desk in Washington for three years. Picking up the receiver drowsily, Ausland heard "This is Dave"—the duty officer at the State Department Operations Center. "We have just received a news agency report that something is going on in Berlin. But it is not clear what." Although the East Germans had by then been busy for three hours with the noisy handiwork of sealing the border, Ausland was unable to elicit a solid assessment of the fragmentary facts. "Call me again when you have an official report," he told the duty officer and went back to sleep.

1:00 A.M. Even *The New York Times* was half asleep. Its fat Sunday issue was out with a pedestrian three-column headline at the top of the front page: EAST GERMAN TROOPS SEAL BORDER WITH WEST BERLIN TO BLOCK REFUGEE ESCAPE. The subheading made it sound like local squabbling: COMMUTING ENDED. The story came from Reuters, not one of the *Times'* own correspondents, and failed to report anything about physical obstacles until the twenty-sixth paragraph.

There, at the bottom of the runover on page three, the article finally got around to mentioning that "East German troops began to stretch a wire fence . . . and to drive stakes into the soil."

The *Times'* editors obviously considered the news less than momentous, and students of the signals emitted by the paper's front-page layout could spot the downplaying at a glance. The headline across only three of the available six columns signaled that the story was important, but not overly so. The most revealing tip-off was its placement on the left-hand side of the front page. The news on the right-hand side was always the day's lead, the story considered most important. That Sunday the right-hand headline said, GOVERNOR TO CALL SESSION OF LEGISLATURE

2:00 A.M. Steaming with impatience, Lothar Loewe drove to the apartment of his friend Jimmy O'Donnell, who worked for Under Secretary of State George Ball. Jimmy, a founding father of the old Berlin gang, had an apartment on Sheridan Square, close to the department. Together, they phoned Berlin to question Albert Hemsing, the chief of information at the U.S. Mission. They talked forty-four-dollars' worth. "What the hell is going on, Al?" Loewe demanded. Hemsing, delighted to hear from an old crony in Washington, eagerly shared details of the slowly unfolding situation. He knew what was happening at the elevated and subway lines and which border crossings were still open. Loewe scribbled notes and then helpfully called the State Department Crisis Center. No, he was told, they didn't have that information. "I'll give you the rundown," said Loewe and began dictating. He did not stop to reflect upon the oddity of what he was doing: a German civilian transmitting military information from one American government office to another. Somebody had to do it. Everybody knew about the constipation of bureaucracies, especially on Sundays in mid-summer.

4:00 A.M. Remembering that it was mid-morning in Berlin and that his mother must be up by now, Lothar Loewe phoned her in her suburban Marienfelde apartment. She sounded excited and said that everybody she had talked to that morning was worried. Loewe had once attended the University of Oregon and loved Americans, no matter how inefficient they could be. He had confidence in them. He also wanted to calm his mother. "Don't worry," he told her. "You're safe. The Americans will take care of you."

4:00 A.M. John Ausland, the State Department duty officer, had been sleeping only fitfully when his Operations Center called for the second time. According to an urgent message just in from the CIA in Berlin, the East Germans "were cutting off movement into West Berlin," but "there had been no interference with movement between West Berlin and West Germany." The message included a code word denoting the CIA's opinion that the President should be informed at once.* "I will be right in," Ausland told his office.

4:30 A.M. Only the duty officer was present when John Ausland hurried into State's seventh-floor Operations Center, but the lack of alarm did not surprise him. The center had existed for only a

---

* This deepens the never-resolved mystery of why the President did not receive the news until about nine hours after Ausland heard about the CIA message. Contacting the President was the responsibility of White House communications channels, not those of State.

few weeks. It consisted of little more than press service teletypes and one telephone without secure lines,* and at this hour it had no information that Ausland hadn't already heard on the phone and on his car radio.

7:00 A.M. "This is the White House duty officer," said the voice on the phone of the State Department Operations Center. "Is there anyone from the German Office around there?" The phone was handed to John Ausland. "I just received a call from Hyannis Port," said the man at the White House. "I need some suggestions regarding what Pierre Salinger should say to the press."† Within a few minutes, Ausland had drafted three "talking points" for the presidential Press Secretary to make to reporters traveling with Kennedy. These comments (1) summarized the night's events, (2) protested the violation of Berlin's four-power status, and (3) held the Soviets responsible for the split of the city. As a junior man, Ausland did not feel comfortable about releasing his draft without clearance from the Task Force Director, the crusty Assistant Secretary of State Foy D. Kohler. Only after he tried phoning Kohler at home and getting no answer, did he dictate his points to the White House. Shortly afterward Ausland heard from Walt Rostow, who was in charge of the National Security Council in the weekend absence of Mac Bundy. "I have added a fourth point," said Rostow —namely, that the closing of the Berlin border "showed the failure of Communism in East Germany."

· · ·

---

* Secretary Rusk did have a line equipped with a KY9 scrambler, but it was rarely used because it didn't work when it was most needed.

† The circumstance of junior level White House staff failing to keep the President informed was not unusual for a vacation Sunday. The free time—especially the sleep—of high-ranking dignitaries was not interrupted without some risk. To make this point, Bromley Smith, the longtime executive secretary of the National Security Council, liked to tell of General George Marshall, then Secretary of State, being awakened by a junior officer while on an arduous mission in Moscow. Marshall sat up and asked, "Is the President dead?" Once he was assured that the President was alive and well, Marshall put his head on his pillow and went back to sleep. It is also standard procedure for the Press Secretary, at his regular briefings, to feed reporters innocuous comments on routine news developments without troubling the President personally.

7:00 A.M. The Berlin Mafia, that band of hard-line Cold Warriors who had treasured Berlin as the world's number one cause since 1945, was moving into action. Jimmy O'Donnell, recovering from hepatitis, was awakened by his first call from Berlin at 7 A.M. "All hell has broken loose here," said his longtime pal Peter Boenisch, the editor in chief of *Bild*.

Not everyone approved of Boenisch or of *Bild*. Both were loud, pushy, opinionated, simplistic. Both were also powerful opinion makers. With its huge, garish red headlines, *Bild* (national circulation: 3.6 million) was the largest publication between London and Moscow, the flagship of that feared, self-made media tycoon, Axel Caesar Springer.

Boenisch, thirty-five, was a boyish rabble rouser with a nose for the local mood. The West Berliners wanted blood. Boenisch wanted to give it to them. But how?

As his visitor Lothar Loewe listened, O'Donnell schemed with Boenisch on the phone. Boenisch wanted to know what the Americans were going to do. O'Donnell of course had no idea. Maybe nothing. Boenisch wondered: How about tearing down the barbed wire at the border?* O'Donnell liked that. He'd see what could be done. Whereupon he and Loewe sat down to a breakfast of waffles, biscuits, and further scheming. Each would stir up his best contacts at State. And both began to think of recalling into service the erstwhile supreme leader of the Berlin Mafia, General Lucius D. Clay, the former Military Governor and hero of the 1948 airlift.

8:00 A.M. Having been joined by Frank Cash, a senior officer of the Berlin Task Force, Ausland tried phoning Foy Kohler again. This time the Assistant Secretary picked up. He had heard the Berlin news on the radio. Ausland asked if Kohler was coming into the office. "Oh," came the relaxed reply, "you and Frank seem to have the situation in hand. I don't think it will be necessary." To Ausland, Kohler's casual mood was a meaningful tip-off. The department would not be doing much about events in Berlin Mitte.

---

* While the political implications of such action could have been grave—the fencing having been carefully put down so as not to encroach on Western soil—the physical problems would have been negligible, at least on that Sunday. Photographs document that the wiring was initially so low and loose in many areas that children could have pushed it aside.

8:30 A.M. Ausland thought it was time to review the contingency plans. What had the government thought to do if the Communists sealed the border to stop the refugee flow? Ausland had asked to see the plans the week before but had been told, "Don't worry. There is a file on that, too." He had assumed that it was a bulky document, carefully sequestered with the department's other top-secret papers. So he asked Frank Cash now, "Did you get the contingency plan from the safe?" This produced an embarrassed silence. Eventually Cash pointed to his briefcase. Concerned, Ausland reached for it and, as he later told the historian Honoré M. Catudal, "I opened it and took out a file folder. It was empty." The department had planned for a crisis over access to West Berlin, not for the crisis that arose in actuality.

Hyannis Port, Massachusetts, 8:30 A.M. At the Yachtsman Motel, an Army sergeant rapped on the door of Major General Ted Clifton, the President's military aide, and handed him the morning's messages from the Teletype machine in the motel basement. It was the night's traffic from the Situation Room in the basement of the White House. As always, Clifton studied the yellow papers with care; they were the President's lifeline. More than twelve and a half hours had elapsed since the border closing, yet there was no mention of Berlin.

9:00 A.M. Lothar Loewe was making himself useful to Roger Tubby, the Assistant Secretary of State for Public Affairs, hoping that Tubby might make himself useful to Berlin. Tubby still had not seen the intelligence on the situation at the Berlin border, which Loewe had dictated to State's Crisis Center hours before. Fascinated, Tubby too took down the information by hand and inquired where Loewe got it. "From your Mission in Berlin!" said Loewe, starting to get exasperated. His beloved Americans didn't seem to be taking Berlin seriously enough, didn't seem to realize that their credibility was at risk. Tubby couldn't see what the excitement was about. "The West Berliners aren't affected," he said. Loewe exploded. "But it's *one city*," he exclaimed. "This is like barbed wire running down Wisconsin Avenue and dividing Georgetown! Imagine what that would be like!"

. . .

10:00 A.M. Foy Kohler had changed his mind and decided to come to the office after all. In the Operations Center it took Ausland very little time to bring the director of the Berlin Task Force up to date and to hand him a copy of his own White House "talking points." Kohler glanced at them, shoved them in his pocket, and departed without further conversation. Taciturnity was Kohler's way. "He rather gives me the creeps," Robert Kennedy once said.

10:00 A.M. Jimmy O'Donnell felt he controlled a solid pipeline into the top level of the United States foreign policy apparatus. This morning was the perfect time to use that clout. He would persuade George Ball to stiffen the collective backbone of the appeasers who were trying to sell out Berlin. These cowards were about to convene in an emergency meeting with Secretary Rusk and peddle the line that the seal-off of the border was a defeat for the East, a show of Communist weakness. What bull!

"This is bigger than the Bay of Pigs," O'Donnell exploded at Ball. O'Donnell urged the Under Secretary to recommend that the United States tear away the barbed wiring; unarmed GIs from the Army Signal Corps could handle the job with pliers in no time! Ball was intrigued by the idea. He was something of a hard-liner, and he knew Europe, having lived for years in England. O'Donnell was mainly a speech writer, true, yet no American knew Berlin more intimately. Still, Ball harbored reservations. While the O'Donnell scenario was worth exploring, it raised obvious questions.

"Look," said Ball, "what if they [the East Germans] have orders to drop back a hundred yards?"

"Then we go in," said O'Donnell.

"Then they drop back another hundred, then what?"

"We go in some more."

"And they drop back another hundred, then what?"

"Then the Soviet Army comes rolling in."

"Then what?" Ball asked again.

"Then we call for a four-power conference and make them own up to their responsibilities [as the true sponsors of the Wall]."

At this point the Under Secretary promised to propose the wire-cutting scheme to Rusk's conference. Even this decision required courage, because tempers were rising. Ball was about to go into his meeting when George McGhee, the head of State's Policy Planning Council, stopped in the corridor and began to argue that the West had no rights in East Berlin.

"McGhee," snarled O'Donnell, "you and your crowd of mandarin idiots are trying to put a fourth color in the American flag!" At once McGhee moved to become physical. Nobody was going to get away with calling him yellow! Ball separated the two schools of Berlin thought, recognizing that he faced another fight inside the conference room.

10:15 A.M. Berlin was not the subject that Secretary Rusk was discussing with Deputy Under Secretary U. Alexis Johnson when the Secretary routinely began his day's first meeting shortly after reaching his office about 10 A.M. on a leisurely Sunday schedule. Germany was not one of Johnson's areas of responsibility or expertise. Moreover, fully twelve hours after the border closure neither man had the slightest inkling that it had taken place. And when word reached them about it at 10:15, their reaction was relaxed. "There was nothing we could do about it," Johnson reflected years later. Rusk asked Under Secretary George Ball and Foy Kohler to come to his office at 10:40. Meanwhile, calmly and methodically, as was his custom, he finished old business with Alexis Johnson.

10:40 A.M. Rusk listened carefully as Kohler propounded the proposition that the new situation was not confronting the United States with a new problem at all. The West, said Kohler, had "never considered" going to war over *East* Berlin. All that mattered was that the location of the border remain unchanged. We should "not contemplate changing the lines of demarcation" or permit "anyone else to change them by force." This stance suited Rusk. The lack of advance warning from the CIA was not ruffling his equable nature.* He viewed the border closure as a flyspeck incident in a large and continuing crisis in which "tension was mounting so high

---

* The Secretary held intelligence efforts generally in small esteem. In a 1986 interview he reminded me that he had worked in Army intelligence at the time of Pearl Harbor. This frustrating experience had left him with a quaintly philosophical, resigned, and remarkably unsophisticated view of espionage. He told me pleasantly, "The good Lord has not given us the capacity to pierce the fog of the future."

that there was a great risk of war." Given the cautious attitude of
the Allies and the "overwhelming" military vulnerability of West
Berlin, the United States should do nothing to create an attitude
of muscle flexing. Everyone in the administration still felt chas-
tened by the catastrophic results of the military initiative that had
blown up at the Bay of Pigs. Rusk did want to explore "what actions
were available if action be wanted by the President" in Berlin. So
when Kohler left the room, Ball brought up O'Donnell's idea of
whisking away the barbed wire. The Secretary would have none of
it. "It would have been futile," he said years later. "How far into
East Berlin do you go?"

12:10 P.M. Kohler having returned to Rusk's office, it was decided to phone Allan Lightner, the ranking American diplomat in
Berlin, to check for any late developments. Kohler did the talking.
Lightner sounded excited ("Lightner was always excited," Kohler
would recall), but he had nothing major to report. He did mention
that the three Allied missions had been working on a strong protest
statement which was about to be released to the press in Berlin.
Kohler told Lightner to hold the phone so he could confer with
Rusk. Momentarily he was back with Lightner, emphatically informing him that the Western Allies "were not to issue any statement whatsoever." The situation was too "serious." Washington
would issue a statement.* The Berlin missions should draft a joint
protest to the Soviet commandant, and that document should be
cleared by all three capitals. When Alexis Johnson returned to
Rusk's office at 12:16 to take up other matters, the Secretary had
not yet resolved his most urgent immediate problem. He knew he
had to phone the President in Hyannis Port, but he didn't know
what to tell him. And so he decided to wait, hoping that more
information might come in. "The President was the kind of fellow
who wanted to know details," he explained much later. "You had
to have your ducks in a row."

---

* The statement, released later in the afternoon, dutifully rehashed how the East
German refugees had "voted with their feet," and recited a long-standing litany.
The border closure violated the four-power status of Berlin, the right of free
circulation throughout the city, and a four-power agreement of 1949. The present American response to these violations was confined to one sentence: "These
violations of existing agreements will be the subject of vigorous protest through
appropriate channels."

· · ·

1:00 P.M. Having finally been informed of the Berlin news by his military aide, General Clifton (see page 26), the President was much annoyed that he was being compelled to seize the initiative and phone Rusk only to learn that the State Department had no ducks for him, much less any ducks all lined up for action. He was not surprised. His struggle with Rusk and the department, over style as well as substance, was gathering momentum. He determined to make still another, firmer try to get better performance out of Rusk. The Secretary was not particularly upset at the President's annoyance. He was used to it. The President was always lecturing, cajoling, demanding, complaining. That was *his* style. So Rusk decided to take in the Yankees-Senators ball game at Griffith Stadium, as he had planned. He figured he would cause eyebrows to be raised in the hypersensitive capital if he canceled a public appearance at the last moment. Rusk did not like causing eyebrows to be raised at anything he did. That was *his* style.

16

ZERO HOUR:
A PERSONAL REMEMBRANCE

How did it all begin, the estrangement between East and West that turned into separation, divisiveness, and undeclared hostilities? How? I knew. I saw it happen, for by coincidence I had been present at the creation. Berlin was the place, 1945 was the year.

It was the onset of the Cold War, but nobody knew it then,* and I never led a more exciting life. I was twenty-two, a technical sergeant in the United States Army, returned to Berlin after an absence of eight years, this time as city editor of a major newspaper, the *Allgemeine Zeitung,* published for the Berliners by our Military Government. We set up shop in the Ullstein skyscraper printing plant near Tempelhof Airport and suffered no German competition. All German media had been ordered shut, pending—in the argot of the day—de-Nazification. In the American sector we were the source, the law.

I had helped stage Ben Hecht's play *The Front Page* back at City College in New York and had learned that city editors were ex-

---

* The term "Cold War" is usually attributed to the financier Bernard Baruch, who launched it in a 1947 speech. Its principal popularizer was the columnist Walter Lippmann. However, the term had been coined earlier by that formidable phrasemaker George *(1984)* Orwell in his writings for British socialist publications.

pected to be tough. So I was tough. I bullied my staff of very young Germans—we never called them anything but "Krauts"—to write news objectively and briefly, dear God, please, briefly.

"*War and Peace* we don't need!" I snarled at one of my apprentice reporters, tossing back his impassioned yard-long production about a no-injury manhole accident on the Alexanderplatz. The writer was Egon Bahr, eventually a minister in the West German cabinet and de facto author of Willy Brandt's *Ostpolitik,* the policy of rapprochement toward the East. (Bahr still told the manhole story forty years later, roaring with laughter.)

In that summer of 1945, the summer of beginnings, most of our deadline nights were like New Year's Eve. The lead story of our paper's first issue reported the bombing of Hiroshima. The third issue headlined the end of World War II.

Our local coverage was less lively, but not for lack of my familiarity with the territory. For once, the Army's madcap personnel assignment system had not hammered a square peg into a round job. It was baffling. I fit the role of city editor because I was at home in Berlin, born in the Charlottenburg district, Kantstrasse 128, lately become the British sector, and I grew up there until I was thirteen. Nevertheless, a useful sense of detachment ruled my reactions to my return; heaven knows where I got it. I had a feel for the city, but I no longer felt that it was home.

Along with all Jewish youngsters, I had been expelled from public school under the Nazis. We were not allowed to infect "Aryan" classrooms. My parents possessed the good sense to emigrate in 1937, well before Crystal Night ushered in the Holocaust. Now, with five battle stars on my Eisenhower jacket, I had come back to test my sense of self against the burned-out shell of our Kantstrasse apartment house.

No, this was no longer home. Home was on East Twentieth Street in Manhattan, above the riding academy that smelled of horse manure. I knew my place right away, standing in front of Kantstrasse 128, a safe distance from the crumbling facade that was soon razed for a parking lot.

I next visited the loft building, abandoned and perforated with shell holes, where my father had worked in the textile manufacturing business founded by my great-grandfather and where the coaster-equipped stock carts made fabulous racing vehicles for me when my father had to work on weekend afternoons. I also returned to the brooding darkness of the Jewish cemetery in Weissensee, where my antecedents lay buried and my father grew up because his father was the resident manager. These way stations of my childhood seemed even less connected to my adult self than the apartment house on Kantstrasse, because they were in gloomy, deserted East Berlin, always a blue-collar area and now called the Soviet sector.

With my roots in both camps, I could sense that something, something seismic, was happening. While no physical barrier impeded passage between the two sides—it was a generation before the Wall and almost a year before Winston Churchill coined the term "Iron Curtain"—Berlin was already the weathervane, the stage where, as my colleagues and I watched in confusion, heroes were suddenly villains and vice versa.

How were we to perceive back then that ideological glaciers were cracking, that the big powers were choosing up sides for a world split into new camps, East and West, and that we were present at the creation because the fresh lineup first became visible in Berlin? German scholars would eventually single out this period as *Die Stunde Null*, zero hour, when the clock first began to tick, the first hour of the first contemporary day. But that insight came later, much later. In the Berlin of 1945 we looked at the world from a foxhole perspective. We only saw cherished beliefs popping like balloons; that was perplexing enough.

Weren't the Germans the bad guys? How could they suddenly have changed into victims? They had stolen my father's business, killed my Aunt Marie in Theresienstadt, and shot at me in Normandy, the bastards. In our prisoner of war stockades in France my friends and I laughed out loud when German generals claimed to know nothing about Nazi misdeeds.

"Ich bin ja nur ein kleiner Mann," they insisted, "I am only a little man."

Nazis? Where were there any Nazis? Nobody seemed to know a single one. So if the Berliners were on starvation rations now and out of firewood for winter, I supposed it served them right. A pound of black-market butter cost a month's wages and cigarettes were worth their weight in gold. So what? Let the sons of bitches go without.

In our annoyed view they all had to be Nazis, or almost all, and they were making themselves additionally objectionable by trotting out a new scapegoat. Germans were fond of scapegoats. They used to blame their troubles on the Jews. Now they blamed the Russians, which was equally hard to credit at first. The Russians? Our allies who did so much to help us defeat Hitler, dying by the millions at Stalingrad and Leningrad?

We *liked* the Russians. Indeed, our policy directives in Military Government *ordered* us to get along with these new neighbors, just as the Allied leaders had tried to make peace with them. When Germany was divided into four occupation zones, the Soviets received the Eastern slice, with twenty million people. When Berlin was cut up into four occupation sectors, leaving it adrift as a curious island artifice 110 miles within Soviet territory, they got their share, east of the Spree River.

But it was transparent even in 1945 that they acted very possessively about Berlin. Their troops took the city on May 2. The Jeeps of my detachment were not admitted until mid-July, after endless delay along the Helmstedt Autobahn, the one fragile road link to Berlin authorized by the Soviets.

How did we, the great General Eisenhower's victorious troops, manage to turn ourselves into supplicants dependent upon Soviet indulgence? Why did we ever agree to consign Berlin to the vulnerability of an island encircled by Communist forces?

This was much more than a momentary inconvenience for me and my stranded colleagues. *Access to Berlin* would become the name of a historic game. The issue was the stuff of East-West crises for decades and would remain worrisome toward the end of the century, although trouble had been predictable from the start and was in fact predicted.

In 1945 the origins of the Berlin access game were buried in the secret files and memories of diplomats who would soon slip from the ranks of the obscure to the forgotten. When I looked into the record much later, I wondered, as I had on other occasions in other contexts, how American voters would have reacted if they had known that the future of Berlin, along with other pieces of Occupied Germany, was being shoved back and forth across negotiating tables like so many slices of pie. I suspect people would not have held still for the official confusion and butterfingering.

It had been a heartbreaking, largely unknown affair, mismanaged at the top of the top, by Franklin Roosevelt, the man for whom I cast my first vote for President in 1944 and for whom I would gladly have voted a few more times if he had lived.

One American did smell trouble and protested while the game

was still fluid, but he was not early or persistent enough and he failed to make himself heard where it might still have done some good. The man was Robert Murphy, a smooth, hardheaded veteran State Department troubleshooter just appointed as Eisenhower's political adviser for Germany with the rank of Ambassador.*

When Murphy quietly checked in Washington during early September of 1944, he was shocked to find that while many plans existed for Occupied Germany, there was no agreement, not even on basic policy. The War Department had a plan. So had the State Department. And so had Treasury, which, under Secretary Henry Morgenthau, Jr., was proposing the radical Morgenthau Plan, calling for the pastoralization of the country. The departments were deadlocked and wrangling because President Roosevelt had not made his views known, and when Murphy was called to the White House, FDR told him he was in no hurry. He had his eye on a higher objective. He instructed Murphy to act so that the Soviets would be convinced that America really wanted to cooperate with them, that Germany must be the proving ground of this cooperation, that world peace would be impossible without it.

On arriving in London in mid-September, Murphy found that a three-nation committee, the European Advisory Commission (EAC), meeting at Lancaster House in nine months of frustrating bickering, had already finished hammering out a program for the occupation. This was a minor miracle, for even the Americans and the British could not agree among themselves (both sought the ports of northwest Germany), and the French had not yet been cut in at all. The protocol was signed by representatives of the United States, Great Britain, and the Soviet Union on September 12 and, amazingly, contained nothing about access to Berlin. It was called a first draft, but it would never be altered in any vital respect involving the Soviets.

Murphy was upset all over again, though not nearly as fervently as the American negotiator, John G. Winant, the Ambassador to

* I always had a high opinion of Murphy during my postwar time in Germany, but his record as a political prophet was spotty. He was the United States Consul in Munich on November 9, 1923, and present on the main square, the Odeonsplatz, watching Hitler march in the Beer Hall Putsch that gave birth to the Nazi movement. Like almost all other observers Murphy found it impossible to believe, as he recalled, that "the demagogue Hitler, so unconvincing to me, would ever amount to much."

Britain, a tense and volatile loner who had become a supporter and friend of Roosevelt after having served as three-term Republican governor of New Hampshire. Winant, a shy idealist of deep convictions, was privileged to communicate directly with the President via the naval code and hoped for the vice-presidential nomination in 1944, although the relationship cooled that year.*

Consistent with FDR's wish to cooperate with the Russians—the President's confident phrase "I can handle Stalin" was circulating among insiders—Winant had performed patiently and effectively to pacify the Soviet delegate, Ambassador Fedor T. Gusev, a glum, stubborn diplomat of limited intellect who resisted social amenities, referred the most minute points to Moscow for weeks of indecision there, and sometimes capriciously ended bitter arguments by suddenly yielding with the surprising statement, "I have no objection."

The buffeting that faced Winant in Washington was just as frustrating. To no avail, he traveled there in search of guidance. In vain he told the War Department in May that he wanted to "propose detailed provisions safeguarding American access to Berlin by highway, railroad and air," that Gusev had assured him the Soviets would not object. The Pentagon negotiators declined to involve themselves in what they considered relatively minor details.

In the absence of instructions, Winant kept defending the EAC plan, which left Berlin isolated 110 miles within the Soviet zone, and he rejected an ingenious solution offered by a State Department adviser in London. The adviser wanted the occupation zones to converge upon Berlin like slices of a pie, thus providing each zone with frontage in the city. Winant now took the position that the American right of access was implicit in the right to be there. He wanted nothing to upset the hard-won cooperation of Ambassador Gusev.

The vehemence with which Winant defended this stand surprised even Ambassador Murphy, who knew that Winant was given to occasional temper outbursts. At a two-hour private luncheon in the Embassy on Grosvenor Square, Murphy argued that the American right to access of Berlin ought to be defined,

---

* Winant wired FDR in despair over having been excluded from the Yalta Conference of February 1945 and was essentially unable to cope with Roosevelt's death and various personal reverses. On November 3, 1947, suffering from mental exhaustion and a severe depression, Winant shot himself in the right temple with a Belgian automatic pistol in his Concord, New Hampshire, home.

that in his experience the Soviets were tough bargainers and expected others to act the same way. Winant finally exploded: "You have no right to come along at this late date and make such a proposal just after we have agreed upon a draft!"

Murphy folded. He was too little in rank, had arrived on the scene too late, and was probably in violation of presidential policy. "I felt it would serve no useful purpose to appeal to higher authority in Washington," the Ambassador wrote in his memoirs. "The President himself, in his recent talk with me, had emphasized that he thought the most important thing was to persuade the Russians to trust us, a sentiment which apparently motivated Winant's negotiations."

Monday-morning quarterbacks would eventually launch postwar historical excavations under such slogans as "Who lost China?" and "Who lost Korea?" Nobody asked, "Who lost Berlin?"—probably because the situation there, as always, was too complicated.*

By the time we were permitted to proceed into Berlin in July, all but the heaviest of the Ullstein plant's printing presses had vanished. While they had stalled, keeping Westerners from entering the city, the Soviets had spirited just about every piece of movable industrial equipment to Russia.

Understandable, if vengeful. But rape? Rape was something else. We didn't believe the stories when the Berliners told us the Soviet occupation soldiers had tried quite systematically to sexually attack German women even though many of them had disappeared into hiding. Recitations of such stories, as I heard them, sounded authentic enough, usually beginning with imitations of the heavily accented call *"Frau, komm!"* (Come, woman!). Surely such incidents had occurred. But I did not accept weeks of uncon-

---

* Another national hero, General Eisenhower, also let Berlin down. In the fall of 1944 Ike had said, "Clearly Berlin is the main prize." By April 1945 he had changed his mind. Soviet troops were thirty-three miles away from the city, the Americans fifty miles. Eisenhower thought that he would not win a race and that other objectives were militarily more important. He was also appalled by a hysterical estimate that an American drive into the Nazi capital would cost 100,000 casualties. "A pretty stiff price to pay for a *prestige objective*, especially when we've got to fall back and let the other fellow take over," said General Ike (emphasis added). An American retreat was of course inevitable because Berlin was well within the occupation zone assigned to the Soviets by the EAC in September 1944 and confirmed by the Yalta Conference five months later.

trolled sexual rampaging. That had to be a Nazi fabrication, more paranoid German scapegoating.*

I would always retain a memory of the rank-and-file Russians as startlingly childlike. They hung like grapes from their antique trucks and horse-drawn carts—we had never seen such vehicles— and seemed to have journeyed to the West mainly to acquire watches, especially Mickey Mouse watches, and our PX candy. *"Uhri, Uhri!"* was their war cry (*Uhr* meaning "watch" in German); even the stonelike Zagnut candy bars, which we refused to consume, fetched enormous stacks of occupation marks from these earthy consumers.

I would have loved to run stories about such local color in our paper. We did not. It would have been unfriendly, hence contrary to American policy. Nor was it fit to print that Soviets ranking above the level of the *Uhri* traders did not behave like allies.

Fraternization with Westerners was against their rules, and so one couldn't talk to them except rarely, when our Soviet counterparts absolutely could not avoid contact with us. I had shed military status and worked for a while as a civilian for the War Department before it became the Defense Department. Over drinks, I cornered a ranking Soviet information officer before an official dinner. His small talk focused upon the greatness of Karl Marx, no kidding. He also told me that my personal politics were motivated by my "fear of Bolshevism." I felt I was in a bad play.

Secrecy was the passion of our colleagues from the East. They would not tell their American partners how much food was produced in their zone, traditionally Germany's breadbasket. They would not say how many occupation marks they were printing. They would not tell our cartel busters what factories they were dismantling in their territories. They permitted no Western publications to circulate in their zone and, in effect, closed their domain to Western Allied travel.

I had to test this to believe it and drove my Jeep to Klein-Machnow, a few miles from our headquarters. Though God has yet to make a village of lesser importance than Klein-Machnow, I was

---

* It took time to authenticate these events and assemble them into a pattern. A convincing account, including frank admissions by Soviet authorities, is by Cornelius Ryan in *The Last Battle* (Simon and Schuster, 1966), pages 484–93. For a reliable contemporaneous version from the Communist perspective, see the recollections of a defector, Wolfgang Leonhard, in *Child of the Revolution* (Regnery, 1958), pages 295–97.

stopped by a red-and-white barrier across the road. A grinning Russian soldier with a tommy gun offered a regretful shrug. The secrets of Klein-Machnow were safe from prying American eyes.

The Germans under Soviet control were learning to live with the rule of the people, Eastern style, back in those days. Docile editors who submitted to the Soviet censors a feature story about a girl picking strawberries and reminiscing about better strawberries in her far-off hometown found the passage blue-penciled.

"That's chauvinistic propaganda," the censor explained. "Strawberries are the same everywhere."

The parallels with the Nazi order had already emerged. Instead of summoning *Parteitage* (party days) in Nuremberg in the fall, the Soviet Germans unfurled their red banners everywhere on May Day.

"Workers of all plants will march in closed rank and file," I read in a smuggled copy of orders to union leaders for that holiday. "The plants are to be decorated with banners and red flags. Other than red flags are forbidden. Every comrade [*Genosse*] will be responsible for decorating the windows of his home. Plant chiefs will report those who did not participate in the demonstration."

To act as enforcers, we learned, the Russians had imported their own brand of housebroken Germans, who had waited out the Hitler era in Moscow. These were dependable *Genossen* with Communist Party records dating to the 1920s, and their George Washington was Walter Ulbricht, fifty-one, already known as "the Goatee."* Before Hitler he had been a Communist member of the Reichstag. On April 30, 1945, he left home, the Hotel Lux in Moscow, at the head of a ten-man delegation of his chums and flew in an American-made Douglas aircraft to Soviet headquarters twenty miles east of Berlin. His papers identified him as "Walter Adolphovich Ulbricht." Fighting for the city was still audible, but the Soviets were eager to be prompt in installing their own backbone of civilian government in East Berlin. Within days, Ulbricht had his apparatchiks functioning as if they were locals. They were placed into key departments as number two men. The more visible top positions were filled by weak but genuine locals, innocents, who served as window dressing.

Fascinated by this efficiency, I assigned myself to interview Ul-

---

* This designation was nothing to snicker over. In 1958, a Dr. Först, a dentist, was sent to prison for a year because he "defamed the state" when he was overheard using this nickname in a restaurant.

bricht. Ex-Communist defectors had briefed me that he was a demon organizer, a totally tireless workhorse with awesome recall for names, utterly lacking in emotion or humor. He did not drink or smoke and kept in shape with daily calisthenics. His only endearing quality was said to be the accent of his native Saxony. Non-Saxon Germans think *Sächsisch* sounds hilarious.

Ulbricht in person was a depressing experience of unexpected proportions. I faced a mechanical voice box, a mask with perfect posture droning out the same phrases that stuffed the Eastern party newspapers. My questions merely elicited more of the same, delivered, click-click, in the same monotone. The fellow looked, no doubt by design, uncannily like busts I had seen of Lenin. And forget his dialect. I, too, had always giggled when I heard *Sächsisch* spoken. My father used to do a devastating imitation of it. Coming out of the robotized Ulbricht it sounded sad.

To face off Ulbricht's machine on behalf of the United States, General Dwight D. Eisenhower, our Supreme Commander, and his bosses in the Truman administration had picked an engineer officer, Lieutenant General Lucius DuBignon Clay, a West Pointer (Class of 1919) from Marietta, Georgia, the son of a United States senator. Compactly built, hawk-nosed, and outwardly courtly, Clay came to Berlin with a reputation for a steely will—some accused him of arbitrariness—a first-class mind, and a wily way of managing politicians in Washington.

I looked upon Clay with suspicion. He had spent most of his life building dams in the American hinterlands. He didn't know Germany, much less German, and I had never heard of a general with competence in civilian affairs, especially abroad. He did seem to realize that much was at stake in our efforts to make the old wartime alliance function in the occupation.

"It's got to work," he told a reporter for a cover story in *Time* magazine. "If the four of us cannot get together now in running Germany, how are we going to get together in an international organization to secure the peace of the world? The test is here."

For a year I attended Clay's Berlin press conferences. I also had several private sessions with him. No question: he understood the Germans, the Russians, and the "test" shaping up in Berlin. He had a mind for complexity, and I was far from the only one who noticed.

One fall afternoon an international press corps of something like one hundred correspondents assembled in front of the long conference table at his headquarters on what would eventually be named Clayallee. The ostensible subject was the steel-producing capacity of Krupp country, the Ruhr. The real subject, everyone understood, was the dismantling of the Nazi arms machine and deciding how much of it to ship to the Soviet Union as reparations.

The room was one of those monumental halls recently occupied by Hitler's air ministry. The rectangular conference table was narrow, gleaming, vacant, its length seemingly endless. The correspondents were, for once, waiting in near-silence. A little door opened behind the table and Clay stepped out alone, looking small and defenseless, without aides or papers of any kind. For the better part of an hour he spoke and answered questions about steelmaking in the Ruhr as if he had never done anything else.* The correspondents, not normally easy to please, went away impressed.

Oh yes, Clay understood what mattered in politics. And what mattered in Berlin was not to be bulldozed by the Soviets and their friends.

I knew Americans who fought with the Lincoln Battalion during the Civil War in Spain. In the 1930s they were dismissed as premature antifascists. East Germany and its Soviet bosses made me prematurely anti-Stalin. When I returned to New York in 1946 and wrote about East Germany's neo-Hitler society and our difficulties with it, editors reacted with suspicion. They thought I exaggerated. They had not met Ulbricht. Or Clay.

---

* After he left Germany in 1949, Clay was named chairman of Continental Can Company at the then royal salary of $96,000 a year.

17

"WE MUST NOT BUDGE":
AN AMERICAN GENERAL AT THE
BERLIN AIRLIFT

**West Berlin,
March, 1948**

The Cold War was heating up and access to Berlin became its most reliable thermometer. Disturbed over almost daily incidents instigated by the Soviets to rattle at the city's fragile road and rail supply lines to the West, the Pentagon high command summoned General Clay to a secret transatlantic Teletype conference. Washington suggested it was time to evacuate American military families. Clay's telecon response was crisp: "Withdrawal of dependents from Berlin would create hysteria. . . . This condition would spread in Europe and would increase Communist political strength everywhere. . . ."

No dependents were moved. The Russians turned up the heat.

March 31. The Soviet Military Administration ordered that all Western military trains to Berlin would be boarded and checked by its soldiers. Clay telexed the Pentagon: "We cannot permit our military trains to be entered . . . to do so would be inconsistent with free and unrestricted access in Berlin. . . ."

The Pentagon responded that a firm stand by Clay could lead to war. Clay telexed back: "I do not believe this means war. . . . Please understand we are not carrying a chip on our shoulder and will shoot only for self-protection."

Military train traffic ceased; no trains were better than harassed trains.

General Lucius D. Clay, the hero of the Berlin airlift, refused to let the Soviets force the Western powers out of Berlin in 1948. "If we mean . . . to hold Europe against Communism," he telexed the Pentagon, "we must not budge."

April 2. In a further teleconference, the Pentagon told Clay that it was coming under increasing pressure to take American families out of Berlin. Clay telexed: "Evacuation . . . is to me almost unthinkable. Our women and children can take it."

The women and children stayed.

April 10. The Soviets having just prohibited civilian passenger trains from leaving Berlin, Washington telexed that it was again reviewing whether the city should be abandoned altogether.

Clay telexed: "We have lost Czechoslovakia. . . . When Berlin falls, Western Germany will be next. If we mean . . . to hold Europe against Communism we must not budge."

June 24. All remaining rail traffic between Berlin and the West was closed by the Soviets at 6 A.M. "because of technical difficulties." A total blockade of two million West Berliners was on. Food stocks would last thirty-six days.

Acting on his own, General Clay ordered all available C-47 two-engine transport planes—the battered "gooney birds" left over from the war—to start transporting food and fuel to the besieged city.

The airlift was on.

June 25. At the next teleconference the Pentagon again urged caution upon Clay. Should dependents be evacuated after all? The general responded: "I still do not believe that our dependents should be evacuated. Once again, we have to sweat it out, come what may. . . . We do not expect armed conflict. . . . Nevertheless we cannot be run over, and a firm position always induces some risk."

June 28. At a secret White House meeting, President Truman shortened debate at the outset by quickly announcing the first pivotal postwar decision on Berlin. Regardless of any Soviet action ("Come what may," he said, echoing Clay), there would be no discussion about the American commitment to the city: "We are going to stay. Period." The President also approved deploying two groups of B-29 Superfortress bombers to Europe. Everyone present understood the intended implication of the move, which was carefully leaked to the press. The B-29 was the only U.S. plane able to carry the atomic bomb, on which the nation still held a monopoly.* Everyone also understood that demobilization after

---

* The balance of power would soon begin to change: on September 23, 1949, the Soviets successfully tested their first nuclear bomb. Even in the summer of 1948

1945 had weakened conventional forces so severely that no military gesture (and no airlift) would carry credibility for the Soviets unless backed up by the bomb.

July 10. General Clay concluded that although the Soviets did not wish to risk war, they had convinced themselves that the West would give up a great deal rather than risk conflict. He telexed Washington his personal plan to call the Soviet bluff. He would advise them that on a specified date he would move an armed convoy down the Autobahn to Berlin, carrying engineering troops equipped "to overcome the technical difficulties" that had allegedly prompted the blockade.

Washington rejected the idea as too provocative.

July 19. General Clay cabled the Pentagon that he was convinced the proposed convoy would have reached Berlin and that the issue was nothing less than America's willingness to assume world leadership against Soviet aggression. His telecon said: "Only we have the strength to halt this aggressive policy here and now. *It may be too late the next time* [emphasis added]. I am sure that determined action will bring it to a halt now without war. It can be stopped only if we assume some risk."

No convoy was authorized.*

July 20. Recalled to Washington for consultations, General Clay assured President Truman, Secretary of State George C. Marshall, his revered mentor, and the assembled National Security Council in the White House that the United States could stay in Berlin "indefinitely without war" if he was given enough planes. He asked for 160 C-54 transports, which could carry loads four times greater than the C-47s.

The President made the decision: the American commitment to Berlin stood firm. Clay got his planes.

July 28. With sixty B-29s having arrived in Britain and thirty

---

the "atomic" B-29s were a bluff. The planes were not modified to carry the bomb, and they couldn't lift enough fuel to reach Soviet targets and return.

* In a 1971 interview Clay still sounded wistful about the convoy idea but hinted that he might have had second thoughts about it. He also conceded that ego had been his motivation and that in 1948 he had not thought the consequences of the convoy proposal all the way through. He said: "I still wish we had tried. I wanted to do so for pride. I don't know what we would have done if we had gone through and the Russians just let us go through and then had stopped the next group of German trucks. . . ." Clay further recalled that President Truman told him he would have approved the convoy but that all his military chiefs had been against it.

more to come shortly, Defense Secretary James Forrestal complained to his closest advisers that he felt frustrated: President Truman would not issue a firm order to employ the A-bomb against the Soviets if the airlift led to hostilities. (Forrestal would have other conferences with Truman in July and August about using the bomb, all inconclusive.*) If Forrestal was left in the dark, so were the Soviets. Still, the mere deployment of bombers capable of dropping the bomb could have sufficed to convince them that America would stand firm in Berlin.

September 13. Fearful of a Soviet tank attack on Western Europe, the United States was quietly organizing for war. Secretary Forrestal again asked President Truman whether he would consent to drop the A-bomb in case of such an assault. "The President said he prayed that he would never have to make such a decision, but that if it became necessary, no one need have misgivings but that he would do so," Forrestal wrote in his diary. The President's assurance was credible. It was he, after all, who had not hesitated to drop the bomb on Hiroshima and Nagasaki to end World War II. But the burden of the crisis triggered by the Berlin blockade did not rest easily on him. In his diary, the President noted: "A terrific day. Berlin is a mess. Forrestal, etc., brief me on bases, bombs, Moscow, Leningrad, etc. I have a terrible feeling afterwards that we are very close to war."

Late September. Clay remained convinced that his airlift had outwitted the Soviets, but Tempelhof Airport in downtown Berlin, hemmed in by apartment houses and often inaccessible during central Europe's winter fogs, could not handle the subwaylike shuttle traffic of up to 1,000 daily flights operated by the combined American and British air forces. Clay ordered construction of a larger, new airport at Tegel in the French sector. His engineers reported the new base would be ready in March.

"I found it necessary to tell them that it would be completed in December," the General wrote later.

It was—Clay having ordered the work to be assisted by 20,000 Berlin men and women working three shifts a day by hand.

---

* Later in 1948 the chief of the U.S. Secret Service advised the President that Forrestal had been moving toward "a total psychotic breakdown." But the Secretary's resignation was not requested until March 1, 1949. Shortly after 1:45 A.M. on May 22, while under treatment for melancholia at Bethesda Naval Hospital, Forrestal copied several brooding verses by Sophocles onto sheets of paper, climbed out of the window, and died four floors below.

Winter 1948–49. Berlin was living largely on dried potatoes, dried eggs, and dried milk. Electricity was turned on only a few hours in late evening. Gasoline was not sold for private cars. Public transport stopped at 6 P.M. School classes met in three shifts. Offices and factories were unheated.

April 15–16, 1949. The airlift set a record. Nearly 13,000 metric tons of food and fuel arrived in 3,946 starts and takeoffs—one every 22 seconds. But unemployment had risen to 17 percent of the labor force.

May 4. After eleven months, 277,728 flights, and 78 accidental deaths, it was announced in Washington that the blockade was over. The negotiations had been so secret that General Clay learned of his ordeal's end from the newspapers.

"I was somewhat chagrined to hear the story this way," he wrote with sarcastic understatement later.

The story of the settlement could have come out of suspense fiction. The first tip arrived well hidden on January 31. A journalist from a news service had submitted a list of written questions to Stalin in Moscow. This was a routine maneuver. Answers came only on rare occasions. Even more rarely did such responses make headlines. Usually, nothing happened. This time Stalin did reply. To a question about currency reform in Berlin, one of the precipitating causes of the blockade, Stalin failed to respond directly, but he acknowledged that the long deadlock in Berlin was economically damaging.

The admission aroused the curiosity of the canny Chip Bohlen, the State Department expert on the Soviets. He sensed that Stalin just might be receptive to a deal. He went to see his old friend and new boss, Dean Acheson, the veteran diplomat who had become Secretary of State earlier that month. Acheson agreed that it was time to test the waters. Shortly, the United States Ambassador to the United Nations stopped to chat with the Soviet Ambassador about the New York weather and casually inquired whether Stalin had only accidentally failed to mention currency problems in Berlin.

After a month of Soviet silence, the Soviet UN Ambassador called. Bohlen had read the signal correctly. Stalin was willing to give up his blockade. In the week of wheedling that ensued, Acheson stood firm. When word of the final agreement arrived on the State Department Teletype, the Secretary and Bohlen toasted each other and their colleagues on the spot.

The crisis in central Europe had passed, at least for the time being. It had been Acheson's first exposure to the Berlin problem. The next time, Berlin would prove more nettlesome to him, but at least for now the siege of the city was lifted.

Winston Churchill issued one of his Olympian dicta: "America has saved the world."

Having learned not to trust the Soviets, Washington ordered that enough cargo planes be kept in readiness so that the airlift could be resumed without advance notice, the next time for up to three years.

In the West, the airlift was celebrated as a victory—evidence of American ingenuity and the resolve to honor the commitment to Berlin. Some old Berlin hands in the American contingent scoffed. Nothing had been won, according to their theology. On the contrary: the Russians had demonstrated to the world that they could endanger Western access to Berlin at their whim. The United States was able to resist only at great risk, expense, and not indefinitely. We should have called the Soviet bluff instead of turning chicken, the old hands preached. We should have let Clay ram his convoy down the Autobahn. It would have worked, so the old theologians mourned, thinking ahead to "the next time."

There was no disagreement, however, about two results of the blockade. General Clay had become the hero of the Berliners, their patron saint. And his tough stand had magnified the internal difficulties that plagued the East Germans.

18

ENTER ERICH HONECKER

East Berlin,
Wednesday, June 17, 1953

Erich Honecker hurried into his main conference room toward noon. "It's getting serious," he told his assembled department heads, his voice rapid, its pitch high. "We will defend the building. Weapons are at hand."

Honecker was forty-one, unknown in the West, a little fellow with peacock posture and tall ambition. Officially he was no more than the leader of the Free German Youth (FDJ), a uniformed party auxiliary much like the Hitler Youth movement, where many FDJ functionaries received their training.

But Honecker's political pedigree was flawless. Active in the Communist movement since the age of ten,* he represented the new generation of DDR bosses. A roofer by trade,† he had risen to

---

* That was the tender age when Honecker entered a Communist children's group known as Jungspartakisten (Young Spartacists).

† The roofer's trade always held a significant psychological meaning for Honecker. His 1980 autobiography contained this almost poetic flight of fancy that offered surprising insights into the emotions of this normally dry and taciturn organization man: "I came to love the trade because it allowed for a certain freedom of movement. It gave one an opportunity to get around, to see the world from above, and always to strive upward. And I felt a thrill because the work was not without danger and always demanded alertness, circumspection, precision

become Ulbricht's principal protégé and junior partner, in part because he had spent the Hitler years in the Nazi prison at Brandenburg Görden, not safely as a refugee in the wartime Valhalla of the party leaders, the Hotel Lux in Moscow.

Now, unbelievably, the workers of the workers' state were rioting. Honecker and his party associates had to fear for their lives, had to reach for guns, and as his FDJ colleagues scattered to take their defense posts at the windows along the four floors of their East Berlin headquarters, Honecker was called into his deputy's office. His wife, Margot, who worked with him, went along. Just then a call from the party's central committee brought shocking instructions: the families of leading comrades were to be immediately evacuated to the Soviet Union. The leaders themselves were certain to be next.

Honecker's deputy said he would refuse to leave his post. Honecker was furious. He feared that the deputy might be killed or fall into enemy hands. The implications for the party's future were intolerable. What if the rioters were to succeed? That appeared to be a real possibility. "Who is going to rebuild Communism if we become victims of the counterrevolution?" he demanded.

The argument was unresolved because the other *Genossen* in the room were making Honecker even angrier. They were busy listening to news coming in over RIAS, the United States–sponsored Radio in the American Sector.* This preoccupation with a forbid-

---

and adroitness." In March 1945, his trade brought Honecker freedom to escape prison. In the war's final days he had been detailed to lead a group of prisoners who were repairing the roof of a prison in the Lichterfelde district of Berlin. He simply walked off the job and went into hiding. Within days of their arrival in May, he joined Ulbricht's group of Communist apparatchiks, fresh from Moscow.

* The Communists never ceased claiming that the events of June 17 were organized and fomented by RIAS and the CIA. It wasn't true. Gordon A. Ewing, a circumspect former *Business Week* editor who ran RIAS, operated under instructions from Washington "to do nothing that could provoke the Soviets," and he refused to let his aggressive German staff use the inflammatory term "general strike" on the air. At the height of the riots he was phoned by one of his State Department advisers in Berlin, Charles Hulick, who reiterated the obvious: "My God, Gordon, be careful! You could start a war with your station." The CIA base chief, Henry (formerly Heinrich) Heckscher, a colorful and venturesome refugee from Germany who had served in the OSS during World War II, was eager to intervene but was also handcuffed. He cabled Washington for permission to distribute rifles and sten guns to the rioters. CIA Director Allen Dulles being unavailable, the request was denied by two senior operators, Frank Wisner and John Bross. When Dulles heard about it the next day, he acquiesced but was

den source of Western propaganda provoked another outburst from Honecker.

"Unbelievable!" he snarled. "You're falling for just what the enemy wants you to hear!"

His wife, who was twenty-six—they had been married only earlier in 1953—laughed. "But, Erich," she teased, "where will we get information? The DDR radio is playing operettas!"

Honecker was not overreacting to the news that was in fact breaking on that rainy Wednesday, June 17. The government of his protector, Ulbricht, was shaking under an assault more embarrassing than any other police state experienced in those times except in Hungary, three years later.

The DDR workers' unrest had first erupted in mid-April when price increases were announced for meat, sausage, and baked goods. In late May morale dropped further because production quotas went up by 10 percent. The ensuing brief work stoppages elicited an unprecedented conciliatory government response on June 9. A Politburo communiqué conceded that "errors" on the part of the government had caused "numerous people to leave the Republic." The food price increases were canceled. Migrants were promised restoration of their property and civic rights if they returned from the West. But the hated new production quotas stayed in force, scheduled to go into effect on Ulbricht's approaching sixtieth birthday.

Massive defiance began to spread on June 15, starting among construction workers along the DDR's monumental showplace, Stalinallee, the broad "first socialist avenue of Germany." Stopping work, the men marched—many in wooden clogs—to the House of Ministries, brandishing crudely lettered signs demanding repeal of the production norms.

"Down with the quotas!" came the cry through bullhorns. "Free elections!" "This is revolution!" And, unheard of, Ulbricht came under personal attack: "The Goatee must go!"

The government announced cancellation of the quotas but ignored the unrest. Ulbricht told his ministers that the leaderless workers would tire and disperse. They did, but the dictator greatly underestimated the depth of their resentment. As the men broke

---

unhappy. In those days, he and his brother, Secretary of State John Foster Dulles, still talked gamely of "rolling back the Iron Curtain."

ranks, the word spread: everybody out on general strike, Wednesday, June 17!

Wednesday morning many factories stood silent throughout the DDR. In central Berlin, tens of thousands marched on the Alexanderplatz, the Marx-Engels-Platz, and the great square before the Brandenburg Gate. A red flag waved from the gate's roof. Two young workers cut it down from its mast but it got stuck. One of the men—some in the crowd knew him as Horst—climbed back and tore it loose. It sailed slowly to the pavement amid thunderous applause.

Old-timers were reminded of the civil-war street fighting after World War I. This morning, signs marking the sector borders were torn down. Party offices, newspaper kiosks, and a Russian bookstore went up in flames. Vehicles carrying party officials were stopped and overturned. Here and there the mobs broke into songs of freedom ("Brüder zur Sonne, zur Freiheit") and, incongruously, the "Deutschlandlied," the old anthem celebrating the Kaiser's expansionism. Rocks flew. The *Vopos* started shooting. Dead and wounded fell on both sides.*

By 1 P.M. the Soviets had seen enough. They proclaimed martial law. Their T-34 tanks swept down Unter den Linden, not firing but scattering the workers, hundreds of thousands of them by this time. The *Vopos* were withdrawn and replaced by motorized Soviet troops. At the newly proclaimed 9 P.M. curfew time the streets were deserted except for Russian patrols. Unorganized, lacking any semblance of leadership, the rebellion collapsed. Ulbricht received word of its end while hiding under the protection of Soviet troops at the party summer resort in Kienbaum, thirty kilometers to the city's east; Honecker had fled westward, to suburban Babelsberg, and was also under Russian protection.

The economic hardships that triggered the revolt of June 17, 1953—a date that would be well remembered as a landmark in both Germanys—also accelerated a long-term evolution with a devastating fallout for the DDR leadership. The trend was seminal:

---

* The toll was never reliably ascertained. The *Stasi*'s figures of 25 dead and 378 wounded were undoubtedly too low.

the DDR's population of seventeen million was all but melting away.* Dissatisfied and forbidden to express their views by ballot, people voted with their feet, migrating westward in astonishing numbers.

Suddenly, from 1952 to 1953, the one-way traffic almost doubled: from 182,393 to 331,390. And Honecker suffered a most particular personal shock: about half the refugees were under the age of twenty-five. They were the alumni of his FDJ movement. If the DDR (and Honecker's career) were to have a future, something innovative had to be done to keep the young people at home. How? Honecker decided that the government's response would have to be unique to be effective.

To his deputy, Heinz Lippmann,† the Second Secretary of the FDJ, Honecker confided the theoretical underpinnings of what would become the Berlin Wall eight years later. Only a "radical" sealing of the Berlin border could stem the population drain, he told Lippmann. To support his argument, Honecker cited an episode that was hallowed like a catechism in the minds of European Communists: the fate of the Paris Commune.

Every good Marxist could recite the story. For about two months in 1871, a besieged Paris was ruled by the insurrectionary workers' Commune, the first dictatorship of the proletariat. When government troops moved in from Versailles to crush the dream, the last 147 Communards, already taken prisoner, were slaughtered with machine guns at the "Wall of the Federals" in the Père Lachaise Cemetery and promptly became celebrated as shining examples of bravery.

---

* In most years until the Wall was built, defections exceeded 250,000 annually, and this reflected only refugees who registered for emergency aid with West German authorities. The full count was estimated to be as much as one third higher. The quality of the migrants was, from the beginning, even more revealing than the numbers. Between 1954 and 1961, 17,082 engineers and technicians, 17,476 teachers and academics, and 3,371 physicians registered for assistance.

† A Berlin Jew who had survived four years in Auschwitz, Lippmann fled to West Germany in September 1953. Political disenchantment was one of his motivations. Financial irregularities also played a role. In 1956, a West German court sentenced Lippmann to nine months in prison and a fine of 5,000 marks for having embezzled funds from Honecker's FDJ. In subsequent years Lippmann rehabilitated himself and became a researcher for the Bonn government's All-German Institute, working on DDR affairs. He also wrote what is still the best biography of his onetime boss: *Honecker* (Verlag Wissenschaft und Politik, 1971). He died in 1974.

Karl Marx, still an unknown writer in London, made them famous and they did the same for him. Within two weeks of the massacre Marx hailed the heroes in an address that finally brought him headlines. "History has no comparable example of such greatness," he pronounced. "Its martyrs are enshrined forever in the great heart of the working class."

To Honecker, the Commune was more than gospel; it was part of his own youth. In June 1933, with the Nazi regime less than half a year old, he led an already illegal group of young Communists from his native Saarland to a world congress of antifascists in Paris. They made the trip crowded into an old Mercedes because it was cheaper than the train and less likely to risk arrests by the Nazis. Honecker never forgot how moved he was when he visited the Père Lachaise, but he told Lippmann that the Communards had brought certain defeat upon themselves.

He compared their situation to that of the DDR in the Berlin of the 1950s. The Communards should have erected "solid" defenses against the government troops. Similarly, the DDR should seal off the drain of refugees. They would have to be more radical than the radicals of 1871.

Honecker's colleagues in the government became intrigued by the possibilities, and the State Planning Commission was ordered to come up with technically feasible methods for cutting a modern metropolis in two.

19

THE INSIDERS:
A PERSONAL REMEMBRANCE

**West Germany,
Fall 1957**

Every crisis has its insiders, a core of obscure, usually unremembered early birds. For the West, the discoverer of the Berlin Wall was an eager-beaver double agent, a precocious junior functionary of the SPD, the Social Democrats, Fritz Schenk, twenty-seven.

In October 1957 Fritz and his wife, Rosemarie, twenty-four, were hidden away, laboring twelve to fourteen hours daily in a rustic little mountain guest house owned by the SPD in the Eifel Mountains. Together they were reconstructing the story of the double life Fritz had been leading for the preceding five years.

Bright, clean-cut, well-organized, and polite to a fault, Fritz was thought to possess leadership potential back home in East Berlin. His tender age notwithstanding, he had been appointed executive assistant to the director of the State Planning Commission in 1952. The DDR security authorities had missed one flaw in his makeup: he was secretly disenchanted with their regime. At heart he had remained a Social Democrat, loyal to the party of that rising star, Willy Brandt, the Mayor of West Berlin.

With access to his boss's safe, Fritz kept borrowing the most important papers overnight and copying key passages by hand at home. In his neat, methodical way he incorporated these secrets in manuscripts that appeared to be drafts of his boss's future speeches. Periodically, he spirited the pages to the Ost-Büro (East Department) in Bonn, the intelligence arm of the SPD, long rumored to be financed by the CIA.

Schenk's smuggled intelligence included key fragments of plans that fulfilled Honecker's dream to improve upon the Paris Commune of 1871. The studies showed how the East Berlin authorities could cut off West Berlin's electricity; disrupt subway and elevated train service; and turn the sector border into "security belts" with barriers and guard towers. To Schenk these no-man's-land belts looked remarkably like the Nazi concentration camps he had read about as a teenager.

On Sunday, September 8, 1957, suspecting imminent arrest, Fritz, Rosemarie, and their two young sons, equipped with a volleyball, a blanket, and sandwiches to make them look like picnickers, boarded an elevated train to West Berlin, and were flown to West Germany by a U.S. Army plane. Their family cover name was "Rose." It turned out to be the last time the Americans would do anything special for Fritz.

Enchanted by the gift of three months in the mountains to put his spy experiences on paper for the SPD, Schenk and his wife poured their energies into their own debriefing. A highlight of their report was a five-page reconstruction of proposed "permanent measures" by the DDR to stop the exodus of refugees.

Soon, however, the couple's enthusiasm dimmed. Fritz had begun to commute to the Ost-Büro in Bonn to refresh himself on the documentary materials he had smuggled out over the years, and his exposure to the archives was depressing. His work had evidently not been forwarded to the SPD leadership. It had been "evaluated" and filed away.

Then he hit upon the internal comments of the SPD experts. They were unkind, especially in their judgment on his five-page memorandum about stopping the refugee flow. Schenk would not forget the wording: "This is where the author's fantasy really ran away with him."

His vacation over, Schenk was received by the chief of the Ost-Büro with obvious embarrassment. The chief did not know what to do with Fritz. Since he had once learned the printing trade, Schenk was offered work as a typesetter at the party newspaper in Bonn. Fritz was disappointed. He did not mind too much starting from the bottom again. But his goal had eluded him. He had come to the West, the promised land, to warn of grave danger to Berlin and no one seemed to care.

**East Berlin,
Spring 1959**

The East Germans did care, of course, very much, and from time to time they undertook physical preparations for a secession that might someday divide the German universe. Bahnhof Friedrichstrasse, the main zonal train and elevated station in central Berlin, would have to become a watershed in any such scheme. In 1956 a new switching system was quietly installed so that the East/West through tracks could be made to dead-end there on a moment's notice, but most of the time Honecker's dream of Communard defenses remained in abeyance.

By the spring of 1959 the DDR leadership had convinced itself that there was no need to go to the trouble of closing the Berlin border after all. It had fallen victim to an uplifting fantasy. The Communists thought that they had discovered another way to deal with the migration westward. They had convinced themselves that the flow could be greatly reduced by painless—even enjoyable—internal means. All that the government would have to do was to improve living conditions enough so people would see little point in leaving.

This euphoric theory became formal policy at the Fifth SED Congress in July 1958, when Ulbricht announced a dramatic goal to be attained by 1961: "The West German per capita consumption of food and the most important industrial consumer goods is to be reached and surpassed."

This astounding target had been encouraged by an 8 percent increase in industrial production during 1957. In 1958, output increased another 12 percent in the first half of the year, and still another 12 percent in the second half.

The effects on the quality of daily life were gratifying and visible. In May 1958 ration cards disappeared. For the first time since before World War II, almost twenty years before, meat, fat, and sugar were not rationed.

The migration fever promptly calmed. In 1957, 261,622 East Germans went West. In 1958, the figure fell to 204,092. In 1959, 143,917 would leave, the lowest figure since the founding of the DDR. The link between the downtrend and better living conditions was unmistakable.

Alas, the economic improvements were reached at the price of breakdowns in the system and could not be maintained. The country came nowhere near reaching the output of its West German competition, and would still not attain anything approaching the same level even thirty years hence. Ulbricht's goal had been illusory, a conceit. The refugee figures began to increase again. Plans for closing the Berlin border became topical once more.

Some East German documents about the proposed sealing of the East-West border found their way into the hands of Mayor Willy Brandt in West Berlin. Brandt turned this intelligence over to his analysts to judge whether the plans were feasible. The experts said that they were, but reported that the Russians had rejected the concept.

Brandt considered this secret so improbable that he even discussed it publicly.

In May 1959, Jim O'Donnell interviewed him for a *Saturday Evening Post* article to be called "Mayor Under the Soviet Gun." Ever since he started covering Berlin in 1945, the city had been O'Donnell's spiritual home, so the article was a labor of love.

"What about the refugees that flow through West Berlin?" he asked Brandt. "Many see in this the true origin of the crisis—a sealing-off operation."

"I very much doubt that," Brandt responded. "East Berlin had a kind of Chinese Wall project to run through the heart of the city. But the Soviets vetoed it. . . ."

The word "wall" was out in the open for the first time—barely. Fritz Schenk's insight remained valid; the West did not take the concept seriously. Not even when it was spelled out plainly in the pages of an American magazine by O'Donnell, a charter member of the Berlin Mafia.

Jim O'Donnell was one of the Berlin insiders who made me feel like an alumnus being dropped into the middle of a class reunion. The cast of characters—and, oh, what characters!—made me remember the time when my older son, Ron, was little and couldn't pronounce the word "group." He used to point at some other youngster and announce, "That boy is in my *groof!*" Well, the Berlin Mafia of August 1961 was my *groof.* We felt a bond because we had met at the fork of history where East turned East and West became West. We were the Class of '45, the graduates of Year Zero.

Jimmy O'Donnell, with his light blue eyes, his earnestness, and his uninterruptible logorrhea, had joined *Newsweek* so recently that he was still wearing his army officer's uniform when I met him at the American Press Club in Zehlendorf in the summer of 1945. A

Harvard man with a notoriously low boiling point, he had studied in Germany before the war and spoke German with a strong accent but considerable fluency. He flaunted the profanity of a sailor and the intellect of a Talmudic scholar.

Many years afterward I attained the status I had always envied Jim; I became a correspondent for *Newsweek* too. When Jim moved to *The Saturday Evening Post,* he fingered me for a spot on that magazine, then a journalistic Valhalla with influence that impressed even John Kennedy. Over the years I worked in Washington, Chicago, New York, and elsewhere. Jimmy left Berlin only occasionally for brief periods in a span of almost forty years. Fiercely—better: desperately—he wished to influence United States policy toward his own unyieldingly hard-line views. When his fling as a bureaucrat for the State Department ended in frustration, he turned back to his typewriter and to the black-and-white of the past, to our days together in the Berlin of our youth when it was still possible to tell the heroes from the villains.

His other friends and I worried about him. Jimmy was a brilliant and facile writer, yet after he broke with the *Post*'s editors (over what looked to me like picayune squabbles), he spent years slaving at his magnum opus, his only big hit. *The Bunker,* published in 1978, was a deservedly big best-seller, a minute-by-minute excavation of Hitler's final underground days during the spring of 1945. It is a mesmerizing tour de force, researched with an obsession that only a Germanophile like Jimmy could bring to the subject of *Götterdämmerung*.

Jimmy and I had lunch in New York after he finally wrenched himself away from his adopted home city in the 1980s. Relentlessly he talked German politics as if I still belonged to the Mafia and we were resuming a conversation of the day before. He was still a prisoner of Berlin.

I was not surprised that Jimmy dedicated *The Bunker* to Marguerite Higgins, by then long dead.* Maggie was many things, but she was not forgettable. Jimmy and I met her as she was about to

---

* She died at age forty-five of a tropical disease she contracted while covering the Vietnam War.

become Berlin bureau chief for the *New York Herald Tribune* at the age of twenty-six. I was lucky. I never had a job that forced me to compete with her. Maggie was a five-foot-eight blonde with a baby face, delectable proportions, and a voracious sexual appetite. Everybody knew that she slept with news sources, but I always hoped that she did so because she enjoyed it, not because she considered it necessary.

It wasn't. While Maggie was no fine stylist, she was a sensational reporter, totally without fear, more competitive than a tennis champion, a war correspondent whose wars did not stop because it was peacetime. She never seemed to cease darting around for exclusives, and the most productive feature of her anatomy was not her shape but what O'Donnell called her three elbows.

I don't believe there ever was a woman journalist more spectacularly successful, more ruthlessly manipulative, more famous, or more resented. O'Donnell's wife-to-be, Toni Howard, wrote an erotic novel about her. It massacred a female bed-and-business correspondent and was titled *Shriek with Pleasure*. When Maggie married and became pregnant, her *Tribune* archcompetitor, the great Homer Bigart, who also roamed Berlin in the 1940s and was afflicted by a stutter, asked, "Who's the m-m-mother?"

Though I cannot picture that Maggie managed to get the patrician General Clay into bed, she did almost as well. One of her best news sources (whom she eventually married) was Clay's director of intelligence, a tall, handsome major general named Bill Hall. They met in Berlin. He had a wife and four children in the U.S. It was during the airlift, the world's hottest news story at the time, and Maggie had grown possessive and partisan about the city.

For her, as for most of the Class of '45, the romance with Berlin began during the earliest American rivalry with the Soviets in the Year Zero. Berlin became another of Maggie's loves because it needed protection from the Russian wolf. It wasn't difficult to become a hard-liner under Clay's tutorship back then, and to turn more fiercely protective during the hunger of the airlift. Maggie was more relentless about it than most. Her passions were not confined to bed.

A lot of people underestimated Maggie. They thought she lived only for excitement. The brilliant Mac Bundy, Kennedy's man for National Security, in a memo to JFK during the 1961 Wall crisis, dismissed her as a "firebug." Bundy had also trivialized the Bay of

Pigs fiasco, as "a brick through the window." It was Bundy's job to protect the President from bricks and fires. For Maggie, Berlin was no fire. It was religion.

Peter Boenisch, the editor of Axel Springer's raucous tabloid *Bild,* brought to the Berlin Mafia his exuberance, which was infectious, and his irreverence, which was total. In speech and mentality Peter was like the old-time Berlin cabbies, half ego and half *Schnauze* (loudmouth). Absolutely nothing was sacred to these cynics—or to Boenisch—except Berlin. They lampooned Berlin, they reviled it, they shrugged off its traumas with a jab of sarcasm or a roll of the eyes; that was bravado. In truth, Berlin was their mantra, it was untouchable.

As a tall, handsome, tousle-haired reporter—he was nineteen when I met him—Peter was a city editor's New Year's Eve. Grinning broadly, his huge black eyes sparkling, Peter would march in anywhere and ask anybody anything. His mother had been born in Russia, so he knew Russian and could talk himself into the drinking bouts—and wonderful news stories—at Soviet headquarters, a rare skill.

Although I'm certain that the characteristics of a great tabloid editor lay implanted in Peter's genes, he told historians years later that he owed his shamelessness to me, his first city editor. He told them that I punished his journalistic lapses by lobbing ink bottles at him across the newsroom, neglecting to mention that this occurred only once and that the bottle was empty (at least according to my memory). He also told interviewers that he borrowed a leaf from my skeptical attitude toward news sources, including generals—even, so Peter would recall, toward the sainted General Clay.

This may be accurate, and I'm glad if it is. In German journalism, even pre-Hitler, personages of rank and title belonged to the exalted class of authorities. Authorities were holy. In the journalism that we taught in the U.S. Military Government of 1945, crude as it was, we tried to convince young German reporters that news sources were liars until proved otherwise. This was received as a logical and liberating fact of life by young Peter, my irreverent disciple.

Tactfully, I never asked him how he managed his cat-and-mouse game when he became chief spokesman for the Kohl government in Bonn and, perforce, the most colorful and most quoted news source in the country.* Nor, in my numerous encounters with Peter over the years, did I take him to task about his journalism or his politics, although my tastes are, to put it gently, distinctly *more* conservative in journalism and much *less* so in politics.

For years I couldn't understand my acceptance of Peter's waywardness. His errant public life would have scandalized me in someone else. Sentiment played a role, of course. He and I had been green beginners together in the newspaper business during Berlin's first arctic postwar winter. The trees in the parks had vanished as firewood, and the currency of the realm was the cigarette, at 100 marks the carton. Most civilians were hungry most of the time. For our German reporters the democratic editorial diet of our occupation newspapers meant less than did the one hot meal we dished out daily to keep the staff, literally, from collapsing.

(Necessity makes odd bedfellows: while we served army rations to our prodigies and taught them to disrespect our generals, General Eisenhower's "nonfraternization" regulations officially still prohibited social contacts with our recent enemies, a rule ignored by almost everybody.)

Nobody would forget that first winter. By the time I reached Berlin, the shouts of the Soviet soldier rapists ("*Frau, komm!*") had subsided, but their cries of "*Uhri! Uhri!*" were still going strong. Though my Army colleagues and I did not share the hunger of the Germans, we knew something of our readers' discomforts. Commuting distances forced us to spend the winter in a typical unheated flat in Tempelhof, sleeping under mounds of blankets in two sets of long winter GI underwear, producing little clouds every time we exhaled.

Our bond to that downtrodden Berlin did much to make me tolerate Peter, even to defend him against those of my German friends who considered him a cannibal. Eventually I understood that only the Berlin bond could have withstood the tests of his outrageousness for decades. It was an alliance inviolate—like one's inability to fire a relative. How could I turn against anybody who defended the gates to the Center of the Universe against the Huns?

---

* Boenisch resigned this post in 1985 over a temporarily unpaid personal income tax obligation. Characteristically, the attendant dustup did not affect his friendships among high or ranking reactionaries or his employability.

Indeed, I was a bit guilt stricken because I had been AWOL, busy elsewhere since the war.

Berlin is *überparteilich,* above party politics, which can be said of hardly any other major issue in the lives of Germans. They politicize anything. Party affiliations even become criteria for the employment of editors on TV networks. And so, while nobody could be more alienated from Peter Boenisch (the very voice of the CDU conservatives) than the Social Democrat Egon Bahr, Willy Brandt's confidant and philosopher, it would not occur to these two enemies to exchange anything but warmest agreement about the sanctity of Berlin.

Bahr, too, was one of us boys from the Year Zero. At twenty-three, pale, grim, perpetually in a hurry, he was a year older than I was when he came to work for my city desk. He, too, told interviewers years later that I taught him the essentials: keep the lead paragraph of a news story crisp; do not, on pain of strangulation, mix political views into the facts. We wanted the facts plain, no gravy, a novel notion for the Germans.

Not that anything was wrong with Egon's politics. His father had lost his job because he was a defeatist; he voiced the view, much too early, that Germany would lose World War II. On his mother's side, Egon got in trouble because his maternal grandmother was Jewish. When the authorities uncovered this flaw in Egon, they expelled him from the *Wehrmacht* and made him lug heavy goods in a steel factory. He survived because he never lost sight of his father's counsel: "Son," the old man used to say, "always keep your ass to the wall."

When Egon walked into our newspaper, he was that rarity, an experienced hand without a Nazi past; he had spent several months as a freelance reporter (at 35 *Pfennig* per line) for the Soviet-licensed *Berliner Zeitung* in his own East Berlin neighborhood. Trouble hit him there quickly too. Having talked himself into becoming the only journalist to attend East Berlin City Council meetings, he was eventually spotted by Karl Maron, who snapped, *"Der muss raus!"*—He's got to go!

In a way this was quite an honor because Maron, then Deputy Mayor, was the same apparatchik who became Minister of Internal Affairs and thus a chief hatchet man for Walter Ulbricht and Erich Honecker when the Wall went up. Maron had been in the inner circle of the Communist immigrants who were flown in with Ulbricht from Moscow after the fall of Berlin. And, unfortunately for Bahr, the editor of his *Berliner Zeitung* had been in the same clique.

When Bahr assigned himself to cover Berlin's most formidable local story, the attempts to clear up some of the rubble from the bombings, the editor complained that Egon's reporting lacked "the viewpoint of the class struggle." Bahr got the message. He possessed some of the fictional good soldier Schweik's flair for bamboozling authority; so when he next wrote about Berlin's socialist efforts at reconstruction of the flooded subways, Bahr took only a brief peek underground. He then composed an article awash with rote adjectives of the class struggle jargon. His editor was thrilled and remarked: "This is taken authentically from real life! You're on the right course."

Egon inferred instead that his ass was no longer close enough to the wall. It was time to defect to the Americans.

His later move to Willy Brandt's staff and the plunge into politics came just as naturally to Egon and again he did brilliantly.

In a 1963 speech at a church conference he launched the *Ostpolitik* that would win the Nobel Peace Prize for Brandt. Almost simplistically, Bahr called for *Wandel durch Annäherung* (change through rapprochement). It didn't ring like much of a battle cry, yet the phrase became famous and remained the leitmotiv of West German foreign policy into the 1980s. It was revolutionary because it focused on realities that the West had long denied. Bahr was saying: the East Germans and their Soviet backers are hardly cozy people, but they won't disappear. One had to deal with these difficult new Germans.

Into the 1970s, Bahr practiced shuttle diplomacy with East Berlin and Moscow. Having become a minister in the Brandt cabinet, as we shall see later, he enlisted Secretary of State Henry Kissinger to help him negotiate a series of breakthrough treaties regulating such essentials as East-West highway and rail traffic. In the 1980s, still in a hurry, Bahr made himself the West German parliament's prime authority on disarmament.

Egon remains furious at what he calls the *Scheissmauer* (Wall of Shit). It no longer preoccupies his life because Berlin seems secure now. We talked about that late one evening in 1986 at his office after most of the lights had gone out in the Bonn skyscraper of the Bundestag. I asked Bahr what would happen to politicians of the right or the left if they criticized the enormous expenditures for subsidies that West German taxpayers still shell out every year to keep Berlin alive.

Willy Brandt *(left)* and his longtime confidant and adviser (and erstwhile member of the "Berlin Mafia"), Egon Bahr.

Alumna of the "Berlin Mafia," veteran foreign correspondent Marguerite Higgins *(below)* played a key role in getting Lucius Clay back to Berlin in 1961.

"Political suicide," snapped Bahr.*

And so our little Berlin Mafia would eventually grow up. Its brand of stubborn *Lokalpatriotismus* (parochialism) would never become fashionable, but on at least one occasion its passion was pervasive. During the week following the border closure of 1961, the emotions of the Berliners threatened to boil over and Washington felt compelled to take notice.

**Washington,
Sunday, August 13, 1961**

It was a slow, painful lurching and it got under way after lunchtime on that fateful Sunday in mid-August.

Glumly, Under Secretary Ball and Jimmy O'Donnell were leaving the State Department Building. Having followed through on O'Donnell's idea and proposed at Secretary Rusk's meeting that the East German barbed wire be cleared away, Ball could not even get a discussion going. It was like firing cannons after white flags had already been hoisted. Ball felt he could not insist. He would become the number two man in the Department the following month, which would give him general responsibilities. At the moment he was only handling economic affairs. The officials running political and military matters did not want to risk raising international temperatures over Berlin.

As if to dramatize the department's business-as-usual stance, Secretary Rusk stepped through the building's door while Ball and O'Donnell were taking leave of each other outside. Rusk wore a seersucker suit but carried no papers. "He's off to Griffith Stadium to watch the ball game," Ball said.

O'Donnell, having disgustedly given up his plan to energize the State Department, had not abandoned his search for allies elsewhere in government. He told Ball he would try to mobilize the CIA. No way. When he reached the Chevy Chase home of Seymour Bolton, his highest-level contact in the agency, there was no evidence of international crisis. Bolton was mowing his lawn and invited O'Donnell inside for a drink. All was quiescent among the spooks.

---

* In a 1968 poll, 49 percent of West Germans voted for *more* aid to West Berlin. Ten years later the vote was 52 percent.

By 3 P.M. the Berlin Mafia had stepped up its footwork. Luck was helping the conspirators along. "Guess who my neighbor is up here?" asked Marguerite Higgins. She was phoning Jim O'Donnell from her vacation house on Cape Cod.

Fortuitously, Clay was vacationing at Square Top, his summer home in Chatham. O'Donnell and Higgins conspired to put him to work: Maggie volunteered to walk down the street and persuade Clay to return to Berlin. The role of the recruiter fit her. She had become an influential columnist with close connections to the Kennedys. In the 1960 presidential campaign she had helped raise money for JFK and advised on cabinet appointments. Attorney General Bob Kennedy was godfather of her daughter, Linda.

Still, Clay might resist a Kennedy lasso. He was not only a corporate powerhouse as chief executive of Continental Can, he had also become a Republican kingmaker, the key money raiser for Eisenhower. Ike might not have become President without his sidekick Lucius. As a sixty-four-year-old retired four-star general, would Clay accept a front-line post and serve a forty-four-year-old President of the opposition party?

By evening the Mafia had struck: Clay had signed on. When Maggie Higgins called upon the general he had already been thinking of volunteering his services to the President. He had lost four fifths of his stomach in an ulcer operation, but he was feeling scrappy once again and of course Berlin remained the great sentimental cause of his life. Higgins reported the great news to O'Donnell, and they agreed on their next move: Maggie would call Bob Kennedy and suggest that the President name Clay as his personal representative in Berlin.

O'Donnell had barely hung up when Clay was on the line to confide a personal caveat. "I'm a President's man," he said, "but I cannot abide that little brother of his." O'Donnell said he was certain that the general would not have to deal with the brash young Bobby. When Maggie called once more to say that Bob had agreed to recommend the general's appointment to the President, she said she understood Clay's sentiments about the Attorney General. The President would have to be briefed: unlike most "personal" presidential appointments, this emissary would really have to be managed by the President himself.

On balance, O'Donnell concluded that he had salvaged something from a disastrous day. The administration was writing off East Berlin, but at least his own bunch had again shown loyalty in an emergency. He phoned Peter Boenisch at *Bild* in Germany to tell him in confidence that Clay would probably be coming. Peter should pass the word to their old friend, Willy Brandt's confidant, Egon Bahr. The old network was in operating order, though its influence would prove minimal. Washington was bent on pursuing its own ways.

20

THE WEEK AFTER THE DISASTER, DAY BY DAY

West Berlin,
Monday, August 14, 1961

Morning. "Small numbers of East Germans are continuing to break through the Communist cordon to West Berlin," Dan Schorr broadcast to CBS audiences. "Some of these had stories of spectacular escapes, such as a young engineer who kicked a policeman in the stomach, another man who grabbed a policeman's carbine, one who stepped on his car gas pedal and rammed through, still another who put West Berlin license plates on his car and simply drove through unhindered. . . ."

Washington,
Monday, August 14, 1961

Morning. The New York Times had woken up. SOVIET TROOPS ENCIRCLE BERLIN TO BACK UP SEALING OF BORDER, said the four-column headline on the right-hand (lead) side of the front page. The article, by Sydney Gruson, characterized the border closing as "sudden and dramatic" and reported ominously that the Soviet troops were "battle ready." There was no more talk about the plight of Berlin's "commuters."

· · ·

7:30 A.M. "What the hell do we do now?" Mac Bundy asked Robert Amory, Jr. They were alone in Bundy's White House office. American policy for Berlin had obviously been knocked into disarray over the weekend. Amory, like Bundy a crisp, aristocratic Bostonian, was the CIA's veteran Deputy Director for Intelligence, the chief of the intellectual—the analysts'—side of "the House." He had been at his office in Langley, Virginia, since 5:30 A.M., as usual, assembling the "morning briefing book" that contained the night's intelligence reports for the President's exclusive consumption. Shortly before 7 A.M. Amory had shaved, and was driven to the White House to deliver the briefing book, also as usual.

A World War II combat Marine officer, the urbane Amory was an activist, a mover. He had never quite forgiven the Eisenhower administration for failing to come to the aid of the Hungarian freedom fighters when Russian tanks cut them to pieces in Budapest in 1956. The East German border closure this weekend was no reason to alter his morning routine, however. It was the umpteenth Berlin crisis Amory had been through and this one looked like no emergency. The Soviets had mounted no new blockade of West Berlin, as had been feared. One strand of barbed wire had been strung. What did that amount to? "Nothing," said Amory later. It was obviously a defensive, not an aggressive, move. He thought the United States should seize the opportunity to take a firm stand.

"Mac, there is one thing you can do right here and now," he said, "and that is to vividly enhance your commitment to Berlin." He suggested sending a combat team of Army troops down the Autobahn to reinforce the West Berlin garrison.

"What do you think about that, Max?" Bundy asked General Maxwell Taylor, the President's military adviser, who had just arrived.

"That's a hell of a bad idea," Taylor snapped. "We're in a dangerous situation there. This would further [increase] maldeployment. Any troops that we have in Berlin will be casualties in the first six hours of fighting." The NATO shield throughout Europe was too thin to risk the senseless annihilation of reinforcements for a hopeless outpost. Bundy disagreed. He favored sending some troops.

Amory withdrew discreetly—he was an analyst, not a policymaker, after all, and he was conscious of his status as a technician —but since Bundy's office doors were not soundproofed, he could hear the argument continue inside. He was not surprised that Gen-

eral Taylor opposed a military escalation. Role reversals between
spokesmen for military and political foreign policy responses were
common. Generals were often particularly conservative about the
use of force unless the odds were superb. Nobody liked major
risks. As the standard motto had it, "CYA" (cover your ass).

Only the President could pass the buck to no one else, and that
Monday morning, having returned from Hyannis Port the night
before, Kennedy had been questioning his Berlin policy since before breakfast. He was still in his pajamas and getting out of bed
when Assistant Secretary of State Foy D. Kohler arrived to report
as directed. Kohler was tough as the proverbial nails and not as
circumlocutious as his boss, Secretary Rusk.

That morning Kohler was of no help. When the President inquired what was being done about Berlin, the State Department
man did little more than sympathize with the President's renewed
irritation that there had been no advance intelligence about the
East German move.

Should the Berlin garrison be reinforced? As so often, the President felt most comfortable sharing his thoughts with his assistant
Kenny O'Donnell of his Boston Irish Mafia.

"He leaned back in his chair and tapped his teeth with his fingers
the way he always did when he was reflecting," reported O'Donnell. "And then he said: 'This is the end of the Berlin crisis. The
other side panicked—not we. We're going to do nothing now because there is no alternative except war. It's all over, they're not
going to overrun Berlin.' " Not at the moment anyway.

**West Berlin,
Monday, August 14, 1961**

Afternoon. Still playing his Paul Revere role, Murrow shook up his
own domain, the USIA, back in Washington. He phoned his deputy director, Donald M. Wilson, a relaxed old hand from Time-
Life, and directed in a voice "vibrant with emotion" that the Berlin
crisis be given "absolutely the maximum treatment imaginable."

"Bottling up a whole nation" was an act of Communist desperation and a gift of priceless propaganda value, he lectured Wilson.
Murrow wanted plenty of film sent around the world to make
certain that the ugliness of the border barricades would be lost on
no one.

"We were slow to react," Wilson admitted later, and lassitude was not the reason. One cause of the limp response all over Washington was psychological and had been part of the impression Erich Honecker hoped to create. "Nobody thought the border closing would be permanent," Wilson said. "We cranked up because the boss called."

And it was the boss's emotional punch that rocked Wilson. He knew Murrow as an icy old pro. This time the boss was "outraged."

The intensity of these feelings steered Murrow back to Axel Springer, who also had come to Berlin over the weekend. When they met in the publisher's home on Bernadottestrasse, Murrow challenged his host at once: since Springer had proved himself such a spectacular prophet, what advice did he have for the United States?

"You have to clear away the barricades," Springer echoed his editor Peter Boenisch. "I'll guarantee that the Russians will accept it."

Murrow was not so sure, and neither was everyone else in the room. Boenisch was already doubtful himself. He thought that the idea would have worked on Sunday morning, but that the hour had probably already grown too late.

Feeling that he should nevertheless do more, Murrow decided to capitalize on his personal standing with Kennedy and to reinforce his cabled recommendation for more empathetic American action. He'd phone the President. After he had made the call, from the U.S. Mission, his aides thought that Murrow appeared relieved and pleased with himself.* The President had told him he was sending Vice President Johnson and General Clay to Berlin to wave the flag on behalf of American prestige.

Although he had been a bureaucrat for only a few months, Murrow had learned to appreciate how difficult it was for the President to pick his course from a flood of often conflicting advice. The State Department people in Berlin were too cautious to suit Ed. He thought the President should hear from the one German ally who had most at stake in a tough American stance—Mayor Willy Brandt. Calling on Brandt in Schöneberg, Murrow showed him a copy of his cable to JFK and urged the Mayor to contact the President too.

Brandt asked Egon Bahr to draft a lengthy letter to the White

---

* It isn't known whether Murrow asked the President to remove the border obstacles.

House that night, but decided to set it aside. There would be no Western military action anyway, and the political complexities deserved further reflection.

Evening. Konrad Adenauer was not going to allow Willy Brandt to shine as the saintly martyr of Berlin. At an election rally in Regensburg, the Chancellor lashed out against his challenger as "Herr Brandt alias Frahm." This unseemly police jargon referred to Brandt's birth as Herbert Frahm; his mother had been an unmarried saleswoman in a Lübeck department store. German politics traditionally resembled mud wrestling, but this slur was too low a blow and old Adenauer was widely criticized for it. Brandt tolerated it poorly. Informed of the attack during a session of the Berlin senate, the Mayor was too distressed to continue and left.

Evening. Dan Schorr of CBS was again patrolling East Berlin on foot. "Five times in half an hour I saw small groups approached by plainclothes police and told to keep walking, regardless of what they were talking about," he broadcast later from the West. "Mostly the people reply with a look of sullen hatred and walk off. Sometimes they have to be pulled or pushed. At the Friedrichstrasse elevated and subway station there were still people trying to board trains to the West. Many of them came out dazed or in tears. . . ."

**West Berlin,
Tuesday, August 15, 1961**

Morning. The New York Times was tracking developments at the border carefully, but correspondent Sydney Gruson admitted, "The purpose of all this was not yet entirely clear." No permanent, concrete construction was yet in sight.

Morning. In a CBS news analysis, Dan Schorr sent this wrap-up of the American policy dilemma: "We might have been willing to go to war to defend our right to stay in West Berlin. Can we go to war to defend the right of East Germans to get out of their own country?" Events were answering the question with an unequivocal no.

. . .

Afternoon. Dan Schorr of CBS was at hand when the first hint emerged that a permanent structure, a *wall,* was about to go up. He was keeping watch on Bernauer Strasse, subsequently the notorious scene of breathtaking escapes and deaths, all because of an administrative fluke: the ancient apartment houses on the Eastern side of the street were in Communist territory; the opposite side belonged to West Berlin.

After lunchtime something new began to stir on the Eastern side. A large construction crane rumbled toward the edge of the sidewalk that constituted the frontier. Suspended from the noisy machine hung the first segment of the Berlin Wall: a slab of concrete 1.25 meters square, 20 centimeters thick.

"Look at it," a tobacconist exclaimed, heaving a sigh at Schorr. "Look at what they are doing! Force, force, force! And what are we to do about it?" The old Berliner sighed again.

Schorr was fascinated and slightly incredulous. Sounding somewhat tentative, he used the operative word for the first time: "We notice slabs of concrete being moved into place as though to build a *wall,*" he announced into his microphone. He said he was reminded of the wall built by the Nazis in Warsaw to isolate the Jewish ghetto early in World War II.

On Bernauer Strasse, workers were stuffing mortar into the cracks between the slabs. Somewhat later all of the huge Potsdamer Platz—once Berlin's busiest traffic point—was divided in the same way: a wall went up under floodlights, 1.25 meters high, unpolished, pockmarked, forbidding. Only at this stage, as the third day ended, was the true character of the nightmare slowly starting to become apparent.*

4:00 P.M. The border closure was triggering unexpected restlessness in DDR citizens who had never before thought of quitting their country. Among those newly troubled was Conrad Schumann, the nineteen-year-old baby-faced sergeant who had arrived with the first unit to close the Brandenburg Gate early Sunday morning. He was patrolling the schizoid Bernauer Strasse, trudg-

---

* All during that week, concrete was used only on a nebulous scale as the Communists cautiously continued to test Western reaction. Concrete construction did not appear in large volume until the following week, Tuesday, August 22.

ing ten paces up, then ten paces down. He kept looking straight ahead, yet he absorbed much to distress him.

"You pigs!" yelled West Berliners in Schumann's direction. "You traitors!" "You concentration camp guards!"

That was bad enough. Out of the corners of his eyes he observed scenes that hit him harder. A young woman handed a bouquet of flowers across the barbed wire. The old woman who grasped the bouquet in the West was obviously her mother. Schumann heard how the daughter wished her a happy birthday and apologized for not being able to visit. Pointing toward Schumann, the daughter said, "Those over there, they won't let me across anymore."

That made Schumann feel terrible. He was a simple country lad, a sheepherder from the hills of Saxony like his father. When Conrad was seventeen years old he had volunteered for the better life of a professional soldier. He still stood ready to defend his country against "Western military aggressors" and "provocateurs," who, according to his instructors, threatened his people. The facts at the border taught Schumann otherwise, and as he continued to pace up and down he had plenty of time to contemplate the lessons of life in the real world of Bernauer Strasse.

He saw no military aggressors on the west side of the street, just an occasional cop. There were tanks at the border, but only on his side, in the East. All he was doing was imprisoning people like the young woman who wanted to wish her mother a happy birthday. Was that how he should spend his life?

Toward noon, another incident shook him severely. Within hearing distance, at the Arkonaplatz, more than one thousand demonstrators assembled and shouted slogans. The words were indistinct, but occasionally Schumann heard *"Freiheit"* (liberty). Then he froze.

"Suddenly this mass of people moved toward us like a living wall," he recalled later. "I thought: they're going to run over us right away. I was nervous and didn't know what to do. I didn't want to shoot and I wasn't supposed to."

There was no need. Armored cars poured out of the side streets. Soldiers jumped off the vehicles. Holding rifles with fixed bayonets, they pushed the demonstrators back. Some were slow to move. Others stayed put.

"They stood still with their arms folded," Sergeant Schumann remembered, "and they called out: 'Go ahead and shoot! Shoot, you cowards!' "

Eventually the protesters were shoved back.

Schumann was beginning to think that he ought perhaps to leave a country where such oppression was practiced. The notion remained vague in his mind until shortly after the demonstrators were dispersed. Then another shock made him think that he had best hurry and make up his mind. He saw trucks pulling up with concrete posts and plates, and one of his buddies ruminated, "Are they going to build a wall?" Pretty soon, Schumann concluded, escape would be infinitely more difficult.

When he thought nobody was watching, he pressed the hip-high fencing with his fingertips. It gave way, but one of his colleagues had seen him.

"What are you doing there?"

"The wire is rusting already," said Schumann, trying to sound casual.

During the next couple of hours he managed to stop at the same spot occasionally to press the wire down farther. After a while he spotted a man with a camera loitering on the west side of the street. The photographer was watching him manipulate the wiring.* Schumann was delighted. The more people were within view of the other side, the less likely his comrades were to start shooting. He even had a chance to build up his audience. When a young man happened to approach from the West, Schumann shouted, "Get back at once!" But he also whispered, "I'm going to jump!" and he watched while the young man ran off to alert the West Berlin police, which shortly arrived in a van.

At about 4 P.M., with the wire pushed down to knee height, Schumann jumped off with his left foot, pulled his head into his shoulders and his flat steel helmet into his face, hit the top of the wire with his right foot, threw his Russian submachine gun to the ground, and ran into the open door of the waiting police van.

A cop slapped him on the shoulder and said, "Welcome to the West, young man."

Schumann trembled all over. His decision had ripened quickly, but he never regretted it. The evil of the Wall had made him switch sides.

---

* The Western press photographer who patiently kept watching Schumann was Klaus Lehnartz, and his camera clicked the very second the sergeant's right foot hit the top of the fence. The dramatic shot, with Schumann's boots and gun flying, made front pages throughout the world and was frequently reproduced over the years as a symbol of resistance against DDR authority.

Washington,
Wednesday, August 16, 1961

Morning. President Kennedy was furious at Willy Brandt. The letter that Egon Bahr had drafted for the Mayor on Monday and that Brandt had revised on Tuesday had been telexed to the White House and was provoking an entirely unexpected interpretation. It prompted JFK—a politician first and foremost—to suspect Brandt of covert election campaigning.

Brandt's letter conveyed tension and his criticism of Western inaction was straightforward: "While the commandants used to protest even against parades of the so-called *Volksarmee,* they have contented themselves this time with a tardy and not very powerful step. . . . The illegal sovereignty of the East German Government has been acknowledged through acceptance."

West Berlin was becoming a ghetto, Brandt warned. The refugee movement into Berlin might be replaced by a flight out of the city.

Brandt suggested a protest to the United Nations and a strengthening of Berlin's Western garrison. In conclusion he switched to a personal note: "I assess the situation to be serious enough to write you this frankly, as is possible only among friends who trust each other fully."

"Trust?" Kennedy exploded. "I don't trust this man at all! He's in the middle of a campaign against old Adenauer and wants to drag me in. Where does he get off calling me a friend?" The President turned even more incensed when he heard that Brandt had confided to a mass rally of Berliners that he had sent a private appeal to the President. Turned off by these pressure tactics, Kennedy instructed Press Secretary Pierre Salinger to tell White House reporters that the President had not yet decided whether he would reply to the Mayor.

The annoyance was brief. Marguerite Higgins asked to see Brandt's letter and, after Kennedy, sitting in his famous rocking chair, handed it to her, she defended the Mayor. "Mr. President," she said, "I must tell you frankly: the suspicion is growing in Berlin that you're going to sell out the West Berliners."

The President was taken aback. He muttered that Brandt should not have indulged in grandstanding and resort to written declarations. He should have phoned or flown to Washington. But slowly the anger toward Brandt's tactics gave way to the realization that the United States was looking cowardly in Berlin.

**West Berlin,
Wednesday, August 16, 1961**

Afternoon. Would the Berliners riot, perhaps uncontrollably? In East Berlin, the authorities were firmly in the saddle; American fears notwithstanding, a repetition of the June 17, 1953, workers' riots seemed blocked. But the West Berliners were boiling mad. Slogans were egging them on. The situation was incendiary.

THE WEST IS DOING NOTHING, shouted the banner headline of the tabloid *Bild,* and as thousands of riot police with water throwers assembled in the side streets, 300,000 Berliners flocked to the square in front of Willy Brandt's City Hall, the Schöneberg Rathaus. Their mood was reflected in their inflammatory homemade posters: BETRAYED BY THE WEST. WHERE ARE THE PROTECTIVE [WESTERN] POWERS? And most ominous: THE WEST IS DOING A SECOND MUNICH!* Cold wind gusts swept the square.

The first speaker, representing Willy Brandt's conservative CDU opposition party, inflamed the crowd further when he cried, "The barbed wire will vanish again!" As principal speaker, Brandt now faced an assignment worthy of a magician. He had to hold the Western Allies' heels to the fire. He had to make his fellow citizens feel secure. And he had to send them home without rioting.

Visibly strained, his voice scratchy, he brought it off. While the crowd yelled, "Come to the point, Willy!" and "Bang the drum, Willy!" he pointed to the essential effectiveness of the Western powers ("Without them, the tanks would have rolled on"). He also challenged the Allies ("Berlin expects more than words!"). It was an elegant feat of crowd control. Applause rang out only once— when he announced that he had written to Kennedy ("I told him our views in all frankness").

As Brandt finished, his shirt sweat stained, shouts erupted demanding that the crowd march to the border. Egon Bahr, Brandt's principal adviser, having expected such an invitation to disaster, ordered the ringing of the City Hall's big bell. Ironically, it was an imitation of Philadelphia's Liberty Bell, a gift from America. As planned, the sound drowned out the protests. The throng dispersed. With trembling hands, Brandt asked for a cognac.

---

* A painful reminder of 1938, when the Western powers appeased Hitler at Munich, thereby making World War II inevitable.

Disaster was averted, the problem remained. On East Berlin tele-
vision, a commentator made the point with a joke that night:
"Did you hear that Brandt called the Allies for help?"
"Yes, I heard about it, but the Allies didn't."

6:00 P.M. Ed Murrow had concluded that the very existence of
Berlin was threatened. In a priority cable to the State Department
he warned: "There is a real danger that Berliners will conclude
they should take themselves, their bank accounts and moveable
assets to some other place. What is in danger of being destroyed
here is that perishable commodity called hope."

Evening. Bill Graver of the CIA had concluded that the United
States was guilty of a fundamental error. It was getting very late to
attempt a correction, but perhaps not too late for a demonstration
of who was doing what and to whom at the border. Graver had an
idea. It was the same idea that Wolfgang Leonhard, the defector
from the DDR, had proposed the previous Sunday on the "Frühschoppen" television program in Cologne, but the CIA base chief
had a more useful audience for it. At 2 A.M. Graver caught up with
Allan Lightner, the U.S. Minister, who was pacing in his office.
"Allan, we've got to get American troops to the border," said El
Supremo. Lightner vetoed the notion at once. "But we've got to do
it," said Graver. "The Russians are claiming they have nothing to
do with any of this." Graver was convinced that political mileage
could be won if the Soviets could be smoked out, could be made to
admit that they, not the East Germans, were the real power behind
the Wall. "No," said Lightner, "it won't fly." He did not have to
spell out where it wouldn't fly. By then the Americans in Berlin
had seen enough evidence that Washington was in no mood to
rattle the fortifications at the Berlin border.

**Washington,
Thursday, August 17, 1961**

Morning. Responding to Mac Bundy's request that the White
House staff submit suggestions for administration action, Jay W.
Gildner, an assistant presidential press secretary with diplomatic

experience in Berlin, wrote up an imaginative memo outlining fifteen ideas. None created a stir, not even the suggestion to reactivate a forgotten electric news sign. It faced East at the sector border and could have flashed bulletins to the news-starved East Berliners. The President had other plans.

Evening. Vice President Lyndon Johnson was never an enthusiastic recruit when he had to represent President Kennedy on public relations errands to dangerous places abroad.

The Kennedys—Jack and his brother Bob, the Attorney General—seized every opportunity to get the Vice President out of Washington. Johnson was inconvenient ballast. His southern political clout had made him an unfortunate necessity in the close 1960 presidential race, but the Kennedys neither liked nor trusted him.

The Vice President was at dinner Thursday when the President called and told him he would be going to Berlin with General Clay.

"Is that necessary?" asked the Vice President unnecessarily.

"Yes, it's necessary," said Kennedy. Let Johnson spend the weekend placating the pesky Germans. That's what vice presidents were for.

Informed that his arrival in Berlin was to coincide with the dispatch of 1,500 GIs to reinforce the Berlin garrison, LBJ was reduced to wailing like a sacrificial lamb: "There'll be a lot of shooting and I'll be in the middle of it. Why me?"

En Route to Berlin, Friday, August 18, 1961

9:00 P.M. In one of the four booths of their Air Force Boeing 707 en route to Berlin, General Clay held his own against the uncharacteristically subdued Lyndon Johnson. As if trying to make the Vice President feel more martial about Berlin, the normally modest general regaled the Vice President with stories about his own record for standing up to the Russians in the divided city.

Just about single-handedly, Clay recalled, he had persuaded President Truman to hold Berlin in 1948 and to supply planes for the historic airlift that the general had already started on his own. If he had been allowed to ram an armored column down the Autobahn then, Clay insisted, the Korean War never would have taken place. If he were President now, he'd tear the Wall down.*

Tactfully, Clay did not bring up the fact that one of the advisers listening in on this conversation, Chip Bohlen, the State Department's top Soviet expert, had advised Truman in 1948 to pull out of Berlin. Bohlen had been sitting by quietly, but when Clay counseled an attack on the border obstacles, he remarked that this would be a good way to start World War III. The more the Berlin scene changed, the more the old arguments remained the same.

**West Berlin,
Saturday, August 19, 1961**

Afternoon. Vice President Lyndon Johnson was determined to make the most of his unwanted weekend in Berlin, and the Berliners cooperated jubilantly from the moment he climbed out of his U.S. Air Force Constellation at Tempelhof. As soon as the police band had finished "The Star-Spangled Banner" and the unofficial Berlin anthem, "Das ist die Berliner Luft, Luft, Luft," the crowd of more than 100,000 exploded in an unrestrained roar of welcome. *The New York Times* correspondent cabled home that the triumph resembled the liberation of Paris in World War II, and so the exuberance continued.

Crowds speak a universal, emotional language that Lyndon Johnson understood, and these Berliners were whooping it up like Texans at election time. The Vice President was supposed to in-

---

* By then it was probably already almost a week too late for any such Western action. General Clay conceded the point in 1970 and 1971, when he addressed the crucial question of Allied *timing* in the course of a series of thirty-one oral history interviews (1,106 pages of transcript). "I think we might have been able to have stopped the Wall from having been built that night" (i.e., early Sunday morning, August 13), he speculated wistfully. "If the American Commandant had acted, even if he had been in violation of his instructions, he would have succeeded and he would have been forgiven and he would have become a great man. All he had to do, in my opinion, that night, was to have run trucks up and down the [East Berlin] streets unarmed. . . . We never would have had a war. But you got to do these things at the right timing. . . . " In a secret ["Eyes Only"] cable to Secretary Rusk on January 17, 1962, Clay had already begun to indulge in hindsight wishful thinking about possible "unilateral" action by the American commander on August 13, but in January he conceded, "It would not have stopped closing of the border a few blocks farther back."

spect the Wall at Potsdamer Platz, but he never got there. Sitting next to Willy Brandt, he had his Cadillac stop again and again so he could wade into the crowds to shake hands, accept flowers, kiss babies, pat dogs. The spectators quickly identified the hawk-nosed American in the second car as General Clay (*"Der Clay ist hier!"*) and the shouting never ceased: "Bravo Johnson!" "Bravo Clay!" "Bravo Willy!" A big bunch of thorny roses hit Clay in the face. It was a love feast.

Lagging behind schedule, the triumphal procession changed course and inched directly toward the Schöneberg Rathaus. As on Wednesday, some 300,000 Berliners crowded the square, but what a difference! It was Paris all over again. Clay was near tears. Looking overwhelmed, Johnson vowed, "To the survival and to the creative future of this city we Americans have pledged, in effect, what our ancestors pledged in forming the United States: 'our lives, our fortunes, and our sacred honor.'"

The Berliners roared their feelings of deliverance. Only insiders knew that Johnson's speech had been dashed off at the last moment in Washington by the loquacious Walt Rostow of the National Security Council to prevent the Vice President from—as Attorney General Bob Kennedy phrased it—"talking nonsense," and that every word had been mulled over by the President.

The White House, Washington, Saturday, August 19, 1961

Night. "It was his most anxious moment during the prolonged Berlin crisis." So President Kennedy's confidant Theodore C. Sorensen would remember. Another aide told *Time*, "There was the feeling that this mission could very well escalate into shooting before morning."

Since the President did not know that Khrushchev feared war as nervously as Washington did, the anxiety spreading through the White House seemed amply justified. Both of Kennedy's most senior generals, Maxwell Taylor and Lyman Lemnitzer, the chairman of the Joint Chiefs of Staff, had opposed sending reinforcements to the beleaguered West Berlin garrison. British Prime Minister Harold Macmillan was also against such a provocative move. "Militarily, it's nonsense," he recorded in his diary. Indeed, no more than a flick of the Soviet wrist could wipe out the convoy that was about to embark from West Germany.

The President decided not to leave for his usual summer week-end in Hyannis Port and ordered his military aide, General Ted Clifton, to check on the progress of the convoy every twenty min-utes throughout the night. It was his only protection against the nuclear war that could be started, as he had put it earlier, "by a trigger-happy sergeant on a truck convoy at a checkpoint in East Germany." Now he would have to await the fate of the GIs on the road to Berlin. As so often before, he was still the de facto Berlin desk officer.

West Berlin,
Sunday, August 20, 1961

6:30 A.M. Might war still break out over Berlin a week after Honecker rolled out his barbed wire? Throughout that second Sunday morning the answer rested with Colonel Glover S. Johns, Jr., a professional fighting man with a theatrical flair. A peacock-proud Texan, Johns never walked; he strode. He was a parachutist who packed a sixty-year-old Colt pistol. As Commandant of Cadets at the Virginia Military Institute he had ruled with a feared spit-and-polish swagger stick. As a World War II battalion commander, he was decorated with three Silver Stars and three Legions of Merit, a record of extraordinary bravery.

Johns was not all guts, however. He spoke four languages, in-cluding German, and combined his swagger with a feel for history. All told, he seemed a fortuitous choice to command the 1,500 GIs of the First Battle Group, Eighth Infantry Division, who were to dash down the Autobahn from Helmstedt to Berlin, thereby test-ing Soviet willingness to keep American land access open to the city.*

Johns was selected for this crucial command by another feisty war hero, four-star General Bruce C. ("the Sergeants' general") Clarke, who was vastly annoyed by the mission. The Pentagon was carrying on as if the fate of the universe depended on Johns.

---

* A Battle Group was picked for this highly sensitive mission because it was the smallest self-sustaining unit in the Army. President Kennedy, anxious not to provoke the Soviets, wanted to keep the operation's "noise level" as subdued as possible. During the preceding April the same desire had led the President to reduce the forces for the invasion of Cuba at the Bay of Pigs. On that occasion the Lilliputian size of the American intervention helped to contribute to military disaster.

The colonel's service record had been personally approved in Washington by the ranking "Berlin desk officer," President Kennedy, though not without misgivings. The Commander in Chief phoned Clarke at his Heidelberg headquarters and said he hoped Johns had a cool head. Trigger-happy colonels were as dangerous as the trigger-happy sergeants who were so conspicuously on the President's mind. Clearly worried, Kennedy also used his call to interrogate the crusty general. What sort of battle could the White House expect if Colonel Johns ran into trouble? Where would the front run in such an engagement?

"Fifty feet on either side of the road," snapped General Clarke, candid but hardly offering much comfort.

For two days the Pentagon bombarded Clarke with orders covering such minutiae as the Battle Group's rest stops. Was there anything at all that Washington would leave to the discretion of the local commander?

There was. As Clarke was quick to notice, his instructions failed to include so much as one word about the most critical item, ammunition. The oversight was so glaring that Clarke did not question it. As an old hand at the game-playing of command, he knew what was expected of him. His superiors were passing the buck.

At the last moment and on his own authority, Clarke ordered ammunition boxes stowed in each vehicle. Then he passed the buck on to Colonel Johns. He did this silently by giving Johns no instructions on what to do if his column was attacked, although the hasty issue of ammunition suggested that the colonel was not expected to surrender without a fight.

Appropriately, Johns was quite prepared to die a hero's death in what Army reports always euphemistically described as a "battle incident." He later said, "Everyone knew: if anything did start, we were in for certain destruction." How many others might then have been destroyed, soldiers and civilians, East and West, depended on the President and the colonel's tenuous phone connection to the White House. The Signal Corps link was, like all technology, ever subject to failure.*

---

* "I did not tell the Colonel what to do at 4 A.M. Sunday when I had him break out the ammo," General Clarke, then eighty-five, wrote me on April 30, 1986. "In fact, I did not know what to tell him. I have found that in a crisis do not tell a responsible commander what to do, if you don't know what to do. He can make better decisions in his crisis than you . . . I am sure the Pentagon did not wish me to ask them about ammo and such a contingency." Colonel Johns died in Austin,

Some of the coolest heads in Berlin thought that Johns's hot line would be needed that Sunday; "I had a deep fear the Russians would attempt to intervene," remembered Sydney Gruson of *The New York Times*.

11:00 A.M. "You've been asking us for action instead of words," Vice President Johnson told Willy Brandt, grinning. "I'd like to see whether you can act too."

The two men were standing in a Mercedes convertible, waving to the crowds lined up along the way to the Marienfelde refugee camp. Brandt was startled by Johnson's challenge. It had escaped his notice that the Vice President had been eyeing the Mayor's elegant loafers.

"Can you get me a pair like that today?" Johnson asked. Aware that Johnson would leave Berlin before stores opened Monday, Brandt promised to do his best.*

The transfer of possessions evidently constituted an act of friendship for this Texas primitive; at Marienfelde he handed the refugees ballpoint pens marked LBJ as well as admission tickets to the congressional visitors galleries in Washington.

Brandt's elated spirits could not be dampened by gaucheries. The visiting Americans were obviously a huge hit. His own reputation was enhanced. Even President Kennedy was paying attention to him; earlier that morning Johnson had handed him a three-page response from President Kennedy to his letter. Typed on light green White House stationery and marked SECRET, it was conciliatory in tone and ended with "warm personal regards." It

---

Texas, on May 19, 1976, and I could not ask him how he would have responded to Soviet interference. I expect that he did not know. He probably would have dodged the question like my own infantry platoon lieutenant in World War II. When we asked him something unanswerable he used to say, "That depends on the situation and the terrain." At issue for Colonel Johns in 1961 was the master threat of the nuclear age. Before nuclear weapons were widely dispersed, General Clarke's reliance on local responsibility entailed few irreversible risks. Today, when nonnuclear local military decisions can quickly escalate into nuclear action, dependency on the judgment of a local commander with fallible communications to the top command is the chilling weak link in the chain known as "command and control."

* Within hours, the owner of the Leiser shoe store reported to the American ambassador's villa with dozens of samples. After vigorous rummaging, the Vice President helped himself to two pairs.

promised no action to challenge Khrushchev's nuclear bluff, but the pro-Berlin advice from Ed Murrow, Marguerite Higgins, and other Cold Warriors had loosened one presidential concession: Colonel Johns and his GIs.

"This brutal border closing evidently represents a basic Soviet decision which only war could reverse," the President wrote Brandt. "Neither you nor we, nor any of our Allies, have ever supposed that we should go to war on this point. . . ." Nevertheless, as a token of American determination to stand by the Berliners, the President promised a "symbolic" reinforcement of the Allied garrison.

Brandt realized: if the American soldiers reached Berlin, the four-power status of East Berlin would remain lost, but at least his West Berliners would feel more secure. That was worth a couple of pairs of shoes.

Washington

Morning. Great news was phoned to the White House from Colonel Johns. The first sixty trucks of the American reinforcements had crossed into Berlin without mishap at 12:30 P.M. (6:30 A.M. Washington time). The President relaxed. This was a major milestone. "He felt that a turning point in the crisis had been reached," recorded his counsel, Ted Sorensen.

West Berlin

Evening. "Wake up, Sarge!" yelled an officer of Colonel Johns's Battle Group. Like many of his fellow defenders of Berlin, the sergeant was so bushed that he had fallen asleep in his Jeep during the colonel's jubilant victory parade down Kurfürstendamm. Startled, the sergeant shook himself awake and snapped to attention just as he passed the Vice President of the United States, who was proudly acknowledging the cheers of the Berliners in the reviewing stand.

Lyndon Johnson had adjusted nicely to his unexpected hero's role. Never mind that Colonel Johns's liberating troops looked— so Dan Schorr of CBS remembered—"as if they'd just been gotten out of bed." Awake or not, the men had brought off their performance as symbols of American power.

At the Helmstedt Autobahn Checkpoint Alpha in the morning, a nerve-wracking three-hour delay had heightened tensions in Washington while Colonel Johns and the Soviet captain in charge straightened out a disagreement over the head count of the troops. Along the march route, a Soviet fighter electrified the convoy by buzzing directly overhead with its bomb bay open. But inside was only a camera. The dreaded march was just an exhausting picnic.

By the time Colonel Johns's troops had dragged themselves through their parade duties—four GIs were hospitalized with heat prostration—all Berlin wallowed in relief like a reprieved prisoner, Willy Brandt taking the lead.

"I am completely satisfied," he exulted in a formal statement. "We have the full confidence of the President. The President is determined to keep West Berlin secure." Brandt's punch line echoed Kennedy: "I do not believe we are facing a war."

The most relieved man of all, Vice President Johnson, resumed his quest for rewards. After taking delivery of his new loafers, he had ordered half a dozen electric shavers, which the harassed Mayor Brandt also extracted from a closed store. It wasn't enough. En route to a celebratory fried chicken dinner at the rooftop restaurant of the Berlin Hilton, Johnson informed the Mayor that he had heard of the famous Royal Prussian Porcelain Manufactory and would like to stop there for souvenirs. The manager was summoned by radio phone, and had opened his establishment when Johnson arrived to pick out a large light blue table service for delivery, to the Hilton later that evening.

When the porcelain executive made his delivery while Johnson, Brandt, and their aides relaxed over drinks, the Vice President had another assignment for him: could he also have the initials "LBJ" engraved on some ashtrays, to be sent to Washington? Absolutely. Delighted, the Vice President ordered several hundred.

"Why so many?" asked Brandt.

"They look like a dollar and cost me only twenty-five cents!" What a productive weekend it had been!

For Johnson's 5 A.M. farewell ceremonies at Tegel Airport, a band played a reprise of "Das ist die Berliner Luft, Luft, Luft."

The air over Berlin had indeed cleared during the weekend, though not nearly as much as its heroes claimed in public.*

* In his private report to Kennedy, Johnson cautioned, "We can't close our eyes to one fact: as long as the people of Berlin remain separated, doubts about the resolution of the Western powers will remain."

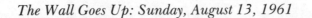

Vice President Lyndon Johnson didn't want to go to Berlin in the middle of the crisis, but once he got there he basked in his unexpected hero's welcome—and found time to load Air Force Two with souvenirs.

PART IV

AFTERMATH

21

LOOKING BACK:
"WE LAUGHED LIKE MAD"

West Berlin,
Tuesday, August 22, 1961

Bill Graver and his Cowboys of the CIA base were beginning to wonder whether maybe, just maybe, the other shoe was not going to drop. It was difficult to believe. Ever since Sunday the thirteenth, the men of the American intelligence community in Berlin had been cogitating and bickering about little but one question: how did we miss this? It was a dreaded conundrum because, no matter how one viewed what happened, the CYA ("cover your ass") potential vis à vis Washington, the room for credible alibis, was small.

At first the Cowboys thought they might be living on borrowed time. But the questions (critiques? denunciations?) that operations director John Dimmer expected to pound in from Washington headquarters as early as the morning of the thirteenth never materialized. Next, our spies waited for the usual Washington investigating committee to sharpen its hatchets. Perhaps it wouldn't operate on the grand scale of the Bay of Pigs postmortem—for which CIA Director Dulles, General Maxwell Taylor, and Attorney General Robert Kennedy sat in judgment, taking testimony for weeks, with Taylor producing a report as big as a phone book. Still, an inquisition with lots of embarrassing questions seemed unavoidable. "Walking back the cat," it was sometimes called.

But no, nobody seemed interested in walking back this cat.

And so the local CIA crew and its peers from the State Department and military intelligence convened with each other almost nonstop, in committee and informally, trying to figure out how Erich Honecker and his *Einsatzstab,* the special staff at the East Berlin police headquarters, had pulled off one of the neat military hat tricks of recent times.

Security had been perfect, of course, aided not only by Communist discipline and secret police, but by the convenience of the very short distances within a country as small as the DDR. The compact geography made it unnecessary to tell even participating unit commanders anything about the operation until almost zero hour. The proximity of Berlin to sources of supply in the provinces also made it possible to delay bringing up construction materials until *after* the operation was under way. Indeed, since even the rudimentary beginnings of a wall were not embarked upon for three days after zero hour, the bulk of the materials did not have to be in place at the border for quite some time after the need for secrecy had ceased.

Considerable discussion erupted among the intelligence officers about the construction materials that the East Germans did have to have on hand before the "go" signal was given. It turned out that good-sized supplies of barbed wire were scattered around military *Kasernen* in the Berlin area. The CIA men heard that vast quantities of building material were cleverly distributed among sites near the border as if needed for civilian construction.* The crucial fact was that relatively little was needed until the cat was out of the bag. As news photographs would record forever, much of the barbed wire strung on the thirteenth was so thinly laid that children could (and sometimes did) shove it aside. The commitment to a wall came only after it was clear that the Allies were not reacting.

Inevitably, fingerpointing ensued about who, beforehand, should have called attention to what. The chief of Army intelligence in Europe, Major General Stanhope B. Mason, sneered that "only Merlin" could have hidden the DDR's preparations under "a veil of invisibiilty." Bill Graver's defenders argued, on the other hand, that El Supremo was in charge of *strategic* intelligence only; petty *tactical* details like barbed wire were not part of his brief.

---

* This was denied by the DDR insiders I interviewed in 1988. It must be remembered that the CIA never did learn how Honecker and his team pulled off the August 13 surprise.

Although I heard no one bring up General Marshall's plea for twenty-four-hour notice of Soviet moves, I was retrospectively treated to reminders of Pearl Harbor, the Battle of the Bulge, the invasion of the United Arab Republic in 1956, the North Korean invasion of South Korea, and so many other examples of successful surprise attacks that the Berlin Wall was made to look like a trifling fluke, something of a Ripley "believe-it-or-not" caricature, not worth taking too seriously.

And that was how official Washington came around to viewing it. "Why should there have been a postmortem?" I was asked, with some astonishment and slight indignation, by Richard Helms, nearly a quarter of a century later. It sounded as if the man who was deputy director for operations at the CIA in 1961 and subsequently the director of the agency, wanted to brush me off as a troublemaker who was trying to elevate a flyspeck into a true annoyance for men who were busy public servants at the time.

At the scene, guilt feelings were minimal. "So what?" I was asked by Tom McCord, the Army intelligence officer who did predict the Wall. "We were not going to do anything about it in any case."

This was also the message explicitly communicated by the VIP group that had accompanied General Clay and Vice President Johnson on their quick cheerleader stop during the past weekend. The Washingtonians felt sorry for men like Allan Lightner, the United States Minister, who was taking the border action very much to heart. "Cool it," Lightner was told by Ambassador Chip Bohlen as the delegation arrived at the airport. "This is not a big issue in Washington."

And Bill Graver's links were so close to the CIA's German hands whom he had left behind in Washington so recently that he could tell soon after the event that he had little to fear from his superiors. The Communists had built a wall, so what?

"It was so absurd a measure it was difficult to take it seriously," I was told in the 1980s by John Huizenga, one of the agency's highest-ranking analysts, eventually chief of the Office of National Estimates.

Only President Kennedy could have initiated a meaningful investigation of this intelligence failure, and he did not do so. He had already fired the agency's entire top leadership after the Bay of Pigs. General Taylor, his military troubleshooter, was preoccupied with a new theater of intense worry, Vietnam. The President himself had written off East Berlin weeks ago. Maybe it was more productive to worry about new surprises than to hash over an old one that knowledgeable people were calling absurd—and treating accordingly.

But the Berlin Cowboys had rejoiced prematurely. The Wall was making trouble after all. Career trouble. Washington just about wanted to close Berlin down. With the refugee flow to Marienfelde almost stopped and communications to most of the BOB's agents in the East cut off, Washington overreacted and decided that Berlin was suddenly worthless as a collection center. The fear over who would get blamed for failing to warn of the Wall was replaced by a more personal apprehension: "Who is getting shipped out next?" An ignominious retreat from Berlin was on.

For a brief time, Joe K. flourished as the hero of the base. Joe, a particularly compulsive case officer, had long been ridiculed by his associates for the care he lavished on setting up complicated "alternate commo" with every one of his agents. It had been a devilish effort and everybody had considered it useless. The Wall made Joe look terrific; every one of his agents reported for duty and stayed on tap, so the base could show Washington what it hoped would be career-saving news: the take from Berlin would slow down but it would not dry up.*

The maneuver didn't work. Washington wanted the staff cut down from more than one hundred to thirty five. This was the sort of situation that drove Bill Graver, the fighter for office turf, to sparkle. The Wall became a boon for underemployed CIA officers. They were merely shifted to Munich, to a special new unit that would prepare for a catastrophic war contingency, stashing away underground caches of arms and supplies, recruiting Germans who could survive as "stay-behinds," agents who would supply intelligence even if all West Germany were to be overrun. The war never came, but nobody could say that Graver and his Berlin Cowboys hadn't helped to get the agency set for it.

One policymaker who did want to learn from the intelligence failure of the Wall wasn't inhibited by guilt feelings, for he hadn't been in the government at the time. John McCone, a hard-faced Republican industrialist, had been picked only in November to

---

* In fact, the base did recover surprisingly well. It took a year of painstaking effort, but an estimated 95 percent of the pre-Wall agents were recovered for further efforts.

replace the disastrous Allen Dulles as DCI (Director of Central Intelligence).

McCone had not yet been confirmed by the Senate when he arrived in Berlin ("in black"—that is, under a false identity) and asked to be driven to the Wall. The local CIA people took him to the Brandenburg Gate in a green military staff car with a uniformed driver because, even in his black homburg, McCone did look like a general. Nervously, they watched their new chief climb up the observation tower.

Looking about, McCone was livid and asked the correct questions. "How the hell could this have happened?" he demanded. "Are you trying to tell me they had all this stockpiled?"

Nobody had satisfactory answers. Nobody ever would. One of the escorting CIA men remembered: "The DCI looked depressed and incredulous." And back home, the staff that McCone was about to inherit still had no idea how to deal with this "absurd" phenomenon.

CIA Headquarters, Langley, Virginia, late August, 1961

The Wall had finally become real to CIA headquarters: it didn't help the image of the Communists, but it hardly made the West look good either; it was an enemy of the United States, and word had gone out in Langley—can anybody figure out a way to get rid of the damned thing?

That question was on the agenda of a desultory bull session of middle-level planners attended by Ted Shackley, the Bill Harvey protégé in Berlin during the 1950s, the "blond ghost" whose name would pop up during the Iran-Contra hearings of the 1980s. Shackley, invariably keen for direct action, thought the Wall should be sabotaged somehow. Somebody in the group, forgetting that chemicals had failed to work against even a lone vulnerable human being, Fidel Castro, mused that perhaps the Wall could be dissolved by chemical means.

Nobody could think of how to make this creative notion work. The meeting broke up without hitting upon any brainstorm that seemed worth pursuing. The next step would be up to the novelists.

**Checkpoint Charlie, West Berlin,
late August 1961**

David Cornwell, thirty, had become a frequent visitor to the Wall, shuttling to Berlin on most weekends. The expense was something of a nuisance because he earned only $6,000 a year as an intelligence agent using the cover of a second-string diplomat at the British Embassy in Bonn. Nevertheless, the Wall seemed a promising investment. Cornwell was fascinated, obsessively so, by the psyche of spies. He had written some spy stories that had not done too well. Now he was researching a new book. He had hopes for it. Berlin and the Wall offered precisely the foreboding backdrop for the intricate plot of treachery he was weaving in his mind. What better scenery than the very capital of espionage?

Cornwell took pride in the authentic trappings of his fictional action, so when he observed the taut scene at Checkpoint Charlie and went for long, slow walks along the Wall, taking photographs as he always did so he could refresh his memory later when he would be at the typewriter, his practiced eye soaked up the ugliness of an environment that seemed tailored for his purpose. For several nights he went without sleep.

Nobody paid attention to him. Hardly anybody ever did, not even later when he became very famous. He was a tall, gentle-looking type, conservatively tailored in London, schoolmasterish in manner, dark blond hair brushed from the left with no visible parting, lighter eyebrows, blue eyes, no pronounced British accent, no ring. He might have been any educated American or European from anywhere, even one of those Scandinavian-looking Russians. Mr. Anonymous.

He did have the right kind of eye for that summer's job of literary spying in Berlin, and in the final scene of the book he would write, when his loyal British spy hero, Alec Leamas, and his girl, Liz, want to come in from the cold of East Berlin only to be shot in the last moment at the border, betrayed by an ex-Nazi DDR double agent, it was the Wall that blocked their way to freedom. The Wall was the ultimate villain.

"Before them was a strip of thirty yards," Cornwell wrote. "It followed the wall in both directions. Perhaps seventy yards to their right was a watchtower; the beam of its searchlight played along the strip. The thin rain hung in the air, so that the light from the arc lamps was sallow and chalky, screening the world beyond. There was no one to be seen; not a sound. An empty stage.

"The watchtower's searchlight began feeling its way along the wall toward them, hesitant; each time it rested they could see the separate bricks and the careless lines of mortar hastily put on. As they watched, the beam stopped immediately in front of them. . . ."

The book, of course, became *The Spy Who Came in from the Cold*, published in 1963. The anonymous visitor to the Berlin Wall was, of course, the novelist who called himself John le Carré.

The men of the CIA base in Berlin scoffed at the tradecraft practiced by the book's characters.

"We laughed like mad," remembered one of the Americans. "Right at the opening he has a case officer waiting openly for an agent at the border, which would identify him. . . ."

Le Carré (French for "the Square") had the last laugh. His book sold more than twenty million copies worldwide.

The Wall of its early days would be the silent star of many other books and movies, works by Leon Uris, Len Deighton, William Buckley, and players with less box office appeal. But, strangely, one element was missed by all these chroniclers, and it was crucial. That was the role of the Wall as a pawn in the deadly game of the new nuclear weapons.

22

THE NUCLEAR DANGER MOUNTS

Washington,
Wednesday, August 30, 1961

Kennedy had new reason to fear nuclear war. Khrushchev unexpectedly announced that the Soviets were resuming atmospheric tests of nuclear weapons. "Fucked again," said the President.

Clearly the Wall was not enough to mollify the Soviet premier. He was still furious that the Allies were remaining in West Berlin. How far would he go to challenge that foothold again?

At the gloomiest White House meeting in a long time, the President's military advisers and his brother Bob weighed what they should do if the Soviets tried to shoot down Allied planes in the air corridor to West Berlin. The President asked: Should the Americans fire back if they were attacked by Soviet antiaircraft fire? Generals Lemnitzer and Taylor said yes. The President wanted to retain personal control. Eventually the conferees agreed with Defense Secretary McNamara: no land targets should be attacked without permission.

The meeting generated further pessimism in the Kennedy brothers.

"I want to get off," said the Attorney General after the others had left.

"Get off what?" asked the President.

"Get off the planet," said the Attorney General.

Was "no use" truly the unconditional American nuclear policy at the time of the Berlin Wall crisis?

In fact, the matter was ambiguous. The answer rested mostly in President Kennedy's head. No one would ever know how he settled it, not even in theory. And this was one case where theory and practice might differ radically. No matter how firm a leader's resolve might be not to use nuclears, who was to say what he might do minutes or seconds before the presumed impact of Soviet missiles?

Who indeed? On one occasion during that summer the President stayed behind after a meeting in the Cabinet Room about contingency planning for Berlin. Only his national security adviser, Mac Bundy, and former Secretary of State Dean Acheson were with him. The President chose the occasion to ask Acheson under what circumstances he would have to issue the order to use nuclear weapons. Acheson said that Kennedy should consider the point of no return most carefully, make up his mind in private, and tell *no one* what he decided.

The President thanked the cagey old diplomat for this Solomonic wisdom. Appropriately, he gave no indication of any reaction. Bundy thought that the Acheson counsel was wise, but also said nothing then or later.

And the President apparently never brought up the subject openly again.

By implication, it arose yet again in June when a decision had to be made about the question, never to be absolutely settled, of delegating the President's authority to command and control nuclear weapons. In a somewhat desultory way, the issue had come up before, principally during 1954 when the Eisenhower administration discussed the defense of the Nationalist islands Quemoy and Matsu off the Chinese coast.

"If we defend Quemoy and Matsu we'll have to use atomic weapons," said Secretary of State John Foster Dulles at a White House meeting. Eisenhower agreed, even though the CIA estimated that the civilian casualties on the mainland would probably run between twelve and fourteen million people. At that time there was excellent reason to delegate the authority to launch nuclears to American naval commanders on the scene, since communications between Washington and the theater of action were often out of commission, sometimes for hours every day.

In the summer of 1961, Carl Kaysen, a Kennedy assistant on nuclear questions, located a notebook containing letters by Eisenhower specifying the contingencies when his nuclear authority would be automatically delegated to military commanders in the field.

"What has Kennedy done about this?" Daniel Ellsberg asked Kaysen.

Kaysen said the President had weighed the question carefully and decided to do nothing.

Why not?

"This is not a good time for *Lieutenant* Kennedy to reverse the orders of the great general," said Kaysen.*

All of which made it more urgent than ever to put into place a workable version of Lieutenant Colonel Dee Armstrong's baby, the "flexible response" doctrine.

Armstrong's civilian bosses would eventually promote him to brigadier general, but that summer he remained under attack by his Army peers. A major general, the powerful Joint Chief of Staff representative to the Western NATO alliance, a rugged character who had taught Armstrong military topography at West Point, barged in on him to protest Armstrong's detailed scenario for flexible response, his famous poodle blanket.

"We had a high-pitched emotional discussion," Armstrong recalled. "He said, 'You can't do this!' and all but accused me of treason for pulling the nuclear rug out from under NATO."

"I know what my oath is," replied the then lieutenant colonel, a descendant of Chief Justice John Marshal.†

---

* According to Kaysen, the President wanted principally to avoid a fight with the military, which would certainly have been triggered by a presidential directive to withdraw the Eisenhower letters. Whether the letters remained legally binding from one administration to another remained ambiguous, just like the question of whether nuclear weapons should be used at all.

† Dee Armstrong was not one to shirk risks that he considered patriotically desirable. In the autumn of 1962 he advocated an American occupation of Cuba as a preventive afterthought to Kennedy's "flexible response" for extracting Khrushchev's missiles from the island. Nitze did not buy the final step of the Cuba blanket, which risked the trading of Cuban-based Soviet missiles for Soviet mis-

Kennedy, too, knew his oath. During the campaign culminating in his inaugural address ("Ask what you can do for your country") he had sworn again and again that he would protect the nation by closing the Soviets' presumed lead in intercontinental ballistic missiles (ICBMs).

Since the CIA's new Discoverer satellites still had not furnished incontrovertible evidence of the nuclear balance of power,* two of the President's "defense intellectuals" had hit upon the ultimate defense, the scenario of all nuclear scenarios.

Like more and more of their brainy tribe, these coauthors, Henry Rowen and Carl Kaysen, were no longer tucked away in think tanks or universities. Having smelled power, they had been allowed to join it. Rowen, from RAND Corporation, was Paul Nitze's deputy in the Pentagon. Kaysen, from Harvard, was on the White House staff. Together, they had scrutinized the early Discoverer photos and drawn their own conclusions. Having pinpointed the bases of Russia's 190 strategic bombers and spotted four ICBMs ready at the Plesetsk testing grounds, they scribbled onto a few sheets of paper what they called their "plan to show we could have a successful, clean first strike."

"First strike." This supposed no-no of warfare in our nuclear times would still be discussed as a seductive possibility in the 1980s. Behind closed doors, that is. In plain language, it translated into a sneaky nuclear Pearl Harbor designed to surprise the enemy and kill off his nuclear capability, or most of it, before *he* could make a

---

siles hitting the United States from the Soviet Union. Nor was Armstrong a "purple suiter"—one of the few policy-drafting Pentagon officers who, figuratively, wore the uniform of no particular branch of the military and were supposedly immune to the epic interservice rivalries for top-dog role in budgets and war plans. (I once covered such Cain-versus-Abel battles during a brief tenure as a Pentagon reporter; they were occasions when one could practice how to duck for cover.) Armstrong never forgot that his bread was buttered on the Army side and that he therefore could not qualify as a major league player in a large-scale nuclear war; that was an Air Force–Navy ballpark.

* The defense establishment and the CIA had supposed that the Discoverer's predecessor, the U-2 spy plane that had become so embarrassingly public by getting shot down over Russia, had to have done an incomplete reconnaissance job; according to conventional wisdom, there absolutely *had* to be far more than the four known Soviet ICBMs hidden somewhere. Ironically, the same CIA executive primarily responsible for the disaster at the Bay of Pigs, Richard Bissell, had masterminded the entire brilliant photo reconnaissance program from the beginning.

similar move. Rowen and Kaysen would later say that their scenario started out as an intellectual exercise, and they did keep it
secret from even the highest military planners for fear that the
generals might embrace it.

Initially, though, the scheme claimed some fans among the civilian intellectuals. It was indeed "clean." It minimized civilian casualties because it targeted no cities. And, if it went off as sketched
on paper, it would catch Khrushchev with his nuclear pants down.
No wonder the plan held attraction.

"We could really dust them up," said one of the thinkers, and as
the Berlin problem heated up when the Wall was built, the scenario
would be trotted out for closer consideration.

How would a public debate have tilted the squabbles between
the insiders if I had had access to all this drama in 1961 and had
opened it for inspection in the (then highly influential) *Saturday
Evening Post?* Twenty-five years later the thought still made my
colon twitch. And back at the time of the Wall the internal debate
was ferocious.

"You're crazy!" Kennedy's counsel Ted Sorensen shouted at Carl
Kaysen, the nuclear planner. "We shouldn't let guys like you
around here." And one of Mac Bundy's National Security Council
staff men exploded at Kaysen, "How does this make us any better
than those who measured the gas ovens or the engineers who built
the tracks for the death trains in Nazi Germany?" This man had
been Kaysen's friend but never spoke to him again.

Propelled by the appearance of the Wall, the sneak-attack "first
strike" scenario hastily sketched by Kaysen and Henry Rowen in
June had resurfaced, this time fleshed out by military planners
down to the altitudes and flight tactics of the attacking American
bombers. It still looked feasible but no longer quite so "clean."
According to the likeliest calculations, some Soviet bombers and
missiles would almost surely survive and retaliate, resulting in two
to three million American casualties ("best case") or possibly ten to
fifteen million ("worst case").

So-called soft-liners like Sorensen were mortified, and even cool
defense intellectuals who were "fascinated" did not stay pleased for
long. "Very quickly they'd come to understand that if you're honest, then there may be a ninety percent chance of success, but there
was also a ten percent chance it will all go haywire," said one of

these experts, William Kaufmann, and "they'd lose interest in fifteen minutes."*

The advent of the Wall also prompted Paul Nitze's Pentagon contingency planners to stage two weekends of "crisis simulation" war games that played out a lexicon of attack-and-defense scenarios with Berlin as the prize. One set of games was played on the secret floor of a Virginia office building near the Pentagon, another series in the privacy of the presidential retreat at Camp David.

The games were disappointing because the superiority of conventional forces commanded by the Warsaw Pact nations made the Western cause hopeless. "No matter what we tried in these hypothetical cases, the Soviets stomped on us," one planner said.

For three days at a stretch, with only a few hours of sleep at night, the players, divided into "Blue" and "Red" teams that included such influential thinkers as Mac Bundy, Henry Kissinger, and Dan Ellsberg, were put through grueling situations by the referee, Tom Schelling, the Harvard professor whose musings about Berlin the President had found so stimulating. Schelling turned up the heat of the Berlin battle with ease.

Blue was flying East German refugees out of West Berlin. Red told Blue to stop. Blue persisted. Red shot down Blue planes and killed dozens. Riots erupted in East Berlin, then in the rest of East Germany. Two Soviet divisions cut off Berlin from the rest of the DDR. A battalion of Blue troops broke through the barriers. Red aircraft attacked the Blue force. . . .

"The game made you very pessimistic," remembered Ellsberg. "There was no way to defend Berlin without threat of nuclear weapons. What the game made so vivid was how quickly you were confronted with the choice of using nuclear weapons or giving up."

Ellsberg was not the only game-player to be depressed by Schelling's sport. At the end of one day's session, Ellsberg walked into the rainy darkness with Abram Chayes and heard the State Department counselor utter heresy.

"We've got to get out of Berlin," Chayes said. "It's absolutely untenable."

Ellsberg was shocked to hear the words uttered out loud, even in private.

---

* In the 1980s, the fatal specter of even the narrowest failure margin similarly beset—but failed to shut down—President Reagan's "Star Wars" scheme. Even at its unlikely best, it too could not be a fully effective shield against a nuclear assault.

The icy Professor Schelling was undeterred, however. In the real-life contingency planning for Berlin, he came up with what he considered a foolproof brainstorm to demonstrate American resolve. He proposed exploding a harmless nuclear "warning shot" over an isolated Soviet location such as an island called Novaya Zemlya.*

The demonstration idea was short-lived. Nitze dismissed it as a "mug's game." He thought the Russians might respond by firing their own warning shot or shots. "If we used three they might use six," he reasoned. The test of will could backfire because one side or the other might eventually direct a bomb at one real target. "When that happens," Nitze pointed out, "then you know that you're in for keeps and you've lost a hell of a lot."

Mac Bundy also declined to play the demonstration game, pointing out that the Russians were entitled to misunderstand the intention behind the first firing of a nuclear-tipped demonstration missile from the moment of launch. How was the enemy to know whether an incoming missile was aimed at a remote island or at the Kremlin?

Later Bundy would say it would have been "irresponsible for the administration not to have considered the possibility of using nuclear weapons in the crisis, but even more irresponsible to have actually used them."

While the United States had weathered the immediate nuclear debate over the Wall, Kennedy had not settled the underlying question, at least not overtly: at what point would a "flexible response" end?

"Everyone agreed that we might *eventually* have to go on to nuclear war" (emphasis added), wrote the historian Arthur Schlesinger, a leading Kennedy soft-liner at the time. When would "eventually" become "now"? The question was raised over Berlin but was never settled. Except perhaps, as Dean Acheson had recommended, in the stillness of the President's conscience.

---

* Shades of nuclear decision-making just before the bombing of Hiroshima in 1945! My book *Day One—Before Hiroshima and After* (Simon and Schuster, 1984) includes a chapter on the scheming of the American scientists who proposed a demonstration that might have persuaded the Japanese to call off World War II. The project's leader, J. Robert Oppenheimer, preferred to watch what his bomb could do and failed to inform the Washington decision makers of the—great many and varying—proposals for a demonstration.

23

PRESIDENT KENNEDY: "THE FOUL WINDS OF WAR ARE BLOWING"

The White House,
late October 1961

The word "miscalculation" had never left President Kennedy's mind. More than at any time since the onset of the Berlin crisis in the spring, he had been fretting over the risk that Khrushchev could be blundering into nuclear war; consistently, the Soviet Premier seemed to underestimate the American resolve to stand firm on its rights in West Berlin, if not beyond the city's newly sealed border.

Continuing the practice he adopted after the Vienna Summit, the President used the Washington press corps to transmit word from him in two directions: first, to warn the American public about the great seriousness of the international situation; second, to caution the Soviets that their threats were being taken at face value, that any provocative misstep on their part might escalate into war.

Almost every week, Kennedy met privately with his old friend Ben Bradlee, the Washington bureau chief for *Newsweek*, to talk about pressing presidential concerns of the moment. After each session, Bradlee briefed his editors in New York with a memorandum of editorial guidance. The editors knew that the information came directly from the President and could be used in the magazine, but entirely for background purposes and not to be attributed to anyone.

Bradlee's memo of September 8 contained an unusually somber note. Talk of war had preoccupied the press and the public all summer—the recall of so many civilian reservists to active military duty had seen to that. Yet the President had carefully kept his language from sounding dramatic, much less inflammatory.

Bradlee found him in a grave mood.

"The President believes that 'The foul winds of war are blowing,'" the *Newsweek* man's internal memo reported, "that Khrushchev is really moving inevitably toward the brink. . . . " Bradlee added that the President repeated the "quotation" about "the foul winds of war" several times, and he suggested that his editors look it up in Bartlett's *Familiar Quotations.**

No doubt was possible: war was on the President's mind.

Suddenly, in October, everything changed. Technology had come to the President's rescue, and, in a bizarre twist, a spy had also helped—an *American* traitor who would never make headlines.

JFK couldn't fail to notice that somehow Khrushchev had been "reached," because on October 17, without earlier indications, the Russian executed an about-face. He totally changed his Berlin tune and delivered a conciliatory six-hour speech to the Twenty-second Congress of the Soviet Communist Party. The Western powers, he allowed, were "showing some understanding of the situation, and were inclined to seek a solution to the German problem and the issue of West Berlin." If this was a fact, "we shall not insist on signing a peace treaty absolutely before December 31, 1961."

Kennedy and his advisers were delighted. The immediate crisis over Berlin had evaporated, but why?

Assuredly, the administration had been maneuvering doggedly to undo Khrushchev's picture of Kennedy as a weakling. Earlier in October, by way of recent example, JFK tried to plant a strategic correction in the mind of a neutral messenger, Urho Kekkonen, the President of Khrushchev's little neighbor Finland.

"You must be aware of the melancholy state of mind induced in West Germany by the Wall," the President said. "We do not want

---

* The "quotation" is not in Bartlett's, nor in any of several other reference works I consulted. The President evidently made it up. There was a precedent for his casual way with "quotations." After the Bay of Pigs disaster he commented that "Victory has a thousand fathers, defeat is an orphan." He said it was a familiar quotation, but nobody ever found it.

to spread that state of mind by legitimizing the East German regime and stimulating a nationalist revival in West Germany." The
President dismissed Soviet guarantees of the Western presence and
access to West Berlin. He made this point adroitly by telling Kekkonen, "The Soviet Union is asking us to make concessions in
exchange for which they will give us again what we already have."
Nothing doing, Kennedy said.

The President escalated his psychological warfare by approving
the text of an article he had leaked to the columnist Jim Wechsler.
Miscalculation was again the text of Kennedy's sermon, but his
tone had grown sharp and personal. He had a tremendous stake
in convincing the Russian leader that he was no pushover but that
he could nevertheless be dealt with. As the son of a rich man, he
noted, he was the perfect caricature for Communist propagandists
who argued that wealth spelled war.

"If that doctrinaire rubbish is what Mr. Khrushchev believes, he
is mad, and we are all doomed," Wechsler wrote. Kennedy would
not be pushed around, he continued. The President had even
managed to achieve "a certain composure about the brutal nature
of the choice he may face in the solitude of some ghastly night."

Wechsler came very close to revealing outright that Kennedy was
his source for this insight into the President's nocturnal anxieties.
On the basis of these confidences the columnist concluded: "I have
no trace of doubt about the authenticity and depth of his desire
for rational settlements in the world that has trembled on the brink
so long. Russian papers please copy."

To the amazement of the White House inner circle, the Soviet
press did precisely that. It even printed the suggestion that
Khrushchev was crazy if he thought Kennedy was an imperialist
from Wall Street.

Khrushchev's turnaround on Berlin was in part the work of an
inside source that the Soviets had created for themselves, a pudgy
Army lieutenant colonel in the Pentagon, William H. Whalen,
forty-six, who worked for the Joint Chiefs of Staff. Whalen was in
debt. He was also afflicted by alcoholism, heart trouble, and a so-
cially ambitious wife. Ideology meant nothing to him. Soviet diplomats in Washington had already made it their business to learn
about these weaknesses by the time the colonel approached the
Soviet assistant military attaché at a party before Christmas in 1959
with business on his mind.

Later that month Whalen met the attaché and the First Secretary of the Soviet Embassy at a shopping center in Alexandria, Virginia. The diplomats brought along the colonel's first cash payment of $1,000, and over the next four years, for pay adding up to something over $30,000, the faceless spy Whalen gave away an astonishing wealth of military secrets. His position with the Chiefs and his friendships with key staff officers gave him across-the-board access to the crown jewels of the defense establishment. His disability retirement in early 1961 slowed him down little. He kept in touch by pumping his old friends and poring over papers spread across their desks.

When the colonel finally was arrested, indicted, and convicted in 1966—he aroused suspicions by acting too chummy toward some Soviets at a party—he was officially charged with practically giving away the store. The stunning catalogue in the indictment listed "Information pertaining to atomic weaponry, missiles, military plans for the defense of Europe, estimates of comparative military capabilities, military intelligence reports and analyses, information concerning the retaliation plans by the United States Strategic Air Command, and information pertaining to troop movements."

Investigation disclosed that Whalen had possessed knowledge of almost all the national intelligence estimates of Soviet strategic military capabilities during the period of the mythic "missile gap." Almost incidentally, he had, of course, had access to strategic planning for contingencies concerning West Berlin, and these spelled out that the United States planned to hang tough.

The CIA internal "damage assessment," an autopsy performed by two senior analysts, John Hyland and Victor Marchetti,* came to two conclusions.

"Whalen was the most damaging spy we had in the postwar period," Marchetti told me, "but it's my firm belief that the Russians couldn't understand the [most important] information. He was into the heart of defense planning and they didn't know what to do with it. It was too sophisticated, the analysis was on too high a level, there wasn't the minutiae they loved. I think the Soviets didn't trust their good fortune, they had no way to corroborate it."

The Soviets, then, also had trouble reconciling fieldwork with

---

* Hyland became the editor of the scholarly journal *Foreign Affairs*. Marchetti broke with the CIA and coauthored a 1974 best-seller—*The CIA and the Cult of Intelligence*—so revealing that the CIA's censors were driven to near apoplexy.

analysis so as to mine the most out of information they excavated by covert means. And yet: mixed in with the esoteric product of the Pentagon's strategic thinkers, Whalen also handed the Russians access to the holiest mission of intelligence: an advance tip-off of enemy *intentions*. In the Whalen case, the United States was the enemy, and according to the colonel's stolen information the American intention clearly was to stand firm on Berlin. No ambiguity about that.

Marchetti concluded that the Soviet analysts told Khrushchev: "These guys are really serious. We better go slow." And Khrushchev listened.

Even more intently, Khrushchev had to pay attention to the actual balance of nuclear power, the long-standing riddle of who owned what hardware. The truth as to which side was in a position of superiority in intercontinental ballistic missiles—and therefore ruled the world—finally became revealed to Kennedy. And Khrushchev knew that Kennedy knew. It was probably the most historic discovery of the decade, certainly the central fact of the historic year 1961.

An effective investigation of the famous "missile gap" by American spy satellites had begun on August 10, 1960, with the launching of Discoverer 13. Its photographs, showing the presence of four Soviet ICBMs, the SS-6 model, at the missile-testing site of Plesetsk in the northern Soviet Union, were unmistakable because these missiles were huge, heavy, extremely cumbersome weapons requiring extraordinary support and security systems and railroad tracks or extra-heavy roads.

More satellites were dispatched as rapidly as possible to discover more Soviet missiles, and within a week of the launching of Discoverer 17, on November 12, the Khrushchev government disclosed that it was tracking the American aerial spying. Its authoritative journal *International Affairs* published a rundown of the operations by the Discoverer and other satellites. It warned that the overflights were illegal and that the Soviet Union would "protect its security against any encroachments from outer space." In point of fact, the satellites kept orbiting unscathed.

When Kennedy moved into the White House on January 20, 1961, the Soviet missile count had been inconclusive, and Defense Secretary McNamara made it his top-priority business to resolve the problem. All of the administration's defense and foreign policy planning depended on the intelligence that the satellites were photographing from their global orbits.

For three weeks, McNamara and his Deputy Secretary, Roswell (Roz) Gilpatric, trooped to the Air Force photo intelligence office on the fourth floor of the Pentagon and spent hours at a time bent over the Discoverer photos. Since pictures came in by the thousands and no further Soviet missiles showed up, McNamara formed the opinion in early February that there was no missile gap. But he could not be absolutely certain. It was an old dilemma: how does one prove conclusively that something doesn't exist, particularly in so vast a territory as the Soviet Union?

The definitive answer came from Discoverer 29, launched on August 30. It eliminated several suspected Soviet missile sites, confirming that Plesetsk was the Soviets' first offensive launch complex. By mid-September, analysts reduced the estimated number of existing SS-6s to between ten and fourteen. Khrushchev's bluff over Berlin had run its course. The United States nuclear arsenal contained 188 ballistic missiles.

It was all over but the politicking. En route to the Pentagon in a White House car, the precocious defense strategist Daniel Ellsberg showed presidential assistant Carl Kaysen some notes he had made, hoping that Kennedy would transmit them privately to Khrushchev. (The President had just launched a regular personal correspondence with the Soviet leader; JFK's first letter ran ten pages, single spaced, drafted by speech writer Ted Sorensen.)

In his firebrand way, Ellsberg suggested, in effect, that since Khrushchev couldn't put up, he should be instructed to shut up. He proposed that Kennedy tell the Russian the precise coordinates of the Soviet missiles at Plesetsk and perhaps even send him copies of the Discoverer photos.

Kaysen thought that this approach was much too provocative.

"John Kennedy isn't going to talk that way to Khrushchev," he told Ellsberg.

Shortly afterward, McNamara's assistant, Adam Yarmolinsky, asked Ellsberg to draft a major policy speech that would make unmistakably clear to the Soviets that (1) the United States enjoyed a *wide* and rapidly *growing* nuclear superiority over the Russians and (2) the administration's confidence in making that claim was unequivocal.

The speech, delivered by Deputy Defense Secretary Gilpatric before the Business Council at The Homestead in Hot Springs, Virginia, on the evening of October 21, consequently bristled with the enormity of American nuclear reserves. "The total number of our delivery vehicles, tactical as well as strategic, is in the tens of thousands, and of course we have more than one warhead for each vehicle," Gilpatric told Khrushchev and the world. Then he advanced a claim so colossal that it could not have been proved unequivocally valid.

"We have a second-strike capability which is at least as extensive as what the Soviets can deliver by striking first," Gilpatric asserted, implying that the United States could survive not only enormous casualties of a Soviet first strike but the elimination of the President and his entire nuclear command and control structure. This was a fragile postulate, but America's nuclear muscle had been convincingly flexed.

A further Gilpatric claim was more to the point. It took aim at Khrushchev's nuclear saber rattling, now exposed by the Discoverer satellites to have been enormously exaggerated. Said the Deputy Secretary, "While the Soviets use rigid security as a military weapon, their Iron Curtain is not so impenetrable as to force us to accept at face value the Kremlin's boasts."

Hopefully, the possibility of a nuclear miscalculation had been laid to rest. The makings remained for conventional warfare, perhaps right at the Berlin Wall.

24

THE TANK CRISIS: "MR. PRESIDENT, WE'RE NOT WORRIED ABOUT OUR NERVES"

**Checkpoint Charlie, West Berlin,
Friday, October 27, 1961**

The opening of Dan Schorr's broadcast to CBS that Friday evening was a heart stopper: "The Cold War took on a new dimension tonight when American and Russian fighting men stood arrayed against each other for the first time in history. Until now the East-West conflict had been waged through proxies—Germans and others. But tonight, the superpowers confronted each other in the form of ten low-slung Russian tanks facing six American Patton tanks, less than a hundred yards apart at the Friedrichstrasse crossing point between East and West Berlin."

Schorr was broadcasting from this hot spot and he had made certain that his facts were unassailable. The identifying marks of the Russian tanks had been obliterated. They could have been East German, which was a crucial point. Schorr knew that General Clay was staging this confrontation to draw the Soviets into admitting that they, not the DDR, were the real power behind the Wall.

To the West Berliners this was no technicality. They were fleeing from the city to West Germany at the rate of over 1,700 a week.

"There is resignation and a great deal of bitterness," Sydney Gruson cabled to *The New York Times*. Confidence in Western steadfastness was in urgent need of a boost. Clay's tanks were the symbol of American resolve.

So Schorr walked across the border, talked to one of the crew of

On October 27, 1961, Soviet tanks, stripped of Red Army markings, confronted U.S. Army tanks at Checkpoint Charlie in a tense stalemate. It was the first time in history that American and Russian troops had faced each other as adversaries. In the end, the Soviets backed down.

the unmarked tanks in German, and when he replied in Russian he knew he had his story. Schorr cold have spoken in Russian, too; he had worked in Moscow.

Now his broadcast to America tried to capture the incongruities he was seeing, the prosaic side by side with the threatening: "The scene is weird, almost incredible. The American GIs stand by their tanks, eating from mess kits while West Berliners gape from behind a rope barrier and buy pretzel sticks, the scene lit by floodlights from the Eastern side. On the Communist side, in three-two-two-three formation, the Russian tanks stand in the gloom, their wiry little black-uniformed crews hardly visible. . . ."

Although hundreds of civilian spectators, many with binoculars, were watching on either side, the incendiary nature of the tableau was unmistakable and trouble could start from East or West. The American lead tank was equipped with a bulldozerlike scoop designed to remove obstacles; a company of *Vopos* formed a human chain facing east toward their own people.

Weird scene or not, Schorr thought World War III might be close at hand, and so did such other seasoned eyewitnesses as Gruson of the *Times.*

"I had a moment's twinge when the tanks started rolling," he recalled years later. "I didn't expect Russians, I expected East Germans. I always thought that when push came to shove, the U.S. and the Russians would not fight, but Clay was running an intense, high-stake game. An accident was always possible."

Schorr, Gruson, and the rest of the public did not realize that Clay was not running this show. The Commander in Chief in person was secretly in control in his self-assigned role as Berlin desk officer, and nobody knew this better than Clay did that night.

The retired general was monitoring the action at Checkpoint Charlie from the Command Room of the U.S. Mission. Its location had long ago been renamed Clayallee in his honor.* Otherwise his surroundings were familiar to him from the years beginning in 1945, when the headquarters was known as OMGUS and he had been Military Governor.

Shortly before midnight, with tension at its peak, a call for Clay came from Washington. Supposedly, Mac Bundy wanted to speak to him, but the voice from the U.S. was clearly the President's. Clay

---

* No one else had ever been so honored by Berlin in his lifetime.

told him that a stalemate had been reached at the border and that he expected the Russians would soon withdraw.

At that moment Clay was handed a slip of paper advising him that twenty more Soviet tanks were rumbling toward Checkpoint Charlie.

"There is a variation, Mr. President," said Clay. "There are twenty more Russian tanks coming up. This proves that they are good mathematicians."

"What do you mean?" asked Kennedy.

"Well, we have thirty tanks in Berlin," said Clay, "so they brought up twenty more tanks so that they will have a tank for every tank that we have. This is further evidence to me that they don't intend to do anything."

"Well, I'm glad of that," said the President. And then: "I know you people over there haven't lost your nerves."

This would have been a curious display of machismo if the President, always anxious not to be considered "chicken," hadn't been addressing a general who tended to think that everyone was chicken except himself.

And so Clay lobbed the ball right back at Kennedy for an extraordinary macho volley: "Mr. President, we're not worried about our nerves, we're worrying about those of you people in Washington."

"I don't know about those of my associates," said the President, "but mine are all right."

To a CIA observer in the operations center, Clay, dressed informally in a houndstooth jacket but looking grave, explained himself.

"If the Soviets don't want war over West Berlin, we can't start it," he said. "If they do, there's nothing we can do to stop them."

The Soviets, while not wanting war, kept pushing their campaign of bluffing. Almost thirty years later, an eyewitness disclosed that the American tanks had made Khrushchev's military very nervous.* Khrushchev calmly upped the ante. When Marshal Koniev bustled in to see him agitatedly and reported that the engines of the American tanks were running in high gear, the Soviet leader paused only briefly.

---

* The insider, Alexei Adzhubei, Khrushchev's son-in-law, described the scene in a Moscow interview.

"Take our tanks to the neighboring street," Khrushchev instructed, "but let their engines run there in the same high gear. And put the noise and the roar from the tanks through amplifiers."

"They may rush forward," said Koniev, hesitating.

"I don't think so," Khrushchev replied, "unless, of course, the minds of the American military have been made blind with hatred."

Clay had been facing much frustration since he entered Berlin so triumphantly with Vice President Johnson in August. Secretary of State Rusk disliked the general's direct access to the President. White House staffers feared the general's aggressive ways, and even the steely Mac Bundy conceded that Clay's temper made him "difficult."* There was always the danger that the general might resign noisily. The vigilant Bundy warned JFK as early as August 28, "You want no risk of setting up another MacArthur-Truman affair."

Clay was also feuding with his former friends in uniform. The American generals in Europe resented his incursion on their turf (and on the military chain of command). They went on strike, refusing to be bossed by a cocky hybrid who had once been one of their own but had fallen prey to civilian ways.

Clay didn't mind fanning the fires under his own feet. Among the members of the Berlin Mafia, his case of Berlinitis was probably the most advanced. His power base with the Berliners was overwhelming: his "very good" rating in the polls exceeded that of the sainted Willy Brandt by 58 to 48 percent.

Clay's experience was hopefully predictive: he was convinced the Soviets were again bluffing in Berlin and he alone had called their bluff once before, with his airlift, and made them crawl.

Most important, perhaps, was the personal element. Despite their differences in age, in domestic politics and at times in foreign policy Clay's personal chemistry with Kennedy made an excellent mix. The two men liked and respected each other.†

---

* A New England banker once exploded at Clay when both were working for President Eisenhower: "Jesus Christ, Lucius, there's a word *maybe* in the English language! Don't you ever use it?" The general's response is not recorded.

† In private, JFK expressed admiration for the willingness of a conservative Republican to stick with such a difficult mission in Berlin. In turn, Clay gave historian Jean Edward Smith this uncharacteristically glowing appraisal of the

Barely settled in his Dahlem villa, Clay unilaterally enlarged his portfolio. The President had dispatched him to buck up the Berliners; Clay decided that his prime mission was to slap down the Soviets.

The fiercest resistance against his private agenda came from his erstwhile cronies in the United States military establishment. When Clay asked the American Commandant, Major General Albert Watson, to have a concrete wall built on a military reservation so that engineer troops could practice tearing it down, Watson's boss, the pugnacious General Bruce Clarke, countermanded the order. And when Clay wanted two companies of GIs to punch through a narrow neck of East German territory to an obscure Western exurb called Steinstücken* (population: about three hundred families), Clarke ordered the already assembled troops back into the barracks and confronted Clay furiously.

"He acted like I had caught him with his hand in the cookie jar," Clarke reported. "I told him he could call the President on the telephone if he disagreed with me. Otherwise, I told him, 'You can take your cotton-picking fingers off my troops.' Clay then responded, 'Well, Bruce, I can see that we are not going to get along.'" The animosity between these men of great rank was surprising, since Clarke had long been an admirer of Clay and had once been his student at West Point.

Clay's personal crusade of brinkmanship picked up momentum on the night of Sunday, October 22. En route to see a performance by an experimental Czechoslovak theatrical company in East Berlin, Allan Lightner of the U.S. Mission and his wife were harassed in their Volkswagen by the *Vopos* at Checkpoint Charlie. The Lightners were asked for their diplomatic passports. In accordance with

---

President: "He was a very stimulating man to talk with. He had a brilliant mind, he listened well, he asked pointed questions and it was exhilarating to be with him . . . I never met with him on any subject that he hadn't done his homework [on]. . . ."

* Steinstücken, an outlying flyspeck previously unknown even to most Berliners, continued to inspire quixotic missions by Clay. He flew there in a helicopter to assure citizens of American support. Then he flew military police to the village to establish the United States presence. The DDR made outraged noises but did nothing. Remarkably, an entire book celebrates the charade over the soul of this hamlet: *Steinstücken: A Study in Cold War Politics* by Honoré (Marc) Catudal, Jr. (New York: Vantage Press, 1971).

precedent and their instructions, they refused. To have done otherwise would have signified diplomatic recognition of East Germany and recognition of East Berlin as belonging to East Germany.

The Lightners demanded to see a Soviet officer. None came. After being stalled for half an hour, Lightner tried to gun his car through the border post. *Vopos* surrounded him, so eventually he turned back. When he shortly approached the border again, this time surrounded by a squad of MPs with bayonets fixed, the *Vopos* made no attempt to stop him.

The next day the State Department advised the American diplomats to "go slow" in entering East Berlin, but Clay appealed the issue to the President and prevailed. More American diplomats were escorted through Checkpoint Charlie by MPs. On Wednesday, the first American tanks took up their positions at the border. On Thursday, the first Soviet tanks rumbled up to face them at the border.

That night more Soviet tanks bivouacked off Unter den Linden; when they rolled up at the Friedrichstrasse border on Friday, Clay told a press conference, "The fiction that it was the East Germans who were responsible for trying to prevent Allied access to East Berlin is now destroyed."*

Shortly after 10:30 A.M. the next day, without ado, the Soviet tanks retreated, as Clay had predicted to Kennedy during the night. Thirty minutes later the American armor left. The confrontation had lasted sixteen hours. Except for the President, who kept silence, official Washington was incensed over Clay's "melodramatizing." The senior British diplomat in Berlin assured Soviet officials in East Berlin that Clay would soon be recalled, which never happened.

Clay had been correct again: the Soviets were bluffing, and Khrushchev—who was all along acting as the Berlin desk officer

---

* According to Robert Kennedy, it was his brother, the President and Berlin desk officer, not Clay, who defused the inflammable tank incident by appealing to Khrushchev personally. The President asked the Attorney General to arrange for the intercession of the latter's friend, Georgi Bolshakov, a press attaché at the Soviet Embassy in Washington who was representing himself as Khrushchev's personal emissary. In 1964 Robert Kennedy told the historian John Bartlow Martin: "I got in touch with Bolshakov and said the President would like them to take their tanks out of there in 24 hours. He said he'd speak to Khrushchev and they took the tanks out in 24 hours. So he [Bolshakov] delivered when it was a matter of importance." If the President offered inducements, admonitions, or conditions, these were never reported.

for the Russians—told Kennedy's Press Secretary Pierre Salinger about his role the following spring in Moscow. Throughout the tank confrontation the Premier was getting telephone reports from Marshal Koniev at the scene and was conferring with his Defense Minister, Marshal Rodion Malinovsky, in the Kremlin. Khrushchev told Salinger that it was he who gave the order for his tanks to withdraw because he wanted no conflict.

"If the tanks went forward, it was war," he said. "If they went backward, it was peace." Khrushchev was willing to make considerable concessions to avoid war and he sized up the American macho psychology shrewdly. "They would, so to say, have been in a difficult moral position if we forced them to turn their backs on the barrels of our cannons," he remarked on another occasion.

He did detest Clay for having detected the Soviet bluff. "Clay is as much a general as I am a shoemaker," he blustered at Pierre Salinger. And Clay was one shoemaker who stuck to his last.

**Washington,
late December 1961**

President Kennedy's record for generalship suffered a further setback before Christmas 1961, the watershed season when he committed the United States to back the South Vietnamese with American troops, knuckling under to the demands of his advisers.

In November he had still been resisting them and had compared their entreaties to the clamor he had faced when they pleaded for a commitment to Berlin, which he had made but with an embarrassing result, the Wall. The Vietnam prospects seemed equally uninviting and inconclusive.

"They want a force of American troops," he warily told Arthur Schlesinger, the historian on his staff. "They say it's necessary in order to restore confidence and maintain morale. But it will be just like Berlin. The troops will march in; the bands will play; the crowds will cheer; and in four days everyone will have forgotten. Then we will be told we have to send in more troops. It's like taking a drink. The effect wears off, and you have to take another."

Kennedy's prediction was prescient. Yet even in 1961 Vietnam was a tar baby whose pull he was unable to resist.

The one halfhearted attempt to apply the efficiency of the Berlin Wall to the Vietnam theater was doomed by lack of attention. Its instigator was the principal military adviser in Kennedy's inner circle, General Maxwell Taylor. When Taylor was dispatched to Saigon in October to assess the American position, he gave his traveling companion, Ed Lansdale, the intelligence general who specialized in unconventional warfare, the strange assignment to design an electronic version of the Wall.

"I want you to figure out a defense line so we can put American genius to work and have an electronic line" (across the 17th parallel), Taylor instructed Lansdale.

"That's not my subject," Lansdale protested. "I'm no good at that."

Taylor insisted, so Lansdale made a perfunctory stab at the task by telling some Saigon staff officers:

"You guys are good at figuring. This is going to cost us several billion dollars. Tell me how many billions and I'll report it."

It is not known whether the notion was pursued further.

25

KHRUSHCHEV WON'T LET UP

Ogoryevo, Soviet Union,
May 1962

Khrushchev's feelings about Berlin had not cooled. Pierre Salinger discovered to his dismay that the Premier's preoccupation was in fact a "fixation" when the presidential Press Secretary, of all people, was thrust into the unlikely position of having to represent the United States in an eyeball-to-eyeball confrontation with the formidable Russian. East and West were still practicing brinkmanship in the arena of nuclear decision making.

Still searching for ways to reduce the risks of "miscalculation," President Kennedy had sent Salinger to the Soviet Union to try to open up better channels of communication with the Soviets. There had been no hint that Salinger might see the number one Russian. Kennedy had nevertheless had reservations about his unconventional ambassador. The portly, cigar-chomping Salinger, known to the Washington press corps as "Plucky Pierre," was considered a bit of a buffoon figure. The reputation was undeserved, but the very shrewd Salinger was no policymaker and Kennedy had instructed him to talk only about communications. Under no circumstance was he to be drawn into substantive discussions.

To his amazement, Salinger was whisked to Ogoroyevo, a birch and pine forest area twenty-two miles outside of Moscow where the Kremlin maintained a guest residence. There the Press Secretary found himself at lunch with Khrushchev and a group of cronies on a patio with a grand view of the Moscow River.

Khrushchev was relaxing under a straw hat with a big brim to protect his huge bald head against the sun. He offered "Gospodin" Salinger alternate bites of his shashlik and gulped at least five cognacs.

The talk was trivial until the Premier suddenly glared at Salinger and said, "Your President has made a very bad mistake for which he will have to pay! He has said that you will be the first to use the bomb."

I had known Salinger for almost a decade—he had been a respected investigator when I covered Robert Kennedy's racket investigations committee and the President was still a very junior senator—so I was not surprised to learn, long after this private summit meeting, that Khrushchev intimidated him no more than the Mafia used to.*

Salinger realized that Khrushchev's tirade had been set off by an article written by my *Saturday Evening Post* colleague Stewart Alsop, entitled "Kennedy's Grand Design." Stew had talked to the President and the article had made people all over Washington see red, though not as crimson as Khrushchev's face, now glowering at the ridiculously outranked Press Secretary.

West Berlin remained free, Alsop had written, because Kennedy managed to convince Khrushchev that a grab in that direction might well trigger global thermonuclear war. In the *Post* interview Kennedy had said: "Khrushchev must not be certain that, where its vital interests are threatened, the United States will never strike first. In some circumstances we might have to take the initiative."

Khrushchev was enraged. "This warmonger Alsop, is he now your Secretary of State?" he challenged Salinger. "He now forces us to reappraise our own position."

Kennedy, McGeorge Bundy, and Salinger had all gone over the *Post* article before publication—and had miscalculated. None had read into it a threat to trigger the great taboo, a "first strike," or "preemptive war." They had meant to deal only with American options to retaliate against a *major* conventional attack on Western Europe. Some worriers in Washington had misunderstood the President much as Khrushchev had, and the White House, so Sa-

---

* In the 1980s Salinger would remain visible as an ABC-TV news executive in Europe.

linger reminded the Soviet Premier, had already issued a clarifying statement.

"I have seen that statement," said the Russian, "but I take the President's words literally in the article. This is clearly a new doctrine."*

Had Khrushchev lured Salinger into the Moscow woods because he was worried about miscalculating Kennedy's real intentions? Or was he fishing for fresh data? Was he fully reassured by Salinger's reassurances? Had he perhaps given up on his sparse supply of missiles and was really rattling his tanks, his overwhelming superiority for conventional warfare? Would he really change his position? Who could be sure? The answers might lead to yet another miscalculation.

Khrushchev could be thankful for one definitive development. His least favorite general was giving up the fight.

**West Berlin,
Tuesday, May 1, 1962**

General Clay had not been scheduled to speak. But Berliners knew that he would be on the platform, that he was leaving Berlin, and that this would be their last chance to see him. And so on May 1, the German equivalent of Labor Day, more than 700,000 came to the Platz der Republik to stand before the charred ruins of the Reichstag, cheering and weeping. Mayor Willy Brandt, sensing the emotions of the crowd, beckoned the general to the microphone.

Clay greeted the throng—he was facing one of every three West Berliners—on behalf of President Kennedy ("I need not remind you of his commitment to you") and closed on a personal note, which he almost never allowed himself: "I shall not now, or ever, say 'good-bye.' For Berlin is too much a part of me to ever leave. I shall only say, as we say in America, 'So long, thank you, and God bless you.'"

. . .

---

* Khrushchev left Salinger in no doubt that he was talking about Berlin as a priority cause of possible war. He went over the 1961 crisis in gleeful detail and bragged, "I personally ordered the construction of the Wall."

Clay's steadfastness was true only in his heart. His influence had run its course. He *was* saying good-bye to Berlin, because Washington had said good-bye to him.

Soon after the frightening tank confrontation that Clay had provoked at Checkpoint Charlie in October, the Soviets started proposing new curbs upon the Allied hold on West Berlin. The Kennedy administration stood its ground, but barely. Clay complained, but his increasingly combative cables got him nowhere and his initiatives were reversed or ignored.

To keep the Soviets from nibbling at the Autobahn access route, Clay had instituted armed patrols between the Berlin and Helmstedt border posts. Washington ordered these runs canceled. In February the Soviets announced restrictions on Allied air traffic. They buzzed Western commercial traffic in the long-established air corridors and dropped strips of metal foil along the routes to disrupt Western radar.

Clay, furious, wanted to run fighter planes daily between West Germany and Berlin by way of protest. He also suggested that Western planes begin to fly above the traditional 10,000-foot ceiling. But Secretary Rusk was about to enter negotiations on Berlin issues with Foreign Minister Gromyko and wanted nothing to interfere, so Clay was again overruled.

The President wrote him long, soothing personal letters on March 1 and again on March 15 ("I do want you to know that we continue to count on you"), but Clay decided to resign. The anti-Clay forces in Washington leaked the news as soon as the general boarded the plane for the trip to inform Kennedy.

Not long afterward Khrushchev again wanted the West to know that he would not have permitted war to erupt because of disputes over such issues as access to Berlin, and the Soviet Premier had his bag of options ready.

In Moscow, the West German Ambassador, a professional diplomat named Hans Kroll, had developed a personal relationship with Khrushchev that made for some surprisingly frank conversations. Kroll asked the Soviet leader what he would do if he blocked the Autobahn and the Americans would try to rush through with tanks. Khrushchev said the American tanks would face Soviet tanks; if the Americans started shooting, he said, the Russian tanks would shoot back.

"But, Mr. Prime Minister," said Kroll, "then we'll have war!"

"No," said Khrushchev, "even then we wouldn't have war! I would phone the Security Council of the United Nations, I would personally fly to New York and would settle the conflict in direct talks with President Kennedy."*

**West Berlin,
August 1962**

A year after the Wall went up, John Kennedy was still the acting Berlin desk officer.

"Mr. President, an escapee is bleeding to death at the Berlin Wall," reported his military aide, General Ted Clifton. "Watson is asking for instructions."

Recognizing the incendiary implications of this particular refugee's tragic circumstances, Major General Watson, the cautious Commandant of Berlin's American garrison, had overcome a career soldier's lifelong worship of the chain of command and, remarkably, reached out straight for his Commander in Chief.

At stake was the life of a nobody, one Peter Fechter, an eighteen-year-old mason. At 2:04 P.M. on August 17, 1962, he climbed over the border's wire fence, dashed across the "death strip," and almost managed to reach the Wall at Zimmerstrasse. DDR soldiers started shooting. Fechter cried out and fell, hit in the stomach and back. His shirt and pants turned red. He screamed.

While the area's eastern side was deserted, it was a busy place in the West. Publisher Springer's finally completed skyscraper stood a short distance to Fechter's left. Checkpoint Charlie with its troops and tourists was 150 meters to the right. As Fechter's cries grew weaker, passersby and West Berlin police gathered, eager to help. The police threw him packets of bandages, but Fechter lacked the strength to use them.

At 2:17 the young American lieutenant in charge at Checkpoint Charlie called General Watson for instructions. Watson: "Send a patrol but stay on our side." When six MPs arrived at the scene, some 250 West Berliners were yelling toward the East: "You murderers! You bandits!"

Fechter was growing constantly weaker and was obviously bleed-

---

* Was Khrushchev speaking the truth or singing a lullaby of psychological warfare? During the Cuban Missile Crisis that October, Kennedy and his advisers would face this question over higher stakes.

ing to death. He was the victim of a horrifying East-West impasse. The Communist guards did not dare carry him from the death strip because they feared getting shot by the Western police. The Western police could not help because they were strictly forbidden from—literally—setting foot in the East. It was the Cold War in a freeze-frame.

Tension was mounting. The DDR border officers tried to disperse the Western spectators with tear gas. The American MPs retreated to Checkpoint Charlie, which became the scene of an angry confrontation with the lieutenant in charge. The assembled Berliners grew increasingly strident in their demands that the Americans carry Fechter to safety. The lieutenant, not about to violate his orders, uttered a widely reported—and clumsily phrased—turndown.

"Sorry, but this isn't our problem," he said.

Of course it was. The lieutenant knew it, General Watson knew it, and President Kennedy knew it. Fechter did not. At 3:05 P.M. six *Vopos* and an officer dragged him away by his arms and legs. He was obviously dead. Cameras clicked and indignation was worldwide. Much emotion was directed at America's apparent impotence and indifference—Berliners, in particular, never forgot—although in fact the President never had the chance to prevent Fechter's death.

General Watson had again called the White House, where Kennedy had barely begun to consider Watson's first report.

"The matter has taken care of itself," Watson said. Even the acting Berlin desk officer could not be quite close enough to the scene to make a difference. Sometimes he depended on deputies in distant outposts, including his one secret ally in the heart of Moscow.

**Moscow,
Saturday, July 7, 1962**

Greville Wynne, the courier from British intelligence, was shocked when Oleg Penkovsky met him at the Moscow airport. The once so ebullient colonel looked pale, tense, exhausted. For a long time this normally effusive extrovert remained silent. When he finally began to speak, his news was depressing.

He thought he had been under observation from time to time since January and had taken extra care not to be detected in his contacts or drops. He had concluded that it was the KGB that had him under surveillance, not his own GRU, which was an important distinction. The KGB would not risk an arrest on GRU turf until there was plenty of physical evidence or, better, a red-handed arrest.

"Which they will never get," said Penkovsky, smiling. "Don't worry, I'll be all right now."

Wynne thought that his friend's optimism was fake even though the latest trip was going well. In Wynne's room at the Hotel Ukraine they exchanged a large batch of films that night. Over dinner at the Gorky Park Restaurant, Penkovsky even managed one of his sly jokes. He reported the birth of a baby daughter and said that she sometimes kept him up all night.

"That's bad," said Wynne.

"Yes, she's worse than British intelligence," cracked Penkovsky.

Two nights later there were no more jokes. Instead of entering the Peking Restaurant, where they were supposed to have dinner, Penkovsky signaled Wynne to follow him. In an alleyway he hissed, "You must get out quickly! You're being followed. Be at the airport by six o'clock. I'll be there."

Wynne had booked a flight for noon, but he showed up at 6 A.M. Penkovsky told him to get out at the earliest opportunity, the 9:15 flight to Copenhagen, and handed him a thick envelope.

"Look after it," he said. "It's the best."

It was. In the package were up-to-date operations manuals for Soviet missiles, including the SS-4 and SS-5 systems that Khrushchev would deploy to Cuba three months hence. Penkovsky's package enabled President Kennedy and his advisers to follow the progress of the Soviet installation efforts on an hour-by-hour basis. They knew the range of the missiles so precisely that they could make an appalling calculation: Seattle was the only major American city that was not threatened. On the other hand, the refire rate of the missiles was slow ("several" hours). Most important, the Pentagon could figure out when the point of no return would be reached, the crucial hour when the country would be in immediate mortal danger. Thanks to Penkovsky, Kennedy and his men knew exactly what even the most revealing aerial photography could not tell them: the moment the missiles would become ready to be fired.

26

THE CUBAN MISSILE CRISIS: "THEY'LL CERTAINLY DO SOMETHING IN BERLIN"

**The White House, Washington,
Saturday, October 27, 1962**

President Kennedy faced the crisis of his life. He had to get the Soviet missile bases out of Cuba. If he failed, it seemed certain that Khrushchev would attempt some form of nuclear blackmail against the West—or a nuclear attack. If Kennedy succeeded in some move against the missiles, the Soviets might well retaliate. Where? When the President's advisers—they called themselves "Excom" for "Executive Committee"—made individual lists of where Khrushchev was most likely to strike back, all of them placed Berlin first.

A crisp, blue Wednesday, October 24, might have been the day for West Berlin to fall. Then there would no longer be a need for any Wall.

Timing is everything in nuclear crisis management—timing truncated, timing finite and irreversible. The Cuban Missile Crisis came to a boil in thirteen days, but thirteen days is an eon in the life of missiles, ample time for counterplanning, especially since Khrushchev's actual missiles were not yet in physical evidence when the President received his first warning of the threat. American spy planes had supplied aerial photos showing only four slashes in Cuban soil, plus other highly suggestive details of the configuration for a Soviet missile launching site.

It was shortly before 9 A.M. on Friday, October 19, when Mac

Bundy found the President sitting on the edge of his bed, in pajamas and dressing gown, scanning the morning papers.

"Mr. President," said the security adviser, "there is now hard photographic evidence, which you will see a little later, that the Russians have offensive missiles in Cuba."

Outwardly calm, Kennedy was angry and surprised. He had not expected such a reckless, high-risk Soviet move. Reports of Communist missiles in Cuba had been floating through the political rumor mills for weeks, but the President had believed that only defensive antiaircraft weapons were involved. The new aerial photos, however, showed a threat of a totally unprecedented order. Kennedy was no longer dealing with Castro militia, as at the Bay of Pigs; or Khrushchev bluster, as at Vienna; or concrete, as in East Berlin. In each of these challenges the Communists had gambled and won. Demonstrably, Khrushchev felt encouraged to try pulling off yet another bluff. This time both sides were toying with Armageddon. Kennedy knew: the Soviets must not be allowed to win again.

For thirteen days, reminders of the threat to Berlin ran through the Excom discussions like a catechism. From the first day, the President agreed with those of his advisers who thought that Khrushchev was launching a maneuver in Cold War politics. He expected that confronting the Americans with his missiles in Cuba would produce nothing more than protests, another show of weakness, and in that event he would apply pressure to American overseas bases or, most likely, to his top-priority target, Berlin, to weaken or eliminate the Allied hold on the Western sectors of the city.

Until Thursday, October 18, much of the almost ceaseless discussion had centered on the recommendation by the Air Force for a "surgical" strike to eliminate the bases with bombs.

"How will the Russians respond?" the President asked General Curtis LeMay, the bulldog-aggressive Air Force Chief of Staff.

LeMay said the Russians would do nothing.

Kennedy bristled: "Are you trying to tell me that they'll let us bomb their missiles and kill a lot of Russians, and then do nothing? If they don't do anything in Cuba, they'll certainly do something in Berlin."

To encourage brainstorming for new solutions, the Excom formed a special subcommittee on Berlin. It met about half a dozen times but could not agree on recommendations because it was headed by two co-chairmen, each representing a different orientation. Chairman Paul Nitze argued for tough action, Chairman Llewellyn Thompson wanted to avoid provocation of the Russians. The division remained sharp and unresolved.

In the Excom itself, the President brought up the danger to Berlin again and again. Attorney General Robert Kennedy at one point suggested the possibility of installing missiles there. A television correspondent walking through the Cabinet Room after an Excom meeting sneaked a look at the President's scratch pad. What he saw scrawled was "Berlin, Berlin, Berlin."

Reports directly from Berlin were not alarming. Housewives were laying in extra supplies of soap, candles, and canned goods, the routine reaction every time the Soviets flexed their muscles against the city. In some chain supermarkets business was as much as 50 percent above normal. A few people left hurriedly for the West, although airlines said that some seats were vacant on almost every flight.

The Communists sounded untypically restrained. Foreign Minister Andrei Gromyko, stopping in East Berlin, made the usual demand for negotiations toward the "withdrawal of the Western occupation troops," but he was careful not to link it to the Cuban situation. He said nothing about Cuba at all. Later it became known that the Russians stopped publication of a militant statement, actually an ultimatum, by DDR Premier Ulbricht, on Saturday, October 27, demanding "speedy" removal of the Allied troops.

In Washington, President Kennedy's Excom was now favoring a blockade of Cuba to keep Khrushchev's missile-bearing ships from landing on the island. But "blockade," the advisers thought, was an unfortunate word; it might invite another Soviet blockade of Berlin. "Quarantine" was better. As Ted Sorensen went to work on the nationally televised address the President would give at 7 P.M. on Monday, October 22, informing the public of the missile threat for the first time, he emphasized that the "quarantine" would not deny "the necessities of life as the Soviets attempted to do in their Berlin blockade of 1948." Yet we would resist "any hostile move anywhere in the world against the safety and freedom of people to whom we are committed—including in particular the brave people of West Berlin."

By the time the Excom's 10 A.M. meeting had gotten under way on Wednesday, the twenty-fourth, two Soviet ships were within sight of the quarantine line. In underground sites beneath the

Washington area, computers of the Damage Assessment Center stood ready to report which American cities had perhaps escaped attack. Key White House staff members had been issued special pink identification cards allowing them to be whisked out of the capital with the President and the First Lady.

A clash of naval forces seemed inevitable. So did retaliation by the Soviets against the American interference with the advancing missile fleet. West Berlin's moment of doom might have been at hand.

"We must expect that they will close down [take over] Berlin," said the President in a tone of resignation. "Make the final preparations for that." The advisers around the table understood. Kennedy wanted to double-check that enough food, gasoline, and cargo planes would be available to break another Berlin blockade.

It was the turning point. Moments later, at 10:25, a messenger handed John McCone a note. "Mr. President," said the CIA director, "we have a preliminary report which seems to indicate some Russian ships are stopping." The report could have many meanings. The Excom men waited. At 10:32 came confirmation. Six Soviet ships had stopped or turned back.

"We're eyeball to eyeball and I think the other fellow just blinked," said Secretary of State Rusk quietly to Mac Bundy.* It was true. Khrushchev was calling off his ultimate test of the American will.

Oleg Penkovsky, the colonel in Soviet intelligence who had slipped his Western controllers the missile manuals that enabled Kennedy's advisers to track the progress of Khrushchev's move into Cuba, may never have learned how he helped the West. He had been arrested in Moscow two days earlier, just after Kennedy went public with the story on television.

---

* During the tensest days of the Excom's deliberations, Rusk's behavior puzzled his colleagues even more than he had perplexed them during the Bay of Pigs operation. At first the Secretary favored a bomber strike against Cuba, then he lapsed into silence. Frequently he absented himself even from critical meetings, pleading other work. "One wonders what those 'other duties and responsibilities' were, to have been half so important as those they displaced," wrote Rusk's former boss and admirer Dean Acheson later. Acheson was disillusioned by his one-time acolyte, but not as much so as Attorney General Robert Kennedy. In 1965 RFK told Arthur Schlesinger that he thought Rusk "had a virtually complete breakdown mentally and physically," probably a hyperbolic outburst.

Penkovsky's end as a spy was as flamboyant as his brief career. When agents burst into his apartment, he had just enough time to send a telephonic emergency signal to his controllers at the American Embassy. By error or grandiosity, he decided to send the signal announcing an imminent Soviet attack.

Raymond L. Garthoff, one of the evaluators of Penkovsky's output in Washington, disclosing this episode in 1987, believed that the colonel tried to play Samson and wanted to bring down the temple on the world by igniting a nuclear war.

"Normally, such an attempt would have been feckless," Garthoff wrote. "But October 22, 1962, was not a normal day. Fortunately, his Western intelligence handlers, at the operational level, after weighing a dilemma of great responsibility, decided not to credit Penkovsky's final signal and suppressed it. Not even the higher reaches of the CIA were informed of Penkovsky's provocative farewell."*

The analysts of intelligence had triumphed over another collector in the field, but the arrest of Penkovsky, the collector, was a victory-in-defeat for him. Penkovsky may have been one of the reasons why Khrushchev backed down from Kennedy's quarantine. The disclosure of the knowledgeable colonel's betrayal probably frightened the Kremlin even more than the facts warranted.

"The arrest must have shaken the Soviet government greatly," Penkovsky's highest-ranking CIA handler told me. "After all it was possible that Penkovsky may have kept us informed of every detail of their planning since 1961."

In another aftereffect of the affair, Chief Marshal Varentsov, a "Hero of the Soviet Union" and Penkovsky's protector, was demoted to major general "for lack of vigilance" and dismissed from candidate membership of the Communist Party Central Committee.

Cuba, at last, was quiet. But in Berlin, little had changed.

**West Berlin,
Wednesday, June 26, 1963**

"How in the hell could they build that without our knowing about it in advance?" Tense and angry, President Kennedy was confiding

---

* Penkovsky pleaded guilty to charges of treason. He was convicted on May 11, 1963, after a brief trial, and shot shortly afterward.

Soviet intelligence officer Oleg Penkovsky (right) not only provided his Western controllers with the missile manuals that enabled the White House to track the progress of Khrushchev's move into Cuba, he also had advance knowledge of the Kremlin's plans to erect the Wall—though he never passed that knowledge along to his CIA handlers. Arrested by the KGB on October 22, 1962, Penkovsky was convicted of treason and shot.

his frustration to General Ted Clifton, the same military aide who had brought him the first news of the border closing during their Hyannis Port weekend nearly two years earlier. The question was unanswerable then; it still was.

Again acting as the ranking Berlin desk officer, the President had just climbed down the wooden stairs from the observation tower at the Brandenburg Gate. The view into East Berlin had been blocked by enormous vertical bloodred banners that the Communists had suspended between the columns of the Gate to keep Kennedy admirers from glimpsing their hero. But the Wall stood out, stark as a scar in its crass ugliness; like everyone viewing it for the first time, the President was shocked and furious.

His trip had been ruffling nerves from the start. General Clay, accompanying the presidential party, had advised against it altogether because he feared for the President's life. Kennedy had waved away such warnings fatalistically, as he always did, but he had issued orders not to allow his sister Jean Smith onto the observation tower. And before he made the climb, he broadened these instructions by telling Clifton, "Don't let any woman go up there with me!"

While it was clear that the East German authorities wanted to keep their citizens away from the handsome young President, they did not quite succeed. As Kennedy left the Brandenburg Gate, a guard handed him a bouquet of flowers with a note asking that it be given to him. It had been thrown over the Wall for him. And at his next stop, Checkpoint Charlie, a small group of East Berliners was visible beyond the barriers. They waved and cheered.

All along, the President had been determined to find the most convincing possible way to identify himself with the Berliners, to demonstrate his admiration for their steadfastness. After his arrival he was still searching for the right words. To his old friend and assistant Ken O'Donnell he said, "What was the proud boast of the Romans—'*Civis Romanus sum*'?* Send Bundy up here. He'll know how to say it in German."

And so the former Harvard dean did. He suggested, "I am a Berliner," and after the President asked for the German translation he took it down as "*Ich bin Berliner.*" Bundy corrected the President and then JFK got it right, "*Ich bin ein Berliner.*" Having written the line down, the President next asked Bundy, "Now tell

---

* "I am a Roman citizen"—Cicero.

me how to say in German, 'Let them come to Berlin.' " Again the National Security Council's ranking intellectual supplied the correct words.

After ordering the phrases typed phonetically into the manuscript of his speech—it came out as "ish bin ine bear-LEAN-ar"—the President set stubbornly about rehearsing the pronunciation. Facility at foreign languages had never been among his talents. His German sounded woeful and he knew it.

"Not very good, is it?" he asked Robert Lochner, the director of the RIAS radio station, who had been sent over as his interpreter.

Lochner grinned. So did Mayor Willy Brandt, who was watching the proceedings.

"I'm not as bad as my brother Bobby," Kennedy said. "I guess I ought to leave the foreign languages to Jackie."

But he didn't. He kept rehearsing until it was time to greet the people of Berlin. Three fifths of the population had poured into the streets, and most of them seemed to be jamming Rudolf Wilde Platz, where, in a more dangerous time two years before, they had sought assurances of support from Brandt and Lyndon Johnson. Some men of Kennedy's entourage had tears in their eyes as the throng set up its gigantic chant, "Ken-nah-dy, Ken-nah-dy, Ken-nah-dy!" It was the greatest reception of the President's career, absolutely overwhelming.

His response was inspired: "Two thousand years ago the proudest boast was *'Civis Romanus sum,'*" he began. "Today, in the world of freedom, the proudest boast is *'Ich bin ein Berliner.'*" Three times he then challenged the doubters who don't understand the difference between freedom and Communism; who say Communism is the wave of the future; who claim Communism makes for economic progress. And three times he shouted out his refrain, "Let them come to Berlin, *Lasst sie nach Berlin kommen!*"

The address was brief and built to a tumultuous and heartfelt climax: "All free men, wherever they may live, are citizens of Berlin," Kennedy called across the square, "and therefore, as a free man, I take pride in the words *'Ich bin ein Berliner.'*"

Nobody had any trouble hearing through his accent that time. The crowd's response was pure hysteria.

"Why didn't you tell me it was going to be like South Boston?" Kennedy asked his fellow Harvard man Jim O'Donnell at Tegel Airport on his departure that evening. O'Donnell just laughed.

"We'll never have another day like this one as long as we live," Kennedy told Ted Sorensen as Air Force One flew west over East

Germany. The President would leave a note about it to his successor, he said. On the envelope it would say: "To be opened at a time of some discouragement." In it, he would leave three words: "Go to Germany."

After the exhilaration came some second-thought reflection. Crowds were too irrational, the President mused to his staff historian Arthur Schlesinger, back in Washington. Perhaps German crowds were especially so. He thought that if he had ordered, "March to the Wall and tear it down," the mob would have marched. "The reception reminded him of Hitler," Schlesinger said.

Were these reactive afterthoughts only fleeting? No one will know. Less than five months later Kennedy was dead. In the White House after the funeral, Jacqueline Kennedy thanked Willy Brandt for having had Rudolf Wilde Platz renamed for John F. Kennedy. She told Brandt how often they had played the film of Jack's triumphant appearance there and of his identification as a Berliner.

Then Robert Kennedy escorted Brandt to his car.

"He loved Berlin," said Bobby.

PART V

FIRST CRACKS IN THE WALL

27

GETTING OUT:
THE TUNNEL BUILDERS

East Berlin,
October 1961

As soon as the barbed wire first appeared, tales of hair-raising escapes over the border—and even right through it—became Topic A in East Berlin. Meek, ordinary citizens felt motivated to become adventuresome escape artists. Desperation turned these perfectly respectable people into daredevils. You could never tell when one of your friends would suddenly prove capable of gambling with his life and the fate of his family.

Bärbel Grübel of Reinhardtstrasse experienced such a transformation one tranquil Sunday afternoon while taking the sun with her family in the Invaliden Park near the border. A couple of their acquaintance stopped at their bench to chat. They had known these people for years; the husband drove an ambulance for the hospital where Bärbel's father worked.

These were the mildest of plodders, so Bärbel and her parents were incredulous when they confided that they were planning to flee the country. Did Bärbel and her family want to go along? Coming from these people, the proposal sounded unbelievable. Bärbel's parents gave them no opportunity to relate by what scheme they would attempt to get away. They laughed the whole business off, leaving Bärbel to wonder how much of this parental response derived from incredulity and how much from the fear she knew so well and hated so much.

Two days later these friends, with their children, were citizens of West Berlin. They had piled into the father's ambulance. Closing in on the border, he pushed the gas pedal hard, turned on the emergency siren and his blue emergency light, and crashed through the control point at top speed before the guards figured out what was happening.

For East Germans of college age, the Wall was no great obstacle during those early days. Students of the Freie Universität (Free University) in West Berlin organized committees to rescue friends from the East. Scouting through rooming houses and dormitories, West Berlin students borrowed West German identity cards from non-Berliners as well as foreign students. Other West German or foreign students were recruited to visit East Berlin, using their own documents and tucking an extra set into underwear or shoes. If an East Berlin friend even vaguely resembled the photo on the borrowed papers, he or she would simply walk out. Sometimes a single document with a murky photo became the escape vehicle for a dozen students.

Inevitably, some of the young people were caught smuggling the extra documents over the border, whereupon the *Vopos* searched defectors for West German pocket litter, matches, cigarettes, clothing labels. Thereupon the defectors were outfitted with some such evidence of supposed West German residence. This made the system work reasonably well until late October. After that, controls were further tightened so that escape required luck or considerable organization, preferably both.

West Berlin,
Summer 1962

To help ensure absolute secrecy, the American TV executives had agreed never to show themselves at the underground site of the filming. But nobody had said anything against driving past the spot and aboveground. So at 11:30 P.M., when his two German cameramen were more than four hours overdue, Reuven Frank, the producer for NBC Television, could no longer tolerate his inactivity in his office across the street from West Berlin's posh Hotel Kempinski.

Picking the shabbiest NBC car he could find, Frank, a scrappy, streetwise little New Yorker, had an assistant drive him past the partially bombed-out five-story redbrick factory on Bernauer Strasse, the famous street of two nationalities where the houses on the East side lined the new East-West frontier. If his secret project had encountered serious trouble, police activity would have been noticeable. Reuven Frank instructed his driver not to slow down as they passed by.

The producer remembered the neighborhood well. This was where he had filmed with David Brinkley on August 13, 1961.

Bernauer Strasse now lay deserted. The factory loomed dark and silent. Frank was relieved.

His two cameramen, the brothers Peter and Klaus Dehmel, showed up at the NBC offices at 2 A.M. They were in a triumphant mood. Their delay had not been caused by any disaster. They brought along the climactic scenes showing the completion of Reuven Frank's tunnel, four months in the digging. While he had waited in suspense, twenty-one adults and five children had crawled through it from the DDR. On December 10, 1962, the ninety-minute documentary "The Tunnel" was shown on the network. Its ratings beat Lucille Ball's "I Love Lucy" hit show on the rival network, CBS.

In the United States, the Berlin tunneling was a short-lived curiosity. In Berlin, it was an industry that flourished as an open secret for more than three years after the Wall went up. The CIA's great Bill Harvey had been the pioneer of this specialty with his communications spy tunnel in the 1950s. The diggers of the 1960s were a very different breed.

Tunneling came into its own because the Wall did not fully accomplish the objective of Erich Honecker and his builders. The border still wasn't sealed tightly enough. Though the tide of escapees from the East had greatly diminished, the *pressure* to flee appeared not to have abated much. Occasional opportunities to scale or to break or swim through the border hurdles were far too few to accommodate even the most determined DDR citizens seeking exits. Ways had to be devised for organized *groups* to get out in sizable numbers.

The first, most obvious routes under the Wall ran through the municipal sewer system. Idealistic, politically motivated students were the principal labor force, especially students from abroad. They could move legally and effortlessly across the border, which helped them to round up potential refugees in the East and make arrangements for escapes. Student groups quickly acquired maps of the sewer routes and chased through the dark, odoriferous tunnels like the spies in Graham Greene's novel and movie *The Third Man*.

The underground freedom lasted only a few months. The Communists fitted heavy metal grilles across the routes and connected the barriers to sensitive alarms. Now tunnels had to be freshly excavated, a delicate task of engineering. Many of the crews, liberal arts students from the Free University, were hopeless amateurs, bedeviled by cave-ins, floods, or sloppy organization. Poor locations or other mistakes led to the discovery by DDR patrols of many tunneling attempts.

Reuven Frank's diggers were different. The group's motives were endearingly personal. It wanted to create an exit for a friend, an East Berlin student, Peter Schmidt, and his wife and baby; the Wall had cut Peter off from his West Berlin art classes. But the methods of Frank's tunnelers were coldly professional. These were engineering students from the Technical University. They also happened to be perfectionists. While they were at it, they wanted to build the perfect tunnel.

The darkly handsome leader, Luigi Spina, an Italian, believed that concealment would work best if he and his German crew became part of a relatively busy urban setting. He considered tunneling under Checkpoint Charlie (on reflection, the access from the East side was considered too dangerous) and underneath the Reichstag, the parliament (the route was too long).

Ironically, he settled on the notorious and fairly busy Bernauer Strasse, the site of fatal leaps where 1,300 windows had by now been sealed and grass and weeds grew out of the rarely used eastern sidewalk, the border. The distance of 140 yards from there to the basement of the dilapidated factory on the western side, where plastic swizzle sticks for cocktails were manufactured upstairs, seemed manageable. NBC's terminus was under the largely bombed-out and deserted ancient apartment house at Schönholzer Strasse 7, which ran parallel to Bernauer Strasse in East Berlin.

Burrowing fifteen feet underground, Spina and his crew had run out of money when the tunnel was one-quarter done. The financing of such projects was a chronic headache, because in those early, relatively romantic days, tunnelers usually did not take money from refugees. Much of the financing was ideologically motivated. Capital came from right-wing political parties, anti-Communist groups, and media organizations such as the Springer chain and magazines like *Stern*. Sometimes funds were secretly channeled to tunnel builders from West Berlin government agencies. In one case a West Berlin police inspector contributed a supply of pistols and ammunition; he had checked up on a tunnel operation and was scandalized by the poor protection the diggers had organized for themselves.

Spina had exhausted his covert underwriting resources because of his exquisite building standards. His tunnel measured three by three feet, and he equipped it with wooden floors and ceilings. The roof supports were held up by twenty tons of wooden beams. Lighting was as ample as a living room's. Compressed air was piped in to the diggers, who shoveled dirt around the clock in three shifts, eight volunteers at first, later twenty-one students. All of the excavated dirt—eventually it filled seven large basement rooms—was pulled out by electrically run carts, and there was a phone for dispatching each load.

"They're trying to build a subway!" yelled Reuven Frank, pained, when he was first approached for $50,000 of NBC's money.

Frank, who still produced the "Huntley-Brinkley Report" and would eventually become president of NBC News, had been shopping for a tunnel since before there were tunnels. Right after the Wall went up, he instructed Piers Anderton, the Berlin correspondent: "Give us anything you get on this problem of refugees trying to get out under these new conditions. Don't worry about getting any permission. Go ahead and do it. I'll pay the bill."

Anderton put out word that NBC was in the market for a tunnel. Spina learned this from an American student friend. Frank was ecstatic, and not only because he bargained Spina down to $12,000. The NBC man relished the frontier action of Berlin, had loved the city ever since his network opened a bureau there in the 1940s. In Berlin, the Cold War was no abstraction. Here the nonstop East-West confrontation produced what television lived on: action pictures, action film.

"Berlin was made for television," Frank shouted twenty years later, still glowing at the memory.

Though Frank was a fierce journalistic competitor, he was not of the old blood-and-blackmail Front Page school. He was careful. He did not want to drag NBC into an international incident. He did not want to get diggers or refugees killed; many were getting betrayed and murdered all along the border all the time. And he kept turning down unqualified volunteer workers.

He remembered: "All that summer I felt a little like the captain in *Dawn Patrol,* who kept telling the Major, 'You can't send those kids up in those crates.' " Also, he did not want his diggers to get discovered by rival networks, which were likewise on the lookout for tunnels to film. Tunnels were high drama. Every tunnel entrepreneur was a Scarlet Pimpernel.

Frank's security rules were drastic. Nobody was allowed to discuss the project on the telephone anywhere, including the United States. Only Frank's boss in New York knew what was happening, and the project used an "out of channels" accountant. No film left Berlin until Frank hand-carried the final product out of the city. Frank himself stayed in London until all segments were ready to be edited in September.

For weeks it looked as if the digging would never be finished. June was unusually cold and rainy. It poured for days at a time. Some of the tunnel's four-by-four support beams threatened to buckle. Suspicious puddles were forming along the floor. Late that month, when Secretary of State Rusk toured Berlin and made another of the hapless routine statements that the Wall had to go, the tunnel was half done but the diggers were pumping out eight thousand gallons of water in one week.

Then the water seeped in faster than they could pump it out. They investigated. A nearby West Berlin water main had broken. The diggers tipped off the municipal repair crews, but tunnel operations had to be suspended for three weeks while the main was being patched up. In July they were inundated by a second flood. This time forty thousand gallons of water had to be pumped out.

Most of the time, the diggers bent every second and every muscle just to dig and to sleep. Chipping and chipping away at the outer end of their shaft, now well under enemy soil, they were monopolized by their own narrowly claustrophobic universe. In August, the outer world intruded. Young Peter Fechter bled to death on the Wall and the incident upset the diggers deeply. They posted newspaper photos of Fechter on their tunnel walls. Then came bad news of friends, other students, who had been building other tunnels. They were captured by the East Germans.

August 1962, the time of the Wall's first birthday, was an evil month.

About midday on September 14, the German fiancée of one of

the Italian diggers—she was a West German, not a Berliner, and thus held valid papers—went to the East to round up the tunnel's original clients, Peter Schmidt and his family, as well as others who had been accepted for passage through the tunnel. Originally, nine such couriers had been recruited. Only this young woman hadn't chickened out.

At 3 P.M. the two Dehmel brothers left for the tunnel with their cameras to film the escapes. The pictures spoke volumes. One by one, the refugees clambered up a wooden ladder to the Bernauer Strasse basement, mud-splattered, their clothes torn, some barefoot because they had lost their shoes on their twelve-minute crawl. One of the diggers watched not only his wife climb to the surface but his baby, who had been born in prison and whom he had never seen.

The following Sunday, thirty-one more refugees used the tunnel, up to their faces in new floodwaters. Late that day, a final avalanche of water closed it forever.

Reuven Frank would always be proud that the film did not use a single interview. None was needed, and Frank knew it when he viewed the footage. He recalled, "We knew we had found what we had always insisted the best journalism should be: the specific event that illuminates the general condition of man, an action taking place in a defined and identifiable time and place which is an adventure of the human spirit."

The script was muted. The pictures did tell almost all. When Frank showed the footage to a producer friend in New York, the old showman looked at the refugees—some had their faces blacked out at their request because they had left relatives behind in the East—and said, "What must they be leaving to risk this?" Frank adopted that line for his script.

The showing of the film was announced for October 31, but it didn't happen. The State Department, finally aware of the film's existence, announced that it was "not in the national interest." The nervous West Berlin government had become upset. Nobody was more upset than Reuven Frank, although the latest world news had provided him with an excellent excuse for delaying the film. The Cuban Missile Crisis was on. It wouldn't do to inflame East-West tensions.

Furious, Frank wrote out his resignation and handed it to Bill McAndrew, his boss. He did not wish to continue in an industry that held such tenuous convictions. McAndrew persuaded him to wait a bit, and two weeks before Christmas the program was aired.

"The climax of the documentary was the arrival of many mothers, infants, and elderly persons on the free side of the Wall," said the review in *The New York Times*. "In their wet and mud-spattered clothing and in their expressions of relief there was a telling indictment of life under Communism. That they would take such risks and hardship to escape spoke for itself."

The *Times* had adapted Reuven Frank's favorite line. He had been right. This film needed no interviews. But the escape story was far from over. Berlin needed many more tunnels.

**West Berlin,
October 5, 1964**

They called him "Tunnel Fuchs." *Fuchs* means "fox" in German, and since everybody knew that foxes hide in burrows, and Wolfgang Fuchs was the founding father of the Berlin tunnel mavens, the nickname fit him perfectly. Fuchs was a large, comfortable, articulate soul. He could think and speak like a poet, and, miracle of urban miracles, he was utterly selfless.

Everyone in West Berlin knew and applauded Tunnel Fuchs—the police, the CIA, the press, which delighted in reporting his capers. The students who did his dirty work on their hands and knees absolutely worshiped him because he was not in the game for money. He wanted to help people in the East; they were neighbors.

When Fuchs began his seventh tunnel—it was his last and most ambitious dig—in the spring of 1964, the elaborate techniques refined by Reuven Frank's diggers for NBC Television two years earlier had become the standard of the "escape helper" profession. Money was still scarce. Sometimes the political parties could be talked into underwriting tunnels. Sometimes wealthy West Germans made contributions. This time Tunnel Fuchs was financed by a magazine, and he too was digging under Bernauer Strasse.

He had negotiated for the use of a bakery that was going to be demolished. Eventually its cellar and ground-floor rooms would all become solidly filled with the earth that Fuchs and his forty helpers excavated from 430 feet of tunneling. On the Eastern side, his couriers located a terminus under an apartment house on Strelitzer Strasse. Ironically, the entire block had been vacated because it was too close to the Wall and the DDR authorities were determined to discourage escapes.

Security had been further tightened over the years. Some border areas could be entered only with special permits. The *Stasi* had infiltrated more and more of its informers into the ranks of students. Rival diggers were giving tunnels away. Fuchs's very first tunnel had been literally blown up. His men were completing a scarecrow at the end of their shaft—they were going to pop it out of the exit as a shooting target during their final breakthrough into the East—when waiting East Germans blew them flat with a bomb.

These days, Fuchs and his volunteers were armed, and the workers were living on-site to reduce traffic around it. They had not lost their nerve, however. Working underground, Tunnel Fuchs always sang songs. And once their shovels hit the East Berlin border, the diggers followed the mocking example of the CIA's Bill Harvey and put up a sign saying YOU ARE LEAVING THE AMERICAN SECTOR.

Prospective DDR users of the tunnel had to be thoroughly known to Fuchs's men. Refugees were met by couriers at the Friedrichstrasse station. Code words were exchanged. Nobody was admitted into the tunnel until Fuchs gave the okay by radio transmitter from his post atop a roof on the Bernauer Strasse side.

No hitches developed, so on October 3 the first of fifty-seven mud-stained refugees crawled out. As Fuchs recalled, they looked "like mice." One of the diggers was reunited with a wife he had not seen for three years. Another had been digging every weekend for six months to free his brother.

"The marks of their knee prints in the tunnel floor looked like the ripples on a beach left behind by the receding tide," Fuchs told the British historian Anthony Kemp. "It does not matter what may become of me, I will never forget that. That is beautiful. . . ."

The scene changed tragically shortly after midnight on October 5. Four students, awaiting more refugees at the Eastern end of the tunnel, got careless. Two civilians appeared who did not know the password but looked scared enough to be legitimate refugees. Suddenly they were joined by a third man who was in uniform and brandished a machine pistol. One of the diggers fired a shot into the air to warn his friends. The soldier opened fire at the student, who aimed seven shots at the muzzle flash. All the students escaped, but the DDR soldier died. The East German press furiously charged he was murdered, and tunnel building as an industry, in effect, came to an end.

Escape fashions changed. The West German authorities, eager to make deals with the DDR for visitors' passes so that their citizens could visit relatives in the East legitimately, began to discourage tunnels and started prosecuting some escape helpers. The East Germans did their part by stepping up their demolition efforts; rows of houses and entire blocks of apartments facing the frontier vanished to make room for the rapidly expanding death strip. More streets near the Wall became a prohibited zone. Patrols were increased. "Unreliable" tenants were moved. Only Communist loyalists remained. Tunnels became rarities.

Tunnel Fuchs stayed in the escape business by switching methods. He was obsessed by the Wall. He owned a drugstore, later two, but for thirteen years his real business was to contrive new ways to outwit the East Germans at the border.

Applying the techniques of a famous British prison escape that he had read about, he mounted a hinged ladder onto a truck and pulled refugees across the Wall at a deserted spot in a cemetery. His Trojan Horse scheme to hoist refugees by crane in a bullet-proof water tank was foiled by the West Berlin police, increasingly eager not to provoke the authorities in the East. So Fuchs turned toward devising new schemes for making use of ordinary cars.

Among the diplomats accredited to East Berlin, he found an impecunious Syrian who owned no vehicle but yearned for a Mercedes. Fuchs presented him with a secondhand model. In exchange, the Syrian made numerous runs past Checkpoint Charlie carrying refugees in the trunk. Diplomatic immunity kept the border guards from searching the vehicle.

In the six months before his retirement from the tunnel vocation, Fuchs and his colleagues created a "supercar," which also made many border runs. "It was a large American vehicle that could be subjected to the most rigorous search, including virtual demolition," the historian Anthony Kemp learned. "The hiding place was most uncomfortable. The car still exists and is in honorable retirement at a secret location. . . ."

Fuchs himself likewise withdrew from the game with body and respectability intact, a rare ending for an escape helper. His whereabouts and his unreconstructed views were no secret, however. In his drugstore he enjoyed reminiscing about the neighbors, hundreds of them, whom he had rescued over the years. "It enriched our lives," he said.

28

PUNCHING HOLES IN THE WALL: THE TRADING IN BODIES BEGINS

The scene on the Autobahn was charged with drama, and attorney Wolfgang Vogel of East Berlin was adept at making the most of such occasions, especially when he was the star. The deserted countryside and the dilapidated state of the DDR bus at the roadside would have made John le Carré feel at home. Only the worn, anxious faces of the twelve male bus passengers in ill-fitting clothes would have given a camera a hint that something out of the ordinary was about to happen.

Of course there was no camera. The transaction was a state secret, and everybody knew that the DDR was exemplary at keeping state secrets. Besides, in these open fields near the villages of Wartha and Herleshausen, close to the isolated East-West border post in the DDR's rural southwest corner, no one was around who could give anything away.

On this hot, sunny day, August 14, 1964, Vogel's Mercedes came along as scheduled and stopped behind the bus. Vogel and his partner, attorney Jürgen Stange of West Berlin, got out and climbed into the ancient vehicle, where Vogel, his chest out and looking immensely pleased, made a little speech to the twelve tense passengers. In the ensuing years, invariably trailed by his Western echo, the little Jürgen Stange, Vogel would make the same trip and the same speech dozens of times. But today was for history. The passengers were the first political prisoners ransomed by the West German government under a just-completed agreement. Progress had been difficult and the outcome had looked uncertain. The suspense never ceased, it never would, not in all the many years to come. Any whim on the part of either of the participating governments could derail Vogel's work.

"The fact that you are sitting in this bus is a miracle," Vogel told his small audience solemnly. "But the real miracle will happen when it repeats itself."

He warned the discharged prisoners that they would have to maintain absolute silence about the circumstances of their release. Then Stange spoke up, welcoming the men on behalf of his government, and the bus, without the lawyers, drove off to the refugee reception center at Giessen, north of Frankfurt.

Why lavish so much ceremony upon a fait accompli? Surely some anonymous police or customs officials could have supervised the transfer of the prisoners. And why did the two governments insist on acting out the charade of secrecy? Did they really believe they could bury these dealings forever, especially since the release of hundreds and then thousands was contemplated?

Vogel knew. The two governments, each troubled by ideological and moral reservations, were as nervous as ever. They still didn't trust each other, really wanted not to have anything to do with each other, treated each other like patients with communicable diseases. As a further complication, a new team was running the Bonn government.

The Minister of All-German Affairs, a noisy, egocentric Christian Democrat named Erich Mende, was surrounded by conservative diehards known as "concrete heads." Any dealings with "Ulbricht's people" were rejected by these advisers as downright sinful and, worse, as dangerous politics. The voters would scream bloody murder if they found out.

Mende did not think so. The voters would respect a minister who broke blameless citizens out of enemy prisons. They would recognize that mud was apt to fly in dealings with the Communists. What of it? The men in East Berlin held the keys to the prison cells. If one got stained by a little dirt, so what? The voters would understand. They would appreciate any gains their government could wrestle from the Communists. The *Passierschein* agreement of December 1963, providing for special temporary passes allowing West Berliners to visit East Berlin, was a good example of progress that was possible.

To free prisoners, the DDR would furnish lists of its needs—butter, coffee, fruit, medicines, machine tools—and the names of inmates it was most eager to dismiss. The Bonn government would bring to the table lists of people it most wanted to have released and a credit, at roughly 40,000 marks per prisoner, to be maintained in a special account with a Lutheran charity, the Diakonisches Werk, in Stuttgart. The church, in effect, would launder the credits. Vogel and Stange would administer the details.

Only twenty minutes were needed to complete the arrangement when Minister Mende finally met with Wolfgang Vogel for the first time in the ministry's West Berlin office on June 12, 1964. Vogel announced that he was instructed by his principal, Josef Streit of the DDR Justice Ministry, to offer the release of an astonishing number of prisoners: 650. Mende was impressed by Vogel. He would later write that he did not mind working this odd Communist "who gave the impression of a British diplomat."

The twelve bus passengers shepherded by Vogel and Stange from East to West in August may have maintained the silence that was asked of them. But in the free society of the West Germans the secrecy couldn't last. On August 26, less than two weeks after the first bus arrived in Giessen, a veiled leak was dropped on the public. Surprisingly, it appeared in *Die Welt,* the flagship of a man sworn to keep the secret, the passionate press lord Axel Springer, who had been a key link in the chain that got the entire process started. His insider status may explain why the story was devoid of embarrassing details. It disclosed that "numerous political prisoners" had been freed by the DDR but claimed that it was done by way of an "exchange." No numbers were given, no payments were mentioned.

Other newspapers followed with similar bland items. It was nothing to get excited about and nobody did.

On October 7, Joachim Bölke decided that the voters deserved to be treated like adults. Hypertense, bulky, and chain-smoking, Bölke was editor in chief of *Der Tagesspiegel,* an independent Berlin daily of enviable intellectual standards, originally licensed by the American occupation authorities. Editor or not, he had never stopped cultivating the prime asset of a street reporter, his sources. Bölke maintained superb sources in Bonn, and they were talking to him and to his staff.

In a front-page editorial, Bölke pulled the money rabbit out of his hat. "In effect," he wrote carefully, the Bonn government had "stooped" to pay "a high *Kopfgeld*" (head money) for every prisoner released by the Communists.

That was major news, and *Kopfgeld* was a highly charged buzz word. The news agencies picked it up and made inquiries in Bonn. Nobody would confirm the truth, but former minister Rainer Barzel, now chairman of the Christian Democrats in the parliament, offered a revealing argument for silence. His words could just as well have come from Wolfgang Vogel and Jürgen Stange; all were eager not to offend the functionaries in East Berlin so that business would not suffer.

"The other side," Barzel said, had to be "given the opportunity to save face."

What? Editor Bölke was outraged. He was a quiet writer, some said a bit pedantic, but what was this nonsense about letting the Communists save face? Surely that was not *his* responsibility. His job was to expose the facts to the public without artifice. On October 9 he wrote that he viewed the deal as a "dreadful slave trade"; his government had no business "descending to the level of the opposition."

He did not attack the laudable purpose of liberating innocent prisoners. He questioned whether it was the business of government to use public money, and secretly at that. Bölke called attention to the solution recently engineered by the Americans for dealing with Castro's offer to ransom dissident Cubans taken prisoner at the battle of the Bay of Pigs. An exchange for money and medicines had been arranged, but the United States government had not dealt with Castro. It had appointed a private negotiator on behalf of a private fund-raising committee. And as Bölke's editorial noted with emphasis, the Americans had made the deal public from the outset.

The politicians in Bonn could have followed that example, but no, so Bölke thundered, they felt called upon to "protect Ulbricht's face and prestige." Ridiculous!

"In the end," the editor charged, "such a policy is no policy at all. It robs us of all political and ethical legitimacy. That is why each of us has to have the opportunity to know what is happening."

Lofty words, and they suited Bölke's *Tagesspiegel* audience, a thoughtful minority. His thundering produced very little agreement elsewhere. The main response came from Springer's mass-circulation daily, *Berliner Morgenpost*. Springer had ordered the comment personally and it was venomous. Wolfgang Vogel loved it and framed it for his office walls.

Some newspapers were publishing too much about the freeing of prisoners from the DDR, Springer bristled. The majority view had a loftiness of its own: "Our readers will understand when we —in the interest of political prisoners who are still awaiting release and regardless of the behavior of other media—will maintain silence in this matter."

And then the dagger punch line: "There are news that kill while they pretend to inform."

In the manner of politicians trapped, the men in Bonn sought to defend themselves of further odious reports, especially charges that the prices placed on the heads of the prisoners differed, differed widely: that 40,000 marks* was paid for a blue-collar prisoner while the ransom for scientists and doctors ran into hundreds of thousands. Always unconvincingly denied, these stories would never die.† Their implications of elitism were political poison.

No, no, one flat price applied for all—so Minister Mende insisted in a vain defense that earned him contempt from his nominal political ally, Axel Springer. The publisher appointed him "Minister for Gossip," and the *Berliner Morgenpost* issued what turned out to be the final majority report on the morality of the ransoming arrangement: "These releases, it must be clearly said, do not carry the stamp of a trade in slaves. The released prisoners do not go into slavery but into freedom. . . ."

The complexities of exchanging political prisoners for value received had begun to take shape in the summer of 1963. Ludwig Rehlinger, who ran the Berlin bureau of the All-German Ministry,‡ was in charge on behalf of the West German government, yet the historic negotiation that was hanging in the balance was out of

---

* Inflation spares no one. By 1988 the price per head had risen to 90,000 marks.

† In 1984, the Springer newspaper chain would report that the West Germans paid 180,000 *dollars* to free the niece of Willi Stoph, chairman of East Germany's Council of Ministers, after she and her family took refuge in the West German Embassy at Prague.

‡ In deference to the DDR's yearning for autonomy, the name was changed to Inner German Ministry in 1969, which suggested a modification of the West German claim to the East German territory, at least semantically.

East Berlin attorney Wolfgang Vogel *(left)* and his West Berlin associate Jürgen Stange *(below left)* pioneered and monopolized what came to be known as *Freikauf*—the grotesque business of exchanging East German political prisoners for hard Western cash.

Though troubled by the morality of *Freikauf*, Ludwig Rehlinger *(below)*, the dapper chief of the Berlin bureau of the All-German Ministry told his superiors, "We've got to try it."

his control, and that made him nervous in the extreme. The deal was dubious on several grounds, he believed; even its opening phase offended his Prussian rectitude.

He had kept weighing the risks, immediate and long-term, ever since his minister had telephoned him from Bonn. The facts looked unappetizing. Everything depended on two lawyers about whom Rehlinger knew next to nothing and whom he did not trust. Large sums of public money had to be handed to strangers in cash without receipts. Any hint of a leak to the public would have triggered a crisis for the government, could conceivably have led to its fall.

Silk-haired, meticulous in manner and speech, flawlessly tailored, Rehlinger was an unusual civil servant: his old-fashioned sense of responsibility had not deadened his enterprise. A born Berliner, forty, he was a lawyer, definitely not a figure who looked at home on the grimy platform of the Lehrter elevated station in a dilapidated section of downtown, too close to the Wall, with its deadening effect on neighborhood life.

It was the money that troubled Rehlinger the most—180,000 marks (about $100,000) in bank notes that produced a prominent bulge in the Din-A1 manila envelope he was clutching. Officials like Rehlinger were not in the habit of carrying cash, unaccompanied, to train stations. It seemed an illicit act, and Rehlinger recalled that in the first conversation he had about the money with his chief, Rainer Barzel, Minister of All-German Affairs, the two of them had sounded like bank robbers.

"I've got to get the money," Rehlinger said.

"How are we going to do that?" the Minister asked.

"You'll have to write a chit for it."

"And you'll get it from the cashier people?"

"They're going to drop dead," Rehlinger predicted.

They almost did and Rehlinger felt uncomfortable ever since. What if someone were to rob him on his way to the Lehrter station? What if the deal was actually a plot by some DDR officials to swindle the West Germans out of money? Was he justified in blithely handing the envelope to Jürgen Stange, thirty-six, the West Berlin lawyer he was to meet on the platform?

The very fact that Rehlinger had chosen this particular train station for the transaction suggested that he had little faith in the small, pink Herr Stange and his every-ready smile. Lehrter Bahnhof was the last stop in the West. At the next station, Friedrichstrasse, a little more than half a mile to the East, the DDR border authorities were in control. Curving gently, the track ran above the Spree River and the Wall. Short of a suicidal plunge, there was no way for Stange to leave the train and disappear with the cash.

Nevertheless, Rehlinger was ridden by doubts. He had never heard of Stange until Minister Barzel had phoned with the bombshell news that the DDR might be willing to release as many as ten thousand of its political prisoners, some of them jailed since 1945. Nor was Rehlinger then familiar with the name of Wolfgang Vogel, the attorney who had offered himself as middleman on behalf of the DDR and now was supposedly waiting at Friedrichstrasse station to receive Stange and the Bonn government's money.

Most distasteful of all was the concept that Rehlinger was being asked to activate: *Freikauf*. Eventually the term would become commonplace in post-Wall Germany. Before the Wall went up it was rarely used. Literally, it meant "to buy someone's freedom." Its unadorned meaning was less benign: "ransom." The DDR was demanding *Kopfgeld,* head money, 45,000 marks per prisoner being the price on which Vogel and Stange agreed after intensive wheedling and repeated consultations with their principals. The concept was reminiscent of the Nazis, who had traded the freedom of Jews in concentration camps for hard foreign currency.

In the current pragmatic era of the Cold War, the *Freikauf* notion appeared somewhat more respectable. Certainly the initial idea could not have come to Minister Barzel from a more eminent source. Barzel was a Christian Democrat, a member of Chancellor Konrad Adenauer's conservative government, and Axel Springer, the conservative media baron, had a mighty voice in Adenauer's circle. So when Springer phoned Barzel and said he wanted to talk about a matter that could be discussed only in person, Barzel left at once for Springer's headquarters in Hamburg.

That same afternoon, in Springer's thirteenth-floor office, the publisher related a tale that at first struck the politician as bizarre. Springer said he had had a visit from an unknown young West Berlin attorney, Jürgen Stange, who claimed he could negotiate the release of political prisoners for cash. Springer was enthusiastic and hoped that Barzel would act without interposing negative bureaucratic legalisms.

For his part, the publisher would guarantee silence. The scheme was obviously a potentially explosive political issue. Such news did not belong in media controlled by a publisher for whom ideology

—he viewed it as the national interest—rated as the overriding concern.

Barzel's head began at once to whirl with questions. His career was at stake. He was thirty-eight, aggressive, and ambitious—was such a scheme politically defensible in the event of a press leak? How could he hide the money in his budget? What would his associates say? What about Adenauer, his political godfather? And what about the fundamental issue, the morality of trading in human flesh?

Back in Bonn, Minister Barzel's senior staff man, State Secretary Franz Thedieck, a seasoned old-timer, was horrified. "*Menschenhandel!* Trading in humans!" he exclaimed. "A horrible system! And which prisoners are we to ransom? Who would choose them?"

The crusty Chancellor Adenauer nevertheless approved the deal by phone from his vacation in Candenabbia, and Barzel convinced himself that humanity would be best served by freeing prisoners who were innocent of true offenses. Their freedom would be a defeat for the "suppression machinery of the DDR dictatorship," or so went the Minister's argument and the opposition Social Democratic leadership agreed. Barzel hoped that his Berlin man, Rehlinger, would also go along. Rehlinger was cautious but he got things done.

"What do you think?" Barzel asked him on the phone after summarizing the proposition and the cast of principal characters.

Rehlinger weighed his scruples on the spot. It was a filthy business, no doubt about that. But didn't the moral flaw lie with those who did the selling? And wasn't it his government's absolute duty to do its best to get those innocent citizens out of prison?

"We've got to try it," he told Barzel, and shortly before Good Friday of 1963 the two officials met with Jürgen Stange at the Hotel Deutscher Kaiser in Munich. The smiling little attorney reported that the DDR had asked for lists of those prisoners in whose release Bonn was most interested. The Communists also demanded absolute secrecy for an indefinite period. Stange was to let Vogel know whether the West would agree to go to the bargaining table. What was the Minister's decision?

"Get moving!" Barzel told Stange, and then, in Berlin, it became Rehlinger's job to spend weeks poring over the names of twelve thousand political prisoners known to the West German government. It was a curious bag of cases: farmers who had resisted collectivization; persecuted church and union members; students and university professors; Social Democrats who had resisted their party's forced marriage with the Communists; Jehovah's Witnesses; spies; and escape helpers.

Menschlichkeit, humaneness, was the cause that motivated the Adenauer government, concern for these helpless fellow Germans who were cut off *drüben,* over there, on the other side; no doubt of that. But another factor was not lost on the politicians. Those twelve thousand citizens behind bars were, for the most part, not waiting out their sentences in a vacuum. Most of them had relatives, friends, and other well-wishers in West Germany who were trying to get their loved ones out, who kept many cases alive by pressuring legislators and government and private aid organizations, and by hiring lawyers. It would have been foolish to ignore these supplicants; they were voters.

"Playing God" was Rehlinger's description of the sifting job he had to do. He hated the power that had been assigned to him, and his minister's exacting instructions turned the selection process into a series of judgments worthy of Solomon. The first list had to be a masterpiece, Barzel decided. Future prisoner releases would depend on its success.

No name could go on the initial list if its inclusion would suggest to the DDR that Bonn had secret reasons for wishing to recapture that particular prisoner. No noisemaker should be picked who was likely to ask a lot of questions and give press conferences after his liberation. And the selected prisoners had to come from several penal institutions, not just one, so that Barzel and Rehlinger could be certain they were dealing with the DDR government, not with a cabal that had gone into business for its own benefit.

Similarly, Vogel's principals in East Berlin wondered whether they were about to blunder into a partnership with dubious Western enterprisers. Was the ingratiating lawyer Stange really an official representative of the Federal Republic in Bonn? It seemed too weighty a role for such a bouncy, eager little figure, a man without stature or record of achievement.

How to endow Stange with credibility? Minister Barzel pondered the problem. Stange wanted his authority spelled out in writing. Barzel refused. The two Germanys were literally not on talking terms; even phone calls between East and West Berlin were not possible. And as for written communications, these were expressly out of bounds and reserved exclusively to the Allied occupation powers.

So the imaginative Barzel hit on primitive but effective demonstration of his official involvement. He took to strolling periodically up and down Kurfürstendamm in the company of Jürgen Stange. Communist agents lurked everywhere in West Berlin. Barzel figured that it would suffice for him to be thus seen with his lightweight representative cozily in tow. Word would get back to the right places in the DDR, and so it did.

The distrust that pervaded the post-Wall relationship between the Germanys—contempt was a more accurate term—would not begin to diminish for another decade. It was extraordinary: two countries, united by language, culture, and tumultuous past, treating each other like thieves, each needing an obscure private attorney to substitute for the performance of official functions, to supply, in effect, a miniature secret government.

Ludwig Rehlinger, handing Stange the manila envelope with the 180,000 marks at Lehrter station, took satisfaction in just one aspect of the deal up to this hour. He had asked for delivery in advance. Four "politicals" had already been released by the Communists, the first having been a carpenter, imprisoned since 1945, who broke down in tears when he arrived in West Berlin and kept demanding why he, he of all people, had been privileged to be freed ahead of all others. Having delivered four prisoners, the DDR demanded payment before releasing more.

Stange got on the Friedrichstrasse train, in those days chronically near-empty. He, too, felt all but crushed by the responsibility of being the carrier of such a ridiculously large amount of cash. All went well. In the police booth at Friedrichstrasse, Vogel awaited him with a group of officials from the DDR Justice Department.

"It was the longest ten minutes of my life," Stange would reflect, yet the importance of his achievement, much less its long-term implications, had not dawned on him. Neither he nor his partners, Rehlinger and Vogel, would have taken seriously the idea that the *Freikauf* procedure that they had just initiated would be institutionalized and still thriving in the late 1980s, having by then benefited nearly twenty-five thousand "politicals" at a cost to Bonn of well over one billion marks (about $600 million).*

. . .

---

* In the official budget, the *Freikauf* item was described as "support of special aid measures of an all-German character."

Other secret moves to reach some small measure of accommodation between East and West had been afoot for more than a year before Rehlinger's appearance at Lehrter station. The first feeler was doomed by West German politics.

In the spring of 1962, with the Wall less than a year old, West Berlin Mayor Willy Brandt called in one of his assistants, Dietrich Spangenberg, and said he wanted to do something about some of the family tragedies caused by the Wall. West Berliners were looking to their mayor for help in cases involving deaths, marriages, and alleged political offenses. Brandt said he had heard of a West Berlin attorney, Jürgen Stange, who might be helpful. Stange was supposed to have connections in the East. Spangenberg should look him up.

Spangenberg called upon Stange, who smiled and bobbed his round, fleshy little head and said, yes, he had been doing certain business with a Wolfgang Vogel of East Berlin. Vogel would be unusually qualified to help Mayor Brandt. A devout Catholic, Vogel was well connected with politically influential church officials of the West as well as of the East and possessed relevant experience. In February 1962 he had presided over the most spectacular spy exchange of postwar times. His opposite number had been a prosperous, politically well-connected Catholic attorney from Brooklyn, James B. Donovan, who remembered Vogel better than it suited him.

Making his way to seek out Vogel in East Berlin for the first time, Donovan glanced apprehensively over his shoulder.

"At such moments," he wrote later, "one is comforted by the thought that there is no point in worry since there is no place to run."

Vogel's office "seemed strangely situated for a supposedly prominent lawyer in any country." The neighborhood of Friedrichsfelde was remote, dingy, and residential. The hallways were barely lighted, and Donovan knew that the two people who walked behind him were not who they said they were.

The young East German woman, who too frequently staged obviously fake attacks of sobbing and asked too many knowledgeable questions, couldn't be his client's "daughter." The client's shabbily dressed "cousin," who refused to walk ahead of Donovan up the dark steps, kept clenching his very powerful-looking hands. He obviously represented the East German police. The Brooklyn lawyer classified him as "an Otto the strangler type."

The case that had lured Donovan to Friedrichsfelde was no shabby matter. His allegedly East German client, Colonel "Rudolf Abel" (it was never revealed whether any of his many aliases was authentic), was serving thirty years for espionage in a Texas federal prison. Abel spoke five languages, including perfectly idiomatic English, and had spent eight years in the U.S. as a much admired artist, photographer, and amateur gourmet chef. The U.S. government unmasked him as a Soviet master spy who dispatched microdot messages to Moscow in the bindings of *Better Homes and Gardens*.

Whatever secrets Abel ferreted out for the Soviets were never disclosed, but his star status became apparent when Moscow showed interest in exchanging him for a most celebrated personage, Francis Gary Powers, the American pilot shot down in 1959 from 60,000 feet over Soviet territory, where he was spying in one of the CIA's U-2 aerial reconnaissance planes. The incident set off a sufficient tumult to torpedo a summit conference scheduled between President Eisenhower and Premier Khrushchev.

Donovan, Abel's court-appointed defense counsel, was contacted by Vogel in a "Dear Colleague" letter accompanied by a $3,500 bank draft, earnest money toward Donovan's fee.*

Purportedly negotiating as private lawyers, Vogel and Donovan were actually representing the Kremlin and the White House. And Donovan, who had a flair for the dramatic and harbored political ambitions in New York State, enacted his part in the charade with the bravado of Humphrey Bogart facing down Sidney Greenstreet.

The bulldog-faced Donovan, an intense chain-smoker out of Harvard Law, had another reason for taking himself and his James Bond status very seriously. He had experience for the role. As a Navy commander, he had spent World War II as general counsel

---

* Donovan received a total of $10,000, which he divided up as gifts among Fordham, Columbia, and Harvard universities. In December of 1962 he volunteered his horse-trading skills again and obtained from Fidel Castro the freedom of all prisoners taken in the Bay of Pigs invasion in exchange for $2.9 million cash and $11 million in medical supplies and baby food collected from private American sources with help from the Kennedy brothers. The final $1 million was raised by a personal note from General Clay, the hero of Berlin, then acting as a member of the Cuba rescue committee.

to General William (Wild Bill) Donovan, no relation, the gung ho founder and spy master of the OSS (Office of Strategic Services), predecessor of the CIA.

En route to East Berlin to see Vogel, Donovan had recalled the heady war days when he traveled with his namesake, the general, in spy-infested Europe. Still vigilant, Donovan had lately registered as "Mr. Dennis" at the Claridge during a stopover in London. He knew the hotel well. In the war he received spies in Wild Bill's suite there.

Hunting down Vogel in East Berlin, Donovan was entitled to feel lonely. His government "contact" in Washington, whom he never identified further, had wanted to send him to the East accompanied by an American diplomat fluent in Russian and German, since Donovan spoke neither. The coming of the Berlin Wall caused a change in plans.

The Wall had made Washington jumpy. "There have been too many incidents," said Donovan's contact, using a gentle euphemism in alluding to the chronic shootings. Nobody could be certain that the Communists would really open a crack in the Wall, even for such celebrities as Powers and Abel. Donovan began to wonder whether he was embarking on a kamikaze venture.

"If anything went wrong on your mission and an American Mission officer were involved, it would be diplomatically embarrassing for our government," the contact said. "After all, we don't recognize East Germany." Then came the clincher. "You will have no official status at all." Donovan responded with a quizzical look, whereupon the contact assured him that if anything "went wrong," Washington would take a very serious view "on the highest level."

"Bob,"* Donovan's American handler in Berlin, was no more encouraging. He said conditions at the border were arbitrarily var-

---

* "Bob" was actually the CIA base chief, Bill (El Supremo) Graver, and he too relished the power of his functions in the stage management of the affair. Since CIA rules kept Graver from traveling to East Berlin to negotiate the preliminaries with Vogel, a State Department officer, Francis J. Meehan, was detailed as the advance man. Meehan was much impressed with Graver. They were sitting in the CIA man's office one day, and upon hearing a plane outside, Graver cocked an ear and announced, "That's Abel's plane." Meehan believed him. El Supremo usually had that effect on people.

ied by the Eastern authorities day by day. Sometimes visitors were stripped; sometimes they were endlessly delayed; sometimes nobody was permitted through. Despite a raging snowstorm and his sinister forebodings, Donovan's border crossing via the elevated S-Bahn at Friedrichstrasse station was uneventful. Deciding to buy a round-trip ticket, he even ventured a wisecrack.

"For good luck," he told Bob.

Donovan had been in East Berlin in 1945 as a Navy officer and it looked unchanged: "The streets were strangely deserted and seemed filled with an oppressive fear." And at his first scheduled stop, the Soviet Embassy on Unter den Linden, the reception was one of unconcealed suspicion.

"This is very good work," said the tall Russian with rimless spectacles in the manner of an expert unmasking an art forgery; Donovan had handed him, in addition to his professional calling card, another card, identifying him as vice president of the New York City Board of Education.

In impeccable English, the Soviet diplomat introduced himself as Ivan Alexandrovich Shishkin, second secretary of the embassy. Donovan assumed he was dealing with a high KGB officer, and it became clear that Shishkin also had a masquerade role to play.

He was, he said, merely taking pity upon the unfortunate "relatives" of "this East German," Abel. Colonel Abel's fate actually rested in the hands of Wolfgang Vogel. Shishkin insinuated that he knew this lawyer only via hearsay; it would be highly improper for a Soviet official to do business with such a "private" East German attorney.

Fed up with all the posturing, Donovan held Vogel in disdain before he ever encountered him, in the tiny but comfortably furnished Friedrichsfelde law office. Instead of finding an oily Sidney Greenstreet, the Brooklyn negotiator was taken aback when he faced an extroverted, elegant figure with a quick smile and a smooth, cosmopolitan manner. Vogel's gray flannel suit was plainly a hand-tailored import, his silk tie and white-on-white shirt also of Western origin.

"He looked like many successful sales executives in the United States," Donovan reported later—a most incongruous presence in the Friedrichsfelde setting. (Vogel spoke no English, however; Colonel Abel's plainclothesman "cousin" interpreted.)

Donovan had become suspicious that he was being set up for failure. The thicket of details still blocking the Powers-Abel exchange would not yield. Vogel explained the impasse with a frankness both disarming and just about unheard of in the East.

"What is happening is a competition between Soviet Russia and East Germany, a sort of wrestling match for obtaining the release of Abel," he said.

"Nonsense," Donovan blustered. "If Shishkin told the Attorney General of East Germany to walk across this floor on his hands, he'd get down and try."

Both lawyers were right in these assessments. But each was wrong in sizing up the other. It was a collision of egos. Vogel underestimated Donovan as a melodramatic stuffed shirt. Donovan underestimated Vogel as a mindless Soviet puppet. The American did not know that this East German was a high-wire virtuoso, a survivor of intrigues that had brought down many other careers in purges typical of Communist regimes during the postwar years.

Vogel had barely escaped with his professional neck intact after Soviet tanks broke up the workers' revolt of 1953. The Justice Minister wanted to grant East German workers the right to strike. The disgusted party leaders placed him under house arrest for this weakness. Vogel, who headed the ministry's Criminal Department (Department I), was in danger. His immediate superior went to prison for fifteen years, Vogel being told that the fellow spied for the CIA. Vogel was fired, but his skill at befriending the right people enabled him to turn the disaster into a lifelong bonanza.

He had made himself the protégé of a rising star in the ministry, Josef Streit.* Streit thought it would be handy to have a personal (and vulnerable) alumnus available in private practice to handle delicate "intra-German" conflicts. At Streit's "suggestion," Vogel in 1954 became one of a handful of Eastern attorneys who were not

---

* Streit's career curve is illuminating. An apprentice printer, he joined a Young Communists group at age fourteen. After spending most of the Hitler years in the Dachau and Mauthausen concentration camps, he became a lay judge, held a succession of posts in the Justice Department, and was "elected" National Attorney General for the DDR in 1962, two weeks before the Abel-Powers exchange; he still held the job in 1986, at the age of seventy-five. He did not receive his law degree until 1965.

full-time government employees. In 1957, he was licensed to practice before the West German courts as well, a privilege that he shared with only two other lawyers. So when Shishkin asked Streit in 1959 for someone to rescue the "East German" Colonel Abel from American prison, Vogel was the logical choice.

It was Vogel's debut as middleman licensed to traffic above all walls. Even then, he played the role with charm and skill. Donovan finally got him together with Shishkin in the Soviet Embassy, where Vogel introduced himself as if he had never met the Russian. The difficulties over details promptly melted away. The East Germans even threw in a bonus: they would release another American accused of spying.*

Shishkin and Donovan were standing by at the Glienicke Bridge border crossing at 8:20 A.M. on Saturday, February 10, 1962, ready to trade Abel for Powers. While waiting for telephone confirmation that Vogel had, as arranged, released Pryor at Checkpoint Charlie, Donovan could not resist a farewell jibe at the fellow professional whose importance he so underrated.

"Perhaps Vogel is arguing with Pryor about his legal fees," Donovan told Shishkin with a smile. "This could take months."†

It took only a few minutes.

Twenty-five years later Vogel would still be trading spies across the same bridge‡ and he would function as middleman in East-West trades involving tens of thousands of ordinary citizens as well.

---

* This second Vogel client was Frederic L. Pryor, a Yale student who drove around East Berlin in a red VW bug researching his master's thesis on the DDR economy and then proudly showed it to his Communist sources. The *Stasi* decided that he had done his job so thoroughly that he had to be a CIA spy and threatened him with the death penalty. When it developed that Pryor was the son of politically influential parents, who came from Michigan to West Berlin to pressure the authorities, he became too much of a nuisance to his jailers. The CIA was also annoyed at Pryor. It didn't know him and considered it insulting to be accused of employing such an ingenuous spy.

† Donovan eventually lost his race for the United States Senate and died of a heart attack. Powers died in an aviation accident. Abel became an honored senior instructor of Soviet spies in Moscow.

‡ The Glienicke Bridge, renamed "Bridge of Socialist Unity," occupies an exclusive status in the bewildering system of ten Berlin border crossings designated by

the DDR authorities partly to facilitate traffic but mostly to assert their authority. The bridge is reserved for official traffic of the occupying powers. The Friedrichstrasse S-Bahn station handles pedestrians of all categories. Checkpoint Charlie does the same for foreign pedestrians and motorists. Of the rest, some serve only West German visitors from the Federal Republic, and the others are for local residents. Even many sophisticated West Berliners have never learned to untangle this labyrinth.

29

WHEN GOVERNMENTS WON'T TALK: THE CASE OF THE TWO LAWYERS

Vogel's partner, Jürgen Stange, was not in fact without qualifications for the delicate role that was thrust upon him.

Struggling to build up a law practice in West Berlin, he had represented students of the Free University who found themselves in legal difficulties when they helped East Berlin students escape through sewers and tunnels and by illegal identification documents. He had proved himself a relentless, unflappable negotiator who clung to his causes like a terrier attached to a shoe. Most valuably, Stange possessed a passport issued in West Germany, not in Berlin. That was another of the subtle nuances that made Berlin unique. Unlike other West Berlin attorneys, Stange could pass through the Wall unhindered.

It was late in 1961 that Stange and Vogel began the odd collaboration that was to endure for more than twenty roller-coaster years. While they invariably represented fiercely combative clients, East and West, they came to behave like partners. They called each other *Du,* they drank and joked and traveled together. Over the years, they were twice trapped in cars that were totaled in collisions with deer on remote rural roads. The second time both lay unconscious for three hours, gasoline dripping upon Vogel the entire time.

Theirs was a friendship cut to the cloth of unconventional needs created by unconventional times. If Vogel and Stange had not existed, the East and West German governments might have had to invent them. And so the two attorneys lived charmed lives protected from more than deer. Both were often accused of cutting ethical corners, yet no one seemed to question their interaction, the propriety of their relationship.

The Vogel-Stange team had risen above the rules governing the conflict of interests as they apply to mortals. Both lawyers seemed to take their exemption for granted, a well-earned compliment to their integrity. Their employers, on the other hand, would trivialize the significance of both lawyers, at least out loud. The authority granted to the negotiators when they were closeted to hammer out agreements was not nearly as broad as both liked to claim, or so it was said in the ministries on both sides.

Perhaps. Or perhaps the entrenched officeholders, East and West, were offended, even envious, because they were so dependent upon the pizzicatos played by these two freewheeling spirits who lacked official status and stooped to *Menschenhandel,* a trade disdained by accredited diplomats.

"We have no competence in these matters," said Ambassador Karl Seidel, Ludwig Rehlinger's opposite number in the DDR Foreign Ministry. His tone was icy.

Ethics and protocol aside, Vogel and Stange did bring East-West relations to life, although back in 1961 the DDR would not yet demand money. The Abel-Powers spy trade was the only model when Stange was asked to represent Engelbert Nelle, the chairman of the German Catholic Student Association. Nelle had wired his DDR brethren in Halle confirming a date at "Aunt Hedwig's." The *Stasi* figured out that Nelle was actually arranging a meeting at Saint Hedwig's Cathedral, near the Wall in East Berlin. The delegates from Halle were arrested when they arrived there. Nelle was taken in custody as he entered East Berlin at the Wall.

Vogel and Stange went to work. The key proved to be a DDR scientist who had been arrested for espionage in West Germany. After months of dickering, a trade was arranged. The Abel-Powers formula still worked, but it was cumbersome and to some degree dependent upon luck; it was unlikely that prisoners of roughly equal "value" would always be available on both sides at the same time. And for groups of prisoners held in the DDR, let alone large groups, the Abel-Powers principle of tit for tat was impractical.

This lack of a better formula emerged as the crucial issue when Brandt's man Spangenberg, calm and diplomatic, met with Stange and Vogel to talk about the hardship prison cases that were troubling the Mayor. The atmosphere was collegial. Spangenberg took to Vogel instantly. Vogel was intrigued by the challenge of the problem. To him the key was quickly obvious: money. Why had no one brought that up before?

"Kinder," said the man from East Berlin, weighing his words with care, "you know that our economy is not in the best of shape. Maybe you could pay to regulate this traffic."

Spangenberg liked this simple notion at once, although obvious reservations hit him right away as well. How would Brandt raise the money? Who would need to be informed of such a deal? Who would sign the receipts? On the other hand, perhaps this was a way to resolve even politically sensitive cases. Spangenberg knew of a man who had been arrested for participating in the June 17, 1953, workers' riots in East Berlin. Might it be possible to get him out?

Vogel promised to see what he could do. Spangenberg would consult with Brandt and the Mayor's closest aides.

Spangenberg found his colleagues "uneasy" at the morality of the proposal, and they wanted to know how much money might be required. But first, he was to sound out State Secretary Thedieck at the All-German Ministry in Bonn, and he did so through Ludwig Rehlinger, who was amazed and pessimistic.

Thedieck, then as later, was indignant. "How can you equate people with money?" he exploded. "We don't want to have anything to do with it. We'll tolerate what you want to do, but there will be no government assistance."

Spangenberg reported back to Vogel during the first of several walks they took in the Volkspark of Wilmersdorf, the park being a security measure.

"Vogel was taking a much bigger risk than I," Spangenberg would remember. The East German was convinced that Stange's office was bugged by the Americans. And he wanted neither government to hear him explain the details of why a certain prisoner could not be released because he was a *Geheimnisträger,* someone whose occupation in the DDR had once entitled him to become privy to so-called state secrets.*

And so it was up to the lawyers to probe the limits of the possible.

---

* The definition of *Geheimnisträger* took in vast territory. Even in the relatively liberalized mid-eighties I knew an elderly East German woman whose privileges were restricted by this personnel classification because many years ago she had been a typist in an office concerned with environmental problems.

In months of negotiations Vogel and Stange managed to reach agreement for the ransoming of six prisoners. The man arrested in the June 17, 1953, riots was not allowed to leave, but the package price for the six lucky cases was surprisingly reasonable, only 25,000 marks for the lot. Possibly, the DDR was deferring to the limits of the Western funding, a relatively modest municipal account maintained by Mayor Brandt to aid the needy.

Money was thus established as the medium of exchange for people. Stange picked up Brandt's cash. Brandt and his men waited in suspense. They were not at all certain that the DDR would make delivery in accordance with the agreement.

The deal did go through without further complications, and Spangenberg shared a bottle of champagne with Vogel. Unhappily, the new channel of accommodation was already dry. Without financing by the federal government in Bonn, ransoming on a major scale was not feasible, and the men in Bonn would not unbend.

"Brandt was of the wrong political party," Stange explained later. "In Bonn he was a foreigner. He was the wrong guy."

So the Mayor was, very much so. Brandt's Social Democratic Party competed with Chancellor Adenauer's Christian Democrats in an oil-and-water atmosphere. The personal rivalry between the two leaders aggravated the relationship further. Adenauer's dislike for Brandt had, if anything, grown since the men clashed during the Wall crisis. The old Chancellor would do nothing that might boost his rival's chance at the chancellorship.

Having scented a promising business opportunity, Stange and Vogel were encouraged to search for alternative ways to get the Bonn government interested in larger-scale prison deals. Stange considered that Axel Springer, the media baron, would make an ideal middleman. Springer's patriotism, his passionate hatred of the Wall, and his inclination for direct action would be helpful.

"Springer is the father of all things," Stange liked to say.

Unfortunately, this father had been inaccessible to Stange in the past, at least directly. Indirectly, the bustling little lawyer had been involved with Springer since the earliest post-Wall days. Stange's connections with student tunnel builders having become known, Springer's editors used the attorney as a channel for getting money to tunnelers, who sometimes yielded big exclusive stories for the

Springer press. Still, during these dealings Stange was kept at a distance from the big boss.

"I was too small to be received," he would eventually concede.

Nimbly, Stange now conceived of a way to reach Springer so that this powerful personage could be enlisted in the new, more lucrative cause. In the course of his representation of potential resettlers in the East, Stange had come to know a marvelous woman in Hamburg, Dora Fritzen, the congenial and rich owner of a freighter fleet, who had for many years operated the Hilfswerk Helfende Hände (Aid Project of Helping Hands). As early as 1951, Dora Fritzen had raised money and organized a group of women to dispatch food packages to prisoners in the DDR on a regular basis. Even the Red Cross had declined to help; in those days it was widely felt that the East Germans could not be trusted with so much as one sausage.

So, early in 1962, Wolfgang Vogel appeared at the baronial old estate of Dora Fritzen, who was not unaccustomed to receiving petitioners in the cause of charities, especially good works concerning East-West relationships. Fritzen had never heard of Vogel, but she had grown to like his friend Stange, and it was immediately obvious that this stranger from the East was not a conventional supplicant, certainly not the pallid, down-at-the-heels sort who customarily came begging out of the DDR.

Vogel's discreet gold watch and cuff links were of the finest, his toilette perfect, his manner courtly. Most arresting was his thick, supple camel-hair coat, a sign of opulence not given to citizens of the East in the early 1960s, not even to big-time lawyers. Fritzen was duly taken with Vogel's entrance, and his ensuing presentation lived up to his external trappings.

Rapidly and modestly, if not too modestly, he sketched his participation in the Abel-Powers exchange, with its cast of American and Soviet diplomats. Then he took Dora Fritzens' breath away with a dramatic statement: "What we did for the *Amis* we can do for ourselves."

It was masterful wording, precisely the right note to strike with Fritzen, a rich patriot like Springer and a businesswoman who recognized the need for the meshing of personal chemistries in complicated deals—which was Vogel's text topic.

"I have no partner," he lamented, "and I'm not leaving West Germany until we find a partner."

Vogel's switch to the first person plural was another quiet mas-

terstroke. It ensnared Dora Fritzen personally in the *Freikauf* enterprise. By unspoken agreement she had bought into the problem
of the Vogel-Stange team, had become part of the insider quest for
the right connection to the government in Bonn.

Fritzen liked Vogel from the start, as people usually did. The
lawyer was not only impressive and adroit, he exuded dedication.
He talked of having looked hard at political prisoners in the jails
and how he could not forget the hopelessness he saw in their eyes.

"He has a heart for people," Fritzen remembered thinking. She
knew; she had such a heart herself. And while Vogel gave her no
specific indication that he was anything other than a collaborator
of the DDR regime, she picked up hints suggesting that he was no
robotized apparatchik.

Occasionally, Vogel would throw into the conversation some platitudinous Communist Party line remark—once he praised the
DDR constitution—while at the same time staring meaningfully at
the ceiling. Evidently he performed this maneuver in deference to
possible bugging devices.

Might there really have been bugs tucked into the ceiling, and,
if so, was Vogel really concerned about them? If bugs were listening, would a platitude or two have constituted a defense against
perceived anti-DDR indiscretions? Or was the insinuation of danger perhaps a careful charade acted out by Vogel in order to hint
that he might be placing his neck in a noose? Or to offer Dora
Fritzen the thrill of drama, real or imaginary?

Such questions were not discussed in the divided Germany.

Likewise unmentionable, at least in ordinary conversation, was a
danger that, for a high-wire walker between the two systems such
as Vogel, was real beyond any doubt. What if he ventured further
than *saying* something offensive to his DDR bosses; what if he *did*
something that they would find objectionable?

Frau Fritzen confronted Vogel with this eventuality.

"What if you fall into disgrace?" she asked.

Vogel's response showed that even in 1962 he considered himself, rightly or wrongly, an international figure, someone who
could only be trifled with at the risk of arousing public attention
and possible diplomatic annoyance for the DDR.

"Then you can only go to the world press," he said.

Since Vogel and Fritzen experienced no trouble airing these
delicate questions, they proceeded easily to discussing the personalities who might be approached to swing the government behind
the cause of *Freikauf*.

Instinctively, they both started at the very top.

"We need Adenauer," said Fritzen.

"We need Springer," said Vogel.

The circle had closed itself. Stange had led to Vogel, Vogel to Fritzen, Fritzen to Springer, Springer to Barzel, Barzel to Adenauer. It was a wearisome reach, but it worked and it was, withal, the kind of wearisome wrangling that enabled democracies to get things done, if necessary, without taking the taxpayers into their confidence right at the start.

Still another team was maneuvering to open up an additional channel for making deals with the DDR. This group was uniquely qualified to tuck the morality of the *Freikauf* process under a cloak dear to Germans of all persuasions: respectability. The sponsor of the effort was the Lutheran Church. Nobody could accuse it of reprehensible ethical conduct, especially not the conduct of its elderly bishop, Kurt Scharf.

During the time of the Nazis, Scharf had become known as "the father of the prisoners"—Hitler's prisoners. With the relentlessness that was the Bishop's trademark, he kept calling upon SS headquarters to plead for the release of persecutees. He was forbidden to speak in public or to publish his writings. Seven times he was arrested. Other resisters also rose among the clergy—some, like Pastor Martin Niemöller, were banished to concentration camps—but consistent campaigning by clerics like Scharf was rare.

After Hitler, the Bishop's life mirrored the new inhumanities of the Cold War. He worked and lived in East Berlin. His family lived in the Western section. Permission for them to move to the East was denied by the DDR. While such a separation was not unusual, the Scharf family symbolized a cause around which much of the Protestant as well as the Catholic clergy was rallying—the cause of *unity,* unity among churches of East and West, equal church responsibility for parishioners in both Germanys, a caring for all, regardless of geography. Since Hitler's day, involvement by churchmen in politics had been an honorable activity. The German clergy was a worldly clan. Shrewd politics would help God to help the believers.

There was much to do. As early as the 1950s, Lutheran congregations in the DDR faced severe economic hardship, and the DDR authorities interposed increasing obstacles to block the affluent Western brethren from helping with money. Bishop Scharf conceived an idea and negotiated with the DDR authorities. He persuaded *them* to support the Eastern congregations. In return, Scharf arranged to supply the DDR with Western foodstuffs, oil, steel, and other goods that were in chronically short supply. Accounts of these barters were maintained in the values of a new currency, *Verrechnungseinheiten* (exchange units).

When the Wall throttled all East-West accommodation, reducing contacts even between the churches of the two countries to occasional runs by couriers, Bishop Scharf was incensed. Together with two other Lutheran leaders he dispatched a telegram to Chief of State Walter Ulbricht, requesting that the border be reopened at least for family members. On August 31, 1961, this audacity got the Bishop banned from the East altogether. He moved to West Berlin.

For an inveterate oppositionist like Scharf, bureaucratic chicanery constituted a personal challenge. Greater ingenuity was called for. He needed a new plan for parishioners and clergy, more and more of whom were being jailed in the DDR for alleged political offenses. To get them out, the Bishop thought he should try to revive and modify the barter pattern that the East had found acceptable in the fifties. This time he would propose *Freikauf,* cash for imprisoned believers.

Since he was no longer admitted into East Berlin, the Bishop required a deputy for his negotiations; luckily, the right man was already in his employ. He was the West Berlin lawyer in charge of the Department of Prisoners at the Council of the German Evangelical Churches, Reymar von Wedel.

Von Wedel was not everyone's favorite. A tall, spare figure, cold and aristocratic in manner, he walked with a limp, the result of a World War II injury. Generally he was thought to be much interested in making money. He was a loyal son of his church, however —discreet, persistent, a technician who got things done in his own unemotional way. There wasn't much that deterred von Wedel. Also, like Jürgen Stange, he possessed that asset made suddenly valuable by the Wall, a passport issued in West Germany, not in Berlin.

As early as November 1961, von Wedel began to reconnoiter opportunities for working in the East. He began circumspectly by meeting with a friendly DDR attorney on Federal Highway 5 on the outskirts of Berlin. By the summer of 1962, when Bishop Scharf was ready to launch *Freikauf* for his prisoners, von Wedel had briefed himself impressively. In particular, he had scouted the influential roles played by Vogel and Stange and knew that these two had already been working together.

Under instructions from Bishop Scharf, von Wedel presented himself at the office of Wolfgang Vogel on June 21. The Vogel premises were still at shabby Alt-Friedrichsfelde 155, where the Brooklyn lawyer James D. Donovan had turned rubber-kneed on the spooky stairway en route to negotiate the Abel-Powers exchange a few months earlier.

Since communications by phone or mail did not exist, von Wedel had not announced his visit in advance. Nor was he supposed to disclose his identity until he could gauge whether Vogel was perhaps a functionary with a lack of vision that would become part of Bishop Scharf's problem. Von Wedel knew of no reason why Vogel would be of assistance or whether he could even be entrusted with information of any kind.

Vogel was out of his office on an appointment, and von Wedel had to wait more than an hour.

Once Vogel appeared, the air changed within minutes. Von Wedel made his rehearsed speech. He said he was a lawyer from faraway Stuttgart, that he had come on behalf of an industrialist in that city who was interested in paying cash to effect the release of political prisoners in the DDR.

Vogel was skeptical. Von Wedel's story smelled phony to him. Why would an industrialist from Stuttgart, of all people and of all places, have an interest in such a deal?

The sour reaction convinced von Wedel that he had better come clean if his mission was to bear fruit. He spilled his real story.

The change in Vogel's attitude was instantaneous. Von Wedel was impressed. "He could shift gears *very* quickly," the emissary from West Berlin recalled. Before long, von Wedel handed Vogel the first of many "church lists" to come—names of hostages whose liberation was close to the hearts of Bishop Scharf and his people.

Vogel was pleased. He welcomed the chance to spread his wings over more people in need; nor was he averse to the new business for his practice that von Wedel's affluent client might generate. There would also be an attractive bonus. The participation of the church would yield more than volume; it would add some much needed dignity. Unfortunately, so Vogel thought, the scheme almost certainly wouldn't work. He doubted that he would be able to sell *Freikauf,* a concept so unconventional and so reeking of capitalism, to the hidebound officialdom of his own side.

Personally, the morality of the arrangement left Vogel in a philosophical frame of mind. "If there are no buyers, then there are no sellers," he observed to a friend, the Swedish church representative Gustav Svingel. "Who is worse?"

As was his custom, Vogel went to see his old mentor, the man who had set him up in business, Josef Streit, whose position ranked just below that of the minister in the DDR Department of Justice. Streit's principal claim to prominence derived from his diligence in persecuting dissidents. And while Vogel knew him to be capable of compromise, occasionally even humane procedures, Streit did not seem likely to embrace a deal designed by an unreconstructed oppositionist like Bishop Scharf.

Surprisingly, Vogel's protector bought the *Freikauf* proposal immediately. He recognized that the ongoing discharge of so many political prisoners back into the DDR kept heating up internal opposition; these people were bitter and they talked too much. Besides, his party was interested in easing the restive mood that the Wall had quite generally stimulated in East and West, resentment that might lead to some form of aggression, perhaps another workers' riot, as had happened on the abominated and much feared day of June 17, 1953.

Freikauf, Streit recognized, was a convenient outlet of steam, of political pressure. It would bring a cleanup among malcontents. And the hard currency it would yield, the *Devisen*—yes, surely the *Devisen* would help squelch opposition in the party. Nobody could overlook that the hunger for *Devisen* bordered on desperation, what with the black-market value of the East mark at only one fourth or one fifth of the West mark's exchange rate instead of the official quotation of one to one.

Streit perceived yet another justification for advocating acceptance of Vogel's scheme. He advanced a creative bit of reasoning, serviceable to defend *Freikauf* against moral doubts in the West as well as against anticapitalist compunctions in the East. The ransom money could be treated as a refund of the DDR's investment in the education and professional training of the people it would lose, plus partial compensation for the loss of future productivity by those ingrates.

The DDR politburo bought the deal, its internal debate protected by the usual total secrecy of its proceedings. The DDR would never acknowledge participation in the scheme. Years after the deal leaked to the public in the West, Vogel would justify it there as simple compensation for the DDR's economic loss. He would claim that this was the DDR's *only* reason for going along.

The Wall, then, was not unbreachable. Holes could be negotiated into it. Money was equally helpful in East and West. Money spoke a language understood by all.

Freikauf was no soap opera, no hostage drama. The prisoners were family, like children of divorced parents. The parent nations had split, were no longer on talking terms. That was politics. Politics was deniable. The children, the prisoners, could never be denied. Their future tied East and West together in a commonality that no ideology could cancel, no Wall could split. The parents were compelled to talk, to negotiate, now and forever.

As in divorce cases, lawyers had their uses in hustling to bridge the East-West gap. A lawyer with a sense of mission could do much, and Vogel was acquiring a mission. He wanted to make the Wall porous.

**East Berlin,
Autumn 1963**

Trust, the other ingredient essential to the buying and selling of people, had been nonexistent when the trading began. With the entry of the church as a partner, the unofficial agents found that their hands had turned cleaner. Their ambitious little circle was coalescing.

Streit trusted Vogel. Encouraged by von Wedel's favorable reporting, the church certified Vogel's reliability to the Bonn government's man, Ludwig Rehlinger. Taking comfort in his relief that Jürgen Stange had not run off with Bonn's money, Rehlinger became reconciled to using the smiling little attorney as his liaison man. Stange introduced Rehlinger to von Wedel, who of course was accredited to Bishop Scharf, the unassailable.

By luck or by meshing of personalities and self-interest, the three lawyers hit it off and soon forged a brotherly bond.

"We were three musketeers," von Wedel recalled, "along with our wives and not without alcohol."

At the urging of his church, von Wedel acquired an office in the new Reilerstrasse headquarters of the expanding Vogel law firm. Von Wedel's private practice prospered; he specialized in the administration of large fortunes and estates, as he liked to point out. In the *Freikauf* business he would remain a sideshow. For a generation, the principal dealers were only two musketeers, Stange and Vogel.

They made a very odd couple, these two, especially since one of them, Stange, was no match for the other. Vogel's connections were already enviable. He exuded hauteur, his style was cerebral. Stange fraternized with cronies in the Lions Club, and his practice was so fragile that at the time when he first ran into Vogel he was thinking of giving up the law and returning to his native Braunschweig to become a police detective.

And Stange's style was, well, histrionic. He rarely walked. He dashed, he danced. His emotions were not always under control. Talking to an American rabbi about his life under Hitler, he burst into tears. Privately, he was adept at mimicking an opponent at the negotiating table. When he was under the gun himself, Stange could become uninterruptible. He talked and talked, acting out his considerable emotion, simply not responding to repeated interjections—the soliloquist.

When reporting to his superiors in the West German government on deadlocks in negotiations—perhaps over prices or the unavailability of a sensitive prisoner for ransoming—Stange turned into a wounded lion. Such occasions were frequent, and the drama was of high velocity.

"I fought hard," the little lawyer exclaimed, "but nothing worked." Nobody ever heard Vogel extolling his own pluck or conceding impotence.

Whether he realized it or not, Stange was cast in a useful if inglorious role. "He became a punching bag," said one of the negotiators. "The others cursed him so that they could feel strong."

The price Bonn paid for this privilege was high. As Brandt's man Spangenberg recalled years afterward, Stange and Vogel started out with each collecting 8,000 to 9,000 marks a month from the West Germans. These were lavish fees, especially in Germany, where attorney compensation tended to run radically lower than levels customary in the United States. According to Spangenberg's memory, the payments included reimbursement for expenses except travel, which was refunded separately. All monies were paid into Western bank accounts. In Western currency, of course.

Over the years, the financial fortunes of the Vogel-Stange partnership would diverge. With publicity came criticism of *Freikauf*, especially from human-rights groups, and the elegant Wolfgang Vogel proved to be afflicted with surprisingly thin skin. The role of punching bag did not suit him.

"They're peeing on me," he complained to Spangenberg. "I've got a bellyful of it."

He wanted the West Germans to stop paying him, and they did. Vogel told them that he had made other arrangements with his own people. "His government made it possible for him not to take money from the capitalist *Ausland*," Spangenberg remembered. Instead, Vogel began to enjoy certain tax advantages at home. According to his own account, often repeated in a hushed tone, he refused to take pay for any of his humane endeavors or his spy trades.

When his name first appeared in the press, Vogel gave an interesting explanation of his finances in an interview for a British magazine. "I know that some people would not believe it," he said, "but my only pecuniary advantage from these [government] deals is that I am given tax concessions because I can prove that I am spending a great deal of my time on these negotiations. I have been paid by the families of prisoners on both sides, for instance by Americans whose sons were in custody in Russia, but never by a government or an intelligence service. I am earning good money from my clients in the West, commercial companies and so on, and I do not mind spending some of this income on my idealistic pursuits."

Stange, on the other hand, seemed none too troubled by his vulnerability, although friends thought he was drinking more than was wise. Receptive to new ways of ingratiating himself with clients who would eventually make him rich, he became a shopper for leading figures in the DDR government, picking up shavers, radios, and other scarce items for them in West Berlin. Christmas became a busy time for him, and he deputized Mrs. Stange to select perfumes for the wives of his Communist patrons. Jürgen Stange had a talent for appearing indispensable.

All the while his fees climbed, ultimately reaching an enormous 50,000 marks *per month*, not including such items as the 20,000 marks his government paid for refurbishing his law office. When the latter item was brought up in a court proceeding, the judge was told that the expense had been essential because Stange's clients had complained about their attorney's seedy surroundings.

Some observers wondered what was keeping Vogel so loyal to his lightweight sidekick for so long. Was it mostly personal affinity, a sense of brotherly loyalty, perhaps even pity for a lesser talent? Might the wily Vogel have been content not to have to wrestle with a more formidable opposite number? Or was theirs a marriage of convenience kept alive by successes that a divorce could have endangered?

Later, when West German federal prosecutors questioned Stange's honesty in court, accusing him of dipping into the millions of public money earmarked for *Freikauf* ransom, Vogel stuck by his partner, even after the Bonn government fired Stange and before the charges against the younger man were finally dropped.

"Stange has a character of integrity," Vogel told me. "Somebody else might have asked for a divorce, but I never would have told him: 'I don't want you anymore.'"

Most relationships between husbands and wives are less complex than the professional accommodation between Vogel and Stange. No doubt, ordinary affection, the similarity of backgrounds, and some shared tastes helped to keep this alliance afloat. Both men had emancipated themselves from petit bourgeois provincial homes. Together they were running up a series of achievements that both, until mid-career years, would have considered beyond their power.

Understandably, their exotic missions abroad caused them to reel like country bumpkins. When I asked Vogel what had impressed him on his first secret visit to New York to negotiate an exchange of spies, he conceded that the tall buildings gave him pause—and for a distinctive reason.

"Who would come to make repairs if something went wrong with the outside of a window on the thirty-sixth floor?" he wanted to know. "It's unimaginable!"

Stange recalled with warmth and drama how he and Vogel, on another spy mission, this time to Paris, absented themselves from their business like students playing hooky so they could rush to the Palais de Justice to view Daumier caricatures of excitable French lawyers at work. Both men hung copies of these witty sketches of their imaginary colleagues in the waiting rooms of their respective offices.

Stange played host to another fantasy in his law office, revealing the overextended little attorney in an appealing light. Thanks to the interior decorating financed by his government, Stange's premises on Bundesallee, near the ministries, were impressive. The waiting room could seat fifteen comfortably. The way to Stange's enormous private office led through a steel door. A conference table for eight people was lost in open spaces.

The most pervasive figure under the cavernous ceilings was the fictional antihero of the early seventeenth century, Don Quixote.

Sculptures, drawings, and paintings of this addled warrior were spread across walls and coffee tables. The old crusader had to be Stange's patron saint, and he was.

"I love him," Stange explained eagerly. "I feel close to him. He wanted to change the world with love. I wanted to do that."

It would have been rude to suggest that Stange was fooling himself if he was taking his self-casting seriously; that his dream was too grand; that he was engaging in a role reversal. Students of the Vogel-Stange relationship have noted the obvious: that Stange was in fact living the part of Sancho Panza, the hapless little helper fated to trail Don Quixote through his battles.

It would have been inappropriate to ask this affluent idealist how his windmill-tilting idol would have felt about *Freikauf*.

Across the Wall on Reilerstrasse, partner Vogel presided over another surprising private world. It was a setting of a very different order. Sleepy Reilerstrasse, never paved, was one short block in Friedrichsfelde-Ost, near the rural eastern edge of East Berlin; the New York equivalent is northern Yonkers. Here were no ministries, no other offices of law firms, just a grocery, an army barracks with the usual red banners and their tired exhortative slogans, fields jammed with weekend shacks, where the *Bürger* grew always-scarce vegetables. And, huddled close together, rows of drab two-story homes.

One of these, a small, relatively cheerful light green stucco structure with a neatly pruned garden, stood out because its garage housed an object as alien to this environment as a golden calf: the ultimate exhibit of West German capitalist success, a gold Mercedes 300E that Vogel drove on his rounds, often at speeds that petrified his passengers. At a time when ordinary citizens had to wait fifteen years to buy a tubercular buggy of socialist manufacture and an occasional visiting Western vehicle was still a curiosity on the streets, Vogel's transport with its East Berlin license plates was a dazzling symbol of power and wealth.

Yet inside Reilerstrasse 4, it would have come as no surprise to find a sign saying HOME, SWEET HOME. Instead, there were signs with jokes. SMOKING IS PERMITTED ONLY FOR THE IMPOLITE, said one of these. Another announced the house rules. Rule number one was THE BOSS IS ALWAYS RIGHT. Rule number two stated, IF HE ISN'T, REFER BACK TO RULE NUMBER ONE. What other international law offices displayed such uninhibited folksiness?

All the rooms were small, cramped, overflowing with files, including the boss's sanctum. In his space there was hardly room to move. The massive dark furnishings with their lace doilies and brocades, and the Oriental carpets were reminiscent of a living room fashionable during the Weimar Republic. Favorite paintings, along with bursts of clippings and photos of friends, clients, ceremonials, and statesmen left few vacant spots along walls covered with dark, heavy fabrics.

This was the private territory of a man unashamedly yearning for coziness as *he* wanted to allot it; who couldn't care less what outsiders might think of his outdated tastes; who wanted to be at home while at work in this niche where—so he said—Vogel spent most of his life. This notion of his hours isolated at the workplace was not much overdrawn. Often he toiled past 9 P.M., interrupting himself briefly to have dinner, which his wife cooked for them in the basement kitchen.

While this ambience hardly fit a high-velocity lawyer, it was in keeping with the mind-set of the arriviste who craned his neck in wonder before thirty-sixth-floor skyscraper windows in New York and whose formative years were cocooned in a setting that even small-town Germans would describe as confining.

The lonely mountain village of six hundred souls, Wilhelmsthal, where Wolfgang Vogel was born on October 30, 1925, did give the boy a taste of the divisions, occupations, and annexations, the Sturm und Drang of Eastern Europe between World Wars I and II and since. Wilhelmsthal was in the province of Silesia, south of Breslau. It now is part of Poland and has been rechristened with one of those Polish names difficult for Germans to pronounce. During Vogel's boyhood it was German, but barely so, because the areas that almost surrounded it with their exhausted iron mines happened to belong to Czechoslovakia, at least at that time.

Nobody could grow up in the ebb and flow of Wilhelmsthal in the middle of the twentieth century thinking that Germany was a country of immutable borders.

The Vogel home, however, was rural bedrock. The father, stern, with a vision of life as a duty, was *the* village teacher in the one-room school where bright young Wolfgang unenviably spent his first years of classes before going off to a Catholic boarding school in Glatz, the county seat. The Vogels took their Catholicism very seriously, and not just on Sundays. His father went to confession almost every day. His sense of religious duty turned him into a lay missionary, and the boy would retain scenes of father making rounds.

Dire poverty was a permanent house guest in Silesia, especially during the depression twenties and thirties. *Herr* Vogel, the teacher, would call on the downtrodden and the sick, would get them help if he could, console them if he couldn't. He would take Wolfgang along, grasp his hand, as a country doctor took his child on house calls to patients. "In my parents' home I was very insistently educated to help other people," Vogel said in his sixties. "Perhaps something of that stuck to me."

Also unforgotten were hungry years in the Nazi Labor Service, as a teenage flak trainee during the Nazi army's final collapse, as a law student under the new Marxist regime, first at Jena University, then in Leipzig. Initially he learned without books, because available texts were infested with Nazi ideology and forbidden. Financial independence came early; while at the university, Vogel earned his keep by managing a window-cleaning service.

It was no accident that the Vogel office on Reilerstrasse was run like a cottage industry. Vogel acquired secretaries and an associate, later two, but his only close aide, his true inside partner, was his wife, Helga. She swam with him twice every day in their home pool. She drove him to the office and back while he worked in the car. She was his counselor when he wanted advice, and he was not embarrassed to acknowledge Helga's role to outsiders. Also, she was in charge of the accounts, his money.

She was a West German, this tall, quiet, exceptionally attractive and sensual woman—from Essen—and she had a sister in Texas. All of Vogel's family ties were to the West—unique for an influential personage of the DDR. His first wife settled there when they divorced, as did his married daughter, Lilo. His son, Manfred, became a lawyer in West Berlin. Helga, the second wife, originally came to Vogel seeking help for her boyfriend of the time, a West German swimming instructor who had run into legal problems in the DDR. She married the lawyer *after* the case was settled, as her husband would point out even if the question arose only by inference.

Vogel's most Westernized characteristic was his pace. By standards of the profit-conscious West Germans, most work in the DDR moved at a gentle rate. Not Vogel's work. He drove himself like a man hounded. As do many brilliant lawyers, he possessed a computerlike brain capable of retrieving, without help from papers, fine points of cases dead twenty years in the files. Vogel enriched this technique: he was *possessed* by his love of organization; a file-card memory was a tool, not a philosophy. Vogel's credo was peculiarly German. It was *order*.

"Order is half of life," he enjoyed telling me when I asked how he applied personal attention to thousands of cases, tens of thousands of cases, rivers of papers that flowed into Reilerstrasse 4 and out on a scale that would baffle American law firms.

When Vogel came to do business with huge legal factories in New York or Washington, he was amused by the way these colleagues, working in platoons, tossed time and money around. Fees of $300 or more per hour for routine matters were so impossibly enormous that they made him smile. And with what abandon those Americans wasted time! They worried for three hours over a problem that would rate no more than a few minutes on Reilerstrasse.

Admittedly, issues were not always weighed in great depth on Reilerstrasse. The pressure of Vogel's work load was so compelling that he had disciplined himself in ways clients in the West would find unacceptable. Unless a file held exceptional implications—so Vogel had decided when the two German governments became his chief concerns—he would spend no more than half an hour with it. That was his deadline, the limit. Period. Any questions would *have* to be settled within that time.

"I'd rather be wrong than waste time," he explained.

Time. Many executives and professionals make a fetish of managing their time, treating it as the precious, finite commodity it is. Vogel was *possessed* by time. It surrounded him. He was enveloped by time. He collected clocks, his only hobby; eight of them ticked away from every direction in his little office, many more at home.

"They are living things" (*Lebewesen*), he said softly. They were his masters.

And so he scurried about at his near-trot, almost always tense and working hard not to show it, almost always late for outside appointments, often *very* late, the Mercedes churning, his wife driving as fast as he did. At his desk, Vogel sat coiled, ready to deliver responses before a questioner had his words out. Rarely did one get a chance to tell him more than he wanted to know.

"Just the phone number!" he snaps when a fellow attorney on the phone wants to volunteer addresses and other details.

Such pressure, taken for granted in New York or Los Angeles, came as from outer space in East Berlin. Phone conversations tended to be unhurried in the DDR. Personal appointments were measured by the hour, even in the highest places.

Startlingly, Vogel began building up time pressure from the moment a caller asked for a meeting. "How much time will be needed?" would be his first question, followed by serious haggling, not about hours but for the minutes to be allotted. To overstay one's time quota in Vogel's office was to feel like a thief.

Riddles remained. Friends and longtime students of the Vogel phenomenon never stopped wrestling with the great conflicts of his life: his simultaneous service to East and West; his capitalist income (and tastes) versus his self-characterization as something of a philanthropist in his work for the two Germanys; and, most confusing, his simultaneous loyalty, pledged with equal fervor, to the Catholicism of his upbringing and the Marxism that ruled his state.

His religious belief was unquestioned. Vogel says prayers every day—he told me so himself. He keeps a vessel filled with holy water at home; the local priest refills the supply frequently. He believes in the hereafter. God is quite real to this believer. Vogel's faith in Him is so open, so apparently guileless, that friends have called it mawkish. That fits: Vogel can be a piece of ice in a legal matter, but underneath dwells softness, acceptance of sentimentality. He has been known to ask men, near-strangers, "When was the last time you cried?"

His Marxism is less conventional.

"Are you actually a Communist or an idealist, a humanist?" a French interviewer once asked him, not realizing that Vogel embraced a formal religious faith as well.

"Above all I'm a Marxist," the lawyer replied. "Marxism doesn't exclude faith or a humanistic attitude. Quite the contrary, it requires them. The reality is that I attempt to be both Marxist and humanist. That's possible, but it's not always easy. . . . " He did not mention that he had not joined the SED (Communist) Party.

Years later, amid the clocks of Reilerstrasse, I brought up the discrepancies—at the very least—between Catholicism and Communism, and still this practiced middleman saw no conflict, except for the Marxist belief that life ends at the grave. With the brevity that was his trademark, he proceeded to dispose of an issue that would have deadlocked a convention of philosophers.

"Marxism opposes the exploitation of man," he lectured me. "I don't call that Christian either." Vogel smiled.

"I was looking for a middle way," he went on, "something I could relate to my childhood."

So Marxism was the middleman's middle way. This was not the doctrine according to Engels and Lenin, but it pleased Vogel's capacious conscience and seemed to settle any questions in far less time than the half hour he allotted to routine matters.

It was not the occasion to bring up the moral fine points of *Freikauf,* which had continued to make distasteful news.

Herleshausen, East-West German border, Friday, February 14, 1969

In the guardroom of the West German frontier station, Wolfgang Vogel and Jürgen Stange were settling another of their undercover transactions. This one was out of the ordinary even by their unconventional standards. The West German government was trading a single prisoner for twenty-one Western spies who had just been transferred from an East German to a West German bus that was waiting out of sight down the road in the freezing night.

Presiding personally at the shabby border post was Ludwig Rehlinger, the Bonn official who had started all the prisoner exchanges with Vogel. Today's deal had been in the making for more than five years, and the snags had almost torpedoed all future trades.

The lone prisoner who stirred so much fuss was Heinz (Fiffi) Felfe, the supermole from General Gehlen's BND "Org"—a KGB double agent for a decade. The Soviets had started to make moves to bring in Felfe the moment he was sentenced to fourteen years at hard labor in 1963. At first they offered to trade two clumsy Heidelberg students whom the CIA had dispatched to the Soviet Union to photograph military installations. The West Germans refused. Felfe was a "dormant crater." He had worked too long in too sensitive a spot in counterintelligence. He still had too much to spill about Western espionage methods and personnel.

A point of professional philosophy also troubled the KGB. Western intelligence agencies by and large thought of captured agents as disposable pawns. The Soviets showed more attachment to their blown undercover people; at least they displayed greater eagerness to get them back. Such loyalty boosted the morale of agents still in the field, and it kept imprisoned operatives from feeling abandoned and therefore tempted to give away too much information under the pressure of enemy interrogation.

So the Soviets had kept pushing for Felfe, offering to trade him for eighteen prisoners, fifteen men and three women. These were BND spies, agents of the West German Social Democratic Ost-Büro, plus some choice "politicals." Herbert Wehner, the West German Minister for All-German Questions, a controversial ex-Communist himself, informed the West German Chancellor. The proposition was turned down.

Wolfgang Vogel had developed a friendship with the crusty, pipe-puffing Wehner, and eventually the East Berlin negotiator appeared in the Minister's Bonn office to offer the West Germans an interesting choice in the game for Felfe. They could have the group of eighteen. Or they could get three thousand "politicals" from DDR prisons who were hoping for release to the West.

"And if we don't agree?" asked Wehner.

"Then there'll be no more prisoner exchanges," said Vogel.

"If I hadn't known you for such a long time, I'd call that blackmail!"

"It *is* blackmail," said Vogel. "But I have no other choice."

And so it was done. The West Germans got the group of eighteen plus the two Heidelberg CIA spies still languishing in prison in Moscow, plus one more Heidelberg spy arrested in Leningrad in 1967. In Karlshorst, Felfe was greeted with Soviet-style kisses by "Alfred," his KGB controller, and settled down to teach criminology at Humboldt University.

The three thousand "politicals" stayed in jail. Spies commanded priority in the scheme of governments, though not always in the life of lawyer Vogel.

East Berlin

Dieter Borkowski had no idea why he had been summoned to the interrogation room of the Magdalenen Strasse prison in the East Berlin suburb of Lichtenberg. He had served only fifteen months of a seven-year sentence for "hatemongering" against the state. In plain language, he had been writing pseudonymous articles for Western media.

Borkowski had no reason to expect gentle treatment from the Communist leadership. He belonged to that hated species, one of their own who had turned against them. In the 1950s he had worked for Erich Honecker in the Free Youth movement. Rambunctious and irreverent, Borkowski was too outspoken to keep his contempt for his increasingly rigid and self-important former bosses to himself. In the DDR, noisy ingrates like Borkowski wound up in dark, dirty places like Magdalenen Strasse prison.

The interrogation room, however, was large and airy, and at the window, smiling, stood a civilian whom Borkowski recognized. This was the man who visited prisons in his famous Mercedes, the magician whom the prisoners called "Deputy Jesus," Wolfgang Vogel. Much of Vogel's business was not in government offices, going over lists of unfortunates he never had to meet. Many of his duties were personal and difficult. Like the business with the troublemaker Borkowski.

"In three days you'll be free and I'll take you to West Berlin," said Vogel, shaking hands.

Once he had recovered from his initial surprise and joy, Borkowski asked what he could do about his house.

"You want to go West," said Vogel. "A sale is out of the question. You'll have to give your house to the state."

"But what about my library, my research materials?"

"Make a list of what's most important. Maybe I can save a suitcase or two for you. But I can promise nothing."

The words were spoken harshly, and Borkowski did not like this spokesman for his enemies, who was in such a hurry, so eager to push on, but he sensed that Vogel was not enjoying the scene.

"I didn't envy him," Borkowski would remember.

At the appointed time, Vogel, again in a hurry and nervously checking his watch, pulled up to a sudden stop before the Wall at the deserted Invalidenstrasse control point, glanced casually out of the window of the Mercedes, but offered to show no papers. Borkowski sat next to him. The guard just looked dumbly at them. The lawyer addressed him in a military tone. "Don't you know who I am? I'm Dr. Vogel!" No further formalities were required.

Another Mercedes was waiting in the West. Vogel introduced the driver, Jürgen Stange. Then he opened the trunk of his car and pulled out two worn suitcases crammed with Borkowski's prized memorabilia and a few clothes.

"This is what I was allowed to take out of your house," Vogel said. "Perhaps it will give you some pleasure." It seemed to Borkowski that the lawyer looked ever so slightly embarrassed.

30

CROSSING OVER:
TWO PERSONAL REMEMBRANCES

**Weissensee, East Berlin,
August 1965**

"Today we went to the parking lot where Daddy was born," my younger son Jeff wrote with his accustomed precision on a post-card to a relative in California. We were on our private "roots tour" of Berlin: Jeff, his older brother, Ron, and my wife. That day we had inspected the middle-class Western suburb of Charlottenburg, where I had been born on Kantstrasse and where the bombed-out skeleton of our ancient, gloomy apartment house had given way to a slickly paved parking lot for a Neckermann department store.

The bizarre truth was sinking in: my very own childhood world had been partitioned! The places where I had been at home and school were safely tucked into the West. My father's business and the graves of my antecedents were part of the East.

For the rest of the day we had leased a special taxi, one of a dozen or so then licensed to carry foreign tourists in West as well as East Berlin. We wanted to visit the Jewish cemetery in the Eastern suburb of Weissensee, where our ancestors lay buried and where my father, Erich, grew up in the cottage of Max, the superintendent, who was *his* father.

Like most travelers crossing the Wall for the first time, I had pictured a wall, period. I had imagined that there would be a guard checking passports. I was dazed by the profusion and complexity of the fortifications rising—somehow unexpectedly—out of the asphalt on the East end of Checkpoint Charlie: the warrens of fences, gates, mirrors, searchlights, posts, barricades, and whatnot into which the Wall seemed to have been dropped almost as if by afterthought.

And surely I had not imagined such swarms of armed, impassive-faced East German soldiers patrolling, probing, peering, glowering, tapping, stubbing their fingers into every orifice of our taxi, poking under the chassis, looking our bodies up and down as if they wanted to pick apart the seams of our underwear.

In a dank wooden hut we received our initiation into that epidemic socialist activity: waiting. And waiting. And waiting. Passports were pawed and studied like religious objects by relays of guards. A baby-faced trooper then examined our faces through a wall opening perhaps twelve inches square. He peered from his side. We had to peer back at him from ours. The idea was to authenticate the passport photos. My wife wore her hair in bangs and they aroused suspicion. Her passport picture showed a previous hairdo, without bangs. Baby-Face motioned her to lift her bangs so he could assure himself that he was not dealing with an imitation wife.

I was instructed to count out my cash at a table in front of another baby-faced soldier—all of it, every penny. I habitually carry quantities of small change for phone calls and happened to be traveling with coins from three other countries we had visited, so the accounting took a while. Baby-Face stared stoically at the mounds of near-worthless metal while I kept counting, feeling like a fool and further delaying the queue of fellow capitalists pushing into the hut behind me.

Weissensee Cemetery was, as it had always been, a forgotten universe. Our taxi driver had never been there and had trouble finding it, although it is surrounded by well-known and heavily settled residential areas. The street with the entrance gate is now called Herbert-Baum-Strasse, no longer Lothringen Strasse, as in my father's time.*

---

* The wholesale renaming of streets is one of the more visible barometers of ideological warfare in both East and West Berlin. The huge square in the West that was known as Reichskanzlerplatz in my youth was relabeled Adolf-Hitler-Platz during the Nazi era and now is Theodor-Heuss-Platz (after a postwar president of West Germany). Herbert-Baum-Strasse was named for the leader of some thirty-five World War II resistance fighters. Their average age was twenty-two, and at least thirteen were women. Almost all were executed by the Nazis in

Weissensee is the largest Jewish cemetery in Europe, one hundred acres, more than 115,000 graves, yet we saw no other visitors, just as in 1945 when I had come as a GI. My grandfather Max supervised two hundred caretakers plus a funeral staff of seventy back in the 1920s. Now fewer than half a dozen looked after the barest necessities. Only about two hundred Jews were left in East Berlin, and the cemetery was almost penniless because the Jews of West Berlin preferred their own burial grounds, opened in 1955.

The yellow brick superintendent's cottage where my father lived stood unchanged. Some of the damage done to trees and graves by bombs and vandals in the war had been cleared away, though not nearly all of it. The enormous grounds were as dark and damp and sheltered as I remembered from childhood, sealed like a space capsule by their unbroken umbrella of enormous treetops. Except for plots near principal paths, almost all the graves lay shrouded behind thickets of head-high weeds and brush obscuring the inscriptions on the tombstones—lettering that spelled out a century of Jewish history in central Europe.

Here lay the naïvely proud who "fell for the fatherland" in World War I; the assimilated tycoons and the professional elite from between the wars; the three thousand who took their own lives to escape deportation to the camps, husbands and wives often together on the same day. Here my sons could be witnesses to the Holocaust because a disproportionate number of the suicides dated from 1942, the year Hitler set in motion his death machine, "the final solution of the Jewish problem."

We located the graves of our family, including those dating to the 1800s, and cleared them with our hands as best we could. On our way back to the Wall, I told my sons how their Grandpa Erich —he was then still living—used to leave his home on the cemetery in the evenings for a life of laughter. As a young man he sang humorous tunes and performed card tricks in the workers' bars of Weissensee; there was such a *Kneipe* at almost every corner then.

At the Wall, we and our taxi were again ransacked as if we were prisoners, this time presumably because we might have been smuggling (or trying to help) escapees out of the DDR.

My sons and I had often talked about our West European roots, though, for some reason, never about those in the East. That day

---

1942 and 1943. Without exception, Baum and his people were Jews as well as Communists, and several are buried in Weissensee.

we made up for this omission. I have photos of the boys at the Wall. They were wearing their best clothes and expressions as deeply shaken as I have ever seen on them.

It was a far from unique response to the Berlin border experience.

**East Berlin,
Summer 1965**

Eric Bentley had passed through the Friedrichstrasse elevated station before. In the forties and fifties he had gone frequently to visit his patron, Bertolt Brecht, the great and eccentric playwright who wrote *The Three-Penny Opera* and lived near the station, on a continuation of Friedrichstrasse, at Chausseestrasse 125.

Bentley, the lanky American dramatist and critic who translated many of Brecht's works into English, particularly remembered the freezing night in January 1949 when he crossed the border to East Berlin to see Brecht's riveting new play, *Mother Courage.* While there was yet no wall to be crossed, the train trip and the passage through the station had been problematic. The Berlin blockade was on, the fuel shortage was severe, trains and stations were totally unlit.

Tapping his way past the rubble and ruins remaining from World War II, Bentley barely made the curtain at Brecht's theater, the Berliner Ensemble, a short way from the station. Bentley had a reputation for punctuality, so Brecht was waiting for him in the lobby. Muttering *"pünktlich, pünktlich"* (punctual, punctual), the great man seized a chair and pushed it and Bentley into a box just above the stage.

In the summer of 1965, Bentley was back for an appointment with another resident of Chausseestrasse, and by then it would have been impossible to make an imminent theater curtain. Friedrichstrasse station had changed from a point of ready passage into a monstrous roadblock, the principal opening in the Wall, a miserly aperture, a filthy, evil-smelling symbol of separation between the power blocs of the Cold War.

Brecht, a Communist of the rare irreverent kind, had died in 1956. Now Bentley was on his way to meet another artist, a Communist considerably more restive than Brecht, the singer and composer Wolf Biermann, and Friedrichstrasse station was standing in his way, making him wait—wait interminably.

"The Friedrichstrasse *Bahnhof* feels like a jail," Bentley wrote in a reminiscence. "You have the sensation that you may never again see the light of day. . . . It is pure nightmare." He was especially troubled over what he was waiting *for:* "You are waiting to be ajudged harmless."

Harmless. "Is that good?" Bentley asked. "Or should you rather be a very person they wish to apprehend—one who is plotting mischief, arranging to build tunnels through the Wall, or to bring people through the checkpoints on other people's passports?"

If Bentley, born in England, had grown up in Berlin, he would have been struck by a more glaring incongruity. Before Hitler's time, the neighborhood of Friedrichstrasse station was anything but a place of pain. It was the epicenter of the gaiety for which Berlin was famous. This was central Europe's old Broadway. The intersection of Friedrichstrasse and Unter den Linden was Broadway and Forty-second Street. Here, starched ladies and gentlemen of the establishment took their cakes, whipped cream, and gossip at the Konditorei Kranzler or the Bauer. Across the street, Max Reinhardt, producer of epics, started his first theater in the banquet hall of the Victoria Hotel.

Reinhardt lived at Friedrichstrasse 134. At number 216 lived the elegant Paul (Gorgeous Paul) Lincke, the father of Berlin operetta, the composer and lyricist of Berlin's anthem, "Das ist die Berliner Luft, Luft, Luft." The song was first played at the Apollo, located next door to Lincke's residence, Friedrichstrasse 218. The Admiralspalast, the Wintergarten, and dozens of other musical theaters, cabarets, and cafés kept the area jumping with song and dancing.

Friedrichstrasse was the place where everyone went for what the Berliners call *bummeln,* carousing around, preferably a cruise through several establishments in leisurely succession. It was the center of the center, the *Treffpunkt* where people met people. It was natural that the young boy Emil, the hero of Erich Kästner's enchanting classic *Emil und die Detektive,** traveling to Berlin from the provinces for the first time, was to meet his grandmother and cousin at the flower stand in Bahnhof Friedrichstrasse.

---

* The book, published in 1928, is still used as a German text in schools all over the world. My 1985 copy is from the one hundred thirty-first edition.

· · ·

When Bentley was finally released from his purgatory in the station and emerged into the street, another chilling sight assailed him. Could this be the center of a major city? The place looked dead. "Why are there no people around?" he would write later. "One would think it was five in the morning . . . a setting of uncertainty and ghostly unreality."

The emptiness was another spooky paradox, for Bentley was walking through the streets once famous as the site of central Europe's first traffic jam. By the 1870s the onrush of locals and visitors had made the building of major public transportation an urgent necessity. In 1882 the Friedrichstrasse station became the major stop for the city's first elevated trains. Linking the eastern with the western districts, steam engines served 11.25 kilometers of tracks, viaducts, and bridges, an achievement not long before dismissed by some politicians as "technically not feasible."

The trains helped, but not enough. With automobiles competing against horse-drawn streetcars, cargo carriages, tidal waves of pedestrians and bicyclists, accidents became epidemic. In 1902 the intersection of Friedrichstrasse and Unter den Linden became the station of Berlin's first traffic cop. Soon he was a desperate man. The roaring traffic refused to respond to his whistle signals, so he showed up one morning with a new instrument for making his directions known: a trumpet.

Bentley did not have far to walk through the silence into which the Communist regime had plunged this historic neighborhood. Chausseestrasse, Bertolt Brecht's old haunt—by coincidence now also Wolf Biermann's home—was only five minutes from the station on foot. Having been a Brecht collaborator since 1942, when he first met the master (then making movies in Hollywood), Bentley was a guest in good standing in East Berlin, welcome to Communists as well as dissidents. His way to Biermann also led through Brecht, Biermann having apprenticed at the master's theater.

Bentley was aware that Biermann was a rapidly rising star and was becoming a political cause in both Germanys.* He knew that

---

* A little later in 1965, on December 15, Erich Honecker would deliver a trend-setting address on cultural standards before the Eleventh Convention of the SED's Central Committee. Honecker used a remarkable amount of time to denounce Biermann, foremost in the land, as a "petit bourgeois anarchist," a traitor who was promoting "damaging tendencies" by his rebellion against "alleged flaws

Biermann was the child of a Communist working-class family in West Germany. The father, who was Jewish, was murdered in Auschwitz. Wolf immigrated to the DDR as a teenager, acquired degrees in philosophy and mathematics, and spent many years defending the DDR. He did it backhandedly, calling it "the better German state," the lesser evil.

Bentley was also informed about the other incarnation of Biermann: the rebel. In this role Biermann started to write political songs and poems, protesting the DDR's dogmatism, ridiculing its oppression. As a singer, Biermann was pounding on raw nerves, especially among DDR youth. Sales of his works (published only in West Germany) were enormous. It was as if, in the United States, the young Frank Sinatra had decided to use his music for a private war on Washington. The Honecker government prohibited Biermann from appearing in public or traveling abroad, which made him even more of a hero.*

At Biermann's home, the singer sang some of his songs for Bentley. The American agreed to make a recording of Biermann's work in the United States.† He also came away with a better appreciation of the guts that was required in order *not* to become a defector.

"It is staying that counts now," he would write, "but staying not as a hired man of a regime but as a thorn in the flesh. So one does not cross the Wall to make headlines, one stays on one's side of it —to make trouble."

Walking back to Friedrichstrasse station with Biermann that evening, Bentley had to pass through an elaborate system of outgoing border controls that had recently been shifted into a shiny new annex especially constructed for this purpose. It blended into the neighborhood about as quietly as a Taj Mahal. In a sea of dirty

---

and mistakes" of Communist society. This was the speech in which Honecker also damned my friend the writer Stefan Heym (see Chapter 50).

* Biermann unquestionably stung the Honecker regime harder than any dissident. He came across more plainly and to larger audiences than the more intellectual rebels. Changing its course against this opponent, the government desperately tried to get Biermann to quit the country. There were frequent grotesque encounters at his home with *Stasi* officers, who sometimes arrived at 6 A.M., arguing heatedly to persuade him to go. Biermann wouldn't budge. He wanted to work against the authorities from within. Finally, in 1976, he was allowed to appear at a major concert in Cologne—and then denied reentry. Since then he has been living in the city of his birth, Hamburg.

† Bentley on Biermann: *Wolf Biermann's Songs Sung by Eric Bentley*, Folkways Records, New York (FH 5432).

stone, its tall shed roof and its shiny walls leaped out because the sides were of glass, an astonishing sight.

"They call this 'the Palace of Tears,' " said Biermann.

Departing visitors from the West were saying their sad good-byes here to relatives and friends staying behind. An old woman was selling scrawny flowers from a basket.

When I talked to Biermann many years afterward about the Palace of Tears, he remembers having gone there often in the early time of the Wall, making himself a Peeping Tom in a populist cause.

He reminded me that the Berlin authorities suffered from a chronic weakness for palaces. Ten such edifices were still standing in East Berlin, and the government's Palast der Republik on Marx-Engels-Platz was yet to be built. It was a form of megalomania. The nickname Palace of Tears (*Tränenpalast*) therefore came naturally to local humorists.*

The tears were not born equal. Biermann said that most of the weeping done at the palace was no doubt authentic, but not all. Maudlin sentiment was not Biermann's favorite key, and he'd seen plenty of crocodile's tears at the Friedrichstrasse glass house. They would well up in the eyes of certain local girls (*"Ost-Mädchen"*) who were taking dates back to the border. The men would be blue-collar people, often foreigners on temporary jobs in West Berlin.

"They'd come over to fuck," Biermann said. "Then they'd take the girls to the intershop and give them twenty marks *Westgeld* and maybe a carton of cigarettes." Western girls did not go to the East to have sex with men there. "Girls fucked only for *Westgeld*," Biermann explained. He had also noticed that visitors from the West rarely cried when they left the DDR at Friedrichstrasse. Tears were an Eastern product.

Bentley was mesmerized by the *Tränenpalast*. To him, it suggested that the authorities wanted to make everything and everyone totally visible, to strip people of their secrets, their privacy. It reminded him of a design for a prison he had heard about. It was entirely of glass so that it could be kept under control by a single guard perched high up in the center. Presumably, nothing could be hidden from him. He would be all-knowing.

Having eventually shuffled through the glass house, Bentley found himself waiting endlessly again, this time in a filthy gray-

---

* The structure was also known as *Tränenbunker* and *Tränenpavillion*.

The author's sons, Jeff and Ron Wyden, at the Wall, August 1965.

In a sea of dirty stone, the glass-walled East German border control station known as "the Palace of Tears" blends into its dreary East Berlin neighborhood about as quietly as a Taj Mahal.

brown corridor, one of the way stations toward being let out of this prison. The corridor never left his mind. It seemed somehow central to the East German experience. He would write an epitaph to it: "To this corridor all the aeons of evolution have led." Over the years I have spent quite a bit of transit time in the corridors of the station, and I resist Bentley's appalling judgment. No. Friedrichstrasse can't be the end of the line.

31

VOGEL GOES INTERNATIONAL

**London,
November 1969**

By 1969, lawyer Wolfgang Vogel's business of trading spies was running as smoothly as a commodities exchange.

In February, he witnessed the West Germans' release of his client Heinz Felfe, the KGB master mole at the top of General Gehlen's West German intelligence service. In June, Vogel and Jürgen Stange were in Paris completing the exchange of three DDR spies for three Frenchmen caught by the Soviets—a deal that had to be approved by General de Gaulle. In July, the British freed Helen and Peter Kroger, two American agents of the Russians, for whom Vogel had been bidding for five years.

And in November he set a record. He got a Soviet spy sprung from a West German prison ten days after sentencing, even though the agent, an electronics engineer, had smuggled eight hundred documents out of the top-secret West German Nuclear Research Institute.*

Impressed by so much success at such a novel specialty, the editor of London's *Daily Telegraph Magazine* decided to assign an author experienced in matters of espionage, E. H. Cookridge,† to

---

* By 1987, Vogel had been responsible for the freedom of more than 150 spies from fifteen countries.

† Real name: Edward Spiro.

write about this business and to interview Vogel. As an Austrian-born intelligence officer in World War II, Cookridge was intrigued and willing. Vogel's constant insistence on secrecy, however, had left the lawyer with such a dark reputation in the West that the writer was not about to endanger himself by appearing in East Berlin. His apprehension was specific.

"I told the editor I had no desire to put myself in a situation where I might have to be exchanged as a hostage," he would write later.

It was prudently decided that Cookridge would establish contact with Vogel by phone; any interview would then be conducted by a German reporter, Peter Schmitt from the *Telegraph*'s Bonn office.

Surprisingly, Vogel agreed and rewarded the *Telegraph*'s enterprise with a stunning degree of frankness. Other East Germans would have shunned Vogel's bragging as frivolous, possibly suicidal. But unknown to the West, the attorney had—and would always be troubled by—a frustrating public relations problem. A prophet without honor in his own country, he was also no prophet anywhere else. Many years later, when the DDR honored him with the title of "professor," the papers there carried a tiny item. It was a rare public appearance. Since Vogel's most colorful vocations, *Freikauf* and spy trades, were not acknowledged by his government, *he* was not acknowledged either.

The role of unsung hero did not suit Vogel. As an extrovert whose ego needed stroking and whose exposed position at home left him in need of a constituency, he knew that it would be risky but probably rewarding if he presented himself somewhere as a powerful and colorful public personage. West Germany was not ideal for that. It was too close to home, too subject to internal political gyrations. The public would be too apt to write him off as a *Menschenhändler,* a trader in human bodies. Besides, he was already somewhat known there, mostly as a mystery figure on television, skulking around the edges when spies were dispatched to East and West across the "Bridge of Socialist Unity." Not a masterful image.

The best place to build stature was abroad. An international reputation was the safest accident insurance. Vogel was sufficiently sophisticated to recognize that; he had mentioned it to Dora Fritzen, the shipping magnate, back in 1962 when she asked him what she should do if he fell into disgrace in the DDR and he told her to appeal to the world press.

England was a good place for a Vogel publicity splash. The British did not care for injustice. Let them get to know him. He had been doing a brisk business there for years, and they didn't even care that he couldn't speak English. Well, he did business with the Russians and the French, too, and he couldn't speak a word of Russian or French.

The representative of the *Daily Telegraph* was startled by his discoveries at Reilerstrasse 4. Instead of the sinister apparatchik, he found Vogel "a charming host," "dapper," "handsome," free with every sort of Western alcoholic beverage, and as talkative as a salesman, utterly disarming, although the dead eyes of a bust of Karl Marx seemed to glare disapprovingly at the outside interrogator from its perch atop a bookcase.*

Vogel described himself as just another very busy lawyer.

"I have to deal with more than two hundred court cases a year," he said. "Looking after prisoners accused of espionage and negotiating their exchanges is only incidental." The same held true of political prisoners who were "exchanged" with his assistance, he said; these transactions helped to improve relations between East and West. He was proud to contribute his services without charge and delighted that no one doubted him these days when he made a commitment.

"I have never made a brass penny out of these barters," he asserted, as he always did. "I am an idealist and I believe in helping people."

The host of Reilerstrasse was also happy to parade his Western life-style before his British audience. "I do not need to take my holidays in [the popular Czech spa] Karlovy Vary or on the Baltic," he scoffed. "I can spend them on the Côte d'Azur, in Switzerland or the Tyrol."

Cookridge found little to criticize in the rendition of the Marxist whom he had originally shunned like a mobster. The author came away praising the "agile brain" that lets this negotiator "deftly walk the tightrope" of satisfying his Communist employers while keeping himself reasonably sanitary to Western governments.

. . .

---

* I looked for this symbol of Vogel's Marxism on my visits to Reilerstrasse in 1985, 1986, and 1987 but it seemed to have vanished.

Vogel's public relations job on Cookridge paid off further for the "deft" lawyer. The author later wrote a book called *Spy Trade*, in which Vogel starred as a principal character. Cookridge analyzed some of Vogel's cases, and again the treatment was generally admiring. Fair was fair. One could not look at Vogel's virtuoso performance in the Lonsdale case, for example, without noting that the East Berliner was no coarse horse trader. He enlisted unlikely allies. He orchestrated. He darted all over London, lobbying, maneuvering, undeterred by barriers of culture and language.

Gordon Lonsdale had posed as a jukebox salesman until he became a resident in the maximum security section of Winsor Green Prison near Birmingham, England, sentenced to twenty-four years as a spy for the KGB. Though he pretended to be Canadian, he was Russian, with a wife and child in the Soviet Union. His original name was Conon Molody and he was heavy goods. He bossed a ring of six agents, including four Americans, who had for years stolen American, British, and NATO military secrets.

When Vogel arrived in London in July 1963, the Canadian fiction had been dropped. Much as he had represented "Mrs. Helen Abel" in the Abel-Powers trade, Vogel had papers showing that he was acting for "Mrs. Halina Lonsdale" and her daughter, Liza. Displaying his pleasant smile at the Foreign Office, the lawyer requested Lonsdale's release in exchange for Greville Wynne, the British "businessman" who had just begun serving his sentence in Moscow for having acted as a courier to the great (and by then executed) Colonel Oleg Penkovsky, the spy who knew in advance about the Berlin Wall.

Negotiators at the Foreign Office remained cool. Lonsdale was a professional who had done a lot of damage. Wynne was only a delivery man, a handholder. He was, however, something of a civilian, almost a victim, someone who could arouse sympathy among British newspaper readers. Wynne was one of their own.

Vogel converted him into a humanitarian cause. He advised Mrs. Wynne to petition the Foreign Secretary. Smiling, he called upon London politicians and journalists, counting on the British sense of fair play, not for Gordon Lonsdale, the pro, but suggesting that it was less than just to let poor Greville Wynne rot in a Moscow jail. A call for a Lonsdale-Wynne exchange was heard in the House of Commons.

The KGB helped. It told British correspondents in Moscow that Wynne's health was deteriorating. Articles were allowed to appear about the unhealthy life in Soviet prisons. But it was Vogel who kept carrying his client's ball, returning to London for a second lobbying trip, visiting Lonsdale in prison to boost his morale, beating the humanitarian drum until the Foreign Secretary in London and the Deputy Foreign Minister in Moscow struck the deal in April 1964 amid elation on both sides.

The pro had been traded for the amateur. This was textbook stuff for all negotiators who want to get more than they give.

The year 1969 marked more than Vogel's public relations coup in Britain, his entrance on the international stage. Whether by coincidence or not, it was also the time of his first *official* recognition by his employers. Although he had acted for them for almost a decade, he was never backed by more than the verbal say-so of Chief Prosecutor Josef Streit, his political godfather. This was no legalistic detail; it was a reflection of Vogel's airy status in the DDR establishment. It made him uncomfortable. Lawyers like commitments and want them set out on paper, German lawyers even more so than those elsewhere. Vogel had no paper legitimizing himself.

Now he did. On August 1, Streit handed him a two-paragraph "authority" certifying that Vogel was a "permanent legal adviser" of the DDR government, charged with representing its interests vis-à-vis "the Federal Republic of Germany, the special political territory of West Berlin and other states."

Vogel considered this document wondrous, and it was. Authorities in Communist countries abhor committing themselves on paper about anything. It is a pervasive allergy, never wanting to be held responsible, not knowing how today's action will appear in the light of tomorrow's perhaps radically altered conditions. Even if your name was Stalin or Khrushchev, it was preferable not to sign anything.

Nobody knew this better than Vogel. He also knew that his cheerful gossip to the *Daily Telegraph*, especially about his capitalist life-style, had been noted in East Berlin and had not aroused excessive offense. He had tested the limits of his exceptional status and had not fallen off the tightrope—increasingly the workplace of the powerful.

. . .

The two diplomats in the White House Jetstar, both speaking in heavily accented English, were en route to Cape Kennedy for the Apollo 14 moon shot, although neither man was remotely inter- ested in the space event. The junket had been arranged as a cover by one of them, Henry Kissinger, President Nixon's National Se- curity adviser, so he could talk privately with the other: my onetime City Desk reporter Egon Bahr, the confidant and emissary of Willy Brandt, who had become Chancellor of West Germany.

The topic of the two incognito travelers was the status of Berlin. Kissinger was hiding from his own State Department. Bahr was undercutting the equally ponderous bureaucracy of his Bonn For- eign Office.* Both men disliked and distrusted each other but were united in their distrust of their true opposition, the Communists. Kissinger's fear of State Department sabotage was so obsessive that he had arranged to communicate with Bahr secretly through a U.S. Navy officer in Frankfurt. The CIA was briefly contemplated as a middleman but was rejected as unreliable.

The problem under discussion in the Jetstar was formidable and chronic. "Berlin exceeded even SALT in its intricacy and esoteric jargon," Kissinger would remember. "The legal positions had grown up over the decades of Berlin crises, encrusted with tradi- tion and hard-won consensus."

The result was chaos. West Berliners still could not travel to East Berlin. There still was almost no phone service. Civilian rail and road traffic was under the arbitrary control of East Germany, whose existence the West did not recognize. And periodically, still, the Communists threatened Allied air and road access to West Berlin.

Though Kissinger was a frantically busy geopolitician—he was

---

* The Kissinger-Bahr underground diplomacy had started up during Brandt's first visit to Nixon, in October 1969. Already the State Department was Kissinger's great enemy. "Dealing with each other like two sovereign entities," as the ascend- ing wheeler-dealer described his relationship with his hated rival, Secretary of State William P. Rogers, the two Nixon officials negotiated a compact: Kissinger could receive Bahr but wouldn't negotiate with him. According to his memoirs, Kissinger violated the deal immediately: "Bahr, after leaving the White House by the front door, reentered it through the basement for a private talk with me, primarily to establish a channel by which we could stay in touch outside the formal procedures. . . ."

about to open up China for Nixon—he remained at heart a German-born authority on Europe, convinced that nobody knew more about Berlin than he. It irked him to have to deal with Bahr, whom he considered too friendly to the Communists, but Bahr represented Brandt and Brandt had become the new principal mover of Europe because the Soviets welcomed his *Ostpolitik*, and *Ostpolitik* was the first new thought in Europe since the Marshall Plan of the 1940s.

Kissinger detested *Ostpolitik*. It implied a long-term division of central Europe by the Wall and ultimate recognition of the DDR as a legitimate state. Those were the realities, however. To energize the "three-dimensional chess" (Kissinger's term of the negotiations), Nixon's National Security man recruited another conspirator: Kenneth Rush, the American Ambassador to Bonn. Rush was signed up in the Watergate apartment of his good friend John Mitchell, then the Attorney General. Rush agreed to negotiate the details in Europe with Bahr and with the Soviet Ambassador in Bonn. The State Department would not be filled in.

"It was an odd way to run a government," Kissinger conceded in his memoirs. "The miracle is that it worked."

In April, Kissinger and Bahr pushed the German deal ahead when they met under the cover of a conference of business leaders in Vermont. In May, the East Germans turned themselves slightly more flexible by edging the unreconstructible Walter Ulbricht into retirement, replacing him with the somewhat more reasonable Erich Honecker. Compromises were struck. The Soviets granted West Berliners the right to travel with West German passports. Kissinger agreed to let the Soviets establish a consulate in West Berlin.

White House muscle was required to persuade Secretary of State Rogers to go along with the agreement that was announced on September 27. Under it, the Soviets guaranteed the West unimpeded access to West Berlin from West Germany. West Berliners received the right to travel to East Berlin and East Germany. The Bonn government would refrain from running presidential elections and other constitutional business from Berlin, further reducing the city's slipping stature as quasi-capital of the West. And the Soviets gained Western acceptance of de facto East German control of East Berlin.

The "Quadripartite Agreement" (the title coyly made no mention of Berlin) was signed September 3 after yet another controversy was shoved under the rug. The East Germans had produced a translation that varied considerably from the English, the Russian, even the West German. So it was agreed that there would be only French, Russian, and English "official" texts. The Germans had to live under the agreement and to implement it, but not according to a German text, because there would be none.

Bahr went to work immediately to bargain out the contractual details with the DDR. His talks with the East Germans had been stalled while the overall four-power agreement was unresolved. Suddenly the hurdles were ready to be whisked away. By December 1971 an agreement on the Western transit traffic along designated major DDR highways had been signed. (It took ten minutes just to initial the seventy pages of documents.) By June 1972 telephone dial service between East and West Berlin had been put in place. In October, travel by West Berliners to East Berlin was regularized. On December 21, the two Germanys signed an agreement placing their "basic" relations on a formal and equal footing.

No further acute international crises have shaken Berlin since that time, but the impact of the Wall on private lives kept proliferating as the DDR gained in status.

PART VI

UP AGAINST THE WALL

32

THE BOOK OF BÄRBEL: IN SEARCH OF ALLIES

East Berlin,
1971

As Bärbel Grübel grew into her teens, her confrontations with teachers became more pointed, especially in her history classes. The greatness of Marx and Lenin was extolled as if no thinkers had existed before them. Recent events bore small resemblance to the experience of the students. Long before the Wall sealed off Reinhardtstrasse, the teachers tried their best to legitimize what Bärbel knew to be a blatant lie. The instructors insisted that the DDR was the ideal society, which hardly meshed with everybody's shabby clothes, the empty stores, the daily queuing, the deserted streets, the shortages. Anybody could separate the proclaimed truths of the classroom from real life outside.

The West, so the teachers insisted, was a hotbed of exploiters who victimized working people. In the patois of the DDR these nations were collectively dismissed as the "KA"—the abbreviation for *kapitalistisches Ausland* (capitalist foreign countries), the home of *Klassenfeinde* (enemies of the people), criminals less likely to reform than common crooks and therefore more despicable.

Bärbel and the more intelligent of her classmates could hardly be expected to swallow this instruction. They knew West Berlin; people over there didn't look or act exploited. The kids watched Western television, although this was forbidden. And they knew from experience that those of their teachers who had fled to West Berlin assuredly were not criminal types.

Teachers who remained in the school system needed expert assistance to persuade their charges to accept the official version of life in the East, so in the years after the Wall the political drills were frequently buttressed by emissaries dispatched from the party's Central Committee.

Bärbel hoped to embarrass these functionaries with her nervy questions. She had heard that a workers' revolt had paralyzed all East Berlin on June 17, 1953.* How had that come about? Why would workers revolt against a workers' state? And why were fortified borders required to keep people from going wherever their work or family life might take them?

The lecturers were well drilled in the party line responses and delivered the phrases with patient condescension. Accordingly, the events of June 1953 had been no rebellion; they were fleeting excesses committed by "rowdies," a favorite locution to label oppositionists. The secret services of the capitalist countries had stirred up these antisocial elements.

The sealing of the border was a defensive stop to frustrate the "warmongers" infesting the Western nations—essential protection against aggressions being plotted to destroy the DDR. The Wall was a widely misunderstood socialist measure to secure peace, and was never identified as a wall. In the official Orwellian nomenclature it was an "antifascist protective rampart" (antifaschistischer Schutzwall).

To encourage acceptance of the indoctrination or at least to stanch the flow of uncomfortable questions, the school authorities ordered the children to affix their signatures to documents attesting support of the party positions and vowing to ignore capitalist versions of the world. Bärbel and her classmates signed and signed. They had to sign a statement promising not to watch Western television or listen to the enemy radio (even though this prohibition was violated nightly in all but the most blindly Communist households). They signed a protest against the CIA invasion of Cuba at the Bay of Pigs.

Bärbel dodged as many signings as she could. She particularly resented being asked to sign a statement denouncing John F. Ken-

---

* See Chapter 18.

nedy and his policies. It made her furious to the point of tears. She admired the President more than any living person.

Bärbel could not understand Kennedy's words when she saw him on television, but his youth, good looks, and vigorous manner matched her vision of America as an open society, the home of *Freiheit,* liberty. *Freiheit* was a holy word in Bärbel's lexicon, and it would have been difficult to find anyone anywhere who worshiped the President more ardently. Magazine and newspaper photos of her hero covered the walls of her room. Somehow she had managed to scrounge an American flag and had mounted it above the display that she, years later, half-mockingly remembered as her "Kennedy museum."

Kennedy's visit to Berlin was no vague inspiration for Bärbel. It gave her a sense of obligation. To see the President in the flesh was a point of honor, the more so because the Ulbricht government was trying to discourage popular interest and flex its own muscles. DDR fighter planes patrolled the border at altitudes so low that the roar made Bärbel instinctively flatten herself to the ground. At the Charité Hospital the vibrations shattered windows and the shards injured many patients.

When Bärbel heard that Kennedy would visit the Brandenburg Gate, she ran there—only to find the view obstructed by gigantic red flags covering up the spaces between the columns. According to rumors circulating in the crowd, Kennedy would also visit Checkpoint Charlie. Bärbel raced there, only to be blocked by *Vopos* who had cordoned off the area. By the time she had run back to the Brandenburg Gate, people there said that Kennedy had already left. She never did manage to catch the glimpse she longed for.

And then her hero was assassinated. Much like Americans, Bärbel could never forget the instant the news lit into her like a blow to the stomach. It was early evening in Berlin. She was on the bus going down Unter den Linden, en route to the opera, half listening to her little battery radio. Young Kennedy dead? How could it be?

In school the next day she proposed to her classmates that they all come dressed in black the following morning. The others agreed. What changed their minds? Bärbel did not care. It was enough to know that she was the only student dressed in black. Never had she felt more starkly alone.

The school authorities were not surprised to see Bärbel so strongly affected by Kennedy's death. Not long before, her classroom teacher had visited her home on an official inspection tour and asked to see her room. Stunned to be confronted by Bärbel's "Kennedy museum," the teacher passed along word of this aberration and made relevant entries in the school records. These comments were the most telling of the verdicts already pronounced upon Bärbel over past years. Her pattern was unmistakable: Bärbel would never make an upstanding socialist. She was a troublemaker and would need watching.

As she approached the age of fifteen, Bärbel Grübel was asked to sign up for the government-sponsored ceremony called *Jugendweihe* (Youth Consecration), a secular, made-in-the-DDR novelty meant to take the place of church confirmation as a step signaling the advent of adulthood.

Bärbel refused. To have gone along would have meant lining up in a public formation and taking an oath, reminiscent of old Nazi vows, to "live, work, and fight in the spirit of proletarian internationalism and for the good of the socialist fatherland." Communist clichés were not for Bärbel. Never!

She decided instead to be confirmed in church. Though not a believer, she continued to yearn for a means to demonstrate—even flaunt—her opposition to the Ulbricht regime; confirmation was one way to take a public stand. It did entail personal risk; religion was suffered in the DDR but not gladly. Attending her preconfirmation classes in church, Bärbel winced and ducked when gangs from Erich Honecker's Free German Youth heaved rocks through the windows; on the way in and out of the building she ran a gauntlet of catcalls.

That was not the worst of it. While the DDR nominally guarantees a free higher education to all intellectually gifted youth, and Bärbel's schoolwork reflected a first-rate mind, church confirmation and her other displays of disaffection with official doctrine placed a college education automatically off limits. Sure enough, when she was summoned to appear for the DDR's draconian equivalent of high school graduation counseling, her counselor snapped, "What will it be for you: salesgirl or secretary?"

"Secretary," said Bärbel with a sigh. Years later she would write, "My thoughts of anarchism date back to that time."

She was surprised to be assigned a job in a government ministry near Checkpoint Charlie. Was this a slipup, bureaucratic sloppiness? Or a deliberate maneuver to keep an "unreliable" hothead conveniently under observation? Or was the government willing to take surprising chances to get hold of intelligent office help?

Bärbel never found out, which was just as well, because her antiauthoritarian instincts drove her to take dreadful chances. Not that she wasn't warned. Superiors ordered her not to bring her prized Western shopping bag to work, because an ad of a capitalist department store was printed on it. At an indoctrination briefing she was told that two other fifteen-year-old apprentices had been sentenced to prison for life because they allegedly smuggled some ministry papers to the Americans. From files in her own office Bärbel learned that adults caught at such activities were executed —and by guillotine.

Like the anti-Nazi resistance couple in the Fallada novel she had admired as a child, Bärbel felt challenged by dictatorial constraints. On the rare occasions when she was not watched in her office, she made for herself copies of sensitive papers. One document detailed the effects of sabotage upon a Soviet-DDR oil pipeline. She hid her collection under her mattress at home or, in summer, under the wood and paper in her parents' stove, where she could have burned her secrets instantly in case of emergency. She was hoping to run, somehow, somewhere, into a trustworthy American, to whom she would hand her hoard. Such an American never materialized and eventually Bärbel turned her documents to ashes.

She also started to hang about Checkpoint Charlie and the Bahnhof Friedrichstrasse border crossing at lunchtime so she could stop foreign visitors, especially tourists whom she could question about life in the West and whom she would guide along the Wall, kilometer upon kilometer, down to Heinrich-Heine-Strasse, up to the Walter Ulbricht Stadium. Visitors were fascinated by the Wall, and Bärbel recognized the forbidding role that the Wall had taken on in her life since she first watched this monstrosity taking shape from Petra's apartment on Reinhardtstrasse.

"The Wall, the Wall, the Wall," she wrote after escaping to the West. "Everywhere soldiers and the Wall. I was always near it, worked near it, lived near it, I was suffocated by it, obsessed with it."

Except for her friend and neighbor Petra, Bärbel still knew nobody with whom she felt free to talk. Her parents turned more and more unworldly. Her brother and two sisters seemed to care about little except having fun, an attitude that Bärbel envied and at the same time disdained. Her figure filled out, and she was a decidedly pretty girl, but melancholic, her huge dark eyes brooding. Increasingly she viewed herself as withdrawn, a bookworm, an isolate.

Almost all the males in her environment seemed to be in uniform. They made her feel as if she lived in wartime. More and more soldiers swarmed into the Reinhardtstrasse neighborhood. One evening a fire broke out in the Charité Hospital, and within minutes machine-gun posts and tanks blocked streets and lawn areas. The authorities lived in a state of constant alert, afraid that malcontents would use the hubbub of a fire as an excuse to storm the Wall.

Closer to home, the soldiers stationed in the onetime café on the ground floor of her apartment house began to show sexual interest in Bärbel. She thought they displayed illusions of grandeur; she was supposed to be flattered that they would notice her. They filled her with disgust. One day she spat at one of the men and immediately worried that this might cause her serious trouble. But the soldier said and did nothing. The DDR encouraged very prudish mores; Bärbel assumed that the man was concerned because he had approached an underage female.

Another breed of male took an interest in Bärbel, especially on Sunday afternoons, when she, along with casual acquaintances from her neighborhood, pursued the classic German Sunday afternoon activity: walking. Often the teenagers were followed by men in long leather coats who made themselves obtrusive by elaborately trying to act unobtrusive. The overcoats gave them away as *Stasi* agents; Bärbel thought they looked just like the Gestapo bloodhounds she had seen in movies about the Nazis. It amused her that teenagers in the DDR could, by catching a little Sunday exercise, stimulate the suspicions of their government.

Bärbel had just celebrated her eighteenth birthday, and was old enough to cast her vote for the first time. Like all DDR voters, she knew, of course, that elections were invariably rigged. Effective opposition was not tolerated. Non-Communist candidates were never listed on any ballot. Still, Eastern elections were not totally unanimous. A vote of 98 percent for the Ulbricht Communist slate was normal, and Bärbel had become accustomed since her schooldays to being part of a tiny minority of naysayers.

Short of committing some suicidally crazy act, she lacked almost any opportunity to make her opposition public, and still she was determined to stand up and be counted among the 2 percent who refused to knuckle under when they faced the Ulbricht steamroller. Voters were known to dare such rebellious gestures on occasion. Going to her assigned polling place, she made sure to take along a pen. She was determined to cross out some names and enter others.

Not a chance! Unlike the lines that took up so much of her time in the food stores, the queue of docile voters moved with astonishing rapidity. The election officials made no effort to stage a pro forma air of secrecy. Two women stood at the ballot box. One pressed a ballot into Bärbel's hand, the other tore it away and stuffed it in the box. The entire process took seconds. Bärbel never voted again.

Something was bound to happen sooner or later to break the logjam of her life. For Bärbel it finally came when she was nineteen, and the encounter produced a bombshell impact. In a café one Sunday she met Ota Grübel, thirteen years older, much taller than herself, overflowing with bubbly charm, expensively dressed, obviously experienced with women, and very attractive to the young females at the surrounding tables. He was a nonstop talker, words pouring out of him, words without end, always more words, and what that man was saying!

At first, Bärbel barely absorbed Ota's light blue eyes, his well-formed sensitive round face, the fluffy haircut, the pleasure that this polished, much older, burly teddy bear of a male took in her. Forces more surprising than sexual chemistry fused an instant bond. For Bärbel the rush of feelings was all but hypnotic. At last, after all the lonely, silent years, she had happened upon another free spirit, a product of the DDR who detested the Ulbricht regime and the constraints of Communism with a passionate revulsion matching her own. And, sitting among friends, Ota possessed the nerve to wax articulate about his hate, to talk and talk, even to rant about it. It was wonderful, this merging of hate at first sight, quite inseparable from love.

Ota was a salesman, extroverted like all of that breed. He sold carpets and fabrics for furniture and curtains at the Haus der Stoffe (House of Fabrics), the government establishment on Karl-Marx-Allee, and in the idiosyncratic economic hierarchy of East Germany his position conferred status and prosperity. What Ota had for sale, subject to very erratic shipments, was *Mangelware*, merchandise in chronically short supply, and since he could offer it along with his excellent taste and his appealing manner, privileged customers of the supposedly "classless" society—doctors, engineers, party functionaries, actors—flocked to him for favors and spoiled him with tips, sometimes even in the form of that most prized *Mangelware* of all: foreign currencies.

Foreign currency was the DDR's Open Sesame; it could buy anything, anything except freedom.

Freedom was Ota's personal *Mangelware*, he told Bärbel during their first long nights of mutual confessions. It had already been his problem back on the notorious weekend of August 13, 1961, when the Wall entered their lives. Ota had served three months of a one-year sentence in jail at suburban Rummelsburg when, in the early Sunday morning hours, the prison guards and their officers announced *Alarmzustand,* a state of alarm, and rushed about, pulling on their steel helmets and dragging machine guns onto the roof.

Ota and the approximately thirty other prisoners in his cell were fairly certain that war was either about to be declared or already raging. The prison personnel told them nothing. The inmates had no radio. Even the vigorously censored local newspapers were withheld until Wednesday, and then their accounts were sketchy. It was not until Ota's release that he learned what had risen at the border. He went there to see for himself. His reaction was the universal one.

"I couldn't believe it," he recalled years later. "I said to my friends, 'That'll never stay! The *Amis* [Americans] will take it down.' We were always waiting for Santa Claus."

Not Ota, not actually. In small ways he tried to provide some freedoms on his own, and it was one such enterprise that had landed him in prison. Even though many DDR citizens shared vicariously in the capitalist way of life by way of Western television, Ota, working as a waiter in 1961, lacked the necessary 1,000 marks to buy a used set; the price amounted to a month's wages. So he had gone to West Berlin, bought an old TV set for 180 marks, carried it home on the S-Bahn in an unmarked carton, and found himself denounced for this illegal act by an envious neighbor, which put him in his Rummelsburg cell.

Intermittently questioned and often kept under surveillance after his release, Ota lived in a state of restlessness, nursing his rising resentment. Continuing his education was not allowed. Changing jobs was not allowed. And his sense of basic justice kept getting him arrested. He told Bärbel how, downtown one Sunday the year before they met, he saw the police holding up traffic to let Walter Ulbricht's black Volvo limousine pass. Through its curtains Ota could see the Goatee in white shirtsleeves, a fresh rose peeking from a vase mounted near the window. An ambulance was being blocked with the rest of the traffic, although it had hoisted its little pennant to show it was carrying a patient requiring immediate care.

Ota confronted two traffic cops. "Can't you see?" he yelled, pointing at the ambulance. "You have to let him pass!"

The officers did not move. Ota kept shouting.

"Do you want to provoke an incident?" one of the cops growled.

Ota protested until he was hauled away and held for four hours, his Sunday ruined.

Bärbel was enchanted by Ota's tales of his small revolts, so similar to her own. They began to live together and, after handing out money in the right places, found an apartment with a big living room on Hermann-Matern-Strasse, around the corner from Bärbel's parents on Reinhardtstrasse. Bärbel felt uncomfortable about remaining, in effect, a captive of the Wall, but her life was turning agreeable, downright plush.

"In some respects you could buy yourself freedom," Ota remembered, and by the time they married and the children came along, little Ota and then Jeannette, they could buy and buy because they were adrift in money.

Mobilizing his ambition, his innate artistic sense, and his formidable energy, Ota free-lanced as an interior decorator for some of the affluent customers of his store. He often left home at 6 A.M. to call on clients before regular working hours. Since the shop was so short of merchandise, he could sometimes leave and start hustling for himself by 3 P.M. Sometimes he worked until 2 A.M. Eventually he earned an incredible 9,000 to 10,000 marks a month, about as much as Ulbricht's ministers. Once a customer stuffed a $50 bill in his hand. Dollars!

The Grübels dined in the finest hard-currency restaurants on filet Stroganoff and flambéed apricots, shopped for delicacies in Exquisit stores, and purchased appliances in the intershops, those oases of luxury inaccessible to most citizens because only foreign money was accepted. They frequented theaters, concerts, and the opera. They acquired a "Hawaiian-blue" Opel Rekord, used of course, for 20,000 marks, and Bärbel got her driver's license within five days, although the normal waiting period was three years or more. No driving test was required, just a written examination and a bribe of 1,000 marks—the customary arrangement for those who could afford it.

What young couple could want a better life?

Bärbel and Ota could and did. There was more to living than their affluence. They were prisoners. In public, they had to whisper whenever a remotely sensitive subject came up. Downtown, *Vopos* paced at almost every street corner; they felt watched, constantly watched, whether they were or not. Petty functionaries were everywhere, looking askance, making them feel like what they really were, outsiders, because they wore better clothes, mostly Western styles, not the lapel button of the SED, the ruling "unity" party. Quite consciously, the Grübels withdrew from their environment and replaced it with what they saw on Western television.

The TV programs were their true home until their first vacation together set off a flicker of hope, a breath of freedom from the world beyond the Wall, though not from the West. In the fall of 1968 they drove to visit friends in Czechoslovakia. Strange things happened to Communism there during the brief, golden time known as the "Prague Spring." A new Communist premier, Alexander Dubček, had tolerated a surprising degree of personal freedom until, on August 21, the Soviets rushed in with tanks to make certain that the East Berlin workers' rebellion of 1953 and the full-scale Hungarian Revolution of 1956 would not repeat themselves.

Dubček was still nominally running the country when the Grübels came to vacation in Prague (he was not purged until the following year), and for the tourists from East Berlin the atmosphere was heady. "The workers could talk and curse," Bärbel remembered. "That's what we'd been dreaming about for years. You could actually curse Ulbricht, and we did. Right out on the street!"

They also wondered about the security measures prevailing at the Czech border. Could they reach the West via that route?

"If only you had come a couple of months earlier," said their friends. "It would have been simple then, but not anymore."

Feeling like wild birds stuffed back into their cage after a quick fling in the open, Bärbel and Ota returned to their fine apartment at the Wall more depressed than when they had set out.

In the Theaterkeller, the basement restaurant of the Deutsche Theater, around the corner from their apartment at the Wall, Bärbel and Ota Grübel discovered stimulating company: stage people, students, intellectuals. More than sociability made these contacts significant in their lives. They needed to talk, to let off steam, to float their opinions, to test their ideas in dialogue. Socialist existence was suffocatingly dull, and they couldn't very well talk back to the television set.

The discussion partners who assembled over schnapps and steins of watery DDR beer on many evenings after the theater were not all kindred souls. Bright people with a variety of views joined in, and so did middle-level Communist officials from government offices in the neighborhood. Bärbel and Ota found some of these apparatchiks immune to reason in matters of politics, which sometimes made conversation awkward, because absolutely everything in the DDR could be manipulated to give off political odors.

Some party people who were immutably *linientreu,* faithful to the party line, were nevertheless of interest to Bärbel. One of the women from the Ministry of Education worked at censoring novels and short stories. Her duties kept her up to date on trends and gossip in literature all over the world, which made her a valuable informant and eased some of Bärbel's sense of isolation.

For Ota, the voluble one, the evening round table was a smorgasbord supplying what he craved so much: an audience. Forever wound up and ready to persuade, he tried to sell his idealistic populist outlook, scoffing at official doctrine, philosophizing and lecturing loudly and long. After Bärbel became a mother, she was fearful for her husband. Sometimes she was tempted to restrain him. She never did. She understood his need. So did his other listeners, friends who enjoyed him and foes who used him.

For a long time Ota burbled away unrestrained, as if the *Stasi* had decided to set him up as a propaganda show horse and as bait, to have him demonstrate that freedom of speech was not dead in the DDR after all—and to watch the reactions that his heresies released in others.

The freewheeling talkfests stretched longer and longer into the night, often winding up early in the morning with the entire circle trooping to the Grübel apartment. The Grübels were night people and loved the conviviality, the absence of intellectual restraints, the feeling of being free to speak their minds.

At the Theaterkeller, Bärbel and Ota also formed several solid friendships with young people who shared their opposition to the regime. Among them was a student couple from the Uni, the Humboldt University, Erich and Hannelore Schmidt. After Erich was evicted from the Uni for making critical remarks about the government, the Schmidts subsisted precariously on his earnings as a stagehand.

They had a youngster of little Ota's age, who attended kindergarten; the children often played together. Unlike the Grübels, the Schmidts had Western connections and had devised ways to smuggle in regular supplies of forbidden books and magazines that they loaned to their friends. The two couples also baby-sat for each other, there being no such convenience in the DDR as paid baby-sitting.

In the West later, Bärbel and Ota reminisced that they and others had found a special depth and warmth in these friendships, an emotional quality that seemed to flourish only within relationships in the East and was universally missed by refugees once they left the DDR. Was this a case of misery loving company so much that it generated unusual selflessness? Did poverty encourage altruism? Or was there something real in the one-for-all-all-for-one doctrine of camaraderie proclaimed by the slogans of the fatherland? Bärbel and Ota wondered: should they stick it out at home for a while, at least until the children were old enough to be safely moved?

Elsewhere in the DDR, the decision to get out had already ripened.

33

THE BOOK OF VOLKER: "I'M ENTITLED"

In the building of the Riesa County Council, Department of Internal Affairs, all doors except one were marked by signs showing the functions being performed inside. Behind the unmarked door, in Room Number 10, sat the officials who handled emigration applications. It was an activity that the authorities did not wish to advertise. However, Volker Seifarth, twenty-one, a steel roller in the huge state-owned Riesa steelworks, had been briefed about Room Number 10 and knew where to go.

"What do you want here?" barked a clerk when Seifarth's turn came.

"I'd like to emigrate," said Seifarth politely, placing a neatly typed voluminous application form on the clerk's counter.

"You've got to be dreaming!" said the clerk.

"No, I'm entitled," said Seifarth. "The law says so."

"How do you know that?"

Seifarth responded that someone had told him so. At once the clerk displayed interest. Who told him so? Where did that person live? Seifarth, a short, stiffly erect man with powerful, thick shoulders and arms, made his bright blue eyes go blank. He shrugged. He didn't know his informant's name, he said.

"Rejected!" snapped the clerk, tossing the application back on the counter.

"How come?"

"You have no right to ask questions here!"

"But the constitution says I'm allowed to change my domicile," Seifarth remonstrated quietly.

"Out!" yelled the clerk, tearing up the application into small pieces and flinging them ostentatiously into a wastebasket.

Seifarth knew how to make himself appear dull and servile when it suited him for a manipulative purpose, and his quiet performance at the Department of Internal Affairs was a tour de force worthy of a character actor. He was anything but calm; as he left the Department of Internal Affairs he was in fact seething. He was a proud and fiercely stubborn type. He also hated waste. It had taken considerable time to cope with the numerous pages of the emigration application, and now all the typing would have to be done again.

As a child of the DDR, Seifarth knew that patience was a requirement in dealings with all authorities, yet he could hardly have guessed that in the ensuing years the Department of Internal Affairs would become something of a second home to him. He had just launched a quest that would not end for a decade.

Berlin was responsible for Seifarth's determination to quit the DDR. More precisely, he was motivated by a particular vision of life in West Berlin, experiences reported to him by peers, young people he could trust.

When he was a child, Volker did not distinguish between East and West Berlin. Berlin was Berlin, the noisy big town two and a half hours north of Riesa by train. Berlin was the rich place that had everything, the mecca for shoppers where adults went to stock up on goodies before Christmas. Volker's grandparents had taken him along on such a holiday junket when he was seven or eight years old. That was before the Wall, and Volker was permitted to select a wristwatch for himself, with an armband that was too wide for him. Much later he realized that they must have bought the watch in West Berlin. You couldn't walk into a store and buy a watch in the East.

On his next trip to the capital Volker had been thirteen. He was on a high school class excursion. The group spent a week touring museums, the Brandenburg Gate, and other historical sites. The Wall was up. Nobody mentioned it. Volker would remember riding past a stretch of it on the elevated train and asking the teacher why barbed wire was strung at the top. The teacher said he'd discuss that later; he never did. Volker didn't mind. He assumed that all national borders looked that way. East Berlin was his Berlin and that was that.

At the age of fifteen his indifference toward the city's division had remained unchanged. He had become an apprentice steelworker in the VEB Rohkombinat Stahl und Walzwerk Riesa, the town's principal enterprise, where his father was chief crane operator. And in this closed Communist workers' society Volker caught his first reliable glimpse of the West, his first picture that didn't come from Western television, a source that was slightly suspect as possible propaganda.

His education came from some older apprentices who worked at his plant, fellows aged eighteen and nineteen, who went to Berlin on weekends. They were trainees temporarily in the DDR from Venezuela, Cuba, and other third world countries. All were certified Communists, and the DDR authorities were obviously anxious to treat them elegantly. The foreign apprentices received half their pay in Western currency, and when they returned from Berlin they were loaded with great clothes, chocolate, and tales of fabulous girls.

At first, Seifarth did not catch on. With his Eastern blinders still in place, he assumed that his foreign friends had caroused in East Berlin. He did not realize that the Wall was penetrable for holders of foreign passports. Once it dawned on him that the reported pleasures were available only in West Berlin, a dream took hold. Someday he would leave the East. It was no place for a young man who was aware of his intellectual limitations, and accepted them, but whose innate love of an unshackled life was incompatible with the dreariness and the handcuffs, unseen but real, of the DDR. He wanted to go places, to see places, and he didn't want to ask for permission every time, like a kid in school asking the teacher to let him go to the bathroom.

He hated Riesa. It was not as hopelessly provincial as Goltzscha, his native village, ten miles away in the countryside of Saxony, where his grandmother ran the inn and his grandfather was the mayor and leading Communist. Still, for an industrial center of 50,000 people, an inland port of consequence along a bend of the Elbe River, Riesa was plainly disgusting, a monument to the DDR's indifference toward the practically uncontrolled environmental pollution that prevailed throughout the country but was at its worst around concentrations of heavy industry.

Nobody hung up laundry within miles of Riesa's steel plant because it would turn gray in minutes. In warm weather the Elbe did not smell, it stank. A chemical plant upriver dumped all its waste into the water, and it was not the sole offender. At Riesa the Elbe was a chemical smorgasbord, sometimes running solid green and sometimes red.

Riesa did have a regional reputation for an expensive and excellent brand of salami, but talented people did not usually live in the town longer than absolutely required. The hospital, for instance, had a dreadful reputation. It was widely rumored that wives of party bosses refused to give birth there; these privileged mothers would seek out one of the few surviving small hospitals run by churches.

Economics and aesthetics were not Volker Seifarth's principal motivators, nor was he given to any political or religious persuasion. And though politics bored him, his ripening decision was chiefly political; he was beginning to recognize that he couldn't stomach the DDR system. Its hypocrisy offended him.

He was supposedly living in a classless society; all the media said so. What bull! Volker liked his grandparents in Goltzscha, but he couldn't see why they should profit from preferential treatment simply because they were party big shots. That wasn't the equality the media mouthed about. In school the teachers kept referring deferentially to the status of his grandfather as if he were some superior being. They also fussed about an uncle, a party functionary who belonged to one of the *Kampfgruppen* militia units that were mobilized when the Wall went up on that celebrated weekend of August 1961.

Volker thought the fussing was absurd. He preferred the independence of his father, an apolitical worker who placidly accepted the system and kept out of trouble, but whose freedoms could not be encroached upon beyond his personal thermostat setting for tolerance.

Volker would always admire how the old man had stood firm when a band of Free German Youth (FDJ) teenagers in their blue shirts appeared at his house one weekend to haul down the family's television antenna. The youngsters were part of a nationwide government campaign to deprive DDR viewers of the capability to tune in Western stations. The effort was a particular hardship for audiences in Saxony. The province was known as "the Valley of the Innocent" because atmospheric conditions often made the reception of democratic stations impossible without an antenna.

Eventually the scheme was abandoned because almost nobody would give up Western TV. The defeat turned into a major domestic embarrassment for the government, but that came later. When the Blue Shirts arrived at Volker's house, resistance could spell serious trouble. Regardless, his father didn't hesitate to tell the party youths to get the hell away from his home or else, so he shouted, he'd sic the dogs on them.

Volker's father had shown himself supportive toward his son's career choice. He had not insisted that Volker enter the steelworks. The father was an avid do-it-yourselfer with a basement full of tools, and he appreciated his son's manual skills. As a boy, Volker shaped his own toy soldiers out of lead. When the time came for him to decide on a profession, he said he wanted to be a plumber and his father agreed.

A master plumber was found who accepted Volker as an apprentice, but the government's efforts further to centralize and collectivize the economy blew up the boy's plans. A few days before he was to start work, the plumber's shop was expropriated, the master went into retirement, and the *Abteilung Volksbildung,* the educational authorities in charge of such assignments, summarily ordered Volker into the steel mill after all. His skills would be underutilized there, the working conditions in the plant were hard, and Volker resented that his career choice was ignored by a bureaucracy whose rulings were beyond appeal.

By 1973 he had decided that he had kept his decision to go West in abeyance long enough. He had not mentioned his intention to a soul until one evening, apropos of nothing in particular, he began to talk about it to his girlfriend, Gisela—a Riesa native, twenty, one year younger than he.

"I want out," he simply said. Gisela understood at once, but she thought he was not serious. For a young man with a most conventional working-class background Volker sometimes harbored unconventional impulses involving long hours of travel. At least his wanderlust seemed exotic to Gisela, a rather shy, easily intimidated young woman out of an equally colorless working-class environment.

"This is one of your silly things, isn't it?" she asked.

"No, I've been thinking about it for a long time," he said. "Listen, how do you feel about it?"

Gisela was scared. She had been together with Volker for more than five years, which seemed pretty much forever. She could not readily picture life without him anymore. They shared a lot of interests, especially in sports. Volker was on the boxing team at the steel mill, and when they had first met, at a party for sports-minded teenagers, Gisela was a full-time student at a special school for gymnasts.

She was working as a waitress nowadays, angling to get into the restaurant management field. Her life seemed set. Now, all of a sudden, Volker wanted to leave his family, his town, his work, everything, in exchange for an unpredictable fate in the West, and he wanted her to do the same. It seemed farfetched, downright crazy.

"There are disadvantages," she told him cautiously. "Over here we know what we've got. Over there everything is unknown."

They discussed some of the obvious pros and cons, but not long. Volker was not much for conversation once his mind was made up.

"I'm going to go in any event," he announced.

Gisela was shocked but said nothing.

Volker felt abandoned. His urge to leave the DDR was undiminished, but somebody had to help him figure out how to do it. He didn't want to wind up like his brother-in-law, who was serving a six-year sentence in Brandenburg prison for an escape attempt. So when his sister mentioned that the family had hired a prominent attorney, Wolfgang Vogel in East Berlin, to get the brother-in-law's sentence reduced, Volker decided to see this influential man on his own behalf as well.

He never met Vogel. It took him three months to get an appointment, and he was favorably impressed when he found forbidden Western magazines casually displayed on the coffee tables in the great man's waiting room on Reilerstrasse. But he got to meet only with one of Vogel's associates and received advice that he considered unhelpful.

"Nothing will happen unless you get yourself arrested," the lawyer said with a perfectly straight face.

It was true. In the Orwellian culture of the DDR, a well-behaved citizen was pretty much stuck in place. The most efficient way to get an exit permit was to commit a crime. Then you went to prison, your name would go onto Vogel's lists for *Freikauf,* and eventually the West German government would ransom you out of the country. That was the normal drill.

The prison route did not appeal to Seifarth. Jail was for criminals and for bumpkins who allowed themselves to get caught, as his brother-in-law had. Volker proposed to join neither category, so, feeling lost and isolated at the steelworks, he turned during one lunch break to a crony, a young fellow he had known most of his life.

He began with extreme caution, simply ruminating about the joyless ways of the DDR, much like a foot soldier griping about life in his foxhole. When his pal responded on a similar note, Volker grew bolder. After a few more exchanges of grievances he finally came out with it: he admitted that he had been thinking about leaving the country.

"Is that really what you want to do?" asked his friend.

"You're damned right," said Volker.

By instinct or perhaps just by tremendous good luck, he happened to have shared his dream with a kindred spirit knowledgeable about the techniques of *Ausreise,* or "exit travel," the official euphemism for emigration.

"Did you know that you can submit an ordinary legal application?" asked the friend.

Volker had never heard of such a thing. It seemed incredible. He was delighted.

"I'll take you to someone who'll help you," the friend said, and right then it developed that this "someone" was a man Seifarth had long known and trusted: his doctor.

Volker knew Dr. Karl-Heinz Nitschke as a most untypical medic. He was an internist, forty-three, the plant physician at the steelworks. Unlike most doctors, even in the supposedly collegial DDR, he was not a bit stuffy. He expected to be addressed with the familiar *Du,* not as *Herr Doktor,* and he tended to side with employee-patients rather than factory management. When Volker had sustained a burn injury to his foot, Dr. Nitschke made sure that he received plenty of convalescent time.

The doctor welcomed Seifarth warmly to his second-floor apartment in a new suburban block at Schwerinerstrasse 26, but here a sterner and more cautious side of the older man emerged. What did Volker want to leave the country for? Seifarth talked about his appetite for new experiences, for a "free life," for wanting to see more of the world.

Dr. Nitschke sounded skeptical.

"Here you're part of the system," he said. "A lot gets done for you. What do you think it'll be like to live over there? Don't think it'll be so easy! You have to shift for yourself and the job market is very different."

For Volker the lecture was almost like listening to Gisela's warnings all over again, but again he was not dissuaded. The doctor's wife typed his exit application, and after the document wound up in the wastebasket at the Department of Internal Affairs, she typed it another time.

It was the typing that aroused the suspicion of the Internal Affairs clerk when Volker appeared for the second time. It was the following Tuesday, the only day of the week when Room Number 10 and the emigration people were accessible to the public.

"Who wrote this?" barked the clerk. "You don't have a typewriter!"

"My sister does."

"But you can't type!"

"Yes, I can, with one finger."

In the course of the ensuing discussion Seifarth cited relevant paragraph numbers of the DDR constitution as well as references to human rights resolutions passed by the United Nations, rattling off these legalisms word for word, as he had been coached by Dr. Nitschke.

"You mean you really want to pursue this?" asked the clerk.

"I'll be here every Tuesday, you can depend on it!"

And so he was, with only occasional unavoidable lapses, month after month, year after year. His reception varied. In the early days the clerks simply barked that they had no developments to report and told him to get out. When Volker asked questions, the clerks became abusive. Who in hell did he think he was, anyway, making demands that they work on his papers? They were not accountable to him, they said. Once, one of the older bosses came out from an inner office and called him a *Knallkopf,* a quaint term slightly more insulting than "dunderhead."

In time, as the iron quality of his determination could no longer be ignored, Seifarth was frequently invited into an inner office. Seated at a conference table, the little steelworker was interrogated by the official who called him *Knallkopf;* he was invariably accompanied by a second official, who never said a word.

The first question was always the same: "What's your motive?"

Right at that point Seifarth committed an unfortunate tactical error. Two principal motives drove dissidents to leave the DDR. Generally, they wanted to get out either for economic or political

reasons. Seifarth told the truth. He said his reason was political—
he detested the DDR government, its system, all its works.

More than a decade later, in the West, he learned what even the
well-informed Dr. Nitschke did not realize: the emigration functionaries were under instructions to stall politically minded applicants, preferably forever. Such rebels were considered ingrates
who deserved to be subjected to as much frustration as the system
could dispense. Potential emigrants with economic motivation were
vulnerable to very different treatment. They tended to be more
approachable. Often they could be moved by negotiation.

Eventually, Herr Knallkopf and his silent cohort tested Seifarth
for his responses to economic incentives, a strategy that brought
about a startling change in the atmosphere that faced him on Tues-
days in the Department of Internal Affairs. When Seifarth arrived
in Room 10 either before or after his shift at the mill, a clerk
welcomed him cordially. The familiar *Du* form of address, which
the clerks had employed with him to put Volker in his place as a
half-grown whippersnapper, was not longer applied to him. He
was treated circumspectly, a little like a land mine.

"*Ach, Herr Seifarth,*" said the clerk, all but bowing in the manner
of a salesman, "do come in and have a seat!"

By then Herr Knallkopf was thoroughly briefed about Volker's
private life. He knew that Gisela had moved in to live with him.
Two government men had dropped in on her for a chat when she
was not at work one day. They had been elaborately polite, com-
miserating about the deplorably small size of Volker's apartment
and picking up that she and Volker were talking about getting
married. They knew that she had not filed an emigration application of her own. No doubt they guessed that she was less than eager
to leave the country.

Herr Knallkopf was equally friendly in his negotiations with
Volker.

"I think we can get you a new apartment," he said with a slight
smile at the opening of another session in Room Number 10. He
mentioned the new condominium complex where the apartment
was located and expressed confidence that satisfactory financial
terms could be arranged.

Seifarth realized that he was being blackmailed and said he
wasn't interested.

Why don't you look at the apartment anyway?" suggested
Knallkopf. "After all, you want to get married."

"I know the apartments," said Seifarth and departed.

Next he was summoned by the secretary of the party unit at the steelworks. This dignitary, too, exuded smiles and goodwill. He praised Volker's record at work and said that he deserved a promotion. The secretary had different, less arduous work in mind for him, something that could be done in street clothes. Volker thanked him but said he was not looking for different work. He was looking for a different country to live in.

As he well knew, this bizarre turnaround in the attitude of the authorities and their smiling courtship of him were not set off by concern for his personal plans. More was at stake. He had become identified as a follower of Dr. Nitschke, and the doctor was a dangerous enemy of the state whose conspiracies had to be stopped, preferably before word of his activities became widely disseminated.

Seifarth was taken aback when he discovered that his old friend the doctor was fomenting civil disobedience in, of all places, Riesa. The doctor was calling on like-minded citizens among his neighbors and acquaintances to stand up for *Bürgerrecht* (citizens' rights), a concept unheard of in the DDR. Dr. Nitschke was speaking out at meetings, mostly of young couples, that convened in his apartment, sometimes in the apartments of others.

Volker attended more than a dozen such meetings over three years. He was not a joiner. Nature and the DDR society had made him, if anything, suspicious. He found the gatherings nevertheless congenial and informative. At his first get-together about fifteen people were in attendance and he knew at least ten of them, which was comforting. Sometimes there would be thirty or more. All were trying to leave the DDR, which made Seifarth feel less lonely, less like an oddball. Some meetings adjourned in an hour, some lasted all evening with the doctor doing most of the talking. Usually he had new information to help the potential emigrants advance their cause with the authorities.

The gatherings were illegal and dangerous, as they all knew. Everyone realized they were under observation. The fact that they were not stopped was surprising and encouraging. It suggested that the government had not yet decided how to deal with Dr. Nitschke, and this was true. He was a vexing case. The *Stasi* had never experienced anyone quite like him. He could be put away in an instant, of course, but word would get out to the Western press. He would become a hero, a martyr.

An estimated 150,000 DDR citizens were chafing to quit the

country, possibly tens of thousands more than that. If something happened to turn that many malcontents into clamorous demonstrators, perhaps at the Berlin Wall, the DDR would look like a prison state again. Honecker, in office for only two years, was determined not to lose face that way.

No, precipitous steps against Dr. Nitschke could cause trouble. The man needed careful watching. In time, he could perhaps be tripped up quietly, very quietly. Once he was out of business, small-time followers like Volker Seifarth could be taken care of. For the DDR authorities, the disposal of individual cases did not accomplish much. The trouble was systemic.

34

WALL SICKNESS: A CURABLE PSYCHIATRIC ILLNESS

East Berlin, Spring 1972

Mrs. E. S., a forty-year-old saleswoman, had been referred to the Department of Psychotherapy in August 1962. The transfer was requested by dentists at the Leipzig University Clinic for Nervous Diseases because the patient could open her mouth only less than one inch. She was highly agitated and depressed. No physical causes could be found.

DDR psychiatrists treating her with sedatives soon discovered that the woman's problems were directly traceable to the building of the Wall one year earlier. After marrying a West German citizen in the spring of 1961, she moved into his fine apartment in West Germany, where he had a good job. Having become a West German citizen, Mrs. E. S. returned for a brief visit to her native town, a small community near Leipzig, to sell and give away her remaining household belongings there. Her disposition was sunny, the outlook for her life blissful.

On Monday, August 14, her chores completed, Mrs. E. S. went to the rail station and blithely asked to buy a ticket for the interzonal train home. She was refused. Her West German passport was no help. The railroad employee, an old acquaintance of hers, patiently explained that DDR citizenship is never lost. Since the weekend border closure, she would need a special permit. Mrs. E. S. went to the police and local government offices with the same results. It was an excellent idea for her to rejoin her husband, the officials told her, but the couple ought not to be living among the imperialist West Germans. Her husband should come East. Together they should help "build socialism." These were the events that signaled the onset of her illness.

Increasingly depressed and irritable, Mrs. E. S. turned to higher and higher bureaus and finally to Walter Ulbricht's Council of State in Berlin. Everywhere the response was the same.

She was keeping her husband informed by phone and mail. At first he found it difficult to take their problem seriously. The DDR authorities must be engaging in "dumb jokes," he said. How could they refuse him permission to live with his wife in his hometown, where they had been legally married and had established legal residence?

Once he realized that the obstacles to his marriage were real, the husband became warmly supportive and applied for relief by bombarding various DDR authorities with letters, again without success. His wife, meanwhile, became deeply depressed and required medication regularly in order to be able to work. In the summer of 1962 she acquired her jaw closure problem, clearly of psychogenic origin.

The psychiatrists at the university clinic treated Mrs. E. S. with induced sleep to calm her. She was further given hypnosis, autogenic relaxation exercises, occupation therapy, group therapy, and group gymnastics. The doctors deliberately ignored the jaw problem. Once they had determined that there were no emotional problems in the patient's background, they kept psychotherapy to a minimum, because the sessions invariably led Mrs. E. S. to restrict herself to railing against her fate at the hands of the bureaucrats, which was hardly a psychiatrically treatable condition.

After a hospitalization of six weeks, Mrs. E. S.'s jaw problem had vanished. Her spirits were much improved. Her old energy and normally optimistic outlook had returned. "Things are looking up for me," she said, "so now I finally want to get back to my husband."

Again she tackled the government offices. Again she was refused. Again she became depressed. This time the condition turned extreme and did not improve with more intensive treatment. In October she threatened suicide.

The case interested the director of the clinic, Dr. Dietfried Müller-Hegemann, trained at the famous Charité Hospital in Berlin and now also Professor of Psychiatry and Neurology at Leipzig

University. Patients with emotional problems caused by life circumstances were hardly unusual, and sometimes politics played a role.
The condition troubling Mrs. E. S. was uncommon because it came
on virtually overnight (*"blitzartig,"* like lightning) and the building
of the Berlin Wall could be pinpointed as the precipitating event.

Were there many such cases? Dr. Müller-Hegemann decided to
keep his psychiatrically trained eye on the Wall.

Mrs. E. S. recovered as if by a miracle as soon as the Wall was
made porous for her. The clinic had written to the district physician in her hometown refusing to accept responsibility if her exit
permit were to be delayed further. The permit was issued, she
rejoined her husband, and wrote to the clinic that she was doing
fine.

From 1964 to 1971, by then as the director of East Berlin's largest psychiatric institution, the Wilhelm Griesinger Hospital, Dr.
Müller-Hegemann investigated the new clinical syndrome that East
Berliners had come to call "Wall sickness." Usually, this was a
depression of varying severity, sometimes a psychosis that occasionally led to suicide. It was explicitly set off by the Wall and it
was a risky field of study.*

The doctor was able to take notes only surreptitiously and only
in a private code. The fact that he had undertaken the research at
all had to be kept secret because he had been officially advised that
the use of the term "Wall" in connection with psychiatric work was
taboo. He had to do all his own legwork because he could find no
way to circulate questionnaires about this too-hot topic among his
colleagues. And despite the doctor's rank, he could not break loose
any statistics about suicide, traditionally a DDR state secret.†

Eventually Dr. Müller-Hegemann would publish a book in the
West,‡ discussing thirty-six of his sample case histories of Wall
sickness in some detail, although he admitted that he was dealing

---

* Among precedents for psychiatric conditions caused by political events are
barbed-wire sickness, first chronicled among long-term prisoners of war in World
War I, and *KZ Syndrom,* a cluster of mental aberrations troubling World War II
concentration camp survivors.

† An emergency-room doctor at the Charité Hospital, Dr. Wolfgang Hoffmann,
reported that the total caseload of suicides in the East Berlin area increased by
some 200 for the year following August 1961.

‡ *Die Berliner Mauerkrankheit* (Nicolaische Verlagsbuchhandlung, 1973).

with no more than a fragment of the phenomenon. Not even all of his own research was available to be included in his report. The doctor left the DDR in 1972 to become a visiting professor of psychiatry at the University of Pennsylvania Hospital in Philadelphia. He worked on the book there but had been unable to take along all his notes.

Fairly typical was the 1968 case of a forty-eight-year-old saleswoman, Mrs. F. Z., admitted by the doctor's Berlin hospital in a psychotic state and suffering from a severe depression and paranoia. The staff treated her with large dosages of psychopharmaceutical medications and eventually traced her condition back to Sunday, August 13, 1961.

Her husband and the older of her two sons happened to be visiting her mother-in-law in West Berlin. As news of the border closure spread along Mrs. Z.'s street, the neighbors became enormously agitated. Not Mrs. Z. She was not the excitable type then. She recalled that the border had been closed once before, during the June 17, 1953, riots, and had quickly been reopened. She also felt confident that she could depend on her level-headed and resourceful husband, with whom she had enjoyed a close marriage for twenty years.

Listening to the radio she became upset after all. The border action was said to be permanent. Mrs. Z. breathed easier with the further announcement that all DDR citizens who happened to have been caught in the West would be allowed to return.

When it became very late there still was no sign of her husband. Distraught, she dashed to the nearby border with her twelve-year-old son. It was a most distressing scene. Thick crowds of citizens were milling about, venting their indignation. No information was to be had.

Since no phone lines existed, Mrs. Z. telegraphed her husband and spent a sleepless night. A wire came from him shortly, asking her to wait for a letter from him. It was this letter that ended her marriage and life as she had known it. The husband said he would not return. He reminded his wife that they had often talked of moving West. It was time to do that. He was certain that the DDR authorities would not wish to split up a family. He would take the required legal steps. She should do the same.

As Mrs. Z. made her rounds of government offices, her mental state deteriorated markedly. Though she had once been so placid, her excitement became extreme. Her temper was in constant explosion. Faced with officials, she screamed at them as loudly as she could. It made no difference. Patiently, monotonously, the officials lectured that her family could easily be reunited. Her husband would simply have to come home.

Throughout this period, Mrs. Z. had to seek medical help in order to be able to work at her job. Her doctor prescribed sleeping pills and tranquilizers. Her husband's letters—they were loving but adamant—made clear that he was sick of the DDR. As time went by Mrs. Z. slowly became resigned. Her energy left her. She refused to see old friends and permitted herself no relaxing pleasures.

Over the ensuing years, her state worsened steadily. She became increasingly withdrawn, then suspicious, then paranoid. She thought her neighbors were plotting against her, that her apartment had been searched, that her bed sheets had been moved. She had a "fine nose" for that sort of trickery, she said. At her workplace she got in trouble because she kept muttering imprecations at "the Wall."

When her inner turmoil became as acute as it had been in August 1961, her doctor ordered her hospitalized. After a ten-week stay, Dr. Müller-Hegemann found an improvement of her symptoms but concluded that her prognosis was "not favorable." Her Wall sickness would have been treatable only by a reunion with her husband—a cure that her government would not allow.

The doctor's overall prognosis for psychiatry in the DDR was also poor. As coeditor of the journal *Psychiatrie, Neurologie und medizinische Psychologie,* he was being accused of "objectivism" and of allowing himself to be seduced by "Western" influences. In the fall of 1970, the country's psychiatrists and psychotherapists were summoned by the party's Central Committee to a policy conference in Brandenburg. The doctors were informed that theirs was the only medical specialty being elevated to an "ideological discipline," whose theory and practice would be guided by the party line.

Dr. Müller-Hegemann made up his mind to leave the country. Wall sickness in its acute form was ebbing, but the doctor took little hope from that. What he had heard at the Brandenburg conference sounded painfully familiar. As a longtime socialist, he had belonged to the anti-Nazi resistance, and when the Nazis were solidifying their rule in the 1930s, they had gone through similar steps. They called it *Gleichschaltung,* coordination, meaning centralization and no deviation. The buttons were pushed at the top, and in the DDR the top was reachable by only very, very few.

35

INSIDE THE VIP GHETTO: THE CASE OF THE UNDERESTIMATED COMRADE

**Wandlitz, East Germany,
Summer 1973**

Wolfgang Vogel was slowly rising in the DDR hierarchy, but his first contact with the new East German head of state, Erich Honecker, the architect of the very Wall that the lawyer sought to weaken, was formal, in writing.

Walter Ulbricht, old and outdated like a battleship, unpopular with the Soviets, had been shoved into retirement in 1971 with the aid of "the friends," the Russians. Honecker, who succeeded him as General Secretary of the SED,* was different: a more subtle,

---

* His power fully consolidated, Honecker acquired his second title, Chairman of the DDR's Council of State, in 1976. For each of these functions he maintained an elaborate set of offices in a separate setting, as if to demonstrate physically that he was at least twice as powerful as any other mortal. Most of his working time Honecker spent in Suite 2010 of a gloomy old gray five-story colossus on the Werdersche Markt square. It once housed the Reichsbank of the Nazi period. Here, surrounded by the "ZK," the national political apparatus, the Central Committee (*Zentralkomitee*) of the SED with its staff of more than two thousand, he presided as head of the party. This was the true pinnacle of the government; a ZK department head (*Abteilungleiter*) wielded more power than a minister in the state apparatus. In his second incarnation, as head of the state, Honecker officiated in the relatively cheerful, ornate, and more modern (1964) Staatsrat (Council of State) building, with its face of natural stone. This anchored a huge square, the Marx-Engels-Platz, the government center at the foot of the Unter den Linden

somewhat less insular type, less inclined to wave away realities. For instance, he did not look upon the West German brethren as anachronisms doomed to extinction.

If Honecker's thinking was a shade less blindly doctrinaire, his actions were no less steely. When the West Germans in 1972 publicized a DDR amnesty for citizens who had resettled in the West and then said that they wanted to stop paying East Berlin ransom for the release of future prisoners, Honecker reacted drastically. He ordered a strike. There would be no further exits. Not even dissidents who already possessed their permits would be allowed to emigrate. These unfortunates became known as *Kofferfälle*, luggage cases, because they were all but left sitting on their packed bags.

In Bonn, too, the governing cast had changed. Willy Brandt was Chancellor. The new Minister for All-German Affairs, another Social Democrat, Herbert Wehner, was very different from his noisy and ambitious predecessors. Crusty and independent, his pipe seemingly cemented into his craggy face, Wehner was a widely trusted old-timer. Characteristically, his nickname was "Uncle Herbert."

Wehner, an insider not yet appreciated by history, was a thinker. Like Brandt, he thought deeply about "the distant neighbors."* The two crotchety colleagues fought a lot about *Ostpolitik*, too, but unlike the early Christian Democrats, both acknowledged that the geographically nearby strangers *had* to be dealt with, and Wehner had the advantage of knowing them firsthand. He was a shoemaker's son from Dresden, right in the SED's Saxony stronghold. In his youth he had been a Communist, one of the wartime emigrants to Moscow, where he had become well acquainted with Wal-

---

Boulevard. The Staatsrat was flanked on one side by the antiseptic white Foreign Ministry and on the other by the monumental, starkly glassed-in Palast der Republik, which housed the Volkskammer (parliament) and was popularly known as "the lamp store" because of the many lights inside. The arrangement of the buildings conveyed a meaning: the showy Parliament, Council of State, and Foreign Ministry fulfilled largely ceremonial functions. The power rested in the drab Central Committee building, looming like a sentinel directly behind the others, alone, on its own square.

* *The Distant Neighbors* was the wonderfully descriptive title of a shrewd book about the DDR by Klaus Bölling, once spokesman for West German Chancellor Helmut Schmidt and West German representative in East Berlin from 1981 to 1983.

ter Ulbricht and the DDR's founding fathers. He was an authority who had been present at the Creation, and in the earliest Hitler years he had helped Honecker with Communist Party organization work in the General Secretary's native Saar region. Though Wehner was only six years older, he was already a major party leader and Honecker looked up to him.

Wolfgang Vogel's personal radar, scanning for productive contacts in the West, had picked up Wehner as a prospect years earlier. The lawyer had cultivated this much older ex-Marxist, visiting him often in Bonn, taking up hardship immigration cases, exploring the fratricidal strife between their two countries, nurturing a personal relationship that ultimately came to resemble a father-son kinship. No doubt about it: Vogel had a knack not only for making himself indispensable, but making himself liked and building unquestioned trust.

Honecker's strike was an unpleasantly public setback for Wehner. As the responsible minister, he could not afford to let future West German citizens sit on their suitcases in the East. It looked too much as if they were being abandoned. He had to get to Honecker personally. Eleven years after the Wall, the leaders of the two Germanys still were not talking to each other; so Wehner asked Vogel whether he could arrange a meeting with the number one East German.

Vogel turned to Streit in the Justice Ministry. The request was so touchy that Streit—quite possibly not wishing to be in the position of having to make the sales pitch to the top—asked Vogel for a letter.

Vogel, habitually mindful of everyone's time pressures, composed only a few lines. *"Grossen Leuten muss man wenig schreiben"* was one of the rules he once shared with me ("To great people one must write little").

"You'll hear from me," said Streit. Vogel heard nothing for two months, but the approach worked. Honecker had never forgotten Wehner's Communist past and had heard reports of this ex-colleague's ruminations about the two German futures. Moreover, there continued to be excellent reasons why the DDR should continue the *Freikauf* process.

The public in both Germanys seemed not to object to it. Western goods continued in very short supply in the East. A safety valve for expelling malcontents was still convenient, and the DDR had added a wrinkle: into the flow of political refugees it had quietly mixed some real criminals. Since they, too, were Germans, the Bonn government decided it could not keep these undesirables out.

Nor had it escaped Honecker and his Politburo colleagues that they were in control of *Freikauf* because they could regulate the supply of prisoners at will. If they wished to increase their income from this trade, they only had to let more "politicals" go West. The more they let go, the more they could restock their prisoner supply by rounding up more dissidents. More than enough were always at hand, because the reasons for arrests, as set out in the DDR's catch-all statutes, were plentiful and richly varied. Almost anybody could qualify as a "hatemonger" or be considered guilty of seeking "illegal contacts."

While Honecker eventually decided to receive Wehner, he made sure to keep his distance by ordering that the occasion not be dignified by an official atmosphere. Accompanied by one aide each, the two leaders convened May 31, 1973, on the veranda of Honecker's lakeside home at Wandlitz. Nibbling that all-German between-meals snack *Kaffee und Kuchen,* coffee and cake, they were shown in news photos perched on garden chairs around a tiny white outdoor table, wearing business suits, with coats and ties to match their grave expressions.

News accounts did not mention that the first of the waiting refugees were allowed to cross the border on the following day and that Western payments resumed as well.

Such rare glimpses of Honecker at home also failed to reveal the sense of superiority and the paranoia that characterized the DDR leadership, all of whose members resided in luxurious regimentation at the shores of the lovely Lake Wandlitz, in the fir woods off the Bernau Autobahn about twenty-five kilometers north of Berlin.

Theirs was a quasi-collective, its core taking up more than seven square kilometers. Despite its sylvan surroundings this retreat was a fortress, encircled by two widely separated concrete double walls, each about twelve feet high. The double gates were of thick steel, and the entire complex was patrolled around the clock by an elite military unit of 160 volunteers.

Its goal was to protect the rulers from the ruled, and it was secrecy itself. I once met a *Genosse* who was invited to the home of a VIP resident there, an old friend. It was an exalted privilege, and my informant didn't tell a soul about it. To talk about the inside of Wandlitz was an invitation to the *Stasi* to investigate.

Begun not long before the Wall went up, the roads and excavations for this ghetto were so unusually elaborate and obviously costly, and the layout looked so military, that CIA headquarters in Langley, Virginia, grew alarmed, then frantic. Encoded messages began to bombard its BOB, the Berlin Operating Base.

To Langley, the preparations for the large, rigidly lined-up homes—thirty-two of them, mostly in rows of six—looked suspiciously like the excavations for missile launching platforms that American spy satellites had been photographing in "denied" (Soviet-controlled) areas around the Communist world. Langley wanted Wandlitz investigated at once. Close-up details were needed from the ground.

The CIA officers were stumped. What area was more denied than Wandlitz? No ordinary civilian—and certainly no agent—could get near the place. Suddenly miraculously, phenomenal luck struck at the Marienfelde Reception Center. Among its many refugees, at first it was almost impossible to believe, was the architect who had designed the Wandlitz settlement!

Delighted, the Americans sequestered the architect in an office of his own, got him a drafting table and all other equipment he might need, and asked him to recall his plans from memory as best he could. In due course the man produced a book-size document. The CIA agents shipped it off to Langley with a sigh of relief. Rarely had they managed to rid themselves so elegantly of so sensitive a task.

Or one involving so much detail. The architect's renderings had to be extensive because Wandlitz was an autonomous little city. The homes were nothing special by Western standards: largely identical, three stories of beige stucco, three or four bedrooms, the upstairs floor set aside for servants. The interiors varied with each resident's tastes. Ulbricht was content with heavy upholstering on his sofas and lace doilies on his tables. Honecker, beginning to assert a measure of worldliness, had acquired valuable paintings, including a Picasso.

Within the ghetto walls, a store catered to daily needs. Other conveniences included a clinic, a gymnasium, half a dozen tennis courts, a pistol range, and a kindergarten. The Kulturhaus contained a restaurant, a theater, a banquet hall, and a heated pool whose movable windows let in the outdoors during summer.

The service personnel, numbering more than three hundred,

lived in their own village of apartment blocks, outside the walls, with its own shopping center, repair shops, and beach, within easy walking distance of Lake Wandlitz.

Alas, this paradise was not without figurative worms gnawing in the apple. At various times, at least in the early 1970s, the leaders' homes were infested with cockroaches, and the water often contained silverfish. Other complaints were heard. At least one of the VIP residents enjoyed motoring and was unhappy because she was not allowed to drive her car to work. She was Ingeburg Lange, one of two female candidates for membership in the Politburo. It annoyed her that security rules made it necessary that she be chauffeured from and to "Volvograd" in the customary dark blue Volvo limousine, surrounded by cars containing the men she called her "sputniks," her bodyguards.*

Even before terrorists and assassination commandos became worrisome, the Honecker government was obsessed with its safety.† The rulers' vehicles from Wandlitz enjoyed the right-of-way to Berlin automatically. Honecker, the only one in the group to use a silver-gray Citroën, used two identical models to throw gunmen off the track. The very passage from Wandlitz enjoyed royal privileges. After leaving the Autobahn en route to the min-

---

* I am indebted for these household details to Katja Lange-Müller, Ingeburg Lange's daughter. A frequent Wandlitz visitor in the 1970s, the daughter resettled in the West in 1986, and her fiction at once began winning prizes—a rare turn for young authors raised in the stultifying East. The mother, a onetime protégée of Erich Honecker in the Free German Youth, was a minority on two counts, as a woman and as a Jew. To describe her relationship with her brilliant, rebellious daughter would require a Tolstoy. I learned of other DDR leaders who frantically struggled but failed to keep their sons and daughters in the East. These were poignant tragedies with political and personal motives irretrievably intertwined.

† In the late 1970s, the Wandlitz group would acquire its own rural atomic bunker, forty miles northeast of Berlin. The supplies stockpiled in this hideout were meant to let the leaders ride out a nuclear attack for up to two years. Although the bunker was supposedly supersecret, its existence was well known to residents of the nearby villages, Möglin and Schulzendorf. They called the place "Honecker's *Wolfsschanze*," Honecker's Wolf's Hole. Reportedly measuring nine hundred feet in diameter at ground level and dug two hundred feet deep into the ground behind concrete walls twelve feet thick, the oval area was well defended against domestic as well as foreign intruders. A set of three fences surrounded it. The innermost fence could be charged with up to 35,000 volts of electricity.

istries in Berlin, the limousines passed through the business district of Pankow, and the shops there were ordered to take special precautions. They had to stuff their windows with goods not actually available, since the Wandlitz stretch was a *Protokollstrecke,* a "protocol road"—an environment where the republic's best foot had to be put forward. It was a matter of face. Face was terribly important to Honecker and his *arrivistes.* Everything had to look right, hopefully to look as rich as in the West.*

In his early years as the number one resident of Wandlitz, Erich Honecker was still imprisoned by his unpromising past. He moved awkwardly, looking fragile and painfully stiff, like a toy soldier. He lacked flair and all other outwardly leaderlike qualities.

The "GS" (General Secretary) was a lackluster speaker, peering blankly from behind thick horn-rimmed spectacles and given to the swallowing of syllables. He managed to seem pale even when tanned. Somehow he could never fill up a television screen. His smile looked forced. But there was nothing grim about him, none of the sinister air that had hovered about Ulbricht.

Honecker appeared to be a bland party hack who had made it to the top by slogging ahead tenaciously, cautiously, engaging in no intrigues, following in Ulbricht's shadow, utterly reliable on crucial assignments like the Wall, above all *linientreu,* a steadfast follower of the party line.

And hugely underestimated.

Self-confidence came very slowly to Honecker. No wonder. The poverty in Kuchenbergstrasse 88, Wiebelskirchen, the Saarland home of his coal miner father, a lifelong Communist, was palpable —and easy even for a child to trace to the source. The reactionary owner of the local industry, the ironworks, founded the "Association to Combat Socialism," and his workers were allowed to get

---

* This is no generalized interpretation. The DDR leadership is extremely sensitive to appearances in general and to the implications of shop windows in particular. When Ambassador Karl Seidel, the Foreign Office official in charge of relations with West Germany, lectured me about the "ideological drumfire" to which the DDR was daily exposed from Western television, he grew especially bitter about the seductive influence of the *Schaufenster Optik* (the optics of the display window) and the *Glanz des Schaufensters* (the glow of the display window). I gathered I was being asked to accept the notion that the display of luxury on TV amounted to mean-spirited anti-Communist psychological warfare (see Chapter 62).

married only on days authorized by this personification of the capitalist system. The underdogs knew where they stood and so did their children.

The Saarland also transmitted a measure of cheer to young Erich. It showed itself as gemütlich, a cozy retreat of relaxing beer gardens where menfolk gathered in summer, protected from the sun by a certain simple, solid kind of straw hat, worn slightly off the forehead. Half a century later, a writer from the area noted that General Secretary Honecker was still wearing a Saarland-style straw hat. He wrote a profile of Honecker, inferring that the GS retained a secret longing for his deeply German petit bourgeois origins. A Western diplomat asked Honecker whether this was true; the number one East German said that he had read the article and agreed with it.

This was a meaningful confession, for at the age of eighteen, already a full-time functionary of the Communist party, Honecker was further exposed to another, a very different, infinitely more exciting environment. It inspired him, and perhaps he adopted it as temporary roots at the time. He was sent to the Lenin School in Moscow, the cadre training ground for world revolution. Decades later, in his autobiography, he would describe his excitement at the moment when his train crossed the Soviet border and soldiers of the Red Army jumped aboard.

"For me," he or his ghostwriter exulted, "the land of Lenin was my fatherland."

Not for long. In his government, Honecker would naturally maintain amiable relations with his numerous Soviet contacts and on occasion was overheard conversing with them at length in their own language. Communism was his religion. Nevertheless, he would confess to a surprising degree of independence from the occupiers, once lecturing a West German negotiator, "You had better keep in mind that the policy of the German Democratic Republic is not made on Unter den Linden" (the location of the Soviet Embassy in East Berlin). The same diplomat learned that Honecker looked upon the Soviet invasion of Afghanistan with foreboding and was severely troubled by the Soviet push for more missiles during the 1970s.

At heart Honecker remained an arch-German, an admirer of Bismarck and Prussian royalty, a sentimental son of the Saarland, and—most significant by far—an authentic, certifiable, anti-Nazi who did not sit out World War II in Moscow but spent almost ten years, nearly one third of his life at the time, incarcerated in a brutal German place, the Brandenburg Görden prison. There he worked with a cell of resisters, all during the period when the local guillotine decapitated two thousand inmates, sometimes thirty-five per day.

It was a time of fear, courage and for honing the arts of survival, not for building self-confidence, not yet, not even when the Nazi nightmare was over. When Honecker was placed in charge of the Free German Youth movement, his faith in the Communist cause was firmer than his dialectical skill. He was genuinely embarrassed in 1945 when he took an apprentice colleague to lunch at the party's Central Committee and the young man, a newcomer, asked why there were three lunchrooms for three grades of comrades (Honecker ate with the middle echelon officials in the second room).

The young man challenged the system; it did not fit his picture of socialism. After a pause, Honecker recovered and said that only enemies of the state thought of Communism as an equalizer. In practice, the movement treated everyone according to his achievements.

Other postwar eyewitnesses pictured Honecker as absurdly eager to kowtow to superiors. Hermann Weber, who would become a professor of history in West Germany and author of the most authoritative history of the DDR, worked for Honecker in the Free German Youth after the war. He would remember that Honecker stooped so low as to court acceptance of his bosses by adopting their favorite phrases and imitating their speech patterns.

"At that time I thought he would never amount to anything big," Weber said. "He always looked to the people above him, and so did a lot of others. As his self-confidence has grown, so has the man."

Once Honecker himself rose to become the word from above, his considerable self-discipline could not control his pride and his great vanity. He loved to be considered fast on his feet and witty. At a large dinner, he was not above calling the attention of a guest at another table to a pointed remark that he, the GS, had just delivered and that the other might have missed.

Even his highest-ranking associates were expected to defer to him in the most informal circumstances. While they were presumably at their ease, it was Honecker who staked out the conversational themes, who interrupted with unscheduled remarks, who drew others into the circle of discussion at times of his choosing.

Rigid order, unvarying protocol, deliberate formality, unhurried pace—those were the trademarks of Honecker's operating style.

Over the years his almost aristocratic bearing encouraged a deification that could embarrass him to the point of remonstrating. When an elderly Saarland editor claimed that Honecker had been something of a model youth who neither smoked nor drank, the General Secretary entered a public correction. He wanted to be known as a regular guy.

"I was no saint; I used to enjoy a beer even though money was tight," he recalled. "Later I smoked, too, although I stopped on the advice of my doctors when I got older." Back in Wiebelskirchen, he said, he belonged to a workers' gymnastics group and played handball. Pig's knuckles and sauerkraut was his favorite dish in adulthood, and beer would always remain his favorite drink.

Honecker's brief descent off his pedestal may have been superfluous. Gossip flourished in the DDR, inadvertently encouraged by the lofty dullness of the media. Thus it was no secret that Honecker's love life failed to follow the puritanical model preferred by the Politburo, at least as it presented its members to the public. By those lights, Honecker was a playboy.

Not always. In 1947, as a thirty-five-year-old bachelor, he married his first wife, Edith, three years older and his deputy in the Free German Youth. Their idyll—Erich built some of their furniture himself—lasted two years, until he met the girlish, blond Margot Feist, a Free Youth functionary from Halle, eighteen years his junior, very bright, ambitious, and possessed of considerable charm.

Their affair, launched in the summer of 1949, quickly became known in their circle. Colleagues noted when Erich came to see his girlfriend and talked about the way he promoted her career. Edith resisted a divorce for four years, but in 1953 Erich and Margot could marry. Margot rose to be his deputy, as Edith had been, and her husband's government appointed her Minister of Education in 1963.

The year of their separation is not known. They kept up a married front, appearing as a couple at some official functions, but nobody was fooled. Reportedly they were divorced by the court of Berlin-Lichtenberg in 1970, though documentation is lacking.

Honecker's bachelor fun was purely German—hunting, sometimes, surprisingly, in the company of a Western supercapitalist like Berthold Beitz, the Krupp steel baron; and singing. After a hunt and on other relaxed occasions the General Secretary chanted the old *Volkslieder* of his childhood, gustily, in a strong, high voice, and poked fun at those who, unlike himself, remembered the lyrics of only the first stanzas.

Honecker's cult of personality would erupt in the DDR media in startling ways. A joint communiqué by the General Secretary and the Romanian Prime Minister or other visiting dignitaries received an envoi of biblical proportions, pages and pages of print and pictures. It was at the end of one Romanian courtesy call that I counted eight photos of Honecker in *Neues Deutschland,* including three on the front page. There he was, smiling, waving, looking grave, signing documents, watching the presentation of flowers, admiring an electronics demonstration, basking front and center in his archangel role,* a picture editor's Saturday night.

After the Wall went up, the personality cult was institutionalized by the official introduction of *Eingabewesen,* the right to make "submissions." Any citizen who considered himself unjustly treated by the authorities could complain in writing.†

Naturally Honecker was the recipient of the largest number of submissions, and these were studied by a sizable staff. Not infrequently, Honecker ruled against his bureaucracy, which threw its machinery into instant reverse gear. The process reminded Western diplomats and correspondents of court procedures practiced by Prussian kings. Certainly they were just as arbitrary.

One reason why Western critics of the DDR often underestimated Honecker was that they applied inapplicable yardsticks: their own. DDR citizens naturally tended to compare their present

---

* Readers who find their credulity strained are referred to pages 1, 2, and 3 of *Neues Deutschland* for May 31, 1985. This was no record. In the June 2, 1987, issue Honecker was pictured twelve times.

† The East German industrial regulators (though not their West German counterparts) also reintroduced the *Beschwerdebuch,* the complaint book, officially known as the *Gästebuch* (guest book), a hallowed pre-Hitler tradition in restaurants. Under Ulbricht and Honecker, diners could again formally register gripes about food and service in a big book that had to be kept available by management. Under the Communists this outlet for frustrations became an instrument of government punishment. An establishment that finished the year with too many complaints was penalized financially.

state with the recent past of their Communist world. And measured against Ulbricht, Honecker meant substantial progress. There were no more purges and intrigues. He ruled softly and in a reasonable, collegial manner. He *listened*. He maintained stability: there were no more 1953 riots, no strikes, few protests of the noisier sort, not for some time. Honecker was learning that it sometimes paid not to assert one's power in matters of small moment— as long as everyone was left in no doubt about who was in *control*.

If the economy remained shaky, the nation met its obligations on the dot, and the world had at last taken note that it *was* a nation; even the United States and the United Nations had so agreed. If it still took seven years to get a telephone installed, at least housing was hurriedly getting built and fruit was in the stores slightly more often.

Another dimension worked in Honecker's favor and kept most of his citizens placated; this factor, too, was largely overlooked by critics. Through their prisms, Westerners tended to see the East Germans cut off, in isolation. Not at all. The Wall did much to separate them from the democratic world, but the East was a huge place, and it was wide open to them. If one couldn't play in the sun on Majorca, one could get tanned on the beaches of the Black Sea. The bus tours to the playgrounds of the East were incredibly cheap, and during their stay in other satellite nations the East Germans made a consoling observation: they were better off than the Soviets, better off than any of the East bloc countries except Hungary. Like all else, poverty was relative.

At home, meanwhile, life was getting better steadily. The trend was hardly visible from month to month, but living standards were definitely beginning to improve under the ministrations of this much underestimated Saarlander with the straw hat.

That satisfied some of his citizens, but far from all.

Shy as a young girl *(left)*, the independent-minded Bärbel turned into a rebellious teenager *(below)*. Bärbel's mother, Eva *(below right)*, was too timid to flee West.

Bärbel grew up at 37 Reinhardtstrasse *(above)*, just a few yards from the Wall.

Ota, Bärbel, and Sulamith in 1987.

POWER PLAYERS

Walter Ulbricht *(left)* trusted his protégé, Erich Honecker *(below).*

West Berlin Mayor (later West German Chancellor) Willy Brandt *(above)* was let down by his ally, President Kennedy.

AUGUST 13, 1961:
A QUICK AND EASY COMMUNIST VICTORY

With water cannon and a wall of troops, the East Germans sealed the Brandenburg Gate —and Khrushchev and Ulbricht celebrated.

In the early days, when the Wall was merely a strand of barbed wire over which neighbors could still shake hands, East Berliners were able to flee merely by climbing out of their windows.

Even the *Vopos* weren't immune to temptation. Conrad Schumann *(above right)*, a nineteen-year-old sergeant attached to the first unit of East German troops to close the Brandenburg Gate, hurdled his way to freedom two days after East Berlin was sealed off.

Escaping could sometimes be as simple a matter as running across the street.

But it wasn't long before the East Germans began to brick up the gaps.

THE NET TIGHTENS

With families split, newlyweds began to make appointments at the Wall so relatives in the East could see them in their wedding finery.

By the autumn of 1961, the thin strand of barbed wire was being replaced by far more formidable construction.

Vopos carry off the body of Peter Fechter *(above)*, who bled to death near Checkpoint Charlie after being shot in a widely protested August 1962 escape attempt. Where troops weren't visible, "death automats" *(above right)* were.

As the Wall fortifications grew, houses were knocked down to make room.

Three fifths of the city's population jammed into the streets to greet John Kennedy when he visited West Berlin on June 26, 1963. "Two thousand years ago, the proudest boast was *'Civis Romanus sum'* ['I am a Roman citizen']," he told the huge crowd. "Today, in the world of freedom, the proudest boast is *'Ich bin ein Berliner.'*"

One American official after another came to inspect the Wall at close hand: General Lucius Clay *(above),* national security adviser McGeorge Bundy *(above right),* and NSC deputy chief Walt W. Rostow *(right),* who was accompanied by the ranking U.S. diplomat in Berlin, Allan Lightner.

As border security grew stricter, ingenuity became the order of the day for would-be escapers. Hidden compartments could be fitted into the most unlikely places—from automobile radiators to cable reels.

Despite the difficulties of construction and the constant risk of discovery, tunnels under the Wall were long a favorite mode of escape.

Sometimes all it took was boldness and poise. This East German family, dressed in their own homemade Soviet army uniforms, managed to drive unmolested through a Wall checkpoint.

After one aborted attempt, Günter Wetzel and Peter Strelzyk built and flew an eight-story-high hot-air balloon that carried them, their wives, and their four children West in September 1979.

But countless thousands didn't make it. This bullet-riddled bus failed in an attempt to crash through the Wall.

DEN OPFERN DES STALINI...

AN DER MAUER ERMORDET

West Berliners erected this memorial to the many who died trying to escape to freedom.

THE GRÜBELS LOSE THEIR CHILDREN

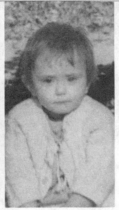

Little Ota and Jeannette were taken from their parents on August 6, 1973, when the Grübel family was captured by Czech border guards as they attempted to escape into Austria. The Grübels have not seen their children since.

Bärbel in the Grübels' "Hawaiian-blue" Opel just before the abortive escape attempt.

Bärbel and Ota in happier times with Ota's mother. Both grandmothers later operated a determined campaign to discover what had become of their grandchildren.

Though Bärbel and Ota Grübel were finally allowed to emigrate West, the toll of their years in prison and the loss of little Ota and Jeannette is still evident in their faces.

THE SEIFARTHS LOSE THEIR MARRIAGE

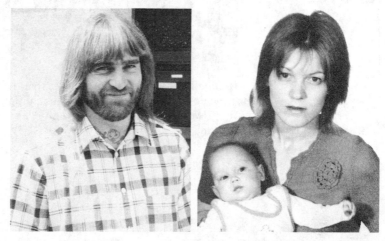

Volker Seifarth's desire to move West cost him his wife and daughter.

A facade reminiscent of a Hollywood movie set hides the stark devastation that surrounds the Wall.

Despite Erich Honecker's promises that the Wall will come down soon, the East Germans continue to "improve" the barrier, making it more escape-proof all the time.

In the West, graffiti, a U.S. Army patrol, and the modern Checkpoint Charlie.

There is nowhere to hide around the Wall today. Much of its eastern side is preceded by a death strip: anyone caught in this no-man's land is liable to be shot on sight.

36

THE BOOK OF BÄRBEL: SHOTS AT THE FRONTIER

**East Berlin,
September 1973**

The small freedoms enjoyed by Bärbel and Ota were fading. Gradually they had to admit it to themselves: their liberties were illusory. The freewheeling talkfests with their friends in the Theaterkeller had to have been monitored by the government. The DDR was letting them live on borrowed time. Their freedoms had been arbitrarily bestowed by the party, and the party could cancel the privileges at will.

The first warning came through their friends Erich and Hannelore Schmidt. The young students were arrested, their apartment searched, their Western literature confiscated. Upon their eventual release, Hannelore was fired from the university, as Erich had been kicked out earlier. Their child was dismissed from kindergarten. The last student subsidy payments stopped. Saddest of all, the Schmidts were shunned by their friends. They had become nonpersons, too risky to associate with.

Not so for the Grübels. Bärbel and Ota made it their business to care for the Schmidts' little son whenever possible. They asked Erich and Hannelore over for meals more often. They gave their friends clothing and money. Honecker & Co. were not to sit in judgment over their friendships.

What the *Stasi* thought of their unconventional behavior the Grübels of course never learned. The possibilities were interesting.

Were Bärbel and Ota diagnosed as bizarre intellectual isolates? Might there be many such fearless malcontents hidden throughout the DDR? Could the Grübels lead the authorities to other nuclei of potential unrest? Or could people like them be turned and persuaded to use their obvious sincerity on behalf of the regime?

Obviously puzzled, the *Stasi* decided to uncover what this odd pair was about, and so, early one warm summer morning, a pleasantly wrinkled-looking man with an ingratiating smile and a big briefcase appeared at their apartment on Hermann-Matern-Strasse. The visitor looked cozy, grandfatherly, in his sixties, and said he had been with the *Staatssicherheit* but was "retired." He had come over to chat a bit.

Bärbel and Ota liked this emissary's warmth and apparent understanding. His very curiosity was attractive, disarming. He was an audience.

"What don't you like about our society?" he inquired softly. "What's really so bad?" Bärbel and Ota told him they would never feel fully alive as long as they were muzzled, and then they went on from there. Ota in particular lectured expansively, as usual.

"It was just open and honest—it made me feel good to come right out and tell him what I thought," he recalled much later, still with the innocence and naïveté of the righteous.

The "retired" *Stasi* type was sympathetic. He told the Grübels that they were "clever" and "interesting," that Ota plainly had a promising future. It would be a shame for them to freeze themselves rigidly into negative attitudes. And so unnecessary. Everything that they disliked about the country would change in time. Meanwhile, he would personally be willing to help by interceding in their behalf with higher authority. . . .

At this point, little Ota, insatiably investigative like all boys of three and a half years, opened the visitor's briefcase and exposed a hefty-sized tape recorder. Which abruptly ended the visit, although still did not shut up the irrepressible Grübels.

Later that week they were visited by their *Abschnittsbevollmächtigte*, their sector controller, the same sort of official local snoop who had spied under the title of *Blockwart* (block warden) during the Nazi period. This one was a simple type. He wanted to know what in the world was wrong on Hermann-Matern-Strasse.

Ota gave him a cognac and complained that there were too many cops in the streets. And why did the troops of the People's Army have to march in goose step like the Nazis—hadn't Germany had enough of that kind of thing? And why did consumers have to have "connections" to squeeze scarce *Mangelware* out of the shops?

The *Blockwart* who was no longer called *Blockwart* gulped another cognac and withdrew. The Grübels congratulated themselves. It felt great to be open and honest.

Two days later a distant relative of Bärbel's was at the door, sweaty and with a bad case of jitters. Bärbel had never liked this man, mostly because he was a government bureaucrat.

"You've got to leave and right away," the relative whispered. He confessed that *Stasi* agents had visited him the year before. They wanted to be filled in on the Grübels. The relative had told them what he knew and had kept them informed from then on. Now he had a guilty conscience.

"It's getting critical," he murmured. "They're ready to come and get you!"

Bärbel and Ota parked their Hawaiian blue Opel in the woods and scampered off toward the Czech-Austrian border, less than five hundred yards away. They were unencumbered by possessions except for a pair of wire cutters and a small flashlight. Their local guide, young Hanuš, was trotting ahead.

It was shortly before midnight, Monday, August 7, 1973, surprisingly cold, cloudy, and totally dark—no lights visible anywhere. Ota was carrying his sleeping little son on his back, wrapped in a dark cloth, papoose style. Jeannette, clutching her favorite doll, was stirring awake in Bärbel's arms.

Panting from exertion, the parents could not, of course—not in their worst nightmares—imagine that punishment perhaps worse than death was about to befall them. It would be a living death: they would have only one more day with their children. After that, they would be forever separated from little Ota and Jeannette.

It had taken a month to determine a time and place for escape. To friends and relatives back home in East Berlin, Bärbel and Ota had said they were going on vacation at the summer house of friends near Prague; this cover story burdened nobody with any guilty knowledge; there would be nothing to confess once the men in the long leather coats came around with questions. And questions were inevitable, because Bärbel and Ota had made a firm decision: under no circumstance were they coming back home.

Since they doubted the trustworthiness of all experienced "escape helpers," they had to do their own planning. How? They had no idea. Their chief concern was the comfort and safety of their children. The kids should not get too frightened and would have to keep still at the critical moments. Ota, senior, occasionally took Faustan tablets, a mild tranquilizer. From friends at the Charité Hospital, Bärbel learned that two tablets were perfectly safe even for small children, so some Faustans would come along on the trip. Both kids were delighted when they heard that they were going to the country on holiday.

The friends in Prague also were not told of the impending venture. This couple used their cottage only on weekends, so the Grübels had plenty of time to study maps for the likeliest border crossings. But the maps proved misleading; they made difficult terrain look too easy. For five days the Grübels inspected the border area with depressing results. Taking care to make themselves look like vacationers in search of a picnic site, they tramped through woods and fields checking for accessible approaches to the frontier. They found none. Mountains, rivers, and excessive distances barred the way.

Finally they drove into Slavonice, and the outlook brightened. The outskirts of the pretty village could hardly have been closer to the frontier; the nearest guard tower was about one third of a mile distant and easily visible.

At the gas station they met an elderly widow who spoke German and offered to rent them a room in her home. Chatting with her that evening the Grübels steered the talk to politics and the Wall, and they mentioned that in the DDR the border guards operated with "shoot-to-kill" orders. The landlady responded that nobody had ever tried to flee across the border at Slavonice.

The next day Ota went to the police station, and told the officer in charge that he and his family were vacationing in the village and that he would like to do some fishing. He said he had heard that the most promising ponds were in the immediate border territory, so he assumed he would need a permit. With a friendly smile the officer wished Ota a pleasant vacation and told him of an elderly townsman who belonged to the fishing club and could get him the permit.

For several afternoons Ota went angling at various fishing holes and had plenty of time to study the topography and defenses of the border. His observations were cheering. The two fences marking the frontier did not look insurmountable. He saw no dogs or cleared-off "death strip." The guard towers, about 250 yards apart, were each manned by only one soldier. The scene looked almost bucolic. Would they face worse at night?

Bärbel and Ota realized they would need local assistance, so with some trepidation they decided to take their landlady into their confidence, step by step. Once Bärbel had told the children their usual bedtime story and they were asleep, she began by remarking that the family did not enjoy living in East Berlin. Their hostess said that if she were younger she wouldn't want to live in Czecho-slovakia either.

Bärbel took the plunge.

"We really want to get across the border," she confessed.

"I understand you well," said the old woman. "I'll help you as much as I can, just don't tell me too much."

Relieved, Ota asked her whether he could borrow the key for the little church across the street; the steeple looked like a good spot for night reconnaissance. The old woman did even better. She brought the key as well as binoculars for better daytime viewing, too.

The elevated observation post yielded no fresh information except the good news that the border was not lighted at night.

Time was running out. Any day now the Grübels' employers back home would report them missing. The children had to be prepared for the perils ahead. Bärbel and Ota had held gentle rehearsals for the kids by taking them along to the church tower and telling them that they had to keep absolutely quiet while observing the border, that border country was dangerous and full of bad soldiers. Jeannette was too small to understand more, but little Ota would have to be told additional details.

His father took him aside and revealed that the family was not returning home; they would move to a place with fewer restrictions.

Little Ota, having undoubtedly picked up earlier signs of his parents' dislike for the constraints of the DDR, listened attentively and said: "That's okay. Things are pretty stupid at home anyway. Anytime we play on the lawn out in front of the house some police-man says we have to play someplace else." His father's warnings about the border did not trouble the boy either. They sounded like rules for some cops-and-robbers game.

The Grübels' method of raising their youngsters was paying off. Although they recognized that they were given little freedoms unknown to other kids, little Ota and Jeannette knew very well when to mind their parents. In Slavonice, the Grübel children loved to throw some of their small plastic toys into the shallow town fountain just to fish them out again. The local kids were aghast and said that their parents would never permit such nonsense. Bärbel and Ota were delighted. Their kids were uncowed, but in a tight spot they were likely to handle themselves sensibly. Certainly they did not behave like uprooted youngsters fearful about their future.

The shears needed for wire cutting remained a problem. Ota made inquiries around Slavonice and all surrounding communities. Finally he had to drive to Brno, a large city 120 miles distant, to locate this crucial item. And promptly upon his return the Grübels' escape plot acquired its last, indispensable component: Hanuš, the son of Ota's old fishing companion, offered to act as guide.

Hanuš was another miraculous find. He had been stationed at the local sector of the border during his military service and possessed a country dweller's intimacy with the terrain. He told Ota where to look for trip wire that could set off the alarm system. He pinpointed the safest possible spot for skipping into Austria. He warned that dogs might be used against them after all, but that the animals could be thrown off by the scent of ordinary pepper.

On Sunday, August 6, Bärbel and Ota played all day with their children and did not put them down for their usual nap; they would be tired by evening. At 8 P.M. they said farewell to their hostess and gave her all their Czech currency. The old widow kissed each of them on the forehead. She promised to light candles that night and pray for their safe journey.

At Hanuš' house a garden party was in progress. Hanuš was playing the guitar. The Grübel children squealed as they threw wood into the blazing fire. Then their parents gave them the Faustan tablets and watched them fall asleep in the back of the Opel, snugly wrapped in their blankets, Jeannette holding her doll tightly.

From the church steeple their marching route had looked short and simple. On the ground in the dark it was an interminable obstacle course. For several hundred yards they stumbled across fields and meadows until swampy woods slowed them greatly. Mud gurgled above their ankles. Both children were awake now. Should they have been given more pills?

Jeannette insisted that her father carry her as well as her brother. She clutched his neck and clamped her legs around his chest. She kissed her brother and whispered, "Psst, we've got to be very quiet so the soldiers won't hear us!"

Bärbel had lost one shoe in the swamp and then abandoned the other in order to walk better. Systematically, she left a trail of pepper behind. Every few steps Ota turned to her and whispered, "Can you keep going?" Silently, Bärbel plowed on, the ground turning wetter, softer. The party's progress slowed still more until they reached firm ground and an open field. Hanuš motioned that the border was just ahead. He would leave them at this point. He waved good-bye and vanished.

Breathing hard, Bärbel and Ota leaned against a haystack and peered about. A guard tower loomed in front of them. Earlier they had heard cows. Now all was silent.

Ota moved on alone to reconnoiter, passing through a field of chest-high cornstalks that he could not completely keep from rustling. Fortunately they slowed him down so much that he had no trouble locating—and stepping carefully over—the trip wire running along the ground about ten feet before the first fence.

Stopping to study his last obstacles, Ota located guard towers to his left and right, each more than one hundred yards away. The fence he faced was about eight feet high. And—he froze—there was a death strip after all, just beyond: a stretch of light, neatly raked sand, narrow, not enormous, as in Berlin. This one was some ten yards wide. The final fence, behind the sand, seemed not forbidding either, perhaps seven feet tall.

Returning to report to Bärbel, Ota couldn't tell her what he had seen. It was already too late for words. A signal rocket popped into the sky from the direction of Hanuš' departure route. Had they caught him? Would he give them away? Time had run out.

Pleading with the children to stay absolutely quiet, Ota swept both into his arms and took off on the run through the cornfield, Bärbel trailing close behind, still barefoot.

This time the cornstalks could not be silenced. To Ota the noise sounded like an audience of a hundred people applauding.

At the first fence he clipped away the top three wires, stretched his overcoat lengthwise over the fourth and rolled himself across. Bärbel handed over the blessedly silent children. Ota helped her over the fence. They all stood still to listen. Nothing. It was past 3 A.M. At this time of year dawn would break before long.

"Come on!" Ota hissed excitedly, picking up the kids.

They raced across the sand strip to the final fence obstacle. Not wanting to take time to wield the wire cutters, Ota used hands and feet to press apart two fence strands, enough to create an adequate opening. Ota crawled through first, his clothes repeatedly getting stuck and tearing. The kids followed, Ota pulling and Bärbel pushing. Then Bärbel snaked across. It all seemed to take forever.

A flat, vacant cornfield stretched in front of them. Ota picked up his son, Bärbel swept up Jeannette, and together they ran headlong toward Austria until Ota threw himself to the ground and motioned Bärbel to do the same. They had to catch their breath.

Suddenly the entire area was alight as in daytime. A signal rocket exploded overhead. What did it mean?

They ran on for a stretch and again flopped to the ground. They *had* to be in Austria, and, as if in quick confirmation, they heard voices in the distance. The words sounded German.

Two panting soldiers and a dog raced past. Ota thought they had not been spotted, but the soldiers stopped, pointed their submachine guns at the stunned family, and yelled something, evidently in Czech. The Grübels could not make out the words but understood the meaning well. They were to get up and raise their hands high.

It was not over. From the Austrian side shots rang out. The Czech soldiers returned the fire. Though they had obviously advanced too far, it was equally apparent that nobody wanted an international incident. The Austrian fire had been warning shots. Signal rockets popped next. Then the shooting abruptly ceased. The Grübels and their wide-eyed children were surrounded by soldiers and an officer who gave unmistakable signals with their flashlights: they were to head back to the Czech border, to Communism.

At the Slavonice police station, Ota and Bärbel, exhausted, their clothes torn and mud-covered, focused their worries on the children. What would happen to the kids while their parents served the inevitable jail sentences? It was by far the most foreboding of the many questions they asked themselves that day.

The kids zeroed in on the villains around them.

"Why did the soldiers shoot?" little Ota asked his father.

"Because they're dumb and don't know what they're doing," he said.

A military guard was sitting on a chair nearby. Jeannette jumped up and hit him on the head with her doll. The man jumped up, frightened, and yelled, "No talking! No talking!" in poor German.

Ota quieted the kids, and they fell asleep on a shabby couch. The room smelled of tobacco and sauerkraut.

The ensuing interrogation covered the predictable ground predictably. Yes, they had acted entirely on their own. No, absolutely nobody in the village had helped. Yes, they realized the law called for them to be handed over to the DDR authorities. Still, how could the Czechs sit by and send a family to its destruction?

The interrogators were apologetic and brought bread and lemonade for the children, who had awakened and had questions of their own.

"Why can't we go outside to play?" little Ota wanted to know.

His father explained that the soldiers would not allow it and that the kids would have to accept other changes, too. Mama and Papa would be going to prison and would not be seeing them for a while.

Luckily, the meaning of the word "prison" baffled the children, and so the prospect of a temporary separation did not seem to frighten them at first. They were secure in the knowledge that parents were people who sometimes went away for a while but always turned up again quite promptly.

"We'll just wait for you at Oma's house," said little Ota cheerfully, and Jeannette repeated his words in her normal little-echo style. Oma was their grandmother, Bärbel's mother on Reinhardtstrasse.

Then all four of them sat on the floor to play. Jeannette babied her doll. Ota had a pencil and made drawings on the linoleum floor.

The Grübels' next stop, en route back to the DDR, was at Budweis, the Czech town famous for its beer.* Ota was transported there in handcuffs, two officers watching his every move. Bärbel and the children were driven in a separate car without guards. She arrived in front of the Budweiser prison moments before Ota was to be taken inside.

She jumped out of the car and raced toward her husband. His guards pushed her away. She tumbled onto the cobblestones. Little Ota and Jeannette now made a dash for their father. He tried to pick them up. Since his handcuffs made this impossible, the chil-

---

* Budweiser Pilsener, widely sold in Europe, East and West, is not the brand of the same name made by Anheuser-Busch in the United States.

dren clutched him by the legs. As the guards pulled them away, he lifted up his hands as if in supplication and cried out, "You pigs! You're just as rotten as the Nazis!"

The Czechs continued to treat husband and wife very differently. While they seemed to think of Ota as a criminal, they were relatively gentle with Bärbel and the children, almost as if they had been bystanders of Ota's evildoing. Bärbel could easily have run away with the kids. The thought did not occur to her. Never would she separate herself voluntarily from her husband.

Ota having been marched off to jail, Bärbel and the youngsters were taken to an unguarded, comfortable double room of the local hotel. Little Ota turned on the radio. Jeannette bathed her doll. The boy asked why his father wasn't there. Bärbel explained again that Papa and Mama were going to prison, that the kids would be going to stay with Oma in Berlin.

"Well, once we're at Oma's, you and Papa will come soon," said the boy confidently, still clinging to the comfort of his past experience. Quickly he fell asleep for the night, lying next to Jeannette on the big bed.

Bärbel sat at the edge of that bed and watched her children for hours. She had to extricate them from this nightmare very, very quickly. Her mother or Ota's mother had to help.

Strangely, nobody interfered when Bärbel took the children to the post office the next morning to call her mother collect in East Berlin. She paced two hours waiting for the connection to come through. Her mother was not in. Neither was the other Oma.

Back at the hotel Bärbel again reminded the children that they would be staying with the family in Berlin.

"You've got to take good care of your sister," she said to little Ota. "But you're smart and you're not afraid, right?"

"Sure, Mama," said the boy, "and you're not going to stay away long, are you?"

She could not respond.

"What's a prison?" asked Ota. "Why can't Jeannette and I go there with you?"

Bärbel told him something, she could never recall what, and eventually the children fell asleep, Ota cradling his sister in his arms. This time Bärbel sat with them all night, dozing occasionally but spending hours studying their faces, intent on absorbing every detail. She would have to remember, she *would* remember.

. . .

"Is Papa in there?" little Ota asked Bärbel.

The boy knocked at the metal walls of the odd-looking little truck with its five narrow cells for transporting prisoners.

The family had reached the DDR textile manufacturing town of Plauen, fifteen miles north of the Czech border, and Bärbel suspected that her husband had been crammed into this fearsome vehicle that did not even seem to be equipped with air holes. Not wanting to upset her children, she said she thought that their father must be in another car.

Within, Ota followed the same protective scenario. Having listened to the conversation outside, he, too, feared that it would be too traumatic for his children to find out that he was caged in his traveling prison like a zoo animal. So he listened silently. He heard his son knocking. Then the boy clawed at the metal doors. He heard Jeannette talking to her doll. These were to be the last sounds he would ever hear from his children.

Bärbel had been perched on a cot in a cell of the Plauen State Prison for about an hour when, around 10 P.M., two uniformed men and one woman noisily unlocked the iron door.

"We've come to get the children. Tell them good-bye." It was the moment Bärbel knew would come, the moment she dreaded most.

Jeannette, tired and hungry, did not realize what was happening. Bärbel prayed that her son would not cry; she did not think she could handle such a scene without losing control. Equally important, she must not cry herself. If she did, the boy would refuse to leave and the wrench would become unbearable for all.

Little Ota embraced his mother. He volunteered that he would take his sister to their Oma and tell Oma to contact a lawyer, just as Bärbel had instructed him. He headed for the door, then he turned to come back to Bärbel, doubts written on his face after all.

He kissed her and asked, "When may I come back?" She said nothing. He did not cry.

Alone, Bärbel climbed on a stool and looked out on the prison courtyard. A hundred windows stared at her under the bright floodlights. They looked like the blank eyes of a hundred people.

"Ota! Ota!" she screamed. And again, "Ota! Ota! Ota!" Her husband did not respond. Nobody responded. She threw herself into a corner of her cell and wept at last.

. . .

Her interrogation began in a dark, windowless room at about
midnight. The officer said that her husband had already undergone questioning. Now her side of the story had to be heard. After
taking Bärbel through each step of their attempted escape, he
asked whether it wasn't true that her husband had been responsible for instigating this criminal venture, that it had been necessary
for him to persuade her to attempt *Republikflucht,* their flight from
the Republic.

Bärbel replied that there was not a trace of truth to this theory.
Theirs had been a joint decision, she said. From then on she tried
to make herself sound more convincing by wording her responses
in the first person, singular. She wanted the interrogator to know
beyond the slightest doubt that her mind was her own.

"But you're a mother," he persisted. "Clearly your husband had
to persuade you!"

"Just *because* I'm a mother I wanted to spare my children the
kind of life that I experienced in the DDR," said Bärbel defiantly.
"I want my children to live, not just to breathe."

The interrogator nevertheless persisted in his efforts to drive a
wedge between Bärbel and Ota until she demanded that he stop
trying to intimidate her. If he refused, she would report him to his
superior. Startled by the prisoner's effrontery, the interrogator
switched to other lines of questioning.

All forty new women prisoners were lined up along a corridor
awaiting medical examinations. Bärbel saw a doctor for only a few
moments.

"Any problems?" he demanded.

"Yes, I have pains in the area of the heart."

"If I were in your place," he snapped, "so would I. Next!"

Bored and desperate, Bärbel measured her new cell with her
toothbrush. The space was fourteen brush lengths long and eight
brush lengths wide.

She had arrived in late August at East Berlin's Barnim Strasse
prison, bringing along an almost romantic picture of the ram-
shackle old place, as if she had been there before. Rosa Luxemburg, the Communist revolutionary and heroine of liberated
German women, had been a prisoner in Barnim Strasse during the

Kaiser's time of World War I, and she had written about her stay in one of Bärbel's favorite books, *Letters from Prison.*

From her cell Bärbel looked down upon the same courtyard where Rosa, soon to be assassinated and dumped into the Landwehr Canal by renegade soldiers, went for walks every day from 7 to 10 A.M. or sat reading a book on a bench next to a bed of roses. Bärbel remembered the scene so well that she could almost smell the roses.

A bench was still there, but the roses were gone and so was the serenity that Bärbel longed for. She was allowed only to march up and down the yard in neatly aligned rows with some forty other women, twenty minutes per day. Reading in the yard was forbidden; even talking was forbidden.

Bärbel decided to address a personal appeal to Erich Honecker. She had heard rumors that a despairing letter sometimes stirred the bureaucracy into taking notice. She wrote asking for the right to determine for herself where she should live and questioning the government's right to incarcerate citizens because of their political views.

An indirect reply came three days later by way of a female captain who wanted to know how Bärbel had formed her views. The captain could not have been more elaborately sympathetic.

"My goodness," she exclaimed nearly three hours later, "how well I understand you now! How could you have acted otherwise? You acted according to your conscience! You'll be placed on probation with a reprimand or a fine. I can't tell you exactly when it'll be, but you'll be reunited with your children soon."

The captain said she would have Bärbel transferred to a larger cell, a promise that was fulfilled three days later. For the next 641 prison days, by Bärbel's painstaking count, nothing else positive happened to her.

For the first of her innumerable questioning sessions in the Berlin prison an interrogator appeared in the company of a woman attorney from the state prosecutor's staff. The interrogator again tried the sympathetic approach. Bärbel was so young, he said, a child of the DDR; she could be helped to make a fine new start in life. He had inspected her apartment and admired its lovely furnishings. Surely Bärbel would not have left all this unless her husband had put her up to it. She had to be his victim, the interrogator insisted, since Ota had long been identified as an enemy of the state.

Bärbel countered that she would not remain in the DDR for as much as one day longer than necessary. She would never stop trying to get out, she said. And nobody had put her up to her resistance. The experiences of her own life had solidified her outlook many years before she met her husband.

The woman prosecutor, leafing through the transcript of Ota's interrogation, said, "Well, your husband says here that you had an intellectually intensive marriage. I guess you didn't get along in bed."

That went too far for Bärbel. What gave the authorities the right to snoop around her sex life? She peered at the ungainly attorney, with her ugly, wart-encrusted face, and exploded: "You know something? As far as I'm concerned you're a dumb cow!"

Without a word, the lawyer left.

Bärbel asked her interrogator where her children were.

"They're with your mother," he said.

Ota Grübel was the first to learn that his son and daughter had vanished into the Kafkaesque labyrinths of the government bureaucracy. The news confirmed a recurrent dream that had been awakening him, bathed in sweat, during the night. In this nightmare, little Ota and Jeannette had fallen into deep water. The father jumped in after them and swam as fast as he could, yet no matter how desperately he tried to reach them, they drowned every time he dreamed the dream.

Ota had nightmarish thoughts about his own fate as well, for he was back in the same Rummelsburg prison of East Berlin where he had served time when the Wall went up, and on September 26, 1973, a date he would never forget, he was notified on a form postcard that his children had been placed in a state institution as long ago as August 8.

Having previously received assurance, like Bärbel, that the children were with his in-laws—an interrogator had confirmed this comforting word by reading Ota a formal entry to that effect from an official document—he thought at first that the postcard of September 26 must be an error.

When finally a state-appointed defense attorney appeared, he brought much news, all of it awful. Their case would go to trial on November 15. A three-year prison sentence was very probable. Ota should behave submissively in court, the lawyer instructed, no matter how difficult this might be for him to bring off. Under no circumstances was he to bring up that he still wished to leave the country. The Grübels should leave everything to him and hope for the best. It might be possible to request a reduced sentence for Bärbel. He would try.

Yes, the children had been placed in an institution, the lawyer confirmed. They would not remain there. A vendetta against the Grübels seemed to be in progress. A woman attorney from the prosecutor's office had called their attorney, and it was evident that she was furious at the family. (Later, when Ota and Bärbel were permitted to communicate briefly, it turned out that this was the same woman whom Bärbel had called a cow.) The woman had made the Grübels' lawyer a vengeful promise: little Ota and Jeannette would be put up for adoption.

Adoption. It took time for the word to sink into Ota's brain. It seemed impossible. Even the meek defense attorney was thunderstruck. He had never heard of parents being punished in this way.

"That's inconceivable," he told Ota flatly. "Don't worry about it."

37

THE BOOK OF BÄRBEL:
THE TWO CHILDREN ARE GONE

**East Berlin,
late October 1973**

Bärbel had been transferred to still another jail. Along with several dozen other women prisoners she had been moved in a convoy of vans that were not painted the usual police green but were camouflaged with a pleasant pattern of blue and white stripes. The signs on the trucks advertised local businesses. The windows were covered by curtains with happy flower patterns. The government was transporting prisoners incognito.*

Bärbel's cell was windowless and freezing. No one would tell her the whereabouts of her husband. Contacts with relatives were not permitted. Nothing that was happening to her—not her heart pains, not her self-accusing fury at having been yanked away from freedom at the very last moment on the border, not her nightmare-ridden sleep, her awakening each morning feeling confused, decimated, destroyed, wondering where she was—none of that mattered when she thought about the children, the children, and she thought about them nearly every waking moment.

Were they really safe at her mother's apartment on Reinhardt-

---

* This was not an unusual practice. The DDR did not like its enemies publicly seen. These outcasts were inconvenient symptoms of opposition and best kept invisible.

strasse? She found that increasingly difficult to believe. Something in the manner of her interrogators, in the expressions of their faces when she questioned them again and again and they said, yes, the kids were with her mother, something made her suspicious. She kept on questioning her questioners until one of them sighed and said she was welcome to write a letter to the office of the General Prosecutor of the DDR.

Bärbel wrote at once, demanding to know the whereabouts of little Ota and Jeannette. Surely, she said, the parents should not be deprived of *all* rights; weren't the mother and father entitled to know the whereabouts of their children and whether they were well? The reply reached Keibel Strasse prison relatively fast. It was a copy of an order dated August 8 from the Youth Aid Office of the Council for Berlin Mitte, stating that the Grübel youngsters had been assigned to a children's home. The two-month-old notice provided no details: not the name or location of the institution where the children were being kept, nothing about their physical or emotional state. The covering note from the General Prosecutor merely referred Bärbel to the order of the Youth Aid Office, adding that the case was thereby closed.

She felt her world crashing in. At first she tried hard not to believe the devastating news about her children. The notice had to be an error. That had to be it. Then again, the bureaucratic locutions of the notice—she studied and studied it—looked coldly authentic. Very likely this was no error. She had to *do* something, anything. Unable to think of any other way, at least to call attention to her despair, she decided to appeal to the top again, to write once more to Erich Honecker.

By now she could not contain her fury. She accused the government of inhuman conduct. And she needled Honecker. How could the party keep preaching about the sanctity of the family and advertise how much it was doing for the nation's children? It was tearing the Grübel family apart! Bärbel wrote that she was sick of the hypocrisy. She wanted her children back, and if she couldn't have them right away she wanted them to be with her mother. This time Bärbel had trouble persuading her guards even to accept the letter. She never heard what became of it and assumed that it was "lost" in the prison. Utterly cut off from the world, she felt lost herself.

. . .

Meanwhile, both grandmothers were frantic. Their children and grandchildren had vanished. Ota and Bärbel having told their mothers nothing of their plan to flee the country—what the grandmothers didn't know couldn't be held against them—the elderly women guessed what had to have happened as weeks went by without word. Had the foursome made it to the West? It seemed most unlikely. Had they been safe, they would certainly have phoned.

One August morning Bärbel's mother, Eva, found a postcard from the Youth Aid Office of Berlin Mitte in the ground-floor mailbox of her house on Reinhardtstrasse. Her grandchildren were at a children's home, the card said. She could pick them up there after attending to certain formalities for the youth authorities. Eva and Bärbel's father, Franz, wept tears of joy and immediately phoned the news to Ota's mother, Meta Kraal, in Karlshorst. The grandmothers agreed: once the grandchildren were free, the kids would tell what happened to Ota and Bärbel.

Eva appeared at the Youth Aid Office anticipating no problems. She would have to fill out papers, of course; government bureaus always had papers to fill out. To her immediate distress, no papers were waiting for her at the dingy office with the latrine odor. Instead she was ushered into the presence of the chairman of the Youth Aid Committee, a certain Herr Voss, and Herr Voss, who was livid, launched at once into a lecture about Bärbel and Ota.

They were totally unfit parents, he yelled. They were enemies of the state, the worst, the most stubborn sort of troublemakers! Never could such scum be expected to bring up children as decent socialists; it was a preposterous expectation.* What kind of upbringing had she, Eva, imparted to *her* daughter to turn her into such a *Klassenfeind*?

Eva was too stunned to respond. There wasn't much opportunity to speak up anyway. Herr Voss obviously was not interested in an answer. If anything could be done on behalf of Bärbel and Ota, Eva realized, this wasn't the time and the Youth Aid Office was not the place. She wanted nothing but to gain custody of her little

---

* Under DDR statutes, Herr Voss was correct in applying "socialism" as the guiding light of child-raising. Paragraph 42 of the Family Law calls on parents to encourage their children's "*socialist* attitude toward learning and work, respect for working people, acceptance of the rules for *socialist* living and solidarity toward *socialist* patriotism . . . " (emphasis added).

grandchildren, as she had been promised on the card she had received in the mail.

Herr Voss quickly made clear that the routine notice did not apply to her family. Someone had had a change of mind. Herr Voss never mentioned the notice, and gave Eva no opportunity to bring it up. She had been manifestly derelict by not raising Bärbel as a good socialist, Voss shouted. Having failed as a mother, she could not be given access to her grandchildren. The children's own parents were beyond hope. What would be the point of burdening the state's institutions by keeping the youngsters in a home? Red-faced, Herr Voss spoke his verdict: he personally would make certain that little Ota and Jeannette would be permanently adopted before the end of the year by some deserving couple. That was final.

"Those parents will never see their children again!" he ruled. He could promise Eva that much—and absolutely.

Eva was so close to collapse that she could barely make it back to Reinhardtstrasse. She had been physically and emotionally fragile throughout her life. Her small, finely featured face, the creamy complexion, the beautifully brushed black hair held in a bun, the delicate long neck, the tall, bony body held erect with effort—her features made her look like an ailing aristocrat. Her physical ailments were sketchily defined, but the bombings of World War II, a tragic love affair, and then the scrabble for existence in the DDR had left her badly frightened, unequipped to cope with authority, certainly not able to challenge it.

Meta Kraal, on the other hand, the other grandmother, could hardly be accused of excessive delicacy. Stocky, big-boned, her face furrowed like a potato field, she was never at a loss for comment. She was the prototypically sassy Berlin *Arbeiter,* the worker type, and her profession had endowed her skin with extra protective layers. Meta drove a streetcar. On her feet all day, sometimes much of the night, she was accustomed to getting pushed around by her *Arbeiter* customers, and she knew how to shove back, verbally and by elbow.

How Meta loved and adored little Ota and Jeannette! She had taken two weeks off from her job when their parents had gone on the first "vacation" to Czechoslovakia and the kids had stayed with her. She took them to the zoo because Jeannette was crazy about animals, and they had all gone to the playground at Pionier Park in Oberschöneweide. Long after Meta would cross over to the

West, she still thought that the authorities in the East did a lot for kids; you couldn't take that away from those fanatical Communists, the party leaders.

Not all the party people were crazies like that terrible Herr Voss, the diehard whom Eva had told her all about on the phone. Meta had been in the tram business twenty-four years, and in her garage they were "like a big family." Everybody knew about the disappearance of her grandchildren, and even the party secretary was sympathetic.

Meta knew she was considered an excellent worker, so she felt perfectly secure in changing her shift one weekday and standing in line for more than an hour at the Youth Aid Office to inquire for the whereabouts of her beloved grandchildren.

"Can't tell you," snarled the clerk when it came Meta's turn.

"Why not?"

"None of your business!"

She turned next to her party secretary at the tram garage, and he promised to try his best to find out.

"Meta, I can't get anywhere," he reported a couple of weeks later. He had heard rumblings that the secret police, the *Stasi,* was somehow involved. Nobody would tell him details.

Meta returned to the Youth Aid Office and this time found a kindly young woman clerk.

"I'll try," she said. "Come back in three days."

When Meta went back, the clerk looked scared. "Can't tell you," she said. "I don't know where they are."

"What's such a secret?" Meta wanted to know. The clerk would not say another word.

Whereupon Meta set about to search for the grandchildren on her own. She knew that the government's homes for children were located in the outlying suburbs. Sure enough, near the final stop of her usual tram route, Johannistal, she spotted groups of young children at a fence. As casually as she could manage, she described her grandchildren to these youngsters.

"I'm their aunt," she said. "I'm just passing through on a trip. I hear they're here. Have you seen them?"

Her grandchildren were not in Johannistal. Nor were they at Königswusterhausen. Nor were they at the youth home in Weissensee, an outlying destination serviced by one of her fellow drivers, another elderly woman, whom Meta had enlisted for help.

Banking on her unblemished reputation as a worker, she marched right into the district office of the *Stasi.* Why not go directly to the source of her difficulties? At least these were officials who would have no trouble making inquiries in the right places.

When she was summoned, after a long wait, to see a clerk, her latest audacity quickly evaporated.

"Who sent you?" the clerk demanded.

Meta didn't understand. "Who sent me?" she asked indignantly. "I'm the *Oma!*"

The clerk told the old streetcar conductor to get out.

Having covered all the children's institutions she could find, Meta still did not cease her detective work. She stopped her streetcar whenever she spotted large groups of children near a likely-looking building and pursued her quest. Nothing. Eventually she told Eva on the phone that she could think of nothing else to do. The grandmothers agreed they would have to wait until the government showed its hand. The bureaucracy had swallowed their grandchildren; only the bureaucracy could disgorge them.

PART VII

THE ESCAPE HELPERS

38

ERIKA: LEAVING FOR NEW YORK

New York,
August 1973

Inevitably, the Wall had become a challenge to an army of Wall-breakers. Adventurers, profiteers, heroes, and villains invented surreal schemes to outwit the Communists, and ordinary citizens like Siegrid Manolo had to cope with these entrepreneurs.

Siegrid was startled by the call she received one evening at her apartment in the modest Forest Hills suburb of New York.

"I'm a friend of . . . ," said the voice with the German accent.

The caller mentioned a West German name, a friend of friends. "Erika can get out," he said, "but we'll need money: fifteen thousand dollars in a bank draft, but not on a Berlin bank."

Siegrid, who had left the DDR before the Wall went up, had dreamed for years of being someday joined by Erika, the last of her sisters still in East Berlin. But $15,000? They'd have to borrow it. And should they send it blindly to some stranger? What if a swindler ran off with it? What if Erika got caught? Siegrid told the caller to hang on while she quickly told her husband of the proposition.

"That's great!" he said without hesitation. Johnny Manolo was a born New Yorker, but he knew about his wife's sisters and the Wall that divided them. Siegrid had taken him to Berlin to see the Thing for himself, and it had given him the shivers.

. . .

In East Berlin, Erika, twenty-six, was feeling more and more like an outcast at her secretarial job. She had been told that advancement was out of the question for her. When she inquired why she was no longer being shown office files dealing with international conferences, the response was unnerving. Her family ties were incriminating. Her boss told her, "You have sisters abroad"— which was of itself considered a symptom of doubtful loyalty.

So when the husband of a friend who had legally left the DDR came for a visit and offered to make contact with an escape helper in West Germany, Erika assented.

Eventually, Hans, a law student, materialized from Tübingen. Erika's eerie relationship with him frightened her the longer it developed. The man was extremely nervous. For weeks at a time, he failed to show up for meetings. He was petrified at the thought that she might tell someone, anyone, anyone at all, merely that she might be *thinking* of leaving. Even her mother absolutely must not be told! Anyway, did Erika think she'd have the nerve to go through with it?

Erika was not at all certain. Could this shaky student be trusted? How good would *his* nerves turn out to be?

Hans's disposition improved after his money arrived from New York. Erika's mood didn't. She developed something of a guilty conscience about leaving her family and her friends at work. When Hans said he'd come to her house on Saturday with her exit instructions, and she happened to win a trip to Bulgaria in a contest at an office party Friday night, she was tempted to tell her boss to give the prize to someone else. She managed to keep quiet, however, realizing that undue generosity would have aroused suspicion.

On Saturday, Hans arrived at noon and announced, "Okay, it's tonight!"

He sounded more anxious and security-conscious than ever. She was to burn all her letters, pictures, and other possibly identifying materials. Since she had a cold and was coughing, she was to take along cough pills but nothing else, nothing, not even a handbag.

Erika was momentarily stunned. She had not pictured her physical getaway. "I can't just leave here like that," she stammered. Later she would reflect, "I couldn't see myself locking the door for the final time."

If Hans was worried that she was getting cold feet, he didn't show it. She was to take a nap; it would be a long night. "I'm going to tell you very little," he said, "but you'll be fine." Erika was not so sure at all.

Hans said he would pick her up shortly before 7 P.M. They would walk to East Berlin's equivalent of Times Square, the Alexanderplatz. There they would meet a young East German, an accomplice, and Hans would leave them.

"You'll see me again after two A.M.," he assured Erika. "The other fellow will make sure we aren't being tailed."

"What am I going to do with him?"

"Don't ask him questions," Hans instructed. "Talk about the weather. Go window-shopping. Then he'll drive you way out to Grünau and he'll buy you dinner. You'll sit until it's time to get going."

The young East German turned out to be shabbily dressed, nicelooking, and very, very quiet. In his white Trabant they drove for about forty-five minutes to one of the large beer gardens on the shore of the Müggelsee, where they dawdled over dinner for more than three hours. Erika's escort insisted on sitting indoors, in a corner, from where he kept watching the door. He must have participated in such missions before, because he moved with assurance and seemed unusually alert to all that was going on around them.

The conversation was sparse and casual. The man told Erika of his wife and child and gave her a name, perhaps his real one.

At 2 A.M. they were at a table in the nearly empty twenty-fourhour rest stop at Michendorf, south of Berlin on the Autobahn. The place smelled of urine, as they all did. Erika's companion ordered a glass of milk and said he was waiting for a signal.

"I want to thank you for taking a risk like this," Erika said.

"It's worth a lot of money," the young man replied drily.

Erika realized how much her sister and brother-in-law were sacrificing financially. She also knew the precise seriousness of the gamble she had undertaken. Hans would drive her south, down the "transit" Autobahn to the border of the DDR. Discovery at the control point, while not probable, was entirely possible. Under the traffic agreement signed by the East and West Germans in 1972, the DDR border guards had been required to modify their practice of ransacking every car leaving their territory. They were, however, entitled to conduct spot checks, especially if they sniffed any hints of illegal activity.

From worrisome DDR newspaper accounts describing show

trials of escape helpers who had been caught, Erika knew that the *Stasi* was adept at tracking and infiltrating organizations that employed people like Hans. Often the drivers of escape vehicles, arriving at the border with clients hidden in the trunk, were greeted by an official welcoming party that had clearly been tipped off about the mission.

At the *Raststätte* in Michendorf, Erika's escort was stirring to rise. "This person is here," he said.

Erika had seen no person or signal.

"There will be a blue Opel Ascona in front of us," the escort said. "We have to catch up with it. We'll be looking for a flat spot that has no bushes where the police can hide."

At a likely-looking place the Opel would slow down to a crawl. They would drive up behind it. It would be Hans who would stop and get out, pretending to check a tire but then drive quickly on.

Erika was to jump out of her car while it was still in moving along, and *run* to get into the moving Opel. Its door would be open for her.

Erika was very tired. It occurred to her that she was lucky to be unencumbered by possessions of any kind. She took pride in her athletic fitness, but her exercises had hardly included dashing from a moving car into another moving car. It sounded crazy.

She did it. "It that you?" asked Hans, at the wheel of the Opel, as she puffed into the seat next to him. There was no other greeting, just a curt "You'll have to get into the trunk."

Wanting to be sure they hadn't been spotted and were being followed, he drove up and down a short stretch of Autobahn three times. All transit roads teemed with *Vopo* patrols around the clock. It was pitch dark, raining, and nearly 3 A.M. The road lay deserted. Quickly, Hans stopped and stowed her in the trunk under a scratchy woolen blanket.

Erika had been feeling too rushed to get frightened. Now she would have four hours of immobility until they reached the border at Hof. Still she wasn't scared. None of this seemed real; it was too much like a movie.

Hans said he would keep the radio on except at times when he might need to talk with her. He said nothing all night. Around 7 A.M.—rays of light had been penetrating the trunk ever so slightly for some time—the radio went off. Hans said they were five minutes away from the border. He would be getting gas.

With civilization suddenly materializing, Erika got frightened with equal suddenness. She heard Hans talking to the gas station attendant—a creepy experience. And as Hans resumed driving, reality with its dangers crowded in on her. She started chewing on her blanket.

Hans told her they would make three separate stops for East German controls, then a fourth, manned by the West Germans. She said nothing. He started playing soft music on the radio.

In her trunk, Erika was talking silently to her mother back in her home village deep in the rural DDR. She would never forget what she told herself under her blanket: "Mother, Mother, Mother, be at my side, I don't want you to visit me in jail. . . ."

The first stop was brief. The second stop lasted for an eternity, at least five minutes. The third stop was short again. Erika heard no conversation, nothing until after the third stop, when Hans spoke up just loudly enough so she could make out the words under her blanket.

"We made it," he said. "The next one is nothing. Just be quiet."

At the fourth stop, the West Germans, Erika heard a pleasant male voice say simply, "Good morning."

Hans pulled away and said calmly, "Congratulations!"

She could say nothing except to ask him to stop right away. She had to urinate and did so in some woods. Then they sat together on the ground for a long time even though it was foggy and raining. Erika drank in her surroundings. She thought that she had never seen trees of such a luxuriant green or roads so richly paved.

Hans finally let his guard down and identified himself as a first-time amateur at the escape trade. At the long second stop, he said, the guard had taken hold of his West German passport. Though Hans knew that this was normal procedure, the act of giving up his precious document unnerved him.

"When the guy walked away with the passport I thought I'd drop dead," he told Erika in their euphoric postmortem.

Within hours, the phone rang at the home of Erika's sister in Forest Hills. Siegrid picked it up.

"Hold on, here's someone who wants to talk to you," said an unknown voice.

At first Erika couldn't say a word. She only cried.

"You're out!" Siegrid shouted.

"Yes, I'm out!"

The amateurs had triumphed. So would others, using less conventional means.

39

BARRY: SNATCHING REFUGEES BY HELICOPTER

Traunstein, West Germany,
August 1975

Approaching the Czech border on that sleepy summer Sunday afternoon, Barry Meeker took his rented Bell JetRanger helicopter down to treetop level to avoid Communist radar and revved up his speed to the maximum of 120 knots. His mission was moving ahead on schedule. Landmarks came into view exactly where he expected them. Precisely at 5 P.M., roaring past the wooden guard towers that dotted the frontier, he crossed into enemy territory from Austria northeast of Aigen. He had become a target for the Communists.

By 5:03 P.M. Meeker had passed over the Stausee, the large artificial lake formed by the Moldau River. At 5:03:12 he was hovering a meter or two over the narrow dirt road near the chapel where his passengers were supposed to be walking, preparatory to being picked up and ferried to the West. They had been instructed to wear red jackets so that Meeker could not possibly miss them, but as he looked up and down the road he could spot no one.

He was not seriously disturbed. Not yet. He estimated that he had about four minutes to spare before the alarm that had surely been triggered by the tower guards would become effective among police units stationed throughout the area. Four minutes was a reasonably favorable grace period to Meeker, a strapping thirty-three-year-old New Yorker who had routinely flown U.S. Air Force

American helicopter pilot Barry Meeker flew three daring rescue missions into East Germany in the early 1970s. "I thought, 'Here's a really good thing to do with a helicopter,'" he said.

helicopters behind the lines in Vietnam, had been shot down seven times, wounded twice, and was decorated for bravery with the Distinguished Flying Cross and other medals.

Meeker also had confidence in his employer, Heinz Heidrich, an unconventional Munich attorney. The American pilot had flown two previous border missions for the bouncy little Heidrich. Both flights had been prepared meticulously and had been successful. This time Meeker was to rescue four Heidrich clients trying to escape from East Berlin: a middle-aged couple, their teenage daughter, and a twenty-year-old student.

Teddy, a Polish physics student who had volunteered to ride along with Meeker as a helper, spotted their refugee passengers hiding under some trees at the lakeside. (Later they reported that their East German contact had failed to instruct them to walk along the road.)

The hilly terrain forced Meeker to land sixty meters from the anxiously waiting group. Worse, the refugees had to puff uphill to reach the copter. The two men made the race swiftly. The two women hit trouble. The older one, severely overweight, quickly ran out of breath. Meeker heard shots. The teenage girl was felled by a shot in the thigh and started to bleed heavily about twenty meters away from the whirring aircraft. By the time Teddy had dragged her onto the copter, Meeker's grace period had run out.

A shot came through the left rear of the cabin, went through the pilot's left elbow with a thud, and skinned his chest. Five seconds later the chopper was hit. Meeker could feel the fuselage shudder. By this time Teddy was running to get the woman who had failed to reach the plane. She had collapsed from exhaustion. Meeker yelled for Teddy to come back. But the young student could not hear the pilot over the rotor noise. Assuming that he had five seconds between shots—so Meeker quickly calculated—he could no longer spare the thirty seconds or more that it would take Teddy to move the heavy woman aboard.

The pilot had lifted his craft to a height of twenty to thirty feet. If he hesitated any longer, he and his people in the chopper could count on getting blown up. More shots were hitting the aircraft.

"I thought, Jesus Christ, maybe I should surrender before anybody gets killed," Meeker said later. "But then I realized that I would have to set the helicopter down somewhere and probably get out and wave. How the hell do you surrender from a helicopter?

"My idea was not to get anybody killed. Then I realized that surrendering wouldn't work and I knew I couldn't get back to Teddy or the woman. I was gushing blood all over the place, so I decided to go."

And so he did, regretfully leaving behind Teddy and the heavy woman (who were later sentenced to six and three years in prison, respectively).

En route back to Munich, where he had been living since he left the military, Meeker instructed his male passengers to bandage his wound as well as the teenage girl's injured thigh. Discovering that he lacked enough fuel to reach Munich, he remembered the helicopter pad on the roof of the nearby Traunstein hospital. He used to fly ambulance rescue missions to the place. Needing medical help himself, he landed with ninety seconds of fuel left.

Heinz Heidrich, fifty-five, the Munich lawyer-entrepreneur sponsoring Meeker's escapade, had immigrated to West Germany only two years earlier, and he, too, had to resort to unconventional transportation to make it across the border from the DDR.

Back home in East Berlin, Heidrich hadn't seemed the type to go in for extralegal stunting. For decades he had been a servile member of the DDR legal establishment, a member of the ruling SED, an *Oberregierungsrat* in the Justice Ministry, a judge, and an author of technical treatises in official legal journals. Then he had enjoyed the special privilege of private practice.

Like Wolfgang Vogel, Heidrich had the right connections to procure exit papers for dissidents wanting to move to the West. Lacking Vogel's personal access to Premier Honecker, Heidrich was frankly jealous of his "good friend" and competitor Wolfgang. Heidrich felt certain that Wolfgang had to have connections in the *Stasi*.

Withal, Heidrich made vast amounts of money—"more than a cabinet minister," he liked to brag—and his financial acumen may have led to his downfall among East Berlin's stodgy socialists. He began to pick up hints among members of the legal society that they envied him. So Heidrich had not been overly shocked when he phoned his office one afternoon to discover that his files had been seized; he would not be permitted to reenter his own premises.

The hidden side of the little lawyer's personality moved promptly to the rescue. At heart, Heidrich was no establishment hack at all. Under his bureaucrat's skin lurked a jolly, hyperenergetic persuader, roguish by nature, with a talent for uproarious imitations of pompous authorities. Heidrich rarely walked; he danced. His survival among the DDR's officialdom had left him with a sharp nose for incipient disaster, and when the *Stasi* took possession of his files, Heidrich's dancing feet turned itchy.

Within hours, wearing only bathing trunks and clutching an air mattress and his briefcase, the little lawyer had swum across the Elbe to freedom. He didn't think that the wife and two small children he had left behind in East Berlin could cope with the river's strong currents, so why not leapfrog across all border trouble in a helicopter? He had not heard of anyone using such a craft for a private airlift out of Erich Honecker's possessive domain. The idea appealed to his preference for direct action.

And why entrust the pilot's job to some stranger who might give the plot away? No, the lawyer would run the chopper himself, even though he had no flying experience. While Heidrich was a rascal who might have stepped out of a Till Eulenspiegel fable, he was not really a fool. After some twenty hours of lessons on an Enstrom helicopter, he decided it would take him too long to master rotary-wing flying. Cautiously, he began to ask around at his suburban Munich airport for the requisite talent, and was shortly introduced to Barry Meeker, whom he liked immediately.

Barry seemed the quintessential American: a bronzed, burly chain-smoker with thick, curly hair, huge sideburns, and a blond walrus mustache. He was quick to quip and to smile. He spoke superb German—only the faintest trace of an accent was audible. And while this American shared Heidrich's exuberance and lust for adventure, he was no mindless mercenary.

After graduating from Columbia University with a degree in English literature, he grew bored with the dreary sameness of his chores as a junior editor in a New York book publishing house, shipped out to Vietnam as a helicopter pilot, and there he found himself.

"He underwent a real transformation when he was in the army," said one of his brothers. "Before he went in, he tended slightly to the left, and he came out as a real right-wing jock, very gung-ho, distinctly a hawk."

Barry was also wild about helicopters. He adored choppers as other men love women or automobiles. Settling in Germany, where he lived with a good-looking woman doctor, he ran choppers to rescue mountaineers; transported documents as a courier; and served as an airborne base for film camera crews. He had not used a copter as a getaway vehicle, but he reveled in risk-taking for a good cause. The liberation of innocent civilians from a Communist dictatorship appealed to his hawkish inclinations and his humanitarian instincts.

"I just really thought it was a good idea to get those people out," he said. "And I thought, 'Here's a really good thing to do with a helicopter.' "

Barry also had good use for the 10,000 D-marks (then about $4,000), payable in cash, that Heidrich offered him for one round-trip behind the Iron Curtain. Less than two and a half hours of flying were involved. Free-lance air jobs were fairly scarce, and Meeker was trying to amass capital to start a helicopter transport business.

Finally, the pilot appreciated Heidrich's lawyerlike thoroughness in setting up the rescue mission. Dismissing the area around the Berlin Wall as far too risky, Heidrich had spent every weekend during the summer of 1973 investigating the East-West border, especially the Austrian-Czech frontier, where it seemed most likely that he would find a lightly guarded spot without a history of recent escapes. Near Aigen and the nearby town of Saint Ulrich, where the Moldau becomes the border for a stretch of about ten miles, he climbed on an observation tower and approved the terrain. So did Meeker, who later visited the tower to take photographs from which he could memorize the major landmarks.

With Heidrich sitting in as copilot, Barry flashed past the border at an altitude of one meter, the JetRanger's nose and landing skids canting down. Its identifying emblems were masked with yellow tape. It was a lovely Sunday in late July of 1974. Heidrich's wife and his children, aged nine and sixteen, were posing as picnickers. Spotting them within moments, Barry set down right next to their blanket. Heidrich jumped out, helped his frightened-looking family aboard, and they were all off within seconds, the passengers crying and celebrating with the champagne that the lawyer had brought along.

Nobody seemed to have noticed the rescue team's visit and there was no publicity. At the Munich airport the party got on a bus as if they were returning from a sight-seeing jaunt.

Heidrich told Meeker that he would need his services again, because he wanted to bring out the secretary who had worked at his East Berlin law office. It took a year to arrange that mission, and Barry spent much of that time in Iran, training pilots for the Shah's air force. The second mission did pick up the secretary, as well as two of Heidrich's clients and a fifteen-year-old girl. The rescue was staged at the same place as the first flight, again on a Sunday afternoon. It also went off without problems.

Only the third mission, when two people had to be left behind in the East, resulted in shooting and injuries, probably because Heidrich and Meeker had pushed their luck too far. They had picked the identical escape route for the third time and had run the flight on the Sunday following the second mission. They had gambled that the border authorities would not expect escape attempts on successive Sundays. They were wrong.

Meeker's career as an escape helper was finished. His third mission made him a hero briefly on the front page of *The New York Times,* but in adding up the income and losses of his rescue missions he was forced to conclude that he could not afford further such investments of his pluck and skill. While he had collected the total of $12,000 from Heidrich—who always paid up promptly in 500-mark bank notes—Barry wound up responsible for a $16,000 bill to repair the helicopter damage plus an $800 fine from a West German court for "illegal touchdowns outside public airports and the unauthorized transport of persons."

For Heidrich, whose role remained secret for some time, the enterprise was no great bonanza either. It did yield a modest profit. Each flight set him back $4,000 for the pilot plus $8,000 for plane rental. According to testimony before a Czech court, he collected slightly over $5,000 for each passenger. With total costs at $12,000 and income at more than $20,000, the last mission netted him enough money to whet his continued interest in the border business.

Money was not his sole motivator. The conventional side of his legal practice was nicely remunerative; the escapes offered more seductive incentives. They allowed him to play tricks on former colleagues in the East who had turned against him. The game also seasoned Heidrich's life with the excitement he craved. He had an evocative word for the thrill: *Nervenkitzel,* tickling the nerves. For Heidrich the gamesman, the existence of two Germanys provided a tantalizing adult version of a child's hide-and-seek.

Deciding to abandon helicopters as too risky, Heidrich hit upon the imaginative scheme to smuggle refugees via horse transport. He had a horse trailer rebuilt to provide a closed space large enough to hide five people. And he moved operations farther south, all the way to Bulgaria, for a safer border crossing. The guards in that area were less fussy. They appreciated the beer and skin magazines handed out by Heidrich's drivers. Expenses ran high because real horses had to be ferried as decoys each time ("What those horses cost!" Heidrich exclaimed disgustedly), but every mission brought a profit and the trips continued into the 1980s. Heidrich was not the type to stop dancing.

For Meeker, the daredevil missions he flew for Heidrich would be the peak experiences of his short life and his last taste of high adventure. Ultimately, his great love, the helicopter, betrayed him.

Finding work scarce in Europe, he returned to the United States and signed on for a prosaic career as pilot with an Oklahoma City helicopter service. Mostly he taxied busy rich oilmen. He married a local woman and had a son.

Barry was forty years old in April 1982 when his Bell Model 222 copter, carrying him and two oilmen, blew apart over a wheat field in rural Caddo County, killing all three men. The Oklahoma City broadcast media, smelling East German revenge because of Meeker's past, launched rumors of sabotage. Investigators for the National Transportation Safety Board laughed at this theory and ruled that technical problems with the aircraft had led to its crash.

Meeker's Oklahoma pilot buddies were relieved that neither Barry's flying nor his colorful history could be faulted. "The only mistake he made was getting up that morning and going to work," one friend said.

Barry never did think much of routine jobs. Neither did another escape artist, named Micha.

40

MICHA: BLOWING UP THE DEATH AUTOMATS

**Hamburg, West Germany,
May 1976**

Like a match, the sealing of the Berlin border on August 13, 1961, had struck a streak of rebellion in tousle-haired Michael Gartenschläger, seventeen. Together with four teenage friends in the Strausberg suburb of East Berlin, he went on a rampage. The boys threw paint at government propaganda posters. They painted antigovernment slogans on walls: OPEN THE GATE! and GERMANY TO THE GERMANS! And to light up a dramatic "beacon protesting the Wall," they set a barn on fire.

On August 19 Gartenschläger was arrested. In court he declared, "I'm not in agreement with this state because there is no freedom." Branded as a "criminal against the state" who would have to be "permanently isolated from society," he was sentenced to life in prison. Between 1963 and 1971, the lawyers Wolfgang Vogel and Jürgen Stange tried to get Gartenschläger ransomed again and again. The DDR kept refusing to release him until he had served nine years and ten months. Then, trained in prison as a lathe operator, he was allowed to settle in Hamburg.

"Micha" Gartenschläger did well enough financially by leasing and operating a gas station. It didn't satisfy him. His hatred against the DDR had been further inflamed by his treatment in prison and he wanted revenge. Without assistance, he smuggled six East Germans to the West, one by one, and organized other escapes in the Balkans. His sense of adventure aroused, he plotted to kidnap the East German Defense Minister. Instead, the November 3, 1975, issue of the newsmagazine *Der Spiegel* inadvertently presented him with his ultimate challenge.

Beginning in 1971, the DDR had installed 45,000 (later there would be 60,000) *Selbstschussgeräte* (self-firing devices) on every fourth fencepost all along the East-West border.* Officially, the weapons were known as SM-70, unofficially as "death automats." Over the years, new, more sophisticated models, M-501 and An-lage 701, caused less trouble for the border guards; they were not as readily set off by thunderstorms and roaming animals.

A human being trying to pass through or over the fencing would automatically release ninety jagged-edged, dice-shaped steel pellets. Scattered through a funnel, these shrapnel fragments disintegrated on penetration much like the dumdum bullets that were declared illegal under international law in 1899. West German doctors often found it impossible to stem the resulting blood loss.

"Until this day West German border forces do not know exactly how the SM-70 functions and how escapees might disarm it." So Micha Gartenschläger was reading in the *Spiegel*. The article became an assignment to him. He was thirty-two, his hair all but gone from his forehead, his waistline expanded since his prison days, but his mind was set. He would steal one of the "comrades"—as he had come to call the death devices—so that its precise workings could be analyzed.

The history of the SM-70 made it particularly worthy of being disarmed and defeated. According to a West German arms specialist, the device had been designed by the SS for the guarding of fences around Nazi concentration camps. The end of World War II halted final development until the *Stasi* found eight technicians in its special prison for *Intelligenz* (intellectuals), who readied it for mass production.

At about 3 A.M. on March 30, 1976, having spent six months to spot a stretch of the border only thirty miles east of Hamburg

* The devices were not installed in Berlin. There, guards, towers, and other security measures made the machines unnecessary. Conceivably, the DDR also did not want them there because of public relations reasons.

where thick fir woods provided good cover, Gartenschläger parked his car, blackened his face and hands, and proceeded across the border, leaving a trail of pepper to ward off any dogs. Having located an SM-70, he used his pliers to snip what he—correctly, as it turned out—took to be the two thin ignition wires. He loosened the screw of the gear that fastened the device to the fence. The death automat did not budge. Fumbling further—the night was moonless and totally dark—he found a second holder, loosened it, grabbed the SM-70, and ran like hell.

A friend was waiting for him and together they made as much noise as they could. Gartenschläger's drive for revenge was let loose. He was keen to alarm the border guards. "I would have loved to photograph them standing dumbfounded by the empty fencepost," he said later. But his luck had run out. Nobody came. No matter. Gartenschläger had other ways to embarrass the masters of the death automats.

He took the captured "comrade" to the Hamburg editorial office of the *Spiegel*, sold it for 12,000 marks, and was delighted to see it fully analyzed in print, with charts and X-ray photos, in the April 12 issue. Presumably, the new intelligence would enable anybody else to render the dreadful gadgets harmless.

Gartenschläger wasn't satisfied yet. The thrill of the chase had snared him. And he was determined to annoy the DDR still more. Back for a walk at the border, he spotted some East German guards, and when he was separated from them by only four yards, he called out, "I'll take a third one away from you and then a fourth!"

His friends pleaded with Micha not to risk it. Manfred Müller, the *Spiegel* correspondent covering the story, urged him not to do it. "Leave things alone," Müller said. "We've got one of the things. We don't need another." Rainer Hildebrandt, the chief of the Checkpoint Charlie museum in Berlin, had befriended Gartenschläger and made the young man promise with a handshake that he would suppress the urge to kidnap another SM-70.

Micha was not interested in sane counsel. On May 1 he was back at the same spot in the woods where he had succeeded earlier. He had decided to make his next attempt farther south, together with two friends. First, he wanted to retrieve a ladder he had hidden. After the men did so, Gartenschläger motioned toward the border and said, "I think I'll go up there and see what things look like." The friends urged him not to go. He went.

"Shit," he said, "before we go I'll just blow up one of these things. It'll be fast."

The friends heard and saw the firing of four machine pistols. Micha tumbled backward, riddled by bullets.* It had happened very fast.

---

* Eventually Gartenschläger would win the war against the automatic "comrades." The publicity generated by his daredeviltry, his murder, and the horror of the death devices themselves created strong revulsion in both Germanys, and by November 1984 all these devices had been removed by the Honecker government. This success followed years of pressure and secret negotiations initiated by the West German government, culminating in some very sizable loans to the DDR by a consortium of West German banks. By 1984 the border fencing with its electronic signal system, along with other fortifications, had become so effective that the removal of the automatic killers did not result in more escapes. It did make the border controls more humane.

41

THE WALL BECOMES BIG BUSINESS

The WANTED poster on the Eastern side of Checkpoint Charlie in Berlin held out juicy bait: the apprehension of Hans Ulrich Lenzlinger would be worth 500,000 marks to the DDR secret police. They described him as a "trader in people." His company, grandly calling itself Aramco, of Zurich, had spirited an estimated four hundred East Germans to the West between 1971 and 1979, including a sizable number of physicians and nurses desperately needed in the DDR.

Among the entrepreneurs of the escape-helper industry—with its lineup of idealists, gangsters, primitives, and con men—Lenzlinger, fifty, was arguably the most public and unquestionably the most controversial and colorful. So the Zurich police were not surprised that sometime between 8:05 and 9:40 A.M. on February 5, 1979, he welcomed a man of about thirty, who had rung the bell at Lenzlinger's eleven-room suburban villa, Ackersteinstrasse 116, and had shot him repeatedly and fatally in the chest in the Aramco reception room.

Lenzlinger had been adhering to his accustomed morning schedule, which was obviously known to his caller. The Aramco chief was normally alone during this time. As usual, he was wearing his green rubber apron, having just fed the private zoo caged in his garden: two lions, two leopards, one puma, and two jackals. Lenzlinger had no close friends except his animals.

The son of an architect, he had come to the attention of the police more than one hundred times previously. "Irregularities" in his chinchilla-raising business had sent him to jail for a year. The operation of a "massage" parlor, in partnership with his wife, Bernadette, a former beauty queen, netted him another eight-month sentence, for prostitution. He served more jail time after he suspected one of his sixteen-man escape-helper staff of betraying his operations: Lenzlinger tied this unsatisfactory employee to a garbage cart that carried a banner reading THIS IS A SPY FROM THE EAST and dropped him off at the gate to the building housing the Swiss parliament.

Aramco's affairs were astoundingly public. Lenzlinger advertised for escape sponsors in West German newspapers. He issued press releases extolling his "most modern technical methods." His prices were not unreasonable: $10,000 to $12,000 per head, with "quantity discounts" for families, payable into a blocked account of the Swiss Kantonalbank. If an escape attempt failed, the sponsor would get most of his money refunded.

If any clients became disenchanted, they didn't speak up. Lenzlinger produced stacks of recommendation letters listing names and addresses of satisfied customers. Sometimes he posed with groups of them, freshly liberated, for West German magazine spreads. His faith in the rewards of publicity never wavered.

Like any market-conscious executive, Lenzlinger kept adapting his techniques as conditions in his industry changed. At first he used specially rebuilt cars or horse transports or fake "emergency aid" cars to hide refugees and whisk them over the interzonal Autobahn transit roads, which the DDR border guards were not supposed to check except in cases of blatantly obvious violations. When these routes became too risky, he switched to fake passports and ran customers through Prague and rural Hungary. Once he took a week to ferry fourteen defectors by rubber raft across a lake that linked Hungary with Austria. He used a dachshund, in heat, to deflect the attention of Hungarian guard dogs.

Personnel headaches were Lenzlinger's abiding sorrow. A grudge that he developed against one of his assistants was so virulent that he caused the man to be evicted from his apartment. Aggrieved, the staffer complained to the *Stasi* in East Berlin, and it gladly accepted the disloyal Aramco man's offer to spill dirt about his boss. According to subsequent court testimony, Lenzlinger, having been tipped off to this outrage, recruited another assistant to equip the defector with fake documents. When the traitor was about to board a plane for Berlin, Lenzlinger called in the police, and the "thief" of the fake documents was arrested. It was not advisable to fall from Lenzlinger's good graces.

Most of Lenzlinger's helpers were Swiss, but in 1976 one of his West Berlin operators, twenty-nine-year-old Rainer Schubert, was caught and sentenced in East Berlin to fifteen years in prison. He had helped Lenzlinger bring eighty-six East Germans and one Czech to the West, and he acknowledged earning $200,000 for a year's work. During the five days of a show trial he generated more free advertising for Lenzlinger by testifying in detail about Aramco's trade practices.

While he acknowledged his devotion to his primary cause, money, Lenzlinger's anti-Communist convictions were authentic and ran deep. Toward the end of his days, his hatred toward the East Germans spilled over onto the Swiss authorities; they were "hounding him to death." His seven-page will accused Zurich officialdom of being infiltrated with Communists. He called Zurich "a red city" and bequeathed upon it a large Swiss flag upon which he had affixed a Soviet hammer and sickle.

His murder, clearly a professional job, was never solved. The *Stasi* remained the principal suspect since it had managed to "turn" some of Lenzlinger's henchmen and was known to have paid about $2,500 to one of them for information that would have been helpful with the assassination. On the other hand, my chief consultant on such matters, Rainer Hildebrandt of the Checkpoint Charlie museum, heard that Lenzlinger had in fact been in business with the *Stasi*.

"They came to him and told him they could make him more successful," Hildebrandt said. "They told him: we'll make sure that five out of ten of your clients will get out okay and we'll see what we'll do with the others. Maybe we'll use them as informers." Hildebrandt heard that Lenzlinger agreed because the deal would increase the volume of his business and he needed help to keep his highly paid border-runners (*Schleuser*) busy. He had often been heard to complain about his "immense" overhead.

None of which helped solve the murder. The methodical Swiss authorities checked 150 possible tips and suspects and found Lenzlinger as slippery in death as in life. "We have nothing in hand," said the investigating judge. "Anything is possible." It was an epitaph appropriate for the Wall's villains, its heroes, and those with sufficient ingenuity to require the services of neither.

42

ACROSS THE BORDER BY BALLOON: A FAMILY TALE

**Naila, West Germany,
September 1979**

Petra Wetzel, twenty-four, was a popular, bubbly young wife with a well-developed sense of fun and zero interest in politics. She earned good money as a quality control inspector in a tool factory; collected Elvis Presley records; and looked great in miniskirts, though these were hardly standard items in the dress code of her native Pössneck, a county seat of twenty thousand in Thuringia, the rural southwestern tip of the DDR.

By the criteria of her country, Petra enjoyed middle-class comfort. Her life was pleasant enough. She had two bright sons, aged two and five. Her husband, Günter, also twenty-four, did well as a free-lance electrician. They owned their own car, TV, and washing machine. With the help of the Strelzyks, their best friends, Petra and Günter Wetzel were modernizing their home, an old one-family house that they had lately bought on bank credit.

In their search for a part to fit their new hot-water heater—the special battery for it was unobtainable in their section of the DDR —the Wetzels traveled to Berlin. During a leisurely sight-seeing walk with her husband, Petra was exposed to the Wall for the first time. Its barren ugliness, the forbidding guard towers, and the heavily armed soldiers startled her and changed her life.

"It reminded me of scenes from a prison film I saw on TV," she recalled after her escape to West Germany. "I suddenly felt a tremendous anger rising in me. I asked Günter: 'Why are people allowed to imprison us behind this Wall, and our own government at that?' "

Günter had asked himself the same depressing question for some time. Although he too was apolitical, he had recently become increasingly exasperated with the obvious lies in the government propaganda. It kept celebrating phony production triumphs in factories where he worked, so he knew that the truth was different. And he grew envious when he witnessed the free-for-all of opposing opinions about public issues on Western television.

Lamenting the limitations of life in the DDR at dinner with their best friends, the Strelzyks—Peter, thirty-seven, and his wife, Doris, thirty-two—the Wetzels discovered that the other couple, who had sons fifteen and eleven, had been thinking of leaving the country since early in 1975. It was then that Peter first suggested the notion to his incredulous wife.

"You're crazy," said Doris, who had a fine job as clerk in the Pössneck savings bank. "Why should we do that now when the house is almost finished? And how would you do it with the kids? It'd never work!"

"I don't know how," admitted Peter, "but something will occur to me."

Something did. In the summer of 1975 the family planned to go on vacation to Yugoslavia. While there, Peter was fairly confident, he would think of some way to sneak across the border into Austria. The scheme was never tested. Travel permits to "socialist" nations like Yugoslavia were not as difficult to obtain as visas to capitalist areas; nevertheless, such privileges were granted or refused according to arbitrary and unpublished rules. In the case of the Strelzyks the travel application was turned down and, as customary, without reason. It was like wanting to cross the ocean but not being able to get a taxi to the airport.

In the four years since then, the Strelzyk and Wetzel families had further improved their living standards. They had completed their homes. The men had become business partners and had more electrical work than they could manage. They were saving a lot of money. At the same time, their frustrations with their environment grew. Peter could hardly believe, in retrospect, that he had once been an SED Party member, an officer in the DDR *Luftwaffe,* and that he had been decorated as an "honored activist of socialist competition" in his first civilian employment.

Much as some people devote themselves to working out games

and puzzles, the technical-minded team of Peter and Günter began to examine ways to depart for West Germany, only eighteen miles south of Pössneck. Since they were familiar with the border fortifications, they quickly rejected cross-country methods as too risky. A plane or helicopter seemed promising, but how would they get one in the well-guarded DDR?

Regardless, the aerial route held appeal. On March 7, 1978—they remembered the date but could never recall which one spoke up first—they were eating breakfast in the dressing room of a client, a leather goods manufacturer, and the solution burst upon them: they could build themselves a balloon!*

At the town's biggest bookstore the next day they found nothing about balloon technology, but in the reference department there was a Brockhaus encyclopedia. Here they encountered a helpful entry under "Montgolfier," the name of the French brothers who in 1783 built the world's first hot-air balloon and flew it over Paris. The discovery of the Montgolfiers rested on simple logic: hot air being lighter than cold, it was elementary that a fabric container would rise and turn into a carrier once the air within it was heated.

As Strelzyk returned the encyclopedia, he whispered to Wetzel, "Man, if they could do it two hundred years ago, so can we."

Even for these resourceful do-it-yourselfers, the calculations necessary to guarantee safe air transport for eight people were formidable. They finally decided they would have to build a balloon twenty meters high and heated at 100 degrees Celsius by a homemade device that resembled a flame thrower. Propane gas and an engine they had salvaged from an old motorcycle would lift their contraption and keep it going. One problem remained: where in the shortage-bedeviled DDR could they corner the necessary eight hundred square meters of fabric?

In town after town of the surrounding area they tried their luck to no avail. Then, in the main co-op store of Gera, the provincial capital, they located enough rolls of brown cotton and bought 2,400 marks' worth for cash. (Money was no great problem. Like most DDR families, the Strelzyks and the Wetzels had accumulated ample money in savings accounts because there rarely was much merchandise in the shops to spend money on.) The co-op sales-

---

* In 1981 this family venture was turned into a Disney film, *Night Crossing*, starring John Hurt, Jane Alexander, and Beau Bridges, based on the book *Mit dem Wind nach Westen* by Jürgen Petschull.

woman, astounded by the enormous order, was reassured when the men said they were building tents for their camping club.

All this effort and expense got the men nowhere. They stitched the fabric together on a forty-year-old treadle-operated sewing machine and transported their balloon into the woods one midnight, only to find that they could blow it up to impressive size but it would not rise, not even one meter. And within minutes it began to shrink ingloriously. The seams were not sufficiently airtight. Upset and feeling like fools, they burned up their bulky investment in Peter's basement stove. What next?

Using a vacuum cleaner as a base, they rigged up a testing gadget and tried it on four different fabrics. Umbrella silk and taffeta worked best. Posing as representatives of a sailing club in Gera, the men shopped around in Leipzig and managed to scrounge enough sections of relatively inexpensive green, blue, and beige taffeta to piece together another balloon. This model proved airtight, yet it also would not rise, not one meter. With skill and luck they figured out why: they needed more heat—at least three times, maybe five times, more than they had been generating.

The Wetzels were beginning to get second thoughts, especially Petra. She kept having dreams about crashing in a balloon, with her little sons screaming in terror. So when Günter Wetzel pointed out to Peter Strelzyk that a balloon's chances for success might be doubled if its weight was halved, Peter regretfully acquiesced to his friends' withdrawal.

Once its source of heat was enhanced, the taffeta balloon lifted the Strelzyk family aloft easily at 1:30 A.M. on July 4, 1979, well over a year after the idea was conceived. They were elated. At about two thousand meters they hit clouds. Strong winds kept turning the balloon and its gondola in sickening circles—like a merry-go-round spinning out of control. It did keep moving toward West Germany. After twenty-five minutes it seemed to Peter that the lights below were growing bigger. They were falling. Moments later, his son Frank yelled, "Watch it, Daddy! Trees!"

As treetops tore into the balloon, the gondola sailed gently to the ground.

"Hold tight! Hold tight!" shouted Peter to his family, and thirty-four minutes after takeoff they were safely on the ground. But in which country?

"Maybe we made it," said Peter. He was wrong. As he gingerly investigated the ground, he came upon strange metal spirals. Trip wire! They had to be in the "death strip," the defenses just inside the DDR side of the border.

Ducking through the woods, repeatedly within earshot of patrols, the Strelzyks hiked for eight hours, located their car, gathered up all evidence of their takeoff, and made it back to their home without arousing suspicion—a near-miracle.

When they talked over the experience with their old friends, the Wetzels volunteered to rejoin the balloon enterprise, their change of mind shedding significant light on the reasons for much of the restlessness endemic among DDR citizens.

Petra had turned less worried about her family's safety because she was furious. Three times in recent months she had been denied permission for brief visits to West German relatives: once for a funeral, once for a wedding, and for a farewell visit to her dying stepmother. She had enough of the DDR's lack of compassion.

The motives of her once apolitical husband were very political. Like Peter, he was disgusted with the increasingly punitive laws that were taking effect on August 1, 1979. Any criticisms of conditions in the DDR were becoming punishable by up to eight years in prison. Incredible! Wetzel told Strelzyk he agreed with a prophecy that the new laws had provoked from the dissident DDR writer Stefan Heym. Wetzel had heard Heym's words on Western TV and had been jarred.

Heym had warned, "A great silence will break out in the DDR, but it will be more meaningful than any criticism, no matter how loud."

The ultimate blow to Günter Wetzel had been a notice from the DDR *Volksarmee*. He was to report to his army engineering unit for duty.

As the men set about constructing their third and largest balloon —it had to be as tall as an eight-story house in order to lift eight people—the wives, posing as representatives of a sailing club, scoured twenty-eight shops in more than half a dozen cities to amass 1,200 square meters of taffeta and bed ticking.

At 2:20 A.M. on Sunday, September 16, 1979, winds were favorable, and Peter Strelzyk called out, "Cut the ropes!"

At 2:46, at an altitude of 2,600 meters, the heating unit's gas flame grew smaller and whooshed into silence. With a fistful of matches Wetzel got it going again—for a few seconds.

At 2:50 all propane was gone. The balloon could no longer be steered.

Back on earth after twenty-eight minutes of flight in darkness and silence, the two families were shortly tracked down by two policemen.

"Are we in the West?" they asked.

They were, having landed in the Upper Franconian woods near Naila, a small place not far from the border city of Hof.

The Strelzyks and the Wetzels were feted as heroic figures, elaborate official applause coming from the West and snickering approval circulating surreptitiously in the East. The balloonists heard that a new joke was making the rounds in their old DDR town of Pössneck:

"Question—why do the People's Police now patrol in teams of *three* instead of two?"

"Answer—because one of them has to keep checking the sky!"

At the site of the balloon takeoff, a wag erected a directional sign that was quickly removed by police. It announced FLIGHT TIME TO NAILA—28 MINUTES. The sign was a nice joke, of course, but it was depressing, too. The distance between the two Germanys was as discouraging as ever.

PART VIII

ONE FAMILY'S AGONY

43

THE BOOK OF BÄRBEL: SURVIVING THE PRISONS AND THE COURTS

East Berlin,
May 1975

Pacing frantically up and down her cell, Bärbel Grübel spent weeks almost entirely without sleep. Suspecting that she was near a nervous breakdown, she asked to see a psychiatrist. To her surprise, she was eventually summoned to see such a specialist. His interest, however, remained almost entirely confined to her "crime." After questioning her in detail about her attempt to flee the country, he wrote an order for some sleeping pills and sent her back to her cell.

At about this time her mother was permitted to visit for the first time. Bärbel was elated and shocked all at once: Eva looked dreadful. And she was acutely frightened, cowering, oppressed by the prison surroundings. Tearfully, she related her encounter with Herr Voss of the Youth Office. She repeated his vow that the children would "never" be released, that they would soon be put up for adoption. Both women collapsed in tears. Eva's thirty minutes were up.

A few days later a lawyer called on Bärbel, having been appointed to defend her and Ota. Bärbel was not cheered by his visit. The fellow said he was pressed for time. Besides, he could do very little for them.

And the children?

"*Ja,*" the attorney confirmed matter-of-factly, "your children are probably lost." A trial of Ota and Bärbel would take place shortly.

"You have to count on a three-year sentence," the lawyer said. "Since you're so young, maybe with good behavior I can get you released after you've served half that time."

Bärbel had requested a change of cellmate, and the move to another two-person cell was authorized. A guard was unlocking her new cell—there was a red dot on the door, which meant that at least one of the inmates was a serious suicide risk—and the woman whom Bärbel was to replace was coming out, her head down, her face blank. Bärbel couldn't believe her own eyes.

"Frau Schulze!" she exclaimed. "Don't you recognize me? I'm Bärbel from the Tenth Upper School!"

The prisoner had been her high school teacher for two years, and when Bärbel called out her name, the woman recognized the former student at once. Speechless, she stroked Bärbel's cheek as she was led away.

For her trial on November 15, Bärbel was taken to the courthouse on Littenstrasse in a green Minna (as the police vans were known). As she stood waiting in the guard room outside the court, Ota was led in. In three months she had received only one sign of life from him. He had written her twice before, his note said, but she had not received these letters. And not until they were out of prison much later did she learn that he, too, had written to Erich Honecker and to the General State Prosecutor as well as the Council of Berlin Mitte.

Seeing her husband, even under such depressing circumstances, made Bärbel smile broadly. Ota, almost hopping up and down for joy, moved to shake her hand, in the German fashion, and leaned over to kiss her.

Bärbel's guard jumped between them.

"You pig," she yelled at Ota, "you don't seem to know where you are!"

Ota's male guard grabbed him by the lapels, shook him, and muttered, "If you don't toe the line, you scoundrel, I'll show you a thing or two!"

The guards placed husband and wife in handcuffs and led them into the courtroom. They had hoped to have a quick word with their lawyer, but he only nodded a greeting and returned to the study of his papers.

The trial was the customary DDR-style farce. It was a private proceeding. The prosecutor and the judges did 99 percent of the talking. Mostly they reviewed the details of the crime—*Republikflucht*—once again. The Grübels' lawyer offered a quiet request for leniency, especially for Bärbel. The sentence came quickly: each defendant received two years and five months.

Their lawyer looked relieved. At least Ota and Bärbel had not violated his urgent instructions. Whatever you do, so he had pleaded with each of them from the outset, don't say anything about still wanting to leave for the West. And don't ask questions about the children! They were forbidden territory.

To maintain some measure of physical and mental fitness, Bärbel and her cellmate decided it was essential for them to exercise regularly. They would jog. And so they did, up and down, up and down, up and down, in their little cell. It limbered them up a bit. It also presented them with a new problem. The cell was so small that a few minutes of running made them dizzy. They kept running anyway but stopped for more frequent rests.

The jogging had to cease when Bärbel was transferred into an eight-person cell. Space there was so confining that inmates could barely stand. With this change of domicile came a great gift: Bärbel was reunited with her former teacher, and there was time to learn her story.

The teacher was not one of the "politicals" in the cell, like Bärbel, nor was she one of the "criminals"; she belonged in a third category, an "antisocial," one of the large class of unfortunates not sufficiently stoic to withstand the social criteria prescribed by the government for DDR citizens.

It was a universal story, except that the outcome was dictated by DDR law. The teacher's husband had found another woman. Their marriage collapsed and the teacher had a nervous breakdown. After some months of hospitalization she was assigned to clerical work in a brewery. Bärbel could not determine whether the teacher had remained too depressed to be able to work at any regular job or whether she became discouraged because she was no longer allowed to teach. In any event, the teacher could not rouse herself to appear at the brewery daily and promptly. Against such "anti-social" conduct the DDR applied its standard remedy. It was called "work education," an Orwellian euphemism for prison.

The teacher was serving a sentence of one to two years. Bärbel was soon separated from her and never learned the woman's fate. Did her depression lift? That would be hard to know, because when Bärbel was her cellmate the teacher was mostly depressed about her two children. No one would tell her what was becoming of the youngsters. For all Bärbel ever knew, the teacher might still be undergoing "work education." Whenever one such sentence failed to encourage "anti-social" citizens to reform, they could expect more of the same. The second sentence ran two to five years. Bärbel also knew of three-time "anti-social" losers. They would get five to ten years.

As long as she remained in the same cell as the teacher, Bärbel's boredom with the dreariness of prison routine was pleasantly eased. Two, sometimes three, other well-educated inmates banded together in an informal discussion society. For hours they argued about nonpolitical subjects: philosophers, books, anything that might transport them temporarily out of their surroundings.

One inmate who occasionally attached herself to the group took a special interest in Bärbel. She was about forty and carried the Wagnerian name of Brünnhilde (unusual even in Germany). Bärbel was told that Brünnhilde used to express herself favorably about the DDR. Once Bärbel joined the cell, however, the woman abruptly changed her pitch. Now nothing seemed to suit her about her country.

Brünnhilde told Bärbel that she expected her own release shortly and that she possessed useful connections. She assumed Bärbel would be eventually released to the West. Helpful Brünnhilde would be willing to enlist idealistic friends who could kidnap Bärbel's children and bring them to her on the other side.

Bärbel said she was not interested. She was reasonably certain that Brünnhilde was attempting to buy her own release by performing favors for the secret police, the *Stasi*. Some days later Brünnhilde took Bärbel aside again and confirmed her suspicion. The woman said she had acquired, in ways she did not mention, a certain familiarity with security people and their methods. Would Bärbel be willing to do some work for them in exchange for the return of her children?

Bärbel exploded. She and her Ota needed no such assistance,

she insisted. They were quite capable of using brutality of their own to get their children back. It was her way of getting rid of the woman and communicating her defiance to the agents who were surely manipulating her. In Bärbel's heart, the fear for her children was settling into her like a load of lead. When would she even discover where they were?

Rummelsburg Prison, East Berlin, June 1975

Ota Grübel was not popular with the prison authorities, the "educators." They did not like his unmilitary slouch. They shoved and boxed him around when he refused to attend propaganda movies. They shouted at him when he looked bored at the daily news briefings based on articles in the morning's party sheet and when he protested against the sanitary facilities at the prisoners' workplace.

The men were braiding leather straps for women's shoes in a damp, windowless basement, starting daily at 6 A.M. The toilet equipment consisted of a pail on the floor. It was to be used only for urinating. If one of the fifteen men in Ota's group wanted to move his bowels, he had to ring for a guard, who might not arrive for a half hour or more.

This policy eventually seemed too liberal to the sublieutenant-educator in charge of Ota's guard detail. He lined up the inmates and bellowed: "We're not your servants and this is no hotel! From now on you may use the latrine only at eight A.M.! Train your asses accordingly!"

Predictably, the new system led to "accidents" that did not improve the already penetrating stench in the dank workroom.

Ota lived for Bärbel's letters. They were finally reaching him with some regularity, and no one could have treasured letters more. Bärbel had a way with words and she had a way with Ota. Ota kept all the letters, written on grainy gray prison stationery, accumulating them like deposits of gold in the savings bank of his hopes. It was a difficult hoard to collect and manage. The prison administration was determined to destroy letters from loved ones, as if an inmate's resistance could be subdued by severing this lifeline to the outside.

An inmate was permitted to possess only one letter at a time. Whenever a new letter arrived, an old letter had to be surrendered. Ota beat the system. He was persistent and he was still a talker, and so he managed to find prisoners who had saved old letters but did not feel so sentimentally possessive about them. Ota would persuade such men to give up an old letter, which he would hand to the guards as his own. It was a risky scheme, but Ota did not care, especially at night after the unlocking and locking of cell doors had ceased, when he dug up his collection, savoring the letters in the quiet one by one, again and again.

At other times he was so deeply depressed that his fellow prisoners laid aside their own burdens to console him. The wildly arbitrary hand that seemed to hold sway over Rummelsburg Prison made it easy to luxuriate in false hopes. One day in January a report spread that a man in Building Number 6 had "quite suddenly" been sent to Karl-Marx-Stadt. Ah! The prison there was usually the last stop for "politicals." Westbound transports of ransomed prisoners were assembled there. No doubt the man from Number 6 was headed West. There would be more transports before long, no doubt about that either.

"You'll see," the cellmates told Ota. "It won't be long and you'll also be *drüben*" (over on the other side).

The prospect was not without some foundation in reality. Prisoners were occasionally plucked out of their cells without notice and sent West without trial and, miraculously, without bureaucratic complications of any kind. It was baffling—like the proverbial strike of lightning. The prisoners whispered that Dr. Wolfgang Vogel, the superstar attorney in East Berlin, usually had a hand in such miracles.

Ota, having heard the lawyer's name mentioned by inmate after inmate, had some time ago written Vogel, asking him to expedite his release and Bärbel's, and to make sure they would join the transports to the West. (Not infrequently, prisoners were discharged and ordered to resume life in the DDR against their will. Ota thought that he and Bärbel could no longer survive such a fate.)

Anyway, regardless of how much they detested the DDR, they could never depart without their children, and so far no proceeding about the fate of the youngsters had taken place; their whereabouts remained unknown. Nobody knew whether the threat of adoption voiced by Herr Voss in the Youth Aid Office wasn't perhaps bluster after all.

Ota's fellow prisoners thought so. "You'll see," said one. "Pretty soon you'll hear the order 'Grübel, pack your stuff!' And then it's off to the West with the wife and the kids. You'll see, they *can't* take your kids away! It's unheard of, no way!"*

The authorities did have ways to convince Ota that they were serious about separating him from his children. Three times Ota was summoned to court sessions about the proposed adoption. Each time the date was canceled at the last moment. The strategy behind these on-again, off-again maneuvers became obvious the first time around, on April 5.

A guard came to fetch Ota from his cell at 3 A.M. The court was scheduled to convene at 9:30. The intervening hours, the guard said, were "time to rethink." Toward 9 A.M. Ota was summoned to the office of his "educator." This time the officer sounded fatherly. Ota would do well to reconsider, he said. Why couldn't the whole family make its peace with the DDR and stay there? In that event, Ota could soon be reunited with his wife and children.

"Out of the question," said Ota. "I've no confidence in this regime. I've no alternative but to take my family and leave."

As the educator took him back to his cell, Ota demanded to see his wife. "I've not seen her in six months," he said. "Every thief and sex offender can see his spouse every few weeks. Why am I different?"

The educator said that in Ota's case the decision could be made only by the prison director.

On May 15 Ota was taken to the visiting room of Bärbel's jail and led to a table divided by a three-foot-high glass pane. Bärbel was brought in wearing a threadbare soldier's uniform. She was very pale, but her huge eyes sparkled. A woman guard told the couple that they were permitted to shake hands across the glass. The guard sat down close to Ota and got ready to take notes of the prisoners' conversation.

At first both were too embarrassed by the guard's proximity to say a word. They sat bolt upright and smiled at each other. Finally Ota spoke up.

"How are you?"

"Fine."

"Did you hear anything about the children?"

"No."

"We'll make it!"

---

* In actuality, numerous other cases of forced adoptions were getting under way.

"Yes, we'll make it!"

"Are they making you work here?"

"Yes," said Bärbel and glanced at the guard, who was closing her notebook and rising.

"I love you," said Ota.

"I love you," said Bärbel.

The guard said their time was up. Bärbel and Ota shook hands. As they reached the doors on the opposite sides of the room, each turned and waved.

A few days later Ota received an encouraging letter from Wolfgang Vogel. The lawyer wrote that he had filed a formal application for the Grübels and their children to leave the DDR. He expected a reaction from the authorities within a few months.

At the first court session about the children, the Grübels' attorney questioned the legality of the adoption decision that Herr Voss had disclosed to Bärbel's mother at the Youth Aid Office. How could a low-level functionary order such a radical step before the court had had an opportunity to consider the case?

The judge broke in and signaled the attorney by an annoyed wave of an arm that he should sit down and be quiet. The rest of the session was devoted to the parents' negative attitude toward the DDR. Were they really determined to leave the country? Bärbel and Ota affirmed their wish vigorously. At no time were they allowed to talk to their lawyer or to each other.

At the next proceeding, in June, the court seemed to recognize that the Grübels really couldn't be persuaded to stay in the DDR.

"What would you do if your application to leave is rejected?" asked the judge.

"We'd try to escape again," said Ota.

"I'm sure our request will be granted," said Bärbel when the judge turned to her. She looked exhausted and very frightened.

This time Herr Voss was in court, all business and obsequious. He handed the judge a formal petition from the Youth Aid Office demanding that the Grübels be denied the right to raise their children.

Whereupon Bärbel and Ota were led out of the court to be handcuffed and taken back to their cells. Later they learned that after their departure the judge announced his ruling: they were to be permanently deprived of their children.

. . .

In its plodding way of applying its own notions of justice, the DDR court system was still pondering Bärbel and Ota's fate. Their lawyer had appealed their two-year sentence, and this prompted the appeals court to throw out the sentence as too lenient! The case was returned to the district court, which decided that Bärbel and Ota, having sought to escape together, were guilty of a "group" conspiracy. This aggravated offense required sentences of two years and ten months each.

In September the Grübels were returned to court. Their attorney wanted to talk to his clients. Not a chance. Two guards took positions between them and the lawyer so that communication was impossible. The proceeding was bizarre.

"Do you have anything to say?" the judge asked the couple when they were led in.

"No."

Within two minutes they were led out of the room again. What had this been all about? They did not know and never found out.

In prison, Ota was never out of trouble with his keepers. Every time he had finished his one permissible monthly letter to Bärbel, he was summoned to the educator, who had the job of censoring outgoing mail. The educator did not approve of Ota's letters.

On one occasion Ota wrote, "When will this misery end?"

The educator demanded that these words be stricken. There was no misery, he argued. Ota's housing, food, and clothing needs were being provided. The fact that he was in prison was his own fault; he had violated the law. If Ota wanted Bärbel to receive his letter, the offensive words had to go. There was no way for Ota to win these ideological fencing matches. Some letters he had to rewrite three times.

Overtly, conditions in Rummelsburg Prison were reasonably tolerable. Nobody starved. Nobody was physically abused. Nonetheless, Ota was constantly reminded of the atmosphere in Hitler's times, the terrible days he had heard about from his parents when he was small. The Rummelsburg "educators" might as well have been SS men. "They didn't gas anybody and they didn't beat anybody to death," he said years later, "but psychologically it was just like under fascism."

Tension and sleeplessness got him down. He developed chronic abdominal pains. His appetite was poor. Some weeks after he asked to see a doctor, an X ray was taken that showed stomach ulcers, for which he was given injections. At the same time the prison doctor diagnosed "inflammations" of the kidneys and bladder. After three months in the prison hospital, another doctor told Ota that he was as well as he would get. The "inflammations" would never disappear entirely. They were psychosomatic.

"You think too much," the doctor diagnosed.

Half a year after his last visit with Bärbel, Ota was taken to see her again.

"It'll all be over soon," she said, trying to smile. "The last time my mother was here she said our exit to the West is all set. But you've got to watch your health. Our children need us. Pretty soon we'll have it made."

Both were convinced that their children would be permitted to leave the DDR with them. There had been no more talk of adoption. If Bärbel and Ota were deemed unfit to raise the youngsters as good socialists in the DDR, this surely did not disqualify them to raise little Ota and Jeannette as nonsocialists in the West.

The authorities soon conveyed a very different picture of the family's future. Four weeks after Ota filed a request to see a copy of the court decree concerning the fate of the children, he was received by an officer of the *Stasi* in one of the interrogation rooms of Building 4. The officer was elaborately courteous. He almost apologized. An unfortunate mistake had occurred. Ota should have been given access to the court ruling. He would not be allowed to keep the document, but the officer would shortly arrange for Ota to examine a copy.

"Where are my children?" asked Ota, trembling but making every effort to keep calm.

"I don't know, I can't tell you a thing about that."

"Will our exit visa be approved?"

"I don't know that either," said the *Stasi* man. "In any event it definitely won't be approved for your children. They're going to stay with us. Whether you and your wife will be allowed to leave is up in the air. Maybe you'll be able to go and we'll keep your wife here. Or maybe we'll keep you both. The decision hasn't been made. We've got plenty of time."

When the officer saw Ota's face darkening, he said cheerfully: "I can't understand why you want to go over to the other side anyway. You're an intelligent person. Do you really think you'll live better over there than with us?"

"I finally want to be left in peace," Ota said. "I've been in difficulties for years here, getting threatened and insulted just because I'm in disagreement with your system. That's why we want to leave the DDR; we want to live without fear."

"I can't understand you," the *Stasi* man said. "What are you afraid of? If you do your work and participate in our society you'll live in perfect peace here. Do you think things will be peaceful in the West? Life is not so gentle over there! It could happen that a car runs over you and nobody will know whether it's a genuine accident or not.* You should begin a new life here. We'll help you."

Ota said nothing. The conversation had left him infinitely depressed. He was also baffled. The DDR system did not normally pay so much attention to one case. Why were they lavishing so much time on the case against his family? What was so important about the Grübels? Why were the authorities so keen on changing his mind and having him stay in a country he detested?

A few days later Ota's educator called him into his office, asked him to sit down at a small table, and handed him the court decree taking away his children.

"Take your time," the officer said. "You've got a right to read this."

There were seven typed pages, dated June 20, 1974. The file was number 240 F 780.73 of the district court, Berlin Mitte. The title of the file, running in large print across the top, said, "In the Name of the People!" In contention was the fate of Ota Grübel, born July 12, 1969, and Jeannette Grübel, born September 2, 1970.

The decree summarized the charges of the prosecution that the parents had neglected their duties by giving the children tranquilizers and trying to transport them across the East-West border. The parents had endangered the children's lives; had endangered their future; had "torn them out of orderly living conditions"; and they had done all this only to "pursue their own interests."

---

* This was an allusion to the high crime rate in the West, a favorite theme of Communist propaganda.

The defense had replied that the tranquilizers had been harmless; that the children had not been endangered at the border, because the parents had stopped promptly and followed the instructions of the border guard. The defense also noted that the defendants "felt no sympathy for the DDR and believed they could not be happy here with their children."

The court thereupon ruled that the use of the tranquilizers had been "irresponsible in the highest degree"; that the parents had been swayed by "egotistical goals"; that they were guilty of depriving their children of their "stable social security"; that Ota and Bärbel had allowed themselves to be criminally swayed by their unrealistic notions of life abroad.

"Their irresponsible attitude endangered both minor children to an extreme degree," the court concluded.

When Ota handed the decree back to his educator, the officer said: "You see? You're always saying there is no justice here. Are you satisfied now? You've read the verdict and everything is in order."

Ota remained silent. How could the court have missed the point so totally? The decree seemed to deal with people whom Ota did not recognize; it might have been written in Urdu. There was no way to negotiate with this alien other world.

A new mood overcame Ota. He stopped struggling, protesting, asking questions. He became resigned. He felt like a sleepwalker, shutting out all but Bärbel, little Ota, and Jeannette.

"Those three names, those three faces, I knew nothing else, I saw nothing else," he wrote later. "I kept saying the names, afraid that I might forget them. I shut my eyes so that the three faces would come alive."

His mother found him apathetic when she was allowed to visit in March 1975. He shouldn't worry so much, she said. Everything was going well. Soon he would be reunited with Bärbel and the children.

"Ja," said Ota softly, "everything will go well." He did not believe it. He had heard it too often before.

Six days later, around 10 A.M., a guard rushed into Ota's basement workplace to get him. He was ordered to bundle up his few belongings in a great hurry, then he was squeezed into the tiny cell of a prison truck, the kind he had come to know from past transfers. There was barely room to sit, it was totally dark, and, in keeping with the DDR fetish for secrecy, nobody would tell him where he was headed or why.

Was he about to be liberated after all? He trembled with excitement. Sweat poured down his face. In his jail the men had spread word that prisoners who were about to be ransomed by the West German government were assembled in Karl-Marx-Stadt and transported by bus to a discharge center in Giessen, West Germany, every Wednesday. That was only rumor. Nobody was sure of the facts. Besides, the report might be accurate, yet not apply to Ota.

Twice the truck stopped, and Ota could hear other prisoners climbing aboard to be locked into cells. He guessed that three or four hours had passed when the truck pulled up in a prison yard. Blinded by the sunlight, Ota stumbled into a supply room. Officers in civilian clothes—*Stasi* men—told him to change into new fatigues. He was allowed to retain only toothpaste, toothbrush, soap, comb, and cigarettes. Everything else had to be abandoned in a garbage can, including all notes, correspondence, and other papers. En route to a four-man cell Ota asked an officer where he was. The answer sounded like a reprieve from death. He was in the *Stasi* prison at Karl-Marx-Stadt.

Early that evening, in an office one floor up, an officer handed him a printed form, a request for "dismissal from DDR citizenship." It asked for names of family members who were supposed to leave with him. He wrote in the names of his wife and children. Nobody would tell him when he would see them or when they might leave. Then, to his immense surprise and delight, he learned that Bärbel had already arrived in the same building.

From the adjoining cell Ota and his cellmates heard the faint voices of women. The men bailed the water out of their toilet, and once the women had cleared the toilet in the other cell, the two groups could communicate easily by way of the plumbing. Names and stories were exchanged.

"Do you have anybody there from Berlin?" Ota asked. "Yes," said one woman, "yesterday we had a prisoner from Berlin, Bärbel Grübel, but she was moved."

When silence descended on the prison that night, Ota placed his mouth on the crack of the cell door and called out, "Bärbel!" And from somewhere nearby she replied, "Yes! Soon we'll have it made!"

. . .

Suddenly, they faced an appalling choice. With freedom within their grasp, they were forced to make a momentous decision about little Ota and Jeannette. The issue was cruel: should they consider leaving the country without the children after all?

When they were first approached about this proposition, it seemed unthinkable. Out of the question. Preposterous. And yet it developed that, paradoxically, they might regain the children sooner if they abandoned them for the time being.

It was the sort of catch-22 choice not uncommonly set up by the DDR bureaucracy: arbitrary and loaded with grave risk for citizens who were pawns in the gamble.

For the Grübels the choice was offered in a Kafkaesque setting. Although a joint decision was called for, they were interviewed separately. Each was made to witness the identical strange tableau. Trading notes later, they found that they had given identical responses.

Summoned to one of the prison visitors rooms, they were confronted by lawyer Wolfgang Vogel, representing the DDR, along with his West Berlin opposite number, Jürgen Stange. For once, no guards were present to eavesdrop, although the Grübels took for granted that the room was wired. Vogel faced each prisoner. Stange took a seat in the back of the room. This odd arrangement might have been meant merely to satisfy DDR protocol, but Bärbel and Ota were in agreement that it served a more subtle purpose: neither lawyer was able to observe (or could later be questioned about) the facial expression of the other. The two men were unmistakably operating as a team; their silent signals turned out to be much more meaningful than anything spoken in the room.

Judging by Vogel's words alone, the dismal choice facing the Grübels was no choice at all. If they remained in the DDR, he said, the children might "possibly" be restored to them after "many years of probation." If they left the country without the youngsters, the kids might "possibly" be lost to them for good.

The nonverbal messsages sent by both attorneys were dramatically different. Vogel remained relatively discreet. "By gestures and facial expressions he led us to believe that we shouldn't necessarily give full credence to what he was saying," Bärbel remembered. Stange, however, having said nothing, went all out in disassociating his client, the West German government, from Vogel's words.

"By the way he motioned with his arms he unmistakably gave us to understand that we shouldn't believe what we were hearing and that we should come over to the West," Bärbel recalled.

The Grübels' reaction to this fateful charade was decisive. Each said they still wanted to go West and firmly believed the children would be allowed to join them there. This caused Vogel to rise, smile, and shake hands. Stange's expressive round face danced with pleasure and he gave Bärbel a warm hug.

Reviewing the performances later, Bärbel and Ota agreed that the lawyers' extralegal pantomime was hardly a foolproof guarantee of parental rights. No matter. The Grübels could do nothing for their children as long as they remained in the DDR themselves. Once safely in the West, they could generate pressure to get the kids out. If nothing else, Stange's enthusiastic play-acting indicated that he and his West German superiors would help.

Once they accepted the unavoidability of having to toss dice for the destiny of their children, the Grübels considered their gamble reasonable. Nagging doubts about the loyalties of their East-West lawyer team did trouble them. Whose side were these showmen really on?

A week later forty prisoners were discharged from cells surrounding Ota. He could hear them laughing and joking, and then the lucky ones pounded down iron steps. He heard the outside door open and clank shut. Silence. He had never felt so abandoned.

His turn came on Wednesday, May 21, 1975. Suddenly, crazily, the status of the departing prisoners underwent drastic transformation. They were taken to the prison's top floor, where they faced what looked like a well-stocked department store, a bizarre sight. Spread before them, as in some dream of Christmases past, stood racks and tables overflowing with suits, shirts, ties, suitcases, toilet articles, Western cigarettes by the carton, everything a prosperous traveler required for a comfortable trip abroad. *Stasi* men served as sales clerks, importuning the prisoners to treat themselves generously. It was a bewildering role reversal, as if the guards had become the jailbirds.

Prices were reasonable and the prisoners could pay with the credits accumulated in their accounts from years of prison labor. No money would be exchanged for Western currency, although leftover funds could be transmitted to relatives in the DDR. Few took advantage of this offer, because the *Stasi* salesmen kept urging the men to keep on buying. It became obvious that the authorities wanted their charges to make a decent impression in the affluent West; they were not to appear neglected.

The effect of this incongruous largesse on Ota and his fellow prisoners was profound. Back in their windowless cell they giggled, offered each other cigarettes, smoothed out a neighbor's shirt collar, or straightened out his tie. Nobody strained to hear noises from outside any longer, nobody daydreamed on his bed. Like party guests waiting for the dance to begin, they kept standing, joshing, smoking. They had winning lottery tickets in their pockets —their exit papers.

Then it was their turn to trample down the iron steps and pile into the bus parked directly in front of the prison door. Several women were already inside, and one of them, in a window seat, was Bärbel, looking wan but radiant. Ota bounded up to her and then they were in each other's arms, both of them repeating over and over, "I love you." For most of the trip they held hands, each wanting to be certain that the other was still there, needing confirmation that this strange ride to freedom was not another prison reverie.

On the highway outside Karl-Marx-Stadt the dilapidated old bus stopped, and two smiling, well-dressed civilians climbed aboard. The escort officers greeted them as "Dr. Vogel" and "Dr. Stange" —the lawyers who represented the two German governments for the ransoming of political prisoners from the DDR.

Standing in the aisle, Stange, small, pink, and well upholstered, addressed the expectant travelers on behalf of the West: "In the name of the Federal Republic and myself, I bid you the heartiest welcome. You're free now. You'll be taken to Giessen, where you'll be well taken care of. There's no need to worry. . . ."

Stange reviewed the East-West ransoming process and told them that if they wanted more prisoners to be liberated in the future, they should give no interviews in the West, should tell no one how they came to be freed. He did not explain why they were supposed to keep quiet about a trade arrangement that was by then widely known, and nobody summoned the temerity to ask questions.

Stange smiled his ingratiating smile and wished everybody the best of luck in their "new life." The applause was loud and long. Bärbel and Ota were moved close to tears. They had liked Stange before. He seemed to be a warm, civilized soul, not at all a trader in human flesh; his words sounded heartfelt.

When the more formal Herr Vogel took his turn, the happy bus passengers were less attentive, and he obviously realized that his audience considered him part of the hated government they were leaving behind.

"Please hear me out, I have just a few words," he pleaded. He offered the services of his East Berlin office to help with any remaining legal problems, wished everybody *"Alles gute,"* and sat down.

Bärbel and Ota said little en route to the sleepy border town of Herleshausen. They were still holding hands for reassurance. They felt—so they decided when they talked about it later—as if they had never been separated, at least not for as long as two years. It was a dreary trip down a DDR Autobahn that carried almost no traffic, past fields and woods that looked gray to their disenchanted eyes.

At the multilane border control area, where the obstacle course of DDR passport and security procedures often took an hour to negotiate, an extraordinary thing occurred: nothing! The bus steamed without stopping past the long snake of waiting vehicles, right through the system of fences, gates, control booths, and barriers. The *Stasi* escort officers in the bus waved at the border guard, who grinned and genially waved back. That was all.

The Grübels were stunned. Never had they experienced the artificiality—the essential ridiculousness—of the German-German border so graphically. Never again would this man-made demarcation line figure in their lives in such a weightless way. Never would it part to yield their children.

The children, if only the children had been with them! The absence of little Ota and Jeannette burdened them so severely that they could not bear to talk about it. Herr Stange, the cheery lawyer, brought up the subject when he sat down to extend the Grübels his personal welcome. He put his arm around them, one by one, bussed them both on the cheek, and urged them not to worry about the children; they would come West soon. Bärbel and Ota wanted so badly to trust the bouncy little man that they believed him.

A few minutes past the border the DDR bus stopped at a clearing in the woods. A gleaming Western bus was waiting, and as the ransomed prisoners climbed aboard, a medley of current hit tunes came tootling out of the public address system. Outside, traffic moved in great volume and at high speeds. The fields seemed to look more pungently green than *drüben*, on the other side. People looked healthier and happier.

The reception camp in Giessen pulled them into a depressing contrast. Bärbel and Ota were assigned a private room that didn't seem Western. The iron bedstands and the rickety closet reminded them of their DDR prison cells. Walls and floor were filthy. Bärbel was disgusted.

"Only the bars in front of the windows are missing," she said.

"*Ach,* come on," Ota consoled her. "We're free; this is only for one night and now we're finally alone." He went to the door and locked it for their first privacy.

Having been given some Western spending money in the camp, they went to a *Drogerie* the next day to shop for cosmetics. When the owner learned that they were "politicals" from the camp, she gave them a big bag of free samples.

The children never left their consciousness. To fly to Berlin they had to take a train to the Frankfurt airport, and all the adults in the dining car seemed to be traveling with youngsters. It took Ota and Bärbel a few minutes to realize that they were paying no attention to their unaccustomed (and delicious) coffee and cake. They had their eyes on all these children, watching their movements, trying to catch their every word.

"As soon as we get to Berlin, we've got to look up Herr Stange," Bärbel said.

"Yes, right away," Ota agreed. "I'm sure little Ota and Jeannette will be with us very soon. I'm looking forward to life here! It won't take us long to learn how to use our liberty."

Frankfurt Airport, a labyrinth so mammoth that it intimidates even some American jet-setters, became a bewildering lesson in their new freedom. Why was everybody rushing so? The Grübels felt they were trapped in a space colony. Nothing seemed familiar. They didn't know that the little chrome carts were meant for baggage. When Ota mounted one and tried to ride it, people stared aghast. And where was the gate for the Berlin flights? Even the irrepressible Ota felt too cowed by the twenty-first century ambience to make inquiries.

44

THE BOOK OF BÄRBEL: TUG-OF-WAR FOR THE CHILDREN

**West Berlin,
December 1976**

At the Grübels' first stop in West Berlin, the Marienfelde refugee camp, the realities of Western life, good and bad, materialized quickly. They were fingerprinted, their pictures were taken, and they were interrogated, always individually, by relays of American, British, and French intelligence officers.

The Americans, presumably CIA men, were especially thorough. The fate of the Grübel children interested them in every detail, especially the potential for the kids' being used by the *Stasi* as bait in a blackmail scheme. "Someone will probably contact you and want you to spy in exchange for getting them out," one of the Americans warned. "If you're approached, let us know immediately."

Exploring West Berlin, Bärbel and Ota sometimes felt exhilarated; mostly they turned depressed. Everything was too much: the brightness of so many colors, the pushiness and pace of people, the opulence in the shops, the sheer onslaught of consumer goods in such unending, redundant variety. In the Ka De We, the biggest department store, the escalators made Bärbel dizzy, and the food department—the entire seventh floor, a gustatory landmark famous throughout Europe—made her feel faint.

Who could use more than a hundred kinds of bread, several

dozen different types of ham? It was crazy, obscene. She felt re-lieved when she left.

In the camp her vision became blurred. There was never a night without frightening dreams about the children. Ota, his weight down to 116 pounds, suffered from the stomach and kidney symp-toms he had developed during his prison stay. They looked up lawyer Stange who was smoothly reassuring: it was only a question of time and their kids would come. The Grübels were becoming suspicious, however. The delay did not help their fragile psychic and physical states.

The camp authorities were very understanding. Recognizing that the Grübels suffered from battle fatigue, they sent the couple to recuperate at a little rustic *Pension* in the Bavaria hills. It was a happy time. "Even the cows smiled at us," Bärbel and Ota remem-bered. On their return to the city they were assigned a bright, spacious apartment in a rowhouse of the Lichtenrade suburb, on Pechsteinstrasse, directly at the Wall.

The border location did not trouble them. On the contrary, the everyday presence of the Wall's Western face reminded them of their liberation and of their children's need for help wherever they might be back in the East. Right away, two small bedrooms were reserved and outfitted for them. Ota built two complete sets of furniture, Bärbel sewed fluffy red-and-white-checkered feather blankets for the beds.

When their depression and their physical symptoms failed to lift, the West Berlin immigration authorities sent them to a psychiatrist. The elderly Dr. Rudolf Hampel was a fidgety chain-smoker with a Freud-style beard, hopelessly overworked in the mountainous clut-ter of his office. But he was kind and competent and, having him-self fled from the DDR, he knew what the Grübels were up against.

He prescribed tranquilizers and antidepressants and offered to see them for psychotherapy at government expense. Bärbel went to him weekly for almost six months and took the medication at least some of the time. Ota saw the doctor only a few times and stopped the medication quickly. He could not tolerate reminders of the horrendous past.

Ten years later Dr. Hampel remembered the couple precisely.

"Both of them knew they were running against a wall," he said, referring to an emotional barrier rather then the construction at the border. "She clearly managed to deal with it better and reached some sort of accommodation. He didn't. He was bottled up and stayed stuck in a neurotic depression. He fastened himself onto those missing kids."

While Dr. Hampel affected a gruff manner, his empathy for the Grübels was steadfast. Thanks to his intervention, they were paid substantial sick benefits for one and a half years, which was almost as long as the struggle for the children lasted in its most suspenseful phase. In all that time, again and again, their release seemed tantalizingly close. Every time the suspense was followed by a letdown. The tension would have driven anybody crazy.

With Bärbel spending hours daily at the typewriter, the Grübels unfolded a fanatical campaign. They dispatched long status reports to the office of Willy Brandt, by then Chancellor, in Bonn. They mobilized the Berlin branch of the All-German Ministry. They followed up by seeking out anyone of influence who would receive them. The government people said they were pursuing the case vigorously; Bärbel and Ota should be patient, the kids were sure to be freed.

Not satisfied, the Grübels recruited still more helpers. Vogel was working with his second West Berlin partner, Reymar von Wedel, who was such a unique insider that he shuttled back and forth constantly between East and West, even sharing Vogel's East Berlin office several times a week.

Bärbel and Ota went to plead with von Wedel, and in his cold business manner, he, too, tried to pacify them. It was another unofficial go-between, Carl-Gustav Svingel, the former opera singer who represented the Swedish church authorities, who uncovered the truth and shared it with the by-now frantic parents.

"Your children were adopted last year," he reported in November 1975.

"Impossible!" exclaimed the Grübels' contact man at the All-German Ministry when they confronted him with this devastating information. "Vogel gave me his *word!* He gave me his handshake and promised the children would be let out!"

What was going on? Was the man from the ministry lying to them? Was Vogel lying to *him?* The Grübels felt enmeshed in an impenetrable bureaucratic web; only the most radical measures might stand a chance to sweep it away.

Svingel counselled them not to get desperate. He had confidence in his old friend Vogel. The lawyer was reliable. He had never broken his word. The Grübels, feeling that they had been stalled long enough, became furious at their Swedish friend. They thought his calm suggested insensitivity. Ota became so abusive that the gentle Svingel almost threw the couple out of his apartment.

Feeling hopelessly sandbagged, the Grübels decided to go public, to blow a whistle in the press. Their lawyers had been cautioning them against talking to outsiders about the children. Publicity would upset the DDR authorities. It would result in the one calamity that the paranoid officials in the East were most eager to avoid: loss of face. At a time when other nations were starting to recognize the DDR government as legitimate—it had finally gained admittance to the United Nations after much effort—it wouldn't do to be found guilty of inhuman practices against its own, youngest citizens. Quiet diplomacy was surely the most effective persuader.

Not for the Grübels. They were sick of circumspection and secrecy. Good manners were getting them nowhere. Their supposedly high-powered advisers couldn't even tell them where their children were and whether they were well! Bärbel and Ota were not the docile type to tolerate such treatment indefinitely. And what did they have to lose? Nothing.

The story broke in the December 15, 1975, issue of *Der Spiegel*. While the newsmagazine styled itself in the pattern of *Time,* it also practiced a most aggressive brand of investigative reporting, frequently with an explosive result. Which was precisely what the Grübels hoped for when they talked of their heartache in a dark Berlin pub to Manfred Müller, a quiet, veteran *Spiegel* reporter who had once been a priest.

At first Müller didn't trust his journalistic luck. What he heard sounded like a crazy tale. His magazine had exposed the brutal ways of the DDR authorities on many occasions, but their treatment of the Grübels appeared too extreme to be plausible even by primitive Eastern standards. His editors were suspicious and asked him to investigate further.

To Müller's surprise, the attorneys in the case were by now also so distressed that they violated their own policy of silence.

"What's happening is a tragedy," the pink little Stange exclaimed to the reporter.

"Because of a single mistake [the escape attempt] the defendants are supposed to be deprived of their children for all time," said even the Grübels' normally muzzled East German court attorney incredulously.

"Something is unclear and peculiar in this proceeding," conceded the oracular Vogel.

As Müller kept digging, he uncovered cases of other DDR "politicals" whose children were being taken away from them. Forcible adoption was no isolated event; it seemed to be becoming a secret DDR policy.

The response to Müller's article was spectacular.

"Monstrous," bristled the Governor of Bavaria. "The civilized world hasn't seen anything like this since the days of [Heinrich] Himmler [chief of Hitler's SS]." The Governor canceled his invitation to a high-ranking DDR diplomat who had just arrived in Munich for trade negotiations. The diplomat denounced the Grübel story as "dirty libel by a magazine."

Bavaria was the stronghold of the Christian Democrats (CDU-CSU), the West German political opposition. The ruling Social Democrats (SPD) reacted defensively. They didn't want to upset an about-to-be-signed agreement with the DDR for badly needed improvements of the Autobahn routes to West Berlin. If Bonn fussed too much over the Grübel case, the fragile relations with the East were certain to suffer. The East Germans were already incensed. The day the *Spiegel* article hit the streets, the Honecker government closed the magazine's East Berlin bureau and expelled the DDR correspondent, although he had had nothing to do with researching or writing the article (no action could be taken against Müller, since he was based in West Germany).

The West German minister in charge of relations with the East, Egon Franke, maintained public silence. He was a folksy politico, an SPD wheelhorse, not known for grasp of detail. Later he would be accused of embezzling funds appropriated by the government to ransom refugees (he was acquitted but his principal assistant went to prison). Pressured for a response to the Grübel case when it became public in 1975, Franke assured the West German cabinet that he knew of "only" five cases of forced adoptions.

Attorney Vogel tried to calm the uproar by taking the same line. He confirmed the facts of the Grübel case, along with some others, dismissing them as "not representative."

Triumphant at having drawn so much blood, the *Spiegel* followed up with a devastating ten-page cover story. Much more than the fate of the Grübels and a handful of other families was involved, so the magazine argued. It turned out that some 2,000 children were waiting in the East to be reunited with parents in the West. About 1,200 of them had been held for more than a decade; they had been separated from their West German parents by the construction of the Wall merely because they happened to be in the East on the fateful weekend of August 13, 1961.

As a matter of principle, the Honecker government was tenacious in its possessiveness toward its youth, as the *Spiegel* pointed out. Impressionable kids were national assets prized by the highest levels of government. The law that was applied against the Grübels —withdrawal of their right to bring up their children—was enforced by the Ministry of Education. Its chief was Margot Honecker, the Prime Minister's wife, a notorious hard-liner. It was known that she encouraged her functionaries to use adoptions against "politicals."

The magazine recalled that the government's purpose in ordering forced adoptions, the promotion of "socialism," was spelled out explicitly in the Family Law. So was the next phase in the lives of the affected children. The priority task of the adoptive parents was specific. "The [adopted] child is to be solidly rooted in its new life and education, especially in cases of younger children," the statute ordered.

Now the *Spiegel* reported a very rare occurrence: an open internal conflict at the top of the DDR government. Some officials thought that the law had been too harshly interpreted against Bärbel and Ota Grübel. Moreover, the *Spiegel* disclosures and their context constituted a public relations disaster for the freshly emerging Communist republic.

Lawyer Vogel was obviously among those holding reservations about the handling of the Grübel case; since he was close to Erich Honecker, it was inconceivable that a final decision on little Ota and Jeannette could evolve without the chief executive's making the judgment call.

Events moved with unprecedented swiftness. Only five days later, lawyer von Wedel phoned the Grübels and asked them to come to his office the next day, Christmas Eve. His news was momentous.

"I talked to Dr. Vogel yesterday," he said, "and I'm authorized to tell you that you'll get your children in the first quarter of 1976, possibly earlier."

Bärbel and Ota responded with tears, laughter, embraces. That night they celebrated Christmas for the first time since they lost the children.

The year could not have ended more auspiciously, and for a while the flow of favorable signs continued. Ota kept a diary record of the roller-coaster developments.

January 1, 1976. Summoned back to the office of von Wedel, they found him still briskly optimistic: "I've asked for photos of your children and I'll have further information on the fifteenth."

January 12. Von Wedel phoned and asked, "Would you agree if the children go to your parents [in East Berlin] first?" Bärbel and Ota rejected the proposal. Von Wedel asked them to come to Vogel's office on the fourteenth. The case was still headline news. On television that night the spokesman of the West German government announced that all forced adoptions would be invalidated; all affected parents would be reunited with their children "in the foreseeable future."

January 14. In his East Berlin office Vogel addressed the Grübels with unaccustomed vehemence. The tide had turned against them once more. Under DDR law they were now citizens of another country, and this made it impossible to restore to them the right to raise the children.

Ota exploded. Vogel reddened.

"I don't have to listen to your accusations and insults," the attorney huffed. "I'll stop this conversation at once. I don't get a *Pfennig* for my trouble and I don't have to argue with you. I had a hard enough time getting an exit permit for the two of *you!*"

Once everybody had calmed down, Vogel decided the time had come to tell the Grübels the real reason for asking them to see him. He had already worked out a way to get around the law. He suggested that the right to raise little Ota and Jeannette be awarded to Ota's mother, Meta. She could then ask for a permit to resettle in the West. The request would be granted and Meta could leave the country with the children.

Vogel interjected one condition. "You're to maintain absolute silence about this," he said. "There is to be nothing in the press; otherwise all efforts will cease at once and you won't get the children."

Disgusted and elated all at once, the Grübels said they would put this proposition up to Mama Meta.

Meta had continued her worrying and spying on behalf of her adored grandchildren. Their fate now seemed all the more agonizing because Bärbel and Ota had finally learned their exact where-abouts.

Confidential church sources notified them that the youngsters had been adopted by Ulrich and Anneliese Klewin in Eisenhütten-stadt on the Oder. They lived in a modern six-story apartment house at Chopin Ring 15, on the right-hand side of the ground floor. Mr. Klewin, an engineer and surveyor, was a loyal member of the SED.

As soon as Bärbel and Ota had phoned this information to Meta in East Berlin the old woman took off from her streetcar job and moved into action. She confided in a friend who hated the party and owned an old Wartburg automobile. Together with the friend's husband the women embarked on the four-hour trip to Eisenhüttenstadt, although Meta did not really know what she would do once she got there.

The detective team had been told that little Ota was in the first class of the Alfred Jung Eleventh Upper School, but when they reached Eisenhüttenstadt in the afternoon, school had let out. After driving to the Klewin apartment house, they parked two blocks away, and Meta walked around the pleasant tree-lined neighborhood for three hours, hoping for a glimpse of her grandchildren. As she wandered up and down the deserted suburban blocks, residents were watching. She found the Klewin name sign in the apartment house hallway but was too scared to make inquiries.

Three weeks later the same trio tried the same mission again, this time leaving Berlin at 4 A.M. and arriving in Eisenhüttenstadt just as little Ota blew a kiss to his adoptive mother and left alone for school. What to do? Mother Meta shuddered when the boy walked by within one meter of her car. She could make no move toward him.

It was an instant's decision. She ached to reach out—why had she come here anyway?—yet some instinct restrained her. Any kind of remotely unconventional action tended to provoke trouble in the DDR, and her grandchildren were in enough trouble al-ready. Dejected, the detectives drove back to East Berlin. At least Meta could tell Bärbel and Ota that she had actually seen their son and that he seemed fine. She did not mention the kiss the boy had blown in the adoptive mother's direction.

.   .   .

When Bärbel and Ota reported Vogel's scheme to bring the children home via Meta's custody, the grandmother was taken aback. She had never been among the many DDR citizens who wanted to quit the country. She'd never considered it. Who would employ an old woman in the hypercompetitive business climate of the West? In the East she had numerous cronies and she loved her work. She'd run streetcars for twenty-four years—the *Tramberuf*, she called it, a profession, not a job—and in her garage everybody pulled together like blood relatives.

And still, she didn't have to weigh Vogel's proposition more than a few minutes. "I wanted to save the kids," she said later, her eyes moistening at the memory of what might have been. How could she turn down her son and daughter-in-law? Vogel had made it clear that Meta was the children's lifeline, their only chance.

January 26. Bärbel, Ota, and Meta visited Vogel at his office, and Meta said she agreed to move West. Vogel replied that he expected to know in two weeks when the grandmother would get the children.

January 29. In a debate about the DDR's policy of forced adoptions before the West German parliament, the cabinet minister in charge of All-German Affairs, Egon Franke, in a change of mind claimed flatly that "no such case" existed.

February 9. Meta called Vogel. "I can't tell you anything precise," the lawyer said, "but everything is moving in a positive direction."

February 12. Ota called von Wedel to ask whether they could get help to find an apartment for Meta in the West. "There's plenty of time for that," the lawyer said. "Once your mother is notified that her application is in the right channels, it'll still be at least three months before she gets here." Ota said it sounded as if the kids wouldn't come West in the first quarter of the year, as promised. Von Wedel: "What I said in December was a bit premature." Concerned about the delay, Bärbel called the Berlin office of the West German government. The official was reassuring. She shouldn't worry, "the case is moving."

March 2. Meta called Vogel to ask about the arrival date of the kids and the status of her emigration approval. Vogel parried with a new, more elastic timetable: "I've already told you, it'll be in the course of the year."

April 8. Ota called von Wedel, who said: "Vogel is having major difficulties, but there are no changes in the agreement. Photos of the children are in work; by the end of April you'll get binding information."

April 29. Ota called von Wedel again, who said: "The transfer of your children to your mother is in progress and will take place within the next few weeks. Since you'll be seeing them soon, Vogel is no longer working on photos." When Ota pressed for more details, von Wedel conceded, "Well, there've been lots of difficulties, especially since the DDR authorities had often assured the adoptive parents that they could be certain they'd keep the children."

May 14. Meta called Vogel, who placated her: "Everything is moving in a positive direction. You'll be contacted about the transfer of the children in the next few days. It's important to be calm now, else there'll be sharpshooting." Meta did not inquire into the shooting that was being threatened. It was not a question one asked in East Berlin.

June 24. Ota phoned von Wedel, who announced solemnly: "Dr. Vogel has notified me that the resettlement of the children has been approved by the authorities, and this is final. The children will be staying with their grandmother only briefly, probably only a few days. Things should begin to roll very shortly. The children will probably be with you in July." When Bärbel and Ota got this news, they were overwhelmed with joy. Yes, they had been disappointed before, but this time enough specifics had emerged from the East to make a happy ending of their travail credible.

June 29. Meta was asked to appear at the DDR Interior Ministry. She was given an application for her exit visa, to be filled out and returned as rapidly as possible. And she was instructed about a change in procedure. Suddenly, Vogel's scheme to circumvent the law concerning the transfer of the children was abandoned. For reasons nobody explained, the subterfuge was no longer necessary. Meta was handed an application, to be filled out by Bärbel and Ota on behalf of the children, calling for the youngsters' exit.

For Grandmother Meta these were difficult days. The apparatchiks in the Interior Ministry had frightened her. Their barking and their demands made her feel like an enemy of the people. Constantly they demanded more answers to more questions on more documents. The new documents asked her for still more documents, and she had difficulty obtaining some of these papers. She knew about streetcars, not papers, and she was all alone; nobody helped her. And now she was hit by the ultimate blow, the point of no return; they wanted her to quit her beloved job at once.

Bärbel and Ota immediately sent the children's papers to Vogel, and Bärbel phoned the lawyer to ask him to help Meta. Vogel, smelling trouble, declined: "If you can't come to an agreement with your mother, that's not my affair." Bärbel then asked him about her latest worries. Was it really still necessary for Meta to go West, now that the children could travel with their own papers? Vogel replied that Meta would still have to cross the Wall and resettle with the children.

"What if she doesn't like it here?" demanded Bärbel sharply. "We wouldn't want to be saddled with the responsibility for that."

"I won't tolerate that tone from you," said Vogel. "Don't you make any mistake now—that'd just hit you in the eye!"

Bärbel and Ota understood the lawyer's message: if they made waves of any kind, the children would stay gone for good. In several urgent phone conversations they managed to make the situation clear to the distraught Meta, and she agreed to play out her role. She brought all her papers to the ministry, quit her work, and started living on her meager savings.

August 19. Tortured by their anticipation and out of touch with the lawyers for more than a month, Ota called von Wedel once again. Where were the children? Von Wedel switched the subject. "Are you sure your mother's exit is going to be approved?" he wanted to know. Ota was speechless. How in the world was *he* supposed to know what the DDR was really planning for his mother after the entire affair had gone through so many unexpected twists? Von Wedel said, "Call me next week; I'll talk to Dr. Vogel."

August 26. Von Wedel told Ota: "Your mother would not be allowed to go to the West without the children, but Dr. Vogel is meeting a lot of resistance. If he can't manage this, nobody can, but you'll remember that my church channels are also working hard in your behalf. . . . " Bärbel and Ota went into a tailspin. Resistance? Whose? Why? And why now, at the last moment after so many favorable signs? Whatever was happening behind the scenes in the East, their prospects had obviously deteriorated once more.

September 9. The Grübels' contact man in the West German government's Berlin office was perplexed. "According to my documents, the exit date was supposed to have been September 1. Your case is the most amazing of the lot, but Dr. Vogel is on your side. . . ."

September 13. Vogel told Ota in his office: "There are people in the DDR who don't want your children to move to the West. If we don't get this done by October 22, I see no hope."

A week later the DDR Interior Ministry phoned Meta in her Karlhorst apartment. Three days from then, at 3 P.M., she was to appear at the Invalidenstrasse crossing of the Wall. Her grandchildren would join her there. That was it! Bärbel and Ota were convinced that their hour of deliverance was at hand. Acceding to the Grübels' wishes, the *Spiegel* had been publishing no follow-up articles. Now, as agreed, Bärbel and Ota notified the magazine. A scoop was to reward the journalists' silence.

A reporter-photographer team hid in the pissoir just off the Western side of the Invalidenstrasse crossing, ready to record the reunion. It still was unwise to disclose any interest on the part of the press. Bärbel and Ota waited in the open, directly at the border post exit. They had brought chewing gum and a few small toys for little Ota and Jeannette. The waiting did not trouble them. They were absolutely certain their children were about to come home.

Meta had arrived on her side of the border by 2:30 P.M., carrying one small, bulging suitcase and a shopping bag. Sitting on a bench, waiting for her grandchildren to appear, all but *seeing* them come up to her, she lost track of time. Shortly after 5 P.M. she asked one of the border guards what time it was. Then she drew what turned out to be the correct conclusion: her grandchildren would not show up after all. Invisibly, the DDR had vetoed the reunion.

Meta stepped up to the guards.

"Your name?"

"Meta Kraal."

"Ist gut." She could pass over to the freedom she did not really want.

It was a quiet, chilly day at the crossing, and when the little Meta appeared alone, bent down with the weight of her belongings—all she now owned—she filled up every last measure in Bärbel and Ota's field of vision. Bärbel and Ota had lost another battle—but not, as they vowed yet another time, their war.

Counseling with Manfred Müller, the *Spiegel* reporter, they learned that supposedly friendly forces were resisting them; the government in Bonn was displeased by the publicity and was adopting a we-told-you-so attitude about the dismal outcome. "When these things become public, they go wrong," one of the officials told the magazine.

The *Spiegel* people disagreed. Müller told Bärbel and Ota that the trouble wasn't the publicity; things had gone wrong because they hadn't become public soon enough. This was not the time to withdraw again into silence. It was the perfect time for another push, to take advantage of the DDR's loss of face over its odious practice.

Spiegel reporters had ferreted out some telltale details about the extent of this embarrassment. The DDR authorities were maneuvering hard to quiet down the entire unpleasant adoption controversy. In at least one case—of a ten-year-old boy whose adoption had already been ordered—the court judgment was reversed, and Vogel had restored the child to his parents. The boy was handled like smuggled merchandise. The lawyer handed him over on a West Berlin side street near the Wall. Two other boys who were about to be adopted were instead sent to live with their grandmother while their parents, two Leipzig physicians, served a prison sentence for a failed attempt to flee the country.

In the Grübel case, the *Spiegel* had learned, Prime Minister Honecker had personally authorized a secret memo sent to the West German authorities in Bonn disclosing that the adoptions had been the work of "middle level" administrators, that the top echelon of the DDR government had not known about these moves, and that Vogel had been assigned to spirit little Ota and Jeannette back into the hands of their parents.

Since that memo was now ten months old, the Grübels agreed to cooperate with still another *Spiegel* article. The five-page blast appeared on November 29. It included numerous entries of Ota's diary documenting the Grübels' seesaw negotiations with the lawyers. And it reported an abortive mission by the magazine that would have been routine in the West but violated government regulations for reporters working on the other side of the Wall.

On a Wednesday at 5 P.M. a *Spiegel* reporter rang the bell at the Eisenhüttenstadt apartment of the Grübel children's adoptive parents. When the adoptive father, Herr Klewin, appeared at the door, the reporter said he wanted to ask him some questions "about the adoption of your children."

Herr Klewin refused to say anything, but in making inquiries around the town, the reporter picked up one tantalizing fragment of news: little Ota, now seven years old, knew the basic fact of his life very well and he had no qualms about bringing it up.

"My parents are not my parents," he had been heard to say to some of his friends in his school. "My real parents were arrested."

Bärbel and Ota were not surprised when they heard about the boy's remark—he had always been an alert child—but they inferred that little Ota had not heard of his parents' release to the West, much less anything about their efforts to get the children back. Perhaps the children felt they had been abandoned. It was yet another intolerable thought, so at Christmas 1976 Bärbel and Ota decided to send the youngsters a telegram affirming their abiding love.

It was their last attempt at contact and almost certainly fruitless. According to rumor, the DDR had moved the Klewin family and the Grübel children to another city. They could not be located again. And even if the Christmas telegram had been forwarded to the correct address, it seemed most unlikely that the Klewins would have shown it to the children.

45

THE BOOK OF BÄRBEL: "THE CASE CANNOT BE CONSIDERED CLOSED"

West Berlin,
Summer 1977

Bärbel and Ota Grübel had not given up. All three lawyers who had worked for the release of their children—Vogel in the East, von Wedel and Stange in the West—said they could do nothing further, and so the parents turned toward the West German politicians. Perhaps the rivalry between the ruling Social Democrats (SPD) and the opposition Christian Democrats (CDU) could be stirred further for the benefit of the Grübel youngsters. Bärbel's typewriter worked overtime again.

In response to the continuing stream of the parents' letters and phone calls, the "Grübel case" came up for yet another debate in the West German parliament in Bonn. This time, the responsible minister, Egon Franke, showed signs of impatience. The case had been an embarrassment to him for too long.

"Ladies and gentlemen, we'll pursue each and every case of forced adoption . . . ," he pledged, trying to shut off the subject.

"So how about the Grübel children?" demanded a CDU representative.

"This is one subject I'd rather not discuss here," parried Franke.

The CDU man persisted in pressing for word about the youngsters.

"You'll be surprised what you'll hear [about the case] one of these days," Franke countered mysteriously. "Then you'll never mention that name again. So you'd better be quiet! I'll be glad to assume responsibility."

"Fine!" shouted another CDU oppositionist. "We're going to remember who's responsible!"

Franke could not be shaken. Indignantly, he shouted back, "Nobody will be able to deny that I was willing to involve myself in even the most difficult cases."

This was too much posturing for Helmut Kohl, then the opposition leader and later Chancellor.

"You've got no reason to encourage controversy about this," he called out to Franke. But lacking hard information, the debate petered out.

What surprising data did Franke have about the case? Neither the Grübels nor their partisans found out. Bärbel and Ota were learning about the inner workings of the democratic process. If the West Germans ran their public business less rigidly and with far less secrecy than their brethren in the East, the openness of Western bureaucrats like Minister Franke also had limits. Nor could one call the Western methods speedy. Four years had passed since Bärbel and Ota had last seen their children, and still no one would even say why, after so many favorable signs, the DDR hierarchy had at the last minute changed its mind about letting them go.

A year had gone by since Bärbel and Ota Grübel had requested help from West Germany's last court of citizen appeal. The Petitions Committee of the Bundestag (parliament) acted as a national ombudsman. Anybody with a gripe against the government could seek satisfaction in this forum, and in their petition of October 29, 1976, the Grübels had complained against the government as a whole and specifically against Minister Egon Franke. The authorities didn't "measure up" to the difficulties of the case, the Grübels argued. They pursued it "with insufficient emphasis."

The Petitions Committee enjoyed a good reputation. Although chronically snowed under by paperwork, it usually devoted adequate time to meritorious pleas. The chairperson, Liselotte Berger, was popular and blustery, a longtime legislator, a big woman with a heart to match—anything but a pushover. She was a Berliner, and since she represented the opposition CDU, she was not about to grant special treatment to an SPD minister like Franke.

In its final report the committee applauded the "unceasing sacrifice" of Bärbel and Ota. The committee regretted that "the petitioners have for years been disappointed in their hopes" and pledged its support "to the fullest extent." After examining the information it received from Minister Franke, the committee had to agree that the "rigid attitude" of the DDR was causing "particular difficulties." Mrs. Berger and her team could do no more than urge the government to "accelerate and reinforce" its efforts.

"As long as there is no success the case cannot be considered closed," concluded her report.

This turned out to be the government's last word to the Grübels. Nothing was said about the "surprising" information that Minister Franke claimed to have in his possession.

Having lived most of their lives in a state of alienation, fervently resisting the authorities in the East, the shocking letdown of their recent experience turned the Grübels against the West as well. It was inevitable. As they viewed their situation, two bureaucracies were conspiring against them and their lost children, not just the Communists.

The Grübels' Western contacts turned increasingly irksome. When they managed to push themselves into the presence of officials, the response was cold, sometimes downright fearful. The possibility of further publicity turned everyone off. "Please don't do any more writing in your diary," begged the Bonn government's chief liaison man with the West Berlin authorities.

Bärbel and Ota no longer thought that the supposedly sympathetic officials were suffering from ordinary cowardice; they *had* to be duplicitous, too, or else they'd compel the DDR to give up the children. Or at least they'd try much harder to apply pressure.

The press was no longer helpful. There was nothing new to write about. The story had grown cold and redundant. Even the *Spiegel* found nothing more to expose. Its reporter Manfred Müller had spent a lot of his own time befriending the couple, had taken many meals with them, had sat with them for long stretches in friendly conversation, had introduced them to his wife. They turned against him, too. He was no longer so readily available, he made too much money, he was always preoccupied looking for a new house—another obscene consumer in the disgustingly materialistic West. The opulence of their surroundings was getting on the Grübels' nerves, everything was getting on their nerves, and Müller, the ever-polite ex-priest, seemed an apt target, perhaps because he was so gentle.

To keep himself busy, Ota had started to paint large pictures in oils, and one of his first portraits was a hideous vision of Müller in garish black and red, looking very much like a pig. The rendering could hardly have been less complimentary. Ota loved it, it made him smile, it was satisfying, it struck back at the lot of them, everybody who would no longer lift a finger on behalf of little Ota and Jeannette. A curse on all of them, they were worse than pigs.

Ota looked for no other work. He was fidgety, his physical symptoms from prison persisted, he needed to be alone, not reporting on the dot every morning in a buzzing shop or office. He had little appetite, almost no energy at all; it became incomprehensible for him how hard he had once worked as an interior decorator, moonlighting in East Berlin.

Painting relaxed him—he painted exotic birds, the Berlin Wall with the city's skyline at night, anything that popped into his head. At first he sold a lot of his work. He had met an executive of a bank, the bank had many branches, the banker had businessmen friends, Ota didn't charge much for a painting, and business was great. For a while.

The sales stopped abruptly. Ota had had an argument with his friend—it seemed Ota was arguing with everyone, deep philosophical arguments, never anything trivial—only Bärbel didn't seem to mind what her husband did or what he said to whom. She smiled a small smile, she knew him.

She had taken a secretarial job, she was very good at it, some money came in. Their life seemed to be in yet another transition. Often they talked of moving, away from Berlin, away from their stony neighbor, the Wall, away from that cursed place called Germany.

America seemed too exotic, too expensive, too hectic. For a while they thought Australia might suit them. Not for long. What was life really like out there—wasn't it preposterously far away, and who said it would be a peaceful place? They needed someplace peaceful. Bärbel had heard about Provence, she knew someone who had been there; yes, France was the place where they might settle—not, of course, until they had a sense of certainty about their children.

The children, they were never out of their minds. Their photos, years out of date, were on the apartment walls, and Bärbel and Ota never stopped to speculate what might be in the children's minds. Were they trying to investigate their past? Sometimes Bärbel was absolutely sure of it. At other times it seemed certain that they had either forgotten about their real parents or would want to forget, that their memories would be murky or wiped away.

Bärbel's memories were not fading at all. She thought daily of her children, remembering every inch of their little bodies. With the passage of the years, she conceded to herself that their return was less and less likely. Resettlement might not even be good for them. Perhaps they liked their adoptive parents so much that they would not want to leave. Besides, what could suddenly happen, after such a long time without news, to bring the kids back?

Encountering a politician who volunteered that he had the right connections for having the children kidnapped and brought to the West, Bärbel and Ota shrank away from the notion. It was crazy; they'd never want to assume responsibility for participating in such a scheme.

In retrospect, they wondered whether they should have gone along with Vogel's idea to have Grandma Meta settle in the West so she could bring the children out. Meta hated the West and missed her pals in East Berlin. She had visited them, but the old feelings of friendship had faded. The friends thought that Meta, who lived in a dilapidated flat among destitute refugees from Turkey, had turned into a snooty Western capitalist. They no longer wanted anything to do with her.

PART IX

FIGHTING THE WALL

46

RESISTANCE IN RIESA: A DOCTOR FIGHTS BACK

**Frankfurt, West Germany,
October 1977**

Dr. Nitschke, the rebellious internist in Riesa, had become something of a national hero. For a while, the West German newspapers carried stories about him and his resistance group almost every day, and West German TV spread the word throughout the DDR.

The headlines were dramatic: DOCTOR LOSES HIS TELEPHONE. MASSIVE SECRET POLICE INTERROGATIONS IN RIESA. REPRESSION AGAINST DOCTOR WORSENS. RIESA GROUP GETS NEW SUPPORT. And then in large type: COURAGEOUS DDR DOCTOR ARRESTED.

That had been in 1976. By the fall of 1977 the doctor had made it to West Germany, the press and public lost interest. The International Society for Human Rights arranged a press conference for him at its Frankfurt headquarters; only a handful of journalists appeared. The doctor disclosed that the *Stasi* had planned a show trial for him. They had called it off when he warned them he would speak out on behalf of human rights in the courtroom regardless of what they would do to him or his family.

"I didn't allow them to intimidate me," he said, still flashing his old defiance.

There were no headlines anymore, and that was not the worst of his fate. The doctor's family and his new friends in the human rights movement were very worried about him. Behind his brave front he was no longer his irrepressible self. He was depressed. He had lost almost all his hair. His skin tone was poor, his heart was causing him trouble. His conversation was laced with bitterness and suspicion. He had aged so shockingly that when he came home from prison, his thirteen-year-old daughter, Marion, did not recognize him until he said, "It's me, *Mausi*, your daddy!"

The doctor had good reason to be worn out, for his journey West had begun as far back as 1964, shortly after he started practicing medicine. The Berlin Wall had restricted his freedom to travel and had cut him off from Western books. The supervisors at his hospital complained that he was too involved with his patients, spent too much time with them. The doctor felt "imprisoned," he told his wife, Dagmar, far more regimented than he had been as a member of the Hitler Youth when he was a child. So when the authorities refused to respect his pacifist beliefs and ordered him to conduct physical examinations to screen young men for military service, Dr. Nitschke and his wife decided to flee the DDR.

As enthusiastic practitioners of water sports, they tried to escape on a catamaran across the Baltic Sea to Denmark. An innkeeper near the seacoast gave them away. Dr. Nitschke served two years in prison, much of it in the solitary confinement of a windowless, lightless cell. Mrs. Nitschke was placed on probation for one year. Their relatively light sentences were the result of the couple's detailed confessions, which the *Stasi* elicited by threatening to take away Marion, then four months old.

Dr. Nitschke was, like his disciple, the steelworker Volker Seifarth, a stubborn, methodical soul, and even before he was assigned to the clinic in Riesa in 1971, he spent every summer vacation reconnoitering possible escape routes to the West. Masquerading as carefree tourists, the family searched western sections of Czechoslovakia, Poland, and Hungary for places where loosely guarded lakes or rivers constituted the border to Austria. They still preferred water to land routes.

"We were looking for a hole in the Wall," Mrs. Nitschke would remember later, shaking her head at their innocence in those days. They did more than look around. The doctor arranged army-style maneuvers for his family. Each had a small folding boat and a camouflage-pattern rubber suit, including little Marion once she was four years old. They jumped into ponds to practice swimming in icy water. The doctor did not worry nearly as much about getting caught as about Marion coming down with pneumonia.

In August 1975 they did get caught. All the border spots they had been investigating over the years had been too well watched to risk penetration. When they were arrested in Romania, they were still twenty miles away from the Danube, and they were picked up on the flimsiest of suspicion. The *Stasi* had to let them go for lack of evidence.

Dr. Nitschke decided he had tempted fate often enough. He stopped his border reconnaissance to concentrate on the legal way westward, by way of applications for an official exit visa.

Until August 1976 he fired off thirteen such requests, first on a monthly basis, then at the rate of two per month. He applied to the Department of Internal Affairs in Riesa, to various higher echelons of the government, and to Erich Honecker. Each time he cited applicable paragraphs from human rights declarations of the United Nations, the DDR constitution, and the Helsinki Accords on human rights signed by thirty-five nations in August 1975. Although the DDR had been one of the Helsinki signatories, the details of the agreement had never been made public by the press in the East. Dr. Nitschke possessed—and often cited from—a precious copy of the full text. It had been mailed to him by his sister in West Germany, sewed into a corset.

The authorities did not budge under Dr. Nitschke's bombardment of emigration requests. "An individual just can't get anywhere," he finally told his wife. They would have to enlist enough like-minded citizens in some sort of organization so that the government and the Western media could not avoid paying attention.

"They've got to hear a lot of noise from us," the doctor said.

By 1976 he had been fired from his post at the steelworks, but the shortage of physicians was so acute that he was allowed to practice on his own, at a considerably reduced government salary. The move from the clinic was a lucky break. It created privacy and more time at home. The doctor could identify patients and neighbors who were also trying to leave the country. He advised them about the necessary paperwork, as he had counseled Volker Seifarth. On the wall of his office he hung a framed copy of the basic declaration on human rights which the UN had issued in 1948. In the evenings he conducted more frequent meetings of potential emigrants at various homes and aboard the *Gertrud,* a dilapidated retired ferryboat that one of the men had refurbished for excursions.

Most members of the doctor's resistance circle were married blue-collar workers in their twenties. Roland Dumlich, the rambunctious owner of the *Gertrud,* was a cabdriver. Several others drove long-distance trucks. At first, the talk at the meetings was halting. Nobody trusted anybody. As they began to share details of each other's travail, the atmosphere changed dramatically. A spirit of communion took hold. The dissidents recognized themselves as a fraternity. When some of the men lost their jobs for alleged disloyalty to the state, others helped out with financial contributions. A few of the get-togethers turned into cozy beer parties.

Dr. Nitschke was restless. As word of his efforts got around, he heard from more and more Riesa citizens who had submitted emigration papers and, like himself, were not getting results. "We've got to call attention to ourselves," he told his resisters. He was not going to let himself be quietly ignored. And he knew exactly how to needle his enemies so as to produce maximum noise. He drew up a "Petition for the Full Achievement of Human Rights." In dry, legal language this amateur SOS signal cited a string of international agreements to which the DDR was a party and then it politely requested that the petitioners be permitted their free choice of where they wanted to live and work.

Nothing like this had ever been attempted in the DDR. Whoever signed such a declaration of troublemaking risked serious reprisals. By the summer of 1976, thirty-three Riesa citizens had nevertheless *printed* as well as *signed* their names and addresses to the revolutionary document. Shortly afterward, forty-six citizens from Karl-Marx-Stadt and neighboring communities added their names, and eventually the total was more than two hundred. On July 7 the petition was dispatched to the United Nations Commission of Human Rights; to the governments of all nations that had signed the Helsinki Accords, including the DDR; and to the Western press.

The Honecker regime struck back in August. A *Stasi* car was permanently stationed in front of Dr. Nitschke's apartment house, and the officers in it photographed his visitors. When the doctor or his wife set off in their car, a *Stasi* vehicle followed. *Stasi* men trailed Marion to school and her mother to the supermarket. The doctor's phone service was canceled. All incoming and much of the family's outgoing mail was confiscated. In late August the doctor's wife was interrogated for several hours. The Nitschke apartment was searched.

By August 31 the *Stasi* had obviously decided that all these efforts at intimidation had not worked. Dr. Nitschke was arrested and his wife was picked up in the East Berlin subway for several days of questioning. She had been on her way to the office of Wolfgang Vogel, hoping to enlist the lawyer's aid in getting her husband released.

The other signers of the Riesa Petition (as the doctor's cri de coeur had come to be known) were called in for interrogation. The *Stasi*'s questions were revealing. Had the petitioners called on the West German government for assistance and what had been the response? How had the text of the petition reached the West? Under no circumstances were the signers to discuss the petition with anyone whatsoever.

Dagmar Nitschke and the petitioners remembered the doctor's judgment that only noise—international noise—would get them out of Riesa. So when Lothar Loewe* of ARD, the First (West) German Television Network, came to call on Mrs. Nitschke, she volunteered, after some worried initial hesitation, to go on camera with the story of the Nitschke family, her husband's arrest, their petition and its courageous signers.

Loewe, a blustery, hyperenergetic Berliner, faced a professional dilemma. The DDR authorities had previously issued a general warning demanding that he tone down his freewheeling style of reportage. Loewe had shrugged off this protest as a routine attempt at intimidation, nothing to worry about. That was a misjudgment. At 7:30 P.M. the night before his trip to Riesa he was cited to appear at the press center in nearby Leipzig for a personal confrontation with two representatives of the DDR Foreign Ministry, and the authorities were manifestly greatly upset.

With his hands trembling and his face flushed, the senior official read from a document issued by the Foreign Ministry in East Berlin advising Loewe that his planned interviews in Riesa amounted to tampering with witnesses of an ongoing prosecution, therefore violating DDR legal process. The interviews would constitute sabotage of the DDR's right to investigate probable violations of the law.

---

* This was the same Lothar Loewe who on August 13, 1961, as a West German correspondent in Washington, helped to wake up the State Department to the East Germans' surprise sealing of the Berlin border. Shortly after his filming in Riesa, the DDR revoked Loewe's accreditation because of his aggressive reporting. Later he became head of Sender Freies Berlin, the West German government television station in Berlin.

West German television correspondent Lothar Loewe *(above)* focused international attention on Dr. Karl-Heinz Nitschke *(right)*, the rebellious internist from Riesa who organized East Germany's first open resistance movement.

After consulting with his teammates, Loewe decided on a compromise. He would go ahead with the Riesa story; he would not
ask citizens to go on camera. Their appearance would have done
more than cause trouble for him; Loewe sympathized with the local
people and did not wish to cause more difficulties for them.

When the West German TV crew pulled up in front of the
Nitschke apartment house, the *Stasi* was prepared as if an armed
attack was imminent. Loewe counted at least thirteen male and
female officers with walkie-talkies on the otherwise deserted street.

"High Noon in Riesa," murmured his sound technician. In truth,
neither side considered the tense standoff amusing. Loewe kept
telling himself that he must not lose his nerve, that he must proceed as if on a routine assignment. The *Stasi* officers, for their part,
were eager to stay discreetly out of camera range. As soon as
Loewe's technicians had begun to unload their equipment, the security contingent took cover behind bushes and parked cars.

Mrs. Nitschke came out into the street, and Loewe told her why
he would not interview her after all. She said she understood.
Other signers of the Riesa Petition, crowding onto Schweriner
Strasse, were harder to pacify. Surging upon Loewe and his assistants, they began pouring out the stories of their frustrations on
the spot, in detail, several talking at the same time.

Loewe told them why he had decided not to place them in front
of the camera. The petititoners would not subside. They burbled
on, their accounts becoming increasingly confused in their excitement. Some of the women began to cry. The men cursed. Loewe
could tell that microphones of the *Stasi* officers were picking up
much of what was being said, which further intensified his nervousness. What would the government do to these poor souls?
Moreover, for all he knew, the security people would not permit
him to broadcast at all.

With his determined manner and his commanding voice, the big,
broad-shouldered Loewe eventually calmed the crowd, cleared
some space on the sidewalk, took his microphone in front of number 26, and began: "Here in Riesa, in the house behind me, lives
the family of Dr. Karl-Heinz Nitschke. . . ."

At the conclusion of his step-by-step account of the Riesa Petition, he posed the bottom-line challenge: "Will the DDR leadership
respond to the Riesa citizens' initiative with police intimidation or
will it permit those who are determined to leave the country to exit
in peace?"

Dr. Nitschke's followers were overjoyed by all the attention.

From the way they were tracked and questioned they concluded that they had prodded ultrasensitive pressure points in the DDR security apparatus and that the government would want to eliminate the Riesa irritant by getting rid of its roots: Dr. Nitschke and his petitioners.

Which turned out to be true. Gradually—it took about two years —all the signers were released to the West.* Unfortunately, although the doctor was among the first to benefit from the decision, the DDR had succeeded in defeating him at last.

After his release across the Wall on August 26, 1977, he spent months in a West Berlin government hospital under treatment for an acute heart ailment complicated by circulatory problems—conditions clearly aggravated by the tensions of his harassment over the years and never cured.

Psychologically, too, he was in terrible condition. Driving his car in the free West, he often felt he was being followed. When his fellow petitioners from Riesa held a reunion in West Germany, the doctor, their leader and hero, felt too dispirited to participate. He thought that his public appeals for more attention to the absence of human rights in the DDR were met with indifference. So few people listened to him!

Even sympathetic television producers could not please the doctor. When they asked him to appear on West German programs, he complained that they sentimentalized his pleas into bad soap opera and he was never allowed enough airtime. In the fast-paced West, heroes were too quickly scrapped for other heroes.

Although he found a good job as a plant physician for Volkswagen in Hannover, his wife and daughter saw the doctor experiencing little fulfillment in the freedom for which he had battled so resourcefully for so many years. Almost predictably, he would die in 1984 of a heart attack.

"A broken heart," everyone said.

_____

* I met with a group of six petitioners in West Germany in 1984. All were employed, reasonably pleased with their lot, and in great spirits.

47

THE BOOK OF VOLKER:
THE SYSTEM WANTS HIM TO
GET A DIVORCE

Bautzen Prison, East Germany,
Summer 1979

Volker Seifarth, the stubborn little steelworker, was not among the Riesa petitioners allowed to depart quietly for the West. He was a special case, too sassy to go unpunished. He got too deeply under the skin of the authorities and enjoyed himself too ostentatiously whenever he could thumb his nose at them. The man was a challenge. His spirit had to be broken.

Everybody carries a vulnerable spot through life, and the *Stasi* quickly found Volker's. His weakness was his love for Gisela, his high school sweetheart.

They had married in 1975; their daughter, Rommy, was born the following year; and Gisela no longer opposed Volker's campaign to leave the country. She was hearing from relatives and friends in Hamburg and Munich who were doing well, and so she grew to accept Volker's assurance that not everybody in the West was unemployed, as the DDR media kept suggesting.

Then Gisela had a visitor from the other side, a friend, and this woman proved Volker's case beyond all doubt. Gisela had for years been in school with this traveler, and in 1974, inexplicably, the young woman had been allowed to leave for West Berlin. Gisela trusted her, and their reunion was an eye-opener. The friend's husband was nothing more than a mechanic, yet this freshly Westernized couple already drove a recent-model BMW, and the cheerful responses to Gisela's inquisition about the availability of Western apartments, the rents, the pay scales, and the realities of capitalistic unemployment bordered on the miraculous, at least by Riesa standards.

Gisela had to concede: her resistance against Volker's plans had been grounded in ignorance, needless fear of the unknown.

Right after the wedding, Volker and Gisela went to Room 10 at the Department of Internal Affairs to add her name to his exit application.

"We'll take it under advisement," said the clerk in charge.

"I'll be back regularly," said Volker.

"No need to do that, you'll hear from us."

"Never mind!" Volker shouted furiously. "It's been years and I still can't find out whether you're even working on my papers!"

The encounter scared Gisela badly, and when they left the building she tried to lecture him.

"You better do this more calmly," she cautioned.

"Calmly?" Volker yelled back. "What are you talking about? You don't get anywhere around here by being *calm!*" He spit out the word like a curse.

Volker had absorbed his wisdom from Dr. Nitschke, and the morale-boosting strategy meetings of the doctor's petitioners had also helped. Although Seifarth's ruggedly independent nature made him something of a loner and he disliked joining groups or causes, he did sign the Riesa Petition. Like the other signers, he felt the bond of the group. They were uppity characters like himself, most of them. He felt contempt for those of the signers (nobody knew how many) who withdrew their names under pressure from the *Stasi*.

Not Volker Seifarth. He came right out with the milling crowd on Schweriner Strasse when Lothar Loewe bustled into Riesa with his TV crew to film his commentary in front of the doctor's house. Volker watched the *Stasi* people dash and duck, clearly unsure of how tough they should get with these incensed citizens-turned-criminals. Volker stood leaning against a doorway and laughed out loud at the street spectacle. He thought it was a hilarious show, like a movie cartoon.

There were no other comic interludes. Volker kept calling on the Department of Internal Affairs to no avail, and the *Stasi* kept summoning him to fruitless interrogations. The same scenarios ran their course over and over. The clerks in Room Number 10 would not tell Seifarth what, if anything, was happening to his emigration application, and Seifarth, in his turn, answered the *Stasi*'s questions with escalating impudence.

Why did he want to leave the DDR? What was discussed at the meetings with Dr. Nitschke's group? Seifarth told them to go to hell. The interrogators were only trying to get him down. Everybody suspected that the *Stasi* had planted an informer in the group of dissidents; the cops didn't need Volker's help.

In 1978, predictably, he was arrested. The charges: "agitation" and "insulting the state." For a man as resolutely autonomous as Seifarth, his year and a half in Bautzen Prison could have been a devastating shock, and on some days he felt as if there was no air for him to breathe. Other prisoners could make their peace with the affront of having to refer to their barely literate supervisors as "educators." Seifarth never could. To him, this Orwellian label was an intolerable indignity. It was obviously meant to minimize the prisoners by demoting them to the status of children in need of getting "educated."

By the late 1970s prison life in the DDR was no longer overtly reminiscent of the Nazi past. Nobody had to fear for his life. Physical abuse was uncommon. Psychological pressure was something else. It never let up. It was built into the "education." The lives of prisoners were governed by a compendium of rules carefully crafted to make them bend.

Seifarth refused to buckle. To protest the prison rules, he turned against his own petit bourgeois background and restyled himself as a quasi-hippie. He grew a beard and absolutely would not shave it off. He persuaded another prisoner to cover his torso with tattoos almost up to his chin, an act of defiance that all but drove his guards crazy, because the pictures were ubiquitous reminders of their inability to clamp their authority on little Volker.

Seifarth treasured his small victories over his keepers, and he was further cheered because he kept in mind that in the perverse world of the DDR the road to freedom in the West began for most emigrants with a prison stay; it was the ticket that made them eligible for ransoming. Hadn't lawyer Vogel's associate recommended five years ago that he go to prison? At last Seifarth had made it to first base, a hopeful step.

After a few months in Bautzen, Volker picked up signals that the authorities had earmarked him for special treatment. He had been getting chatty letters from Gisela at the officially permitted rate of one per week, and she had gently commiserated with his lot when she faithfully came to see him every six weeks on visitors' day. Suddenly, her letters and visits stopped, and his parents appeared instead.

"Why isn't Gisela writing?" asked Volker.

"But she *is* writing," his mother said. "She writes all the time!"

"Why isn't she visiting anymore?"

"She can't get the permit."

Seifarth confronted his educator, who gave him a tight smile. The officer found it enjoyable that the impudent Seifarth was finally worried about his lot. All prisoners had their weaknesses; if Gisela was this annoying little man's soft spot, good! It was a sore point to be exploited.

"Your wife is willing to withdraw her exit application," the educator said smugly.

Seifarth did not give away that he suddenly felt hollow. Maybe the *Stasi* had persuaded her to stay in the DDR. He was careful not to show his shock.

"I know her better than you people do," he said. "I don't believe it."

The educator disclosed that officers had gone to the Seifarth home to "reason" with his wife. Later Volker heard that they offered her a better apartment and the opportunity to begin the course in restaurant management that she had long wanted to attend.

Volker recognized at once what the officials had in mind.

"You want to separate us!" he said.

The educator shrugged. "Your wife is more sensible than you," he said. "One can talk to her."

As the months wore on, Volker became increasingly torn about the government's threat to pull apart his little family. He did not question Gisela's loyalty to him, and he could sympathize with her lot. She was very young, unsophisticated, alone, working at her waitress job as well as raising a child, and, suddenly, came the temptations of preferential treatment.

Volker's nights and weekends became longer and lonelier as he brooded about Gisela's ability to deal with her dilemma. What *was* she thinking these days? If he could speak to her for only a very few minutes, they could support each other in their isolation. Which was exactly what the authorities were preventing.

Instead, they tried to shake Volker's faith in Gisela's reliability as a parent. A woman from the Riesa Youth Aid Bureau came to see him in prison.

"It's about your daughter," she said. "The child is being neglected."

Volker laughed at her.

"What are you laughing about?" the woman demanded indignantly. "Your wife doesn't even spend weekends with your daughter."

Nonsense. On the subject of Rommy's well-being Volker was fully informed and needed no reassurance. The child was staying with his parents, and his mother regularly reported that she was doing fine. Gisela often visited her in Volker's native village. Only one of the youth worker's complaints contained a kernel of truth. Gisela could rarely come on weekends. On Saturday she had to work and on Sunday she was usually just too tired to make the trek to Volker's village; she sensibly used the day to get some rest.

The youth worker quickly gathered that she had not succeeded in upsetting Volker. She left, and the charge of Rommy's "neglect" was not brought up again. Instead, the authorities launched their long-planned offensive against Seifarth's marriage. And they made sure to drop the news on Volker with the finesse of a guillotine.*

Seifarth's educator summoned him and presented him with a list of lawyers. He was to select one of them.

"I don't need a lawyer," Seifarth said.

"Yes, you do," said the officer. "You're getting divorced."

"What? You're joking!"

"No, I'm not. Here are the necessary forms. You've got to fill them out."

"What *is* all this?" Volker was totally bewildered, his bravura cracking. The idea was beginning to get to him: they really wanted him to get out of Gisela's life!

"You wife is *asking* for a divorce," confirmed the educator.

"I don't believe it!"

"Well, you should believe me."

"Oh no," Volker said. "She'd have to tell me that herself! I'm not filling out anything!"

---

* The guillotine method was not academic with the DDR authorities. Until 1968, all death sentences were carried out by this ancient device. From then until 1979, capital crimes were punished by shooting. Thereafter, death sentences were dropped. This eleven-year evolution is another yardstick of the DDR's march into the twentieth century.

"That's your business. You'll see what's going to happen!"

To Volker it was an unbelievable development. Yet perhaps it was not altogether unbelievable. In prison one heard unsettling stories. Four months earlier, a fellow prisoner whom Volker had gotten to know well had suddenly been taken before a court. He was *ordered* to sign a divorce application against his will. His wife had been told nothing, but when she was shown the document weeks later she, too, agreed reluctantly to a divorce she did not want.

Since then, Volker had heard of similar cases in Bautzen Prison, and he was beginning to detect a pattern. The DDR was still fighting the battle of the late 1940s and the 1950s, still trying to stem the tide of restless critics wanting to leave for the West. *The Wall had not fully done its job of bottling up the population.* A lot of citizens like Bärbel and Ota Grübel and Volker Seifarth remained eager to wave good-bye to socialism. And the DDR was still resisting them, not wanting to lose workers, especially not energetic young hands, trained hands, most especially not children who might still be converted to the socialist cause.

If one spouse in a marriage had to be written off and surrendered to capitalism, at least the other partner and the child might be salvageable for the DDR system. Ideological pride and economic necessity were persuasive motivators. Why not let the divorce laws cut away the cancers, the individual spouses disloyal to the state?

By isolating Volker in his prison, cutting him off from Gisela, keeping away his parents, often for months at a time, letting him brood and soak up the many true and false rumors and ruminations of his fellow prisoners, the authorities aggravated his growing concerns. It was common to hear of wives turning faithless when their men were in prison and then demanding a divorce. And no solid counsel was available to Seifarth, especially since his one visit to Wolfgang Vogel's East Berlin office had led to his disenchantment with the legal profession. He was becoming as lonely and nervous as the authorities had wanted him when they made their plans for softening him up.

After they had him simmer for a while longer, Volker was taken before a clerk at the County Court at Bautzen, where he was again asked to fill out an application for divorce. Again he refused.

"We'll do it together," offered the clerk helpfully.

"I don't want to."

"But your wife wants a divorce."

"I don't think so."

Volker's educator next approached him like an uncle trying to reason with an obstinate child.

"Why are you making such difficulties?" he asked Seifarth almost plaintively.

"Why don't you let me talk to my wife?" Volker countered. "I want to hear from herself how she feels about this."

"Be reasonable," said the officer. "It ought to be enough for you to be informed by us officially."

"It's not."

Gisela did not come to see Volker, and when his parents were allowed to visit they brought disappointing news. His mother said that Gisela had withdrawn her emigration application. The young wife had been subjected to great pressure, the mother reported. *Stasi* agents had told her that her refusal would entail "serious consequences." If she cooperated, she would be allowed to study "gastronomy"—DDR language for restaurant management.

To a Western visitor, the prospect of managing one of the DDR's depressingly sparse "people-owned" inns would not have seemed tempting. To Gisela, the offer loomed as a great opportunity. She had been scheming for this advancement for three years. Ultimately it would triple, perhaps quadruple, her income. She could wind up making more money than Volker earned at the steel mill. Knowing of her ambitions, Volker was not too surprised at her surrender.

With heavy heart he asked his mother whether Gisela had said anything about a divorce. The mother was astounded.

"That's impossible," she said. "I would know if she had any thoughts along those lines."

Volker told his mother to ask his wife straight out whether she was thinking about a divorce. Not having seen Gisela (or heard from her) in four months, he was disturbed. After waiting six weeks for the next visitors' day, the answer came as a relief. His mother said that Gisela had assured her positively that divorce was nowhere on her mind. She couldn't even understand why the question was being brought up.

Reassured, Volker launched a letter-writing campaign demanding to see his wife. He pleaded with the prison administration, with the *Stasi*, with the Department of Internal Affairs in Riesa. No one responded.

Next he refused to work at his normal prison job of candle making. A *Stasi* officer, acting surprised and indignant, asked him why in the world he would think of refusing to work. Seifarth said he wanted to see his wife. The *Stasi* man looked sympathetic and said he'd see what he could do. Still no sign of Gisela. Seifarth continued his strike, whereupon he was placed in a dark solitary cell. Twice a day he got some bread and coffee; every three days he was given one warm meal.

When he still refused to work three weeks later and the prison still wouldn't let him see Gisela, Volker went on a hunger strike. Twice a day a guard would ask him, "Want to eat?" Twice a day he refused. He did want to drink something. He got no liquids, and when the guard brought him a bowl of water for washing, it turned out to be undrinkable; it had been treated with pine extract. He tried to drink it and it made him vomit.

After six days he was weak enough to be taken to the prison hospital. There he insisted on sitting on the stone floor until a friendly sounding functionary arrived and asked in seemingly innocent astonishment, "Why aren't you eating?"

"I want to see my wife!"

"Well, we'll work on that, but first you have to eat."

"Only if you guarantee that I can see my wife."

The guarantee was given and he ate. A week passed uneventfully. Volker said he'd stop eating again. His educator told him that his wife would visit in a few days.

Instead, his mother arrived. She had been told nothing of Volker's campaign. She had received a card asking her to come, nothing more. She was aghast at her son's haggard appearance and at his agitation. He said he didn't want to talk to her, he wanted to see his wife. He stopped eating again, and this time Gisela arrived within three days.

She was in a dreadful state, distressed, confused, clearly out of control. Volker had seen her like this only once before, when her mother died.

"What's this about your wanting a divorce?" he said.

She could not say a word. She only cried.

At this point the educator, who was monitoring their conversation, commanded: "Leave that subject! Talk about something else!"

"What about your exit application?" Volker asked.

"That subject is not authorized," said the officer.

"Well, you know I always wanted to take the gastronomy course," Gisela finally managed to say.

"Then I guess we have to get a divorce," said Volker despondently.

Gisela trembled and wept. "I don't know what to say," Volker heard her whisper. She continued talking, but for a long time Volker could not understand her through her crying.

The educator broke in: "You can see that you're about to destroy your family," he told Volker. "Why don't you simply suspend your exit application?"

"Then I'll be in prison for nothing," Seifarth argued.

"Your wife is being smart," said the educator, but as the discussion meandered along, it became apparent that he was making no progress. He was trying to blast apart a solid marriage, and the spouses were not buying the idea. When Volker was given the signal that it was time to go, he asked Gisela outright, "Do you want a divorce?"

"No," whispered Gisela through her tears.

"Well, I said no too," Volker responded, and that was the end of her visit.

Stressful as it had been, the encounter with his wife cheered Seifarth enormously. The fact that it had taken place at all was a victory for him. It showed that even as a prisoner and incommunicado he was not bereft of weapons, that the authorities felt compelled to give way to hunger strikes and other forms of determined civil disobedience. And while Gisela was manifestly suffering under the government pressure, her loyalty stood established beyond question. It troubled Volker that he had been even slightly in doubt about his wife's steadfastness. He should never have questioned that she loved him and wanted to stand by him.

How long could a lone young woman be expected to withstand pressure from officials who controlled her environment, her family, her livelihood, her fate for all time? From the scope and persistence of their efforts, it appeared that the authorities felt they had a significant stake in wiping out Volker Seifarth's little island of individual resistance and separating him from his wife and child. What would they try next?

For a week or so, Volker's initial cheer carried him along, reinforced by the arrival of a letter from Gisela, the first in almost half a year. Volker beamed over the envelope as if it were a windfall of unexpected wealth. The text of the letter changed his mood. Though he was hardly a man of literary sensibility, his scent for trouble had been sharpened by the adversities of his recent years.

The letter spelled trouble. It was pleasant. It said not a word about a divorce. It was, well, a shade too formal, a degree cooler in tone than her earlier messages to him in prison.

His keepers did not keep him in suspense long. The educator and a *Stasi* man summoned Seifarth, and they were all smiles.

"You want to know about your divorce?" asked the *Stasi* man.

"What divorce?"

The men laughed. "We're not here for nothing," one of them said, and from a considerable distance a piece of paper was flashed at Seifarth. He could see that it was typed, but he could not read it.

"This is from your wife," the officer said, laughing again. "*You're divorced!*"

Volker felt like crying. At the same time, somehow, he managed to laugh. Having been placed in a preposterous situation, he was determined not to dignify the charade by giving any sign of credence.

The officers' amusement continued undiminished. Volker could not be sure: these fellows either knew that they had really defeated him or else they were determined to play a bluff to the finish. They placed their document directly before Seifarth now, keeping about half of it covered with a plain piece of paper. Volker could see that it was a divorce application form of the County Court.

"Take it away," he yelled. "This doesn't mean anything!"

"Your wife signed it!"

"If she did, then show me!"

"It's valid," insisted the *Stasi* officer. "You have to sign here!"

"I'll sign nothing!"

The men left, and another period of suspenseful inactivity ensued. Volker was permitted no mail and no visitors. Could Gisela have been pressured into signing divorce papers? When he complained to his educator at the lack of news, the officer said mysteriously, "It's your wife's fault." He would not explain the remark. To Volker it sounded as if his wife had incurred the displeasure of the authorities, which had to mean that she was still resisting a divorce.

His mother came to visit and confirmed his guess. Gisela was doing nothing about a divorce, the mother said; the young woman was being punished for her obstinacy by being refused a prison visitor's permit.

Volker told his educator he'd embark on another hunger strike. The officer responded with alarm, most likely because any such demonstration tended to be contagious to other prisoners, thereby causing annoyance to the guards. Volker was asked to desist; yes, his wife would be allowed a visit, and she shortly was, looking worn and distraught. A *Stasi* agent was present.

"Tell your husband the truth," the officer instructed Gisela.

Gisela took a deep breath and said pointedly, "I *had* to apply for a divorce."

"You didn't *have* to," the *Stasi* man interjected.

"Did you *have* to?" Volker asked her.

"Yes, I *have* to appear in court," said Gisela, looking trapped and most unhappy.

"Well, then you just have to go and do it," Volker said, sounding matter-of-fact.

It pained him very much to change tactics on Gisela in such a sudden, cruel way, without the slightest warning. He saw no alternative. They were being too closely monitored for him to tell her what was really on his mind. Gisela would have to live with her hurt at least for a while.

She *was* hurt, terribly so. And startled. She told him she couldn't understand what had suddenly gotten into him. The rest of her words were not discernible through her tears.

Volker felt like the world's lowest criminal, but he could think of nothing loving that was reasonably safe to say. All he could do was to keep telling Gisela, "Calm youself, calm yourself!" knowing well that these bland words were not in keeping with the tragedy of the moment.

Without using up all of her allotted time, Gisela left, weeping, convinced that Volker no longer loved her, that he didn't care she was being made to go to court for a divorce. It was the lowest point of both their lives.

An eternity seemed to have passed before Volker received the next visit from his mother. He had been longing for this opportunity to communicate, thinking that their conversation would be less stringently supervised than his talks with Gisela, and he was right. Having been led into a room with four large tables for visitors, Volker hurried to the place farthest removed from the room's only guard, and he was able to talk with his mother fairly openly.

"My God," she said, "I hear *you* want a divorce now!"

"Absolutely not," Volker assured her. He explained what he had lately picked up from conversations with experienced fellow prisoners, especially an accountant and a dentist of his acquaintance.

Often it was best to go through with a divorce, no matter how unwanted, so that at least one partner could make it to the West. Once free, the liberated partner could apply for an exit permit on behalf of the spouse and any children left in the East, and under a law for *Familienzusammenführung* (family reunion) the visa was often issued within six months.

Volker's mother understood. These were the ways of the DDR. One had to go to prison to win freedom and some people had to get a divorce to keep their family together. Even a simple old woman had no trouble fathoming this logic. It worked out, so who cared that it was crazy? It was like getting in line at the store for onions if you and your whole family detested onions. People got in line wherever they saw a queue forming. A line meant that a scarce commodity had unexpectedly come to market, and anything in short supply could always be traded with someone for something that one really wanted.

It was a time-consuming way of life, which is why most DDR citizens were pale and tired much of the time, but things were much worse not many years ago. So Volker's mother was happy to promise him that she would explain his tactic to Gisela right away; that would reassure her that he loved her as always.

The Seifarths saw each other next in a courtroom in Riesa for a formal divorce hearing that overtaxed Gisela's coping powers. She understood that a divorce could be the next step to getting the family out of the country. That was how the government worked. It didn't enable her emotions to respond to Volker's gesture of love by declaring in open court that she did not love him back. That was more than her conscience could bear, and she refused to follow her husband's script.

"Ich lass' mich nicht scheiden!" she exclaimed defiantly. "I'm not going to get a divorce!"

Volker was touched and fascinated. Gisela's rebellion would complicate his plans. He was moved by the fierceness of her emotions, her loyalty to him. And he was mesmerized by the change in Gisela. She was no longer the weepy, confused child wife. She was a totally different person. She came across as strong, knowing her own mind, and there were no more tears.

The judge and court staff were stunned. In a type of civil court proceeding that produced few surprises in the DDR, Gisela had uncorked a showstopper. Shortly after the proceedings got under way, Volker had been the first to be asked whether he wanted a divorce. He had responded affirmatively. When Gisela went against the script and said no, the court was abruptly adjourned, pending arrangements for a later session.

Back in Bautzen, Volker's fellow prisoners reacted with alarm. The authorities were bound to exploit the new twist in the Seifarth case to their own advantage, they warned him. A few days before his sentence was up, they would probably tell him that he would be released back into the DDR, rather than the West. This had happened to many other exit applicants. It enabled the government to appear humane because it was not splitting up a marriage; and it would keep both partners at home and working for the DDR economy.

Waiting in his cell to learn of the next turn toward his destiny, Volker assumed that the *Stasi* was attempting again to persuade Gisela to consent to a divorce and that her new strength enabled her to put up further resistance. This scenario seemed to be confirmed by the next court session in Riesa, this time before a woman judge. Gisela failed to appear, and the hearing was adjourned. Since all mail to Volker was once again being stopped, he did not know what was happening to her. He continued to suspect that the *Stasi* was still working on her, still not achieving the desired result.

At the third hearing Gisela again refused to agree to a divorce.

"Why?" asked the judge.

"Because of our child," said Gisela, having decided that this was the reason most difficult to challenge.

The judge said she would defer a ruling for one year. During this time the partners were to try to agree upon the fate of their marriage.

The *Stasi* had had enough of the recalcitrant Seifarths. Its agents would not be saddled with them for another year. A final ultimatum was given to Gisela: get the divorce immediately or go back to being a waitress for good.

In tears once again, Gisela appeared at the prison with Volker's mother. The government men had worn her down at last.

"What should I do?" she asked her husband.

"You have to go ahead with it," he said.

"I guess I have to."

So only a few days before Volker's release from prison, the Seifarths were divorced. It was simple. Volker did not have to go to court again. Gisela signed a piece of paper, an attorney brought it to Volker the next day, and he signed it too. The deed was done.

On the day of Volker's release the *Stasi* could celebrate still further. Volker's fellow prisoners had been right. He was being released to return to Riesa, not to the West. Six years had elapsed since Volker first brought his exit application to Room 10 at the Department of Internal Affairs and was not a step closer to freedom. He had accomplished nothing but to lose his wife and daughter in the eyes of the law that ruled their lives, the law of the DDR. It was implacable, this Communist rule book, nonnegotiable except by the most ingenious.

PART X

NEGOTIATING THE WALL

48

WHEN DISTANT NEIGHBORS MEET

**Hubertusstock Castle, Werbellinsee, East Germany,
December 1981**

Only four men were at the dinner in the lakeside guest castle of the DDR's Council of State in the woods thirty miles northeast of Berlin: the host, Erich Honecker; his guest, Helmut Schmidt, Chancellor of West Germany; Schmidt's Chief of Staff; and a supposedly unofficial party, the lawyer Wolfgang Vogel.

All were tense. Chancellor Schmidt, who had arrived in the DDR only four hours earlier and had been reluctant to come to such a summit conference at all, had never met Honecker. No two heads of the two German states had ever talked in person before.

Vogel knew they were facing difficult hours, because Honecker had placed him in charge of the preparatory negotiations and the historic encounter had almost blown up before getting started. It was much like getting together a summit between the United States and the Soviet Union during the more frigid days of the Cold War —and for quite similar reasons.

The prevailing political winds between East and West were unpromising. The Russians had marched into Afghanistan. In Poland, Solidarity workers were rioting and Soviet military intervention was feared. On American television, Chancellor Schmidt had lately characterized all DDR citizens as "hostages of Communism." And at Gera in the DDR, Honecker had made a speech bristling with demands. All were of long standing; all would still be unmet at the end of the 1980s.

The West Germans were to recognize a separate and distinct East German citizenship for *Bürger* of the DDR; they were to upgrade their "permanent representation" offices in the DDR to the status of embassies; they were to adjust the Elbe border to run down the river's center; and they were to disband a hated West German government office that researched illegal acts committed by the DDR.

The negotiators trying to arrive at a summit agenda on behalf of Schmidt and Honecker were giving up, the principal stumbling block being the legal standing of East Berlin. To the East Germans, it was the DDR capital; Chancellor Schmidt was to recognize that status by visiting the city. Schmidt would have none of that. In a last-ditch effort to salvage the meeting, the Chancellor asked Vogel to take a personal letter to Honecker.

Schmidt and Vogel had come to know each other well. Their contacts were secret but fairly frequent. Vogel would travel to meet the Chancellor at his weekend home on Brahmsee. Press inquiries were dodged. It was surmised, correctly, that Vogel was acting as Honecker's emissary on diplomatic bottlenecks concerning the release of spies and critics of the DDR regime as well as tester of the diplomatic weather. The crusty Schmidt grew to trust Vogel fully and sometimes talked to him with a frankness that startled the attorney and the Chancellor's own staff. Another Vogel talent was at work: the man *was* remarkably disarming.

The Chancellor's secret letter to Honecker broke the pre-summit deadlock. It was then that Honecker instructed Vogel to hammer out a compromise agenda, and he did. Schmidt landed at the airport outside East Berlin, avoiding the city.

The Werbellinsee meetings included fifteen hours of talks between the leaders of the divided Germanys. Substantive results were virtually zero. The talks were friendly, however, and the atmosphere markedly thawed. At a large social gathering toward the end, Schmidt referred to Honecker as "my honored friend." At other times and places, the phrase would have been dismissed as an empty courtesy. Under the circumstances, it was practically an embrace.

The event that shed the most revealing light upon the chasm separating the disparate ideologies of these leaders was a tragicomic formality. West German correspondents covered the encounter step by step and the scene became a demonstration of a political fact of life often questioned abroad. Here it became palpably valid: anyone dreaming of a reunification between the Germanys was chasing an illusion. In many respects, it would be as likely as the Soviet Union marrying the United States.

Vogel had seen the trouble coming. At some point during his visit, Chancellor Schmidt would unavoidably have to be shown to the DDR public. The *Stasi* dreaded the prospect for political reasons, and for understandable cause. Ordinary East Germans sometimes ventured slightly beyond the bounds of police control, and few had forgotten that when Willy Brandt had visited the DDR's number two man, Willi Stoph, at Erfurt eleven years before, some people in the street crowds had dared to shout, "Willy! Willy!"

The *Stasi* could not face anything like that again. Another such unauthorized display of affection would make Helmut Schmidt look like a potential liberator right on television.

Vogel, the stage manager, could not stage-manage the *Stasi*. As it was, Honecker's bureaucracy could barely hide its fury at having been shoved aside during the preparations for the summit; it wouldn't have its functions usurped in the detailed negotiations about police arrangements. So while Vogel assured Chancellor Schmidt's staff that he would not allow Schmidt to be hidden (the lawyer used the quaint Silesian dialect word *verkuten*), this became an honorable intention on which Vogel could not deliver.

Schmidt's staff was upset. They could tell that their chief was about to be quarantined. "We couldn't let ourselves be demoted to become compliant extras in a production of [DDR] Security Minister [Erich] Mielke," recalled Klaus Bölling, the West German representative to East Berlin. Perforce, the West Germans did become spear carriers despite hour upon hour of their stubborn bargaining with DDR officials about the most minute details of Schmidt's only public appearance.

All concerned were keenly aware that the fuss wasn't about protocol. It was about *face*, image, the making of a commanding public impression—prizes that politicians live for, especially a vain dictator like Honecker. It was important that there be no second Erfurt, that nobody be allowed to shout "Helmut! Helmut!"

The drama was played out on Sunday, December 13, 1981, in the snow-covered streets of Güstrow, a dreary county seat in the province of Mecklenburg. Since Schmidt was known as a connoisseur of the arts—friends like conductor Leonard Bernstein used to drop in at his home and play the piano—Güstrow had been picked so he could visit the home of the late Ernst Barlach, an anti-Nazi sculptor whose work the Chancellor admired.

Police in fur caps lined the streets massively, in places almost shoulder to shoulder. His public outing having been confined to a brief walk across the Christmas market, Schmidt looked grim. Smiling woodenly, Honecker grasped the hands of nearby spectators. The Western press recognized (and reported) that these fans were actually *Stasi* men.

Did Honecker know this? "It could be that at such moments Honecker is able to activate his ability to mistake a desired reality for the real thing," Bölling would write, still distressed, years later. "Otherwise one can hardly deal with such a situation without being a dreadful cynic."

The *Stasi* handshakers were part of an elaborate charade, Western newsmen discovered. Numerous Güstrow residents had had to sign papers guaranteeing they would not leave their homes on December 13 and that they would not position themselves near their windows. Known dissidents were ordered by their employers to attend "Christmas parties" in outlying areas. And the throngs shouting "Long live Honecker" consisted mostly not of local residents but party hacks who had been imported in buses from as far away as Saxony.

A few isolated shouts of "Helmut! Helmut!" were heard anyway, though not enough for Honecker to lose face.

For Vogel, the summit was a personal triumph of a high order. It did exact an unexpected price from him. The scene was unlikely: the summit's final formal dinner for Chancellor Schmidt. The Chancellor sat facing Honecker. Vogel was placed next to the General Secretary, further evidence of the lawyer's ascendancy and not lost upon the status-conscious DDR delegation.

With Prussian pedantry, the place cards noted each diner's party affiliation. In a rare good mood, Schmidt called Honecker's attention to an oddity: Vogel's card listed no political party. Was this only an inadvertent omission? Betraying no embarrassment, Honecker said that it was not. Then he turned to the lawyer and said, "You'll take care of that soon, won't you?" Vogel soon did.

Honecker was enormously pleased with the performance of his lawyer-mediator and, untypically, didn't mind saying so. He regarded Vogel the way Vogel saw himself—essentially selfless. In one of their one-on-one talks, Chancellor Schmidt had taken the trouble of telling the General Secretary how much he valued Vogel's services. Honecker, visibly pleased, remarked, "Yes, and he doesn't even want me to promote him."

It would have been difficult to elevate Vogel to higher estate, except by bestowing a title upon him, which didn't interest the lawyer.

Much to the continued disgust of the careerists in the DDR Ministry for Foreign Affairs, the relationship between Honecker and Vogel had grown unassailable. In international matters, the relations with those "distant neighbors" in Bonn were all-important, and nobody had built as solid a link to Bonn as Vogel. It was natural for Honecker to have become dependent on this adviser in his dealings with the other Germans across the Wall and to allow Vogel a degree of elbow room.

"You ought to have a strong supervisor," the lawyer was once told by a critic, an official in the DDR Justice Department. Actually Vogel had such a boss. It was Honecker himself, and the General Secretary not infrequently ruled against the lawyer's recommendations.

"You're too soft, too gullible," Honecker cautioned Vogel in one of their far-ranging private talks. "You're too concerned about the human element. You think too little about the political implications."

Vogel told the General Secretary that he was right, so the lawyer informed me. He had no problem to offer such a humbling concession, for his devotion to Honecker was absolute.

"I revere him," he once told a West German writer.

"I pray for him," he said to me.

"Literally?"

"Yes, I say a quiet prayer for him every night."

Cynics, East and West, would counter that Vogel's prayers were meant to encouage a long life for Honecker, because their relationship had grown *too* close. For years, insiders speculated that Vogel's influence would end at the moment of Honecker's departure. Which was possible but doubtful. What Honecker successor would want to forgo Vogel's experience?

Meanwhile, on Marx-Engels-Platz, as in the White House in Washington, access to the ear of the number one leader was what counted, access and credibility. Vogel enjoyed both to a degree that frightened some thoughtful people with experience in both Germanys.

"A man shouldn't have that much power," said Katja Lange-Müller, the defector daughter of the Politburo's woman candidate. "It's too much power for one person. I don't like people who make themselves interesting this way. He's playing a game called destiny, he's too close to God."

It was odd, the way these atheists kept invoking God and worrying about leaders with too much power over people. Wasn't the Communist state supposed to be the people's state? Even the staunchest loyalist I know was reconsidering how this theory was working out in practice.

49

SERGEANT HEYM HAS SECOND THOUGHTS: A PERSONAL REMEMBRANCE

Grünau, East Berlin,
August 1984

The last time I saw Stefan Heym had been forty years ago in the cool, modernistic studios of Radio Luxembourg. We both were technical sergeants in the U.S. Army's Psychological Warfare Division, part of a tiny cell of typewriter soldiers, mostly Jewish refugees, writing long, long, wordy propaganda scripts in German, seven days a week. We were supposed to soften up the morale of the *Wehrmacht.* I thought they were doing the same to us, because ours felt like Sisyphus labor.

We typed and typed and typed until steam came out of our ears. Except for an occasional shrewd German prisoner of war who told our interrogators what we liked to hear and therefore professed to love our programs, we typed without feedback or ratings. We just typed on and on. It was vastly cozier soldiering than getting pounded by the German artillery at Bastogne, all too audible in the distance during the Battle of the Bulge.

My friends and I never felt comfortable with Stefan. He was too impressive. Tall, very broadly built, he affected the stereotypical intellectual's long, wavy hair, commandingly bushy eyebrows, a tight, determined mouth, and a craggy beak of a nose. At thirty-one he was relatively old for the Army. In my earlier infantry outfit such senior citizens were called "Pop," but Stefan did not invite folksiness. He seemed humorless, rarely cracked a smile, and had a stoop suggestive of great burdens piled upon his back. We called him *Dichterfürst,* Prince of Poets, though not to his face.

Our mocking was mostly sour grapes. I was ten years younger than Stefan; I envied and looked up to him. He was a ferocious, driven worker, pouring out a ceaseless flood of artless but fluid, hard-hammering copy on our flimsy yellow and green paper, hunched over his ancient machine hour after hour like a stoker shoveling coal into a blazing boiler.* One could tell from his scripts that he was a real writer, unlike most of us—a published professional!† His novel *Hostages* had been a best-seller fabulously praised in *The New York Times.* "Will be ranked with the finest novels of 1942," said the critic Orville Prescott. Luise Rainer, no less, starred in the movie version.

Everyone in our group of emigrants had lost relatives in concentration camps. We knew that more were still being gassed at that very time. We were eager to exterminate Hitler like a rodent, yet we tended to dismiss the Army as an imposition, a rude interruption of our lives.

Heym was different. In our editorial conferences and mess hall bull sessions Stefan adopted a loftier, more apocalyptic view of our war. He saw it as a mortal clash of ideologies in which we were privileged to make our typewriters sing. And while he was more approving of the military than most of us—he was a spit-and-polish GI and seemed to accept the Army like a church—he fiercely resented the way it conducted its day-to-day business.

I mean: we all griped nonstop in the eternal tradition of soldiers. But we didn't gripe like Heym. To him, the mess sergeant was not despicable because he cooked greasy garbage. The man was a fascist! Our program policy chiefs in Paris were not just ignorant of front-line realities; they were saboteurs, moles from big business. In the large, philosophic sense, Heym worshiped the establishment. Responding to its daily micro-impact upon himself, he

---

* I never knew Heym to throw anything away. The astonishingly sizable inventory of his Luxembourg scripts was published as a 351-page book by Bertelsmann in 1986, entitled *Reden an den Feind* (Talking to the Enemy).

† Other professionals in our ranks were our chief, the brilliant, irascible novelist Hans Habe, a quintessential Hungarian barely converted into an American captain; Joseph Wechsberg, the morose shipboard fiddler, more lately at *The New Yorker;* Morris Bishop, the Princeton professor and author of puckish light verse; and my best friend, Richard Hanser, who later wrote the masterful NBC television series "Victory at Sea."

Heym in 1984, an East German literary lion who enjoyed growling at his rulers.

As a thirty-one-year-old technical sergeant in the U.S. Army's Psychological Warfare Division in 1944, Stefan Heym poured out a ceaseless flood of anti-Nazi propaganda.

stewed in permanent revolt. Heym enjoyed tilting at authority. It brought him to full boil.

I had not known that Stefan was a Marxist until I saw in *The New York Times* in early 1952 that he had mailed back his Army decorations to President Truman with a nasty letter and had appeared in East Berlin requesting political asylum. He was fleeing again, this time from the witch-hunt of Senator Joseph McCarthy, the Wisconsin Red baiter. To me, the escape seemed a demented leap from the proverbial frying pan into a bad fire. For Heym, it spelled fame and fortune of a remarkable magnitude.

Now that I was back in Berlin to investigate the effects of the schizophrenia in the city's double life, Stefan would make an intriguing eyewitness. I called him up. He sounded warm and delighted. We had to see each other. Right away! How about coffee and cake Sunday at his house on the outskirts, in Grünau? He could get us a taxi.

I was very pleased by the reception from this strange Army buddy of two generations past. And I was relieved about the taxi. It's an easy fifty minutes from the Wall to Grünau by elevated train and the fare is twenty *Pfennig*, next to nothing. In the years since then I learned easily how to make the trip; in 1984 Grünau was Tibet. And taxis? You had to be *born* into one.

Not Stefan. He commanded the one asset that makes the DDR run. He had connections. Connections greased almost anything, and Stefan's influence reached into the Inter-Hotel Metropol near the Friedrichstrasse crossing points. His henchpersons there would procure a special taxi for us at their door for 3 P.M. on Sunday.*

I had been divorced since my last Berlin visit, and my new wife-to-be, Elaine, spoke no German and had never been to Berlin. Her impressions would be fresh. Elaine is the director of a public library and hardly timorous. My preparations for the journey into Stefan's world made her nervous. We are both constant clippers of newspaper and magazine articles and keep accumulating these scraps in pockets and wallets. I explained that we needed to divest

---

* Quite possibly, this was one of the numerous ways in which the Honecker regime kept a close eye on Heym and his visitors. The East Berlin hotels are known to teem with *Stasi* agents. Heym had the last laugh. I learned later that he liked to flaunt his extensive contacts among Western journalists and authors. It added to his celebrity status and his immunity.

ourselves of these deposits. All Western "print products" were forbidden. The Eastern border guards often asked explicitly for the surrender of alien *Druckerzeugnisse*. They especially liked to confiscate "pornography" like *Playboy*. I never carried notebooks in the East back in 1984. I also told Elaine to bring only a nominal amount of cash. Heaven knows why, but the East Germans were suspicious of *Devisen*, the hard foreign currencies they so craved. It all had to be accounted for and registered at the border, going in and coming out.

Passing the little wooden shacks at Checkpoint Charlie with their lazily lounging American, British, and French MPs and the wisecracking West Berlin cops, Elaine remarked that the scene appeared far less charged than she had been led to believe by her spy novels. I said I thought that the Western powers deliberately wanted to make the crossing look flimsy and temporary, like a detour, a construction site.

The gray stoniness of the Wall struck Elaine as a more massive, taller presence than she had imagined, and the instant visibility of the schism in *Weltanschauung* between East and West hit her the moment we passed through the opening in the concrete. Nothing pitches the kaleidoscopic mix of the West more vividly against the monotone of the East than the chaotic graffiti sprawled across the Wall's democratic side and the vacantness, the palpable silence on its reverse. Whenever I pass through this exhibition of polarity, I think I am performing a coin toss with one side blank. It is a no-win gamble that produces nothing but a hollow feeling.

A few steps farther into enemy territory, the two-track atmosphere of competition ended abruptly for both of us. Grim-faced military men motioned us and a handful of other travelers into a cage of chest-high iron fencing. As we walked in, a gate clanged shut behind us. Passports were collected from everybody. The effect was profound. We were no longer free persons. We were totally under foreign control.

Intellectually, we naturally realized that thousands of people went through this metallic display of Communist bureaucracy with impunity every day. Emotionally, the impact was upsetting. I always feel naked abroad when I'm even briefly without the dark blue security blanket of my American passport. From time to time, without thinking, I pat the breast pocket where I keep it. Standing like cattle in our cage, waiting for further hurdles to clear in this DDR border obstacle course, we looked anxiously at each other, wondering whether our keepers might find something incriminating about us. If they did, would they just send us back to the West? Or would they hold us for questioning in one of the vacant cubicles in the adjoining barracks obviously designed for that purpose?

There was plenty of time to wonder what I would do if I was asked the obvious question: where were we headed? Should I say we were going sight-seeing? Or should I mention Stefan Heym? I knew that this fellow sergeant of long ago had become a most inconvenient, controversial, highly publicized figure in Honecker country. His name had to be well and unfavorably known at the border. Would its mention harm us? Or possibly him? Luckily, the guards never asked the question.

Standing in our cage tended to stimulate reflection. It made me think of the tall trees on our Connecticut hills. Here, truly, was the Iron Curtain in reality. We literally faced three of them, because we were being sluiced through a sequence of three identical cages.* Each time a gate sprang open in front, another shut firmly in our backs. Prison. At every stage our guards thrust more papers at us to fill out and they retrieved others. After clearing the last pen we got our passports back without a word and were left to move on into the streets of what was again, very visibly, the other world.

Elaine later said she thought she had landed on the moon or perhaps at the site of an epidemic that had wiped out all life. It was Sunday, to be sure, and much of the Eastern side of the Friedrich-strasse neighborhood consisted of office buildings, but I explained that, in my memory, all East Berlin looked pretty much like this every day. The hideous high-rise apartment blocks on the broad but empty Leipzigerstrasse seemed vacant too. Of course they were not. People were working or, on weekends, recovering to work

---

* By the following summer, in 1985, the cages had vanished. Ordinary border crossers without preferential military or diplomatic papers lined up indoors now, shuffling slowly, sometimes with very, very long stops at various control posts, through the hallways of the barracks freshly painted in white. Cheerful sketches of old Berlin decorated the walls. Lacy white curtains covered the windows. Plants were tastefully scattered around. The uniformed keepers no longer barked; they spoke like people. The management had manifestly decided to change face. Despite my repeated energetic efforts with the East German authorities, I was never able to uncover how decisions about the evolving conditions at Checkpoint Charlie were timed or arrived at, nor even what agency (committee?) was in charge of the process. A tape of a discussion among the relevant functionaries would reveal much about Communist mentality. One knows only that nothing official is done lightly in the DDR and that any change whatever at the border, no matter how slight, carries political meaning.

some more. Traffic was a driver's delight; the infrequent buses raced and careened around corners like mad. No danger of grid-locks here.

At the reception desk of the Hotel Metropol they had actually heard of us and miraculously had a taxi ready. The youngish driver was a loyal *Genosse* who beamingly described the larger and sunnier new apartment that the party had recently procured for him. He volunteered that he could never in his lifetime be evicted, the law permitting no such capitalistic exploitation of a worker.

Along the way to Heym's home in the pleasantly wooded south-ernmost outskirts, near Schönefeld, the only international airport in the DDR, and the Müggelsee, the site of water-sports Olympics events, I thought about the advance reading I had done. I had wanted to be briefed on the bizarre turns Stefan Heym's life had taken since his return to Germany—and "the other" Germany at that—more than thirty years earlier.

He had been a celebrity all this time, but for different reasons at different stages. Upon arrival, he was crowned a hero of the pro-letariat.* Despite the then catastrophic housing shortage he had been assigned a snug little villa in Grünau by the government. It was in the peaceful woods of a VIP settlement. Party administra-tors and *Stasi* chiefs were among his neighbors. He was appointed newspaper columnist—the equivalent of becoming a spokesman for the government—and Walter Ulbricht sometimes phoned him with editorial suggestions.

The column was called "Plain Talk" and the government let it run for several years before daring to snuff it out. Heym used this vehicle to set himself up as an ombudsman. Inviting reader com-

---

* Heym's acceptance and glory were a tribute to his stature (even then) and to his talent for persuasion. He had no difficulty in overcoming the paranoia that makes Communist authorities suspect anyone who spent years in the KA (*kapitalistisches Ausland,* capitalist foreign countries). Such a floater could have been "turned"— i.e., to be a Western spy. The Communists find it worrisome that—in the words of a cynic of my acquaintance—a rat should swim out to sea to join a sinking ship. A case in point was Hanus Burger, a filmmaker and mutual friend of Heym's and myself. He was another technical sergeant in the outfit that trained us in World War II, the Second Mobile Radio Broadcasting Company. The Second MRB was probably the only little army unit to sustain two defections to the Communists after the war. Burger, also in the McCarthy days, decided to return to his native Prague. The Czechs initially concluded that he had to be an American agent. He could barely find a furnished room and couldn't buy milk for his new baby. Ultimately, Hanus resettled, in the comforts of Munich.

plaints, he was swamped by letters and wallowed in a huge correspondence, delighted to be trapped by gripers like himself.

All this visibility was a long way from his lot as an unknown
soldier in the United States, where Heym's career had flagged after
the war. He published five novels in six years, including *The Cru-
saders,** a curious version of the Second MRB's adventures, heavily
politicized with left-wing accents. None of these books "worked,"
as they say in publishing. That didn't mean they were bad. They
just weren't commercial; they didn't match the hemlines of prevailing literary fashions.

In East Berlin the muse smiled upon Stefan overnight. He
reigned as the literary lion he had always wanted to be, winning
the nation's three major prizes in rapid succession for new novels
that were extravagantly successful, albeit only in the East.

By 1961, about when the Wall went up, Heym had developed
reservations about the DDR leadership. His relationship with the
United States Army was reenacting itself. He couldn't tolerate authority. The Communist cause seemed just to him; Stefan considered himself a model Marxist, he always would. But damned if
the fucking bosses weren't running it wrong! They were pompous
rhetoricians, rules crazy, paper crazy, they deprived the workers
by gumming up production and flow of goods and services. Worst,
the bosses wouldn't let a good soldier do what a good soldier does
best: gripe. Stefan never joined their party. They were muzzlers.
He didn't belong.

In the spring of 1961, I learned later, a colonel from the Soviet
military administration came to solicit Heym's counsel. Why were
East Germans fleeing to the West in such fantastic numbers? What
should be done to keep them home? Heym said that enormous
alterations in the society would be required. Living conditions
would have to undergo radical change. The leaders in charge *(die
Mannschaft)* would have to be changed.

"That we can't do," the colonel said. He sighed and left.

The same year, for the first time, the authorities accused Stefan
of committing serious political "errors" in a volume of short stories.
In 1965 he managed to publish more criticism of the government,
including a sarcastic article profiling one of the DDR culture czars.
Now the leadership had heard enough out of Heym. Thunder

---

* Boston: Little, Brown, 1948.

descended in manifestos to be enshrined forever in formal histories of his country.

No longer were little literary critics sniping at my fellow sergeant. Honecker himself denounced him on an oracular occasion. Judgment was handed down in the leader's report to the Eleventh Plenum of the Party's Central Committee on December 15 to 18, 1965. I might not have believed this if I hadn't studied the text cramming three pages in *Neues Deutschland*. Stefan was branded a "negative critic"; he was refusing to listen to "advice that had repeatedly been given him"; his books and articles dared to proclaim aberrant "truth as conceived by the West"; his depiction of events in the DDR was "totally wrong" and so on.

Unabashed, Heym responded on Western television. He had always been a loquacious debater, but this change of venue was unheard of chutzpah.

Beginning in the late 1960s, his skirmishing with authority escalated into open war. His books, seven of them, were no longer admitted for publication in the DDR. He had them issued in West Germany, where they were respectfully received. They made him well-to-do in Western (not merely DDR) currency. He had become a literary lion all over again, this time in the enemy camp. He was a resistance hero—a dazzling act of political figure skating.

The government tried for a reconciliation. For Heym's sixtieth birthday in 1973, the Culture Czar appeared at his home with flowers, and Honecker invited him for a private chat. Addressing Heym with the familiar *"Du"* used by the old *Genossen,* the leader proved ingratiating. *Genosse* Ulbricht had been wanting to talk to Heym, Honecker said, but the old man had suffered a stroke. So Honecker had personally okayed publication of Heym's biblical allegory, *The King David Report,* and soon the East German publishers would be granted more independence, Honecker said. His criticism of dissident writers was muted, almost a wail. Why did they have to bring up that under socialism even children sometimes commit suicide?

Nothing changed for Heym except that Western media turned him into an oracle. The *Spiegel* printed long interviews with Heym. He used these platforms to ask questions that the DDR bosses did not want to hear, such as: "To what degree can the Wall be made more porous without endangering the very existence of our society?" He likened the DDR censorship to the practices of Senator McCarthy. Once in a while he managed to sound off even at home.

I had read the last speech Heym was allowed to deliver before the
East German Writers Union on the day they excommunicated him.
It was in June of 1979. "The censorship of the czars allowed Karl
Marx to appear in Russia," he taunted his docile colleagues. "What
critical thinker gets published in our country?" And why should
his own house be watched and his phone be tapped?

June 1979 was his peak month of trouble. On the twenty-second,
Neues Deutschland called him "one of the few bankrupt types who
busily cooperate with the enemies of the people to cheaply call
attention to themselves." The next day the DDR "copyright office"
summoned him and fined him 9,000 marks for having negotiated
book contracts directly with Western publishers and collecting roy-
alties in hard currency from them. Heym paid up, continued his
practices as in the past and was not challenged again. The law kept
hanging over his head. He didn't seem to notice.

Withal, the DDR bosses still allowed Heym to travel to the West
largely at will. Once there, he criticized his rulers with increasing
venom. West German television welcomed him often and with awe,
as if he walked about with a noose around his neck, an interesting
specimen. Not long before Elaine and I went to Grünau to visit
him, he had said in a print interview that his books spoke out for
"a socialism that needs no Wall and where people don't want to
run off." The bosses had forbidden the appearance of another of
his novels. Heym was teasing them about it. He said they were no
longer sure that their cause was pure.

"They are like little boys who got their hands dirty," he remarked, "and now Mommy is asking, 'Where have you been?' "

Having spoken with Stefan from West Berlin, I knew he was not
languishing in the penitentiary, which wouldn't have been surprising. My curiosity was running high. How *was* Heym getting away
with all his impudence? Honecker was not exactly the mess sergeant of the Second MRB, right? The situation didn't add up. I
couldn't fit the griping American sergeant into the mold of . . .
what? A counterrevolutionary? A utopian Marxist? A self-destruc-
tive potential martyr? A wildly reckless publicity hound?

It really was just the old didactic, kvetching Stefan, much mel-
lowed by age and success. At seventy-one, his hair white, his stoop
more pronounced, he moved with great energy. He gave me a tight
embrace and said to Elaine, "He's still the old Peter. His shirttail is

still sticking out." He was speaking English in deference to Elaine's language problem and seemed to be enjoying it.

We met his second wife, Inge, a born Berliner and a former filmmaker; his son, a newly minted physician, Stefan, Jr., and we caught up on old friends and new book projects. He was still writing seven days a week and demonstrated how he nimbly strummed a Siemens computer. The conversation stayed within the bounds of nonsensitive subjects. Once I saw the Heyms exchanging glances, and Stefan rose to close the door to the garden. Elaine and I exchanged looks too. What was out there? Or who?

Stefan suggested a walk through the woods, obviously a move to get away from prying eyes and ears, and the talk did turn political. It became clear: this man was no dissenter, no martyr, no grubber for easy publicity. He was replaying an ancient scenario. Sergeant Heym was railing against Captain Honecker! The level of Stefan's dissatisfaction was no different in these woods than in what I had read from him in Western newspapers and magazines. He believed in the system of the East and wanted to reform it, democratize it, from within. Quixotic? Perhaps, yet: if he wondered in the quiet of the night whether the authorities would leave him alone to carp forever, he gave no sign of nervousness. He acted secure. Why should the regime repossess his villa, for instance, after all these years of tolerating his eccentricities? He was a *Genosse,* a fellow socialist! No peaceful oppositionist was banished to Siberia any longer.

His private brand of socialism certainly appeared comfortable. Taking us to downtown East Berlin for dinner, he drove his distinctly unproletarian low-slung white Lancia roadster. In Ridgefield, Connecticut, this vehicle would get an envious glance or two. In East Berlin cars are an obsession. Any Western-make vehicle, even a VW bug, is a privileged person's plaything. The Lancia was a royal tiara, a maharaja's pink elephant. Stefan, wearing a leather jacket but no bourgeois necktie, explained that he had bought the car for cash, in West marks, at an intershop downtown where Western extravagances such as bathroom fixtures were hawked to the favored few who had gotten their hands on enough hard currency.

I wished I could have seen the intershop salesman's face at the time, but riding the soft pink elephant I only nodded and recalled Marx's maxim: "From each according to his abilities, to each according to his needs." I had known Heym to pull astonishing mileage out of the hat of Army rules during the war and crow about his feats. Since then he had come to relax at his victories. Success became Stefan. He had learned to star as a benign Prince of Poets, a true *Dichterfürst*. Though he never said so, I suspect he was having a marvelous time thumbing his nose at the Communist regime's stuffed shirts who thought they were making the rules.

We were headed for the gourmet roof restaurant on the thirty-ninth floor of the Hotel Stadt Berlin (two thousand rooms), but the main event of the evening took place in the parking lot and on the way into the dining room. Three times Stefan was stopped by strangers who stuck out their hands, grinned at him, offered their congratulations, and told him to keep up the brave work. They were East Berliners who had watched him gripe on Western television. Elaine and I were flabbergasted. Most writers depart from life without arousing a wink of attention. How many novelists get stopped in the parking lots of a police state and slapped on the back for revolutionary outrages?

The ambience in the restaurant was embarrassingly servile. In their rage to look competitive with the West, the service managers of the Communists' choicest restaurants tend to hark back to the imperial Vienna of the Hapsburgs. White tie and tails. Bowings. Scrapings. Singings about exquisite dishes in flowery lyrics. Waiters drilled like ballet stars. Heym, obviously a prized regular, bathed in the reverence, the superb food and wines.

All right, then, so why was he getting away with being Stefan? Why was Honecker letting him blow and gloat and tease? Why was he left alone to live in relative luxury even though he was, locally, a nonperson shunted into isolation, at least officially? Why was he permitted to pound out antiestablishment books in Grünau with the same gusto he had aimed toward the Nazis at Radio Lux in the war? And if Sergeant Heym held Captain Honecker in such low esteem, why didn't he move West like most other malcontents?

"His biography, his biography," I had been told by another East Berlin writer, a woman dazzled by Stefan's chutzpah, and it was true: we hadn't heard about it at the Second Mobile Radio Broadcasting Company, but Heym had built quite a record as a radical spokesman after leaving his native Chemnitz (now Karl-Marx-Stadt) in 1933 and drumming his typewriter for refugee sheets in Prague, then in Chicago, then in New York before joining us downtrodden propagandists of the Army.

Since socialism remained his church—what a reassuring (if quaint) exhibition of loyalty from a free spirit! Why not wait for him to die instead of turning him into a martyr? Let him strut like a *Hofjude* (court Jew) of the ancient German kings, who kept a token Jew on public display as evidence of alleged liberality.

Why should Stefan give up Grünau, lose his hero's stripes, sink to the level of other unexciting defector writers? Why defang himself and lose the gripe artist's exquisite pleasure, an inside seat to bore from within?

It all did add up, more or less. At least the contradictions could be explained away in the context of the DDR hankering for respectability, for Western approval, for Western trade and comforts, for making a show of a tranquil front.

It was getting close to midnight, the end of our visa time. The white Lancia took us to the Friedrichstrasse train and border station. Then we were in front of the *Tränenpalast*, the "palace of tears," so Inge Heym told us. It was the first time I had heard the nickname of the place. People all around were embracing in the dark for their good-byes. A very old woman was selling flowers from a basket, and Inge bought a little bouquet for Elaine. It felt like a scene from a sad operetta.

We said our own farewells and left the Heyms waving. Within a minute or two we were back. Stefan and Inge had not moved. We had been turned away. We hadn't known—and the Heyms had not remembered—that the DDR requires guests to return via the same border post where the country was entered.

Back to Checkpoint Charlie through the dead black streets in the white Lancia. It was three or four minutes before twelve. Elaine was as white as Stefan's car. The checkpoint was motionless, deserted, a vignette out of John le Carré. We got out, headed quickly for the first of the barriers, and turned to wave. Stefan and Inge waved back. They looked lonely. Loneliness was a common condition in the DDR.

50

THE BOOK OF VOLKER:
THE WIFE NEXT DOOR

**Tengen, West Germany,
October 1984**

Despite their elaborate efforts, the DDR authorities had not succeeded in breaking the determination of Volker Seifarth, the
doughty steelworker from Riesa. Five years after he was released
from Bautzen Prison and had divorced his wife, Gisela, against his
will, more than ten years after he first applied for an exit permit,
he had made it to the West, once again in reasonably good cheer,
and he expected Gisela to join him shortly.

What a crazy five years he had lived through!

The Riesa steelworks had been happy to have him back at his
old job when he returned from Bautzen, and his bosses would have
made room for him in the bachelor workers quarters. Volker saw
no reason why he should settle for a life in barracks. He disdained
the offer and took cognizance of the painfully acute housing shortage in the DDR by threatening to pitch a tent on the principal town
square.

After three days of deliberation, during which Seifarth was put
up in a hotel at police expense, the police official who had been
placed in charge of his domestication issued an unexpected and
welcome ruling.

"Well, you've got to live with your wife," he said with a helpless
shrug.

The ensuing entrances and exits at the Seifarth apartment could have come out of an old British bedroom farce. Gisela had agreed to let Volker sleep temporarily in Rommy's room and Rommy would move in with Gisela. That wasn't enough because the Seifarths faced a delicate legal problem. As part of his divorce decree, Volker had been sentenced to *Umgangsverbot* under Paragraph 48 of the DDR penal code. Of course it was understood that this loving husband and his wife would not be allowed to sleep together. *Umgangsverbot* was a more comprehensive constraint. It meant that all social intercourse, indeed all contact, was off limits for the couple.

In his brisk and antiauthoritarian way, Volker wanted to ignore this legal folderol. Not Gisela. Though she was delighted to have her husband out of prison, she was exceedingly frightened by his presence, understandably so. If they were noticed spending any time together, they would both go to jail. And the zeal with which the DDR encouraged its citizens to spy on each other made it probable that they would quickly be spotted and denounced.

"We've really got to keep out of each other's way," Gisela said earnestly. "Nobody must see us together."

That conversation had taken place on Volker's first morning back home in what had once been their joint living room. Volker shook his head. These were demented days. Still, he realized that Gisela was not exaggerating the risks and agreed that the family would do well to follow the rules. From then on, feeling ridiculous, they carefully arranged to come and go at separate times, they talked in whispers if at all, and when Volker was home he almost always remained incommunicado in Rommy's room. After two weeks, to their relief, this regimen ended. The Housing Office had found Volker a furnished apartment of his own.

The Seifarths had further grounds for wanting to stay out of trouble with the police. They were as determined as ever to leave the country and they had learned the game thoroughly: any infraction of government rules would be held against them and would further slow their departure.

Volker had gone back to Room 10 at the Department of Internal Affairs to file a new exit application. Dr. Nitschke and his wife having left the country, Volker struggled with the forms on his own, pretty much remembering how to deal with them.

As the Seifarths began the long, infuriating waiting period all over, they were acutely aware that they could not afford to arouse suspicion by their behavior. The same was generally true for all DDR citizens at all times, and since the laws were written so that

almost any behavior could be interpreted as being illegal whenever
it suited the authorities, everyone constantly lived under a cloud of
fear. For the Seifarths the restraints were cause for special apprehension. Volker had built a roaring record as a *Staatsfeind,* an
enemy of the state. And even though his marriage had been
blasted away, potential evidence was accumulating that his wife
remained in sympathy with him.

Although they did not underestimate the risks, Volker and Gisela were determined not to live totally apart. At first they talked
Volker's reluctant parents into letting them visit together on occasional weekends. His father soon put an end to this privilege.
"They'll put you in jail and me, too," he said. "You can't be seen
together."

Volker next enlisted a former colleague, who let the couple meet
in his apartment and whose wife would pick up Gisela at her home
in the south end of Riesa. This little conspiracy worked three times
before the meetings came to the attention of Volker's police precinct and the Seifarths were summoned for a formal warning.

Gisela now had enough of this DDR version of Romeo and Juliet.
She was too scared to play the role. For a year they did not meet at
all. Only once did Volker run into his wife and daughter in a store.
He followed them into the street and they talked for a few minutes
before Gisela, trembling, seized Rommy and ran off without touch-
ing her husband; fear was written all over her face.

Throughout this time, husband and wife maintained contact.
Their communications were transmitted by Volker's mother and
sister. After twelve months without meeting, Volker arranged
to have Gisela brought to a small, gloomy country inn one night
after 10 P.M. He walked into the place early and ordered a beer
at the bar. When his wife was ushered into another room through
a side door—just as in an Italian opera—the bartender suggested conspiratorially to Volker, "Hey, why don't you go next
door?"

Volker and Gisela barely touched. She had coffee. He had another beer. They entertained no thought of taking a room upstairs.
That would have required them to show their identity papers.
They talked, held hands and left after agreeing they would somehow arrange to go away for a week's vacation.

It never happened. Two days after the rendezvous at the inn,
Gisela was summoned into her manager's office. He was furious.

"You met your husband!"

Taken aback, Gisela confessed and cried.

"I'll let it pass this time, but next time you can count on getting arrested and at least paying a fine!"

Neither spouse was in the mood to take further risks until, still another year later, Volker's parents celebrated their silver wedding anniversary. The young Seifarths used that occasion for another visit and two days of conjugal bliss.

Throughout all that time, Volker kept appearing again and again in Room 10 at the Department of Internal Affairs to inquire about the status of his exit application.

"Es wird bearbeitet" was the bored response each time. "We're working on it." Volker had become about as routine a fixture of the office as its desks.

The fall of 1982 brought a sign of movement. He was summoned to the Department of Internal Affairs and handed new papers to fill out.

"Have things started to break?" he asked.

"Yes." He could dislodge no details.

In January 1983 he was summoned again and told he would leave the country within six weeks. He was instructed to quit his job, close his bank account, and notify the post office.

Having heard nothing further by April, he went back to Internal Affairs to demand his right to leave. The official reaction was non-committal. He said that he planned to go public with his case. It was a desperate alternative that he had threatened to employ before. "If you do that, you won't see the sun for a few years," a clerk had told him then in an unsubtle reminder of the forty days he had already spent in solitary confinement.

This time the men in Internal Affairs merely shrugged. The fact that they had asked Volker to quit his job three months earlier did not interest them. He had brought his troubles upon himself. Nobody had told him he had to leave the country. It was his own idea.

On May 1, May Day, the most martial of the national holidays in all socialist countries, Volker resorted to a stunt never before seen on the streets of tranquil little Riesa. He staged a one-man counter-demonstration, and it went literally against the town's mainstream. While the big official parade worked its way through the downtown area to the tune of military bands, Volker went strutting past the marchers in the opposite direction, carrying a sign that demanded his exit visa. After thus bucking the popular tide for less than ten minutes, he was arrested and incarcerated in prison at Cottbus.

Having expected no other outcome, Seifarth was not distressed. On the contrary. Perhaps prison was the best place for him. If a cell behind bars had not worked for him as a stepping-stone out of the DDR before, perhaps a second stretch would do the job of spiriting him westward.

In September his long-suffering parents were allowed to visit him. They brought wonderful news. Without having been prompted by Volker, Gisela had independently reapplied for her exit visa. Because of this act against the government, and because she had refused to join the SED, she had been dismissed from her restaurant management studies. And she had not been allowed to return to her old work as a waitress in a conventional restaurant, where many customers left tips. She was reduced to selling sandwiches in the canteen of the steel mill.

Volker was elated by Gisela's resilience. He had not doubted her love for him, but he didn't blame her for feeling intimidated by the pressure of the authorities and he had not expected her to take the initiative to push on her own for her exit visa. He could not have hoped for a more encouraging turn in their joint odyssey.

In November, Gisela was granted a permit to visit Volker.

"What should I do?" she asked him.

"Exactly what you're already doing," he said. "You've got to be patient and go to the Department of Internal Affairs as often as you can."

In October 1984, without any further proceeding, Seifarth was summoned before the director of his prison one evening at about 10 P.M. and told that he would be discharged the next day.

"Where to?" Seifarth asked two grim-looking *Stasi* officers who were present. He was extremely apprehensive. There was a fifty-fifty chance that he might be returned to live in Riesa.

The men shrugged and said nothing. It was not their business to make his last night in prison restful.

Volker did manage to fall asleep eventually, and when he was roused at 4:30 A.M. and taken to the supply room to receive his civilian clothing, he realized that his decade of scheming to leave his hated native land had paid off. He had won. Though he was not told whether he would be sent West or East, words were no longer required. According to prison gossip, one's discharge was almost always to the West if one was taken to the supply room before 6 A.M. The rumor was confirmed when Volker was again taken to the warden and was handed his "discharge from DDR citizenship."

A *Stasi* man took Seifarth to the ticket office at the Cottbus rail station, where a ticket was waiting for him. It was valid as far as Wolfsburg, the first major West German city past the Helmstedt border crossing. His bored-looking *Stasi* shadow settled into a compartment with Volker and said he would accompany him to the border control station; Volker was not to make contact with anyone along the way. Seifarth understood: the authorities did not wish to advertise that it *was* possible to leave the country with remarkably little formality; indeed, in style.

The individual treatment, the ease, and the relative luxury of the arrangements all smelled suspicious to him. Never had the government handled him like a person before. Something had to be fishy. It seemed inconceivable that the *Stasi* would suddenly pamper him like a capitalist tourist. They had even given him some pocket money. Were they playing some nasty game, teasing him with psychological torture that he had never heard about? He decided that he had best get rid of his escort. The years of playing cat and mouse with security agents had conditioned him not to trust the breed, especially not when they behaved like civilized people.

At Hoyerswerda, the first stop, Seifarth went to the information booth and asked about the next local train West. The *Stasi* officer did not try to restrain him. A local was about to leave. Volker ran to catch it and dropped happily into the nearest compartment. Within moments his *Stasi* man joined him, looking unhurried, not saying a word.

At the local train's last stop, Magdeburg, a young man asked Volker whether he needed a taxi. The *Stasi* agent was not in sight. Volker inquired whether the taximan was authorized to travel into the border area. The driver said he wasn't, but he was obviously intrigued and sympathetic. Why did Seifarth want to go to the border?

Volker decided to take a chance. The young man could easily have been a *Stasi* employee; taxis were very rarely so readily available in the East. Seifarth had no choice, however. His *Stasi* escort was surely watching. The young driver was Volker's only chance to slip out of a trap that he felt was about to ensnare him.

In a sentence or two, Seifarth blurted out his story. The driver grinned and said, "We'll take care of this!" and they drove off.

Nobody followed. The *Stasi* had not imagined that Seifarth, the prisoner who had dreaded being released into the DDR, would attempt to escape into that same country when he carried valid exit papers.

The driver, clearly enjoying his mission, had to let Volker off at the first border outpost, and Seifarth jogged the remaining five kilometers to the rail station at Helmstedt, the famous old border crossing. Several border guards gathered to ask him for the identification card carried by all DDR citizens. Seifarth said he no longer possessed such a paper. They told him he was under arrest. He blandly announced that he was en route to Wolfsburg. They laughed loudly.

Like a magician slipping a trump card from his sleeve, Seifarth pulled out his discharge paper. The hilarity ceased. After hurried consultations the border officers took Volker to a waiting West-bound train. Ten minutes later he was in Wolfsburg. He could hardly believe that, in the end, the *Stasi* had given up trifling with his fate.

In West Germany he quickly landed a well-paid job assembling chain saws at the internationally prestigious Stihl manufacturing firm in Singen near the Swiss border. Quite a few men from the DDR were employed there, so Volker felt at home from the first day. He wrote ecstatic postcards to his family in the East and lost no time testing his dream of living free as a bird.

"Let's go to France," said one of his fellow refugee colleagues after Seifarth had been in the West just two weeks and possessed no more than temporary identification papers from the refugee camp.

"You're crazy," said Volker. "We'll wind up in jail!"

They went ahead anyway in the friend's new car, and at the border nobody bothered to look at their papers. The police were only interested in waving them along to hurry them up, not to let them slow down traffic. This was the golden West, all right, it was fantastic.

51

THE BOOK OF VOLKER: THE DIVORCE IS FINAL

**Karlovy Vary, Czechoslovakia,
August 1985**

More than two years had passed since Volker Seifarth, the irrepressible refugee, had seen his wife, Gisela, except for the few occasions when she had been allowed to visit him during his last prison stay in the DDR. For months they had schemed to have a happy reunion in Czechoslovakia. When the appointed week was at hand, Volker was surprised at the prospect's unanticipated effect upon him.

He considered himself the least excitable of men, and in his ten-year war against the DDR immigration authorities he had preserved his cool under extraordinary provocation many times. In the Baroque old comforts of Karlovy Vary, Czechoslovakia, the once-elegant spa known as Karlsbad, he suffered from a hefty case of *Lampenfieber,* stage fright.

While Czechoslovakia had become a subservient Soviet satellite in 1968, its citizens retained a benign eye for DDR neighbors who were not enamored of the regime in East Berlin. These disaffected Germans made appreciative tourists, and resorts such as Karlovy Vary, conveniently close to the border, often hosted vacations or get-togethers of DDR *Genossen* who longed for the life of the West but would settle briefly for the slightly less triste brand of Communism in Czechoslovakia (where DDR currency was acceptable).

All of which was why Seifarth had picked the historic watering spot for his long-anticipated romantic interlude with Gisela.

Their date was set for the main railroad station on Friday at noon. Under no circumstances did Volker wish to risk being a moment late. Driving at near-record speeds, he whipped his Audi 100 into town the day before. By 9 A.M. on Friday he had taken up a forward observation post in the window of a café across the street from the station. At noon he was pacing in front, ready to spot the light brown Trabbi (Trabant) in which a friend from home was driving Gisela.

And there she was, running toward him, wearing new black cord pants, a white blouse, and the smile he had not seen shine so brightly on her face in years. Volker's stage fright was instantly gone. It was the first time these lovers had been together away from their grimy home grounds of Saxony. Old Karlsbad, a relic that all too obviously enjoyed better times, might have been Paris, and they relished the dowdy retreat accordingly.

Their lodgings, at the Grand Hotel Moskva, were not listed in the Michelin guide. Still, the place was vastly cozier than the glass-and-steel monument to collectivist labor known as the Hotel am Haus der Stahlwerker (Hotel at the House of the Steelworkers), the pride of Riesa back home.

There was even fun to be had outside of bed. Every day they promenaded through the immaculately tended parks and stopped at the baths to sip smelly, presumably curative *Heilwasser* from huge stone mugs, like the elderly health seekers that surrounded them. In the evenings they made the rounds of discotheques that charged Western-style prices, compensating with capitalistic entertainment of a vibrant order, especially the rock and roll at the *Tanzbar* Sabrina.

And they went shopping. For Gisela, accustomed to the meager pickings at the shops lining Riesa's dreary Ernst-Thälmann-Strasse, the tourist establishments of Karlovy Vary were havens of luxury. Volker bought her a dark blue velvet dress with matching shoes at the Kakadu fashion store. It was one of the standardized government-operated chain of intershops indigenous to all East bloc countries, but Volker loved the prices. They were lower than in West Germany. Sometimes the East had its advantages.

They talked and talked, especially about Rommy back home, who was getting good grades in school and had nice girlfriends. She was nine years old and her postcards had been reaching her father fairly regularly. Her theme never varied: she wanted to go to the West. Volker was naturally pleased. Gisela reported that Rommy's Western loyalties were causing difficulties in her Riesa school. Volker had been sending home some clothes for her, and Rommy's teacher complained that the styles were "ostentatious," that they "bothered" the other children.

Although the teacher did not say so outright, Gisela was given to understand that some of the other kids were jealous of Rommy's high-quality Western possessions. Some were even jealous of her daughters' Western plastic shopping bags and the picture postcards her father sent her from picturesque places such as Switzerland. Gisela told Volker that she had discussed the problem with Rommy. The little girl understood about the discrepancies between life in the East and the West and agreed to do less bragging about her capitalist dad.

Gisela, too, was becoming intrigued with things Western. She marveled at Volker's ability to acquire such a fine car within a year when even the best-connected and most prosperous East German consumers had to wait longer than a decade to acquire a rickety Eastern vehicle and could certainly never, never aspire to an Audi. (Volker had sent Gisela a photo of the car, but she never quite believed that he really owned it.)

Humiliated by her primitive work of dispensing sandwiches, Gisela had been inquiring with numbing regularity at Room 10 in the Department of Internal Affairs about her exit visa. A dozen years after Volker first told her that he "wanted out," she was allowing herself to grow a bit impatient.

When would she and Rommy be allowed to join Volker? They talked about that a lot in their room at the Grand Hotel Moskva and decided that the *Stasi* must be losing interest in them and would let her go soon.

The *Stasi* was, in truth, still much involved with the young Seifarths. Gisela discovered this when she had to appear before her manager the morning after she got back from Czechoslovakia.

"You've been to see your husband!" he said with the air of a judge charging treason.

A trip farther west than Czechoslovakia was not yet at hand for Gisela.

.   .   .

**Hermsdorf, East Germany,
November 1986**

Volker Seifarth was playing a role that was new to him and he was relishing the occasion. He was host at his father's birthday party, spoiling the old fellow with expensive Western gifts, and the event was made particularly piquant by its location.

Volker had conceived another of the creative notions that got around some of the DDR's annoying restrictions. The family's situation was the same as that of many Germans. Their country's split split them up as well. Volker's parents were not allowed to travel West, and the son, as a fairly recent political reject from the East, would have been turned back as an undesirable visitor if he had tried to return to his native Saxony. He therefore scheduled the birthday party for neutral territory.

The night before, he had gone slumming with his girlfriend, Judith, another refugee from the DDR, with whom he lived at Singen, in the Swiss border area where both were employed. Before taking off for the birthday party, they toured night spots in West Berlin. Toward 3 A.M., slightly tipsy, they decided to inspect the Wall near Checkpoint Charlie. Judith had never seen the structure.

Volker had told her that from the East you could not get close to it at most locations. It would not have bothered Judith to keep her distance from the Wall. The very idea of the Wall frightened her. It seemed to protect her by separating her from the security people in the East, yet their mere proximity was intimidating to a refugee.

Judith realized she was safe from possible Eastern incursions. Approaching Checkpoint Charlie, she was nevertheless scared. Volker was talking rather loudly about the crazy graffiti on the Wall and how graphically they showed that the West tolerates free expression. That made Judith even more nervous.

"You'll get hit by a hand grenade for breakfast," she cautioned.

He laughed and told her she was being silly, hadn't learned to appreciate the West.

Later that morning they drove down the *Transitstrecke* from Berlin to the Autobahn crossing at Hermsdorf and stopped at the rest area. This was deep in the DDR, yet they were on tourist territory where the DDR authorities were not likely to interfere except if they were guilty of true misconduct. The four "transit" roads, the fragile feeder arteries between Berlin and the West, were subject to numerous rules of their own. While freedom was grudging along these roads, they were, in essence, neutral corridors for anyone to move between East and West with impunity. Their very few rest areas were international oases.

The crowded Hermsdorf rest area was the mutually accessible spot where Volker had decided to throw a party for his father. When they explained the sentimental occasion to a waiter, he donated a large table and they held on to it all morning. After that they drank beer at tables outside and walked over to the intershop for their birthday shopping.

The government intershops along the transit roads tended to be showplaces where the DDR strove to make a good impression on international traffic and its government entrepreneurs displayed special ambitions to lure hard currency from Western travelers. Numbly, Volker's father stalked counters piled high with pineapples, razor blades, and other luxuries. When Volker bought him a leather overcoat with a collar made of an unspecified fur, the father felt like freshly crowned royalty.

Volker never stopped beaming. The old man surely deserved the temporary good fortune of semifreedom on the transit road. And for Volker, it was a cheering day in a time of sorrow. He led a good life in Singen. He had to labor much harder at the chain saw factory than he had ever worked back home in the Riesa steel mill; that was the expectable function of the pace and competition that helped to make the West more exciting than the DDR. He didn't mind. The money was excellent, and five times the factory had loaned him to its branch in Great Britain. He adored the travel and felt like a cosmopolite when he learned such English words as "breakfast" and "fish and chips."

At home he had become the Autobahn travel expert among his friends and colleagues and on weekends he took off in his Audi, driving *ins Blaue,* into the blue, spontaneously, anywhere at all, France, Switzerland, wherever, giving way to his long-suppressed taste for unfettered movement, physical liberty. He ate sparingly and carefully, and did not overindulge in his new favorite cocktail, Coca-Cola spiked with Armagnac. He all but bathed in the sweet climate of the Swiss border country. Most days he felt as liberated as a traveler through space.

Liberated but not whole. Gisela was the trouble. Gisela and little Rommy. Volker had been certain that they would join him soon. Once Gisela had reinstated the application for her emigration and had been fired from her management training post, the DDR authorities had classified her as a malcontent. She was no longer worth fighting for, no longer an asset to be kept at home. Volker had pushed her application onward by filing supporting documents with the West German government lawyer in Berlin who oversaw such cases. The lawyer had sounded hopeful.

It didn't happen. The decade of separation and upheaval had taken its toll after all. Volker's marriage had disintegrated. At first, Gisela's letters had stopped. Only Rommy kept writing postcards about her yearning to come West. Over time, Volker slowly pieced together the story from his mother and from other members of his family. Eventually Gisela confirmed what had happened.

She had found another man in the East who also had applied to emigrate. They would both go to the West and settle near Nuremberg, and they did.

It was over. Volker's determination had paid off up to a point. He and Gisela and Rommy had made it to the West. By ultimately splitting up a good marriage through years of chicanery and harassment, Erich Honecker and his DDR government crew had won a victory of sorts, though not a total victory, as Volker Seifarth liked to point out. The DDR had eroded a deep bond and a trust. Unable to keep its children home, it scarred them instead. For life, like a sick and grudging parent.

"It's straight out of the Middle Ages," Seifarth said.

PART XI

HURDLING THE WALL

52

THE RABBI WORE A MONEY BELT

East Berlin,
February 1986

A space was somehow made on the crowded walls of Wolfgang Vogel's Reilerstrasse office for another souvenir photo, this one taken very lately right on the couch of the lawyer's premises. The snapshot's central figure was the Soviet dissident Anatoly Sharansky, thirty-eight, smiling, liberated that very morning in Moscow after eight years in a prison cell. Flanking this celebrity were Vogel and the United States Ambassador to East Berlin, Francis J. Meehan. Vogel had his arm around the tiny Jewish leader, who was celebrating his freedom with a poignant gesture. He had grasped one arm away from each of his companions and was squeezing their hands tightly into his knees, the picture of a profoundly grateful man.

Only the final phase of the Sharansky understanding had been an official transaction between governments. The many other turns taken by the case since 1978 were managed by Wolfgang Vogel, assisted by a mostly American cast too amateurish to qualify for any respectable plot of spy fiction.

Perhaps none of the events would have come about at all if Rabbi Ronald Greenwald, forty-five, of Monsey, in rural upstate New York, had not been possessed of so much energy. The rabbi was vice president of the Union of Orthodox Jewish Congregations of America and too restless to tend a single synagogue. He had run a

Rabbi Ronald Greenwald
(left) of rural Monsey, New
York, and East Berlin
attorney Wolfgang Vogel
forged an unlikely but
effective partnership.

The efforts of Greenwald
and Vogel resulted in the
release of Soviet dissident
Anatoly Sharansky *(bottom
right wearing fur hat),* who
walked to freedom across
Berlin's Glienecker
("Socialist Unity") Bridge
in February 1986.

business school in Sullivan County and a summer camp and had organized Jewish groups for President Nixon. Now he was starting an export-import business in Manhattan and remaining active in a lot of Jewish causes.

It was not enough. "Ronnie" Greenwald, a huge bear who looked more like a kosher butcher than a man of God, liked to think of himself as a one-man rescue squad. The world being full of Jews in need of rescue, the rabbi was always involved with interesting people.

Miron Marcus was one of these. He was a young Israeli pilot who had crash-landed in Mozambique, a speck of an African nation under the thumb of the East German *Stasi*. Accused of spying, Marcus had been in prison for nearly two years when his wife called on the rabbi and asked for help. Greenwald, not one of the unworldly members of his profession, recalled the famous Abel-Powers spy exchange and sent a telex to Vogel in East Berlin. Any lawyer who could spring a big American spy out of prison should be able to do the same for a little Israeli lad who probably wasn't even spying. What was to spy in Mozambique?

If Marcus was no Colonel Powers, Greenwald was no James Donovan; the rabbi had no government backing like Donovan, the lawyer in the Abel-Powers trade. Smiling gently, Vogel pointed out these details when the bulky rabbi, wearing his yarmulke and communicating in his own Yiddish brand of German, appeared in Vogel's Reilerstrasse office looking about as inconspicuous in the DDR as a three-headed giraffe.

Vogel also pointed out that Donovan had offered a spy in trade. Where was Greenwald's trade? Vogel could not have been kinder, however. He instantly adored the ingenuous rabbi, perhaps recognizing common ground. Underneath the American's yarmulke, as in Vogel's hideout full of ticking clocks, both men were really still small-town fellows maneuvering so as not to get sandbagged in the big time.

Vogel suggested that the East Germans might be very interested in getting hold of Sergeant Robert Thompson, a former U.S. Air Force code expert convicted in America to serve thirty years as a KGB spy.

Back home Rabbi Greenwald did what so many Americans do when they get bogged down in bureaucracy. He went to see his congressman. He had known this representative for many years, having worked with him for Jewish causes, and happily this politician was another unconventional character in the plot shaping up on behalf of Sharansky and other jailbirds, some of whom actually were guilty of spying.

Representative Benjamin Gilman, fifty-five, a Republican from Poughkeepsie, lately separated from his lawyer wife and a bit sad, was one of a small handful of Jews in Congress. Almost nobody beyond upstate New York knew of him. Unheard of for a politician, Gilman—during his forthcoming role as a spy master his code name would appropriately be "Uncle Ben"—was shy. Not that he minded publicity. He simply was not very good at getting any. He did excel, like his friend Rabbi Greenwald, at rescuing Jews from difficult situations.

Much of Representative Gilman's time on Capitol Hill was spent trying to engineer such extrications, so it was no problem for him to call the State Department on behalf of Rabbi Greenwald, mentioning Marcus, the pilot languishing in Mozambique, and Sergeant Thompson, who was in the penitentiary in Pennsylvania, having served thirteen years.

At State, the request wound up with Jeffrey Smith, an adroit negotiator with a puckish sense of humor who had been part of the Panama Canal treaty talks. Jeff Smith was flexible for a West Point graduate. Lacking experience in getting convicts out of United States federal prisons prematurely, he learned fast. State had experts on everything, and Smith found himself a functionary with relevant knowledge.

"How do we get somebody out of jail if we want to trade him to the East?" he inquired.

It turned out that the most sensitive aspect of the deal was to keep it quiet, which pleased Congressman Gilman and Rabbi Greenwald, eager to measure up to the secretiveness of professional agents.

Gilman had sent Greenwald back to East Berlin to confer with Vogel. On the rabbi's return, he and Gilman went walking in the streets of Spring Valley, New York, after attending a bar mitzvah at the Yeshiva Temple. They were not about to get themselves bugged by the enemy.

"No problems crossing the frontier?" asked Gilman. "I mean, you weren't, umh, you know, spotted?"

"Oh, no," the rabbi assured the congressman. "It was all very smooth. His organization is excellent."

"And you told Wolfgang what I suggested?"

"Yes . . ."

The upshot was real: an exchange of Sergeant Thompson was arranged against two relative lightweights, the Israeli pilot Marcus plus, at Vogel's suggestion, Alan van Norman, a twenty-two-year-old theology student from Windom, Minnesota, who had been caught at the border trying to smuggle an East German chemist and his wife and son into West Germany in the trunk of his rented Mercedes.

Jeff Smith escorted Thompson to Kennedy Airport, where the prisoner was quietly tucked into a holding cell. Vogel, who would accompany the sergeant to Berlin and was anxious not to be spotted, seemed to want to hide by huddling in a lounge chair behind a bottle of Heineken's.

All went off quietly except for an episode during the earlier flight preparations. Jeff Smith had asked Vogel in what class he planned to fly.

"First class, naturally," said the Marxist attorney.

Sighing, Smith managed to wrangle first-class seats, which required special authorization from the Under Secretary of State. No good American wanted to look chintzy in front of the East Germans. Loss of face was not an exclusively Communist fear.

All during this time Rabbi Greenwald was making trip after trip to Berlin to talk to Vogel about Sharansky. The little Russian computer scientist had been convicted of espionage. Actually he had been guilty only of promoting the departure of Jewish dissidents, keeping his Western Jewish contacts stirred up and making noise with Western media, much to the embarrassment of the Soviets.

Jewish organizations in the United States were determined to get Sharansky out and Greenwald was the legman. When he started to think of himself as something more, the turf-conscious Vogel put the rabbi's role in perspective.

"Greenwald can't deliver," he told the State Department's Jeff Smith. "Only I can."

Smith was also making pilgrimages to the overstuffed little Reilerstrasse office, because the Republican administration in Washington was eager to look very active in the Sharansky case. The American motives were partly humanitarian, certainly;

they were also political. Jews tended to be conscientious voters and gave money generously to politicians who support Jewish causes.

Vogel, the obvious middleman, required proper handling. As the ranking member of the agile tribe whom the Germans were calling *Mauerspringer* (Wall jumpers), Vogel needed to be admired.

The Vogel ego had become famous among East and West Berlin politicians. The lawyer sometimes liked to show off how he could get Josef Streit and other top DDR Justice Department officials on the phone right in front of West German visitors and settle some matters on the spot. With Jeff Smith, Vogel was a shade more discreet, but the American negotiator had no trouble admiring Vogel. He was positively stunned by Vogel's speed.

"I could have a meeting in East Berlin in the morning and have an answer in West Berlin in the afternoon," Smith recalled.

At State, officials were impressed by Vogel's alacrity because it was a foolproof indicator of his power. Normally, dealings with the Communists generated mounds of paper that took eternities to get bucked upward through the East Berlin bureaucratic mills, nobody wanting to sign responsible for a decision.

"Vogel was very valuable to the United States," Smith said. "He goes to Moscow. He would talk to Honecker. *I* don't talk to the President!"

At that time Sharansky was immovable—too controversial for the Soviets to touch before the liberalizations of the Gorbachev era. But the cast for negotiations was in place. The unlikely team of Jeff Smith and Ronnie Greenwald kept pushing for more spy trades, and on June 11, 1985, an entire platoon of agents, twenty-nine of them all at once, trooped from East to West, and vice versa, reenacting the Abel-Powers deal as they crossed the "Bridge of Socialist Unity" at Alt-Glienecke in both directions.*

The details had taken years to settle. The two most sensitive Communist agents were Alfred Zehe, a physics professor from Dresden, in federal prison at Lake Placid, New York, whose release would cost the East Germans $200,000 in legal fees and other expenses, and Alice Michaelson, an elderly teacher from East Berlin, serving time at the Metropolitan Correctional Center in New

---

* Mounted at the old bridge linking East to West was a plaque bearing this message of caution: "Those who gave this bridge the name 'Bridge of Socialist Unity' also built the Wall, put up barbed wire, installed death strips, and thus prevented unity."

York City, who would cost $150,000 to get free. Vogel, whose trust in the rabbi was complete, had commissioned Greenwald to hire and pay counsel for Zehe and Michaelson. On one of his East-West flights the rabbi carried a money belt with $50,000 in bank notes. The East Germans believed in paying cash.

Ronnie Greenwald's visits to Reilerstrasse had become occasions for festivity. "The rabbi is coming!" the secretaries would call out gaily at his approach. Greenwald held gossipy social chats with Mrs. Helga Vogel ("a cowboy driver," the rabbi said) and once he slept over on Vogel's office couch until 4 A.M., when it was time to leave for Tegel Airport in West Berlin.

The rabbi had originally felt uneasy to be trafficking in Hitler's former territory. Never mind, he said to himself, he was doing a *mitsvah*, a good deed, working for an innocent prisoner like Sharansky. A live *mitsvah* counted for more than a dead Hitler. Greenwald was also eager to start trading in copper and other metals, and Vogel made invaluable introductory phone calls to the right DDR bureaus. Almost broke and with children in college, Greenwald felt he could not afford to spend life as a full-time charity. Let somebody do a *mitsvah* for *him* for a change.

To stitch together the wholesale swap of twenty-nine agents, Vogel visited New York and Washington in 1978, 1984, and 1986, always shepherded by Rabbi Greenwald or Jeff Smith. He visited his clients in the American prisons, negotiated with his American lawyers and with the government, and took time to inspect the world of the class enemy.

In New York, the rabbi lured him to Moishe's Peking kosher restaurant and hiked with him loyally from Fiftieth Street to Wall Street. Vogel was scandalized by the filth of Times Square but loved to walk.

While Vogel was in Washington, Smith drove him past CIA headquarters, pointing it out, strictly for entertainment. When they were negotiating in the bar of the Capitol Regency Hotel, the State Department man asked his wife, who acted as interpreter, to translate the name of their watering hole for the East German visitor.

The bar was called "The Spy's Eye." Vogel chuckled.

The talks between Smith and Vogel had turned very relaxed. The men seemed to speak the same language. Sometimes the two of them needed no more than to sit silently over their respective prisoner lists, occasionally tapping a name with a pen and peering questioningly at the other.

Vogel was also a welcome guest in the offices of the American attorneys whom Greenwald had retained. For Professor Zehe, the rabbi had selected a firm in Boston, for Alice Michaelson he had chosen one in New York. And in his casual but shrewd way, the rabbi had picked superbly. The world of lawyers was foreign to him, which was no handicap. On television he had admired the performance of a Harvard professor of constitutional law, Allen Dershowitz. He called the professor, asked for referrals, and followed his advice.

In New York he landed with the firm of a famous labor lawyer, Leonard Boudin. This old-timer liked Vogel at a breakfast meeting in the Helmsley Palace Hotel and admired the excellent relationship that the man from Reilerstrasse had managed to build with the United States government.

The Michaelson case did not interest Boudin much. "Spying," he said, shrugging. "It's a game of chess, not a real crime."

He turned the case over to an associate, Judy Levin, who adored games of chess. She found Vogel "beguiling," although he became exceptionally impatient with the minutiae of civil rights procedures in American courts. Levin thought the East Berliner was "ingenuous." She had not expected so much warmth and she was taken by the "little boy quality" that emerged in him, the pride he took in his bright red diplomatic passport from the DDR. After her client Michaelson was freed, Levin traveled to East Berlin to visit the Reilerstrasse office, where she was celebrated as a heroine.

The years of spadework by Vogel and Rabbi Greenwald on behalf of Anatoly Sharansky were paying off. On January 23, 1986, four diplomats convened a conference at the Hotel Gaspinger Hof in Gerlos, a tiny resort village in the snow-blanketed Zillertal, north of the Italian Alps in Austria. In this ski paradise, surrounded by ten-thousand-foot peaks, they were finally settling the Russian dissident's fate. The quartet of liberators consisted of Francis Meehan, the United States Ambassador to East Berlin; an official from the American Embassy in Bonn; Ludwig Rehlinger of Bonn's All-German Ministry; and Wolfgang Vogel.

The three principal negotiators had been good friends for twenty-five years. Rehlinger had been in on every East-West transaction in Germany since the Wall. Vogel and Meehan* had become close since they worked together on the Abel-Powers exchange; the American was godfather to one of Vogel's children. Rehlinger went to Gerlos for the skiing almost every year, and Vogel often took his winter vacations in his company or in the same area. The timing of the Sharansky deal enabled them to mix business delightfully with winter sports.

The deal was largely set. In addition to Sharansky, the West was to get a Czech escape helper and two West German spies. The East would get five espionage agents: one Pole, one Russian, one East German, and two Czechs. Vogel was responsible for the Communist end of the arrangements. The details were complicated, and he had the requisite experience. It was handy to have a negotiator from the DDR, because even at this advanced stage of spy exchanges the Soviets liked to maintain the fiction that they had no agents in the West and therefore could not be expected to negotiate for such nonpersons.

Vogel had worked out agreements with the intelligence services of each of the four Soviet bloc nations involved. Negotiations about the two Czechs in Western hands were irritating.

They were Karl and Hana Koecher, a good-looking couple who had entered the United States in 1965, posing as political defectors. Their records were unusual on two counts. They made many of their spy contacts as members of the Virginia In-Place, a partner-swapping sex club in the Washington suburbs during the mid-1970s. And the husband, Karl, did the supposedly impossible: he infiltrated the CIA. He got work in its AE Screen Unit, a department that dealt with conversations in Russian and Czech, "collected clandestinely" by the agency. It also had access to other "extremely sensitive information." Koecher had remained a contract employee of the CIA up to the time of his arrest in 1984.

The Czech intelligence authorities refused to acknowledge their connection with the Koechers. Once the couple's employers were

---

* Meehan, who retired in 1988, was one of the underappreciated great men of postwar American diplomacy in central and Eastern Europe. Quiet, witty, and very shrewd, he spent seventeen years at various posts in Germany, beginning in Marburg in 1945; he spoke German without accent and with rare idiomatic command. Before taking charge in East Berlin, his last post, he had been the Ambassador in Prague and Warsaw. It was Meehan who first cleared the way for me to see Wolfgang Vogel, a crucial source.

persuaded to change their minds about that, the Americans ruled
that the Koechers would have to confess their guilt in order to be
freed. The pair refused to do that until Vogel flew to the United
States and persuaded them to change *their* minds.

By far the most significant negotiator was neither seen nor heard
as the friendly three-nation diplomatic quartet went to work in the
Austrian Alps. That, of course, was Mikhail Gorbachev, whose new
policies made Sharansky's release discussable. Ludwig Rehlinger
and Wolfgang Vogel drafted an agreement in longhand. Soon the
stickiest point still to be settled was the location of the exchange,
and this was no mere traffic problem.

On security grounds, reservations were expressed about the
Glienecker (Socialist Unity) Bridge. A ceremony there would be as
public as a soccer game and could possibly become a magnet for
crazies with weapons and crazy motives to use them. On the other
hand, everyone at the conference knew that Richard Burt would
love nothing better than a big, murky spectacle on the bridge, with
forests of television cameras recording all. Burt, thirty-eight, an
exuberant former *New York Times* reporter whom women liked to
call "cute," was the United States Ambassador in Bonn, new to the
trade, aggressively ambitious, eager to be seen at headline-making
events that he no longer had to write about.

Frank Meehan from East Berlin, the down-to-earth steady old
hand, said that a massive spectacle on the bridge was "nonsense."
Rehlinger agreed. To their surprise, Vogel disclosed that his clients
were very much interested in giving Sharansky's departure maximum publicity. Moscow hoped to collect credit around the world
for its new liberality. Vogel further said that the DDR would enjoy
a visible demonstration of its participation in the deal. That settled
it. Rehlinger had brought along a secretary, who typed up the final
version of the agreement for the signature of the nations whose
representatives were present.

A little over two weeks later, Sharansky was flown out of Moscow
without knowing his destination until, upon landing at Schönefeld
Airport in East Berlin, he saw a lot of planes from Interflug, the
East German airline. It was the first time in his life that he had
been outside the Soviet Union.

The three Western diplomats in charge of him—Frank Meehan,
who brought him to the bridge from the East, and the two men
who would take Sharansky in tow in the West, Ludwig Rehlinger
from the Bonn government and Burt, the American Ambassador
to West Germany—were interested in more than the little Rus-

sian's safety. They did not want to see him branded as a spy by association. It was important that he not be lumped together, in front of the TV cameras, with the twenty-eight agents being exchanged at the same time. Meehan and Vogel separated Sharansky from the pack, then Rehlinger and Burt made certain that the TV cameras would pick up the face-saving detail: the two Western diplomats spiriting the Russian into the big American limousine, alone.

The little show, so well-scripted, would have been impossible without Vogel's cooperation. Why not? In the spy trade one hand washed the other.

53

INSIDE THE HOUSE AT CHECKPOINT CHARLIE

**Checkpoint Charlie, West Berlin,
Summer 1986**

"I was a failure," said the old man with the dancing dark brown eyes, the bulging belly, and the unruly stack of wavy white hair. Bouncing up and down on his chair in the dingy little pizzeria on the West side of Friedrichstrasse, he laughed loudly and threw out his hands, palms up, in mock helplessness.

I knew that here was a showman putting on a show. Rainer Hildebrandt, seventy-five—he was always called Herr Doktor Hildebrandt, because he held a doctorate in psychology—was no defeated soul. He was a celebrated character among Berlin's redoubtable legends, the founder and leader of the Haus am Checkpoint Charlie, the permanent exhibit that documents the life of the Wall. Hildebrandt was Mr. Wall, the impresario of its records, heroes, villains, and bizarre artifacts, the keeper of its memories.

In the guidebooks, Hildebrandt's Haus, less than fifty yards from Checkpoint Charlie, is listed as a "don't miss it" museum. It is entered through the small storefront of the onetime Café Köln and is probably Berlin's most popular attraction. More than ten million tourists—two thirds of them non-Germans—have shoved their way through its labyrinth of dark, narrow rooms and stairwells.

I had been through Hildebrandt's place several times, and as I

Rainer Hildebrandt, the founder and major domo of Haus am Checkpoint Charlie.

faced the man and the cascade of his recollections over a greasy midafternoon pizzeria lunch—he spoke at incredible speed, as if the world would end in four minutes—it was apparent how much the museum was an evocation of his life and passions.

Like his Haus, his mind was wildly overcrowded, exuberantly disorganized, cluttered with memorabilia, all attached to innumerable stories, all held together by a theme, a celebration of resistance, almost a hymnal, not what one would expect from a Prussian, not even a *Herr Doktor* turned showman.

At first glance, his museum seemed to me entirely devoted to adventure and conspiracy. Here hung the gondola, the instruments, and ten strips of fabric from the hot-air balloon that floated the Strelzyk and Wetzel families out of the DDR (see Chapter 43). Here stood one of Michael Gartenschläger's self-firing execution machines (see Chapter 41). You push past numerous escape vehicles: cars with bullet holes, a homemade chairlift, a homemade one-seater plane, a mini-submarine, the Isetta three-wheeler that seemed much too small to hide anyone but ferried nine DDR citizens to freedom, one by one. There were sample specimens of fake Soviet uniforms, forged passports, machinery and tools that burrowed the famous tunnels, the bric-a-brac of wall-cracking.

Here and there Hildebrandt had smuggled into these primitive relics some linkages with past and future. One display traced the Wall to Hitler and his war, the conflict that led to the partitioning of his Third Reich and the rise of the DDR and the Wall. Other exhibits expounded the passive-resistance philosophy of Gandhi and Lech Walesa, the peaceful revolutionaries who are Hildebrandt's most hallowed heroes, his symbols foreshadowing the day when the Wall could come tumbling down.

I had read that as a student in Nazi days, Hildebrandt had worked with two other resisters, men who had been tortured in the Gestapo cellars of Prinz-Albrecht-Strasse, not far from Hitler's death pyre, the *Führerbunker,* all very much part of this neighborhood, now home of Checkpoint Charlie and its museum. Making my way through Hildebrandt's garish exhibits, I wondered how many of the tourists, most of them young vacationers from West Germany, had ever heard of his anti-Nazi resistance heroes, Albrecht Haushofer and Harro Schulze-Boysen.*

------

* Even according to the rules of inhumanity applied by the Nazis when they murdered their most despised opponents, these revolutionaries died terrible

Hildebrandt described himself as having been only a "mail carrier" for these conspirators. Some mail carrier! He was repeatedly arrested and interrogated, his life hanging in the balance, much as it teetered again when he was threatened with kidnapping by the Communists during his early postwar resistance in his anti-Communist "Fighting Group Against Inhumanity." That group, too, had failed, as Hildebrandt reminded me in our pizzeria, and the violence had appalled him. Yet was his whole life a failure, as he was claiming?

The books he had written, including a lively account of the resisters who staged the East Berlin workers' riots of 1953, had barely kept him alive. His career took a dramatic turn when he stood on Bernauer Strasse in the second half of August 1961. He heard a certain noise, a horrible sound, on this dilapidated street, half West, half East. He was hearing a smacking sound—bodies of jumpers who missed the nets of rescuers and broke up on the cobblestones, followed by the thundering silence of shock from spectators and passersby.

Hildebrandt could not stay away from Bernauer Strasse. Day after day, the fate of his fellow citizens on the wrong side of the street haunted him more urgently. They were being walled in, their windows sloppily slammed shut by bricks, slowly, very slowly. Floor by floor, teams of government masons, *Vopos* watching at their side, worked their way up the street, up and up in each building. Each day people jumped to freedom and each day the risk grew more desperate as the distance to the street kept creeping upward until people were leaping off the roofs. More and more of them paid for freedom with severe injuries or death on hitting the ground.

---

deaths. Albrecht Haushofer, a history professor about whom Hildebrandt later wrote a biography, was one of the conspirators in the nearly successful attempt to assassinate Hitler on July 20, 1944. Less than two weeks before the Russians occupied Berlin, he and seven other resistance leaders were taken from the Prinz-Albrecht-Strasse Gestapo prison and marched to a park, where each was shot in the neck from behind. Harro Schulze-Boysen, a *Wehrmacht* lieutenant and a Communist, led the *Rote Kapelle* espionage ring that furnished intelligence to the Soviets in World War II. Most death sentences for political prisoners were by guillotine. For Schulze-Boysen and other key victims this method was considered too humane. On December 12, 1943, he and his twenty-nine-year-old wife, Libertas, were hanged in Plötzensee Prison at suburban Berlin. Along with six other resistance leaders they were placed on footstools. According to a minister who witnessed the scene, nooses were tied around their necks and then suspended from hooks in a wall, whereupon the stools were removed.

All along this street, Hildebrandt noticed, still photographers and film camera crews recorded breath-stopping scenes. The many miles of barbed wire and wall throughout the city became hunting grounds for cameras capturing the unforgettable: escapes, defections, reunions, wedding receptions, birthdays, all the milestones in the progression of family lives suddenly ripped apart, insisting to continue regardless.

This epic of separation, and the drive to overcome it, cried out to be told in a permanent exhibit of photos and memorabilia, Hildebrandt decided. The showman in him drove him to scout up and down Bernauer Strasse for months, looking for a vacant apartment. In October 1962 he opened the forerunner of his present museum. It lasted for nine years, largely financed by the sale of books and gifts that Hildebrandt managed to extract, mostly from politicians wishing to keep the tyranny of the Wall in the public eye.

After he decided that the stream of tourists from abroad made a move to Checkpoint Charlie desirable, my old friend Egon Bahr got Hildebrandt a government grant. Most of the construction and craft workers who installed the museum were volunteers compensated by no more than their meals, usually working nights. When Hildebrandt started charging an admissions fee it was so nominal that his talents as a *Schnorrer* remained oversubscribed.

He was a persuasive beggar, managing to make even the rich West German State Lottery spring for an occasional subsidy. The West German parliament held a debate affirming the museum's status as a national asset, and when Hildebrandt needed 5,000 marks to buy the only available specimen of the execution devices captured by Martin Gartenschläger, an American diplomat scrounged the funds. Ultimately the Haus became a largely self-sustaining nonprofit agency.

Resisters learn to be patient people and to be optimists, Hildebrandt being no exception, never mind his lament of being a failure. As long as there was a wall, he would be its press agent, relentless, letting its monstrosities speak for themselves. He had created an organization for this purpose, the Cooperative of August 13, and made it a source of public information for every statistic, every change in construction and in enforcement practices, every newsworthy defection. Former political prisoners and deserters from the DDR army, the *Nationale Volksarmee (NVA)*, could count on an opportunity to tell their story at one of his press conferences. Hildebrandt counseled the newcomers, helped get them jobs, and sometimes gave them a little money.

It was hard for Hildebrandt to picture Berlin without a wall, but not impossible. "Hungary already has no refugee problem," he said, pointing to one Communist nation whose people are not fleeing.

In the more than twenty-five years of the Wall's life Hildebrandt had become a principal father confessor to the professional "escape helpers" who made it porous, and he remained a leading consultant on ways of quitting the DDR. These days, his advice was not frequently sought. And it was simpler than in the past.

"It's much healthier to go to jail and come over from there," he said, echoing what lesser authorities on the subject had told me. "That's what we advise now."

For special cases—prospective emigrants with political pasts considered particularly odious by DDR authorities—it was still possible to obtain forged papers, Hildebrandt reported. Holders of such documents were sometimes encouraged to make a detour by flying to Moscow and booking their trip to the West from there. This route was expensive—the exit papers cost up to 50,000 West marks —but it tended to work better than exiting directly from Berlin.

Hildebrandt shrugged. Even special cases did not much interest him any longer. His pet cause was the entire vast DDR army, and his dream was to depopulate it. "Five hundred tanks are unimportant if five men in the tanks will come over," he lectured me, sputtering into the pizzeria, suddenly turned disarmament strategist. "Now! At once! That's the job to be done."

His principal frustration since 1961 had been the caution of Kennedy and his successors in dealing with the Communists. That wasn't the way for the West to gain credibility! Some West German politicians looked upon Hildebrandt as a relic, the last of the Cold Warriors. They were wrong. He was eager to get Red soldiers to climb out of their tanks so they would not shoot at people anymore. It was one job at which he was determined not to fail.

Hildebrandt's style of showmanship allowed for considerable sophistication, so since 1974 his museum incorporated a permanent exhibit of impressive professional paintings, mostly winners of art competitions sponsored by the Haus. All the works attacked the inhumanity of the Wall. On display (and reproduced in a stunning catalogue) was Oskar Kokoschka's endlessly bleak *View of East Berlin;* George Louis's *Day of German Unity,* with desperate hooded figures tumbling across the Wall to reach Western prosperity as symbolized by a plump, vacantly staring, but sexy nude; Matthias Köppel's *Tearing Down the Berlin Wall,* showing an Eastern and a Western worker about to shake hands across the Wall's ruins; dozens of other canvases depicting pain and separation, by such artists as Anton Tapies, and Bernhard Heiliger.

Few of the works dealt with the Wall itself. Many artists told Hildebrandt that they considered the structure too overpowering a subject. "You must have *touched* the Wall yourself to comprehend that it is real," said the painter Michel Butor.

As a canny propagandist, Hildebrandt also knew how to turn the bewildering anarchy of the Wall's Western graffiti against the DDR. He was selling a shocking collection of this populist art in a colorfully illustrated book, *The Wall Speaks,* and he encouraged such artists as Jonathan Borofsky and Richard Hambleton to shout their indignation in paint along "the longest concrete canvas in the world."

In October 1986, Hildebrandt attracted Keith Haring, famous as an illegal decorator of the New York subways, able to command up to $50,000 for a canvas, to contribute a one-hundred-yard mural of acrylic on the cement near Checkpoint Charlie. The Wall was so densely occupied by artistry for so many miles that Haring had to paint over numerous amateur painters. The work took the bespectacled twenty-eight-year-old six hours, and its purpose gratified him.

"It's about both sides coming together," said Haring, echoing his sponsor Hildebrandt's philosophy, "a political and subversive act, an attempt to psychologically destroy the Wall by painting it."

No, Rainer Hildebrandt the resister was not a failure.

Consistent with the circumstance that almost everything in Berlin comes equipped with two opposing faces, I had been privately briefed about the Western graffiti from the Eastern viewpoint during the preceding summer.

The briefing was very private—for me alone—and very official and unexpected. It took place within the East columns of the Brandenburg Gate, in an easily overlooked former guardhouse rebuilt into a surprisingly posh museum with lecture rooms—a counter-museum, a defense against Hildebrandt's propaganda.

This was no public place. It catered to an exclusive crowd. In all my years in Berlin I had never heard of it, nor ever met anybody who had. It served selected guests only—the most privileged members of the supposedly classless Marxist society, especially ranking visitors from the Warsaw Pact Communist nations. I am certain that the DDR government feels uncomfortable about this curious establishment, because it reflects the ambivalence about the necessity of putting up a wall to keep an entire society from collapsing.

For two years I had been appealing to the DDR Foreign Ministry to help me gain insights into the government's true attitudes toward the unmentionable or barely mentionable Wall. The invitation to visit the museum at the Brandenburg Gate was the first direct response. I found the setup spellbinding.

There was nothing ambiguous about the briefer at this tidy and curiously deserted place (nobody came or called while I was there, and I wouldn't have been surprised if I was the day's only visitor). My guide was the museum director, an army lieutenant colonel named Hartmut Beyer, firm-voiced and handsome like briefers all over the world. He had been a sergeant serving at the border on the great day, August 13, 1961, and once he had placed me within a student-type desk-and-chair, taken over the lectern, and seized a pointing stick, I thought I was back in infantry basic training at Camp Wheeler, Georgia, during World War II.

Colonel Beyer's manner changed abruptly. He had been pleasant and relaxed in the early minutes of our encounter. At the lectern, his tone turned hostile as he barked out an obviously well-studied recitation of the West's disgusting disrespect for the DDR's border, down to this very day.

The Western graffiti were a particularly glaring sign of such disrespect, the colonel declared. He said that inscriptions such as *"DDR Verrecke"* (DDR Drop Dead) and *"Alle Roten in die Gaskammer"* (All Reds into the Gas Chambers) vented the spleen of criminals, criminals! Though the colonel did not say so directly, it was clearly his view that the Western powers should permit no such insults.

He represented the presence of the graffiti as evidence of DDR liberality. "We don't resist these things, even though the Wall is on Eastern territory," he said.

Much of the briefing was a tirade, supported by photos and

charts, against border violations perpetrated by Westerners. In German, the term for such violations makes the offense sound more personal. Border violations are *Grenzverletzungen,* and *Verletzung* is a hurt, an injury. A border violation thus becomes an *injury* to the border, inhumane and deplorable.

Colonel Beyer lectured at me on my school chair that 44,000 *Grenzverletzungen* had taken place in the preceding five years, not to speak of "nineteen hundred terrorist acts" in 1985 alone. I was aghast and incredulous, which must have shown on my face. The colonel stopped his rehearsed recitation to remark that "terrorist acts" included *"bewerfen,"* which means throwing things, including orange peels. An excellent example of a border injury, he said, was committed by President Reagan on June 11, 1982, when he deliberately took a teasing step or two across the border, presumably to show his courage in the face of his enemies from the "evil empire."

I said nothing. They had a right to resent the contempt that Westerners often display at Communist ways, and I was not about to defend silly behavior by somebody from our side, not even by a President of the United States, especially not one for whom I did not vote. Should I have protested against the colonel's interpretations of alleged acts against the border? I had learned that such remonstrances served only to cause informants to clam up entirely. Discussions with Communists were possible in informal surroundings.

This weird, silent museum was like signs in libraries of past times. Here the walls seemed to say, "Shhh!"

Communists groomed institutions to suit themselves. And this museum was far from the most forbidding.

54

THE SCHACHT FAMILY OF HOHENECK WOMEN'S PRISON

**Hamburg, West Germany,
September 1986**

Ulrich Schacht and his family, gathering together for the first time ever, were united by a terrible bond: a prison.

His mother, Wendelgard, "dismissed" by the DDR, had joined him in Hamburg. His wife, Carola, had been released from the DDR earlier. His sister-in-law, Bettina, arrived from there later. At various times, all had been involuntary residents of Hoheneck, the institution feared as the DDR's toughest penitentiary. More: it was the only prison set aside exclusively to "educate" women, and it humiliated the female sex in particular. Hoheneck was a microcosm of how the DDR repressed political dissent.

Of the Schacht family group, none had committed any act punishable in Western countries. Only Ulrich, now thirty, had not been formally a prisoner at Hoheneck. He was born there.

Ulrich never knew his father, and no photograph of him survived. He was Vladimir Fedotov, a lieutenant in the Soviet occupation army. Ulrich's mother had met him in her native city, the Baltic port of Wismar, where she was a stenographer and bookkeeper. When the Soviet authorities refused them permission to marry in 1950, they decided to flee to West Germany. A "friend" gave them away, and in November, five months pregnant, Wen-

Hoheneck fortress, perched atop a steep hill in Saxony about fifteen miles north of the Czech border, was used by the Nazis as a concentration camp and then by the East German government as an appallingly brutal prison for as many as a thousand women, about half of them "politicals."

delgard arrived in Hoheneck to begin serving a ten-year sentence for "inducement to commit treason."* She had been guilty of nothing but loving her fiancé.

From the distance, Hoheneck looked like a travel poster for fairy-tale medieval Germany. It was a walled and towered thirteenth-century fortress perched atop a steep hill on the edge of Stollberg, a county seat of thirteen thousand in the Erzgebirge, a pleasantly wooded mountain range in Saxony, about fifteen miles north of the Czech border.† In Hitler's time, Nazi storm troopers, the SA, found Hoheneck a convenient site for a concentration camp. Over the years the two massive wings had risen ten stories high, so that up to eight hundred, sometimes one thousand, women could be sandwiched into the place.

Eventually, about half of them would be "politicals" like the women of Ulrich Schacht's family. The others were true criminals, including nearly one hundred murderers; these received preferred treatment. They acted as straw bosses for the guards and were allowed to harass the "politicals." Twelve or more prisoners slept on three-tiered bunks in rooms usually measuring about twenty-five by thirteen feet, and shared two toilets with twelve additional inmates next door. The sense of total confinement extended to letters the prisoners could write home; they were limited to precisely fifteen lines every ten days.

The commandant during Ulrich Schacht's mother's time did have a soft heart for babies. He inspected Ulrich—born premature and weak—and ordered special injections for him, along with a month's hospital rest with double rations for his mother. Wendelgard, in turn, exercised imagination in guarding her son. When she was asked to fill in the name of his father on an official form, she wrote, "Don't know," realizing that the Soviets might seize the baby once they knew the father's identity, because the offspring of Russian soldiers were "children of the state."

"Better to be branded as a whore than to have my child taken away," Wendelgard said later.

After Wendelgard had served five months, her mother was allowed to visit her for half an hour. "Body contact," even hand-

---

* Her Russian lieutenant was sentenced to twenty-five years in a Soviet "work camp" and was never heard from again.

† The Erzgebirge area is a principal source of uranium for the nations of the Eastern bloc.

shaking, was prohibited. When Wendelgard wanted to hand over her baby to the grandmother, a guard blocked the move like a quarterback. Clothes and toiletries that the elderly woman had brought in her rucksack had to be taken back by her. At the visit's end Wendelgard darted quickly to embrace her mother and received a loud scolding for this breach of the rules.

All of Ulrich Schacht's family were devoted to the Lutheran church, and church services—permitted only once every few months—were great occasions for the inmates. They also became a special experience for the elderly country parson, newly recruited to lead the prayers. He had been told he would be facing hardened criminals. When the "politicals" burst into song, the old man sensed the truth, and tears rolled down his face.

On Reformation Day the following year, the hymn traditional for the occasion, "A Mighty Fortress Is Our God," was not to be sung. At the end of the service the inmates of the Hoheneck fortress spontaneously decided to sing it anyway. They did so with such gusto that the guards paled and looked out of the window in embarrassment. The old parson was never asked to Hoheneck again.

Triumphs were few. Because of her participation in the illegal preparation of costumes for a holiday party, Wendelgard was given twenty-one days in a totally dark solitary cell, with warm meals only once every third day. In 1953 she went on a three-day hunger strike. After Stalin's death an amnesty was declared, and Wendelgard was discharged to her DDR home. That was in 1954. She was not allowed to move West for another twenty-four years.

Her worst day in Hoheneck, always remembered, came when Ulrich was three months old and was carried away by car. Wendelgard had grasped him firmly in her arms and refused to surrender him.

"You pigs," she cried, "you pigs! How dare you take our children away! You pigs!"

She screamed until the effort caused her to collapse. The baby slipped from her arms. The transport nurse barely caught him. Wendelgard had lost possession of her child.

She was beside herself, especially since she knew other mothers in Hoheneck whose children had been taken long ago and who still did not know the whereabouts of their kids. Wendelgard was spared this fate because one woman offered resistance. This mother was to be reinterrogated by a panel of Soviet officers, but she refused to say a word until all the mothers were told where their babies were. The officers surrendered. Ulrich was placed in a Leipzig children's home, soon to be released to the care of his grandmother in Wismar.

Even in the DDR, resistance often got results.

The Berlin Wall was a motivator for the restless "politicals" of the Schacht family, especially for Carola, Ulrich's future wife.

Carola had never seen the Wall until 1975, when she was nineteen. Her mother was a ballet dancer, her father the conductor of the Riesa Symphony Orchestra. Carola studied viola at the Franz Liszt College of Music in Erfurt. Music was her life. Politics as such bored her. The less stultifying ways of the West did not. She grew euphoric whenever she learned over Western radio or TV of successful escapes across the Wall. She fantasized what it would be like for her to risk such an attempt too. The thought never progressed far. Escape was too dangerous. It remained a dream, a vague one.

One hot afternoon in August 1975 the fantasy assumed reality. Carola was on vacation, visiting her fiancé in East Berlin. He was on Army service with an air defense unit in the suburbs. She slept on an air mattress in a hole of a room on Köpenicker Strasse, near the Wall crossing at Heinrich-Heine-Strasse. Walking along the Wall with her lover ("I felt simultaneously attracted and repelled by it," Carola said later), she passed Saint Michael's Church, and her fiancé related that some years earlier many DDR citizens escaped through a tunnel that ran from beneath the church to another church on the Western side.

"If the tunnel were still there, I'd go through it immediately," said Carola.

Her fiancé said he wouldn't. "How do you suppose I'd find work in the West?" he asked. "What would we live on? Besides, the Western secret services would interrogate me about my knowledge of military matters."

Carola was shaken. The question of whether he would go through the Wall with her had assumed new proportions. The issue was: would he go with her through thick and thin?

"I'd go by myself," she said.

"Are you serious?" he wanted to know. It was his turn to be upset. Late that afternoon he told her that he had changed his mind and would go West with her. He did not tell her of the foolhardy crime he was about to commit. Not wanting to start out penniless in the West, he stole some secret DDR military documents that he planned to sell after his escape. Since he was a printer by trade and served with an Army printing unit that produced secret papers, the theft was easy. Naively, he left his loot in his room at his barracks, where it was quickly discovered. He received a six-year sentence, Carola two and a half years.

In Hoheneck she darned socks for eight and a half hours daily, along with a group of prisoners that included spastics, epileptics, and mental cases. Outside their cells, inmates were not permitted to talk. Vegetables were very rare in the diet, fruit almost unheard of. If a prisoner altered her clothing for a better fit, such articles were confiscated; even tucking in a shirt at the waist was an "act of sabotage," punishable by an extension of the guilty inmate's prison sentence. Two incoming letters were permitted per month, no more than one letter could be in a prisoner's possession at any time. Apples were occasionally for sale at a kiosk, which closed at noon—just before Carola could get there from her work shift. Again and again, each day, inmates were counted and frisked, frisked and counted. One visitor was permitted for thirty minutes every three months.

Physical mistreatment was rare, although once Carola heard a prisoner scream from behind double doors and then saw the woman emerge with broken glasses and a blood-smeared face. The daily indignities were so demeaning, however, that Carola sometimes cried hour after hour under the coarse blanket in her cell.

"Of course things were much worse in the concentration camps," she said later, "but I *felt* like a concentration camp inmate."

Since both the East and the West German governments encouraged secrecy, prisoners and their relatives were left in the dark about *Freikauf,* the ransoming scheme for leaving the DDR. Learning about this exit route from the prison grapevine, Carola could not get her name on the official ransoming list until one of her fellow prisoners left Hoheneck, notified her relatives in West Germany, and mobilized them to put attorney Jürgen Stange, Wolfgang Vogel's West Berlin partner, to work on her case.

After eight months in Hoheneck, Carola boarded a bus with eighty other prisoners for the West German reception camp in Giessen. She had met many prisoners who had to serve their sentences in full and others who were inexplicably rerouted back into the DDR—and despair—at the last moment before discharge. Carola was very lucky to be sent West. She never discovered why. Two years later she married Ulrich Schacht, having learned in letters from her former fiancé that he had changed his mind again and did not want to come West.

Bettina, twenty, Ulrich's future sister-in-law, had been vaguely thinking of quitting the DDR. Then she witnessed a scene that left no room for indecision.

It happened in May 1978 in her native Erfurt, a city of 200,000 in Thuringia, famous as a center of horticulture, and the decisive event took place on the grounds of the International Garden Show.

Bettina and her fiancé, Ronald, were sitting on the grass listening to a concert with other young people. Sitting there was not permitted. *Vopos* appeared with dogs to chase the audience away. An argument ensued between the cops and a young woman who wanted to photograph the confrontation. A fistfight followed. One of the police dogs bit into the woman's arm and wouldn't let go. Screams were heard. Fury boiled up, then general fisticuffs that led to numerous injuries and arrests.

Bettina's mind was made up.

"We wanted out," she recalled. "Nothing but out!"

Five days after they were married that fall, she and Ronald sneaked onto a West-bound train while it stood sidetracked and dark during the night at the Erfurt station. They were arrested almost immediately. Bettina was sentenced to two and a half years in prison. Ronald received five years, because he was found further guilty of "treasonable transmittal of communications." His treason consisted of having written a letter to friends in West Germany describing the fight at the flower show.

Bettina felt blessed for having been briefed by Carola about conditions at Hoheneck and she was consequently delighted at one liberalization instituted at the prison since her sister-in-law's confinement. During the outdoor "free hour" in the courtyard, prisoners were now allowed to talk to each other. Sometimes they could even play badminton. The harassment of "politicals" by the real criminals had remained the same. Bettina was treated as a second-class inmate, was instructed by a convict when and where to clean her cell and then clean it all over again. The pace of her work—sewing together parts of men's shirts—was determined by an inmate who had murdered her child.

Yet Hoheneck was evolving. When the tension between the politicals and the criminals grew so intense that Bettina contemplated suicide, friends advised her to appeal to an authority unknown in earlier days: a prison psychologist, and a female at that. Bettina never got to see that doctor, but within a week she was transferred into more bearable company.

In September 1979, after about a year in prison, an electrifying announcement came over the loudspeaker. Certain prisoners would be dismissed as part of a general amnesty to celebrate the thirtieth birthday of the DDR. "Crimes" subject to early release were announced after a suspenseful wait of weeks; they did include attempted escapes from the DDR. The amnesty period was to end December 10. When the day had passed, nobody from Bettina's cell had been freed.

Some of Bettina's friends had long packed. Bettina had not. She suspected that her husband would not be released early and that she would be kept back as well. Besides, the rumor mill reported that the ransoming agreement between East and West had blown up. Inmates were having "reentry interviews" with prison supervisors, which indirectly confirmed the bleak prospect of a return to the DDR.

And so it happened. Bettina was amnestied, as was her husband, but they had to resettle in Erfurt. There they were kept under observation, frequently arrested for short periods, and finally told on April 23, 1981, to leave the country immediately.

Ulrich Schacht's birth certificate stated that he was born at an innocuous-sounding address: An der Stallburg 7 in Stollberg/Erzgebirge. The document left unmentioned that this was the street address of the Hoheneck penitentiary. Ever since he learned the truth at the age of eight, he regarded his birthplace as an obligation to act as an opponent of the DDR regime, and he fulfilled this commitment all through his career as a baker's apprentice, psychiatric aide, dockworker, stagehand, theology student, and ultimately as literary editor of a West German national newspaper.

During most of this time, his poetry and his resistance activities via the Lutheran church kept getting him into trouble. Finally, in 1973, his editorship of an illegal newspaper caused him to have to serve four years in prison, much of the time in the Brandenburg Görden penitentiary, where Honecker was incarcerated during the Nazi days.

Schacht—bald, bearded, soft-voiced, and given to brooding—

saw nothing unusual in any part of this odyssey. "My fate is the fate of many of my generation" was his view of his travail.

With the growth of an illegal peace movement that included many female activists, the total number of women prisoners in the DDR increased considerably beginning in 1983. Hoheneck being full to the bursting point, more women were diverted to other institutions. The authorities made some effort to humanize the old fortress—warm water had been brought into the cells in 1976— but reports from released inmates struck the same old tragic notes well beyond the time when the members of the Schacht family had moved on.

"Hell can't be any worse," said a more recent inmate, Eva Marie Krause, fifty-two, whose asthma brought her "preferential" treatment: a two-person cell that she shared with a woman who had killed her husband by a blow with a vodka bottle. Frau Krause reported that by 1983 soap and toothpaste sent to prisoners by relatives were no longer authorized for distribution.

Doris Wels, a twenty-seven-year-old secretary, got into difficulties with the mail censor because she wrote home that the weather was nice, which was thought to be a coded message. And she reported this bon mot from her "educator": "I will convince you that you will only be free when you have divested yourself of your freedom."

In April 1985, Rainer Hildebrandt of the Haus am Checkpoint Charlie sponsored a press conference at which five recent Hoheneck inmates testified to much the same treatment once experienced by Schacht's relatives. In particular, the discriminatory treatment of "politicals" continued. The visiting mother of one such prisoner found her call at Hoheneck prematurely terminated because she managed to stroke her daughter's cheek.

Few prisons throughout the world treat prisoners with dignity. What caused the DDR, increasingly sensitive about its international reputation, to keep running Hoheneck as a place so unusually awful, a throwback to the age when the fortress was first erected?

Ulrich Schacht believed that the root cause was the Honecker government's lowly view of women. While equality between the sexes was official government doctrine, women in DDR society were greatly underrepresented in leadership and executive slots.

I brought up the conditions at Hoheneck during one of my

conversations with lawyer Wolfgang Vogel, who had called upon clients there many times. He agreed that the standards of the place were not ideal and ventured that prisons for women were more difficult to administer than institutions for men. Not wanting to annoy Vogel, I didn't pursue this dubious thesis. His heart was clearly not in any defense of this prison. In all the contacts I had with him, it was the only time I had seen him slightly embarrassed. Sangfroid was as much part of him as his tailoring, even in the face of scandal, and plenty of that was about to explode around him.

55

EPITAPH FOR THE ESCAPE HELPER INDUSTRY

West Berlin,
July 1987

The witness, Albert Schütz, sixty-three, a corpulent retired pub keeper from West Berlin, appeared flushed and shaky. He was broke, diabetic, and had not long to live. But nothing seemed fragile about his memory of a "Dr. Leistner" who came to see him in March of 1978. Over an excellent dinner at the Berlin Intercontinental Hotel, the "doctor" said: "I'm from the ministry in Bonn. Do you want to bring over some people for us?"

Schütz told the West German court in Bonn that he agreed without hesitation to assist the man from the ministry. Nor was he surprised to be sought out. Arguably, he had become the most successful and longest-serving of the escape helpers, credited with more than one thousand border runs. He had become a millionaire, the 300,000 marks he collected from "Dr. Leistner" in the course of four meetings having helped.

The Schütz testimony managed to pour further enigma into a growing mystery.

On trial were two top-level officials of the West German government: Egon Franke, the folksy, recently retired Minister for All-German Affairs, seventy-two; and his collaborator of sixteen years, the elegant, melancholic Edgar Hirt, forty-eight, his deputy for Humanitarian Affairs. This oddly matched duo was accused of embezzling, between 1978 and 1982, at least 5.6 million marks (about $3 million) of the secret government funds earmarked to ransom DDR refugees and aid church-operated hospitals. The pair supposedly shredded the documentary evidence.

Accused as an accomplice was none other than Jürgen Stange, the cozy little West Berlin attorney who had trailed East Berlin's Wolfgang Vogel as a dogged Sancho Panza for nearly twenty years.

These legal formalities only hinted at the real crime unfolding before the Bonn court. Since much of the trial—in deference to the Alphonse-and-Gaston politesse between the West and East German governments—was conducted behind closed doors, only tidbits of the proceedings became public. These fragments showed that the defendants were all but incidental. On trial was the East-West trade in the bodies of refugees. Corruption was the true issue. In the end, few heroes were left onstage.

Many questions were never settled. Who, for instance, was this "Dr. Leistner" who paid escape helper Schütz? Nobody ever identified him. He may not have existed. The ministry announced that no Leistner was known there. Edgar Hirt testified, "I was not Dr. Leistner." Yet solid evidence was introduced at the trial documenting that large sums from the ministry's "humanitarian" funds wound up at various times in the bank accounts of professional escape helpers.

At the time Schütz testified in Bonn, he was in terminal tax difficulties with his government; he had every reason not to lie or to claim income he didn't earn.

What did Minister Franke really know about the missing millions? Ill, smiling unsteadily under his beret, the moon-faced old Social Democratic Party wheelhorse kept insisting that he knew nothing, having deputized his confidant Hirt to handle all "details." Hirt, a bespectacled, thin-lipped art collector who lived in a $500,000 home, asserted the contrary. "Every single case was discussed with the minister," he testified.

At issue were "problem cases" of refugees whose escapes were financed by special ministry funds and monies appropriated to buy medicines and equipment for church hospitals in the DDR. This was part of the cash channeled through Caritas, a West Berlin church organization, to be "laundered." The Caritas records, which proved accurate, showed that the money was paid back, via the offices of attorney Jürgen Stange, into a special ministry account administered by Franke's man Hirt.

This merry-go-round was stopped by a change in administration at Bonn in 1981. The Social Democrats of Willy Brandt and Helmut Schmidt were voted out. The Christian Democrats of Helmut Kohl came in. Ludwig Rehlinger, the same rectitudinous civil servant who had initiated the ransom arrangements with Wolfgang Vogel in 1963, was placed in charge of Humanitarian Affairs.

Calling on Rehlinger at the new official's office, the Caritas director inquired whether the special cash transactions would continue to be handled as in the past. Rehlinger, not familiar with the unconventional arrangements, was dumbfounded.

"What?" he demanded.

"Well, the cash payments."

"What kind of cash payments?"

"Well, 1.2 million marks in one of the accounts."

Rehlinger ordered an investigation. Witnesses in the ensuing trial shed little light upon the missing money. No receipts or notes about the questionable transactions were found.

Rehlinger was untouched by the scandal, but the friendly Jürgen Stange became his own worst witness in the courtroom. Perspiring heavily in the heat of August 1986, he insisted that he knew nothing about the missing money. His further testimony tended to incriminate Minister Franke while absolving his old friend Hirt.

Under questioning Stange wilted and became mired in contradictions. The prosecutor warned him, "You're talking a rope around your neck" (*"Sie reden sich um Kopf und Kragen"*). Stange pleaded that he was suffering from an attack of "weakness" caused by the heat.

The court, suspecting possible influence of alcohol or pills, ordered a blood test, which proved negative. The charges against Stange were ultimately dismissed, but he never regained the portfolio as a refugee negotiator (he had been fired when the Franke scandal became public in 1982), and his public image was severely tarnished by his inglorious performance in court.

The eighteen-month trial ended in acquittal for the hapless Minister Franke and a three-and-a-half-year prison sentence for his deputy Hirt the art collector.

Another star witness strode cool, smiling, and immaculately tailored from the courtroom, having regretfully testified that he could add nothing of substance to the record, and that was the great Wolfgang Vogel.

His appearance at the trial polished his reputation to a still shinier luster. Although Vogel had negotiated money matters with Hirt

on innumerable occasions, the lawyer testified that when he heard
about the alleged embezzlements his mocha cup fell from his hand.

"Do you have mocha over there?" asked the judge.

"The cup dropped from my hand in West Berlin," said Vogel
smoothly. "But you can rest assured: we've got mocha too."

Pub keeper Schütz, whose escape helper profession contributed
so much to tarnish the trading in refugees, was by then living on
his colorful memories. In 1982, a West Berlin court sentenced him
to a year in prison for forging passports. Barely out of jail, he was
convicted again of a similar offense and fined 30,000 marks, payable in three installments. He sold his assets, even his rings and
gold watch, but did not manage to amass enough to make the final
payment.

Rainer Hildebrandt of the Checkpoint Charlie museum often
saw him idling about at the border, reminiscing for anyone who
would listen. Schütz's favorite story concerned the occasion when
he posed as "Ambassador Spörri" and his diplomatic car ran out
of gas at the moment he passed the border at the checkpoint, a
refugee in his trunk. Imperiously, he waved to the DDR guards to
push him across, and they did.

A onetime waiter in a fast-food chicken eatery, Schütz had acquired diplomatic status of a sort. Shortly after August 1961 he
first ran into CD (consulate) passports in Bavaria. The lettering
normally appeared on the personal documents of the *corps diplomatique*—that is, legitimate diplomats. The passports encountered
by Schütz were for members of a nonexistent "Confederation
Diplomatique." Sometimes Schütz said he came across these convenient escape aids from the hands of another guest at the Munich
Playboy Club. At other times he said that an associate found them
being peddled by a small-time swindler.

Schütz thought he could produce more convincing papers.
Farming out his jobs to printers in Spain, then in Greece, Turkey,
and Scandinavia (he paid 3,000 marks per passport), he ordered
"United Nations" passports bound in rich leather covers, embossed
in gold and adorned with copperplate type. The DDR, then still
hoping to be admitted into the UN, did not want its border officers
to insult representatives of such a respected organization. By 1964,
Schütz had brought more than four hundred holders of fake documents into the West, shuttling through the Wall with his own car
pool of six vehicles.

Success caused his prices to climb to 25,000 marks per escape, and he introduced new gimmicks. Having bought two American uniforms from impecunious GIs, he put them on refugees who passed the border unchecked in the manner of all Western Allied military personnel. It was his subsequent difficulties with his own West German government, not with the bad guys in the East, that brought him down.

On February 23, 1987, the despondent Schütz suffered a stroke and went into a coma. On May 1 he died penniless. On July 6 his widow received a bill from the West German tax officials. It said that he—and now the bankrupt Mrs. Schütz—owed 631,657 marks.

The escape helper industry was reeling, having suffered its most ignominious reverse earlier in the year. It had made itself look ridiculous.

The charade began in London, with huge headlines in the tabloid *Daily Mail* about a "dummy run" through the Wall. Driving the same kind of olive green Lada station wagon used by the Soviet forces, a DDR refugee wearing the uniform of a Russian private first class drove through the border control point at Invalidenstrasse, so the article reported. The guards saluted smartly because the camouflaged defector was accompanied by three "Soviet officers"—actually manikins decked out in homemade Russian uniforms.

The next day Rainer Hildebrandt held a press conference at his Checkpoint Charlie museum. He presented the defector, a middle-aged East Berlin tire dealer, and the plot's mastermind, Wolf A. Quasner, forty-five, for whom the venerable Hildebrandt vouched unconditionally. He had known Quasner for ten years as a "legitimate working escape helper." The *Daily Mail* and the British ITN television network having bought exclusive first rights for more than $10,000, the rest of the press followed right behind. It bought the story without having to pay and with Hildebrandt's authentication.

The yarn was published by media throughout the West: the wire services, *Spiegel* magazine, everybody. THROUGH THE WALL IN SOVIET UNIFORM said the typical headline on the front page in the national newspaper of the Springer chain, *Die Welt*. In East Berlin, the story was denied, which wasn't unusual. Only this time the DDR authorities produced records, and these showed that no Lada passed the border at the time and place given by the escape artists.

Some Western reporters started snooping, and a few days later the conscience of a West Berlin car painter got the better of him. He came forward to tell how he had painted the Lada olive green. The car had never left the West. Quasner confessed that he had fabricated the entire tale. He had only wanted to call attention to the impending twenty-fifth anniversary of the Wall, he claimed.

Hildebrandt, jarred, issued an abject apology. He had been taken in by Quasner and by the man's record of his work in the past. Hildebrandt offered to resign (the supervising committee of his museum refused to accept the gesture). It was "incomprehensible," he said, that a specialist of Quasner's stature would do himself in—Quasner, the trade's most accomplished forger of diplomatic passports, a technical genius who knew ink analysis and chromatography, whose own laboratory daily made the necessary changes in the "official" rubber stamps when the DDR placed its controls on a daily basis.

Quasner's workmanship was even documented in a thirty-minute film shown at Hildebrandt's museum and recording Quasner's masterpiece: a 1984 caper starring an East Berlin railroad worker, bearded and thickset. Quasner turned him into a black diplomat from Ghana. The conversion was accomplished in a Prague hotel by a professional makeup woman whom Quasner had retained. Accompanied by a real Ghanian, the fake black man, wearing dark glasses and a snappy suit, traveled by plane to Schönefeld Airport in East Berlin and took the shuttle bus to the Friedrichstrasse station. A breathtaking moment's scrutiny of his fake Ghanian passport sufficed to let him onto the elevated train to West Berlin's Zoo station, where Quasner was waiting with the man's wife and child.

It required a very nimble quick-change artist to juggle such risks and skills. Quasner qualified for the role. His standard business card identified him as the director of "The Escape Planning Bureau." On an older card he called himself a "Graduate Parapsychologist" who imparted "information on everything you wonder about." He had also been an antiques dealer and the operator of a nightclub in a West Berlin red-light district.

Such men liked to perform the selfless acts of a Robin Hood. They become tempted to milk rich targets like the *Daily Mail*. A little manikin masquerade was fun. Such men also scent when a good thing comes to an end. Wolfgang Fuchs, Albrecht Schütz, and so many others were gone. The *Stasi* lurked all about. The DDR authorities were, legally, letting more dissidents out of the country. The West Germans were taking their laws against forgery and other doubtful habits more seriously. The fun was fading.

"The trade is partly down and out and partly riddled by infiltration," Rainer Hildebrandt diagnosed. "The business of old no longer exists." There were too many other ways of crossing over.

56

THE WALL JUMPERS

West Berlin,
Summer 1988

The German Red Cross operates a small shuttle bus between East and West Berlin that repatriates citizens who have somehow circumnavigated the Wall and are deemed demented. Most of these free spirits are transported in only one direction: westward.

Travelers who crash from East to West rarely get sent back, because the DDR is likely to lock them up as criminals. Mental cases who dash from West to East are automatically classified as crazy by both sides and are sensibly returned to the Germany of their origin for psychiatric care.

A handful of the shuttle bus users were frequent passengers. The chief psychiatrist at the West Berlin hospital that admitted them again and again diagnosed them as "world reformers suffering from the Rudolf Hess syndrome."* Popularly they were known as "Wall jumpers," *Mauerspringer*. This label fit more precisely because these curiously agile shuttlers-between-worlds were less interested in causes, or in the respective virtues of the West and the East, than they were in the *act of jumping,* the anarchism of moving between two universes, the option to cancel the Wall—that absurd

---

* Rudolf Hess was the deputy of Adolf Hitler who flew solo to England during World War II on a maniacal personal mission for peace.

hindrance—to roam at will, switching from side to side, thereby nullifying an insanity worse than the aberrations pronounced upon them by the clinicians. The Wall jumpers battled the insanity of politics.

The notion that some of these crazies might be saner than "normal" people stirred the imagination of a West Berlin writer, Peter Schneider, who in 1982 popularized the concept in his superbly reviewed novel *The Wall Jumper.** Its cast of Berliners, all marvelously clearheaded citizens, unfolded a drama of incessant separation as they jumped and jumped across the Wall.

As if to illustrate Schneider's thesis about sanity, his fictional characters proved steadier than the real Berliners who witnessed the making of the film based on his book. A fake Wall having been built on a vacant lot a thousand feet away from the real thing,† the neighborhood reacted strongly. A drunk lined up at the film's fake Wall crossing, patiently waiting to be allowed across the fake border. Some people thought that the menacing-looking actors running around in DDR uniforms were real and rushed to the phones to notify their next of kin that the worst had happened.

Few were aware that the story of *The Wall Jumper* was inspired by the experiences of a real person, Rainer-Sturmo Wulf, a thoughtful thirty-four-year-old library employee. Nobody had kept track of how often Wulf had jumped (or otherwise traversed) the Wall or how much time he had spent in each of the Germanys at various times. Although he had been mostly resident in the West for some years, he was a child of the Wall, having grown up next to it in the East, in the suburban Potsdam area, using it as a playground and eyeing it as a platform to make a future statement, the way some men join the clergy.

At eighteen, wanting to declare his "private war upon the DDR" and "eager not to let the German question be forgotten," he jumped westward for the first time, just for a weekend.

Finding life disappointing on the democratic side upon his brief initial sampling, he returned home and wound up for six months in a penal construction camp. This did nothing to keep Wulf, the quintessential Wall jumper, away from what he called the "mortal

* Translated by Leigh Hafrey (New York: Pantheon, 1984).

† The construction job, rendered authentic by graffiti and careful architectural detail, was the creation of a firm that specialized in building imitations of the Wall for movie companies.

fear or euphoria, or probably both" that he experienced during the ninety seconds when he knew he had to make good his crossing if he was not to get caught in the act. Each time he jumped, he said, he did it in order to "liberate himself" all over again.

The experience was exhilarating, especially when the *Stasi* interrogated him on tape for eight hours and its officers voiced no objections as he railed against the DDR as being "highly neurotic and repressive." They let him go. The authorities, East and West, were getting used to Sturmo. Four times, in 1973, 1975, 1983, and 1985, he was briefly hospitalized in West Berlin, deemed psychotic, possibly schizophrenic, nobody would say for certain.

The last time he jumped and was returned to the West, the driver of the Red Cross shuttle bus welcomed him with a collegial smile, the way one received any satisfied regular customer. "Well, well," the chauffeur said, "if it isn't Herr Wulf! Been back over on the other side again?"

In my recent years in Berlin, I met three people I liked. They had almost nothing in common with Sturmo or with each other. Except that they, too, were Wall jumpers—like lawyer Vogel.

I was surprised when I heard that Monika Maron had left East Berlin for the West with her husband and son. Hers had been a twenty-year good-bye. She had probably jumped back and forth across the Wall more frequently than Sturmo Wolf, and her latest farewell was perhaps still not final. The DDR wanted her back. It had eased her return in advance by issuing her family a three-year visa, an extraordinary accommodation, almost incomprehensible for such an inconvenient woman now switching worlds with two men needed by the republic: her scientist husband and a nineteen-year-old son who had been due to enter military service.

Even among *Mauerspringer,* the status of Monika Maron, forty-seven, was exceptional. She was a brilliant, widely discussed writer, a public figure. Once a dedicated Communist, for a time even a party member, she had hoped that the Wall would have a democratizing, equalizing effect among East German citizens and keep them happily at home.

"Now we'll have real socialism," she remembered saying in 1961.

Starting with the "Prague Spring" of 1968, and the Russian subjugation of Czechoslovakia, the dream began to fade, and still Maron viewed herself as a deeply rooted citizen of the DDR.

Perforce the SED had to count her as one of its own. Everyone knew that she was the stepdaughter of one of the hardest Communist hard-liners of them all, Karl Maron, the late Minister of the Interior, that this feared founding father of the DDR had raised Monika in his home.*

Monika Maron's seesaw life became a painful family struggle between the state, acting as her substitute father, and the daughter torn by emotional conflicts about her identity.

"Something within me tells me that I belong here, that I must stay here," she told a Western interviewer in her shabby apartment in the Pankow district of East Berlin as recently as 1986.

The DDR authorities didn't always believe her. That year, without apparent reason, she was refused a passport to lecture in West Berlin, Paris, and Switzerland, where she had been allowed to travel many times before. She had been complaining publicly that she didn't want to be told what to do with her life. Perhaps the authorities believed that this temperamental artist, thrice divorced, was playing games with them, that they had to respond by playing their own games with her, if they wanted to tame her. So they kept refusing to have her novels published in the East, books long ago issued in the West to considerable acclaim.

Her choice of topics did not make her life easier. As a young magazine reporter she had written about the pollution of Bitterfeld, a large industrial city, by bituminous coal ashes. This research became the background for her first novel, *Flugasche,* though the plot revolved around the problems of women in the socialist culture. Repeatedly the DDR censors announced that the novel would be published in the East. Repeatedly they said that it wouldn't. It was as if the censors felt compelled to behave like parents vacillating over how to discipline an unruly offspring.

---

* Karl Maron was a late bloomer of exemplary diligence and versatility. During World War II he wrote the military commentaries of *Free Germany,* the newspaper of the German Communist exiles in Moscow. In 1945, at forty-four, he was made Deputy Mayor of East Berlin, rising subsequently to become the deputy editor in chief of *Neues Deutschland,* chief of the *Volkspolizei (Vopos),* and, 1955 to 1963, Minister of the Interior. Maron was one of those relentless administrators whose zeal made the trains run on time for his dictator bosses. One of the few benign facts known about his life was his marriage to Monika Maron's mother, who was half Jewish, of Polish background, and had spent the Hitler years in fear of deportation. She and her parents also were Communists.

In a sad nonfiction piece written for a West German magazine, describing her anxious wait for visiting Western friends at the Friedrichstrasse border station, staring fixedly at the locked, handleless metal doors, Maron's feelings about her homeland's dirt, the toilet smell, the clammy nervousness of the grim, hopelessly overloaded, sweaty travelers were plain, if restrained. A humane witness was conveying a scene of adults reduced to animals—animals or, as she saw it, children.

It was an experience I had briefly shared in the DDR, most transparently at the Friedrichstrasse station, that monument to indignity, that trademark of a system. Much had changed for the better in the DDR since the dramatist Eric Bentley turned away in disgust from the Friedrichstrasse border post in 1965. But not this four-level station. Much third world heroin is smuggled west from here, usually around 250 grams in a condom or toy balloon that a smuggler swallows and turns into an "anal bomb." That was a contemporary innovation. The ambiance remained Cold War frantic.

The exceptionally bright lights everywhere seemed designed to leave every dark spot revealed. You are stuck, trapped in the many lines of sweating bodies shuffling forward at an invisible pace; in the prisonlike confinement of the cells where the faceless *Vopo* officer manipulates his papers and his unseen computer behind a slit and you are surrounded by mirrors and cameras and blank metal walls, unseeing and feeling stripped; in the grotesque competition that the system provokes in the human rats trapped in the maze of control, one control after another and another and another.

You feel childishly tempted to sneak ahead of the laden old lady with the silly German hat, to evade the system of more lines, more papers, more faceless uniformed young men who look like elongated children wearing death masks, their hands moving papers and rubber stamps back and forth, their rubber stamps clicking, their eyes unblinking, watching, watching, for what? For not much of anything except to verify the central fact of the Friedrichstrasse station, to leave absolutely no doubt as to who is in charge. No portraits of Erich Honecker smile at you from Friedrichstrasse station, but they ought to be there.

The childish competition that pitches you against the other border crossers begins upstairs, at the Western elevated tracks, the moment the train doors are released to be opened and you race to enter the control system. Every time I make up my mind in advance. I will not maneuver to get out of the train with the first runners. I will not make a run for the silly *Vopo* controls. I will remember that I am an American citizen in my sixties, on legitimate research business. I carry no East German black-market money or anything else I need to hide, and I have come early enough so that I will not miss my first appointment even if the delay should stretch for more than the usual maximum of something close to an hour.

It doesn't work. I run, I weave ahead of laden old ladies with their silly old hats, I am trying to make Western time against the Eastern system, trying to play hooky from this reform school where I don't belong. That is it. Friedrichstrasse is a reform school. I have not behaved like this, have not run like this, since I ran to beat a cafeteria line in the tenth grade.

Monika Maron experienced the system differently. It was a daily routine. The DDR citizen cannot buck it every moment. That would have meant going crazy, so a Honecker citizen built up a measure of resignation. The DDR subject cannot maneuver like a human with an American passport. The trap is real, the urge to avoid the controls or to strain against them becomes desperate.

"Here you're *always* pushed into the position of a child," Maron told me during a remarkably candid conversation at her East Berlin apartment in 1987. Her most vivid recollections of the border passage at Friedrichstrasse were of her own childish attempts to avoid the experience, at least to postpone it.

Typically, she would have a visa to lecture abroad, perhaps for weeks or months. Her husband would bring her to the station, upset over not being allowed to go with her. She might be traveling to London. He had never been even to West Berlin. The separation was awful, the return home was worse.

"Once I came back drunk at two A.M., two days late," Maron said. "I was with friends in West Berlin and just couldn't leave. I kept remembering things I had meant to do but hadn't done yet. You never know what'll happen, whether you'll ever be back. Leaving is so final. . . ."

She had recently returned from New York, having lived for months in a drafty loft on the Lower East Side. Ill with a kidney infection, she hadn't wanted to leave at all, had wanted to submerge herself in the excitement of the city. She was glowing, bubbling with the remembrance, a middle-aged woman, once beautiful, now worn weary by her schizoid existence, filled with the wonder of a child swept away by the New York experience, feeling she belonged there, had merely been misplaced, assigned to live somewhere else by mistake.

"They forgot to have me get born there," she told me, laughing. She laughed a lot. Her husband had once said that Monika laughed so much because she was so sad.

Resettled in Hamburg in the summer of 1988, Maron seemed to be undergoing a rebirth. She had received an advance and a contract for a new novel, had bought an apartment for her family. Her complaints about life in the DDR were becoming more explicit.

"The listlessness made me nervous," she said, "and the snottiness people use against each other." The limits of life's goals struck her as absurd: "What kind of achievement is it when one has finally managed to corner a sausage and pickle for one's dinner?"

She couldn't stand "living on a leash," she said; "I was incredibly sick of constantly having someone yak into my life." And she could no longer tolerate the "creaky, self-righteous" tones of the mighty, the fathers, the men at the top.

The last theme in particular was familiar to me. It reminded me of a Monika Maron short story called "Herr Aurich." This Aurich, one of the mighty among the Communist boss figures in the DDR, was forced to retire prematurely because of severe heart trouble. Inactivity and powerlessness were impossible for him to tolerate. When he phoned his former office and asked for Herr Aurich and was told that nobody by that name was known, he went berserk. Recovered, he went to a café where Honecker smiled at the customers from the usual portrait on the wall.

Aurich listened as two women talked about the West German teak and marble fixtures recently installed in the bathrooms of the leading rulers in East Berlin. The women tried to console each other about the malfunctioning septic tanks in their own homes.

"My son says he wants to pour two pails of shit across *his* state vehicle," said one of the women, pointing to Honecker's portrait, "so he can smell how bad it stinks."

Aurich, incensed, screams at the women, shouts that he is one of the bosses, that they are to shut their mouths at once!

The women laugh, everyone in the café laughs.

Aurich, beside himself, yells that they are enemies, traitors, revolutionaries, they're to be locked up, locked up, all of them!

More psychotic than Sturmo Wulf or his colleagues riding the East-West Red Cross shuttle bus, Aurich clutches his heart and dies.

I remembered the story so well because Monika Maron had told me that this was her only writing about her stepfather, the Minister of the Interior.*

Peter Feller changed his homeland as swiftly as a conventional *Bürger* changed socks. In late 1987 he was a prosperous young East Berlin City Councilman, running a unique restaurant–cum–art gallery popular with politicians whom Feller amused with his impudent wit. When I met him a few months later, he had moved to West Berlin, was operating a similar establishment there, and was talking of starting up more such places in Bonn and elsewhere.

In his original restaurant, the Friedrichshagener Bilderkneipe in the East Berlin suburb of Köpenick, VIPs like West Berlin Mayor Eberhard Diepgen and big-name parliamentarians from Bonn enjoyed mingling with their DDR opposites. Secretaries phoned to reserve tables, sometimes two or three at a time. Artists and writers from both worlds convened to argue and trade gossip. Food and beer were solid and cheap. Homemade *Sülze* (headcheese) with fried potatoes came to only 3.15 East marks, about $1.75 at the official rate of exchange.

Feller knew he had a nifty setup in Köpenick. He had no intention of abandoning the East when he received a pass to visit an aunt in West Berlin for her birthday. His wife, Elke, and his sons, Martin, eleven, and Peter, five, had to stay behind as unofficial hostages. Feller crossed the border at the Friedrichstrasse station with a light overnight case, like any tourist.

He was preparing to return home when a West Berlin newspaper published a folksy feature story about a party Feller had run at his place in the East a short time before.

It had been a reception for some 150 politicians and media people, sponsored by a Düsseldorf newspaper. The usual crowd of

---

* In point of fact, Karl Maron had to retire from the ministry because of heart trouble and lived in poor health for ten years before dying of heart failure.

Western party leaders from Bonn had included the parliamentary leader of the centrist FDP. Copious toasts were drunk, snapshots were taken, shoulders were slapped. The FDP chief was quoted in the newspaper story as expressing his hope that the convivial restaurateur Feller would drop by to see him if he were to visit in the West.

An innocent pleasantry. Feller, reading it at his aunt's house in West Berlin, was shocked. He had no intention of looking up any Western politician. Under DDR law, this would constitute "establishment of illegal Western contacts." The newspaper story could become a pretext for serious troublemaking by the DDR "organs," the authorities. They had been eyeing the happy scenes at his restaurant suspiciously for some time, hinting they might close the place for trumped-up violations of health ordinances or disappropriate him and run it as a "people owned" state establishment.

He made up his mind on the spot. He would stay in the West. Surely his politician friends would help him bring over his wife and sons.

Feller had never been slow to grasp opportunity. Some years ago he had become thirsty walking around an art gallery while on vacation and asked for a drink. The gallery owner snapped, "What do you think this is, a pub?" Feller, then a gym teacher, wiry and short, reflected briefly on the gallery owner's rudeness—and his first artists' inn was born; it boomed from the moment of its opening until the *Stasi* locked it up when he left.

Once he switched from the Communist to the capitalist universe, he adjusted readily in some respects. His new West Berlin inn, the Rixdorfer Bilderkneipe in Neukölln, maintained a heavy oak East Berlin decor as well as the heavy old menu, although *Sülze* now cost twice as much as before and had to be paid for in hard, convertible Western currency, not East marks worth about 85 percent less on the black market.

Suddenly, a new fever overcame Feller: a drive to amass large amounts of the precious currency hovering within his reach. The prospect tantalized him. He signed up a partner to manage his new inn most of the time; took a job as manager of a country club in the daytime; continued to run his restaurant from 11 P.M. to 3 A.M., seven days a week; assumed a lot of debts; and never had a moment to exercise his humor anymore.

"I can't taste my freedom," he said, looking around nervously. And he was lonely. His old political pals from the West would not come to his new place. "They think I'm connected with the *Stasi*," he said, laughing briefly. His switch of worlds had gone too smoothly. Germans were too paranoid to accept an affluent quick-change artist without deep suspicion.

When I last saw Feller, he was continuing to search for someone to help him bring his family across the Wall. One of his sons had been beaten up in school because his father was a defector. Sometimes, Peter Feller said, he wished he was back in the East.

Karl-Ulrich (Kalle) Winkler said he had changed his name to Charley Wings and wanted to practice his English on me. He had never regretted his move from East to West Berlin, yet he hoped to leave West Berlin soon. What did I think about the pop song scene in Britain? His visits to London had convinced Kalle-Charley that his chances of making it big as a singer, composer, and lyricist, a *Liedermacher,* were better over there than in Berlin, East *or* West.

Kalle had been twenty years old and looking, at most, like fifteen when he went to prison in East Berlin for thirteen months because his songs attracted "the illegal formation of groups"—that is, audiences of dissidents. Teenage *Spitzel,* informers for the *Stasi,* had been planted in his sell-out crowds, memorizing his lyrics, which ridiculed the Honecker government. For days after his arrest, Kalle Winkler faced relays of interrogators who read his texts back to him and asked what he meant by them.

For seven hours at a stretch they went back and forth over the songs that got him locked up, especially the one that went like this:

> They talk and talk their line,
> They pound it into me,
> They've got a lease on truth
> That never will be mine.
> And when I ask my questions,
> They duck and tell me lies,
> They flog and flog their phrases,
> They're nothing, just a guise.*

The accusation about the flogging of phrases annoyed the interrogators particularly. "Who flogs phrases?" they wanted to know. "The newspapers? The socialist mass media?" Kalle kept his replies general. He wanted to make his audiences think, he said, so that they might contribute to the improvement of "conditions." He

---

* Translated from the German by the author.

knew he would never persuade a *Stasi* man to understand him. He couldn't even make his mother or his stepfather understand what he sang about.

The stepfather was a prizewinning scientist, Deputy Director of the national Institute for Physical Chemistry and secretary of this distinguished institution's SED unit. His mother was an editor at ADN, the official government news agency, another bulwark of the Communist establishment. She loved him enough to come to his trial, only to be evicted because the public was excluded so that the "security of the state" would not be endangered. She had hoped to help save her Kalle from his waywardness, although it was much too late.

Even after that she adhered to the universal script of parents. "How can you do this to me?" she wailed when he called to tell her he was in the West, freed by *Freikauf*. "Why kick me in the behind like this, why be so ungrateful?"

Kalle kept asking why his mother and her party friends had to pose as being so infallible. Why could they not stand the slightest criticism? How could any society exist without criticism of any kind?

Winkler was no vacant rocker. At twenty-eight he could still pass for a teenager, pale, with a bird's tiny head. He looked pretty, yet he was masculine in manner, despite his absurdly narrow girlish waist. He was costumed in some tight black uniform full of rhinestones and wore ear jewelry, perhaps to please his agent. I knew this man had written a literate, not ghosted book about his DDR past and had given careful thought to how his rebellion against the lofty ways of his parents had turned him against the authority of his government and, after puberty, into a bullhorn (his term) of his generation.

That was back in Prenzlauer Berg, his home district in East Berlin, a workers' haunt set apart by its distinctive dialect-within-the-Berlin dialect. Prenzlauer Berg was the quintessential home of the proletariat, and the Wall its ultimate parent.

Like Sturmo Wulf and my friend Bärbel Grübel from Reinhardtstrasse in Berlin Mitte, Kalle Winkler was a child of the Wall. He grew up two blocks away from it, on Baumschulenweg, went to school there, went sleigh riding on the embankment where the Wall cut off all the trains. Sometimes the ball went across the Wall when Kalle played soccer with his friends. Sometimes a DDR *Vopo* kicked it back. When a ball remained lost behind the Wall, Kalle and his friends blamed the boy who kicked it out of the country, not their government for putting up the obstacle.

The Wall was a given. Behind it lurked the "class enemy," murky, evil beings whom the teachers couldn't or wouldn't explain, at least not in ways comprehensible to kids. This enemy was invisible. And he didn't matter, not to kids.

Kalle never hated the Wall when he lived in the East, no more than he could hate his mother, no matter how stridently they quarreled. The Wall hadn't separated him from anything that was his. Once he lived in West Berlin this relationship changed. He went walking in the old neighborhood, saw his school from the other side, his old playground, everything just a short distance away, even his house, the house where his mother still lived, the windows of her apartment. Seen from here, the Wall made a difference.

"It goes right through me," he wrote.

About twenty paces from one of the DDR guard towers he stopped and yelled, "You pigs, you murderers! Free the political prisoners! Down with neo-Stalinism!" Then he pissed a high arc in the direction of the tower.

It was his last loud protest. In the West, his music became less political and much less successful. The audiences were loaded up on freedom, felt no need to hear songs about it. "I live on social welfare here," said Winkler. "It's hard. But I do good songs."

As Charley Wings he would do more of them, good songs, perhaps still better songs, in London, separated at last from his Prenzlauer Berg self, his mother, from the Wall he had jumped across and had finally left behind. The border was losing its grip.

57

INCIDENT AT CHECKPOINT CHARLIE: THE BLONDE TURNED RED

**East Berlin,
September 1987**

For the umpteenth time in more than twenty years I was in line waiting to cross the border at Checkpoint Charlie. Even after inching through the same experience so often, I wasn't bored. The mood at Checkpoint Charlie invariably reflected the state of East-West relations. Something new and depressing was always afoot here, and, indeed, trouble was now becoming visible at the head of the line. I hated trouble at the border. It always slowed the slow proceedings further.

A shabbily dressed young man of apparently Near Eastern extraction, having been kept waiting on the sidelines, was summoned to the *Vopo* window and told he could not pass. He argued. He unleashed a lot of body language. He argued some more. Then he left, looking ready to kill.

The *Vopo* sergeant was the usual type. Barely out of his teens, with short-cropped wax-blond hair, frozen eyes, the mouth tiny, the lips tight and razor thin. His tone with the rejected man was like the sound used on nasty dogs.

Ahead of me in line, holding a dark green West German passport, stood an exceptionally attractive medium-blond woman in her late twenties or early thirties, tall and shapely. She not only had an extraordinarily pretty face but was also unusually well dressed. Among the tourists, the salesman types and the flotsam of

Checkpoint Charlie, I'd never seen anyone wearing such an expensive light tan raincoat with a soft little fur collar. Interesting.

The expression on the *Vopo* sergeant's mean little face did not change when the furry blonde's turn came. His frozen eyes studied her, studied her passport, studied her some more.

"I see here you have an appendix scar," he said, his lips hardly moving.*

"Yes."

"Do you have it along?"

I thought I detected some movement in the corners of his mouth, but this could have been because my imagination was being jarred by this remarkable development.

"Yes." The furry blonde was blushing. Very cute.

"Could I see it?" No change of expression.

"I don't think so," whispered the blonde, redder yet, and the sergeant returned her papers, turning blankly toward the next, far less appealing, case, me.

I was flabbergasted. Humor from the border dogs at Checkpoint Charlie? This was more than amusing. This was significant. Nothing happens spontaneously in officialdom in the East. East-West relations really did have to be thawing a little.

---

* German passports contain a space to record any distinguishing marks. When I was little, my mother used to say that my passport should identify me as "Always hungry."

PART XII

LOWERING THE WALL

58

THE DDR CHANGES ITS TUNE

His people were calling him "Honi" now; they were still underestimating their number one citizen, the pale Erich Honecker, ruler of what he liked to call "the first workers and farmers state on German soil."

Hundreds of jokes about him circulated. The cover of one seventy-page collection, published in West Germany, showed him bear-hugging and cheek-bussing Mikhail Gorbachev. The caption said, "As a politician he's a zero, but he sure can kiss!"

It was different among his peers. They thought the man had changed, had matured, was much more relaxed, more secure. "Little is left of the professional revolutionary," wrote Klaus Bölling, the former West German Representative in East Berlin who had come to know Honecker fairly well. "His most longed-for desire is to be recognized or even revered as a caring *German* father of his country" (emphasis added).

Bölling's predecessor, Günter Gaus, whose six years in East Berlin had allowed extensive contact with Honecker, noted another change: the greater "personal satisfaction" and "palpable pleasure" that the GS derived from running the DDR's foreign affairs, visiting with heads of state abroad, and receiving them with graciousness and pomp at home. The mementos in Honecker's principal office used to be the bric-a-brac of a party boss. Most of them disappeared when the office was rebuilt in the late 1970s, to be replaced by expanses of elegant dark brown paneling and an original Canaletto.

The most meaningful change in Honecker was, naturally, his age. Calisthenics, hiking, and the love of the outdoors had kept him in admirable shape, but the official photo of him that hung everywhere, the one with the bare hint of a forced smile and the jacket with the too-wide lapels, was twenty years old. At seventy-five, death or age would sweep him aside in the foreseeable future, though possibly not for some time. Advanced years were no handicap for Politburo service. The leaders were known as the *Alt-Herren Riege* (squad of old gentlemen). Four others were over seventy; Erich Mielke, the *Stasi* boss, was eighty.

Gorbachev was another dreaded uncertainty for Honecker. The DDR citizenry had shown itself crazy about "Gorbi" when he visited East Berlin. The people made it clear: they longed for the fresh air he was breathing into Communism. Feeling their power threatened, Honecker and his old gentlemen were terrified. Perestroika? Their first public reaction tried to dismiss it as old hat. They argued, quite seriously, that they had long ago pioneered similar liberal steps in East Germany. ("We started the multiparty system in 1971.")

American diplomats hearing these fantasies felt their eardrums twitch in disbelief. There was more of the same, and in graphic words: "Would you feel bound to repaper the walls of your apartment because your neighbor was repapering his?" This was not media chatter. It was the official position on the revolutionary Soviet changes as honed by Kurt Hager, the seventy-six-year-old principal ideologist of the Politburo, and it triggered a wave of gags about the shortage of wallpaper in the DDR.

The old gentlemen were not about to rock their own relatively safe little boat. Their gross national product per capita ranked them not far behind Great Britain, not bad for a nation the West had dismissed as nonexistent not too long ago. Why endanger such successes?

They had no fear of being unseated—"security" was too efficient for that. What pained them most about changes in the Soviet Union—so I was told privately by a high East Berlin official—was that the end results of the experiments in Moscow were unpredictable. Gorbachev might not succeed, might be replaced by someone with different ideas; anything might happen. The East Germans were not resilient enough to follow every zig and zag. Their own boat was too delicately balanced in waters with conflicting currents.

What, for example, were they going to do about the Wall? In the West they never got tired of talking about taking it down. President Reagan kept hammering at the theme in statement after statement in Washington, in West Berlin, even before an audience of students in Moscow. George Bush reiterated the chant later. It had become a chorus in chancelleries and on the street. *"Die Mauer muss weg"* (the Wall must go) had long been a slogan shouted by crowds, mostly young people, on the West side of the structure. Increasingly, throngs of youths were daring to shout exactly the same slogan on the East side, and not many were arrested.

More than twenty-five years after it went up, the Wall remained a vibrant cause, a permanent Topic A. The East was compelled to address it.

When I conducted a series of interviews with leaders of the DDR in September 1985, none was in doubt about the Wall, much less embarrassed by it. Far from it.* On the contrary, the Wall was extolled as a miracle, something like a new source of energy. This was a perspective unknown in the West and unsuspected by me.

"August 13, 1961!" exclaimed the director of the Institute for International Politics and Science, Professor Max Schmidt. His enthusiasm suggested that he had been asked to evaluate the invention of the light bulb. "That was the basic breakthrough! The Wall was our graduation exam!"

And how did Honecker feel about it in 1987?

"Honecker is proud of his role," said Schmidt, pink-cheeked and irrepressibly cheerful. "Now he is an international statesman!"

The professor did not look or sound like a traveling salesman, and yet a touch of Willy Loman hung onto him, a Loman who had wheedled a happy end out of life after all. Max Schmidt, too, was still looking for respect. Respect must be shown!

"We want to be respected," he called out, *"and we'll get respect!"*

Karl Seidel, the Foreign Ministry's head of relations with West Germany, dour, clipped, a former ambassador to Moscow, sounded triumphant in his own way. To him, respect was at hand.

---

* My shepherds at the East Berlin Foreign Ministry had done themselves proud in arranging my talks. Although I had not previously known the names of any of my informants, it turned out that they ranked at the policy-making level, just below the reigning Politburo.

"The Wall caused a rethinking process," he said. "It brought us an American Embassy [to East Berlin]."

Did he consider the split of the Germanys permanent? "The [West German] goal of reunification means the disappearance of socialism," Seidel barked. "We have another system; it differs like day from night."

Throughout all my talks, the Wall was shown off as an economic boon. The highest-ranking of my informants, Professor Otto Reinhold, the Rector of the Academy at the SED Central Committee, hit that theme hardest.

"The Wall paid off," said the grandfatherly professor.

He loomed bulky, motionless, seeming almost to disappear in his enormous office, because no light was being turned on in the gathering dusk. "It was a worthwhile investment. Finally we have clarity. It made normalization possible."

How was the Wall financially beneficial? Because it brought stability to the DDR. "Today all the Western banks are ready to give us any credit we want," said Reinhold. "Most recently we asked for $150 million, and they offered us $450 million."

Here was the real rub. With Western loans, the shaky economy could be kept going, could even provide an occasional orange from Italy. Without such support there was the risk of extremely hard times, with riots possibly following. It was a curious irony. Western capitalists supported a system that, at heart, they wished ill, and the Marxists needed to pray at the altar of hard money, which their system could not produce.

My high-level spokesmen had convinced me that there was nothing equivocal about the Wall. I emerged from the dreary, deserted-looking government buildings off Marx-Engels-Platz wondering why phones never seemed to ring there and thinking that the Wall would be as immutable a fixture as the Brandenburg Gate.

I should have guessed better. Only a year later, on January 10, 1986, an eleven-man bipartisan delegation of the United States Congress, calling on General Secretary Honecker, found East Berlin cheerier. The GS said nothing polemical, nothing hostile, nothing self-justifying, nothing in defense of his Wall, much less in its praise.

The delegation's chairman, Representative Tom Lantos, Democrat of California, a Jew born in Hungary and a Holocaust survivor, thought Honecker was "exceptionally likable." The General

In January 1986, an eleven-member delegation of U.S. congressmen *(below)* met with Honecker in East Berlin. "The Wall will come down," the East German leader promised them vaguely—as soon as "conditions" were to change.

Secretary smiled much, took many notes in a little notebook, and kept the astonished congressmen for three and a half hours. They had expected to be given thirty minutes. The next day they were pictured en bloc four times in the coverage by *Neues Deutschland.*

The high point of the session arrived when the ultraconservative Republican Representative Guy Vander Jagdt of Michigan, one of Capitol Hill's noted orators, posed the inevitable question.

"Why do you still find it necessary to maintain a Wall and when will you take it down?"

"The Wall will come down," said Honecker, and then he followed up with the expected qualifier. Economic conditions have to change, he said, without spelling out the ignominious: life in the DDR was still so dreary and relatively sparse that much of the population would run to the West if the Wall came tumbling down.*

Then Honecker waved a carrot. "You can accelerate things by encouraging trade," he told the Lantos group.

Although the congressional visitation changed nothing, it did offer evidence of a slow metamorphosis in Honecker's thinking. No doubt the Wall was needed when he put it up in 1961. Would it be as permanent as electricity?

Perhaps it could somehow be "sold" to the West,† ransomed for loans, somewhat like the political prisoners.

Already, dutiful readers of the monotonous DDR media could scent that their Wall was being converted into something less than a holy shrine. The very word "Wall" used to be unacceptable among East German politicians. It sounded too crass, too flat-footed: it was used only sparingly, in conversations with Westerners and only when failure to use it would have seemed awkward, too defensive.

Instead there was the official nomenclature, a hissing mouth buster even for Germans: *"Antifaschistischer Schutzwall"* (anti-fascist protective rampart). That gave it official perspective, the spin of the German Democratic Republic. By the early 1980s this term,

---

* Honecker's conciliatory-sounding formula, while actually not yielding an inch, blossomed as front-page news in June 1989, when Gorbachev echoed it during his triumphal visit to Bonn.

† Neither Honecker nor any DDR official suggested trading away the Wall for pecuniary gain. The notion was not fantastic, however. The dissenter novelist Stefan Heym (see Chapter 60) had predicted much earlier that the DDR would eventually use it as an economic bargaining chip.

never part of the spoken language, was passé. My official DDR contacts used the next-generation terminology: "border security."

By the time Congressman Lantos sounded out Honecker, "Wall" was creeping into polite society. Once the word actually appeared in *Neues Deutschland,* causing a sensation among those who appreciated that this was no semantic footnote. It was a substantive policy change. The Wall was becoming a secular phenomenon; its future was therefore negotiable.

The negotiations began, sort of, in September 1987 during Honecker's first visit to West Germany in thirty-nine years—but not during the formal part of the program. West German Chancellor Helmut Kohl, addressing a gala group in Bonn's elegant Redoute banquet hall, followed *his* party line by telling Honecker bluntly that the Wall had to come down.

"The people in Germany suffer from the separation," he scolded. "They want to come to one another because they belong together." The Chancellor then blasted the infamous *Schiessbefehl,* the shoot-to-kill order DDR border guards were to obey when they spotted defectors trying to cross the Wall to the West.*

Honecker replied coldly with *his* party line: "The development of our relations is characterized by the realities of the world. Socialism and capitalism are like fire and water."

All that was for the record. Honecker's real travel goal was the beloved province of his birth, the Saarland, which lies as far west as one can travel in Germany. The General Secretary's sentimental attachment to the region was famous. Oskar Lafontaine, its Minister President, recalled how he had first visited Honecker in East Berlin long ago—Lafontaine was still Mayor of Saarbrücken, nobody too important—and the General Secretary had kept him for

---

* For years Honecker took the position that there is no shoot-to-kill order. The facts are less clear-cut. The West Berlin authorities have registered more than 1,700 occasions since 1961 of shots fired at the Wall. Certainly the practice is decreasing. In 1988, weapons were used only twelve times. The applicable law, paragraph 213 of the DDR penal code, vaguely provides that "life be preserved" during border violations "if possible." Also, "if possible," shots should not be fired against women and youths. In 1989, Honecker claimed that border guards were instructed to use weapons only in case of "desertions" or a "direct attack on life and limb." Nevertheless, on February 5, Chris Gueffroy, twenty, a waiter, was killed by seven shots while trying to swim west across the Teltow Canal in the direction of Neukölln. The ambiguity of the DDR policy, in word versus deed, is no doubt deliberate, designed to keep fear alive while displaying a soft public relations line. The point is that gunfire is still reinforcing the Wall.

three hours. All Saarlanders received priority treatment on Marx-Engels-Platz. It was an unwritten rule.

Now it was Lafontaine's turn to greet the distinguished visitor, and he did so in the local dialect right at the airport: *"Fühle se sich wie dahemm"* ("Do feel like you're at home"). Honecker echoed in the same dialect: *"Wie dahemm"* ("Like at home"). He was very moved, and when the band at the luncheon in the Neunkirchen City Hall played the tunes of his childhood Honecker hummed along, his eyes moist.

His journey through the Saar had been an emotional experience along with political overtones. Honecker had visited Karl Marx's birthplace in Trier, where that area's Minister President lectured him about the thousands of tourists who routinely move back and forth between Trier and another country, Luxembourg, every weekend: "The stop at the border takes only a few moments; identification suffices." Then the Saarland's Oskar Lafontaine took over and struck a conciliatory note of commonality: "It may be *your* Weimar, honored guests from the DDR, but it is still *our* Goethe."

Before the luncheon at Neunkirchen, Honecker's sister had cooked coffee for him, and the pair had visited their parents' grave at the cemetery in their native Wiebelskirchen, now part of the city. On the street, some people called out, "Erich! Erich!" In the garden of his birthplace he had picked an apple. He was still holding it when he came to the luncheon.

"Many feelings move me," he said as he began to speak to 450 of his Saarlanders. His forehead was covered with a film of perspiration.

He started with the routine reading of a prepared speech. Suddenly, in the middle of it, he abandoned the text he had been holding like a shield in front of his chest, leaving it dangling in his right hand. Spreading his arms as if in benediction, he began to speak naturally, the way people communicate with a group of friends.

Everybody knew that two German states existed, he said, and that they belong to two different blocs. It was 6:35 P.M. on Thursday, September 10, 1987, as Honecker continued, his voice lifting: "That the borders are not as they should be is altogether understandable." If progress continued as everyone wanted, *"Then the day will come when borders will no longer divide but unite us."* Applause —hesistant at first, then powerful—stopped him.

Obviously aware that he had surprised the audience with his

dramatic message, Honecker quickly added cautionary details. He said he envisioned Western frontier conditions similar to those existing between the DDR and Poland to the east.*

Was Honecker's Polish qualification a quick recovery from a utopian reverie? Was the vision of a borderless border a spontaneous reaction to a pan-Germanic mood evoked by childhood memories? Or a carefully staged trial balloon, bait for the West? Whatever lay behind the maneuver, had it been checked out with Honecker's colleagues of the collective leadership, the Politburo?

Only Honecker and his associates knew, and they never brought up the point publicly. One of my East German sources, a Honecker watcher with decades of experience and excellent judgment, assured me he was certain, having followed the events at Neunkirchen City Hall on television, that the General Secretary's statement about the future of the Wall, however indirect and tenuous, had been spontaneous.

Circumstantial confirmation of this theory came from the large contingent of DDR correspondents covering the occasion for *Neues Deutschland* and the East Berlin news agency ADN. Obviously baffled, they sprinted for the telephones. Anyone could tell that their chief's lines about the border had not been in any script.

The DDR reporters did not rejoin their Western colleagues for an hour. During that time, some West German officials overheard them arguing with their bosses in East Berlin. The correspondents were pleading for guidance and clearly received none. Questioned at the Saarbrücken Press Center later, they were still at a loss.

If Honecker had planned to detonate a surprise bomb, he could not have succeeded better all around.

This man was no "zero" as a politician.

On November 25, 1987, the scent about the future of the Wall was picked up on the front page of *The Wall Street Journal*. GERMANS ARE DEBATING AN UNTHINKABLE IDEA: REMOVING THE BERLIN WALL, said the headline over a lengthy, astutely documented article. Recalling that the Wall had "long been regarded by Germans as an

---

* Border traffic between the DDR and Poland was in fact severely restricted. Travelers had to apply well in advance for permission to travel. Visas were always required. A notarized invitation had to be submitted from someone in the guest nation, and financial restrictions were also in effect.

immutable part of their lives, something that is just *there* and thus not worth discussing," the newspaper said, "that the fate of the wall is under discussion after all these years is striking."

It quoted Germans, East and West, especially West German politicians stirred up by Honecker's tantalizing remarks in the Saar, and added another dimension: Gorbachev's likely attitude toward the Wall, especially its monstrous liability as a public relations reminder of the coldest Cold War, an obsolete relic.

"I would be very surprised if there weren't an offer to dismantle the Berlin Wall in the next two years," former British Foreign Secretary David Owen told the *Journal*. "It's such a ghastly symbol for them. I can't imagine the Soviets won't do away with it."

The article reported a remarkable hint directly from the Soviet Union. Valentin Falin had suggested that Gorbachev might be prepared to do away with the Wall. As the head of the news agency Novosti, Falin was often a spokesman for Moscow. He was also a former Soviet ambassador to Bonn. He knew that he was suggesting news of historic proportions.

No doubt he also knew the most open secret of Honecker's waning years in DDR office: before he had to leave the scene, the former roofer from the Saar wanted nothing more than the respectability of an invitation to visit the White House in Washington.

59

TELLING THE TRUTH AND GETTING AWAY WITH IT

**Ridgefield, Connecticut,
Thursday, October 1, 1987**

"I'm the best known nonperson in the DDR," I was reading at my desk at home. "I don't get mentioned in the press, certainly not on television. . . ."

Stefan Heym was at it again. My former fellow sergeant in the U.S. Army, the Marxist, Jew, eternal refugee, currently Prince of Poets in Honecker country, was crowing away in an interview with *Die Welt*. Come again? *Die Welt*? That was publisher Axel Springer's version of *The New York Times*, West Germany's bible of business and Cold War conservatism, hardly a Heym fan. The interview spilled across two oversized pages along with some new photos that made Stefan look puckish and a little like Benjamin Franklin. It was like the *Times* devoting two pages to the political views of Benedict Arnold.

Heym was doing his shtick with the verve I remembered from his Army days. He was giving hell to his present-day fatherland again, his adopted home, railing openly against its prime symbol of divisiveness, its trademark, the Wall.

In the lofty manner of German interviewers, the man from Springer had asked, "What legitimizes power?"

"If you count on the power of the bayonet and don't have the approval of large segments of your population you'll never get anywhere," Heym responded, pulling his questioner down to terra firma. "Then you've got to have a Wall."

Acknowledging progress that had occurred under Honecker, Heym said, tongue in cheek: "Marx never prescribed the institution of the intershop."

Ouch! Even Karl Marx, his godfather, was no longer sacrosanct to Heym at the age of seventy-four. His interviewer asked why nobody had ever written a major biographical novel about the patriarch of Communism. Might Heym ever take on such a work?

"I couldn't do it," said ex-Sergeant Heym. "I don't think he was a likable personality."

Whew! What about the condition of Marx's world in these times?

"The world is split in a particularly nasty way," said Heym the poet-statesman. "The split is mirrored in Germany and finds three-dimensional expression in this appalling Wall." The sooner the two Germanys learn to get along together, he lectured, "the sooner we'll be able to tear it down."

Tear down the Wall? Could these be the words of an East German? Well, they were Heym's words, and that same week, in an interview with the European edition of *Newsweek,* he predicted some of the interim stages en route to the distant day of the Wall's disappearance. The first steps would have to be economic. The DDR government had finally recognized that it would have to let its citizens travel abroad. Millions of East Germans were already visiting West Germany every year. They were not going to depend on the charity of West German friends and relatives forever. They had to have spending money.

"The next step the East German authorities will have to think about is to make their currency convertible," said Heym the poet-economist. "You have to change all the economic patterns of present-day socialism to do that."

Heym did not seem to doubt that Honecker & Co. would come around to further accommodations, as the *Genossen* had accommodated themselves to his own trouble-making after he ignored their attempt in 1979 to get him to stop publishing books in the West.

"After that, they finally learned the hard way that whatever they did against me worked against them," Heym told *Newsweek.* "From that time on, they have let me do pretty much what I have wanted. The point is that when a government changes its international stance, it also gradually changes its intellectual attitudes. Once you want to be accepted in good society, you cannot go around belching all the time. So you will stop belching."

What about Heym's own belching?

In the *Welt* interview he made the point that he didn't consider himself a "professional martyr." To *Newsweek* he confessed that he was not about to tone down his rudeness, even though—or actually *because*—he was just about the only dissenting literary notable left in the DDR.

"I have no intention of leaving and I'll continue to make trouble," Heym announced.

He was not confining himself to the East. Even many regular readers of *Die Welt* probably didn't notice it, but its Heym interview marked a revolutionary turn in the history of the Springer media domain. All its publications still thumbed their noses at the legitimacy of the DDR government by putting quotation marks around every mention of "DDR." The Heym interview marked the first time that the East Germans had made it into the Springer press without quotes. Heym had told me in advance that he was negotiating with the Springer people about this condition he had set up. I hadn't believed he would bring it off.*

I would have to learn to take old friends more seriously. Heym was taming Honecker and Springer. Another old crony, Willy Brandt's alter ego, Egon Bahr, continued to make history with his promise of change "through small steps." Such as taking the quotation marks off the DDR and making conversation, at least, about the Wall coming down someday.

---

* Almost a year later, in August 1989 the Springer chain announced that it was dropping the anachronistic quotation marks from all its media.

60

INSIDE THE POLITBURO

**Washington,
May 1988**

"The Wall will go," said the tiny, round, red-faced Hermann Axen, his curly hair bouncing like coils, his head slightly cocked.* He jumped up in his fortieth-floor suite at the Helmsley Palace Hotel in New York. My time was up. I had been allotted one hour with Hermann Axen, seventy-two, the foreign policy secretary of the SED Central Committee, member of the DDR Politburo, one of his nation's founding fathers, the highest-ranking East German ever to visit the United States.

The security men at the door were shuffling their feet ever so slightly. Axen was due down the block, at the United Nations. Walking me out, very nimbly for such a heavy man, he made a stab at answering my unasked questions about the when and how of his Wall's predicted departure. Quickly, uninterruptibly, as if puffing steam, he muttered something about "relaxation of tensions," "down-to-earth compromises," then his eyes turned into slits; he grinned and said, "Anyway, I'm a better partner than Richard Perle."

Remembering how Perle, perhaps the fiercest of the Cold War-

---

* As best I could determine, nobody had ever asked Axen his exact height. I didn't want to be the first, because he is remarkably short. At a guess, he may be only a shade over five feet tall. Insiders have speculated that this was one reason why, over the decades, Axen preferred to stay away from television cameras.

Sabotaged by his apparatchik's ways, Politburo member Hermann Axen, the highest-ranking East German official ever to visit the United States, made few friends—for himself or for his government—on a 1988 journey to New York and Washington.

rior holdouts, left his post as a high Pentagon policy adviser because he was too conservative for the Reagan conservatives, I said that I wanted to tell Axen something about how difficult it is for some people "to put themselves in the other person's shoes" but that I could not think of the German equivalent for the phrase. (We had been speaking German, but I had said the words in English, knowing that Axen spoke the language well—if and when he cared to.)

"There is no equivalent in German," Axen said in German, and he was gone.

The inability to step into other people's shoes had been on my mind since I had heard quite a number of people in an American audience of about 250 first giggling and then laughing derisively at Axen a few days earlier. He was giving a talk in the Colonial Room of Washington's Mayflower Hotel, and it was a very embarrassing scene. I had never heard an international political figure being received with such openly rude contempt and disbelief.

Axen brought it on himself. He couldn't help that he looked like an apparatchik left over from the 1950s or that he could barely peer over the lectern. But his talk, which he read off haltingly in German for nearly an hour, was platitudinous, and when the well-informed audience began to ask questions, it became painfully obvious that elderly members of the Politburo, practicing their statecraft in ideological isolation cells, are not adept at the sort of give-and-take that comes naturally to people who circulate in a world without Communist blinders.

Militarism and anti-Semitism* had been eradicated in the DDR, Axen said. Laughter. Russia's glasnost reforms did not apply to the DDR, which launched a multiparty system in 1971.† Laughter. Freedom in the DDR was total. Laughter.

---

* While not publicly in evidence, anti-Semitism is far from dead in the DDR and flourished even among the intelligentsia. In late 1986, Bernd Loewe, a philosophy professor at East Berlin's Humboldt University, was asked by a group of academicians at the Free University of Amsterdam why a defector from the DDR, Professor Franz Loeser (see page 625), was not allowed to speak there. Whereupon Loewe, according to eyewitnesses, called Loeser a *Judenschwein*, a Jew pig. Loeser complained to the DDR National Prosecutor, who replied there would be no investigation, since the witnesses didn't understand the DDR man correctly. Loeser was able, surprisingly, to find a DDR lawyer who took the case and sued for libel. The matter was still pending in 1989.

† On paper, a catalogue of parties does exist in the DDR, but all are effectively

A determined debater, Axen got off some telling responses. The DDR enjoyed the highest form of freedom, he said, freedom from joblessness, drugs, and terrorism. "You won't find any homeless in our country!" he called out. None of this helped him, perhaps because his vocabulary was apparatchik language. The audience refused to take Axen seriously.

Reddening, his Saxon accent becoming more pronounced (K's softening into G's, T's into D's), Axen lost his temper and turned personal.

"There's nothing to laugh about!" he cried, wounded and in fury. "I lost my whole family! My brother was beaten to death by the Nazis, my parents were gassed!"

It was a propagandist's non sequitur, an errant bid for sympathy, a desperate lunge to choke off the dreadful laughter, the loss of face, the indignity that was sure to get back to his Politburo colleagues.

As a tactic, it worked. The laughter ceased.

Embarrassed members of the audience, exchanging notes later, agreed that in exposing the personal pain of his past, Axen had disclosed a truth of today that damaged him and his colleagues back home grievously. This man believed his own propaganda! He could not put himself in the shoes of others, people familiar with the facts.

He could not do it for Secretary of State George Shultz, either, I heard. The Secretary grew noticeably bored during Axen's exposition of DDR virtues. Nor did Axen move the American press; it ignored his presence almost totally, because he made no news that anyone could discern. Only the West German correspondents were delighted. They watched gleefully as Axen made himself ridiculous in America, West Germany's big ally.

The juxtaposition of the elderly Marxist and the Washington of 1988 did have an unreal air. "Rendezvous with an extraterrestrial," the *Frankfurter Allgemeine Zeitung* called it. THE ICE BREAKER CAN'T MAKE HEADWAY, sneered the headline in Munich's *Süddeutsche Zeitung*. I felt sorry for Axen. He was an isolate. What other country's leading "America specialist" had never been to the United States?

. . .

part of the government-controlled system. Minority parties play no independent role whatever.

In my private encounter with Axen, I tried, perhaps naively, to lay out some common ground at the start. Knowing that he was Jewish* and had been an inmate of Auschwitz and Buchenwald, I mentioned my forced departure from Berlin in 1937, that members of my family were sent to "the camps." Aware of his understandable pride in his more than forty years of service to the DDR government, I recalled that during my U.S. Army service in Berlin during 1945, I had interviewed Wilhelm Pieck, Walter Ulbricht, and Otto Grotewohl, the East German equivalents of Washington, Jefferson, and Lincoln.

I should have invested my limited time in other ways, should have had in mind that the Germans have no phrase for someone who wants to put himself into another's shoes. Axen was not listening. Talking with him in 1988 was precisely like talking with Walter Ulbricht et al. in 1945. It was like addressing a tank. Or the Berlin Wall. Or, to put myself in Axen's shoes, somebody who has been ignored for a long time and now absolutely *must* be heard, must get his story out, exactly as he saw it, immediately, in a headlong rush, before some enemy whisks the audience away and he is again talking to himself as he did in the bad old days when everything began, when—he remembered it well—his country was no country, just an occupied military zone in shambles. Only the Russians talked with the German Communists then, often not too politely, and often even they were not listening.

I had experience in questioning uninterruptibles. I once interviewed Castro, but he gave me six hours, so there was time left after he finished making speeches. Besides, I was asking Fidel about one of his favorite subjects, the battle of the Bay of Pigs, which he won in unique style. Talking to Axen about the Berlin Wall was, I realized, like talking about a close relative of his who had bleeding cancer scars.

People like Axen (of course we also know such specimens in the U.S., though not many in high places) have tapes in their heads:

---

* My indirect reference to Axen's religion was a calculated risk. He was in truth a practicing atheist. When asked about his Jewishness during a trip to London in 1980, he said, "For me that is only a religion which I gave up." The concentration camp issue, I knew, was authentic and alive with Axen. Friends had told me that, speaking at Buchenwald, he had appeared genuinely moved by the occasion, and that his text did not sound ghosted.

ready-to-roll speeches on vaguely applicable topics. These filibusters get reeled off to conversational partners, including secretaries of state, regardless whether the text interests the other person.

A straight answer to a straight question, an exchange of views, is rare. As I listened to Axen deal with inquiries that I managed to slip into his monologue now and then, I was reminded of a television coach who taught me how not to answer an interviewer's question. There *is* a way, not too rude, of sticking to your guns rather than picking up the other fellow's bullets. I suspect my coach learned the trick from Communist politicians.

Axen's tape was long and very detailed. His steam-engine delivery at full tilt, he rattled off a set of statistics intended to show that, really, there was no Wall at all. The DDR was no closed society, it was a sieve! His citizens made five million trips to West Germany and West Berlin in 1987, etc., etc.* (No mention that relatives are kept behind as hostages.) From there he took me to Fulton, Missouri, where Winston Churchill started *all* the trouble in 1948 by insisting that there was an "Iron Curtain." As I kept checking my watch, hoping that he would notice, Axen next exposed West German "plans" to invade the DDR in the 1950s and 1960s.

"They were going to march through the Brandenburg Gate with bands playing [*mit klingendem Spiel*]," Axen cried out, reddening. "What were they going to do? Sell ice cream? What an audacity [*Frechheit*]!" †

---

* To my amazement, Axen's shrewd and helpful chief of staff, Manfred Uschner, later handed me eight pages of his boss's personal briefing notes, called "argumentation," covering a mammoth agenda divided into five controversies. It turned out that Axen had spared me much: more statistics; his standard briefing on "humanitarian questions" (bottom line verbatim, "At present there are no open questions"); and a section entitled "freedom of information in the DDR." This freedom was described as "complete," indeed more liberal than in the United States. The proof: we imported only two films from the DDR between 1980 and 1987, while the DDR imported more than one hundred from us. Conclusion: "The DDR is in every respect open to the world. Of course we do exercise control so that no points of view are circulated that glorify fascism and racism or are directed against an understanding between peoples. Glorification of violence and pornography are also not permitted."

† The fiction of a planned invasion of the DDR, supposedly pushed by West German "ultras" (ultraconservatives) prior to the Wall, runs through all East German literature of the period and is still trotted out by Communist propagandists. Amusingly, this fantasy was lately unmasked once again by an authoritative source: Bruno Winzer, seventy-five, the highest-ranking West German soldier to defect to the DDR. Winzer, a major in the West German air force, left for East

My time was drawing to its end. Quickly, I asked what the East Germans would have done if the West had moved against the barbed wire at the border in August 1961.

"We never would have fired the first shot," said Axen.

It was shortly thereafter, as he ferried me out of his suite, that he made his flat prediction, "The Wall will go," which he followed up at the door with the last of several pleas for peace in the world, coupled with a final reminder of his brother, his parents, and the many other dead of the concentration camps.

"I don't have the smell in my nose, but I have the pictures in my head," he said.

Axen never mentioned his own incarceration, although at the National Press Club in Washington he paid gracious tribute to General George Patton's Third Army for liberating him from Buchenwald. Perhaps his modesty was traceable to still-unexplained mysteries left over from his early years.

Axen's experience under the Nazis at first closely paralleled that of his chief, Erich Honecker. Axen, who hailed from Leipzig in Saxony, also had a father active in the Communist Party. He, too, joined the Young Communists early (at sixteen), although his formal education at a *Realgymnasium*, combined with his broad later reading and a brilliant mind, gave him an intellectual base that Honecker would lack. Like Honecker, Axen worked for the Communist underground after Hitler came to power in 1933. Like Honecker, he was arrested in 1935 and sent to prison, where he read about American history, among other subjects.

Unlike Honecker, Axen was released in 1938 and—most unusual for a Communist of Jewish background—was not sent to a concentration camp but was allowed for unknown reasons to emigrate to France. With the outbreak of World War II, he was interned, then surrendered to the Germans, winding up in Auschwitz, where he had to labor in nearby coal mines, then in Buchenwald.

Something significant of a political nature had happened to Axen in France. His first immediate boss after the war was given a hint of the problem. Axen was running the Free German Youth

---

Berlin in 1960 and devoted the rest of his working life to phony briefings, speeches, and TV appearances "exposing" the West German *Blitzkrieg* that never was, as Winzer finally admitted. It "existed only in the heads of a few generals," the old soldier remarked early in 1988 when he redefected, to West Germany— this time, he said, for good.

movement in Saxony. His party supervisor told him there was no need to seek approval "for every piece of crap."

"Do you really need insurance so badly?" he asked.

"I lived through quite a bit, my dear fellow," said Axen. "The party didn't drop me for nothing in France so that I landed in Auschwitz. The party isn't going to mistrust me a second time. . . ."

Shortly afterward, Axen's supervisor learned that Hermann was indeed mistrusted, at least in some quarters of the party. The supervisor's boss said: "Keep your hands off him, he's a murky fellow. Some things are unclear about his immigration to France. He's supposed to have worked as an opposition agent there in two cases."

Whatever the facts, Axen was able to reassure those who counted that he was loyal. He was cleared for party work, and when he first met Honecker in the party's youth office in August 1945, even before the Free German Youth movement was formally launched, it was typing-at-first-sight.

"Can you write?" *Genosse* Honecker asked *Genosse* Axen, who said yes, whereupon he was immediately put to work typing ("with four fingers") an article for a youth publication that was about to go to press. When Honecker was appointed to head the Free German Youth, Axen became his deputy.

During the precarious days of the 1953 party purges, Axen, by then editor in chief of *Neues Deutschland,* reaffirmed his loyalty by informing on an old comrade. In the 1930s he had worked in the anti-Nazi underground with a functionary named Lena Fischer. In 1953, Fischer was expelled from the party's Central Committee for alleged sins committed eighteen years earlier and now conveniently remembered by Axen.

A report of the committee charged: "At the time of her arrest in 1935, Lena Fischer committed treason. She disclosed names of several Young Communist members to the Gestapo and gave the class enemy voluminous information about the development and activities of the illegal Young Communists and the Communist Youth International. Lena Fischer failed to communicate these facts to the Party. . . ."

Axen's tenure at the helm of *Neues Deutschland,* nearly a decade, was a failure in the cosmetic sense. He had been charged with developing "a press of a new type," using prose that would less resemble leather (as one West German diplomat put it). The leather stayed. He did much better as interpreter of the party's will, his experienced nose and a willing pencil tracking changing ideological nuances diligently ("The party isn't going to mistrust me a second time").*

Some of Axen's creativity went rather far. Heinz Brandt, an associate from the Berlin party organization, dropping in on Axen in his office at *Neues Deutschland,* found the pudgy little editor dictating a "secret American document." Axen was making it up as he went along and didn't stop when Brandt entered. Shortly afterward, the government "document" appeared in print.

Axen took pride in being tough. He smiled when a Westerner remembered that Erich Honecker had called him one of the "hawks" of the Politburo. Axen accepted the label as a compliment. Yes, he was tough and loyal and sensitive. He never forgot a slight. And invariably he positioned himself on the hard side of the Communist hard line. A 1968 paper from five Communist nations, warning the moderate Czech leader Alexander Dubček against continuing his reforms, bore Axen's signature. He did things the company way.

With foreigners he sometimes did much better than in America. He could be a charmer, witty in a cynical way, never at a loss for a deft response, his erudition emerging at the right times. In London, newspapers recognized him as a Shakespeare connoisseur. West Germans admired his knowledgeable comments about the personal habits of Goethe and Schiller. At one of Honecker's official hare hunting parties for foreign mission chiefs it was appreciated that Axen, wearing the obligatory fur hat, took over as leader of those who did not care to hunt. He named the group "the industrial-cultural department."

That was his social side. At the negotiating table, Westerners found Axen a relentless, rigid monologuer capable of working impenetrably hour after hour from one small slip of notes, never deviating from his brief by a comma. A photo exists of my old friend and ex-reporter from Berlin and Bonn, Egon Bahr, facing Axen during an East-West negotiating session. Axen looks like a bulldog. Bahr exhibits the tight mouth and slightly puckered cheeks of an ulcer patient who is about to vomit.

. . .

---

* Axen's continuing deep fear of being purged was not grounded in paranoia. In the 1940s, his newspaper had another gifted editor, Rudolf Herrnstadt, also a Jewish intellectual and a devoted Communist. Though Herrnstadt's prose sparkled, he was removed as a heretic.

Why would Honecker dispatch such an elderly Cold War hold-over as Axen to relax tensions with the United States? Again, it helps to place oneself into the shoes of the opponent. Axen was the Politburo executive in charge of foreign relations, and there-fore the appropriate ranking man for the mission. He was also, of the collective leadership's twenty-two members, relatively the most open, the most flexible, the most cosmopolitan.

Which, in turn, reveals something about that ruling body, the men from Wandlitz. Diplomats have joked that the rooms on the second floor of the Council of State Building on Marx-Engels-Platz, where the Politburo meets every Tuesday,* are airless. It *is* demonstrable that this junta runs its affairs as privately as the cardinals of the Curia in the Vatican, perhaps more so. Honecker's group is also known as "the Council of the Gods." Nothing of consequence, nothing, has been known to leak out of its meetings, for which every member is expected to arrive on the dot of 9 A.M. —rigid punctuality being as strict a requirement as a dark suit and a matching face. Not only is the Politburo's power total and un-challengeable. It manages to exude that impression by seeming to decide absolutely everything about everything that needs to be decided.

A former DDR dignitary whom I got to know fairly well, Franz Loeser, a well-connected professor of philosophy, was summoned to give a presentation to the Politburo and head of the DDR Peace Council in the 1970s. The appointment was arranged five weeks ahead of time. Working with his Politburo sponsor, Loeser pre-pared a seven-page briefing exposé. On the appointed day, he had to report at a small side door and was ferried to the second floor, past armed officers standing guard at every corner and via a pri-vate elevator. In an anteroom he waited slightly under an hour, along with more than a dozen other supplicants, each accompanied by a sponsor, like Loeser, and each looking extremely tense, also like Loeser.

The "Gods" sat in a semicircle around a long oval table, Ho-necker in the center. Loeser faced Honecker. The Gods were gentle to the professor, almost deferential. They seemed to be familiar with his preparatory memorandum. The questions were mostly general. "How important do you think this project is?"

---

* On Thursdays, Politburo members with executive functions, like Axen, meet for even more exclusive sessions—a fact that remained unknown for many years.

"How well organized is it?" Toward the end, a crucial point: "Is this going to cost us dollars?" Loeser said no and he was released.

The meeting lasted about fifteen minutes, but its purpose was so trivial as to say a great deal about the operations of the Politburo. All Loeser had wanted was approval to extend an official invitation to the American bass singer Paul Robeson to come to the DDR to sing. In nonsocialist nations, the decision would have been made by the manager of a concert bureau. In East Berlin, an invitation to an American of long-standing left-wing convictions, a hero, was a political decision. The pinnacle of the government, the entire collective, had to find time for it.

Was the DDR still operated like this in the late 1980s? By all available indications, yes. Only the static at the top and in the media had moderated somewhat vis-à-vis the West. Locutions targeting the *"antifaschistischer Schutzwall"* and the *"Klassenfeind"* had largely vanished. Slightly more conciliatory techniques dealt with some of the pressures upon the Politburo, especially the unabated, perhaps even growing, relentless drive of so many frustrated citizens who still wanted to get out from under, to scale the Wall, to leave home.

Among the Honeckers, the Axens, and their old gentlemen's squad, this rear guard of venerable revolutionary soldiers, fighting old age in their seventies, holding on for dear life, changes were paced grudgingly and were largely cosmetic, though not altogether so. Visitors like Representative Tom Lantos and his fellow congressmen were reading the signals correctly. The old guard knew it had to stimulate foreign trade to survive, had to do business with the enemy, whom they did not hate any less.

As an elderly senator in Washington supposedly once said when he changed his vote, Honecker and his old men hadn't seen the light, they felt the heat. And it was economic. The country was still desperately pursuing the same elusive and humiliating rabbit: hard Western money.

In the late 1980s, the DDR was a country waiting for a handful of old men to die. Honecker's likely successor, a younger man out of the Politburo, would be of much the same mold. No German Gorbachev was in sight. Yet the change that had occurred in the government's attitude toward the Wall in just three years was remarkable. Perhaps the Politburo would sell the Wall to the West yet.

And perhaps Honecker was hearing the clamor of those who

wanted to leave and the growing consternation among loyal party *Genossen,* especially middle-aged intellectuals.

I met a man in East Berlin, a professor of history, by his own account a devoted Communist, a loyalist who had had many opportunities to leave the DDR on professional trips abroad but was never tempted to do so, who typified the new restlessness. Unlike Axen, this new generation was opening up to the rest of the world. It was listening.

The history professor to whom I talked was quite literally listening, and in an imaginative way. (Incidentally, while he did not ask me to refrain from mentioning his name here, I feel I should not do so. I'm not at all convinced that he might not get in trouble for taking up an unauthorized Western contact.)

The professor visited West Berlin for historical research. The DDR libraries were not allotted sufficient Western funds to subscribe to some of the more costly Western academic journals. Certain reliable professors were therefore issued visas to visit Western libraries and copy information they needed. For each trip they received a per diem of 14 West marks, enough for a modest lunch and subway fare.

The professor of my acquaintance, reconciled to this indignity, used this travel to broaden his outlook by collecting direct evidence. Every time he was allowed to work in the enemy camp, he went to the Wall and listened to the talk of the crowds who peered toward the East from the sight-seeing towers that line the structure on its Western side.

"It's sad," the professor said. "The Wall hits us like a boomerang. In the West they think we're in a prison."

The professor convincingly denied that he kept his observations to himself. He insisted that he discussed his findings with his classes, his colleagues, even at meetings of his party group. I was so amazed to hear of this openness that I forgot to ask about the reactions of his people. Surely they were *listening.*

Honecker himself appeared to have been gripped by fundamental doubts about the cement handiwork that would be forever associated with his career, would be the key item in his obituaries. An intriguing clue came in June 1988 when an internal SED paper became public after it was distributed to middle-level party functionaries. The document was to help them answer questions from the populace. It abstracted statements made by Honecker on March 3 in a private meeting with a Lutheran bishop of the DDR.

The Wall, said Honecker according to this guidance memoran-

dum, was not built at the urging of the DDR leadership at all! It
was put up "upon the recommendation of the member states of
the Warsaw Pact." If this falsification of history represented Honecker's true and innermost thinking, this denial of paternity was
enormously significant. There could be little doubt that the memorandum did reflect the stance that Honecker wanted his party
leaders to convey to citizens.

In the DDR, the slightest shift of the party line was significant, if
the hint about it came from the top. A denial of responsibility for
the building of the Wall was like canceling George Washington's
ride across the Delaware at Valley Forge.

In old age, then, Erich Honecker himself looked upon the Wall
as a political liability. Having acquired respect internally, international respectability was supremely important to him. Perhaps he
would get invited to the White House yet. Even the lowliest of his
citizens were sampling the West routinely these days, if only at a
distance.

61

WESTERN TV CONQUERS THE DDR: THE NIGHTLY EMIGRATION

**West Berlin,
Summer 1988**

One of my American friends in West Berlin, Bob Lochner, the local ABC correspondent, considers the DDR a delightful source of television entertainment. The Lochner family came from Wisconsin, but Bob's late father, the great Louis Lochner, was the Associated Press correspondent in Berlin during the 1930s and 1940s, so Bob grew up on German movies. He became addicted to the action flicks made at the UFA studios in suburban Neubabelsberg, especially one ancient sci-fi classic about a spooky ocean platform, "FP-1," starring Hans Albers, the Rudolph Valentino of pre-Hitler German films.

This epic was called *FP-1 Antwortet Nicht* (FP-1 Does Not Reply), and I remember it with a delicious shudder because it was a favorite of my own Berlin childhood.

Along with other grainy relics, the film was inherited by the DDR from the Soviets, who seized UFA in 1945, and it now does duty as a bewhiskered rear guard in the DDR's long-lost battle to uphold its dignity in the television war against the West. Desperate to fill its airwaves with ideologically tolerable images, DDR television trots out a lovable old black-and-white soldier like *FP-1* with some frequency, and Lochner leaps on it like an addict finding his fix.

Since not many of today's viewers can call upon such long memories, audiences for these museum pieces are limited. Moreover, in

the politically more sensitive competition over public affairs programming, the DDR fares worse than in the entertainment market.
More than 93 percent of East German homes have TV,* but the
tendency to shun DDR programs is very strong. In 1985 the West
German Ministry for Inner German Affairs estimated that 85 percent regularly watched Western programming. Often, only 7 percent of households turn on the DDR's prime national news
program, "Aktuelle Kamera," shown daily between 7:30 and 8 P.M.

In the East-West ratings war, the losers could hardly slip further.
When a team of academic researchers asked a sample of 162 refugees newly arrived in the mid-1980s at the Giessen reception
center, "How often did you watch DDR television programs?"
the response was shattering: 72 percent said "very seldom" or
"never."

The devastation is not uniform. DDR viewers do not indiscrimi-
nately tune out their home team programmers, headquartered in
Adlershof, an industrial sprawl in Berlin's southeastern suburbs.
Sports programs are highly regarded, even by Western experts,
partly because DDR athletes tend to perform so spectacularly.
DDR children's programs do well, notably puppet shows. So do
some of the self-help counseling programs about (usually rather
innocuous) problems of daily life. And East German viewers do
not accept West German television uncritically as field dispatches
from paradise.

Withal, the demonstrable weaknesses of DDR television add up
to a harsh nightly vote against the government, a mass nose-
thumbing so glaringly rebellious that it must gall Honecker and
his Politburo bitterly. This confrontation on the airwaves is
unique. Nowhere else in the world is the East-West ideological
struggle reduced to such incessant and intimate hand-to-hand
combat. Nowhere else is the verdict so unmistakable. The effects are truly awesome. Western media researchers talk about a
new freedom, "the freedom of the eyes." And how DDR eyes do
roam!

"Most of the country emigrates every night at eight o'clock" is
the way I repeatedly heard the situation described.

· · ·

---

* As of 1981, the last year for which I could find figures, only 17 percent of
households had color sets.

Western TV makes itself felt in the DDR in a most insistent way. It is, first, an acknowledged component of the life-style. When people exchange comments about the news at their workplace, their most frequently cited source is *"Tagesschau,"* the prime Western news program, shown daily at 8 P.M. on ARD, the First German Television Network.

As the long-term effects of the Wall deepened the citizens' sense of isolation, the hunger for Western TV made its nourishment near-mandatory, almost a requirement of life, a pull so strong that Westerners find its urgency difficult to believe until they hear detailed evidence.

Traveling in the DDR during the summer of 1988, my friend Bob Lochner met a friend of an old friend. The political reliability of all concerned was clear; otherwise the ensuing conversation would have been too dangerous. The friend of Lochner's friend, a dentist, said he had just been offered a new, much better post. He had turned it down without hesitation, he said, because he would have to move to Zwickau, a town in the "Valley of the Unaware" *(Tal der Ahnungslosen)* of Saxony where reception of Western TV is nearly nonexistent for technical reasons.

"It would have been a lonely life," the dentist said.

This was a poignant summation of an everyday dilemma. DDR life *was* monotonous, boring, intellectually lonely for most people most of the time. Without the tickle of stimuli from Western TV it would be intolerable for some. The Valley of the Unaware was unmistakable evidence; so widespread was the dissatisfaction over the lack of one of life's essentials that the government was installing cable systems in some Saxon areas to combat critical labor shortages, an expensive admission of defeat.

The authorities had learned the lesson of the 1960s that the urge of the *Genossen* to peek at the TV programs of the *Klassenfeind* (enemy of the working class) was about as easy to root out as the drive for sex and food. It was like Allied radio during World War II all over again. Hitler's men executed people because they listened to the BBC from London under the bedcovers. The listening never stopped. The need to learn the truth about one's own situation and its context is overwhelming. People could not stand it when an outside force tried to close their minds.

With the building of the Wall in 1961, Walter Ulbricht eliminated most eyewitness reports of conditions in the West. Nearly all potential traveler-observers had to stay home. With one additional push he would pull the plug on "freedom of the eyes" and kill off the disgustingly alluring "factory of lies" from the West.

"The *Klassenfeind* sits on the roof," crowed Ulbricht, and his counterpunch was obvious.

This was the era when blue-shirted teenagers from Erich Honecker's Free German Youth clipped the antennae from roofs throughout the country. Not everyone had the nerve to chase them away with the fury of Volker Seifarth's father (see Chapter 34), and Ulbricht's campaign went on for years with waxing and waning intensity.

It was an ignominious failure. Wherever antennae were chopped away, they rapidly sprouted up again, much as in the Greek myth of Hydra, the many-headed serpent.

Honecker was in office less than six weeks when he took the trouble to appoint himself as the DDR's number one television critic in his first major address to the nation. Speaking before the Eighth Party Congress of the SED in June 1971, he promised to apply a new broom to Ulbricht's tired brand of Communism. A fresh social order was under way. To help move the reforms along, Honecker demanded that television "improve the programming" and "overcome a certain boredom."

Boredom. Coming from the Number One Citizen, it was a withering verdict, and it did yield some improvements. To liven up the DDR nights, Western series like "Inspector Maigret" whodunits gunned their way onto the screens. The new fun was in the entertainment programs, not in the news and public affairs shows, which, according to media research, the Communist public in its isolation greatly preferred. The deadliness of the programming in that arena remained unruffled.

It is difficult to do justice, credibly, to the boredom of these shows. Much of the material, tons and tons, celebrates the arrival, the agenda, and the departure of an inexhaustible supply of personalities visiting from abroad, singly or in delegations. No caller hails from a place too tiny or obscure to be honored.

Usually these chieftains appear to be in East Berlin to smile at Erich Honecker and to be smiled upon by him. Proclamations are signed. And many, many friendship treaties. Congratulatory telegrams are read. Factories, laboratories, and other showplaces of the "actually existing socialism" are inspected. Slowly, Honecker strides through all, bestowing his thin little smile, radiating equanimity and satisfaction. This part of the news usually runs first and seems to last forever. Wits call it "court reporting." They mean the kind of court run by Louis XIV.

Why couldn't Honecker's announced ambition to turn his TV warriors into minstrels more competitive with the Western media dazzle stem the nightly yawning over public affairs programs from Adlershof? Was lack of money a major problem? Lack of talent? Lack of nerve? A calcified bureaucracy? Probably. More: Honecker was implicitly asking his rigidified henchmen in Adlershof to make changes that possibly might stimulate controversy.

Such mind bends were abhorrent to the TV bosses. Changes could be dangerous. Livelier programming might have encouraged a diversity of views. It could have rattled the inviolate: the party line, the goose-stepping party techniques that pounded policy into the heads of the public. If the established ways of government TV were dull, at least they did not make heads roll in the home office.

As audiences continued their yawning and the popularity of Western TV grew, Honecker decided upon a move almost never undertaken by a Communist leader wrestling with a meaningful problem: unambiguous surrender.

One morning in 1973, *Neues Deutschland* tucked into its columns a surprising comment that Honecker had pronounced at a meeting of the Central Committee. In the DDR, so he remarked, people "can turn radio and TV on and off as they wish." That was real news! People in both Germanys were amazed. The CIA base in Berlin heard that the East Germans were absolutely euphoric; many people were clipping Honecker's liberating sentence from the newspaper and pasting it on their TV sets.

While the General Secretary could bask in his favorite roles of statesman, conciliator, and kindly uncle, he had really given in to the inevitable. It was senseless to turn an entire nation into scofflaws—like Americans during Prohibition. Besides, some Western TV paid convenient dividends to the Communist cause. Let the *Genossen* wallow in "Kojak" (one of their great favorites). Let them pick up the notion that America is Sodom and Gomorrah with drugs. Let the Western media shoot themselves in the foot with their definition of "freedom": let them spread the word about capitalist cutthroat competition and the inhumane exploitation of workers getting fired and lying homeless in the subway stations.

Never mind what tempests tossed the universe about, TV news

about the DDR exuded good cheer and order. Even ridicule did not jar its steady beat. My old Army buddy, that enfant terrible Stefan Heym, documented this immunity to levity in the February 10, 1977, issue of the West German mass weekly *Stern*. In his role as the DDR's Number One Disturber of the Peace, he published results of a personal "experiment": for a month he had foresworn Western TV and watched news only on the indigenous "Aktuelle Kamera" program. Tongue tucked in cheek, Heym claimed that the local diet produced a profound effect upon his psyche.

A pattern of sameness struck him in the clichés that riddled the news items. He listed sixteen nouns that appeared only in tandem with the same sixteen vibrant adjectives. "Recognition" was always "worldwide," "growth" was never anything other than "dynamic," and so forth.

The usual introductory quarter hour of international hand-shaking, proclamations, and other civilities was always followed by short reports portraying economic well-being in the DDR: factories bustling, production quotas being overfulfilled, no problems in sight.

The second half of the program marked a drastic turnaround, a tour of the world's malignant side: shootings, strikes, arrests, tortures, and other horrors that victimized the unfortunate citizens of nonsocialist countries.

To send the audience into the evening in an upbeat mood, the final fillip would be a reportage from some cheerful factory, school, department store, or other happy place in the DDR or another of the socialist countries. Nobody could mistake the message. The way Heym sized it up, "Everything is moving ahead, all are satisfied, the projections of the Plan are being met, all's well in the world of socialism."

For thirty-three nights, Heym claimed, he felt blissfully relaxed. The monotony of the programs comforted him. Entire sequences of phrasings began to sound so familiar in story after story that he wondered whether the newswriters were using standard forms, troubling to fill in only a few details to distinguish one item from another. In his analysis, Heym juxtaposed the wording in four stories with four stories from the next day's program. While the items dealt with different subjects, the word patterns were stunningly alike.

The program's use of statistics troubled him. Figures were not accompanied by comparisons. Nothing was said about the cost of anything. Suddenly one evening, "Aktuelle Kamera" angrily denied a statistic of which the viewers presumably knew nothing in the first place. Western sources were spreading word, the announcer read, that 200,000 exit applications were pending from DDR citizens wishing to leave the country. The announcer quoted "official sources" as stating that the figure was an invention. That was all. No details of any kind were offered, certainly no suggestion of a more accurate figure.

As his experiment ended, Heym wrote, the program's psychological effect spilled over on his bodily functions: "My right arm falls asleep. My left arm falls asleep. I fall asleep."

More than two years later, in its issue of August 27, 1979, *Der Spiegel* magazine published its own nine-page analysis of television in the DDR. It found that Heym's half-frivolous essay had been no joke. Its own judgment on the television war was: "unchanged." As an occasional viewer of "Aktuelle Kamera" between 1984 and 1988, I came to the same dreary conclusion. Until one has been exposed to "Aktuelle Kamera," one doesn't know how stupefying television can be.

No wonder that the East Germans refuse to do without the offerings of the enemy. Although the act of turning on "enemy stations" was no longer illegal, people were warned that it was wrong, that they were sabotaging themselves—in the words of one Communist ideologist, like "Trojans who wanted to get the wooden horse into their city at any price, even at the price of their own weakening." Nobody paid attention. The indigenous TV was too transparently phony to draw audiences after a hard day's work. Constant barely hidden exhortations to work even harder were particularly offensive and subject of many jokes. An example:

Question: Is sex work or pleasure?
Answer: It's got to be pleasure, otherwise it would have been shown on TV long ago.

To match the Eastern TV product against a sample of public affairs programming from the West, it helps to switch channels to Gerhard Löwenthal and his popular *ZDF Magazin*. From 1969, when he was forty-seven, until his retirement in 1987, at first weekly and then every other week, Löwenthal roared and snarled as the program's ringmaster for an hour and a half on the Second (West) German Television Network, ZDF (Zweites Deutsches Fernsehen).

If "Aktuelle Kamera" snoozed like a dog, Löwenthal careened across the screen like a kamikaze pilot.

I'd heard about him for years. In East Berlin he was a target as prominent as other star "warmongers," such as Konrad Adenauer. DDR refugees and their helpers worshiped Löwenthal as a saint. Conservatives in and out of government, including Henry Kissinger and Richard Nixon, applauded his outspokenness and courage. Two ZDF producers of my acquaintance turned bright red at the mention of Löwenthal's name. He was a Neanderthal throwback to the Cold War, they said—an appalling embarrassment to the network. Everyone with whom these two men worked, they reported, had tried to invent maneuvers to chase Löwenthal off the air before his legal retirement age of sixty-five.

Here was a TV performer whose name was a household word, though he did not sing or act or crack jokes. And his ego matched the image. The press compared him with Muhammad ("I'm the greatest") Ali. Löwenthal himself said, "My name recognition is like the Chancellor's."

Tall, lean, with horn-rimmed spectacles, wavy gray hair, a W. C. Fields nose, and the emphatic voice of a foghorn with sinusitis, Löwenthal stalked grimly about ZDF like Lucifer, waving a large cigar at his enemies, flushed with chronic indignation. According to him, he was practically the only fighter battling Communism.

One by one, his old allies were retreating into silence, not to speak of gutless Social Democrats like Willy Brandt and Egon Bahr, those hopeless appeasers. They were all being taken in by those scoundrels who ran the DDR! His "magazine" program was a nonstop assault on totalitarianism in all manifestations, with Löwenthal and his tiny band of heroes fighting off the Red hordes.

The deeds of the Soviet "evil empire" could leave him apoplectic.

"We're *the* resistance cell!" he shouted at me when I called on him in 1985 at his studio in Mainz.

At ZDF, Löwenthal functioned like a stink bomb at a sorority convention. Along with its sister enterprise, ARD (First German Television), the network is a public institution. Although it ran some commercials, it was largely supported by subscribing TV-set owners and taxes. Operating under a structure of advisory committees elaborately constructed to ensure fairness, it likes to shun controversy.

Löwenthal, loud and constantly enmeshed in feuds, enjoyed immunity, and for a remarkable reason. I never heard or saw it mentioned by him or anybody else, but everybody knew it. Löwenthal was a Jew, and the few Jews remaining in guilt-ridden West Germany enjoyed gentle treatment.

This was especially true for Löwenthal's category of Jew, the unquestioned hero. Löwenthal had survived all of World War II in Berlin. Along with a handful of other Jews, he managed to hide, to find refuge in a job repairing eyeglasses, to be taken to local assembly centers for transport to concentration camps only to get himself released by flimsy ruses. Twice he had opportunity to flee the country. Twice he refused to desert parents and grandparents. It was an odyssey in stealth and courage, and Löwenthal told about it, with unwonted calm, only when he wrote his memoirs upon retirement.*

Such a resister could hardly be denied permission to televise his "Calls for Help from the Other Side." In this regular feature of his TV magazine, Löwenthal named and often pictured political prisoners held in the DDR; he described the trumped-up cases against them and demanded their release. He considered it disgraceful that the government should stoop to *buy* liberty for such dissidents. He wanted to *blast* them out.

Löwenthal based his prisoner appeals on information sent in by viewers, usually the families of prisoners, residents of the West, sometimes of the East. Everybody was aware that the DDR was infuriated by such traffic, that the relatives and the prisoners could find themselves facing fresh retaliation. Löwenthal was undeterred.

"We said on the air, 'Whoever writes us will get in trouble!' " he told me. "But then if they write me, I can't throw the letter in the wastebasket. They know better what's good for them."

The furor over this dangerous drama with audience participation—probably unique in television history—never ceased. West German diplomats said that Löwenthal's televisioned appeals would cause the government efforts at assistance to collapse (which didn't happen). The DDR authorities kept threatening to cease all prisoner releases (which Honecker periodically kept threatening anyhow). Löwenthal kept claiming success by naming prisoners who were released following his appeals, ignoring the possibility that the same people might also have been liberated without his intervention.

The ZDF management, bedeviled by political pressure of every hue, reined in Löwenthal slightly, slowly, over the years, occasionally persuading him to tone down, sometimes canceling a particularly provocative broadcast. Löwenthal's huge fan mail never

* *Ich bin geblieben* by Gerhard Löwenthal (Munich: Herbig, 1987).

stopped. He was one unruly and inconvenient anti-Communist crusader who had built such a large and loyal constituency that he would not be shut up.

Less than a year after Löwenthal's departure, some media authorities already waxed wistful at his memory. "He was a lonely caller in the wilderness," said one expert, Professor Rainer Kabel, in Berlin. "Liberty in journalism doesn't become an issue often enough."

More and more, the East Germans were being fed a picture of West Germany as a mindless never-never land.

"All of West Germany is California," said Kabel. "You ride around in a convertible and you're allowed to do anything."

Löwenthal's partisan clamor was no longer in fashion. Instead, commercials were "in" more than ever in the DDR, especially automobile advertising. With the waiting list for tinny Eastern buggies still about fifteen years long, Eastern viewers had moved away from political nourishment to feast on the millennium of materialism in the shape of gleaming West German and Japanese cars.

The cars were not the ultimate attraction. They represented an idea, the fantasy that in the West everything was for sale and readily acquired. "It's nonintentional propaganda," said one of the experts, looking (at least to me) as if he didn't approve.

Some researchers thought that the content of Western telecasts was so overstuffed with satiety value that it anchored down Communist viewers and, paradoxically, contributed to keeping them content with their home environment. It was an interesting theory.

"Television seems to make political oppression easier to tolerate because it carries within it the insidious persuasion that as long as 'the box' stands, there are easy escapes from the dominion of Communism." So wrote George R. Urban, director of the American station Radio Free Europe, which beams propaganda toward Eastern satellites (but not to the DDR) from Munich. "In other words, 'the medium is the message'; television *is* freedom. The flickering image blots out the reality of oppression."

No doubt television affects some DDR viewers in this paralyzing way. I knew an elderly retired couple in East Berlin who spent about every evening, all evening, watching Western television. They might not have known where Chicago was on the map, but they knew every lyric from *A Chorus Line*. To them, Honecker was a figure to be pitied and ridiculed. Inconveniences and shortages of daily life kept this couple in conversational material. Why, there wasn't even any decent gift wrapping paper to be had! The grousing seemed to make them come more alive.

I once asked these people, very gently, whether they had ever considered leaving for the West. As pensioners, they could have moved across the Wall with nothing to hold them back. They fell from all clouds. What? Leave their cozy little apartment, their phone, their lifelong free medical care, the peace of their crime-free, drug-free neighborhood, and the wonderful, vicarious pleasures of their nightly fix from Western TV? Surely I was joking. TV was what they largely lived for; they didn't have to move to have it waft past their rapt little faces.

These were people in their mid-seventies. Who wants to change environments at that age? Plenty of younger people did not wish to accept the visual freedom of television for the real thing. Their names were on lists for applications to leave the country—750,000 of them by official West German government estimate in 1989.* The population pressure that the Wall was supposed to stop was not letting up.

---

* Between 70,000 and 80,000 DDR refugees were expected in 1989, of whom about one fifth were likely to be illegals and some 1,500 ransomed under the old *Freikauf* formula. According to best guesses, between 1,000 and 2,500 "political" prisoners remained in DDR prisons at any one time.

PART XIII

THE SCARS

62

THE BOOK OF BÄRBEL: "THERE IS A PIECE MISSING FROM ONE'S SENSE OF SELF"

Ridgefield, Connecticut,
Autumn 1988

I couldn't get the Grübel children out of my head. What were they thinking about their parents? Little Jeannette would be eighteen, Ota Junior would be nineteen. Under the East German law children reach majority at eighteen, so they could, on their own, make formal application to visit their real parents in West Berlin; or they could join the hundreds of thousands of East Germans who had applied for permits to settle permanently in West Germany. Whether the DDR authorities would permit these particular young citizens to travel was a question, although I thought that the threat of publicity in case of refusal might melt the government's dread over the revival of the odious Grübel case.

In any event, I thought that one or both of the Grübel children might emerge in the West tomorrow or at any time.

How realistic was this fantasy? I had vague memories of reading about the homing instinct that drives adoptive children to seek out their birth parents. This was said to be a strong and very common emotional manifestation, a compulsion almost, and while child development experts and courts were once adamantly opposed to such potentially painful expeditions into the past, the trend had turned. The curiosity of adoptees was considered inevitable, often irresistible. It was being treated with more sympathy, sometimes with offers of assistance. In the Washington phone book I found two national agencies devoted to helping adopted children discover where they come from.

How much of this might apply in the closed society of the DDR, where the government retained a considerable public relations stake in keeping the Grübel children happy in their adoptive home and encouraging them to forget all about their real parents? And while these kids knew they had been adopted (I remembered how little Ota had said, "My parents are not my parents. My real parents were arrested"), what could they possibly have retained by way of memories of their birth parents and their home lives prior to the spectacular abortive escape across the Czech-Austrian border in the dead of night in 1973?

Not much, I thought. At ages three (Jeannette) and four (Ota), hadn't they been too small to have preserved meaningful memories of that time? Why would they have developed a strong interest in meeting (if not rejoining) their biological parents?

Feeling in need of authoritative counsel, I asked the American Psychiatric Association to nominate two experts on the relevant questions. I was referred to Dr. Jerry Wiener, chairman of the Department of Psychiatry at the George Washington University School of Medicine in Washington, D.C., and Dr. Kenneth Robson, director of the Division of Child and Adolescent Psychiatry at the Institute of Living in Hartford, Connecticut. I briefed both doctors on the available facts and found their reactions stunning. Several of my assumptions about the probable emotional state of the Grübel children had been wrong.

The doctors agreed that the children could be counted upon to have developed an extremely strong interest in finding their parents. Normally such curiosity develops in adoptees between the ages of fourteen and sixteen.

And yes, the doctors agreed, even three-year-old Jeannette would have been old enough to have retained meaningful if fragmentary memories of the biological parents and of life with them in their first home in East Berlin.

And yes, the psychiatrists agreed further, the wildly dramatic movielike scene—the shots, the dogs, the searchlights, the threats of the gun-wielding soldiers at the border on the night of the parents' attempt to escape—would reverberate in the minds of these children forever.

Both doctors brought up "post-traumatic stress syndrome," the aftereffect of very painful experiences that often troubles children lastingly. Dr. Robson thought it was possible that the Grübel children might have expunged this particular trauma from *conscious* memory. Both doctors spoke of "flashbacks," "nightmares," and other likely disturbed reactions as well as likely "definite memories" of positive aspects of life with the real parents.

Finally, the doctors agreed that there was no way for them to assess from the distance how the memories of life with the birth parents, its negative or positive aspects, might have been processed by the minds of the children during the years of presumably secure, supportive, gentle living with the adoptive mother and father.

Dr. Wiener speculated that the children might be feeling much guilt. "It would have something to do with the trouble that they were not suffering while their parents suffered [in prison]," he said, "and possibly guilt over a feeling of relief that 'I'm glad I'm not in prison too.' " Dr. Robson considered it possible, even likely, that the Grübel children might have carried away from the events that separated them from Bärbel and Ota a conviction that the parents for some reason wanted to get rid of their children, that this was the real reason why the parents never came back.

Regardless of how the children might feel—or might have been influenced to feel—about Bärbel and Ota or about their adoptive parents or about life in the DDR, neither doctor doubted that the curiosity of these offspring about the facts of their early lives would be powerful.

"They would wish to connect with what brought them into the world," said Dr. Robson. "They'd want to know the facts, even 'Why did you really not want me?' "

"There would be a persistent, understandable, intense curiosity," said Dr. Wiener. "Its essense is a sense of incomplete identity. There is a piece missing from one's sense of self. 'Who are these people I have genetic continuity with?' "

The need to know the past and the urge to connect with it would persist even if the children were told that both parents and all their grandparents were dead (a not too believable wholesale calamity) and even if they had become convinced that it was considered unacceptable for them to wish to find their kin.

I matched these interpretations against reports about the children at the ages of three and four. While my knowledge had been filtered through the colored accounts of Bärbel and Ota and their necessarily increasingly brittle recollections, I had grown to know these parents well over the years and had absorbed enough solid scenes from them about their old life in East Germany to allow for some conclusions.

There were the scenes of how Bärbel and Ota used to play with the children and how they explained life under the DDR dictatorship to them . . . how these sensitive, alert children must nevertheless have absorbed a sense of the parents' fun and verve and enterprise, even luxury, from Ota's manic life of moonlighting and earning vast amounts of money as a free-lance interior decorator in East Berlin . . . how little Ota must have remembered something of the two whole days after the family's capture in Czechoslovakia when he had intense conversations, incredible scenes, in the hotel and in his mother's prison cell, right up to his separation from her, about the right and wrong of what was happening, about why the father had already been taken away, how his mother and father would never stop loving them. . . ..

These were not forgettable parents, I knew, and these were not forgetting children. Bärbel had talked to me once about the way she and Ota had raised their children in the DDR. It was a remarkable report—remarkable, that is, coming from a young parent describing her private life in backward East Germany. A long time ago Bärbel and Ota had struck up a conversation with a visiting West German architect about child-rearing methods. He had given them a book by the British educator A. S. Neill about the Summerhill School in England. The Grübels had applied Neill's methods to little Ota and Jeannette. Bärbel and Ota had learned how Neill distinguished between freedom and excessive permissiveness, how he developed trust in children and encouraged their self-development.

When other children came to visit the Grübel youngsters, I recalled, they couldn't believe their eyes. Little Ota and Jeannette freely shared their toys with visitors, and although Bärbel encouraged them to take afternoon naps, she wouldn't absolutely insist on it. The Grübel household practices, then, were quite different from the routine of other East Berlin families and were not likely to have left behind unpleasant memories.

If the kids had formed loving attachments to their adoptive mother and father as well, which seemed probable, and were nevertheless ready to upset these people who reared them into adulthood, they would face formidable practical hurdles. They would not know their real parents' whereabouts, perhaps not even their names. They would be unlikely to realize that they had once been, in a sense, briefly famous, that much attention had been given to their case by the *Spiegel* magazine and by the West German parliament, that Erich Honecker in person had issued the final ruling on the disposition of their adoption case, that Western news clippings about them could easily be looked up if one knew the name to look for.

I placed my bet on the Lutheran church. Every East German citizen knew that the church maintained working relationships in both Germanys, that its clergy served as middlemen in hardship cases, and that the ministers knew how to dig out helpful information about family connections. I would bet that if Ota Junior was too unsophisticated to know about the enterprise and freedom of Western media, which he could telephone, especially those stationed in East Berlin, he would find his way to a helpful clergyman, eventually if not soon. Or, like so many adoptive children, he would become something of a detective, return to his original adoptive home in Eisenhüttenstadt to question his neighbors of that time, or hunt up other links with his past. I pictured young Ota as the more worldly and more enterprising of the children. At least that was the impression that his parents had always conveyed.

My responsibilities toward Bärbel and Ota Senior seemed more equivocal. I felt I could use advice. I told my two psychiatric consultants that these two parents were emotionally and financially in fragile shape, principally because of the years of suspense over the fate of their children. Was I morally obliged to pass on to Bärbel and Ota what I had learned about the possibility of the youngsters' reappearance at some indeterminate time, if ever? Might I not increase their woes by setting off another demoralizing waiting period?

In view of the uncertainties, both doctors felt it would be best if I did nothing. I agreed, especially after reflecting over my encounter with the Grübels in Berlin a few weeks earlier.

Since they are not avid newspaper readers, it was I who told Bärbel and Ota at our last meeting about the sudden and surprising happy end of the case concerning the two Gallus girls. There seemed to be no reason why the Grübels shouldn't be informed of the outcome. They were likely to hear about it anyway; and I was curious to learn their reactions.

Jutta Gallus was thirty-six, an attractive, extroverted divorcée, a production assistant for television and theater in the DDR city of

Dresden, when she was arrested with her children in 1982 while passing through Bucharest, Romania, in an attempt to flee to the West with forged passports. Mrs. Gallus served twenty-one months in the Hoheneck prison in a cell with twenty-four other women. Her children, Beate, nine, and Claudia, eleven, were sent to an institution and then placed with the father in Dresden. The mother was legally deprived of the right to raise them in the future.

The case contained one element of high irony. The children were stars in a popular DDR television series, "View over the Garden Fence," portraying a tranquil family idyll under the coziness of socialism. Seven installments had been shown. The Gallus kids had been signed up for seven more when the show had to be dropped because the actress "mother" of the series had fled the country for the West.

In prison, the ubiquitous master attorney Wolfgang Vogel and officers of the *Stasi* warned Mrs. Gallus that she might well be released back into the DDR, where she would then be allowed to submit an application for legal emigration. Mrs. Gallus refused. Like the Grübels, she accepted release to the West by way of *Freikauf*, thinking she would there be more effective in getting the children to join her. The girls, always much closer to the mother than the father, wrote to her in prison almost every day.

Once the mother was in West Germany, more letters came from the children and phone calls filled with heartrending pleas to be allowed to come to the mother. The father was willing, the bureaucracy on both sides was sluggish. Carrying the girls' letters like live ammunition, Jutta Gallus went on a publicity rampage. For weeks she picketed at Checkpoint Charlie, distributing leaflets detailing her plight. For ten days she went on a hunger strike. She cried herself through many interviews, hounded Vogel and the offices of the sympathetic West German authorities. Nothing stirred.

On January 25, 1988, her daughters, grown to age fifteen and seventeen and very self-possessed, seized the initiative. Obviously well rehearsed, they appeared at the Dresden County Council with an exit application for the West. "Our fate was decided against our will," they wrote. "We are not prepared to agree to this any longer." The county officials pointed out that they were minors and therefore not authorized to act on their own. The girls said they didn't care. They informed their mother that they had left one copy of their document and sent off a second copy by registered mail, with a return receipt requested.

Vogel was negotiating details of the girls' release with the punctilious Walter Priesnitz, the new State Secretary in the All-German Ministry, who had succeeded Ludwig Rehlinger, and on August 26 the daughters and the mother were sobbing in each other's arms in the office of a West Berlin attorney. Vogel had brought them there.

Priesnitz commented to the press that he was looking forward to a gradual settlement of more "hard old cases." Vogel assented, observing that times had changed, that he stood ready "to contribute to a satisfactory ending" of such cases.

I phoned Vogel and asked him whether there was renewed talk about the Grübel case, among others. Cordial as always, the lawyer smoothly remarked that it had been a long time since the Grübel parents had manifested interest in their children. I interpreted this as a mild reproof of the parents' perceived indifference toward their kids.

I said that I recalled how he had some time ago informed me of details about Ota Grübel's conduct years ago in the DDR, behavior that caused the East German authorities to conclude that he would be less than an ideal father. Presumably this was the same information that the West German parliament had vaguely heard about in 1977 (see page 484). I had sidestepped the issue in the past because independent authentication of these ancient charges would have been impossible. Now I remarked to Vogel, as pointedly as I could, that the two parents were very different personalities, that nothing negative had ever been mentioned about Bärbel's past.

I suspect that this may have been a point to which Vogel had not given much weight previously. He made no comment. I had been thinking about the differences between Ota's and Bärbel's respective pasts and perceptions for a long time, and they seemed significant, perhaps crucial. Conceivably, the Honecker government could, according to its lights, claim some retrospective right to set itself up as a moral arbiter over Ota's history as a young man; I knew of nothing that might allow the DDR to assert such a claim against Bärbel.

That evening, while the Grübels and I were having a quick Italian dinner at their favorite restaurant, the pizza parlor on the ground floor of their apartment building, I showed them, without comment, a long newspaper clipping about the release of the Gallus daughters. Each read it without expression of interest. Ota offered not one word of comment, Bärbel said very little. I was startled. It was almost as if these people I had come to know so well were asking me why I had shown them the article. It was about other people. It had nothing to do with them.

When Bärbel finally spoke up, looking blank as she rarely did, she said nothing of the Gallus case except, briefly, quickly, how much it differed from theirs. The Gallus children had never been legally adopted; the father, who had custody, did not object to their moving West; and the daughters had been separated from their mother for "only" six years.

If Bärbel or Ota had noticed the reference to new efforts at reconsidering "hard old cases," they gave no sign of it.

The following evening Bärbel and I met at a delicatessen restaurant on their block, and she filled me in about a landmark event in her life, the reunion on her thirty-eighth birthday, which I had missed the preceding autumn. It had been something of a coming-out party for the Grübels, their first organized social event in many years. Bärbel had consciously picked the guests so she could look back on her recent past and gain perspective on her present self.

She scheduled the party to coincide with the opening of an exhibition of Ota's paintings, the stark artwork that brought him almost no money but occupied almost all of the time he didn't require for housework and home improvements. One of the first guests to arrive, Dr. Hampel, the excitable psychiatrist who cared for the Grübels when they came out of prison, picked up at once on the central role that the paintings played in the lives of his hosts and on his own importance as family mentor and cheerleader. Wearing a captain's cap, the old doctor strode in, pronounced the exhibit to be the greatest he had ever seen, and shouted: "You've really made it! I always knew you would!"

The Grübels, who had not seen Hampel for a decade, were immensely pleased.

And Petra came, the little dentist who grew up with Bärbel on Reinhardtstrasse, also invited for the first time in many years. And Clive Freeman, a British reporter who had written about the Grübel case long ago. The most significant guest was Heinz, who had come with his mother and his girlfriend. Bärbel had gone to school with the mother in East Berlin, and the son, a worldly young man well over six feet tall, was nineteen—precisely the age of little Ota.

Bärbel tried to talk to Heinz, whom she had known when he was a small child and who had played with little Ota in East Berlin. It was no use. She could not bring herself to communicate with this young man. He was too unbelievable, this adult, this giant. The thought that her own little Ota was this old and possibly this tall and worldly, with a girlfriend, was not acceptable. Or so Bärbel told herself and me. She could think of her children only as being three and four years old.

"I lost them at that age and that is where they remained to me," she said steadily, without hope.

Next she spoke of one of Bertolt Brecht's last plays, *The Caucasian Chalk Circle*. She had first read it when she was thirteen, she said, this tale of a tug of war between an adoptive and a biological mother. Each mother was ordered to pull the contested child out of a chalk circle to her side. The biological mother let go because she didn't want the child torn apart.

"It's my story," Bärbel told me, "my pain. I know what mother love means."

I thought of previous conversations she and I had had about the missing children. "The past is dead for me," she had claimed on one of these occasions. "The two children don't know where they come from. I don't believe they'll learn the truth. That's why I don't believe I'll ever see them again."

That was the evening when Bärbel, in her husband's absence, shared her beliefs about why she had to be the sole support of her family, why Ota seemed incapable of functioning in the workaday world. "If he wanted money, he'd have it," Bärbel said. "He's never been able to survive the loss of the children."

I asked Bärbel whether perhaps she manages to survive by repressing thoughts about her missing children.

"Yes, I do that," she said after hesitating. "It's essential to keep alive."

Reunions were unkind to the Grübels. These occasions only further underlined the brutality of the separations dictated by the Wall.

Bärbel's party for her thirty-eighth birthday had left the couple more depressed than they had already been. Secretly, they had hoped that somebody would buy one of Ota's pictures, if not on the night of the party then perhaps later. Nobody did. And during the same period they had lived through another reunion, bittersweet at most. This one was with Bärbel's father, Franz, from East Berlin, whom they had not seen for ten years and whom his granddaughter Sulamith had never met.

An elderly aunt had died and Franz, unexpectedly, had received permission to come through the Wall on a week's visit. The aunt was Franz's kin, which meant that Bärbel's mother was not allowed to accompany him. Bärbel's father and mother had never been apart for more than a few hours. The idea of his deserting her, however briefly, and going to the West through the Wall terrified the mother. She could not deal with the separation. On the phone to Bärbel she cried and threatened to kill herself.

Bärbel experienced an ambivalent reaction to her father's fleeting presence in the West. Of course she was happy to see him, yet the encounter was frightening. His voice seemed strange, different from the voice she remembered. He didn't look the same at all. If they had met on the street, she might have passed him by, an appalling thought.

He, in turn, barely recognized his daughter. "You're looking as if you've been through too much," he said. Twice Franz broke into tears about that. Only Sulamith, then six, cheered him. She climbed on his lap and giggled and called him "Grandpa" right away, without prompting. She did not know his voice was not the voice of old.

"Sulamith is me all over again," said Franz, beaming as only grandpas do. And Sulamith understood why Grandpa had to go back to his home behind the Wall because she had been asking questions about the Wall for such a long time.

"Why can't we pull the Wall down?" she used to ask.

"Because there are too many soldiers watching," her mother explained.

Whereupon Sulamith usually wanted to shoot the soldiers, but not always. In her crayon drawings she sometimes showed soldiers cozily having coffee inside the Wall, and often her Wall was gayly striped. She did not always picture the Wall as disruptive. In one of her more elaborate works the Wall was shown very tall, yet the three people representing her parents and herself were positioned beside the structure in such a way that they seemed to stand on both sides simultaneously.

Sulamith maintained a sisterly interest in her siblings although she said she knew that they would probably not want to play with her because they were too old. She had long realized why they were not living in her house. Even so, in their absence she enjoyed showing off a picture of them to her friends.

"These are my brother and sister, they're in the East," she would say. Or: "My brother and sister are behind the Wall." The photo showed little Ota and Jeannette at the ages when they disappeared, but Sulamith never forgot that they had grown to be adults.

In her religion class at school she was asked to place within the inside of a heart all the living things she valued most. In the order of prominence in the drawing, Sulamith produced versions of, first, her father. Then came her cat, Anela, then her mother with a frying pan, then her grandparents Eva and Franz and then, at the very top, Ota Junior and Jeannette as teenagers.

I still wondered whether I had fully discharged my responsibilities toward the Grübel family. I wanted to be careful not to aggravate their fragile situation further. I also did not wish to meddle. Their mute reaction to the news of the Gallus children's return did suggest that Bärbel and Ota were emotionally depleted, incapable of undertaking further initiatives to see their grown children.

Might full knowledge of the facts make a difference to them? What if they had talked, as I had, to psychiatric experts who could interpret so much of what was going on in the heads of young Ota and Jeannette? What if, on the basis of a scientific briefing, they were to make a last effort to contact their children through Walter Priesnitz, on behalf of the West German government, and Wolfgang Vogel, representing the East Germans?

I wrote to both men, told them what the psychiatrists had said, and described my qualms. Both wrote back and said they opposed further moves. Whereupon I finally dropped the matter, still feeling uneasy.

63

DOES THIS SON KNOW HE HAS A MOTHER?

**Giessen, West Germany,
Autumn 1988**

The Grübels were not alone. Some parents knew even less about their children, knew only that their youngsters had been taken from them by order of the DDR, their whereabouts unreported. Like Ota and Bärbel Grübel, these families experienced the West in a state of suspended animation. Year after year, their main purpose in life was to wait, to wait for some sign from the beloved offspring kidnapped by the government.

For Gisela Mauritz, forty-four, the waiting had clouded her days for fourteen years, and she had no reason to believe that it would ever end. It was like sequences from a Kafka novel.

Her mistake had been to entrust her fate to unlucky escape helpers back in June of 1974, when the border controls along the transit Autobahnen between Berlin and the West were still relatively loose. Gisela was a delicately built woman with long, coalblack hair and the youthful air of a college student. Her husband was accumulating the family nest egg in West Germany. Mrs. Mauritz and their lively, flaxen-haired little boy, Alexander, had stayed behind in East Berlin because she was making an excellent living.

Her brains and her graduate degree in chemistry had qualified her for interesting work in the central administration for information technology in the chemical industry; eventually the socialist environment became intolerable, deadening. Several applications for permission to join her husband having been rejected, she wound up inadequately hidden in the back of a truck, clutching Alexander, who was three years and ten months old.

Arrested at the Marienborn border station, Frau Mauritz was sentenced to four and a half years in Hoheneck, the notorious fortress-prison for women (see Chapter 55). Alexander disappeared. Eventually, his mother learned that the boy's closest relative in the DDR, a step-grandmother, had refused to care for him, but that he had not been assigned to an institution. This was the time when the children of the Grübels and of other families were forced into adoptive homes, so the West German authorities assumed that Alexander Mauritz had suffered the same fate—a conclusion that the DDR never denied.

It was five years before Frau Mauritz's travail even became known. One of her Hoheneck cellmates had been freed at Christmas 1979, and brought news of the case to West Germany. That didn't help Gisela Mauritz. Once out of Hoheneck, she was not allowed to go West. She remained, in effect, incarcerated in the DDR; only her cell was larger.

Her prison record relegated her to an underprivileged status. Work in her field of expertise was forbidden to her. Her identity papers were special, temporary, known as "P.12."* A red entry in them barred her from East Berlin and the surrounding area and from many vacation resorts. The only job she could find was a further reminder of her dependent status. She didn't work as a person in her own right. She was an appendage, the below-stage prompter who fed lines to actors in the theater at Döben, a tiny village in the hinterlands of Saxony.

At that, the authorities were not done with Gisela Mauritz. She had retained ideas of her own and she dared to write about them to relatives in West Germany, another serious mistake. The authorities classified this dereliction as "unauthorized contacts." This time her sentence was two and a half years in Hoheneck.

Lacking the slightest hint of her child's fate, Mrs. Mauritz began a letter-writing campaign upon her second release from prison. She wrote to Erich Honecker, as everyone did. She wrote to his

---

* Such glimpses into everyday contemporary German life reveal that guilty memories of Hitler's anti-Jewish persecutions remain alive in the national psychic baggage. The special DDR identity card P.12 is known as *Judenkarte* (card for Jews). In actuality, it is issued to citizens deemed ideologically unreliable.

wife, Margot, the Minister of Education. She wrote to every member of the Politburo and, naturally, to the attorney of attorneys, Wolfgang Vogel. Nobody would tell her anything about her son.

Official pressure from the West finally yielded a measure of action for Mrs. Mauritz. For several years, the Bonn government had brought up her case before the human rights authorities of the United Nations. When Erich Honecker visited West Germany in 1987, one of the leading Bonn politicians appealed to him personally about the plight of Mrs. Mauritz. In its own time, arbitrarily as was its custom, the DDR ventured a first move. From Vogel's law office, Gisela received word that her son was "well"—nothing further.

The ice had cracked, and suddenly, again in the idiosyncratic manner of the German Democratic Republic, time seemed to be measured by a different standard. The regime went into overdrive. Gisela Mauritz had become a tumor to be excised—at once! Kafka gave way to a cops-and-robbers chase.

Gisela was ordered to appear at the Department of Internal Affairs in Döben City Hall at 7 A.M. on July 8, 1988. She knew that her departure for West Germany had been approved, and it was difficult to believe that the officials who received her were the same sluggish types as before. In record time they told her to step forward. It was 7:48. She was to be on the 9 A.M. train to the West.

Gisela was as close to panic as she had ever come in her fourteen years as an alleged criminal. It had not been possible to buy her ticket to the West ahead of time; such documents were not sold to travelers unless they produced what every German in uniform demands to see, the correct *Stempel,* the right stamp. Once Gisela had her *Stempel,* she also had two heavy suitcases, there were no taxis, the trek to the station would take forty minutes, and there was always a slow-moving line in front of the window designated for people who were headed *ins Ausland,* abroad, to the other Germany.

To miss the train would have constituted a further violation of the law. It would not have surprised Frau Mauritz if her tormentors had seized such an opportunity to return her to Hoheneck.

She did make the train to Giessen and its West German refugee reception center and immediately began hunting for ways to contact her son or to make it possible for him to locate her.

Prospects were bleak. Alexander was about to turn eighteen, the age at which he could, on his own, apply for an exit visa. Would he want to do so? No one in the West could say. How would he have processed memories of his birth mother over so many years? Possibly, the young man had never been told that he was an adopted child. He might not know his original name or that his birth mother was still alive somewhere.

Gisela Mauritz was full of fears. At the time of her second arrest, all her application forms and correspondence concerning her son had been confiscated and she was given no receipt. "I wouldn't even be able to prove to my son that I remained his mother all through the years and that I searched for him," she said, her eyes filling with tears.

The DDR officials had tried hard to expunge evidence of her son's existence. Not a trace of him seemed to be left. On Frau Mauritz's identity paper, the entry for "children" was followed by a straight line in ink: no. As if clinging to a life belt, she treasured an entry that the keepers of the records had overlooked on her social security documents. There it still said, "one child."

And she did have a way of recognizing her child. He had scars in the palm of his right hand, reminders of a stove that burned him as a baby. In a country of disconnections even old scars were better than no trace at all.*

Scars. Plenty of them were left from the 1960s. The most dubious heritage was possible miscalculation in the event something happened to the command and control of nuclear weapons.

---

* On February 8, 1989, Alexander was reunited with his mother in the office of Wolfgang Vogel.

64

"LAUNCH-ON-WARNING": A HERITAGE OF THE 1960S

Washington,
Autumn 1988

Having pocketed a doctorate at Yale by studying command and control (or lack thereof) of American nuclear forces, Bruce Blair, thirty, a subdued, reflective scholar, joined the prestigious Brookings Institution in Washington in 1977 to begin a quiet lobbying campaign. Blair wanted to alert the Washington decision makers to the most devastating of the "holes" that riddled the system of nuclear firing "buttons" at the time of the Berlin Wall crisis in 1961.

These headaches remained alive behind the scenes, in the highest and most secret echelons of the United States government. Only the acute manifestations of the standoff in Berlin had faded. The nuclear confrontation continued despite the new emphasis on disarmament. The danger of misinterpreting enemy intentions during the heat of a crisis; the hidden debates about American nuclear strategy, about "first use" and "no use" of nuclears; crucial holes in the command and control system that I had been writing about in the long deceased *Saturday Evening Post* back in the innocent days of 1961; little had changed.

The differences had only sharpened the dangers: more missiles stood poised on both sides. The response times for firing them in a nuclear attack had grown shorter and shorter. The myth postulated by Kennedy's Defense Secretary Bob McNamara—that the country could ride out a major Soviet missile strike and still respond with deliberation—had made national survival riskier than ever, especially during periods of international tension when all missiles would be readied for *instant* launching.

This horror had been sinking in with Blair in very personal terms; it reminded him of his service in the Air Force. During the Yom Kippur War of 1973 he had been a launch officer in the Launch Control Center of a Minuteman Missile base near Great Falls, Montana. He and another officer each had authority over a key that, if both agreed, they would insert into the launch switches of their consoles, thereby firing not one missile but a cluster of them.

While Blair was on duty in an egg-shaped concrete control capsule underground—it swayed a bit because it was suspended from fifteen-foot shock absorbers—word came for the base to go on a global alert stage known as DEFCON THREE (Defense Condition Three). He knew that this signal of imminent nuclear war had been flashed only twice before: once by error during the Eisenhower administration, the other time during the Cuban Missile Crisis of 1962. DEFCON THREE was an intense, provocative form of alert, particularly touchy for nuclear submarines and other naval vessels connected to their bases by relatively tenuous communications lines.*

Blair's Montana alert lasted twenty-four hours. During much of that time he sat upright in his underground egg, agitated, sleepless, having removed his launch key from his safe and placed it on his console for immediate use, as prescribed by standard procedure. (His sealed presidential codes remained in the safe, also according to procedure.)

Blair was not a nervous type and he admired the professionalism of his outfit, the Strategic Air Command. His pride yielded to

---

* If a United States sub is cut off from base, it is authorized to fire its missiles on its own authority, without specific command, as long as three of its officers agree to a launch. Cutoffs from base are usually caused by communications malfunctions and these are common. They were the primary causes for mishandling several international incidents, including the attack on the USS *Liberty* (1967), the seizure of the USS *Pueblo* (1968), and the shooting down of a U.S. EC-121 aircraft (1969) by North Korea. As Blair has written: "Autopsies of these incidents pointed up how difficult it was for messages originating at the national level to find their way into the capillaries of military communications networks. Many were misrouted, misinterpreted and even misplaced. Most arrived too late or never reached their intended destinations."

dismay when he learned about the background of his Yom Kippur War alert. "It almost made a mockery of that professionalism," he said, "for an alert to be declared so quickly and for so little reason."

The scare had erupted at an awkward time: a week after the "Saturday Night Massacre," an explosive spree of purges that preceded President Nixon's resignation. The embattled President was asleep at about midnight when a communication arrived from Soviet Premier Kosygin. It seemed to suggest that the Soviets might dispatch troops to bail out the Egyptian army, which was being mauled by the Israelis. Henry Kissinger, summoned the National Security Council and decided to issue the DEFCON THREE alert. It turned out to be a false alarm. Kissinger had read threats into Kosygin's note that were not there.

Starting out at Brookings four years later, it was dawning on Blair that it would be difficult to change top-level attitudes toward his favorite subject, then becoming known as C³I (for "Command, Control, Communication, and Intelligence"). He was like a doctor trying to practice preventive medicine. His idea for making the C³I system less vulnerable to destruction was considered too expensive; too unglamorous to receive much congressional attention; and too "soft." "Hardware," weapons that kill and irradiate, received far higher priority in budgets.

"Launch-on-warning." In the decade that Blair had devoted to studying missile "buttons," this was de facto American policy for going to nuclear war. The implications were hair-raising. It was not at all inconceivable that the United States would fire missiles on a massive scale on receipt of no more than *warning* that Soviet missiles were en route.

Officially, the policy had been different since Bob McNamara tightened command and control techniques at the time of the Berlin crisis in 1961. In theory, the system was supposed to risk "riding out" a Soviet first strike on the chance that the warning was not the real thing.

Trouble was unlikely to be caused by the alarmingly short fuses of the weapons. The essential weakness was the vulnerability of the 450 "command nodes," the widely dispersed "button" stations that controlled the weapons. These posts were "soft," relatively undefended, and could easily be overpowered by a major nuclear attack, an event picturesquely known as "nuclear decapitation."

"The short endurance and rudimentary design of our control

system makes controlled nuclear war impossible," Blair would tell anyone who listened.

Not many people did. Command and control was still unfashionable, a notion whose time had not yet come, although its sensitivity was recognized. When Blair completed a classified study for the research office of Congress, copies were incinerated, not simply shredded, and congressmen were not permitted to see it.*

As yet, nobody wanted to spend more than $30 billion to build more ground command centers, "harden" existing facilities, and improve sensor and radio links.

Blair advocated a "no-first-use, no-immediate-second-use" strategy. Almost nobody was interested.

Cost was not the only reason for resistance. The Pentagon was unenthusiastic. "It cuts across the lines between the services and strengthens civilian control," Blair noted. Such turf encroachments were distasteful to generals and admirals.

The most stubborn resistance roosted at the very top. Command and control in peacetime was controlled by the attitudes of presidents, and their feelings were guided by the old bromide "After me, the deluge."

Blair heard that President Jimmy Carter, an engineering technocrat who worshiped Hyman Rickover, the nuclear admiral, had secretly okayed a launch-on-warning strategy. The genial Ronald Reagan was rumored to have instructed one of his senior generals casually, "If I'm not available, you know what to do."

The potential catastrophe feared by Kennedy in 1961, when he thought of miscalculating the intentions of the Soviets or causing them to miscalculate American intentions, remained real. In no way could the Kremlin divine when three officers on an American nuclear sub might agree to start World War III on their own, or when a general or two in the Pentagon might set off the apocalypse because the President was "unavailable" and, say, the Speaker of the House was in command but couldn't immediately decide what to do.

The Soviet position on command and control was more rigid, at least on paper. Bruce Blair, researching the subject, had found that the Soviets did not believe in delegating *any* degree of nuclear

---

* The Joint Chiefs of Staff decided that Blair's report should be labeled "SIOP-ESI" meaning "Single Integrated Operation Plan—Extremely Sensitive Information." Such documents may be seen only by the President, the Secretary of Defense, the chairman of the Joint Chiefs, and the Deputy Secretary of Defense.

launch authority whatsoever. At least their writings conveyed this philosophy, and their literature on this subject was surprisingly open and detailed, though possibly designed to mislead. Blair was distressed to discover that the Soviets were well informed—and did not hesitate to write about—American control capabilities, including detailed techniques of underwater sound surveillance.

Did all this make launch-on-warning a more likely prospect on either side? No one could tell. Any scenario was possible into the 1990s, as it had been in 1961.

Miscalculation. The French had a cliché for it: the more things change, the more they stay the same.

65

NEVER THE TWAIN SHALL MEET

Ridgefield, Connecticut,
Spring 1989

In the end it was all for nothing, really: President Kennedy's concerns about nuclear miscalculation, Bärbel and Ota Grübel's loss of their children, Volker Seifarth's divorce, the suffering and sacrifices by hundreds of thousands of others for nearly thirty years. The Wall could have been prevented.

Nikita Khrushchev had been right. When his Wall went up, the West stood there "like dumb sheep." The evidence strongly suggests that his bluff could have been called, that he was poised to retreat, as he did in the abortive tank confrontation at the Berlin border in October 1961.

East Germany could have been saved for the West. Should we care?

The German Democratic Republic does not seem much of a country, smaller in area than Great Britain, with less than half the population, blessed with few tourist sights beyond East Berlin. Even the West Germans are bored with their dreary brothers and sisters. Whenever the *Spiegel* magazine runs a cover about the DDR, newsstand sales dip by about 100,000 copies. Like Honecker, his country lives in obscurity. Like him, it is underestimated.

In the context of risky nuclear times, the Wall is a monument to humanity's tremendous luck, for the head-on clash of Soviet and American power in central Europe—this duel of nuclear muscle constantly threatening a test of strength—has been the central dilemma of our era. It continues. We stand deadlocked, system bucking system, nowhere closer than in Berlin, at the Wall. By sheer great luck, no incident upset the stalemate in almost thirty years.

The price of peace in Berlin remains unappreciated.

By permitting Khrushchev to go ahead with the Wall days after he closed the border (his hesitation to proceed was all but an invitation to the West to resist), we legitimized the creation of a new enemy, a new Communist world power, a society that calmly, officially kidnapped the Grübel children and other youngsters, forced Volker Seifarth and others to get a divorce that nobody wanted, and slaughtered border crossers with automatic death devices because they wanted to leave the country.

The death automats are gone, forcible adoptions and divorces are no longer imposed as punishments by the state, and living conditions are improving, and still the Wall bottles up an encapsulated, rigidly totalitarian culture in the image of Marx and Lenin, not Gorbachev.

With its Western neighbor, this new nation has about as much in common as the United States with Russia. Economically, the gulf remains enormous. Not that West Germany is utopia. Unemployment is high and steady—about 9 percent on average, 10 percent in Berlin—and competition is pervasive and furious. Nor has the DDR worked without notable successes. In the past twenty-five years, its rate of economic expansion matched West Germany's and its per capita gross national product, according to CIA estimates, is about one third higher than the Soviet Union's.

Still, the DDR makes a very poor relative. The West Germans have four times as many telephones (89 percent of households versus 22 percent) and have built twice as many postwar homes (65 percent versus 36 percent). Statistics that are signals of social instability tell tragic stories. The DDR reports two and a half times as many illegitimate children (23 percent versus 9 percent), almost twice as many divorces (3 percent versus 1.8 percent, probably the highest divorce rate in the world), and twice as high a consumption of hard liquor (12.7 liters versus 6.8 liters per head).

Among the gauges of national priorities, the comparative expenditures for defense and education reveal hostile ambitions. The DDR spends about 50 percent more for the military (7.7 percent of the budget versus 5.5 percent. And since it employs education to bind the young to Communism, DDR school classes are kept about 20 percent smaller than in West Germany.

The goal of someday catching up with the West is as tantalizing to the DDR leadership as any idealist's impossible dream. In the interim, the requisite ideological figure-skating has produced inventive dialectics. Since a prosperous socialism is so obviously far distant, the party ideologues try to keep the populace in a perpetual state of gallant striving. In this churning, the word "real" is waved like a new banner, acknowledging the shortcomings of the present while energizing the chase for the millennium.

Instead of "socialism," DDR propagandists promote the phrase "actually existing socialism" (*real existierender Sozialismus*). This terminology, introduced by Honecker at the Ninth Plenum of the Party on May 28–29, 1973, remains very much current. It is meant to convert discontent into ever more valiant effort. In the canny analysis of a leading authority on the DDR, Professor Hartmut Zimmermann of the Berlin Free University, the phrase acts as a simultaneous commitment to push harder for the dream as well as a warning that failure to perform is disloyal or worse.

The East German economic progress is helped by the prevailing highly disciplined Prussian work ethic and some $1 billion a year in Western bank credits and "transfers" for such items as transit roads maintenance and the ransoming of political prisoners. The DDR's rosy performance figures, including those calculated by the CIA, are discounted by some experts because many Eastern goods are of poor quality and because the statistics use the official exchange ratio between Western and Eastern currency of about two to one, the more realistic black market rate running five to one in 1989, sometimes as much as seven to one. No matter: the DDR's showing is impressive.

All the world's statistics do not adequately convey the alienation between these brothers and sisters, and for non-Germans the magnitude of the chasm is difficult to grasp. "They all speak the same language," outsiders say, but even this is no longer quite true. Before me as I write lies a 217-page paperback, a West German *Dictionary of DDR Language*. It lists the differing Eastern and Western vocabulary for fried chicken and tries, in almost two pages, to distinguish between the divergent meanings of "culture."

At that, the rapid-fire format of this painstakingly researched reference work does not do justice to the disparity in national value systems. This novel trend is keeping West German scholars busy. For example, the word *Verpflichtung* (obligation, duty) is an "I" term for West Germans, a self-imposed responsibility. For East Germans, it means a chore prescribed by outside authority.

Refugees emerging from what the East Germans call their *Knast* (slang for "prison") are assaulted by culture shock like welfare clients parachuting into a luxury resort. The West's tumult frightens them. The multitude of colors and lights blinds them. The chaos of the politicians repels them. The multiplicity of personal choices confuses and exhausts them. The competition often defeats them. The standoffishness of people in capitalist society depresses them.

In the DDR, the scarcity of goods and the monotony of available entertainment, along with fear and resentment of the official system, created an isolationist social condition for which Günter Gaus, the former West German representative, coined a clever term. He called it a "niche society," meaning that families tend to withdraw from the mainstream and huddle, figuratively, in their private home nooks, where little interference from governmental authority could reach their lives.

Plunged into the clamorous West, niche dwellers find their new neighbors, shopkeepers, bosses—even their own relatives—less approachable, less sincere, and far more materialistic than back home. Friendships are fewer, harder to forge, more superficial. People do not always rally around to orient confused newcomers.

A full-scale liberation from the niches of the DDR usually requires lengthy and determined effort. The bustlers like Volker Seifarth, revel in the emancipation process. Others, the damaged victims of Erich Honecker—niche dwellers par excellence like the Grübels—never make the adjustment. Employment difficulties exacerbate the passage. Eastern job training standards often are downgraded by the harsher managers of the West; schoolteachers, in particular, find it nearly impossible to make the switch. Of a big refugee wave in 1984, 28 percent of the men and 54 percent of the women were still without work a year later.

For most of the refugees, the most difficult transition is emotional. They suffer from what one wit called "untrained elbows," an unfamiliarity with the need to self-start and to keep on pushing, pushing in order to accomplish anything. Christoph Guera, who had been a pastor in East Germany and became a social worker in the West, told a *Wall Street Journal* reporter how he compared his old life with the new.

"The biggest difference," he said, "is that there your life is lived for you. Here you must live it yourself."

Another social worker who counsels East German refugees reported that her office is often empty. Immigrants are so distrustful of governmental bureaucracy that they will not approach her of their own accord. She has been frisked for microphones and has had her phone taken apart in search of bugs. Many refugees fear they might be spied upon. Many West Germans, in turn, believe that the ranks of new fellow citizens from the East are full of agents. In a 1984 West German government poll, 50 percent of the respondents thought that this infiltration didn't exist, but 47 percent said that they thought it did.

The same survey documented a major reason why DDR immigrants experience difficulties in the other Germany: their new fellow citizens consider them too different, too likely to cause more unemployment and other trouble. The pollsters classified 22 percent of the population as being outright hostile to the refugees, another 26 percent as "tolerant but without involvement," a further 25 percent as "willing to help but feeling insecure and frightened." One percent was "disinterested." Only 26 percent were classified as "friendly toward the settlers."

The West German authorities go to inventive lengths to help the refugees adjust. A self-help booklet called *Compass*, published by the Foundation for Former Political Prisoners, offers no-nonsense advice on ninety knotty problems, not avoiding "Loneliness" and "Small Print" (referring to purchase agreements and other contracts). It lists dozens of addresses and phone numbers where a discouraged new citizen can seek more help, and its large-type introduction is brutally candid:

"The German Federal Republic is not as advertised in TV commercials . . . Many offices want to help you, and will, but not without effort on your part. *You* have to keep after things, *you* have to ask questions, *you* have to inform yourself . . ."

What makes some resettlers succeed and others fail?

At the prestigious Max Planck Research Institute in West Berlin, I encountered an extroverted young sociology professor, Erika M. Hoerning, who was studying the impact of "critical life events" on human "biographies," and I told her the stories of the Grübel and the Seifarth families.

Professor Hoerning, a lively conversationalist who turned out to be a fanatical Humphrey Bogart fan, understood at once. Her case histories showed a similar dramatic dichotomy between "winners" (like Seifarth, who blossomed in the West) and "losers" (like the Grübels, whose lives all but collapsed).

The critical life event of the professor's case histories was the Berlin Wall, and her interest dated to 1982 when she was driving along the border, down Köpenicker Strasse, en route to a party, and spotted several blocks of small businesses, all closed, boarded up and dilapidated. Stopping for a look, Hoerning was fascinated by a fading sign obviously at least twenty years old.

"Will be right back," it said.

What went on here? Hoerning made inquiries in a neighborhood *Kneipe,* one of the thousands of Berlin pubs that serve as institutional memories of the neighborhoods. The closed shops had given up the ghost in the fall of 1961. They had peddled currency, tobacco, chocolate, canned goods, and other edibles hard to get in East Berlin. The customers were visitors from the DDR, the 40,000-plus *Grenzgänger* from the East who commuted to jobs in the West, and West Berliners who raided the East sector in search of cheap haircuts, fried chicken snacks, and other bargains.

The closed businesses along Köpenicker Strasse also served as sources of supply to a border trade that made some practitioners very rich. Much of this commerce amounted to smuggling.

When Professor Hoerning tracked down surviving shopkeepers, their customers, and other border crossers whose lives were radically changed by the Wall, she faced a puzzle that has for decades preoccupied a sizable international literature in sociology.

In 1986, she addressed the Eleventh World Congress of Sociology in New Delhi about this mystery, and from her paper she pointed out to me how frustratingly the problem was summarized by an American researcher, R. S. Lazarus: "The great dilemma is that we have no knowledge either of the ways in which most people cope nor of what ways of coping are efficient for what individuals. . . ."

Professor Hoerning had discovered only one personality clue that the "winners" of her studies had in common. Those who transplanted themselves successfully from the Communist to the Western culture invariably were people of innate enterprise. They displayed a lust for the new, a sense of adventure. Adventure—the German word for it, *Abenteuer,* is evocative of great fresh deeds—was built into these winners like gusto for good food.

Volker Seifarth radiated such a sense of adventure. Ota and Bärbel Grübel had possessed it at one time; the DDR's repressions destroyed it. I thought also of my father, the charming salesman who talked himself into prosperous executive ranks in Berlin before Hitler's time, and went into collapse upon facing the strangeness of America. My father had many assets; a sense of adventure was not among them.

"He wasn't transplantable," said Professor Hoerning, nodding with understanding when I related my father's "critical life event" of immigration and its shattering effect on his "biography." Perhaps he was homesick and went through life in America with an internal sign that said WILL BE RIGHT BACK.

Will East stay East in Germany, and West stay West, never the twain to meet, or are the two parts likely to get together again?

As I've made clear in earlier chapters, reunification is a dead herring issue, at least in any form recognizable from the past. The two German states will cooperate in economic, environmental, and other issues, but their present national identities are fixed for a long time to come. I am convinced that nervous Germanophobes whose justifiably dreaded memories of Hitler make them fret about a merging of the two Germanys are wasting their energy.* It won't happen—not unless cataclysmic events change the European political lineup in ways not foreseeable. Regardless of their wishes, most Germans themselves are convinced that the prospect of a single Germany is a fantasy.

In 1985, pollsters showed a representative sample of West Germans† the following statement: "The world has become reconciled to the division of Germany. It's better that we, too, soberly realize that reunification is no longer possible. There is no point in main-

---

* In the United States, Great Britain, and France, these Nervous Nellies, surprisingly, constitute a minority. When a leading West German polling organization, the Institut für Demoskopie Allensbach, first surveyed public opinion in these three countries in 1969, more than half of the sample said they would support reunification. In 1984, results were similar.

† In East Germany, public opinion research is conducted almost entirely by the government for its own purposes, in secret, and the results are not divulged. The DDR Institute for Opinion Research (*Institut für Meiningsforschung*) is part of the Central Committee of the SED.

taining false hopes." Some 50 percent agreed with this view. Only 30 percent called for patience and persistence in pursuing the obsolescent hopes.

In the last twenty and more years, the prospect of a united Germany has been moving constantly further into the realm of the nebulous. In the 1950s and 1960s, polls showed that between 30 and 50 percent of West Germans considered reunification an issue to which they gave top priority. Since the 1970s, a maximum of only one percent rated this problem so highly. In the mid-1960s more than a quarter of the population expected to live to see the national bond renewed; in 1987, only 9 percent said so.

The very word "reunification" is no longer in the vocabulary of German politicians. Honecker and his people have just about outlawed the concept, taking bizarre steps to make the extirpation stick. The fate of the East German national anthem is a case in point. The music, composed by the DDR's musician in chief, Hanns Eisler, is still in use; the lyrics, written by Johannes R. Becher, the composer in chief, became taboo after the Eighth Party Congress of June 1971, when reunification was officially foresworn. Following the obsolete old party line, the text twice refers longingly to the goal of a "united fatherland." Honecker ordained that the hymn may be played and hummed, but not sung.

In the West, reunification remains part of the CDU majority theology, but the ancient ideal is largely Sunday morning lip service. Helmut Kohl, the West German Chancellor, did not allude to it when he spoke before Honecker during the East German's visit in 1987.

The Bonn politicians do recognize that the *dream* of an East-West remarriage lingers among some rank-and-file citizens. Instead of "reunification," conservative ideologues speak euphemistically of "overcoming the German partition" or "realizing German unity," thereby hoping to stoke the distant vision retained by patriots, many of whom are still alive and voting.

In surveys taken by a variety of polling organizations, between 70 and 80 percent of West Germans have in recent years confirmed their essential support of reunification. They cite four motivations: (1) support of free self-determination, meaning an honest popular referendum; (2) the existence of family ties; (3) "Because we are all Germans"; and (4) "so that Germans won't one day fight Germans."

When feelings are probed indirectly, a consistent longing for

German togetherness emerges unmistakably. Eight times between 1973 and 1985 pollsters from the Allensbach Institute showed West Germans this statement: "Here is a sentence from our constitution. Please read it. What do you think: should the sentence remain in the constitution or should it be stricken?" The sentence reads: "The *entire* German people continues to be urged to complete the unity and liberty of Germany by free elections" (emphasis added). Eight times a large and unvarying majority, around 70 percent, said that this provision should stand.

These are wistful remnants of departed glory. Polls almost uniformly show that these longings are not universally shared. They apply far less to young people, the generation soon to be in charge of the society, and have been consistently dwindling further. It is only a question of time until most teenagers will feel no more affinity for the DDR than for "China or Australia," as a nineteen-year-old girl phrased it in one survey.

The swiftness of time's passage is easy to forget. The DDR has lasted more than twice as long as the Weimar Republic, more than three times as long as the Third Reich. In 1989 it was forty years old. Roughly 60 percent of its people were born after World War II. A united Germany is a fossil to them. Why should they mourn for what they didn't know, for what brought shame and suffering to their parents?

The East-West estrangement is a fact of German life. In 1983, 43 percent of West German students between the ages of 14 and 21 (as against 25 percent of adults) described their fellow Germans to the east as living in the *Ausland*, abroad. Only 6 percent knew the DDR's approximate population size (seventeen million, compared with sixty-one million for West Germany). This ignorance is astounding, because geography is a carefully tended subject in the scholastically rugged German high schools.

Reunification? In 1989 the great diplomat George F. Kennan predicted: "If it ever comes about, it probably will assume forms that no one today can predict."

The Berlin Wall brings out quite another resonance in the West Germans. They want the Wall to go, and the majority believes that the day of its disappearance is not hopelessly distant. The Allensbach pollsters asked in the summer of 1985, "What do you think, how much longer will the Berlin Wall still stand, how many years?"

The average estimate was thirty-four years and the figure did not differ significantly between the age groups. A total of 12 percent responded, "It'll stand always, endlessly, eternally."

A majority thought that it was worth exercising consistent pressure upon the Communists to remove the Wall. The pollsters asked, "Reagan called on Gorbachev to tear the Wall down; do you think one should keep on saying this, or is that really useless?" A positive response came from 53 percent of those polled; only 34 percent said continued pressure wasn't worth the effort. The pollsters commented that the majority's view seemed to "come from the heart."

Today the Wall is received through two sets of lenses. Locals and visitors see it very differently.

The tourists are a mob scene. The city is *the* travel attraction of central Europe ("Berlin is good for you," says the official slogan), and the Wall is its number one sight. Potsdamer Platz offers the choicest view, and ten to twelve o'clock in the morning are rush hours. Enormous long-distance and local tour buses, slickly polished and bulky as houses, disgorge rubberneckers by the thousands.

Once Europe's busiest square, Potsdamer Platz, five blocks north and west of Checkpoint Charlie, is in East Berlin and deserted. The Wall, running along its Western side, is alive with the milling gawkers, souvenir and hot-dog stands, and tall viewing platforms. Each has space for 70 visitors, who line up to take in the wide vistas of East Berlin, the Wall, and the no-man's-land that once was home to Gestapo headquarters and the *Führerbunker* where Hitler killed himself.

The tourists ask their guides questions about Hitler's last refuge, they want to know precisely where among the weeds it was located. They offer no comments, the Nazi time was too long ago. The Wall is something else. It's today. It jars them. The guides want to push on, but they linger.

"I'm depressed, so depressed," a woman from a tourist group of West Germans and foreigners told a reporter for *Deutschlandwelle,* the West German radio network, when the Wall's twenty-fifth birthday was observed in 1986.

"Should this really be a tourist attraction?" demanded another woman in the group. "I don't think it's a good idea."

"Absolutely not," said a third woman. "This is bad enough without sausage stands."

"Awful," a fourth chimed in. "I think it's impossible!"

"Look at how they sell teddy bears and postcards," said a man. "It's like an excursion to Niagara Falls."

"We should make our side more attractive," said a woman. "Maybe with some nice gardens. Let the other side look *triste*. Ours should be beautiful."

Some local householders whose homes adjoin the Wall in quiet, outlying sections of the city installed greenery and play areas long ago to take advantage of the lack of traffic. They enjoy living with the Wall. It is a convenient refuge for parties and Ping-Pong tables. Like the city's cabdrivers, they rarely give the border a thought anymore. "The normality of the abnormal," so the dividing line has been described. A serenity prevails that is extraordinary for a big metropolis.

A few citizens have come to find the Wall downright cozy.

"If you ask me, the Wall is terrific," a jogger said. "You can run quietly here and the air is relatively good. The scenery is pleasant, there's a lot of water around and no traffic, and I think it's absolutely super when the *Vopos* open their windows and stare at you through their binoculars."

In the East the Wall continues to be perceived as a villain. Sometimes it seems as if Honecker and his men accomplished very little to ease the volatility of the eastward exodus when they put it up, so insistent is the popular pressure against this device of separation. Young people want it out of the way. They are still scheming, climbing, running, crashing, swimming to surmount it, and the Lutheran church is their abiding helper.

In the Church of the Samaritan, a capacity congregation of eight hundred burst into a vibrant rendition of "We Shall Overcome" one weekday evening in January 1988. When the pastor took up the collection for the families and legal defense of those who were arrested in the latest demonstrations—on January 17—the parishioners offered up the astonishing sum of 2,500 marks (about $1,300).

The following day, at the Church of Galilee in Lichtenberg, the deacon prayed for God's help against "those who rule us" and then retold the story of how trumpets brought down the walls of Jericho.

On the ensuing Thursday, in the Paul Gerhardt Church of Pankow, Pastor Rudi Pahnke distributed individual lengths of "liberty string" to all one thousand parishioners. They were to tie eleven knots into each string, one for each of the best-known civil-rights demonstrators who had been jailed. Every time one of them would be released, a knot was to be untied.

"If God had not been with us when their homes were searched and *they* then tried to shut our mouths," so Pahnke preached, "we all would have been swallowed up."

Everybody knew who *they* were. They were Honecker's *Stasi*. The churches circumspectly but unmistakably supporting unrest were all in *East* Berlin, engaging in remarkable and very risky undertakings. The rebellious spirit was spreading. In the center of Dresden, more than thirty young citizens waited for the cameras of Western TV to arrive before they shouted (and showed with their fingers) how many years their exit applications had been pending. Several were arrested, if only for a few hours.

Driven by dissatisfaction with the inaction of the Honecker regime in the face of Gorbachev's reforms in the Soviet Union, there had been previous waves of rebellion by young people. The present rumble erupted in East Berlin on January 17—the date would become a landmark for all dissidents—when hundreds of civil-rights demonstrators wanted to march during the traditional remembrance for the assassination of Rosa Luxemburg. The protestors prepared posters bearing relevant quotations from the writings of the martyred Communist revolutionary: "Liberty always means liberty for dissidents" and "If you don't move, you feel the handcuffs more."

Most would-be marchers never reached their starting point. Since they wanted Western media attention, they had made their plans known in advance, and so the *Stasi* moved in, threatening with arrests, persuading people to sign promises that they would not march. On January 17, many were turned back in side streets before they reached the collection area. More than one hundred, including a popular rock star and his wife, went to jail as they unfurled their banners. They were sentenced for "treasonable relations," "attempt at illegal gathering," or the catchall crime of "rowdyism." Some of the most inconvenient of these oppositionists were told to leave the country forthwith, even if they did not wish to do so.

For months, *Stasi* men had been selectively beating up Western TV and radio crews and smashing their equipment because they were delivering bad news. During February 1988, the Communist media renewed their campaign against West German newsmen, accusing them of drawing pay from the Bonn government's intelligence services in order to foment opposition within the DDR.

The Communists are rarely provoked into public comment upon events suggesting that all isn't quiescent in the East. But they had felt forced to do so following the events of the preceding June, when more than three thousand East Berlin youths were barred by police from eavesdropping on a concert by the British rock group Genesis, playing on the West side of the Wall at the Brandenburg Gate.

For hours the young people shouted, "The Wall must go! The Wall must go!" with clenched fists held high. Occasionally they yelled, "Gorbachev! Gorbachev!"

Periodically, *Vopos* would dive into the crowd to arrest demonstrators—about fifty were sent off in paddywagons—who threw cans, bottles, and firecrackers, yelled "Police pigs!" and started singing the Communist hymn, the "Internationale," obviously as a sarcastic challenge.

ADN, the official East German press agency, denied there was a confrontation: "There can be no talk at all of clashes between youths and police. These exist only in the fantasy of foreign correspondents who drive over the border with the aim of creating sensations."

The sensations are created from within, the work of the young and the physically fit, East Germans like Mike Kussin.

This eighteen-year-old apprentice mason from suburban Köpenick, ran into Ulrike Honko, a seventeen-year-old glazier, at the notorious Friedrichstrasse elevated station shortly after 1 A.M. on August 19, 1986. It was escape at first sight.

"How do I get to the Ost station?" she asked him. The Ost station was four stops eastward. Mike liked Ulrike's looks, so he said: "Why go there? It's in the wrong direction. I'm headed for West Berlin."

"I'm coming with you," Ulrike said without hesitation.*

Mike had been giving escape somewhat more thought. He wanted to "live more freely," he said later, and he didn't want to

---

* Improbable as this account may appear, it is based on a carefully verified report released at a press conference by Dr. Rainer Hildebrandt's "Working Cooperative August 13." Both of these teenagers were also interrogated by the West Berlin police.

serve in the DDR army. He was having difficulties with the party secretary at his job. He had no particular plan for making his getaway. He simply decided to approach the Wall somewhere near the Spree River and swim across.

Together, the pair walked north down deserted Friedrichstrasse and turned left in the dark toward the Charité Hospital, walking almost certainly, by bizarre coincidence, down Reinhardtstrasse, the former home of Bärbel Grübel. At the border they found a construction site with a ladder and used it to scale the Wall. Facing the Spree, they could spot no danger except a watchtower near the old Reichstag building.

It would be longer, about three hundred meters all told, but less risky, to swim across the river diagonally, they decided. The guards in the tower were less likely to see them. They took off only their shoes. Mike instructed Ulrike to swim as quietly as possible. Wading ashore near the Reichstag parking lot, they were not sure whether they were as yet in the West. Then they found a beer can with the label "Berliner Kindl." That brand was not available in East Berlin. They had reached the promised land.

Mike and Ulrike were enormously lucky. Near where they landed, the riverbank is dotted with crosses marking the deaths of some of the seventy-seven refugees who perished since 1961 in attempts to leave the DDR from within Berlin. The number of getaway escapades had, after a slump of some years, again been rising rapidly since 1985.* and the ingenuity of the escapees never flagged. They used boats, heavily loaded trucks—and their brains —to outwit the opposition.

On August 22, 1988, at a location very close to the site of Mike and Ulrike's swim to freedom, four more young people used the river to turn their backs on the DDR, choosing a sunny Sunday midafternoon when the Western side was alive with walkers and sunbathers. When the three young men, aged seventeen and eighteen, and one twenty-two-year-old woman, were threatened by a DDR patrol boat, the woman called out that she was pregnant. Angry crowds began to gather along the West Berlin side. The

---

* In 1985, a total of 3,324 East Germans escaped to the West, plus 160 "Sperrbrecher," barrier-breakers who crashed through obstacles at the risk of their lives. In the first seven months of 1988, the comparable figures were 4,785 and 206. Between August 13, 1961, and mid-1988, 213,569 East Germans were registered as refugees despite the Wall. However, some 80 percent of these escapees made the trip via a third country.

DDR guards evidently wanted to risk no public relations repercussions. The swimmers made it.

Other dissidents also decided that their chances stood best at conspicuous locations where Communist watchers were on their best behavior. Some were still using Checkpoint Charlie for their escape.

An eighteen-year-old electronics technician, Falk Mühlbach, from the village of Radeberg in Saxony, spent four days casing the border near the Checkpoint in July 1988. During all of the fourth night he studied the guards and obstacles from under a construction scaffold at Leipziger and Mauer Strasse, a block away. The Wall was relatively low at that location, immediately north of the Checkpoint. Patrols were light because the border was largely blocked by locked buildings. He would try an approach from above.

At 11:30 P.M. on July 24 Mühlbach climbed his familiar scaffolding up to the roof, balanced himself slowly, precariously, across several more roofs toward the West, toward the Wall, until he reached a roof adjoining the last building. From there he cast about for almost an hour, partly to study the patterns of the guards from relatively close up and partly because he couldn't figure out a way to get to street level at the Wall.

Finally he spotted a pipe leading to a barrackslike building that was only one floor high. He climbed down on this pipe, hand over hand, finishing the trip's last floor length distance by sliding down a lightning rod into a deserted courtyard adjoining Checkpoint Charlie.

Pressed against the Wall, he watched a *Vopo* in a nearby small guardhouse until a car arrived that distracted the man. Mühlbach had been getting frightened. He was suddenly convinced he'd never get across the border. Unthinking, he started to run like hell, pulled himself up on the Wall, and kept running and running, not stopping at the guardhouse on the Western side, running blindly on and on, past the next street, Kochstrasse, well inside the West, still running, desperate not to make a mistake by relaxing too early, until he panted into a well-marked West Berlin police station, yet another block farther.

If the Wall crisis of 1961 was for nothing, the daredeviltry of barrier breakers like Falk Mühlbach was not. Without these convincing demonstrations of despair, Erich Honecker and his old guard would not see themselves compelled to open up the safety valve on their gates wider and wider, to allow an astonishing volume of temporary exits—wholesale visiting by DDR citizens to West Germany. In 1987, a record five million East Germans were granted visas to make such trips, and a surprising 1.2 million of them were under sixty-five, the age when practically unlimited travel is permitted. In 1985, only 66,000 citizens below pension age were let out.

The price for such manifestations of humanity was paid over the years by victims of the Wall like the Grübel and the Seifarth families. In financial terms, it is being paid each day by West German taxpayers. The ransom takes the form of billions that the East Germans collect for such privileges as the transit roads through the territory; the *Freikauf* fees for the release of "politicals"; and for subsidies Bonn must pay to the West Berlin government because the isolated island of Berlin cannot subsist on its own steam.

This federal assistance amounts to about $6.6 *billion* annually, 52 percent of the entire West Berlin budget. Campaigns to boost hi-tech industry and employment in the city have been incesssant and moderately successful. So are promotion schemes to make Berlin attractive for conventions and tourists, especially repeat visitors from West Germany. Nevertheless, economic planners assume that the aid from Bonn will not decrease in the foreseeable future.

It is only money. The West Germans have plenty. It's people that count, always people, and Berlin, even as an encircled wallflower kept artificially alive, can live fairly respectably on the record of the Berliners.

The terrible memories are fading. Not many old people are left in the decayed neighborhood around the Sophien Church in East Berlin who remember the pogrom of Crystal Night, though after one of the antigovernment prayer vigils in 1988 the old folks recalled those days under the Nazis, because dissidents, fleeing from the *Stasi*, were knocking for refuge on the same doors where Jews fled from the Gestapo exactly fifty years before.

"*Ja, Ja,*" said one of the old-timers, "it happened like it happened with the Jews."

Not many are left, either, to recall that Kurfürstenstrasse 115 in West Berlin's attractive Schöneberg district once was the headquarters of the Reichssicherheitshauptamt Office IVa, the dreaded *Judenamt* of the SS, the gloomy office building where Adolf Eichmann presided over the paperwork that saw to the "final solution" for more than six million Jews in death camps.

For me, a historical footnote hidden at Kurfürstenstrasse 115 rang an emotional alarm in 1988.

Leafing through a book about the Holocaust, I had come across the fact that the old office building was replaced after the war by the modern Hotel Sylter Hof. I had stayed there half a dozen times recently. It was an excellent place, quiet, friendly; the cheerful young women at the desk, once they knew me, would give me a suite for the price of a double room. Did they know they worked under Eichmann's shadow? Would they care? I never found out. I did not stay there again.

Villains. Heroes. Heroes surviving even in East Berlin. How else can one assess a walker on muddy waters like Wolfgang Vogel, talking Marxism and Catholicism out of the same mouth and rescuing Wall victims by the thousands? Vogel's true religion may be Vogel, no more and no less. He does often get away with working against the rules of his mentor Honecker.

Perhaps I am misjudging Vogel. Perhaps he is less devious than commonly believed. Perhaps Len Deighton defined Vogel best when, in another context, he wrote in his novel *Berlin Game:* "It's only the Jesuit who complains of the Pope. . . . And in East Berlin it is only the truly faithful who speak treason with such self-assurance."

Surely there is nothing ambiguous about that beacon of impudence, my buddy, former U.S. Technical Sergeant Stefan Heym. His survival is keeping many hopes alive in the German Democratic Republic. Our old World War II bosses in the Army's Psychological Warfare Division are long gone, but wherever they are they must be getting big laughs out of Sergeant Heym having turned once more to his rapier, sticking it into the fleshier parts of Honecker and his *Bonzen*. I could picture the endless meetings debating the Heym problem, now a quarter of a century old: "What'll we do with that son of a bitch?" In the absence of our old chiefs, I am laughing their laughs on their behalf.

Who but Heym could graciously receive greetings from the Honecker government for his seventy-fifth birthday while publishing his memoirs, a devastating volume containing, among other gymnastics, verbatim extracts from internal reports of *Stasi* agents who trailed him as he went about his daily rounds in East Berlin and then managed to lose their notes on his front lawn?

The memoirs produced no reprisals. Heym's taunting continued. In a birthday interview with *Stern* he compared the DDR censorship with the practices of Prince Metternich, and ventured:

"That probably still works in Tibet, but not in the DDR." His personal safety didn't worry him. "As a TV personality I'm immune to the catchers of the DDR," he dared to crow.

Why would the DDR leaders insist on attempting to rehabilitate this antihero who refused to be rehabilitated? Were they just waiting for the inconvenient old man to die? Had they gotten used to him, like an itch? Or were they belatedly joining the twentieth century, recognizing, as Heym had lectured them, that in the contemporary international world they can no longer keep belching? I think Honecker and his squad of ancients are recognizing Sergeant Heym of the Second Mobile Radio Broadcasting Company as an inevitable symptom of the times, urgings that they would love to throttle but cannot.

Even at the Grübels' times were changing. Their spirits were finally lifting. At my most recent dinner with them they talked of looking for a larger, less noisy apartment, closer to Sulamith's school. Ota had been selling some paintings. He had stopped drinking and was no longer eating meat. He said he felt much better. He and Bärbel were both planning to give up cigarettes. They were laughing. They were pampering and counseling Bärbel's brother, "Sonny," pronounced "Sony," thirty-four, lately arrived from East Berlin as a legal refugee after years of nonstop campaigning against the Honecker authorities.

A small, pale, fragile-looking figure, Sonny was still wrestling with the breach that nearly scuttled his family, still shaken by the reunion with Bärbel whom he had not seen in fourteen years.

"She was a stranger," he said, cocking his head slightly in wonderment. "You look for the person in the face and it's impossible to find it the way it was."

The way it was. All the family were learning to live in ways different from the old. Bärbel and Ota were slipping out of the Wall's shadow. I remembered that when I first met Bärbel in Bavaria, she had insisted, "Without the Wall I'd lose my identity." When she moved back to Berlin, she sighed in resignation and said, "The Wall has got us back." These days, the Wall was still the monster that kept her apart from her parents, but it no longer figured in her life as a palpable everyday presence.

Sonny would require less time to learn to live with the Wall's western face. Already, he had transformed it into a morale booster, of all things, a reminder of what he had escaped.

"Whenever I feel really lousy," he said, "I'll go over there and look east."

Perhaps the Wall was not for nothing, and in time it will come down. Nobody took Honecker very seriously when he declared defiantly on January 19, 1989, that the Wall was, in effect, forever. "It will still stand in fifty or one hundred years," he said. "That is necessary to protect our Republic from robbers, not to speak of those who are ready to disturb stability and peace in Europe." He was replying to yet another demand from the West to tear the Wall down. The demand and its rejection were becoming a game, a tit for tat that West and East were performing like small children. ("Move your toy out of the way!" cries one youngster. "I won't, I won't, not in a hundred years!" cries the other.)

In actuality, Honecker won the battle, not the war. Neither have we. "Miscalculation," as John Kennedy recognized, was the most dangerous word in the English language during the Berlin Wall crisis. It still is. Our luck can't last forever. Crisis management is no longer enough. Crises—at the Wall and elsewhere—must be prevented, aborted before miscalculation triggers the last alarm.

What have we learned from the Berlin Wall? Not a great deal. As world crises are measured, its outset was perhaps not spectacular enough to leave much of a mark. The preliminary skirmishing had dragged on for too long to qualify as drama. The Wall itself took shape too slowly to produce overwhelming shock. Deaths were few. Overtly, little happened except that the refugee flood came to a halt, which eased tensions to the relief of both sides. No opening gun had sounded, and no end, no last act. The Wall wasn't a crisis, except in retrospect.

"Nobody thought for a minute it would be permanent," said Donald M. Wilson, deputy director of the United States Information Agency, years later.

Only slowly did it dawn on me that the division of Berlin was received as so nebulous an event that it produced near amnesia in the (normally exceptionally communicative) upper layer of the Kennedy hierarchy. High-level eyewitnesses offered excellent memories about the Bay of Pigs venture that preceded the Wall and of the Cuban Missile Crisis that followed it. Of the six Kennedy captains to whom I talked and who wrote big books about their days with Kennedy, not one could recollect much about the early stages of the Wall.

They hardly remembered what they did on Sunday, August 13, 1961. Nor did they make records of that historic day, and I refer to such busy note-takers as McGeorge Bundy, Ted Sorensen, Arthur Schlesinger, Pierre Salinger, and Maxwell Taylor. Walt Rostow, in charge of the National Security Council that day, showed me his appointment book; to his consternation, it was blank.

Vacant memories afflicted not only the Kennedy partisans. Bromley K. Smith, an admired civil servant and longtime executive secretary of the National Security Council, smiled in embarrassment when he could remember nothing of that weekend. I remember asking Richard Helms, who became CIA Director later, why no postmortem had been held into the intelligence failure preceding the Wall, and how this spook of spooks was nonplussed and demanded huffily, "Why should there have been a postmortem?"

Alone among the principals, Willy Brandt voiced regrets. He recorded them almost twenty years after the event. They were no more than a wistful lament, even though close friends earmarked the Wall as *the* key event of the former Mayor's life. Brandt's tardy scolding could hardly have been wrapped in more circumspect terms. "It should be remembered," he wrote archly, "that for three whole days nothing was done which might have prompted the Russians to reconsider their decision." That was as far as this old hand would go with his reprimand.

Today the Wall commands the deference and ennui of most artifacts. Some West Berlin cabdrivers, when they are asked to take a passenger to the Wall at Checkpoint Charlie, mumble, "Terrible thing," mustering as much conviction as one does for the appendicitis of very distant kin. Checkpoint Charlie is another sightseeing stop for tourists, like the Pergamon Museum. Nobody seems to suffer from "Wall Sickness" anymore. Younger people have never heard the term *"Traenenpalast"* ("Palace of Tears"); hardly anybody weeps at the border these days. Daring escapes across the Wall are treated in the press the way the New York papers cover most muggings. And when I went to see the Berlin revival of Billy Wilder's comic film *One, Two Three,* once denounced as heresy, the audience was very young and laughed itself into near exhaustion. If the Wall is not yet a joke, there are occasions when it is not objectionable to laugh at it.

The scene at the border remains an instantly visible juxtaposition. Checkpoint Charlie in the West remains a narrow little shack, a toss-away symbol of temporariness. It no longer faces artless, temporary Communist shacks. Instead, the East looms as a laby-

rinth of barriers, gates, pillars, concrete walls, steel doors, movable
TV cameras, tall and piercing lights. Beige tones suggest inconspi-
cuousness, but all the obstacles are rooted heavily into the ground.
The place is a brooding presence exuding the permanence of a
truck terminal fortified to resist all but the prescribed behavior.

"Welcome to the capital of the German Democratic Republic,"
says a sign. It seems a black joke, a touch from a Billy Wilder film.

Berlin's great jewel value is as a reminder. It is the link between
the Berliners and the virtues of harder and somehow worthier
times: steadfastness, attachment, what the Germans call *Zivilcourage,* an excellent term. It means "civilian courage," which is different from the courage of a soldier. It is an especially sturdy kind of
courage, *Zivilcourage.* The soldier risks getting shot for desertion if
he falters; a civilian's bravery is personal and voluntary.

The memory of Berlin does linger. Everybody remembers the
Zivilcourage of John F. Kennedy, especially when he identified himself with the destiny of the threatened city, proclaiming himself to
be a Berliner. On sentimental occasions the locals still sing of their
"Berliner Luft" and of a certain suitcase that became a hit during
the hard years after the war.

The suitcase song is called, "Ich hab' noch einen Koffer in Berlin" ("I still have a suitcase in Berlin"). It is a cry of longing like
"Lili Marlene," but it is not of men in uniform. It tells of people
with *Zivilcourage* who left emotional baggage behind in the city of
the painful Wall, but can be counted upon not to abandon their
feeling for the place. I know about that suitcase. I left one in Berlin
myself.

CHRONOLOGY OF EVENTS

1958

November 27.   "The Khrushchev Ultimatum": Soviet Premier demands an end to Berlin's four-power status and withdrawal of all Western occupation troops.

1961

January 20.   John F. Kennedy inaugurated President.

February.   Dean Acheson appointed to study Berlin problem.

March 16.   "The Disappearing Satellite," article predicting Berlin Wall, appears.

March 16.   U.S. Ambassador to Moscow Llewellyn Thompson warns in secret telegram that East Germans might close East Berlin border.

March 28–29.   Warsaw Pact leaders reject East German Premier Walter Ulbricht's initial proposal to seal Berlin border as too dangerous.

April 17.   Disastrous CIA invasion of Cuba at Bay of Pigs.

June 3–4.   Kennedy and Khrushchev clash in grimly unsuccessful summit conference in Vienna; Soviet Premier threatens nuclear war.

June 15. Ulbricht asserts at East Berlin press conference that "nobody intends to build a wall."

June 15. Khrushchev declares that a peace treaty recognizing nation status for German Democratic Republic (DDR) cannot be further delayed.

June 16. Kennedy asks Acheson for detailed recommendations on Berlin.

June 29. Acheson delivers recommendations to National Security Council.

July 6. Arthur Schlesinger, Jr., and other presidential aides challenge Acheson's aggressive military options on Berlin.

July 8. Khrushchev announces cancellation of Soviet demobilization and orders one third increase in military spending.

July 25. In a strong national TV address, Kennedy announces detailed program to resist Soviet pressure on Berlin.

July 26–27. In private talks with Kennedy's adviser John J. McCloy at Sochi, Khrushchev replies explosively to Kennedy's speech.

August 3–5. In secret Kremlin meeting, Warsaw Pact leaders give Ulbricht approval to seal East-West border and erect Berlin Wall.

August 7. Khrushchev warns of Soviet nuclear superbomb that could turn all Germany "to dust."

August 9. Colonel Oleg Penkovsky, CIA double agent in Moscow, learns of projected Berlin border closure but fails to notify West.

August 9. Berlin Watch Committee, coordinating American intelligence in West Berlin, concludes that no wall will be built.

August 10. Marshal Ivan Koniev, newly appointed Soviet commander for East Germany, assures Western representatives, "Whatever may occur in the foreseeable future, your rights will remain untouched."

August 11. More than four thousand panicky East Germans arrive in West Berlin reception camps as daily flood of refugees keeps mounting; so far, four million have fled West.

August 13. East German troops seal Berlin border with barbed wire.

August 15. First slabs of concrete are installed at East-West border, signaling Communist intention to build a permanent wall.

August 16. West Berlin tabloid headline: THE WEST IS DOING NOTHING.

August 19. Vice President Lyndon B. Johnson and General Lucius D. Clay arrive in West Berlin for morale-building visit.

August 20. Convoy of fifteen hundred GIs arrives in West Berlin as symbolic reinforcement of U.S. garrison.

September 8. Kennedy glumly tells friend, "The foul winds of war are blowing."

Mid-
September. Tide in balance of power turns dramatically: aerial reconnaissasnce satellite photos prove Khrushchev's bluff; U.S. missile superiority is overwhelming.

October 17. Khrushchev concedes that his nuclear bluff has been successfully called by Kennedy. In six-hour speech, Soviet Premier announces an about-face: he will "not insist" on East German peace treaty.

October 27–28. American-Soviet tank confrontation at Checkpoint Charlie ends in stalemate.

1962

February 10. Francis Gary Powers, CIA U-2 spy pilot, is exchanged in Berlin for Soviet master agent Colonel "Rudolf Abel," thereby launching East Berlin attorney Wolfgang Vogel as key East-West middleman.

Spring. Vogel proposes that West Germany ransom East German political prisoners for cash, a scheme still operating a quarter of a century later.

Summer.   East Germans build glass "Palace of Tears," border control post at Friedrichstrasse station.

October 22.   Expecting Soviet reprisals in Berlin, Kennedy announces quarantine of Khrushchev missile shipments to Cuba (the Cuban Missile Crisis).

1963

June 26.   Kennedy visits Wall, vows, *"Ich bin ein Berliner."*

July 15.   Willy Brandt's foreign policy spokesman, Egon Bahr, launches *Ostpolitik*: "rapprochement through small steps."

November 22.   Kennedy assassinated.

December 17.   First agreement for daily visitor passes between East and West Berlin is negotiated.

1971

Spring   East Germans install first of 60,000 self-firing automatic weapons along East-West border.

May 3.   Erich Honecker replaces Walter Ulbricht as DDR chief executive.

September 27. Four-power agreement settles Berlin's status.

1973

May 31.   Honecker holds first private summit meeting with West German representative at Wandlitz.

1976

Spring.   Dr. Karl-Heinz Nitschke organizes unprecedented resistance petition in Riesa, East Germany.

1981

Dec. 11–13.   Honecker and West German Chancellor Helmut Schmidt hold ground-breaking summit meeting at Werbellinsee.

1983

October 5.   Honecker announces removal of self-firing weapons at border.

1986

February 10. Working with Soviet, American, and West German diplomats, attorney Vogel arranges for release of Soviet dissident Anatoly Sharansky in Berlin.

Summer. "Shoot to kill" orders reportedly no longer mandatory for East German border troops hunting escapees at Wall.

1987

Sept. 7–11. Honecker, in first working visit to West Germany, emotionally predicts day "when borders will no longer divide us but unite us."

NOTES ON SOURCES

PAGE 21

B. Grübel interviews

PAGES 23–26

Anonymous CIA source interview; V. Marchetti interview; Garthoff, *Reflections on the Cuban Missile Crisis,* pp. 40–41, Garthoff interview

PAGES 26–28

Clifton interviews

PAGES 30–43

B. Grübel interviews; Petra interviews; unpublished Grübel notes

PAGE 44

President Kennedy: Salinger, *With Kennedy,* p. 117

PAGES 44–47

Bailey, "The Disappearing Satellite," pp. 20–23; Bailey interview

PAGES 47–48

a wall . . . ": Cate, *The Ides of August,* 62; Catudal, *Kennedy and the Berlin Wall Crisis,* p. 25

build one.": Schenk interview

PAGE 49

nuclear variety: Sorensen, *Kennedy,* p. 513

PAGE 50

making threats": O'Donnell, *Johnny, We Hardly Knew Ye,* pp. 341–42

PAGE 52

C. Sorensen: Wyden, *Bay of Pigs—The Untold Story,* p. 310

PAGE 53

asked Kennedy: Isaacson, *The Wise Men,* p. 594

PAGE 54

the room . . . ": Halberstam, *The Best and the Brightest,* p. 62

played upon.": Catudal, *Kennedy and the Berlin Wall Crisis,* pp. 66–67

on Berlin.": Wyden, *Bay of Pigs–The Untold Story,* p. 294

PAGE 55

a brother: Schlesinger, *A Thousand Days,* p. 391; Sorensen, *Kennedy,* p. 576

of accord." Catudal, *Kennedy and the Berlin Wall Crisis,* pp. 105, 117, 115

PAGES 55–56

cold winter.": Schlesinger, *A Thousand Days* p. 377; Catudal, *Kennedy and the Berlin Wall Crisis,* p. 116

PAGE 56

Times columnist: Schlesinger, *A Thousand Days,* p. 375, p. 374

of me.": Halberstam, *The Best and the Brightest,* p. 76

he said. (Footnote): Bracken, *The Command and Control of Nuclear Forces,* p. 46, p. 48

PAGE 57

shrewd listener: O'Donnell, *Johnny, We Hardly Knew Ye,* pp. 344–47

gap real?: Betts, *Nuclear Blackmail and Nuclear Balance,* p. 166–67; Klass, *Secret Sentries in Space,* pp. 105, 107; Burrows, *Deep Black,* p. 111

PAGES 58–59

by luck: Burlatsky interview

PAGE 60

my life: Wyden, *The Chances of Accidental War*

PAGE 63

"massive retaliation.": Kaplan, *The Wizards of Armageddon,* p. 296

PAGES 63–66

would remember: Armstrong interview; McNamara interview

PAGE 67

Yarmolinsky replied: Halberstam, *The Best and the Brightest,* p. 243

PAGES 68–69

man glowering: Catudal, *Kennedy and the Berlin Wall Crisis,* p. 72

PAGE 69

or wrong: Weintal, *Facing the Brink,* p. 140

and elegant: Isaacson, *The Wise Men,* p. 528

in 1940: Weintal, *Facing the Brink,* p. 162

in 1940.: Isaacson, *The Wise Men,* pp. 5, 85, 464, 594–95

PAGE 70

old hand: Isaacson, *The Wise Men,* pp. 592–94

Pigs expedition: Catudal, *Kennedy and the Berlin Wall Crisis,* p. 44

about Berlin: Acheson Oral History (Kennedy Library)

PAGE 71

and softliners: Schlesinger, *A Thousand Days,* pp. 380–81

landing equipment: Catudal, *Kennedy and the Berlin Wall Crisis,* p. 89

PAGE 72

national emergency: Catudal, *Kennedy and the Berlin Wall Crisis,* pp. 144–46

PAGES 72–73

very well.": Isaacson, *The Wise Men,* p. 611

PAGE 73

at Hyannis Port: Schlesinger, *A Thousand Days,* pp. 386–93

PAGE 74

go along"?): Schlesinger, *A Thousand Days,* pp. 387–88

one third: Catudal, *Kennedy and the Berlin Wall Crisis,* pp. 160–63

PAGE 75

the limit.": Isaacson, *The Wise Men,* p. 612

negotiating table: Isaacson, *The Wise Men,* p. 613; Catudal, *Kennedy and the Berlin Wall Crisis,* p. 177

PAGES 75–76

national emergency: Catudal, *Kennedy and the Berlin Wall Crisis,* p. 176; Sorensen interview

PAGE 77

point out: Sorensen, *Kennedy,* p. 590; Catudal, *Kennedy and the Berlin Wall Crisis,* pp. 180–82

without leadership.": Catudal, *Kennedy and the Berlin Wall Crisis,* p. 182; Sorensen interview

Long Island: Murrow to JFK (JFK Library); Sorensen interview; Sorensen, *Kennedy,* p. 591

PAGE 78

atomic trigger: Rostow, *The Diffusion of Power,* p. 230

PAGE 79

-making loop: Cate, *The Ides of August,* pp. 108–11

Khrushchev's reaction: Sorensen, *Kennedy,* pp. 591–92; Catudal, *Kennedy and the Berlin Wall Crisis,* pp. 113–14

PAGES 81–82

apply it: Schlesinger, *A Thousand Days,* p. 392; Catudal, pp. 197–201

PAGE 85

millimeter farther.": *Spiegel*, August 16, 1976
PAGES 85–86
fruitless: Sejna interview
PAGE 86
Mother Russia: Khrushchev, *Khrushchev Remembers*, pp. 206–7; Mapother interview; Catudal, *Kennedy and the Berlin Wall Crisis*, pp. 49–52
through Berlin.": Catudal, *Kennedy and the Berlin Wall Crisis*, p. 304
PAGE 87
August 3: Cate, *The Ides of August*, pp. 139–45
PAGE 88
discourage refugees: Catudal, *Kennedy and the Berlin Wall Crisis*, pp. 209–12; Cate, *The Ides of August*, pp. 154–61; Sejna interview
PAGE 89
with finality: Cate, *The Ides of August*, pp. 159–61
go ahead?: Catudal, *Kennedy and the Berlin Wall Crisis*, p. 201
Soviet feline: Sejna interview
such agreement (Footnote): Steinert, Hübner, Keiderling, Hanisch, Max Schmidt interviews
PAGE 90
watch them: Cate, *The Ides of August*, pp. 160–61
day indeed.": Talbott (ed.), *Khrushchev Remembers*, 1974 augmented edition, pp. 505–6
watching watchers: Mapother interview
marketplace: Talbott (ed.), *Khrushchev Remembers*, 1974 augmented edition, p. 506; Burlatsky interview
advanced age: Talbott (ed.), *Krushchev Remembers*, p. 459
PAGES 91–93
case officer: von Pawel, McCord, and Dimmer interviews; Catudal, *Kennedy and the Berlin Wall Crisis,* pp. 229–30, 232–35
case officer: Höhne, *Der Krieg im Dunkeln*, p. 547
PAGE 94

along Kurfürstendamm: Taylor, *Swords and Plowshares*, p. 129
Communist territory. (Footnote): Ruland, *Krieg auf leisen Sohlen,* p. 102
Choir boys." (Footnote): Mapother interview
PAGE 95
Soviet attack.": Martin, *Wilderness of Mirrors*, pp. 77–90
Harvey's back: Currey, *Edward Lansdale, The Unquiet American*, pp. 242–43
PAGES 95–96
investigating committee: Martin, *Wilderness of Mirrors*, p. 178; Currey, *Edward Lansdale*, pp. 242–43; United States Senate, *Alleged Assassination Plots*, pp. 83, 182
PAGE 96
nervous visitors: Schlesinger, *Robert Kennedy and His Times*, pp. 514–15; Powers, *The Man Who Kept the Secrets*, pp. 172–73
PAGES 98–99
duplicity broke: Martin, *Wilderness of Mirrors*, p. 103
in awe: Mapother interview
PAGES 100–101
from grace: Hinckle, *The Fish Is Red*, pp. 113–14; Martin, *Wilderness of Mirrors*, pp. 132, 139; Ledeen, *Tinker, Turner, Sailor, Spy*, p. 40; Maas, *Manhunt*, pp. 29–31
PAGE 101
step by step: Martin, *Wilderness of Mirrors*, pp. 97–102
publishing house: Martin, *Wilderness of Mirrors*, pp. 218, 220
PAGE 102
Berlin Cowboys: Martin, *Wilderness of Mirrors*, pp. 178–80
PAGE 103
Washington inspection: Petty interview
PAGES 103–105
to another: Cookridge, *Gehlen—Spy of the Century*, pp. 320–34; Höhne, *Der Krieg im Dunkeln*, pp. 230–37; Felfe, *Im Dienst des Gegners*, pp. 280–95

PAGES 106–108
the enemy: interviews with anonymous sources in intelligence and CIA; interviews Amory, Mapother, Jameson

PAGES 109–116
major enemy: interviews with anonymous CIA sources; Morris, Dimmer, von Pawel, McCord

PAGE 114
of dollars: *Spiegel*, February 20, 1989, pp. 30–49; *New York Times*, May 7, 1989. p. 1

PAGES 117–121
he wished: interviews with anonymous CIA source, Jameson, Garthoff, Rositzke, Marchetti; Rositzke, *The CIA's Secret Operations*, pp. 69–71; Marchetti, *The CIA and the Cult of Counter Intelligence*, pp. 182–84, 254; Garthoff, *Reflections on the Cuban Missile Crisis*, pp. 40–41; Martin, *Wilderness of Mirrors*, pp. 116–17; Powers, *The Man Who Kept the Secrets*, pp. 127, 205, 362; Hood, *Mole*, pp. 265–69

PAGES 122–123
to believe: Catudal, *John Kennedy and the Berlin Wall Crisis*, pp. 226–27

PAGE 123
contradict Fulbright: Catudal, *John Kennedy and the Berlin Wall Crisis*, p. 203

PAGE 124
a wall: Rostow, *The Diffusion of Power*, p. 231
a city: Schwarz, *Berlinkrise und Mauerbau*, pp. 57–58

PAGE 125
a wall: Mapother interview

PAGES 126–127
the crisis: von Pawel interview; Bahnsen, *Kalter Winter im August*, pp. 113–115, 120; Catudal, *Kennedy and the Berlin Wall Crisis*, p. 212; Cate, *The Ides of August*, pp. 173–78; Talbott (ed.), *Khrushchev Remembers*, p. 459

PAGES 127–128
broke away: Seiffert interview

PAGES 129–130
sector border?": Richter, *Die Mauer*, pp. 7–11

PAGES 133–136
page 260): Hübner interview

PAGES 136–143
to digest: Steinert (Löffler), Hübner interviews; Cate, *The Ides of August*, pp. 160, 221–24, 233–35, 236–38; Petschull, *Die Mauer*, pp. 42–47; Bahnsen, *Kalter Winter im August*, pp. 123–24; Lippmann, *Honecker*, pp. 188–91; Thurow, *Kontrollpunkt Kohlhasenbrück*, pp. 3–11

PAGE 143
a shot!": Richter, *Die Mauer*, pp. 12–13

PAGES 143–144
Yuri Vasilyevich: Sigl interview

PAGE 144
West's inaction: Richter, *Die Mauer*, pp. 13–14

PAGES 144–145
isolate themselves?: Heym interview
run off?": Heym, *Nachruf*, p. 668

PAGE 145
to them . . . ": Richter, *Die Mauer*, p. 15

PAGE 146
is over . . . ": Richter, *Die Mauer*, p. 16

PAGES 147–148
their posts: Petschull, *Die Mauer*, pp. 50–51

PAGE 149
that way: Westin, *Newswatch*, p. 21; Schorr and Westin interviews

PAGE 150
West Berlin. . . . ": Petschull, *Die Mauer*, p. 53

PAGES 150–151
reckoned with: Cate, *The Ides of August*, 257–61; Müller interview

PAGES 151–152
like war: Vogel interview

PAGES 152–153
relied on: Bahnsen, *Kalter Winter im August*, p. 11; Brandt, *Begegnungen mit Kennedy*, p. 66; Binder, *The Other German*, p. 185

PAGE 153

into fact: Bailey, *Germans*, pp. 315–16
PAGE 154
of rest: Bahnsen, *Kalter Winter im August*, pp. 11–12; Wistrich, *Who's Who in Nazi Germany*, pp. 93–94
PAGES 154–155
it's happening.": Dimmer interview
PAGE 155
said later: Mapother interview
to sleep: Bahnsen, *Kalter Winter im August*, p. 13
PAGES 155–158
influence felt: Cate, *The Ides of August*, pp. 346–49; Springer, *Aus Sorge um Deutschland*, p. 388; Lochner and O'Donnell interviews
PAGE 158
of war: Von Pawel interview
PAGES 158–159
and truncheons: Bahnsen, *Kalter Winter im August*, p. 15; Binder, *The Other German*, p. 182
PAGE 159
government office: Kennedy interview
crisis began: Cate, *The Ides of August*, p. 316; Ausland communication; Klein interview
PAGES 159–161
box office.: Wilder and Diamond interviews; *Spiegel*, No. 27, 1985; Zolotow, *Billy Wilder in Hollywood*, p. 273; *Morgenpost*, August 13, 1961; *Spiegel*, August 23, 1961
be pushed . . . ": Schorr radio script; Tiffen communication
PAGES 161–164
was empty.": Brandt, *People and Politics*, pp. 16, 26; Trivers, *Three Crises*, p. 33; Bahnsen, *Kalter Winter im August*, pp. 16–18; Cate, *The Ides of August*, pp. 301–4; Binder, *The Other German*, pp. 183–84; Petschull, *Die Mauer*, p. 57; Hammer, *Das Mauerbuch*, p. 68; Brandt and Spangenberg interviews; Müller communication
PAGE 164
underplay events: Gruson interview
PAGES 164–165
War monger: Leonhard interview

PAGE 166
the West: Cate, *The Ides of August*, pp. 347–48; Lochner, Hoofnagle interviews
PAGES 166–167
risky one: Anonymous CIA sources
PAGE 167
political catastrophe.": Cate, *The Ides of August*, p. 348; Petschull, *Die Mauer*, p. 159
PAGE 168
were unauthorized: Bahnsen, *Kalter Winter im August*, p. 127; Catudal, *Kennedy and the Berlin Wall Crisis*, p. 27; Loewe interviews
PAGES 168–169
to sleep: Catudal, *Kennedy and the Berlin Wall Crisis*, p. 22
PAGE 169
OF LEGISLATURE: *New York Times*, August 13, 1961
PAGES 169–170
mid-summer: Catudal, *Kennedy and the Berlin Wall Crisis*, p. 27; Loewe and O'Donnell interviews
PAGE 170
of you.": Loewe interviews
his office: Catudal, *Kennedy and the Berlin Wall Crisis*, p. 23.
PAGES 170–171
car radio: Catudal, *Kennedy and the Berlin Wall Crisis*, p. 25; Ausland communication
PAGE 171
East Germany.": Catudal, *Kennedy and the Berlin Wall Crisis*, p. 28
PAGE 172
the airlift: O'Donnell, Bönisch, Loewe interviews
PAGES 172–173
in actuality: Catudal, *Kennedy and the Berlin Wall Crisis*, pp. 22–31; Ausland, *Foreign Service Journal*, July 1971; Ausland communication; Bromley Smith interview
PAGE 173
of Berlin: Clifton interview
be like!": Loewe interview
PAGE 174

once said: Catudal, *Kennedy and the Berlin Wall Crisis*, p. 31; Schlesinger, *Robert Kennedy and his Times*, p. 540

PAGES 174–175

conference room: O'Donnell interview; Ball communication

PAGE 175

Alexis Johnson: Johnson and Rusk interviews

PAGES 175–176

you go?": Catudal, *Kennedy and the Berlin Wall Crisis*, p. 32; Rusk interview; Ball communication

PAGE 176

ducks in a row.": Rusk, Lightner, Kohler interviews

PAGES 181–184

too complicated: Murphy, *Diplomat Among Warriors*, pp. 21, 22; 226–33; Bellush, *He Walked Alone*, pp. VII–VIII, 192–206; Ambrose, *Eisenhower* (Vol. I), pp. 392–93; Hanser, *Putsch*, pp. 278–79

PAGES 189–195

East Germans: Clay, *Decision in Germany*, p. 374; Davison, *The Berlin Blockade*, pp. 155–56; Backer, *Winds of History*, p. 242; Rogow, *James Forrestal*, pp. 17–18, 306–7; Isaacson, *The Wise Men*, pp. 356, 460, 476

PAGES 196–200

be effective: Fricke, *Opposition und Widerstand*, pp. 88–95; Borkowski, *Erich Honecker*, pp. 312–19; Lippmann, *Honecker*, pp. 152–62; Heinz Brandt, *Ein Traum, der nicht entführbar ist*, pp. 240–42; Bölling, *Wenn der Mann mit dem Strohhut Kommt*

PAGES 200–201

in two: Lippmann, *Honecker*, pp. 188–89; McAdams, *East Germany and Detente*, p. 29; *Michelin Guide*, France (1988), *Père-Lachaise Cemetery*, pp. 187; *Encyclopedia Britannica*, *The Paris Commune*, Vol. 23, p. 576

PAGES 202–203

to care: Schenk, *Mein doppeltes Vaterland*, pp. 124–30; Schenk interview

PAGE 204

in abeyance: "Vor Toresschluss," *Spiegel*, August 9, 1961, p. 13

PAGES 204–205

once more: Weber, *Geschichte der DDR*, pp. 297–99, 325

PAGE 205

Berlin Mafia: Catudal, *Kennedy and the Berlin Wall Crisis*, p. 210

PAGE 213

the spooks: O'Donnell interview

PAGES 214–215

own ways: O'Donnell interview

PAGE 216

through unhindered . . .": Schorr radio script

Berlin's "commuters.": *New York Times*, August 14, 1961, p. 1+

PAGES 217–218

your ass): Amory Oral History (Kennedy Library)

PAGE 218

moment anyway: Hammer, *Das Mauerbuch*, p. 68

PAGES 218–220

further reflection: Wilson Oral History (Kennedy Library); Springer, *Aus Sorge um Deutschland*, p. 388; Binder, *The Other German*, p. 185; Hoofnagle interview

PAGE 220

and left: Bahnsen, *Kalter Winter Im August*, p. 141; Binder, *The Other German*, p. 184; *Spiegel*, August 23, 1961, p. 16

or in tears . . . ": Schorr radio script

in sight: Gruson, *New York Times*, August 15, 1961, p. 1

unequivocal no: Schorr radio script

PAGE 221

become apparent: Schorr radio script; Petschull, *Die Mauer*, p. 154

PAGES 221–223

switch sides: Petschull, *Die Mauer*, pp. 149–53; Westin interview

PAGE 224

in Berlin: Binder, *The Other German*, pp. 185–86; Bahnsen, *Kalter Winter im*

August, pp. 146–47; Petschull, *Die Mauer,* p. 155
　PAGES 225–226
Allies didn't: Petschull, *Die Mauer,* pp. 155–57; Bahnsen, *Kalter Winter im August,* pp. 144–45; Binder, *The Other German,* pp. 186–87
　PAGE 226
Berlin border: anonymous CIA sources
　PAGE 227
were for: Bahnsen, *Kalter Winter im August,* p. 49
why me?": O'Donnell, *Johnny, We Hardly Knew Ye,* p. 303
　PAGES 227–228
the same: Isaacson, *The Wise Men,* p. 615; Clay Oral History (Columbia University)
　PAGES 228–229
the President: Petschull, *Die Mauer,* pp. 167–68
　PAGES 229–230
desk officer: Sorensen, *Kennedy,* p. 594; Gelb, *The Berlin Wall,* p. 214; Hammer, *Das Mauerbuch,* p. 69; O'Donnell, *Johnny, We Hardly Knew Ye,* p. 300
　PAGES 230–232
New York Times: Cate, *The Ides of August,* p. 417; Ellis, *Clarke of St. Vith,* pp. 260–61; Bunting, *"Soldier";* Clifton interview; Clarke communication; Gruson interview
　PAGES 232–233
of shoes: Petschull, *Die Mauer,* p. 175
　PAGE 233
Ted Sorensen: Sorensen, *Kennedy,* p. 594
　PAGES 233–234
in public: Petschull, *Die Mauer,* pp. 173–76; Binder, *The Other German,* p. 190
　PAGES 239–240
his brief: Anonymous CIA sources; Mapother, Dimmer interviews; Catudal, *Kennedy and the Berlin Wall Crisis,* pp. 236–37
　PAGES 242–243

"absurd" phenomenon: Kennedy interview; McCone communication
　PAGE 243
the novelists: Marks interview
　PAGES 244–245
le Carré: *New York Times,* April 21, 1964; le Carré (Cornwell), *The Spy Who Came in from the Cold,* pp. 254–255; *Current Biography* 1974, pp. 332–35
　PAGE 246
Attorney General: Schlesinger, *A Thousand Days,* pp. 462–63
　PAGE 247
openly again: Bundy, *Danger and Survival,* p. 375
　PAGES 247–248
every day: Betts, *Nuclear Blackmail,* pp. 56–57
　PAGE 248
response" doctrine: Ellsberg and Kaysen interviews
John Marshall: Armstrong interview
　PAGES 249–250
was ferocious: Herken, *Counsels of War,* pp. 159–60
　PAGES 250–251
planner said: Kaplan, *Wizards of Armageddon,* pp. 299–300; Herken, *Counsels of War,* pp. 158–60
　PAGES 251–252
President's conscience: Kaplan, *Wizards of Armageddon,* p. 302; Herken, *Counsels of War,* p. 158; Ellsberg interview
　PAGES 253–254
President's mind: Bradlee personal notes
　PAGES 254–255
please copy.": Schlesinger, *A Thousand Days,* pp. 399–400
　PAGES 255–257
Khrushchev listened: *New York Times,* July 13, 14, 27, 30, August 5, 12, 17, 1966; Marchetti, *The Cult of Counterintelligence,* pp. 212–14; interviews Marchetti, Fox
　PAGES 257–258
ballistic missiles: Kaplan, *The Wizards*

of Armageddon, pp. 286–87; Burrows, *Deep Black,* pp. 110–11; Betts, *Nuclear Blackmail,* p. 166

PAGES 258–259

Berlin Wall: Sorensen, *Kennedy,* p. 553; Bundy, Ellsberg interview; Horelick, *Strategic Power,* p. 84

PAGES 261–262

always possible: *New York Times,* August 28, 1961; Schorr radio scripts; Schorr, Gruson interviews

PAGES 262–263

all right.": Clay Oral History (Columbia University)

PAGE 264

with hatred.": Novosti, *Nikita Khrushchev: Life and Destiny,* p. 27

Truman Affair.": Bundy to JFK, August 28, 1961; Smith, *The Papers of General Lucius Clay,* p. XXXI

each other: Gen. Clarke communication; EMNID poll

PAGE 265

West Point: Gelb, *The Berlin Wall,* p. 235; Catudal, *Kennedy and the Berlin Wall Crisis,* pp. 135–35; Ellis, *Clarke of St. Vith,* pp. 268–69

PAGES 265–267

his last: Smith, *The Defense of Berlin,* pp. 319–24; Salinger, *With Kennedy,* p. 228; Talbott (ed.), *Khrushchev Remembers,* pp. 459–60; Kroll, *Lebenserinnerungen eines Botschafters,* p. 514; Lightner interview

PAGE 266

never reported. (Footnote): Schlesinger, *Robert F. Kennedy and His Times,* p. 538

PAGE 267

to resist: Schlesinger, *A Thousand Days,* p. 547

PAGES 269–271

another miscalculation: Salinger, *With Kennedy,* pp. 225–28; Alsop, *Saturday Evening Post,* March 31, 1962

PAGES 271–272

inform Kennedy: Smith, *The Defense of Berlin,* pp. 340–41, 328–32; Gelb, *The Berlin Wall,* pp. 352–53; Clay Oral

History (Columbia University); JFK to Clay, March 1, March 15, 1961 (Kennedy Library)

PAGES 272–273

President Kennedy": Kroll, *Lebenserinnerungen eines Botschafters,* p. 514

PAGES 273–274

of Moscow: Bahnsen, *Kalter Winter im August,* pp. 197–200

PAGES 274–275

the best.": Wynne, *Contact on Gorky Street,* pp. 194–98

PAGE 275

be fired: Garthoff, *Reflections on the Cuban Missile Crisis,* p. 39; Powers, *The Man Who Kept the Secrets,* pp. 422–23

PAGES 276–278

Berlin, Berlin": Abel, *The Cuban Missile Crisis,* pp. 43–44; O'Donnell, *Johnny, We Hardly Knew Ye,* pp. 354, 368; Sorensen, *Kennedy,* pp. 673, 699; Schlesinger, *A Thousand Days,* p. 803; Garthoff, *Reflections on the Cuban Missile Crisis,* pp. 39–41

PAGE 278

allied troops: Shell, *Bedrohung und Bewährung,* p. 76

PAGES 278–279

American will: Detzer, *The Brink,* p. 210

PAGE 279

hyperbolic outburst. (Footnote): Schlesinger, *Robert Kennedy and His Times,* p. 546

PAGES 279–280

provocative farewell: Garthoff, *Reflections on the Cuban Missile Crisis,* p. 41

PAGE 280

since 1961.": Anonymous CIA source

Central Committee: *New York Times,* March 5, 1971

PAGES 280–284

said Bobby: Schlesinger, *A Thousand Days;* pp. 884–85; O'Donnell, *Johnny, We Hardly Knew Ye,* pp. 416–17; Sorensen, *Kennedy,* pp. 600–601; Binder, *The Other German,* p. 204; Clay Oral History (Columbia University); interviews Bundy, Schlesinger, Gildner,

Lochner, James O'Donnell, Clifton, Brandt, Rusk, B. Grübel
PAGES 287–288
was happening: B. Grübel interviews; unpublished Grübel notes
PAGE 288
preferably both: Morris interview
PAGES 289–294
more tunnels: Kemp, *Escape from Berlin*, pp. 68–69; *Newsweek*, October 22, 1962; *New York Times*, December 12, 1962; *Television Quarterly*, Fall 1963, pp. 8–23
PAGES 294–296
he said: Kemp, *Escape from Berlin*, pp. 67–82
PAGES 297–299
couldn't last: Schmitthammer, *Rechtsanwalt Wolfgang Vogel*, pp. 93–95
PAGES 299–301
into freedom. . . .": Schmitthammer, *Rechtsanwalt Wolfgang Vogel*, pp. 96–97; Bölke, *Tagesspiegel*, October 7, 1964, p. 1, October 9, 1964, p. 1
PAGES 299–308
him up: Barzel, *Es ist noch nicht zu spät*, pp. 31–39; Schmitthammer, *Rechtsanwalt Wolfgang Vogel*, pp. 73–77; interviews Rehlinger, Vogel, Stange, Spangenberg
PAGES 308–313
as well: Donovan, *Strangers on a Bridge*, pp. 318, 375, 379, 381, 388, 395, 402–403, 419; de Gramont, *The Secret War*, pp. 224, 263; Bernikow, *Abel*, pp. 298–300; interviews Vogel, Farmer, Meehan, Mapother
PAGES 315–319
eventually concede: Interviews Vogel, Stange, Spangenberg
PAGES 319–321
the start: Interviews Vogel, Fritzen
PAGES 321–334
distasteful news: Schmitthammer, *Rechtsanwalt Wolfgang Vogel*, pp. 79–88; Interviews Vogel, Stange, Kunst, von Wedel
PAGES 334–335
lawyer Vogel: Schmitthammer, *Recht-*

sanwalt Wolfgang Vogel, pp. 124–26; Höhne, *Der Krieg im Dunkeln;* Vogel interview
PAGES 335–336
troublemaker Borkowski: Borkowski, "In der Heimat, da gibt's ein Wiedersehn," pp. 25–27
PAGES 340–342
a trumpet: Bentley, *The Brecht Memoir*, p. 54; Bentley, *Theatre of War*, pp. 215–16, 219–20; Mugay, *Die Friedrichstrasse*, pp. 66–67, 111
PAGES 342–346
the line: Boris, *Die sich Lossagten*, pp. 45–47; Bentley, *Theatre of War*, pp. 224–25
PAGES 347–350
and language: Cookridge, *Spy Trade*, pp. 127, 133; Schmitthammer, *Rechtsanwalt Wolfgang Vogel*, p. 118
PAGES 350–351
the powerful: Martin, *Wilderness of Mirrors*, pp. 99–100; Cookridge, *Spy Trade*, pp. 209–14; Schmitthammer, *Rechtsanwalt Wolfgang Vogel*, p. 133
PAGES 351–357
in status: Hersh, *The Price of Power*, pp. 415–22; Kissinger, *The White House Years*, pp. 410–11, 806–10, 823–32; Garthoff, *Detente and Confrontation*, pp. 119–21; Rühle, *Der 13. August*, p. 186; Binder, *The Other German*, p. 288
PAGES 357–368
already ripened: B. and O. Grübel interviews; unpublished Grübel notes
PAGES 369–379
was systemic: Seifarth interviews
PAGES 380–384
very few: Müller-Hegemann: *Die Mauerkrankheit*, pp. 13–16
PAGES 385–388
as well: Schmitthammer, *Rechtsanwalt Wolfgang Vogel*, pp. 136–39
PAGES 386–387
to him: Borkowski, *Erich Honecker*, p. 69
PAGES 388–389
a task: Anonymous CIA source

to investigate: Franz Loeser interview
  PAGES 389–391
the West: Cate, *The Ides of August,* p.
25–28; *Welt,* May 11, 1986; *Spiegel,*
August 31, 1987; Lange-Müller, Seidel interviews
  PAGES 391–396
straw hat: Jänecke, *Erich Honecker,*
Stern, p. 118; Bölling, *Die Fernen Nach-*
barn, pp. 14–16, 89; Borkowski, *Erich*
Honecker, pp. 185–88, 310; Gaus, *Wo*
Deutschland Liegt, pp. 145, 146, 148;
Wall Street Journal, September 5, 1984,
p. 1; *Spiegel,* August 31, 1987, pp. 31–
32
  PAGES 397–411
about it.": B. and O. Grübel interviews; unpublished Grübel notes
  PAGES 412–417
disgorge them: B. and O. Grübel interviews, Meta Kraal interviews; unpublished Grübel notes
  PAGES 421–425
conventional means: Siegrid Manolo
and Erika B. interviews
  PAGES 426–433
named Micha: *New York Times,* August
19, 20, October 18, 1975; *Hartford*
Courant, August 21, 1975; *Quick,* No.
36, pp. 21–24; No. 37, pp. 71–74,
1975; *Stern,* August 25, 1975; Weeghman, *Flying,* February 1976, pp. 75–
79; *Daily Oklahoman,* April 18, April
29, June 10, 1982; March 15, May 18,
1983; Heidrich, Goebel, Grabe interviews
  PAGES 434–437
very fast: *Spiegel,* November 3, 1975;
April 12, 28; May 17, 1976; *Arbeitsge-*
meinschaft 13. August (press conference transcripts), August 10, 1981, p.
8; August 10, 1984, pp. 18–19, 31–
34; August 11, 1986, pp. 62–66;
Fricke, *Opposition und Widerstand,* pp.
143–44; Interviews Fritze, Manfred
Müller, Hildebrandt
  PAGES 438–441
of neither: *Neue Zürcher Zeitung,* Janu-

ary 17, 1974; January 26, 1974; February 7, 1979; *Stern,* August 16, 1973;
Spiegel, August 20, 1973; *New York*
Times, January 27, 1976; *Bunte,* March
18, 1977; *Frankfurter Allgemeine Zei-*
tung, February 7, 1979; *Bunte,* March
18, 1977; *Welt am Sonntag,* February
11, 1979; *Welt,* September 25, 1979;
Hildebrandt interview
  PAGES 442–447
as ever: Petschull, *Mit dem Wind nach*
Westen, pp. 1–245
  PAGES 451–468
make inquiries: B. and O. Grübel interviews; unpublished Grübel notes
  PAGES 469–482
the children: *Spiegel,* December 15,
1975, pp. 36–38; December 22, 1975,
pp. 19–26; November 29, 1976, pp.
52–61; unpublished Grübel notes; interviews Vogel, Stange, Hampel,
Manfred Müller, Kraal, von Wedel
  PAGES 483–487
with her: Grübel, *Das Beste aus Reader's*
Digest, "Gebt mir meine Kinder zurück!" October 1977, pp. 62–67;
Newsweek, January 17, 1977, p. 11;
Manfred Müller, B. and O. Grübel interviews; unpublished Grübel notes
  PAGES 491–498
everyone said: Ammer, *Bürgerrechts-*
bewegung in Riesa, unpaginated;
Fricke, *Opposition und Widerstand,* pp.
169–72; Loewe, *Abend kommt der Klas-*
senfeind (Book excerpt), *Spiegel,* August 29, 1977, pp. 134–38; *Bild,*
September 4, 1976; *BZ,* August 31,
September 4, 1976; *Welt,* September
4, 1976; *Morgenpost,* August 21, 22, 26,
September 4
  PAGES 499–512
most ingenious: Seifarth interviews
  PAGES 515–520
in practice: Bölling, *Die fernen Nach-*
barn, pp. 158–64, 129–57, 230;
Schmitthammer, *Rechtsanwalt Wolf-*
gang Vogel, pp. 25, 139; Vogel interviews

PAGES 521–533
the DDR: Zachau, *Stefan Heym,* pp. 1–20; Boris, *Die sich Lossagten;* pp. 114–116; Heym, *Wege und Umwege,* pp. 369–70; *Tagesspiegel,* April 18, 1984

PAGES 534–540
was fantastic: Seifarth interviews

PAGES 541–546
Seifarth said: Seifarth interviews

PAGES 549–559
the other: Interviews Greenwald, Gilman, Jeff Smith, Vogel, Rehlinger, Meehan; Schmitthammer, *Rechtsanwalt Wolfgang Vogel,* pp. 156–70

PAGES 560–568
most forbidding: Hoffmann, *Widerstand, Staatsstreich, Attentat,* pp. 634, 739; Hildebrandt, *Maler interpretieren die Mauer,* pp. 11, 13; *New York Times,* October 24, 1986; press release, Haus am Checkpoint Charlie, October 14, 1986; interviews Hildebrandt, Schumm, Beyer

PAGES 569–577
his travail: Schacht, *Hohenecker Protokolle,* pp. 18–24, 75–98, 116–218, 268–88; Boris, *Die sich Lossagten,* pp. 242–43; Schacht, *Europäische Ideen,* pp. 125, 129; Schacht interview

PAGES 577–578
around him: *Welt,* March 14, July 7, 1983; Haus am Checkpoint Charlie, press conference transcript, April 24, 1985, pp. 1–22

PAGES 579–581
were found: *Welt,* October 8, 1986; *Bild am Sonntag,* April 27, 1986; Rehlinger interview

PAGES 581–583
631,657 marks: *Welt,* August 2, 1986; *Tagesspiegel,* December 18, 1986; Schmitthammer, *Rechtsanwalt Wolfgang Vogel,* p. 23; *Welt,* January 23, 1986; *Westfalen-Blatt,* September 7, 1985; DPA dispatch, January 17, 1986

PAGES 583–585
crossing over: Kemp, *Escape from Berlin,* pp. 105–8, 118–22, 123–26; *Spie-*

gel, No. 33, 1986; No. 1, 1985; *Welt,* August 23, 1986; Haus am Checkpoint Charlie, press release, August 25, 1986; press conference transcript, August 1, 1986

PAGES 586–588
side again?": *Spiegel,* No. 33, 1986; Schneider, *Deutsche Ängste,* pp. 8–9

PAGES 588–593
the Interior: Leonhard, *Child of the Revolution,* pp. 290–91; *Zeit,* November 28, 1986, p. 55; June 17, 1988, p. 38; Maron, *Das Misverständnis,* pp. 49–79; Maron interview

PAGE 590
War frantic: Sontheimer, "Das kalte Herz von Berlin," *Zeitmagazin,* September 30, 1988, p. 46

PAGES 593–595
the East: Feller interview

PAGES 595–597
its grip: Winkler, *Made in DDR,* pp. 7, 44, 49, 112, 179, 188–91; Winkler interview

PAGES 603–604
original Canaletto: Bölling, *Leader* magazine; Gaus, *Wo Deutschland liegt,* pp. 151–52

PAGES 604–606
Brandenburg Gate: Interviews Schmidt, Seidel, Reinhold

PAGES 606–608
Lantos group: *Neues Deutschland,* January 11–12, 1986, p. 1; *Tagesspiegel,* January 11, 1986, p. 1

PAGES 608–612
in Washington: *Spiegel,* August 31, 1987, pp. 20–33, pp. 26–29; *Time,* September 21, 1987, pp. 6–7; *Tagesspiegel,* September 11, 1987, p. 2; *Frankfurter Rundschau,* September 11, 1987, pp. 1–3; *Welt,* September 11, 1987; *Wall Street Journal,* November 25, 1987, p. 1

PAGE 609
relations line. (Footnote): *Spiegel,* "Segen des Herrn," June 16, 1989, pp. 31–32; Spittmann, "Sozialismus in

den Farben der DDR," *Deutschland Archiv,* March 1989, pp. 241–44; Hilferufe von Drueben, "Schiessbefehl wurde nicht aufgehoben," *First Quarter* 1989, p. 4

PAGES 613–615
someday.: Heym interviews; *Newsweek,* September 28, 1987 (European edition), p. 56; *Welt,* September 28, p. 9, September 30, p. 6

PAGES 616–620
and Lincoln: *Süddeutsche Zeitung,* May 6, 1988; Kuppe, *Deutschland Archiv, Erkundung eines schwierigen Terrains,* pp. 577–80; Bölling, *Die fernen Nachbarn,* p. 199; Axen, Uschner interviews

PAGES 620–627
middle-aged intellectuals: *Spiegel,* No. 1, 1988, pp. 39–40; Lippmann, *Honecker,* pp. 61–63; Bölling, *Die fernen Nachbarn,* pp. 202, 204, 206, 209; Gaus, *Wo Deutschland liegt,* 108–9, 111, 120–21; Löser, *Die unglaubwürdige Gesellschaft,* pp. 47–54; Axen, Uschner, Löser interviews

PAGES 629–635
long ago: Hesse, *Westmedien in der DDR;* pp. 28, 68, 128; Heym, *Wege und Umwege,* pp. 333–42; Weber, *Die Geschichte der DDR,* pp. 405–6; Bussieck, *Die real existierende DDR,* pp. 150, 154; Informationszentrum, *Ost-Berlin,* p. 88; Urban, "Western TV—Surrogate for Freedom?" *New York Times,* February 7, 1986, p. 27; *Spiegel,* April 24, 1978, pp. 41–44; *Spiegel,* August 27, 1979 pp. 54–72; *Spiegel,* November 4, 1985, pp. 97–99; interviews Lochner, Kabel

PAGES 636–639
letting up: Löwenthal, Schenk interviews; Löwenthal, *Ich bin geblieben,* pp. 40–81; *Deutsche Zeitung,* December 22, 1978

PAGES 643–653
feeling uneasy: B. and O. Grübel interviews; Internationale Gesellschaft für Menschenrechte, *Dokumentation,* pp. 91–98; *Morgenpost,* October 28, 1984; *Welt,* August 26, 1988, p. 1+; interviews Drs. Wiener, Robson; communications Vogel, Priesnitz

PAGES 658–662
the same: Blair interview; *Nuclear Times,* May–June, 1986

PAGES 663–667
the settlers: *Nuclear Times,* May–June, 1986; *New York Times,* September 6, 1987; Penskus, *Zweimal Deutschland,* pp. 44–45; Bundeministerium für innerdeutsche Beziehunge, *Zahlenspiegel,* pp. 58–59; *Wall Street Journal,* November 20, 1985, p. 1+

PAGES 667–670
not sung: Hoerning interview; Ludz, *DDR Handbuch,* p. 720, 759; *Trabbi, Telespargel und Tränenpavillion,* p. 34; *Deutschland Archiv,* November 1987, pp. 1262–64; Röntgen, *Was soll mir eure Freiheit?* p. 229; Kopetzky, pp. 23–24

PAGES 670–671
can predict": Kennan, *The German Problem: A Personal View;* Livingston, "Stop Fearing German Reunification"; Schmemann, "Despite new stirrings, dream of 'one Germany' fades"

PAGES 673–681
the war: *Spiegel,* February 1, 1988, February 22, 1988; *Deutschland Archiv,* February 1988; pp. 227–28, 231; *New York Times,* June 6, 1987; Haus am Checkpoint Charlie, press conference transcripts, August 11, 1987, p. 9, August 12, 1988, p. 21; *Zeit,* January 1, 1988; Informationszentrum, *Berlin im Überblick,* p. 75

ABOUT THE BIBLIOGRAPHY

Since the Berlin Wall cuts across so much more than a city—at first I was staggered by the multiplicity of affected lives, cultures, ideologies, and incidents—the relevant literature is too large and too fragmented for the construction of a bibliography here that might claim anything remotely resembling total coverage.

Moreover, some works that would appear to be helpful are surprisingly unrevealing. To illustrate: two painstakingly researched, well-reviewed biographies appeared recently about Edward R. Murrow, the broadcaster and later the director of the United States Information Agency. A. M. Sperber's *Murrow: His Life and Times* (Freundlich, 1986) is 795 pages long; *Edward R. Murrow—An American Original* by Joseph E. Persico (McGraw-Hill, 1988) runs 562 pages. Yet neither of these excellent studies so much as hints that Murrow played the key role in alerting President Kennedy and his administration to the political and psychological impact of the Wall. This is especially remarkable because of the dramatic circumstances of Murrow's intervention, beginning in the first hours of the border closure on Sunday, August 13, 1961, when this quintessential professional eyewitness happened to be present at the scene, launched incisive inquiries, and phoned the White House.

The researcher's principal problem, however, is profusion of data. The best bibliography about the Wall runs 219 pages without any annotations and is, at this writing, about a decade behind the times and therefore grossly incomplete. Still, this careful, scholarly work, *Die Berliner Mauer,* edited by Michael Haupt and published in 1981 by Bernard & Gräfe Verlag in Munich, with an introduction by former Chancellor Willy Brandt, attempts to be comprehensive through the 1970s. It is a lifesaver, the best point of departure for anyone who becomes fascinated with the troubled life of the Wall.

It was this compilation that led me to an astonishing history by a young American academician, Professor Honoré M. Catudal of St. John's University—no, not the big one in New York but the one in Collegeville, Minnesota. His *Kennedy and the Berlin Wall Crisis* is probably the most informative book on the subject to date. It contains impressive firsthand research, including more than a decade of evidently relentless interviewing, and a thirty-three-page bibliography.

Yet Catudal's effort is almost unknown in the United States. While written lucidly and in English, it was published by Berlin Verlag of West Berlin in 1980 but never in America, possibly because of its curiously truncated form. It covers the diplomatic aspects of the period superbly up to August 1961 but ends there rather abruptly, as if the Wall's history ended that month. Like all other works I consulted, the book makes little effort to appreciate the dimension that most preoccupied Kennedy: the unprecedented *nuclear* dangers of the crisis. Discussion of the intelligence failure suffers from lack of access to contemporaneous principals of the Central Intelligence Agency's Berlin operating base. And data about the East Germans and the Soviets are slight and occasionally wrong, no doubt because Communist sources were silent during the 1970s, the time of Catudal's research.

Other books, including the more recent works, likewise view the Wall so one-sidedly, from the perspective of the West, that its other face, toward the East, and its impact on the DDR are largely obscured. The void is not hard to explain. The literature from the DDR, even the specialized material from military sources, is grotesquely denatured, often substituting paranoid clichés for basic facts that cannot possibly carry security implications any longer.

Not that the DDR historians are suppressing information. Their own government simply has not let them in on much.

I talked at length with the two leading East German scholars in the field, Wilfried Hanisch, a DDR army colonel who wrote his Ph.D. dissertation on the Wall and serves on the staff of the government publishing house for military history in Potsdam; as well as Gerhard Keiderling, a civilian government historian whose masterwork, *Berlin—1945–1986,* runs 904 pages in its latest edition (East Berlin: Dietz, 1987). Both men proved amiable, indeed eager to be helpful and appeared to be quite open.

By the time I met up with them in East Berlin during 1988, I was far enough along in my research to pose meaningful questions. Perhaps these men fooled me with their innocence, but I suspect not. I think they knew little more than I did, even about relatively trivial points. The government archives were closed to them and the state of their knowledge suggested that their interviewing had yielded fewer nuggets than my own. Historian-prophets don't seem to have much honor in their country, and oral history is not a developed art.

Within all the given limitations, the following bibliography is keyed to pragmatism, serviceability. It emphasizes recent materials and the growing body of solid research on the DDR from dependable West German authorities, especially the most savvy, knowledgeable refugees (cf. Fricke, Schacht, Schenk); eyewitness diplomats (cf. Bölling, Gaus, Kroll); and the accounts of Western media representatives once they leave the DDR jurisdiction (cf. Ash, Bussieck, Röntgen, Windmöller).

Week by week, *Der Spiegel* does far, far the best job in covering developments in the DDR. Ulrich Schwarz, the magazine's DDR correspondent, probably understands the country better than anyone, dead or alive. The most illuminating and comprehensive academic research and analysis on the country appear in an unusually lively scholarly journal, *Deutschland Archiv,* published by Verlag Wissenschaft und Politik at Goltsteinerstrasse 185, 4000 Cologne 51, phone (0221) 38 34 40, and edited by another one-time DDR refugee, Ilse Spittmann-Rühle. I cannot recommend this monthly too strongly.

Four other Western sources regularly pour out very useful (if opinionated) material about the DDR. At their Haus am Checkpoint Charlie, Friedrichstrasse 44, 1000 Berlin 61, phone (030) 251 1023, Rainer Hildebrandt and Horst Schumm publish transcripts of their always informative press conferences and summaries of the most up-to-date statistics concerning the Wall and its manifestations. The Internationale Gesellschaft für Menschenrechte (IGFM, International Society for Human Rights), Kaiserstrasse 72, 6000 Frankfurt 1, publishes two magazines that appear every two months: *Menschenrechte* and *DDR Heute.* The aggressive quarterly

Hilferufe von drüben is the work of the publisher of the same name, at Postfach 1770, 4780 Lippstadt. The Brüsewitz-Zentrum publishes *Christen drüben* at Karl-Barth-Strasse 7, 5300 Bonn 1.

For original documentary background on the Wall itself, I particularly recommend *13. August 1961–die Mauer von Berlin* by Jürgen Rühle and Gunter Holzweissig (Cologne: Edition Deutschland Archiv), second revised edition, 1986, as a rewarding time saver.

BIBLIOGRAPHY

Abrasimov, Pyotr. *West Berlin Yesterday and Today* (Dresden: Verlag Zeit im Bild, 1981).

Ackermann, Manfred. "Der begrenzte Blick," *Deutschland Archiv*, August 1987, pp. 823–34.

Ahrends, Martin (ed.). *Trabbi, Telespargel und Tränenpavillion: Das Wörterbuch der DDR-Sprache* (Munich: Heyne, 1986).

Ahrens, Wilfried. *Hilferufe von Drüben* (Huglfing/Obb.: Verlag für Öffentlichkeitsarbeit in Wirtschaft und Politik, 1978).

Albertz, Heinrich. *Blumen für Stukenbrock* (Hamburg; Rowohlt, 1985).

———. *Nachträge* (Hamburg: Rowohlt, 1983).

Alsop, Stewart. "Kennedy's Grand Strategy," *The Saturday Evening Post*, March 31, 1962.

Alten, Antonia von. "Wir wollen endlich nicht mehr von der DDR gegängelt werden," *Frankfurter Allgemeine Zeitung*, February 6, 1988.

Altena, John Van, Jr. *A Guest of the State* (Chicago: Regnery, 1967).

Ambrose, Stephen E. *Eisenhower and Berlin, 1945* (New York: Norton, 1967).

———. *Eisenhower* (Volume I) (New York: Simon and Schuster, 1983).

Ammer, Thomas. "Bürgerrechtsbewegung in Riesa—ein Versuch," *Sonderheft der politischen Studien*, Günter Olzog Verlag, Munich, March 1, 1977 (not paginated).

———. "Menschenrechtsverletzungen in der DDR," *Deutschland Archiv*, August 1985, pp. 949–84.

Ash, Timothy Garton. *Und willst Du nicht mein Bruder sein—die DDR Heute* (Hamburg: Rowohlt, 1981).

Associated Press. "Hartford Native Admits Copter Flights Freed 11," *New Haven Register,* August 20, 1975.

———. "Retired Colonel Pleads Guilty in Soviet Agent Plot," *The New York Times,* December 17, 1966

———. "Spione schickten ihre Kündigung an die DDR," *Berliner Morgenpost,* September 18, 1985, p. 1+.

———. "U.S. Pilot, Under Czech Fire, lifts 3 to West," *The New York Times,* August 19, 1975, p. 1.

———. "Zahl der politischen Häftlinge in der DDR mit rund 10,000 beziffert," *Tagesspiegel,* October 25, 1984, p. 1.

Associated Press/DPA. "Honecker besuchte nach 39 Jahren erstmals wieder seinen Geburtsort," *Tagesspiegel,* September 11, 1987, p. 2.

Ausland, John. "The Berlin Wall," *Foreign Service Journal,* July 1971, pp. 12–16.

Backer, John H. *Winds of History* (New York: Van Nostrand Reinhold, 1983).

Bader, Werner. *Geborgter Glanz-Flüchtlinge im eigenen Land* (Berlin: Westkreuz, 1979).

Badstübner, Rolf. *Die Potsdamer Konferenz,* Illustrierte historische Hefte #36 (East Berlin: VEB Deutscher Verlag der Wissenschaften, 1985).

Baedeker, Karl (ed.). *Der grosse Baedeker—Berlin* (Freiburg: Karl Baedeker, 1986).

Bahr, Egon. *Wass soll aus Deutschland werden?* (Hamburg: Rowohlt, 1982).

———. *Zum europäischen Frieden* (Berlin: Siedler, 1988).

Bailey, George. "The Disappearing Satellite," *The Reporter,* March 16, 1961, pp. 20–23.

———. "The Gentle Erosion of Berlin," *The Reporter,* April 26, 1962, pp. 15–19.

———. *Germans* (New York: Avon, 1972).

Baker, Peter. "His Code Name Is 'Uncle Ben' and He Arranges Prisoner Swaps" (Wolfgang Vogel), *People,* June 19, 1978, pp. 81–85.

Baring, Arnulf M. *Uprising in East Germany* (Ithaca, N.Y.: Cornell University Press, 1972).

Barzel, Rainer. *Es ist noch nicht zu spät* (Munich: Drömer Knaur, 1977).

Bath, Matthias. *Gefangen und freigetauscht* (Munich: Olzog, 1981).

Battle, Hellen. *Every Wall Shall Fall* (Old Tappan, N.J.: Revell/Hewitt House, 1969).

Baum, Karlz-Heinz. "Durch den "Tränenbunker" in den freien Westen," *Frankfurter Rundschau,* July 26, 1986, p. 3.

Beese, Klaus. *Fluchthilfe* (Kiel: Orion-Heimreiter, 1984).

Behn, Manfred (ed.). *Geschichten aus der Geschichte der DDR 1949–1979* (Darmstadt: Luchterhand, 1981).

Bellush, Bernard. *He Walked Alone* (Paris–The Hague: Mouton, 1968).

Bender, Peter. *Die Ostpolitik Willy Brandts* (Hamburg: Rowohlt, 1972).

———. *Wenn es West-Berlin nicht gäbe* (Berlin: Siedler, 1988).

Bennett, Jack O. *40,000 Stunden am Himmel* (Berlin: Ullstein, 1982).

Bentley, Eric. *The Brecht Memoir* (New York: PAJ Publications, 1985).

———. *Theatre of War* (New York: Viking, 1972).

Berliner Morgenpost. "Arzt in Riesa verhaftet," September 4, 1976.

———. "Barbara Grübel: 'Meine Kinder sollten nicht in einer solchen Atmosphäre aufwachsen,' " December 22, 1976.

———. "Nicht einmal Leoparden und Leibwächter konnten Lanzlinger vor seinem Mörder schützen," February 6, 1979.

———. "Ost-Berlin lässt Kinderstars nicht zur Mutter in den Westen," October 28, 1984.

———. "ZDF-Magazin hat 500 Jubiläum," April 4, 1984.

———. "Zwei Welten, zwei Männer und ein lautloses Geschäft," October 4, 1982.

Bernikow, Louise. *Abel* (New York: Trident, 1970).

Bethke, Eckart. *Jubeln nach Dienstschluss* (Braunschweig: Westermann, 1986).

Betts, Richard K. *Nuclear Blackmail and Nuclear Balance* (Washington, D.C.: Brookings Institution, 1987).

Biermann, Wolf. *Verdrehte Welt, das seh' ich gern* (Munich: DTV, 1985).

Bild. "Mutiger Arzt in der DDR verhaftet," September 4, 1976.

Binder, David. *The Other German—Willy Brandt's Life and Times* (Washington, D.C.: New Republic, 1975).

———. "The Wall Is a Decade Old, and Berliners Tend to Ignore It," *The New York Times*, August 14, 1971, p. 3.

Birnie, William A. H. "Berlin's Wall of Infamy," *The Reader's Digest*, December 1961, pp. 73–78.

Birrenbach, Kurt. *Meine Sondermissionen* (Düsseldorf: Econ, 1984).

Blair, Bruce G. *Strategic Command and Control* (Washington, D.C.: Brookings Institution, 1985).

Böhme, Irene. *Die da drüben* (Berlin: Rotbuch, 1984).

Bölke, Joachim. "Eine Begnadigungsaktion," *Tagesspiegel*, October 7, 1964, p. 1.

———. "Der Handel mit Haftlinger," *Tagesspiegel*, October 9, 1964, p. 1.

Bolle, Michael. *Kleiner Gernzverkehr bei Nacht* (Kiel: Arndt, 1983).

Bölling, Klaus. "Der Mann mit dem Strohhut Kommt," *Leader* (Die Weltwoche Supplement), July 1986.

————. *Die fernen Nachbarn* (Munich: *Stern* Buch, 1983).

Boris, Peter. *Die sich Lossagten* (Cologne: Markus, 1983).

Borkowski, Dieter. *Erich Honecker* (Munich: Bertelsmann, 1987).

————. *Für Jeden kommt der Tag* (Frankfurt: Fischer, 1983).

————. *In der Heimat, da gibt's ein Wiedersehn* (Frankfurt: Fischer, 1984).

Boyd, Gerald. "Raze Berlin Wall, Reagan Urges Soviets," *The New York Times,* June 13, 1987, p. 3.

Bracken, Paul. *The Command and Control of Nuclear Forces* (New Haven: Yale, 1986).

Branch, Taylor, and George Crile III. "The Kennedy Vendetta" (Ted Shackley) *Harper's,* August 1975, pp. 49–63.

Brandt, Hans-Jürgen. *Witz mit Gewehr* (Stuttgart: Goverts, 1965).

Brandt, Heinz. *Ein Traum, der nicht entführbar ist* (Munich: Paul List, 1967).

Brandt, Willy. *Begegnungen mit Kennedy* (Munich: Kindler, 1964).

————. *Links und frei* (Munich: Knaur, 1984).

————. *People and Politics* (Boston: Little, Brown, 1978).

————. *Der Wille zum Frieden* (Frankfurt: Fischer, 1973).

Brant, Stefan, and Klaus Bölling. *Der Aufstand* (Stuttgart: Steingrüben, 1954).

Bratke, Andreas. Report of escape, *Arbeitsgemeinschaft 13. August,* November 9, 1988, press conference, pp. 3–5.

Brühl, Reinhard, et al. *Armee für Frieden und Sozialismus* (Potsdam, DDR: Militärverlag der Deutschen Demokratischen Republik, 1985).

Buch, Günther. *Namen und Daten wichtiger Personen in der DDR,* 3rd ed. (Bonn: J.H.W. Dietz, 1982).

Buckley, William F., Jr. *The Story of Henri Tod* (New York: Dell, 1985).

Buhss, Werner. "Liebe ist eine harte Kiste" (Katja Lange-Müller), *Spiegel,* November 17, 1986, pp. 254–56.

Bundesministerium für Gesamtdeutsche Fragen. *Berlin—Friedrichstrasse 20:53* (Bad Godesberg: Hohwacht, 1965)

Bundesministerium für Innerdeutsche Beziehungen. *Auskünfte zur Deutschlandpolitick A–Z* (Bonn: Gesamtdeutsches Institut, 1988).

————. *Reisen in die DDR* 10th ed. (Bonn: Gesamtdeutsches Institut, 1988).

————. *Reisen nach und von Berlin West,* pamphlet, 16th ed. (Bonn: Gesamtdeutsches Institut, 1988).

————. *77 praktische Tips für Besuche in der DDR und aus der DDR* (Bonn: Gesamtdeutsches Institut, 1987).

————. *Zahlenspiegel—Bundesrepublik Deutschland/Deutsche Demokratische Republik— Ein Vergleich* (Bonn: Bundesministerium für Innerdeutsche Beziehungen, 1985).

Bundy, McGeorge. *Danger and Survival* (New York: Random House, 1988).

Bunting, Josiah. "Soldier" (Glover Johns), *VMI Alumni Review,* Summer 1976.

Burrows, William E. *Deep Black* (New York: Random House, 1986).

Büscher, Wolfgang, et al. (eds.) *Friedens Bewegung in der DDR* (Hattingen: Scandia, 1982).

Büscher, Wolfgang, and Peter Wensierski. *Null Bock auf DDR—Aussteigerjugend im anderen Deutschland* (Hamburg: Rowohlt, 1984).

Bussiek, Hendrik. *Notizen aus der DDR* (Frankfurt: Fischer, 1979).

———. *Die real existierende DDR* (Frankfurt: Fischer, 1984).

BZ. "Arzt verlor sein Telefon," August 31, 1976.

Carr, Jonathan. *Helmut Schmidt* (Düsseldorf: Econ, 1985).

Carrington, Tim. "The Ultimate Secret: A Pentagon Report Its Author Can't See," *The Wall Street Journal,* February 18, 1986, p. 1.

Casdorff, Claus Heinrich. "Moderator mit Feuer" (Gerhard Löwenthal), *Deutsche Zeitung,* December 22, 1978.

Cate, Curtis. *The Ides of August* (New York: M. Evans, 1978).

Catudal, Honoré M. *Kennedy and the Berlin Wall Crisis* (Berlin: Berlin Verlag, 1980).

Central Statistical Board (DDR). *Statistical Pocket Book of the German Democratic Republic 1985* (East Berlin: Staatsverlag der Deutschen Demokratischen Republik, 1985).

Christic Institute. "Tony Avrigan, Martha Honey, Plaintiffs, v. John Hull, Rene Corbo, et al. [and] Felipe Vidal Santiago, Raul Villaverde, et al., United States District Court, Southern District of Florida, Civil Action No. 86-1146-CIV-KING, and 87-1545-CIV-KING, Declaration of Plaintiff's Counsel," p. 300.

Clarke, Bruce C. "Should We Have Knocked Down the Wall?" *Officers Review,* January 1982.

Clay, Lucius D. "Begrenzter Krieg um Berlin ist denkbar," *Spiegel,* February 27, 1963, pp. 38–46.

———. "Berlin," *Foreign Affairs,* October 1962, pp. 47–58.

———. *Decision in Germany* (New York: Doubleday, 1950).

Cookridge, E. H. (pseudonym for Edward Spiro). *Gehlen: Spy of the Century* (New York: Random House, 1971).

———. *George Blake: Double Agent* (New York: Ballantine, 1982).

———. *Spy Trade* (New York: Walker, 1971).

Current Biography. "Daniel Ellsberg," 1973, pp. 117–19.

———. "Keith Haring," 1986, pp. 197–199.

———. "Le Carré, John" (David Cornwell), 1974, pp. 232–35.

Currey, Cecil B. *Edward Lansdale—The Unquiet American* (Boston: Houghton Mifflin, 1988).

Davey, Thomas. *A Generation Divided—German Children and the Berlin Wall* (Durham, N.C.: Duke University Press, 1987).

Davison, W. Phillips. *The Berlin Blockade* (Princeton, N.J.: Princeton University Press, 1958).

Deja-Lölhöffel. *Freizeit in der DDR* (Berlin: Holzapfel, 1986).

Deming, Angus. "Child Hostages," *Newsweek,* January 17, 1977, p. 11.

Detzer, David. *The Brink* (New York: Crowell, 1972).

Diederichs, Friedemann. "Ich habe Flüchtlinge für 1 million Mark . . . " (Albrecht Schütz), *Bild am Sonntag,* April 27, 1986.

Diehl, Ernst. *750 Years of Berlin—Manifesto* (East Berlin: Panorama DDR, Auslandspresseagentur GMBH, 1987).

Donovan, James B. *Stranger on a Bridge* (New York: Atheneum, 1964).

Dornberg, John. *The Other Germany* (New York: Doubleday, 1968).

Dörnberg, Stefan, and Franz Köhler. *Sturmglocken der Weltgeschichte* (Leipzig, DDR: Urania, 1984).

Drath, Viola Herms. *Willy Brandt—Prisoner of His Past* (Radnor, Pa.: Chilton, 1975).

Dulles, Eleanor Lansing. *Berlin—The Wall Is Not Forever* (Durham, N.C.: University of North Carolina Press, 1967).

———. *The Wall—A Tragedy in Three Acts* (Columbia, S.C.: University of South Carolina Press, 1972).

Ebert, Friedrich (Stiftung). *Frauen in der DDR,* pamphlet series *Die DDR—Realitäten-Argumente* (Bonn: Verlag Neue Gesellschaft, 1987).

Ebert, Ottomar. *Spionage-Karussell Ost-West* (Bergisch Gladbach: Bastei Lübbe, 1984).

Eckart, Gabriele. *So sehe ick die Sache-Protokolle aus der DDR* (Cologne: Kiepenheuer und Wietsch, 1984).

Ehring, Klaus, and Martin Dallwitz. *Schwerter zu Pflugscharen—Friedensbewegung in der DDR* (Hamburg: Rowohlt, 1982).

Ellis, William Donohue, and Thomas J. Cunningham, Jr. *Clarke of St. Vith* (Cleveland: Dillon//Liederbach, 1974).

Emde, Heiner. *Spionage und Abwehr in der Bundesrepublik Deutschland* (Bergisch Gladbach: Lübbe, 1986).

Farr, Michael. "Berlin Taxi Escape Tale Raises Doubts," *Daily Telegraph,* August 2, 1986, p. 6.

Faust, Siegmar. *Ich will hier raus* (Berlin: Klaus Gohl, 1983).

———. *In welchem Lande lebt Mephisto?* (Munich: Olzog, 1980).

Felfe, Heinz. *Im Dienst des Gegners* (Hamburg: Rasch und Röhring, 1986).

———. " 'In der Sowjet-Union bin ich Staatsgast,' " *Spiegel,* August 11, 1986, pp. 68–87.

Filmer, Werner, and Heribert Schwan (eds.). *Alltag im anderen Deutschland* (Düsseldorf: Econ, 1985).

Finn, Gerhard, and Karl Wilhelm Fricke. *Politischer Strafvollzug in der DDR* (Cologne: Verlag Wissenschaft und Politik, 1981).

Fischer, Peter. *Kirche und Christen in der DDR* (Berlin: Holzapfel, 1978).

Florian, Erik (ed.). *Der politische Witz in der DDR* (Munich: Knaur, 1983).

Frank, Reuven. "The Making of the Tunnel," *Television Quarterly,* Fall 1963, pp. 8–23.

Frankfurter Allgemeine Zeitung. "Aus Hass gegen Fluchthelfer DDR informiert," January 21, 1974.

———. "In der Sondermaschine von Moskau nach Ost-Berlin," January 5, 1967.

Freeman, Clive, and Gwynne Roberts. *Der kälteste Krieg* (Berlin: Ullstein, 1982).

Frei, Gottfried. " 'Diese Leute interessiert alles': Der Staatssicherheitsdienst kontrolliert systematisch den Post- und Fernmeldeverkehr" (Christen Drüben), Brüsewitz Zentrum, No. 1, 1986.

Fricke, Karl Wilhelm. "Anwalt in ganz Berlin," *Frankfurter Allgemeine Zeitung,* November 12, 1976.

———. *Die DDR Staatssicherheit* (Cologne: Verlag Wissenschaft und Politik, 1984).

———. *Ein Mann namens Linse* (Cologne: Deutschlandfunk, 1972).

———. *Opposition und Widerstand in der DDR* (Cologne: Verlag Wissenschaft und Politik, 1984).

———. *Politik und Justiz in der DDR* (Cologne: Verlag Wissenschaft und Politik, 1979.)

———. "Spionage und Koexistenz in Deutschland," *Deutschland Archiv,* October 1985, pp. 1029–33.

———. "Die Staatsmacht und die Andersdenkenden," *Deutschland Archiv,* February 1988, pp. 225–26.

———. *Zur Menschen und Grundrechtssituation politischer Gefangener in der DDR* (Cologne: Verlag Wissenschaft und Politik, 1986).

Fuchs, Jürgen. *Vernehmungsprotokolle* (Hambug: Rowohlt, 1978).

Galante, Pierre. *The Berlin Wall* (New York: Doubleday, 1965).

Ganssauge, Günter. *A Wall of Peace* (Dresden, DDR: Verlag Zeit im Bild, 1967).

Garthoff, Raymond L. *Detente and Confrontation* (Washington, D.C.: Brookings Institution, 1985).

———. *Reflections on the Cuban Missile Crisis* (Washington, D.C.: Brookings Institution, 1987).

Gärtner, Peter. "Es wird eine Freude sein, dort zu bummeln" (Friedrichstrasse), *Volksblatt* (Berlin), December 4, 1986, p. 18.

Gaus, Günter. *Wo Deutschland liegt* (Hamburg: Hoffmann und Campe, 1983).

Gehlen, Reinhard. *The Service* (New York: Popular Library, 1972).

Geisler, Wolfgang. *Seiben Tage DDR—eine Klassenfahrt* (Darmstadt: Luchterhand, 1985).

Gelb, Norman. *The Berlin Wall* (New York: Times Books, 1987).

Geo. "Berlin," special issue (Hamburg: Gruner & Jahr, December 1986).

Geo. "DDR," special issue (Hamburg: Gruner & Jahr, February 1985).

Gerig, Uwe. *Barrieren aus Beton und Eisen* (Krefeld: Röhr, 1986).

Gesamtdeutsches Institut. *13. August 1961,* Seminarmaterial (Bonn: Gesamtdeutsches Institute, n. d.).

Gesamtdeutsches Institut. *Militär in der DDR* (Bonn: Gesamtdeutsches Institut, n. d.)

Gesellschaft für Menschenrechte. "Dokumentation über Bürgerrechtler in der DDR—Petition Riesa," Gesellschaft für Menschenrechte, August 1955, p. 29.

———. "Presse-Konferenz mit Dr. Karl-Heinz Nitschke und Fräulein Bärbel Ludley," Menschenrechte-Schicksale, November/December 1977, pp. 28–29.

Gibbs, Nancy R. "Fire and Water," *Time,* September 21, 1987, pp. 6–7.

Gildner, Jay. "Memo to Mr. Bundy" (re countermeasures against the Berlin Wall), White House, August 17, 1961.

Gill, Ernest. "Foreigners in Their Own Land," *The New York Times Magazine,* February 16, 1986, pp. 46 +.

Gilroy, Harry. "Spy Author Sheds Undercover Pose," *The New York Times,* April 21, 1964.

Glaser, Günther, and Wilfried Hanisch. *Über den Einsatz der Nationalen Volksarmee und der Grenzsicherungskräfte zum Schutze der Staatsgrenze der Deutschen Demokratischen Republik im Jahre 1961* (East Berlin: Deutscher Militärverlag, 1969).

Gnauck, Reinhard. "East Germany Sells Its Citizens for Freedom," *The Wall Street Journal,* November 14, 1984, p. 33.

Gniffke, Erich W. *Jahre mit Ulbricht* (Cologne: Verlag Wissenschaft und Politik, 1966).

Gordon, Suzanne. "Berlin's Mauerkrankheit," *Harper's,* February 1984, pp. 72–74.

Gould, Jack. "TV: Tunnel Under Wall," *The New York Times,* December 12, 1962.

Gräf, Dieter. *In Namen der Republik* (Munich: Herbig, 1988).

Graham, Fred P. "Retired Pentagon Officer Is Seized as Spy for Soviets," *The New York Times,* July 13, 1966, pp. 1 +.

Gramont, Sanche de. *The Secret War* (New York: Putnam, 1962).

Greese, Karl, and Wilfried Hanisch. "Der 13. August 1961. Eine Tat für die Sicherung des Friedens," *Militärgeschichte* (DDR), April 1986, pp. 301–5.

Grübel, Bärbel. "Gebt mir meine Kinder zurück!" *Das Beste aus Reader's Digest,* October 1977, pp. 62–66.

Grunenberg, Nina. "Lust und Last der Leiter" (Politburo), *Zeit,* June 27, 1986, pp. 9–12.

Gruson, Sydney. "Russian Tanks Go into East Berlin; U.S. Shows Force," *The New York Times,* October 27, 1961, pp. 1+.

———. "Soviet Troops Encircle Berlin to Back Up Sealing of Border," *The New York Times,* August 14, 1961, pp. 1+.

Guillaume, Günter. "Memoirs," *Spiegel,* January 4, 1988, pp. 14–38.

Gundermann, Horst. *Entlassung aus der Staatsbürgerschaft* (Berlin: Ullstein, 1978).

Haase, Norbert, et al. (eds.). *VEB Nachwuchs-Jugend in der DDR* (Hamburg: Rowohlt, 1983).

Haffner, Sebastian. "Die Pariser Kommune," chapter in "Im Schatten der Geschichte" (Stuttgart, DVA, 1985, pp. 70–121).

Hage, Volker. "Alles zu wenig, Alles zu spät" (Monika Maron), *Zeit,* June 17, 1988, p. 38.

Hagen, Louis. *The Secret War for Europe* (New York: Stein & Day, 1969).

Halberstam, David. *The Best and the Brightest* (New York: Random House, 1972).

Hammer, Manfried, et al. (eds.). *Das Mauerbuch* (Berlin: Oberbaum, 1984).

Hanisch, Wilfried. "Zur friedenstabilisierenden Wirkung gesicherter Staatsgrenzen zu Westberlin," *Militärgeschichte* (DDR), April 1987, pp. 346–48.

Hanser, Richard. *Putsch* (New York: Wyden, 1970).

Hartwich, Christian. "Ost-Berliner Prominentenwirt hofft auf Hilfe durch Diepgen," *Berliner Morgenpost,* February 7, 1988.

Haupt, Michael. *Die Berliner Mauer* (bibliography) (Munich: Bernard & Gräfe, 1981).

Haus am Checkpoint Charlie. "Wo Weltgeschichte sich manifestiert," an art competition, 71 designs, Haus am Checkpoint Charlie, 1980.

Havemann, Robert. *Ein deutscher Kommunist* (Hamburg: Rowohlt, 1978).

Heinrich, Eberhard, and Klaus Ullrich. *Befehdet seit dem ersten Tag* (East Berlin: Dietz, 1984).

Heitzer, Heinz. *DDR—geschichtlicher Überblick* (East Berlin: Dietz, 1987).

———. "Familienerziehung und Jugendhilfe in der DDR," *Deutschland Archiv,* March 1983, pp. 279–83.

Helwig, Gisela. *Jugend und Familie in der DDR* (Cologne: Edition *Deutschland Archiv,* 1984).

Henkys, Reinhard (ed.). *Und Niemandem Untertan* (Hamburg, Rowohlt, 1985).

Herdegen, Gerhard. "Perspektiven und Begrenzungen, Teil 1: Nation und deutsche Teilung," *Deutschland Archiv,* November 1987, 1260–73.

Herken, Gregg. *Counsels of War* (New York: Knopf, 1985).

Hersh, Seymour. *The Price of Power* (New York: Summit, 1983).

Herzberg, Wolfgang. *Ich bin doch wer—Protokolle aus der DDR* (Darmstadt: Luchterhand, 1987).

Hesse, Kurt R. *Westmedien in der DDR* (Cologne: Verlag Wissenschaft und Politik, 1988).

Heym, Stefan. *5 Tage im Juni* (Frankfurt: Fischer, 1977).

———. "Keep an Eye on the Germans," interview, *Newsweek* (European edition), September 28, 1987, p. 56.

———. *Nachruf* (Munich: C. Bertelsmann, 1988).

———. "Plötzlich hebt sich der Boden,' " interview, *Spiegel,* May 31, 1982, pp. 94–100.

———. "Stefan Heym: Ich mag Kerle, die so tapfer sind wie Robinsons Vater," interview, *Welt,* September 30, 1987, p. 6.

———. " 'Warum kein Sozialismus mit zwei parteien?' " interview, *Spiegel,* October 27, 1980, pp. 54–67.

———. *Wege und Umwege* (Frankfurt: Fischer, 1983).

———. "Wenn sie nur auf das Bajonett setzen, dann brauchen sie die Mauer," interview, *Welt,* September 28, 1987. p.9.

———. "Die Wunde eitert weiter," *Spiegel,* November 7, 1983, pp. 58–72.

Hildebrandt, Rainer. *Berlin—von der Frontstadt zur Brücke Europas* (Berlin: Verlag Haus am Checkpoint Charlie, 1984).

———. *Es geschah an der Mauer* (Berlin: Verlag Haus am Checkpoint Charlie, 1982).

———. "Ist das 'unteilbare Deutschland' teilbar?'" *Tagesspiegel,* August 13, 1981, p. 3.

Maler interpretieren die Mauer (Berlin: Verlag Haus am Checkpoint Charlie, 1985).

———. "Rund 1000 Menschen in den Westen geschleust" (Albert Schütz), *Tagesspiegel,* July 12, 1987.

———. *Der 17. Juni* (Berlin: Verlag Haus am Checkpoint Charlie, 1983).

———. *The Wall Speaks,* 4th ed. (Berlin: Verlag Haus am Checkpoint Charlie, 1985).

Hildebrandt, Rainer, and Horst Schumm. "Frauenhaft in der DDR: Ursachen, Verurteilungen, Haftbedingungen," 64th Press Conference at Haus am Checkpoint Charlie, April 24, 1985.

———. *Ich war Grenzaufklärer* (Berlin: Arbeitsgemeinschaft 13. August, 1982).

———. "Grenzen durch Berlin und durch Deutschland," Arbeitsgemeinschaft 13. August, press conference, August 12, 1988.

———. "20 Jahre Mauer," Arbeitsgemeinschaft 13. August, August 10, 1981.

Hiller, Horst. *Sturz in die Freiheit* (Munich: Universitas, 1986).

Hoffman, Peter. *Widerstand, Staatsstreich, Attentat* (Munich: Piper, 1969).

Höhne, Heinz. *Der Krieg im Dunkeln* (Munich: Bertelsmann, 1985).

Höhne, Heinz, and Hermann Zolling. *The General Was a Spy* (New York: Coward McCann, 1971).

Höllen, Martin. "Der innerdeutsche 'Freikauf,' " *Der Monat*, October/November/December 1980, pp. 62–69.

Holzweissig, Gunter. *Massenmedien in der DDR* (Berlin: Holzapfel, 1983).

———. *Militärwessen in der DDR* (Berlin: Holzapfel, 1985).

Höpke, Klaus. "Wir möchten mehr Streit hervorrufen," *Weltwoche*, May 28, 1987, p. 61.

Hörning, Erika M. "Lebensereignisse: Überhänge im Lebenslauf," chapter in Wolfgang Voges (ed.), *Methoden der Biographie-lund Lebenslaufforschung* (Opladen: Leske & Budrich, 1987), pp. 231–59.

———. "A Sociological Perspective of Critical Life Events: Revitalization of Biographical Resources," address to XI the World Congress of Sociology, New Delhi, India, August 18–22, 1986.

Honecker, Erich. *Aus meinem Leben* (East Berlin: Dietz, 1981).

Hood, William. *Mole* (New York: Ballantine, 1982).

Horelick, Arnold L., and Myron Rush. *Strategic Power and Soviet Foreign Policy* (Chicago: University of Chicago Press, 1966).

Hornstein, Erika von. *The Accused* (London: Oswald Wolff, 1965).

Hurwitz, Harold. "Die politische Moral der Berliner nach dem 13. August 1961 und früher," unpublished

Hyde, H. Montgomery. *George Blake, Superspy* (London: Constable, 1987).

Informationszentrum Berlin. *Berlin im Überblick* (Berlin: Informationszentrum Berlin, 1988).

———. *Ost-Berlin* (Berlin: Informationszentrum Berlin, 1987).

Internationale Gesellschaft für Menschenrechte. "Internationale Anhörung über die Menschenrechtssituation in der DDR," documentation of hearing, December 6–7, 1984.

———. *Politische Haft in der DDR* (Frankfurt: Arbeitsausschuss Bürgerrechtsbewegung und politische Gefangene der DDR, 1986).

Isaacson, Walter, and Evan Thomas. *The Wise Men* (New York: Simon and Schuster, 1986).

Jänecke, Heinrich. "Der Mann aus Wiebelskirchen," *Stern* ("extra"), September 3, 1987, pp. 111–30.

————. "Erich Honecker" *Stern*, September 3, 1987, pp. 111–30.

Jawrocki, Joachim. *Bewaffnete Organe in der DDR* (Berlin: Holzapfel, 1979).

Kahl, Werner. "Franke Prozess: 'Ein Dr. Leistner war der Kurier,' " *Welt*, October 3, 1986.

————. "Das gute Ende einer bösen Geschichte," *Welt*, August 26, 1988, p. 3.

————. " 'Die Hölle kann nicht schlimmer sein' " (Hoheneck prison), *Welt*, March 14, 1983.

————. "Die Leiden der Doris W. im Zuchthaus Hoheneck," *Welt*, July 3, 1983.

————. "Nach sechs Jahren gab DDR der Mutter die Töchter wieder," *Welt*, August 26, 1988, p. 1.

————. "Die vierzehn Leidensjahre einer Mutter," *Welt*, July 15, 1988, p. 3.

————. "Vor Gericht zerbrach die Freundschaft mit Egon Franke," *Welt*, January 23, 1986, p. 3.

————. "Sie warten seit 1143 Tagen auf ihre Kinder," *Welt*, September 25, 1976.

————. "Wolfgang Vogel, der Mann für Grenzfälle," *Welt*, August 31, 1985.

Kaiser, Carl-Christian. "Fremde im eigenen Land?" *Die Zeit*, June 21, 1985, p. 5.

————. "Wo blieb das Geld?" *Die Zeit*, December 27, 1985.

Kaplan, Fred. *The Wizards of Armageddon* (New York: Simon and Schuster, 1983).

Karasek, Hellmuth. "Der k.u.k. King von Hollywood" (Billy Wilder), *Spiegel*, no. 21 (1986), pp. 192–98.

Karutz, H. R. "In Sowjetuniform durch die Mauer," *Welt*, August 23, 1986.

————. "Der Puppenspieler vom Checkpoint," *Welt*, August 5, 1986, p. 3.

————. "SED Papier belegt, was Honecker wirklich denkt," *Welt*, June 15, 1988.

Keiderling, Gerhard. *Berlin—1945–1986* (East Berlin: Dietz, 1987).

————. *Die Spaltung Berlins,* Illustrierte historische Hefte #38 (East Berlin: VEB Deutscher Verlag der Wissenschaften, 1985).

Kemp, Anthony. *Escape from Berlin* (London: Boxtree, 1987).

Kempowski, Walter. *Herzlich willkommen* (Munich: Albrecht Knaus, 1984).

————. *Schöne Aussicht* (Munich: Goldmann, 1984).

Kennan, George F. *The German Problem: A Personal View* (Washington: American Institute for Contemporary German Studies, The Johns Hopkins University, 1989).

Kenworthy, F. W. "Officials Say FBI Agents Shadowed Spying Suspect from 1959 to 1961," *The New York Times,* July 14, 1966, pp. 18–19.

Kessler, Horst-Günter and Jürgen Miermeister. *Vom "Grossen Knast" ins "Paradies"?* (Hamburg: Rowohlt, 1983).

Ketman, Per, and Andreas Wissmach. *Anders Reisen—DDR* (Hamburg: Rowohlt, 1986).

Kissinger, Henry. *White House Years* (Boston: Little, Brown, 1979).

Klass, Philip J. *Secret Sentries in Space* (New York: Random House, 1971).

Kleinschmid, Harald. "Experimentierfeld für Glasnost?" *Deutschland Archiv*, May 1988, pp. 473–75.

Klier, Freya. *Abreiss-Kalender* (Munich: Kindler, 1988).

Klump, Brigitte. *Freiheit hat keinen Preis* (Munich: Knaur, 1981).

———. *Das rote Kloster* (Munich: Goldmann, 1980).

Kohl, Hans-Helmut, et al. "Augenblicke jenseits aller Pflichtübungen," *Frankfurter Rundschau*, September 12, 1985, p. 3.

Köhler, Joachim, and Sven Michaelsen. " 'Ich soll an den grossen Busen kommen' " (Stefan Heym interview), *Stern*, July 28, 1988, pp. 128–30.

Kössler, Thilo. "13. August und Mauerbau im RIAS BERLIN," *Deutschland Archiv*, August 1986, pp. 856–73.

Kopetzky, Helmut. "Die Sehenswürdigkeit: 25 Jahre Mauer," *Deutsche Welle* (radio script).

Kreutzer, Claus J. *Die Rechte der Gäste* (East Berlin: Verlag Die Wirtschaft, 1986).

Kroll, Hans. *Lebenserinnerungen eines Botschafters* (Cologne: Kiepenheuer & Witsch, 1967).

Kuczynski, Jürgen. *Dialog mit meinem Enkel* (East Berlin: Aufbau, 1985).

———. *Memoiren* (Cologne: Pahl-Rugenstein, 1983).

Kummer, Jochen. "Der Katholik, dem Honecker vertraut," *Welt am Sonntag*, July 27, 1986, p. 10.

Kunze, Reiner. *Die wunderbaren Jahre* (Frankfurt: Fischer, 1984).

Kuppe, Johannes L. "Erkundung Schwierigen Terrains," *Deutschland Archiv*, June 1988, pp. 577–80.

Kwitny, Jonathan. *The Crimes of Patriots* (New York: Norton, 1987).

Lange-Müller, Katja. *Wehleid—wie im Leben* (Frankfurt: Fischer, 1986).

Lapp, Peter J. *Wahlen in der DDR* (Berlin: Holzapfel, 1982).

Latk, Klaus-Reiner. "Oskar Brüsewitz," *Christen Drüben*, February 1986, pp. 4–8.

Le Carré, John (David Cornwell). *The Spy Who Came in from the Cold.* (New York: Coward-McCann, 1963).

Ledeen, Michael. "Tinker, Turner, Sailor, Spy" (Ted Shackley), *New York Magazine*, March 3, 1980, pp. 37–42.

Lehmann, Hans Georg. "Mit der Mauer leben?" in *Aus Politik und Zeitgeschichte*, Beilage zur Wochenzeitung *Das Parlament* (Bonn: Bundeszentrale für politische Bildung, August 16, 1986).

Leinemann, Jürgen. " 'Wer sich von Gefühlen fortreissen lässt . . . ,' " *Spiegel*, September 17, 1987, p. 28.

Lemmer, Ernst. *Manches war doch anders* (Frankfurt: Heinrich Scheffler, 1968).

Leonhard, Wolfgang. *Child of the Revolution* (Chicago: Regnery, 1958).

Linke, Dietmar. *Niemand kann zwei Herren dienen—als Pfarrer in der DDR* (Hamburg: Hoffmann und Campe, 1988).

Lippmann, Heinz. *Honecker* (Cologne: Verlag Wissenschaft und Politik, 1971).

Livingston, Robert Gerald. "Stop Fearing German Reunification," International *Herald Tribune,* May 15, 1989.

Lorenz, Ralph. "Die Franke-Millionen," *Westfalen-Blatt,* September 7, 1985, pp. 1+.

Löser, Franz. *Sag nie, du gehst den letzten Weg* (autobiography) (Cologne: Bund, 1986).

————. *Die unglaubwürdige Gesellschaft* (Cologne: Bund, 1984).

Löst, Erich. *Der vierte Zensor* (Cologne: Edition Deutschland Archiv, 1984).

Loewe, Lothar. *Abend kommt der Klassenfeind* (Berlin: Ullstein, 1977).

Löwenstern, Enno von. "Namen, die keiner nennen darf," *Die Welt,* March 25, 1976.

Löwenthal, Gerhard. "Gisela Mauritz, Claudia und Beate Gallus sind frei!" *Hilferüfe von drüben,* Third Quarter, 1988, p. 1.

————. *Ich bin Geblieben* (Munich: Herbig, 1987).

Ludz, Peter Christian, et al. *DDR Handbuch* (Cologne: Verlag Wissenschaft und Politik, 1979).

Luft, Friedrich. "Hier geht Kafka," *Die Welt,* April 3, 1980.

————. "Superklamotte auf dem Glatteis" (review of Billy Wilder's *One, Two, Three*), *Die Welt,* December 23, 1961.

Maas, Peter. *Manhunt* (New York: Random House, 1986).

Maass, Winfried, and Gerd Heidemann. "Fluchthilfe: Der Mann im Hintergrund" (Heinz Heidrich), *Stern,* August 28, 1975, pp. 86+.

McAdams, A. James. *East Germany and Detente* (New York: Cambridge University Press, 1985).

McCartney, Robert J. "Aging East Berlin Leaders Resist 'New Thinking,' " *Washington Post,* January 3, 1988, p. A23.

Marchetti, Victor, and John D. Marks. *The CIA and the Cult of Intelligence* (New York: Dell, 1974).

Markham, James M. "Bonn and Its Many Enemies Within: Spy Scandals Bare Its Vulnerability," *The New York Times,* December 10, 1985, p. A6.

————. "East German Author Thrives on Conflicts," *International Herald Tribune,* July 17, 1984, pp. 1+.

————. "East Germans Pay Their Chief a Subdued Respect," *The New York Times,* September 19, 1984, p. A2.

————. "Germanys Trafficking in People," *The New York Times,* July 29, 1984, p. 3.

————. "Reviving the German Question," *The New York Times Magazine*, December 18, 1983, pp. 53+.

————. "The Spies Who Came from Next Door," *The New York Times*, September 1, 1985.

————. "A Tidal Wave of Germans Is Sweeping Westward," *The New York Times*, March 2, 1984, p. 2.

————. "When Spies Are Traded, Wolfgang Vogel Is There," *The New York Times*, February 14, 1986.

Maron, Monika. *Flugasche* (Frankfurt: Fischer, 1986).

————. "Die halbe Hauptstadt," *Geo*, December 1, 1986, pp. 137–42.

————. *Das Misverständnis* (Frankfurt: Fischer, 1984).

————. *Die Überläuferin* (Frankfurt: Fischer, 1986).

Martin, David C. *Wilderness of Mirrors* (New York: Ballantine, 1980).

Martin, Guy. "The Battle for Berlin," *Esquire*, November 1987, pp. 204–213.

Maschner, W. F. "So endete die Flucht zu Hause," *Die Welt*, April 2, 1986, p. 76.

Maxa, Rudy, and Phil Stanford. "The Swinging Spies," *Washingtonian*, February 1987, pp. 132–40.

May, Antoinette. *Witness to War* (New York: Penguin, 1985).

Mayr, Alexander. "Der Tod des Mannes, der mit Leben handelt," *Süddeutsche Zeitung*, February 7, 1979.

Mazlish, Bruce. *Kissinger: The European Mind in American Politics* (New York: Basic Books, 1976).

Meeker, Barry. "Barry, übernehmen Sie!" *Quick*, August 28, 1975, pp. 19+.

————. "Meine Frauen, Freunde und die Lust an der Gefahr," *Quick*, September 4, 1975, pp. 71+.

Mehls, Hartmut, and Ellen Mehls. *13. August* (in pamphlet series *Illustrierte historische Hefte*) (East Berlin: VEB Deutscher Verlag der Wissenschaften, 1979).

Meier, Bernhard (ed.). *Grenzenlos—Liebe zwischen Ost und West* (Frankfurt: Fischer, 1988).

Mende, Erich. *Die Neue Freiheit* (Munich: Herbig, 1984).

Menge, Marlies. "Das Misverständnis" (Monika Maron), *Die Zeit*, November 28, 1986, p. 55.

Merritt, Richard L., and Anna J. Merritt. *Living with the Wall: West Berlin 1961–1985* (Chapel Hill, N.C.: Duke University Press, 1985).

Merseburger, Peter. *Grenzgänger* (Munich: Bertelsmann, 1988).

Merz, Kai-Uwe. "Kalter Krieg zwischen Widerstand und nationaler Befreiung: Die Kampfgruppe gegen Unmenschlichkeit 1948–1959," dissertation: Berlin, Freie Universität, 1985.

Meyer, Fritjof. "Der Künstler der feinen Töne," *Spiegel*, August 27, 1984, pp. 30–31.

Meyer, Michel. *Freikauf—Menschenhandel in Deutschland* (Vienna: Paul Zsolnay, 1978).

Mielke, Hans-Jürgen. *Die Autobahn Berlin-Helmstedt* (Berlin: Dietrich Reimer, 1984).

Mohr, Brigitte. "Fast die Hälfte der Schüler meint: Die DDR ist Ausland," *Frankfurter Allgemeine Zeitung*, July 28, 1983.

Mörstedt-Jauer, Christa. *Die halbe Hauptstadt—Stadtführer Ost-Berlin*, two volumes (Berlin: Oberhofer, 1987).

Mugay, Peter. *Die Friedrichstrasse* (East Berlin: Berlin Information, 1986).

Müller, Hans Dieter. *Der Springer-Konzern* (Munich: Piper, 1968).

Müller, Werner. "Die DDR und der Bau der Berliner Mauer im August 1961," in *Aus Politik und Zeitgeschichte*, Beilage zur Wochenzeitung *Das Parlament* (Bonn: Bundeszentrale für politische Bildung, August 16, 1986).

Müller-Hegemann, Dietfried. *Die Berliner Mauerkrankheit* (Herford: Nicolai, 1973).

Murphy, Robert. *Diplomat Among Warriors* (New York: Doubleday, 1964).

Naumann, Lutz-Peter. "Honecker's 'Wolfsschanze' liegt tief unter der Erde," *Welt*, May 11, 1986, p. 4.

Naumann, Michael. "Spitzel, Stasi und Spione," *Die Zeit*, February 23, 1979, pp. 9–11.

Nelson, Walter Henry. *The Berliners* (New York: McKay, 1969).

Neue Zürcher Zeitung. "'Fluchthelfer Lenzlinger erschossen," February 7, 1979.

———. "Für und wider Fluchthelfer," January 26, 1974.

———. "Lob Honeckers für die Berliner Mauer," January 22–23, 1989, p. 6.

———. "Die 'Mistfuhr' eines Fluchthelfers," January 17, 1974.

———. "Urteil gegen Sekretärin im Bonner Präsidialamt" (Margaret Höke), September 1, 1988.

Neues Deutschland (DDR). "Du sollst nicht falsch Zeugnis reden," August 31, 1976.

———. "Erich Honecker empfing Mitglieder des Repräsentantenhauses der USA," January 11/12, 1986, p. 1.

Neukirchner, Günther. "Geh doch runter . . . " (Barry Meeker), *Bild am Sonntag*, August 24, 1975, p. 4.

Neumann, Gert. *Die Schuld der Worte* (Frankfurt: Fischer, 1979).

The New York Times. "Cuban Crisis Weighing Heavily on the Minds of Calm Berliners," October 26, 1962, p. 19.

———. "East Germans Let 6-Year-Old Join Parents in West," January 14, 1976, p. 9.

———. "Gen. Sergei Varentsov Dead; Hero Demoted in Spying Case," March 5, 1971, p. 38.

———. "Gromyko Is Silent in Berlin on Cuba," October 25, 1962, p. 22.

———. "Ulbricht Says He Is Ready to Compromise on Berlin," December 6, 1962, pp. 1+.

Newsweek. "Agent of Doom" (Rupert Sigl), May 19, 1969, p. 48.

———. "Filmed Escape," October 22, 1962.

———. "A History of Betrayal," September 5, 1988, p. 8.

Nitsche, Hellmuth. *Zwischen Kreuz und Sowjetsetern* (Aschaffenburg: Paul Pattloch, 1983).

Nitschke, Eberhard. "Die Fluchthilfe AG, Zürich," *Die Welt,* January 16, 1974.

Noack, Hans-Georg. *Frage 7—Entscheidung eines Christen in der DDR* (Seewig: Stephanus Edition, 1980).

———. " 'Hallo, mal wieder drüben gewesen?' " (Rainer-Sturmo Wulf), *Der Spiegel,* no. 33 (1986), pp. 47–55.

Nobel, Rolf. *Mitten durch Deutschland* (Hamburg: Rasch und Röhring, 1986).

Noll, Hans. *Der Abschied* (Hamburg: Hoffmann und Campe, 1985).

Nölle-Neumann, Elisabeth. "Fünf Jahre Regierungszeit Helmut Kohl, Bericht aus der Meinungsforschung" (polls), Institut für Demoskopie Allensbach, 1987.

Novosti. *Nikita Khrushchev: Life and Destiny* (Moscow: Novosti, 1989).

O'Boyle, Thomas F. "Fading Barrier: Germans Are Debating an Unthinkable Idea: Removing the Berlin Wall," *The Wall Street Journal,* November 25, 1987, pp. 1+.

Obst, Werner. *Der rote Stern verglüht* (Munich: Langen-Müller, 1985).

O'Donnell, James P. "Mayor Under the Soviet Gun," *The Saturday Evening Post,* May 30, 1959, pp. 30+.

———. "Statt eines Nachwortes—die Teilung Berlins vorausgesagt," chapter in *Aus Sorge um Deutschland* (Stuttgart: Seewald, 1980).

O'Donnell, Kenneth P., and David F. Powers. *Johnny, We Hardly Knew Ye* (New York: Pocket Books, 1973).

Örtel, Joachim. *Liebesgrüsse an Erich M.* (Berlin: Edition Vespüne, 1984).

Österreich, Tina. *Gleichheit, Gleichheit über Alles* (Stuttgart: Seewald, 1978).

———. *Ich war RF* (Stuttgart: Seewald, 1978).

Oklahoma Information Service. "Barry Meeker," Story 1-9, Data Times Information Service, *Oklahoman and Times,* May 15, 1983, et seq.

Organski, A.F.K., and Jack Kugler. *The War Ledger* (Chicago: University of Chicago Press, 1980).

Ostow, Robin. *Jüdisches Leben in der DDR* (Frankfurt: Jüdischer Verlag/Athenaeum, 1988).

Paar, Jack. *P.S. Jack Paar* (New York: Doubleday, 1983).

Panorama DDR. *Free German Youth* (East Berlin: Auslandspresseagentur GMBH, 1985).

———. *Law and Justice—The Legal System of the German Democratic Republic* (East Berlin: Auslandspresseagentur GMBH, 1984).

———. *National People's Army of the GDR* (East Berlin: Auslandspresseagentur GMBH, 1983).

Panorama DDR—Auslandspresse Agentur GMBH. *The German Deomocratic Republic* (Dresden: Verlag Zeit im Bild, 1984).

Panskus, Hartmus (ed.) *Zweimal Deutschland* (Munich: List, 1986).

Pastor, H. *The Wall Today* (Berlin: Hendrik Pastor, 1982).

Penkovsky, Oleg. *The Penkovsky Papers* (New York: Ballantine, 1982).

Petschull, Jürgen. *Die Mauer* (Munich, *Stern* Buch, 1981).

———. *Mit dem Wind nach Westen* (Munich: Goldmann, 1980).

Pincher, Chapman. *Too Secret, Too Long* (New York: St. Martin's, 1984).

Pittman, Steuart L. "Oral History Interview," John F. Kennedy Library, September 18, 1970.

Powers, Thomas. "Intervention vs. Isolation," *Nuclear Times,* May/June 1986, pp. 30–31.

———. *The Man Who Kept the Secrets* (New York: Pocket Books, 1979).

Pravda. "The Spy Who Came in from the Cold" (George Blake interview) (London: Pravda International, 1988, vol. 2, no. 11/12).

Press and Information Office of the Land Berlin. *Berlin in Brief* (Berlin: Press and Information Office, 1982).

Presse- und Informationsamt des Landes Berlin. *Ost Berlin Information* (Berlin: Presse- und Informationsamt, 1984).

Prittie, Terrence. *Willy Brandt* (New York: Schocken, 1974).

Quick. "Was ist das für ein Staat, der Eltern und Kinder so quält?" December 29, 1976.

Ranelagh, John. *The Agency* (New York: Simon and Schuster, 1986).

Rathenow, Lutz. *Einst war ich Fänger im Schnee* (Berlin: Oberbaum, 1984).

Read, B. M. "Colonel Glover S. Johns, Jr., 31" (obituary), *VMI Alumni Review,* Summer 1976, pp. 58–59.

Reed, David. "DDR: Devisen kaufen Menschen frei," *Das Beste aus Reader's Digest,* October 1976, pp. 23–27.

Reumann, Kurt. "Die meisten jungen Leute können sich die Wiedervereinigung gar nicht mehr vorstellen," *Frankfurter Allgemeine Zeitung,* July 26, 1984.

Reuter/DPA. "Im Blickpunkt: Polens Grenze—keine Reise ohne Visum," *Frankfurter Rundschau,* September 12, 1987, p. 2.

Reuter, Monika. *Ihr da drüben* (Bergisch Gladbach: Lübbe, 1986).

Richter, Hans Werner (ed.). *Die Mauer—oder der 13. August* (Hamburg: Rowohlt, 1961).

Rogow, Arnold A. *James Forrestal* (New York: Macmillan, 1963).

Ronge, Volker. *Von Drüben nach Hüben* (Wuppertal: Verlag 84 Hartmann & Petit, 1985).

Röntgen, Anita. *Was soll mir eure Freiheit* (Bühl-Moos: Elster, 1987).

Roos, Peter (ed.). *Exil—die Ausbürgerung Wolf Biermanns aus der DDR* (Cologne: Kiepenheuer and Witsch, 1977).

Rositzke, Harry. *CIA's Secret Operations* (New York: Reader's Digest, 1977).

Rostow, Walt W. *The Diffusion of Power* (New York: Macmillan, 1972).

Rüb, Walter H. "Der Mörder des Fluchthelfers," *Die Welt,* September 25, 1979.

Rühle, Jürgen, and Gunter Holzweissig. *13. August 1961—die Mauer von Berlin* (chronology and documents, 2nd rev. ed.) (Cologne: Edition Deutschland Archiv, 1986).

Ruland, Bernd. *Krieg auf leisen Sohlen* (Stuttgart: Goverts, 1971).

Salinger, Pierre. *With Kennedy* (New York: Doubleday, 1966).

Salzmann, D. "Hier ist alles so farbig," *Die Welt,* November 12, 1985.

Schacht, Ulrich. "Hohenecker Protokolle (Zurich: Ammann, 1984).

———. "Vita und Bibliographie," text of address, July 3, 1981, *Europäische Ideen,* nos. 54/55 (1982), pp. 118–30.

Schell, Manfred. "Fall Franke, Hirt: Sonderzahlungen an Anwalt Stange," *Die Welt,* February 28, 1983.

Schelling, Thomas C. *The Strategy of Conflict* (Cambridge, Mass.: Harvard University Press, 1960).

Schenk, Fritz. *Im Vorzimmer de Diktatur* (Cologne: Kiepenheuer und Witsch, 1962).

———. *Mein doppeltes Vaterland* (Würzburg: Naumann, 1984).

Schlesinger, Arthur M., Jr. *Robert Kennedy and His Times* (New York: Ballantine, 1978).

———. *A Thousand Days* (Boston: Houston Mifflin, 1965).

Schlomann, Friedrich-Wilhelm. *Operationsgebiet Bundesrepublik* (Munich: Universitas, 1984).

Schmemann, Serge. "Despite New Stirrings, Dream of 'One Germany' Fades," *The New York Times,* May 14, 1989, p. E-3

———. "In Search of a Work of Art to Overcome the Wall," *The New York Times,* November 13, 1987.

———. "Rallying Cry of East Berliners: 'Gorbachev!' " *The New York Times,* June 10, 1987, p. A7.

———. "A Vibrant Berlin Greets the I.M.F.," *The New York Times*, September 24, 1988.

Schmidt, Andreas. "Giessen—und was dann?" *DDR Heute*, July/August 1988, pp. 10–13.

———. *Leerjahre* (Böblingen: Anita Tykve, 1986).

Schmidthammer, Jens. *Rechtsanwalt Wolfgang Vogel* (Hamburg: Hoffmann und Campe, 1987).

———. "Der stille Mittler," *Deutschlandfunk*, transcript of radio broadcast, July 17, 1984.

Schmitz, Rainer. "Der Schock der Verhaftungen hat die Opposition nicht geschwächt" (interview with Stephan Krawczyk and Freya Klier), *Die Welt*, March 10, 1988, p. 6.

———. "Tausend Tage im Westen" (Monika Maron), *Die Welt*, June 6, 1988, p. 17.

Schneider, Peter. *Deutsche Ängste* (Darmstadt: Luchterhand, 1988).

———. *Der Mauerspringer* (Darmstadt: Luchterhand, 1984).

Schorr, Daniel. Unpublished radio scripts from CBS, Berlin, August 10–October 27, 1961.

Schröter, Lothar. "Friedensgefährende Aktivitäten seitens der NATO um den 13. August 1961," *Militärgeschichte* (DDR), April 1987, pp. 343–46.

Schüler, Alfred. "Der Hasardeur von Hoengg," *Die Weltwoche*, September 5, 1973, pp. 5+.

Schulz, Hennes. "Der Osten lässt ihre Familie frei" (Peter Feller), *Bild*, April 13, 1988.

Schulze, Gerhard, et al. *Bürgeranliegen-Bürgerinitiative*, Pamphlet No. 64, series *Recht in unserer Zeit* (East Berlin: Staatsverlag der DDR, 1985).

Schwarz, Hans-Peter (ed.). *Berlinkrise und Mauerbau*, Rhöndorfer Gespräche, vol. 6 (Bonn: Bouvier, 1985).

Schwarz, Ulrich. " 'Es ist wie bei Hofe,' " *Spiegel*, August 31, 1987, pp. 30–31.

Seidman, Steve. *The Film Career of Billy Wilder* (Boston: G. K. Hall, 1977).

Seiffert, Wolfgang. *Das ganze Deutschland* (Munich: Piper, 1986).

Select Committee to Study Government Operations, U.S. Senate. *Alleged Assassination Plots Involving Foreign Leaders* (Washington, D.C.: U.S. Government Printing Office, Report No. 94-465, November 20, 1975).

Seyfferth, Konrad. *Wer meckert, sitzt* (Freiburg: Herderbücherei, 1981).

Seyppel, Joachim. " 'Nur die Wahrheit muss man fürchten" (interview), *Der Spiegel*, August 6, 1979, pp. 75–78.

Shears, David. *The Ugly Frontier* (New York: Knopf, 1970).

Shell, Kurt L. *Bedrohung und Bewährung* (Cologne: Westdeutscher Verlag, 1965).

Sigl, Rupert (pseud.). *In den Klauen des KGB* (Leoni: Druffel, n. d.).

———. *In the Claws of the KGB* (Philadelphia: Dorrance, 1978).

———. " 'This Wall Must Go!' " unpublished article.

Simes, Dimitri K. "Tearing Down the Berlin Wall," *Washington Post,* March 1, 1987, p. D5.

Slusser, Robert M. *The Berlin Crisis of 1961* (Baltimore: Johns Hopkins University Press, 1973).

Smith, Jean Edward. *The Defense of Berlin* (Baltimore: Johns Hopkins University Press, 1963).

———. *The Papers of General Lucius D. Clay* (Bloomington: Indiana University Press, 1974).

Sommer, Theo. "Ein deutscher Kommunist, ein deutscher Realist," *Die Zeit,* January 31, 1986, p. 1.

Sommer, Theo, and Marlies Menge (eds.). " 'Miteinander leben, gut miteinander auskommen' " (Honecker interview), *Die Zeit,* January 31, 1986, pp. 3–7.

Sontheimer, Michael. "Das Kalte Herz von Berlin," *Zeitmagazin,* September 30, 1988, pp. 43–54.

Sorensen, Theodore C.: *Kennedy* (New York: Harper & Row, 1965).

Sperber, A. M. *Murrow: His Life and Times* (New York: Freundlich, 1986).

Sperling, Walter, et al. *DDR* (Stuttgart: Kohlhammer, 1983).

Der Spiegel. "Abschied für immer" (Wolfgang Seiffert), May 1, 1978, p. 111.

———. " 'Altes Schwein, wir knallen dich ab,' " February 27, 1978, pp. 46–49.

———. "Berlin: Lost Weekend" (Billy Wilder), August 23, 1961.

———. "Brandt-Brief: Dank für Entwendung," August 30, 1961, pp. 11–17.

———. "Deutschland-Politik: Feuer und Wasser," September 14, 1987, pp. 26–29.

———. "DDR: 'Das haben wir schon einmal erlebt,' " March 14, 1988, pp. 18–20.

———. "DDR: Die Kinder fest verwurzeln" (cover story), December 22, 1975, pp. 19–26.

———. "DDR-Epionage: 'Das lässt die mächtig wackeln,' " March 5, 1979, pp. 70–83.

———. "DDR-Flucht: Ulbrichts Wahl-Stadt," August 9, 1961, pp. 11–14.

———. "DDR-Grenze: Verrechnet, Bursche!" (Michael Gartenschläger), May 17, 1976, pp. 49–50.

———. "DDR-Grosses Schweigen," August 6, 1979, p. 75.

———. "DDR-Reise: 'Es ist schon etwas Besonders,' " December 21, 1981, pp. 19–21.

———. "DDR-Spionage: Bierdosen für die Stasi" (Erich Ziegenhain), January 11, 1982, pp. 56–66.

————. " 'Die deutschen Dienste sind wie ein Sieb' " (Hansjoachim Tiedge), August 26, 1985, pp. 17–27.

————. "Eine erfolgreiche, komplizierte Operation," February 26, 1986, pp. 118–28.

————. "Entweda Sekt oda Soda" (interview with escapees), April 17, 1983, pp. 92–97.

————. "Fernsehen: kreuzpeinlich" (Gerhard Löwenthal), August 4, 1980.

————. "Fluchthilfe: Das Risiko wird grösser," August 5, 1974, pp. 21–24.

————. "Fluchthilfe: Gezielter Schlag," October 4, 1976, pp. 114–28.

————. "Fluchthilfe, 'Morgen um sechs bist du in Michendorf' " (cover story), August 29, 1973, pp. 24–34.

————. "Fluchthilfe: Nur mit Braut," August 14, 1967, pp. 41–43.

————. "Fluchthilfe: Zum heulen nett," February 16, 1976, pp. 44–46.

————. "Freikauf: Heikle Linie," October 24, 1983, pp. 28–29.

————. "Ganz besonders zwiespältige Gefühle" (Honecker cover story), August 31, 1987, pp. 20–33.

————. "Häftlings-Auslösung gegen Südfrüchte," October 14, 1964.

————. "Krieg der Maulwürfe" (cover story), September 2, 1985.

————. "Krise: Zwischen den Fronten," August 29, 1962, pp. 13–16.

————. "Künftig auch wieder mehr an uns denken—die Bedeutung des Westfernsehens für DDR-Bewohner," April 24, 1978, pp. 41–44.

————. "Lass ihre Politik scheitern," February 1, 1988, pp. 18–27.

————. "Lieber im verborgenen," September 1, 1975, pp. 28–29.

————. " 'Meine Arme schlafen ein, ich schlafe ein,' " *Spiegel* Report über des DDR-Fernsehen, August 27, 1979, pp. 54–72.

————. " 'Meine Eltern sind nicht meine Eltern,' " November 29, 1976, pp. 52–61.

————. "Milkes Unterschrift tut denen weh,' " March 1, 1982, pp. 36–48.

————. "Mindestens noch drei" (Elke Falk), March 28, 1988, pp. 32–34.

————. "Nie wiedersehen," December 15, 1975, pp. 36–38.

————. " 'Schnell, das Ding vom Zaun!' " April 12, 1976, pp. 116–26.

————. "Segen des Herrn," June 16, 1989, pp. 31–32.

————. "Überläufer: Noch eins drauf," January 4, 1988, pp. 39–40.

————. "Verändern, was Veränderung bedarf," August 8, 1988, pp. 16–18.

————. "Die volle Härte unserer Macht" (Erich Mielke), February 26, 1979, pp. 29–31.

————. "Vom Friedhof in die Freiheit," August 11, 1965, pp. 20–25.

———. "Vom Tag X' zu den '5 Tagen im Juni" (Stefan Heym), June 24, 1974, pp. 98–100.

———. "Vor Toresschluss," August 9, 1961, pp. 11–14.

———. "Wahlkampf: Alias Frahm," August 23, 1961.

———. "Warten auf Post" (Stefan Heym), May 21, 1979, p. 115.

———. " 'Würdest du eine Bonner Sekretärin heiraten?' " (Hans-Uwe Ziegenhain), no. 39 (1985), pp. 102–8.

Spittman, Ilse. "Der 17. Januar und die Folgen," *Deutschland Archiv*, February 1988, pp. 227–32.

———. "Sozialismus in den Farben der DDR," *Deutschland Archiv*, March 1989, pp. 241–44.

Springer, Axel. "Dieses Berlin ist ein Glücksfall für die Bundesrepublik Deutschland" (interview by Gerhard Löwenthal), *Berliner Morgenpost*, September 1977.

Steiniger, Klas, and Fred Böttcher. "USA-Aussenminister Shultz empfing Hermann Axen," *Neues Deutschland*, May 4, 1988, p. 1.

Stern. "Bahnhof Friedrichstrasse," October 21, 1982, pp. 143–47.

Stern, Carola. *Ulbricht—A Political Biography* (New York: Praeger, 1965).

Stiftung für ehemalige politische Häftlinge. *Kompass für den ehemaligen politischen Häftling*, 7th ed. (Bonn: Stiftung für ehemalige politische Häftlinge, 1987).

Stiller, Werner (pseud.). *Im Zentrum der Espionage* (Mainz: Hase & Köhler, 1986).

Strack, Gerda. "Minister Franke wegen Veruntreuung angeklagt," *Frankfurter Rundschau*, March 20, 1985, p. 1.

Strohmeyer, Arn (ed.) *Honecker-Witze* (Frankfurt: Eichborn, 1988).

Der Tagesspiegel. "Flüchtling will Grenzposten in sowjetischer Uniform getäuscht haben," August 21, 1986, pp. 1+.

———. "US-Delegation sprach mit Honecker/Abbau der Mauer verlangt," January 11, 1986, pp. 1+.

Talbott, Strobe. "Arms and the Man" (Paul Nitze). *Time*, December 21, 1987, pp. 76–78.

———. *The Master of the Hunt* (Paul Nitze biography) (New York: Knopf, 1988).

———, ed. *Khrushchev Remembers*, augmented ed. (Boston: Little, Brown, 1974).

Taylor, Maxwell D. *Swords and Plowshares* (New York: Norton, 1972).

Thiemann, Ellen. *Stell Dich mit dem Schergen gut* (Munich: Herbig, 1984).

Thurow, Roger. "A Divided People: East Germans Discover It's Hard Integrating into West German Life," *The Wall Street Journal*, November 20, 1985, pp. 1+.

Thurow, Rudi, et al. *Kontrollpunkt Kohlhasenbrück* (Bad Godesberg: Hohwacht, 1963).

Time. "Man of the Year: Willy Brandt," January 4, 1971, pp. 6–20.

———. "Outcasts at the Helm" (Willy Brandt cover story), October 10, 1969, pp. 24–37.

———. "The Siege," July 12, 1948.

———. "25 Years of the Berlin Wall," August 18, 1986, pp. 4–9.

Trivers, Howard. *Three Crises in American Affairs and a Continuing Revolution* (Carbondale, Ill.: Southern Illinois University Press, 1972).

Turner, Henry Ashby, Jr. *The Two Germanies Since 1945* (New Haven, Conn.: Yale University Press, 1987).

Uniewski, Herbert. "Kopfgeld für den Weg nach Westen," *Stern*, August 16, 1973.

Untersuchungsausschuss freiheitlicher Juristen. *Ehemalige Nationalsozialisten in Pankows Diensten* (Berlin: Untersuchungsausschuss freiheitlicher Juristen, 1965).

Urban, George R. "Western TV—Surrogate for Freedom?" *The New York Times*, February 7, 1986, p. 27.

Van Bergh, Hendrik. *ABC der Spione* (Pfaffenhofen a.d. Ilm: Ilmgau Verlag, 1965).

———. *Die Überläufer* (Würzburg: Johann Wilhelm Naumann, 1979).

Vielain, Heinz, and Manfred Schell. *Verrat in Bonn* (Berlin: Ullstein, 1978).

Walker, Ian. *Zoo Station* (New York: Atlantic Monthly Press, 1988).

Weber, Hermann. *Geschichte der DDR* (Munich: DTV, 1985).

Weber, Hermann (ed.). *DDR—Dokumente zur Geschichte der Deutschen Demokratischen Republik 1945–1985* (Munich: DTV, 1986).

Wechsberg, Joseph. "Letter from Berlin," *The New Yorker*, May 26, 1962.

Wechsler, James A. "As JFK Sees It," *New York Post*, September 21, 1961, p. 28, and September 22, 1961, p. 46.

Weeghman, Richard B. "Liberty Bell" (Barry Meeker), *Flying*, February 1976, pp. 75+.

Wegner, Bettina. *Als ich gerade zwanzig war* (Hamburg: Rowohlt, 1986).

Weintal, Edward, and Charles Bartlett. *Facing the Brink* (New York: Scribner's, 1967).

Weis, Otto Jörg. "23 kleine Fische gegen 4 dicke Brocken," *Frankfurter Rundschau*, June 13, 1985, p. 3.

Die Welt. "Niko Hübner gratuliert Anwalt Vogel," July 10, 1980.

———. "Ost-Berlin will zwangsadoptierte Kinder nicht herausgeben," November 30, 1976.

Werner, Ruth. *Sonjas Rapport* (East Berlin: Verlag Neues Leben, 1984).

Wernicke, Kurt. *Sozialistisches Vaterland DDR—Entstehung und Entwicklung* (East Berlin: Museum für Deutsche Geschichte, 1984).

Westin, Av. *News-Watch* New York: Simon and Schuster, 1982).

Whalen, Michael J. "Daring Rescuer Surprises Kin" (Barry Meeker), *Hartford Courant,* August 21, 1975.

Widmann, C. "Hermann Axen in den USA: Der Wegbereiter kommt nicht voran," *Süddeutsche Zeitung,* May 6, 1988.

Wilder, Billy. " 'Wie geht is mein kleiner Zwetschgenröster?' " (interview), *Spiegel,* no. 21 (1986), pp. 198–216.

Wilhelmi, Jutta. *Jugend in der DDR* (Berlin: Holzapfel, 1983).

Wilkes, Paul. "Leonard Boudin: The Left Lawyer's Lawyer," *The New York Times Biographical Edition,* November 18, 1971, pp. 4169–75.

Windmöller, Eva, and Thomas Höpker. *Leben in der DDR* (Munich: Goldmann, 1980).

Winkler, Kalle. *Made in DDR* (Frankfurt: Fischer, 1986).

Wirth, Fritz. "Washington öffnet die Tür für die DDR—aber nur einen Spaltbreit," *Die Welt,* April 28, 1988.

Wistrich, Robert. *Who's Who in Nazi Germany* (New York: Macmillan, 1982).

Wolf, Claus. "Die Gangsterband des H. Dawid," *Horizont* (DDR), April 8, 1983, pp. 5–6.

Wolff, Friedrich. *Vertrauensvoll zum Rechtsanwalt,* Pamphlet No. 35, series *Recht in unserer Zeit* (East Berlin: Staatsverlag der DDR, 1982).

Wolton, Thierry. *Le KGB en France* (Paris: Bernard Grasset, 1986).

Woywod, Georg, and Eckhard Heumeyer. *Menschenrechte in der DDR und Ost Berlin* (Frankfurt: Internationale Gesellschaft für Menschenrechte, 1986).

Wright, Peter. *Spycatcher* (New York: Dell, 1988).

Wroblewski, Clement de (ed.). *Wo Wir sind ist vorn—der politische Witz in der DDR* (Hamburg: Rasch und Röhring, 1986).

Wyden, Peter. "The Chances of Accidental War," *The Saturday Evening Post,* June 3, 1961, pp. 17–18+

———. *Bay of Pigs—The Untold Story* (New York: Simon and Schuster, 1979).

Wynne, Greville. *Contact on Gorky Street* (New York: Atheneum, 1968).

Wyssozki, V. *West-Berlin* (Berlin: Das Europäische Buch, 1974).

Zachau, Reinhard. *Stefan Heym* (Munich: Beck, 1982).

Die Zeit. "Der Spion, der in der Kreide stand" (Hansjoachim Tiedge), August 30, 1985, pp. 3+.

Zimmermann, Hartmut. "The GDR in the 1970's," *Problems in Communism,* March–April 1978, pp. 1–40.

Zitty. Anders Reisen—Berlin (Hamburg: Rowohlt, 1987).

Zolling, Hermann, and Uwe Bahnsen. *Kalter Winter im August* (Oldenburg: Gerhard Stalling, 1967).

Zolling, Hermann, and Heinz Höhne. *Pullach intern* (Hamburg: Hoffmann und Campe, 1971).

Zolotow, Maurice. *Billy Wilder in Hollywood* (New York: Putnam, 1977).

Zschorsch, Gerald. *Glaubt bloss nicht, dass ich traurig bin* (Frankfurt: Suhrkamp, 1981).

ACKNOWLEDGMENTS

The fresh insights into the terra incognita of this book, East Germany, the DDR, were made possible by an unlikely and often very reluctant hero who is bound to detest much of what he will read here. I want to acknowledge and apologize to him for his discomfort. I hope he will not be drawn into difficulties with his superiors on my account. His "crime" consisted of his efforts to placate me for four years of my incessant campaign to request, demand, plead for access to sources in the secretive society of his country.

My hero/victim is Reinhard R. Thost, my East German shadow, the unshakable assigned companion from the Department of Journalistic Relations in the East Berlin Foreign Ministry and a former DDR press person in North Vietnam and Moscow. Closemouthed but ever accessible, this gloomy middleman—his pinched face and hooded eyes made him look slightly sinister—never permitted me to peek behind the scenes of his bureaucratic troubles in his own ministry. Loyally, he never gossiped, or even emitted a gesture, about the obviously formidable obstacles he kept facing in his efforts to supply me with interviewees and information about the Wall, not the DDR's favorite subject. Yet over the years, very slowly, he seemed to acknowledge (no more) some of the standards of Western reporting required by my project.

I was dumbfounded when, toward the end, Thost disclosed his private phone number and permitted me to call him at home late at night, a spectacular concession to an enemy of the people.

Thost does think in such Marxist clichés, yet I feel queasy about his accountability once this book hits East Berlin, more so than about any other government functionary with whom I can remember working. I don't feel guilty, just uncomfortable. I don't believe his chiefs will chop his head off. I do think he'd love to lop off mine, and I can understand his reasoning in the perspective of his government's paranoia.

For more than a year, Thost labored to initiate my contact with the exalted Hermann Axen of his Politburo. For longer than that, he negotiated with the highest military brass and the Central Committee of the party to produce an eyewitness indispensable to this book, Major General Werner Hübner, arguably the best-informed insider on the Wall excepting only the supreme persona, the Secretary General, Erich Honecker himself, whom Thost attempted to produce but could not.

And now plain truth compels me to write here about Axen in ways that Thost and his associates must find upsetting, probably insulting, and I bring up indignities committed by their government in past years. Thost and his people will not accept my treatment as reporting. Or even as the bad manners of a rude guest. They are conditioned to perceive the disclosure of critical facts as hostility, an intent that I can deny with the best of conscience.

I suppose that I must duck behind the lame apology that I am doing my job and Thost was doing his. I grew fond of this hard-shelled ideologue. I miss our excruciatingly polite fencing matches over the phone, his strained smile at my Berlinese jokes from my father's time. I never saw him drink anything stronger than black coffee at East Berlin's invariably deserted International Press Center, but even if he were somehow to appear for an alcoholic dinner at my Connecticut home, I know I could never persuade him to admit that conditions in the DDR are less than utopian or at least heroic. I can only hope that, as history moves along, glasnost might eventually knock on Reinhard Thost's door and nudge him into conceding that bad things cannot be expunged by not writing about them.

· · ·

My West Berlin mainstay, the indefatigable and shrewd Hanne-lore Brenner, spent the same four years grappling with the mountainous library research and directing the accumulation of a sizable private collection of books and periodicals. She conducted nationwide manhunts for eyewitnesses, ran interference through the bureucracies, and established confidence in the project by her warmth and expertise in the initial interviewing of reluctant sources. My debt to her is immense.

I thank Bärbel and Ota Grübel and Volker Seifarth for baring their lives; Wolfgang Vogel, Major General Werner Hübner, Manfred Uschner, and Stefan Heym for lighting up the murky scene in Communist territory from their stations in the East; and Karl Wilhelm Fricke, Egon Bahr, Rainer Hildebrandt, Horst Schumm, and Erhard Göhl for doing the same from the Western side. Shepard Stone and Ernst Cramer, two of my colleagues from the Army Psychological Warfare campaigns against Germany in World War II, as well as Jim O'Donnell from my *Saturday Evening Post* days, provided surefooted guidance. So did innumerable good-humored Berliners, West and East, including some whose names I never learned. Günther Buch located some remarkable sources of information.

Manfred Uschner, the good right hand of Hermann Axen of the East Berlin Politburo, is another source about whom I have regrets. Uschner extended himself energetically to maneuver me into the presence of his very important boss, and here I am having to write things about Axen that he'll dislike a lot. What to do? I apologize to Uschner for my blunt manners, though not for anything else.

I learned long ago that a writer of history is lost beyond all hope without support from librarians. A dozen libraries here and in Europe supplied crucial materials for this volume, none more effectively than the Bryant Library of Roslyn, Long Island, of which my wife, Elaine Seaton Wyden, is the director. The discovery of needles in large haystacks is her specialty and that of her staff, and this time they outdid themselves. Would you expect a community library to be able to tell you the ignoble fate of a Soviet general who was blamed for befriending Colonel Oleg Penkovsky and failing to recognize that the colonel was spying for the CIA? I wouldn't. But Elaine and her librarians came up with a conclusive Moscow news article from *The New York Times,* even though I had not specifically asked for such an item.

. . .

The backbone of this book is built on eyewitness information, carefully cross-checked, source against source. I value the authority of my more than two hundred interviewees. My gratitude goes out to each one, including those who insisted on anonymity. The names of the others follow.

THE INTERVIEWEES

Hoofnagle, James E.
Huizenga, John
Jameson, Donald F.
Johnson, U. Alexis
Kaysen, Carl
Kenney, John
Klein, David C.
Koczak, Stephen
Kohler, Foy D.
Lantos, Tom
Ledsky, Nat
Legere, Laurance
Lightner, Allan E., Jr.
Lundahl, Arthur C.
McCone, John
McNamara, Robert S.
Mallinckrodt, Anita M.
Mapother, John
Marchetti, Victor
Marks, John D.
Martin, David C.
Mautner, Karl and Martha
Merthan, Lawrence C.
Morris, Donald R.
Moses, Hans
Muller, George
New, Ricey S., Jr.
Nitze, Paul H.
O'Donnell, James P.
Owen, Henry
Petty, Clair E.
Pittman, Steuart L.
Pleitgen, Fritz
Rositzke, Harry
Rostow, Walt W.
Rusk, Dean
Safer, Morley
Salinger, Pierre
Schelling, Thomas C.
Schlesinger, Arthur M., Jr.
Schmitz, Clarence
Schorr, Daniel

Sejna, Jan
Sigl, Rupert
Smith, Bromley K.
Smith, Jean Edward
Smith, Jeff
Smith, R. Jack
Sorensen, Theodore C.
Sorensen, Thomas C.
Stanley, Timothy
Stearman, William Lloyd
Steinert, Frank
Stewart, Gordon M.
Talbott, Orwin C.
Taylor, Maxwell D.
Thuermer, Angus M.
Trivers, Howard
Tyler, William R.
Von Pawel, Ernest
Watson, Albert
Westin, Av
Wiener, Jerry
Wilder, Billy

*In West Berlin and
West Germany:*

Albertz, Heinrich
Backlund, Sven
Bahr, Egon
Bailey, George
Biermann, Wolf
Bölke, Joachim
Bölling, Klaus
Boenisch, Peter
Borkowski, Dieter
Brandt, Willy
Brown, Ralph A.
Buch, Günther
Faust, Siegmar
Feller, Peter
Freeman, Clive

Fricke, Karl Wilhelm
Fritzen, Dora
Frucht, Adolf-Henning
Gildner, Jay
Grabe, Hans Dieter
Groebel, Klaus
Grübel, Bärbel and Ota
Hanisch, Edda
Heidrich, Heinz
Hennig, Ottfried
Hildebrandt, Rainer
Hoerning, Erika
Hurwitz, Harold J.
Jope, Manfred
Kabel, Rainer
Kraal, Meta
Kreutzer, Hermann
Kunst, Herrman
Lange-Müller, Katja
Ledsky, Nat
Leonhard, Wolfgang
Lochner, Robert
Long, Wellington
Loeser, Franz
Loewe, Lothar
Löwenthal, Gerhard
McCord, Thomas F.
Mettke, Jörg R.
Meyer, Michel
Müller, Manfred
Naumann, Lutz-Peter
Nietschke, Mrs. Karl Heinz
Nölle-Neumann, Elisabeth
Obst, Werner
Priesnitz, Walter
Pritzel, Konstantin
Rehlinger, Ludwig A.
Salm, Ülo
Schacht, Ulrich
Scharf, Kurt
Schenk, Fritz

Schmidt, Andreas
Schmidthammer, Jens
Schumm, Horst
Seifarth, Volker
Seiffert, Wolfgang
Sicking, Peter
Spangenberg, Dietrich
Stange, Jürgen
Stone, Shepard
Svingel, Carl-Gustav
Thedieck, Franz
Thomas, Stefan
Urban, Ingo
Weber, Hermann
Wedel, Reymar von
Winkler, Kalle
Zimmermann, Hartmut

In East Berlin:

Axen, Hermann
Beyer, Hartmut
Hanisch, Wilfried
Heym, Stefan
Hübner, Werner
Keiderling, Gerhard
Maron, Monika
Meehan, Francis J.
Miller, Cynthia J.
Peet, John
Reinhold, Otto
Rose, Günther
Runge, Irene
Schäfer, Heinz
Schmidt, Max
Schwabe, Ernst-Otto
Schwarz, Ulrich
Seidel, Karl
Uschner, Manfred
Vogel, Wolfgang and Helga

INDEX

PICTURE CREDITS

ABOUT THE AUTHOR

Born in Berlin, Peter Wyden came to the United States at thirteen and has been writing, editing, and publishing since age eighteen. A former Washington correspondent for *Newsweek* and executive editor of *Ladies' Home Journal,* he has been writing and publishing books in Ridgefield, Connecticut, since 1970. Mr. Wyden is author or coauthor of eleven previous books, including *Bay of Pigs—The Untold Story* and *Day One—Before Hiroshima and After.*